More praise for *The Anthology of Rap*

"As ambitious and intelligent as anyone might want, and more enjoyable than anyone might think. . . . If you want to hear how the latter part of the twentieth century sounded, you can't do better than this book."
   —Kevin Young, *Bookforum*

"This mega-anthology strips away rap's performance elements and allows the language itself to pulse, break, spin, and strut in poems of audacity, outrage, insight, sweetness, and nastiness. . . . Electrifying."
   —*Booklist*

"A complete encyclopedia of the history, personalities, beats, rhythm and rhymes of the musical genre from the old school of Grand Master Flash & The Furious Five to hip-hop and Kanye West."
   —*Los Angeles Times*

"Listen along on YouTube and it's a self-taught class on the genre's history."
   —*New York Magazine*

"*The Anthology of Rap* reaffirms the enduring force of the written word—or at least the immaculately constructed freestyle."
   —*LA Weekly*

"The authors have built a poignant collection of rhythm and rhyme. . . . For hard-core hip-hop heads, this book confirms what we have always known: that some of the most innovative writing hails from the imagination of the rapper."
   —Idris Goodwin, *Boston Globe*

"An awesome compilation: 920 pages of some of the baddest, phattest, flyist tracks ever dropped."
   —*Mother Jones*

"Intelligent and authentic . . . written for both the hip-hop head and the uninitiated."
   —James Johnson, *Philadelphia Inquirer*

"Reading *The Anthology of Rap*, which covers everything from Afrika Bambaataa to Young Jeezy, it's hard not to appreciate rap's astounding love of words, of the way they fit together and play off each other, and of how meaning can be layered upon meaning to get at a deeper truth. Which sounds an awful lot like poetry."
—Joshua Ostroff, *The Globe and Mail*

"[The] editors of *The Anthology of Rap* supply a much needed injection of energy and enthusiasm into our analysis of hip-hop's lyricism."
—Quentin B. Huff, PopMatters

"A great, necessary addition to the book collection of any contemporary music aficionado."
—*Creative Loafing*

"As a literary anthology of over 800 pages, this is one of hip-hop's most significant books in the past decade. Arguably, it could even be said it's the most important book in hip-hop literary history."
—*Pound Magazine*

Edited by

ADAM BRADLEY
ANDREW DUBOIS

Foreword by Henry Louis Gates, Jr.

Afterwords by Chuck D and Common

THE ANTHOLOGY OF
RAP

Yale UNIVERSITY PRESS

New Haven and London

Yale University Press books may be purchased in quantity for educational, business, or promotional use. For information, please e-mail sales.press@yale.edu (U.S. office) or sales@yaleup.co.uk (U.K. office).

Designed by Mary Valencia

Set in Minion, Nobel, American Typewriter, and Franklin Gothic type by Technologies 'N Typography.

Interior art and photography by Justin Francis

Printed in the United States of America.

The Library of Congress has cataloged the hardcover edition as follows:

The anthology of rap / edited by Adam Bradley and Andrew DuBois; foreword by Henry Louis Gates, Jr.; afterwords by Chuck D and Common.

    p.   cm.

Includes bibliographical references and index.

ISBN 978-0-300-14190-0 (hardcover: alk. paper)   1. Rap (Music)—History and criticism. 2. Rap (Music)—Texts.   I. Bradley, Adam.   II. DuBois, Andrew (Andrew Lee)

ML3531.A57   2010

782.42164909—dc22   2010023316

ISBN: 978-0-300-14191-7

A catalogue record for this book is available from the British Library.

10 9 8 7 6 5 4 3 2 1

CONTENTS

PART II: 1985–1992–THE GOLDEN AGE   119

viii Contents

x Contents

Contents xiii

PART IV: 2000–2010—NEW MILLENNIUM RAP 559

HENRY LOUIS GATES, JR.

The first person I ever heard "rap" was a man born in 1913, my father, Henry Louis Gates, Sr. Daddy's generation didn't call the rhetorical games they played "rapping"; they signified, they played the Dozens. But this was rapping just the same, rapping by another name. Signifying is the grandparent of Rap; and Rap is signifying in a postmodern way. The narratives that my father recited in rhyme told the tale of defiant heroes named Shine or Stagolee or, my absolute favorite, the Signifying Monkey. They were linguistically intricate, they were funny and spirited, and they were astonishingly profane.

Soon the stories became familiar to me and I started memorizing parts of them, especially striking couplets and sometimes an entire resonant stanza. But every time my dad recited a version of one of these tales, he somehow made it new again, reminding me of all that a virtuosic performer possessed: an excellent memory, a mastery of pace and timing, the capacity to inflect and gesture, the ability to summon the identities of different characters simply through the nuances of their voices.

My father and his friends called their raps "signifying" or "playing the Dozens," a younger generation named them Toasts, and an even younger generation called it "rapping." But regardless of the name, much about the genre remained the same. Since anthropologists tend to call them "Toasts," we will employ that term here. Toasts are long oral poems that had emerged by World War I, shortly after the sinking of the *Titanic,* judging by the fact that one of the earliest surviving examples of the genre was called "Shine and the *Titanic.*" And the fact that the French words for "monkey" and "sign" are a bit of

FOREWORD

a visual pun (*singe* and *signe,* respectively) also points to a World War I origin of the genre as it would have been revised by returning black veterans from the European theater of war. (My father recalls meeting southern black soldiers at the beginning of World War II at Camp Lee, Virginia, who were barely literate but who could recite "acres of verses" of "The Signifying Monkey," underscoring the role of the military and war as a cross-pollinating mechanism for black cultural practices. And of these various forms, none would be more compelling, more popular, more shared than signifying.)

All of these subgenres emerged out of the African American rhetorical practice of signifying. Signifying is the defining rhetorical principle of all African American discourse, the language game of black language games, both sacred and secular, from the preacher's call-and-response to the irony and indirection of playing the Dozens. These oral poets practiced their arts in ritual settings such as the street corner or the barbershop, sometimes engaging in verbal duels with contenders like a linguistic boxing match. These recitations were a form of artistic practice and honing, but they were also the source of great entertainment displayed before an audience with a most sophisticated ear. And though certain poems, such as "Shine and the *Titanic*" and "The Signifying Monkey," had a familiar, repeated narrative content, poets improvised through and around this received content, with improvised stanzas and lyrics that might address a range of concerns from social and political issues to love, loneliness, heartbreak, and even death. The Dozens and the Toasts were, first and foremost, forms of art, and everyone on the street or sitting around the barbershop knew this. Rapping was a performance, rappers were to be judged, and the judges were the people on the corner or in the shop. Everyone, it seemed to me as I watched these performances unfolding even as a child, was literate in the fine arts of signification.

As I listened to my father delighting us in the late fifties with tales of the Monkey and old Shine, I knew at once that there was something sublime, something marvelous and forbidden and dangerous about them. And it was easy to recognize variations on rapping that started emerging in rhythm and blues and soul music in the sixties. I am thinking of James Brown's nine-minute rendition of "Lost Someone" on his *Live at the Apollo* album in 1963, or Isaac Hayes's paradigm-shifting version of "By the Time I Get to Phoenix" from his *Hot Buttered Soul* album of 1969. And H. Rap Brown's emergence as one of the leaders of the younger black militants of the Black Power movement brought the word "Rap" and the lyrics of the

Dozens to a generation of black students because he included his most original raps, as a point of pride in his own artistry, in his autobiography, *Die, Nigger, Die.* (Unfortunately, Mr. Brown did not write as well as he rapped!)

A few years later, I would hear echoes of all of these formal antecedents in the early Rap songs hitting the airwaves in the late seventies and early eighties. Melle Mel's verse on "The Message":

> A child is born with no state of mind
> Blind to the ways of mankind
> God is smiling on you but he's frowning too
> Because only God knows what you'll go through

echoes across the decades back to these lines from the toast called "Life's a Funny Old Proposition":

> A man comes to birth on this funny old earth
> With not a chance in a million to win
> To find that he's through and his funeral is due
> Before he can even begin

Despite all that is different about them, these two verses are bound together by both sound and sense. They each insist upon an unstinting and unflinching confrontation with reality, while somehow staving off despair. Great art so often does this, offering expiation and transcendence all at once. As an art form, Rap is defined, like the Toasts before it, by a set of formal qualities, an iconoclastic spirit, and a virtuosic sense of wordplay. It extends the long-standing practice in the African American oral tradition of language games. Simply put, Rap is a contemporary form of signifying.

By the time I began my first job teaching at Yale while still a graduate student in the mid-1970s, I began to hear about a new music coming out of the Bronx. It was simply called Rap—an old word for those familiar with black slang, but a new form that combined rhythm and rhyme in a style all its own. Like all art—vernacular or high art—it took the familiar and made it unfamiliar again. Rap's signature characteristic is the parody and pastiche of its lyrics, including "sampling," which is just another word for intertextuality. Rap is the art form par excellence of synthesis and recombination. No one could say that Afrika Bambaataa or Grandmaster Flash was not creating something new, but each would be quick to acknowledge his formal debts to other artists, especially to old school musicians from the past.

As we have seen, Rap is the postmodern version of an African American vernacular tradition that stretches back to chants, Toasts, and trickster tales. It connects through its percussive sensibility, its riffs, and its penchant for rhyme, with a range of forms including scat singing, radio DJ patter, and Black Arts movement poets like Amiri Baraka, Nikki Giovanni, and Jayne Cortez. Its sense of musicality, both in voice and beat, owes a great deal to performers like Gil Scott-Heron and the Last Poets, as well as to funk and soul artists like James Brown, Isaac Hayes, George Clinton, and Sly Stone. Rap is, in other words, a multifarious, multifaceted tradition imbedded within an African American oral culture that itself shares in the rich history of human expression across the ages.

At its best, Rap, though a most serious genre, doesn't take itself too self-consciously or try to overburden its lines with rehearsed wisdom, or the cant of ideology. It complicates or even rejects literal interpretation. It demands fluency in the recondite codes of African American speech. Just like the Dozens before it, Rap draws strength by shattering taboos, sending up stereotype, and relishing risqué language and subject matter.

I learned this last lesson firsthand more than two decades ago. In the spring of 1990, after I had published an editorial on the case in the *New York Times,* I was called to testify as an expert witness before a Florida court in the obscenity trial of the 2 Live Crew. The group's 1989 album, *As Nasty as They Wanna Be,* with its provocative single "Me So Horny," had inspired such heated response from civic leaders that copies were burned in the streets. At stake was not simply the songs of one group of young black men, but the very freedom of expression at the core of all artistic creation. In my testimony, I stated that in the very lyrics that some found simply crass and pornographic, "what you hear is great humor, great joy, and great boisterousness. It's a joke. It's a parody and parody is one of the most venerated forms of art."

Rap has always been animated by this complexity of meaning and intention. This is by no means to absolve artists of the ethics of form, particularly in the artist's capacity as a role model for young people, but rather to point out that there's an underlying value worth fighting for in defending Rap—or any other form of art for that matter—against those who would silence its voice. One of the hallmarks of a democratic society should be ensuring the space for all citizens to express themselves in art, whether we like what they have to say or not. After all, censorship is to art as lynching is to justice.

As we have seen, it is not difficult to trace a straight line between the marvelously formulaic oral tales like "Shine and the *Titanic*" and "The Signifying Monkey" and Rap, and, in terms of literary history, it is a short line, too. Rappers often make direct allusions to vernacular culture, as we see on songs like Schoolly D's "Signifying Rapper" and Devin the Dude's "Briarpatch." Even when the connection is less explicit, it is no less apparent. It's impossible not to hear echoes of H. Rap Brown's signifying virtuosity when reading the lyrics to Smoothe da Hustler and Trigga da Gambler's "Broken Language." And there is undoubtedly something of that swaggering folk hero Stagolee in someone like 2Pac, or of that trickster the Signifying Monkey in someone like Ol' Dirty Bastard.

Given Rap's close connection to the African American oral tradition, it should come as no surprise that it also carries with it much of the same baggage. Misogyny and homophobia, which we must critique, often mar the effectiveness of the music. But as with practices like the Toasts and the Dozens, these influences are by no means absolute. Perhaps one of the most bracing things about reading this anthology is the way that it complicates our assumptions about what Rap is and what Rap does, who makes it and who consumes it. In this anthology, we see Yo-Yo going head to head against Ice Cube in a battle of the sexes, or female MCs like Eve and Jean Grae calling attention to issues like domestic violence and abortion that often get left out of Hip-Hop discourse, and artists often associated with gangsta personas or "conscious" perspectives revealing the full range and complexity of their subjectivity.

The Anthology of Rap is an essential contribution to our living literary tradition. It calls attention to the artistry, sense of craft, and striking originality of an art form born of young black and brown men and women who found their voices in rhyme, and chanted a poetic discourse to the rhythm of the beat. This groundbreaking anthology masterfully assembles part of a new vanguard of American poetry. One of its greatest virtues is that it focuses attention, often for the first time, upon Rap's lyrics alone. This is not a rejection of the music, but rather a reminder that the words are finally the best reason for the beat.

One finds in this anthology many lyrics that complicate common assumptions about Rap music. And as we might expect, the reader encounters the brutal diction of Gangsta Rap, but also its leavening humor and parody. One finds instances of sexism and homophobia, but also resistance to them. One finds words seemingly intended to offend, but also, sometimes, the deeper meanings of and motives for this sort of conscious provocation. Rap's tradition is as broad and as deep as any other form of poetry, but like any other literary tradition, it contains its shallows, its whirlpools, and its muddy waters. Our task as active, informed readers is to navigate through the tributaries of Rap's canon, both for the pleasure that comes from the journey as readers, but also for the wisdom born of traveling to any uncharted destinations of the mind. Adam Bradley and Andrew DuBois's superbly edited, pioneering anthology makes such a journey possible.

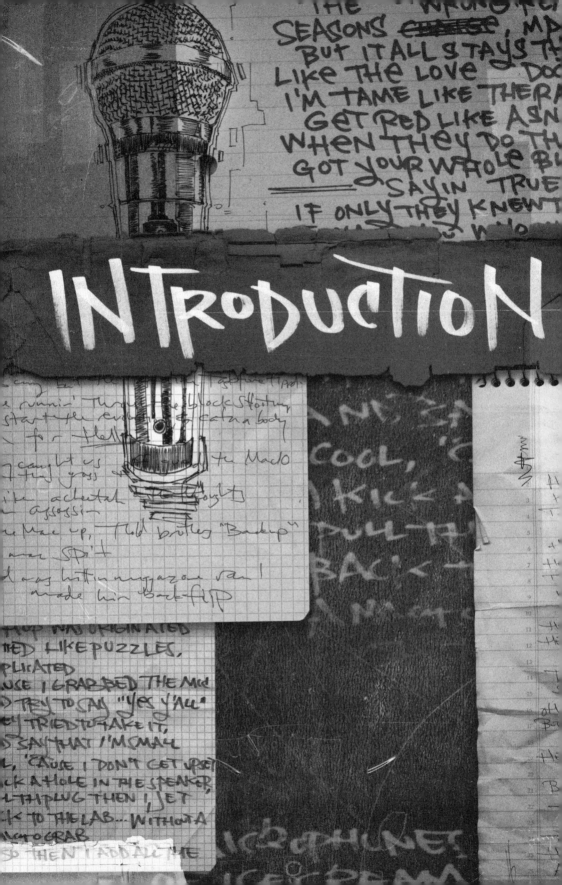

INTRODUCTION

THE ANTHOLOGY OF RAP

is the first anthology of lyrics representing rap's recorded history from the late 1970s to the present. It tells the story of rap as lyric poetry. The lyrics included stretch from a transcription of a 1978 live performance by Grandmaster Flash and (the then) Furious Four to the latest poetic innovations of Jay-Z, Mos Def, Jean Grae, and Lupe Fiasco. The anthology's purpose is threefold: (1) to distill, convey, and preserve rap's poetic tradition within the context of African American oral culture and the Western poetic heritage; (2) to establish a wide and inclusive cultural history of rap on the grounds of its fundamental literary and artistic nature; and (3) to provide tools with which to read rap lyrics with close attention.

Rap and hip-hop are not synonymous, though they are so closely associated that some use the terms interchangeably. Others invest them with distinct values—either rap describes commercialized music and hip-hop the sounds of the underground; or rap suggests a gritty style (as in gangsta rap) and hip-hop a more politically and socially conscious approach (as in backpack hip-hop). At the end of his song "HipHop Knowledge," legendary rap artist and producer KRS-One succinctly explains the distinction: "Rap music is something we do, but hip hop is something we live." Hip-hop, in other words, is an umbrella term to describe the multifaceted culture of which rap is but a part. MCs, hip-hop's masters of ceremonies, are its literary artists. They are the poets and rap is the poetry of hip-hop culture.

Hip-hop emerged out of the impoverished South Bronx in the mid-1970s. In defiance of circumstance, a generation of young people—mostly black and brown—crafted a rich culture of words and song, of art and movement. Rap was the voice of this culture, the linguistic analog of hyperkinetic dance moves, vividly painted subway cars, and skillfully mixed break beats. "Rap was the final conclusion of a generation of creative people oppressed with the reality of lack," KRS-One explains.[1] Hip-hop's pioneers fashioned in rap an art form that draws not only from the folk idioms of the African diaspora but from the legacy of Western verse and the musical traditions of jazz, blues, funk, gospel, and reggae. These young artists commandeered the English language, bending it to their own expressive purposes. Over time, the poetry they set to beats would command the ears of their block, their borough, their nation, and eventually the world.

Rap today bears the legacy of this inaugural generation and, as a consequence, is rightly associated with African American culture. Equally, it is a form of expression governed by a set of conventions available to all and vivified by the creativity of anyone who learns rap's history and masters rap's craft. This helps explain how rap—and hip-hop culture in general—has come to be embraced by people of all races and nations. It is now the lingua franca of global youth culture, varied in its expressions but rooted in a common past.

At the same time, rap has inspired heated debate concerning its explicit speech and subjects. For some, rap constitutes a chorus of welcome voices, previously suppressed; for others, it presents a troubling sign of cultural disarray. Beyond its controversy, however, a hip-hop lyrical tradition has taken shape through poetic gestures and forms that rappers developed over time. The substantial body of literature that has emerged is both related to and distinct from the poetry of the past. In the past thirty years rap has led a renaissance of the word, driving a return to poetry in public life.

Though rap is now widely disseminated in American culture, it has yet to attain adequate recognition as poetry even as universities incorporate it into English, African American studies, and music curricula. Only a few poetry anthologies contain rap lyrics. Those that do, like the *Norton Anthology of African American Literature* and Ishmael Reed's *From Totems to Hip Hop,* do so in a representative fashion. Books like Flocabulary's *Shakespeare Is Hip Hop* and Alan Sitomer and Michael Cirelli's *Hip Hop Poetry and the Classics* offer effective and entertaining tools for using rap to teach canonical poetry to middle school and high school students, but don't illuminate rap's distinct poetic tradition.

This volume treats rap as a body of lyrics that responds to transcription, explication, and analysis as poetry. The lyrics included offer a kind of laboratory of language for those interested in the principles of poetics. Indeed, the study of rap is an effective means of introducing the key forms and concepts that define the poetic tradition: rappers embrace the clear sonic qualities of rhythm and rhyme, make ample use of figures and forms such as simile and metaphor, make storytelling a key component of their art, and emphasize the spirit of competition once central to poetry.

Just as any body of poetry can be studied from many angles, so too can rap. Viable approaches to the aesthetics of rap abound. From a formal perspective, one might look at a song's rhetorical figures, at its local sonic qualities, or at its revisions of conventions of genre. An interest in cultural studies will likely lead one to situate rap in relation to its sociological, geographical, or racial contexts. A range of historical approaches seems relevant in considering rap as an art, whether that means focusing on a song's relationship to African American oral poetry of the distant or recent past, or to English-language lyric poetry from *Beowulf* until now, or to the vast range of commercial popular song lyrics in general—all bodies of poetry with rich and various histories, of which rap is also a part. As the lyrics in this book attest, rap has been and remains many things for many people; perhaps the wisest approach is one as capacious as the art form itself.

Rap's Poetic Form

Raps are lyric poems organized into verses, the standard length of which is sixteen lines. They are performed most often in rhythm to a beat with a vocal delivery that ranges from sing-song to conversational. Their most distinguishing poetic feature is rhyme, which rappers employ in full and slant, monosyllabic and multisyllabic forms at the end of and in the midst of the line. Rap verses make ample use of figurative language, most especially the simile, though other less common rhetorical figures and forms are also used. The dominant poetic voice is the first-person singular, the "I" not only of the MC, but of a range of invented identities that the MC takes on. As poetic practice, rap verses are often confrontational, composed either in competition with an actual rhyme adversary or in mock battle with an imagined one. A dominant theme, therefore, is the elevation of the self and the denigration of the opponent. That said, rap has also developed a complex expressive range, driven by narratives of everything from the street life to the good life and by treatments of themes ranging from love to heartache to speculative projections of alternative realities.

Rap is sometimes conflated with spoken word or slam poetry. In fact, each is a distinct form with a disparate history. Rap grew out of African American oral expressions and took shape in the pressure cooker of the South Bronx in the 1970s. Slam poetry, on the other hand, emerged out of audience-judged competitions held in white working-class Chicago bars during the mid-1980s. The term *spoken word*—which over the years has been used to describe everything from radio broadcasts to beatnik poetry readings—loosely encompasses both modes of expression. Though they differ in their ancestral roots, rap and slam poetry have grown together in creative cross-pollination. HBO's 2002–2007 series *Russell Simmons Presents Def Poetry*, for instance, included many performers who drew heavily from rap influences; the series was hosted by the rapper Mos Def, and MCs occasionally came on the show to deliver their lyrics a cappella (for one such example see Talib Kweli's "Give 'Em Hell"). At the same time, poets such as Saul Williams, Jessica Care Moore, and Sage Francis reflect the aesthetics of rap in the poetry they have performed at slams.

One of the greatest misconceptions about rap lyrics is that they consist entirely of couplets ending with heavy-handed, simplistic rhymes. Certainly, rap in its infancy favored predictable patterns of straightforward rhymes, but this soon gave way to an expanding body of lyrical innovations that would come to define rap in its mature form. The parody of rap as doggerel does not touch truly on much of the music and cannot account for the range and formal dexterity of Rakim, Lauryn Hill, Jay-Z, Nas, and other rap lyricists too numerous to name.

To understand the difference between relative simplicity and sonic density in rap lyrics, consider a couplet from Vanilla Ice's much-maligned but doggedly enduring 1990 hit "Ice Ice Baby," with its infectious energy and rudimentary rhymes:

> Will it ever stop? Yo, I don't know
> Turn off the lights and I'll glow

The rhyme of "know" and "glow" is fairly obvious; though it forges a perfect connection between the two lines in sound, it does little to develop that connection in sense. Certainly, though, there is something of interest in the metaphorical content since Ice, as a white rapper, will "glow" in the dark. Compare that, however, to what Big Pun does with the same end word ("know") in these more complex lines from "Twinz (Deep Cover '98)":

> Dead in the middle of Little Italy little did we know
> That we riddled some middleman who didn't do diddly

Both lyrics share a common end-word in their first line, but where Vanilla Ice employs a plain perfect rhyme, Big Pun eschews end rhyme entirely, instead satisfying the listener's formal expectations with a tongue-twisting series of internal rhymes, assonance, and alliteration. The result is an unexpected and energizing lyric in which the swerves of sound mimic the active confusion of the scene Pun paints. Vanilla Ice's song was the first rap single to top the Billboard charts, selling eleven million copies and helping to launch hip-hop into the mainstream. Yet Big Pun's line is the one rap fans have been repeating now for more than a decade. Both lyrics coexist within the broad expanse of rap's aesthetics.

Rap, like other artistic forms, thrives on constraint as much as it does freedom. Every rap lyric must fulfill certain demands, the dominant ones being the listener's expectation of rhyme and the rhythmic strictures of the beat. In unskilled hands, rap's requirements can prove too much, leading to insipid lyrics that confuse meaning to find rhyme and strain syntax to satisfy rhythm. But in the hands of a skilled MC, rap's formal limitations are a means to eloquence. As David Foster Wallace and Mark Costello observe in their offbeat but visionary 1990 book, *Signifying Rappers,* "The limitations [of rhythm and rhyme in rap] are the invaluable constraints of form that all good new art helps define itself by struggling against from inside them— the formal Other all 'fresh' speech needs."[2]

The MC not only must craft a coherent poetic narrative or create a compelling persona, but must do so while rhyming with some regularity and without ever losing the beat. To quote Foster Wallace and Costello again, "This all means that the rapper's lyric, to succeed, must function simultaneously: as the quickest, interval-inhabiting part, the human part, of the many-geared rhythmic machine that comprises most serious raps; as a powerful, shocking, repulsive or witty monologue, as a defness-in-motion; and as a formally clean and to-the-rhyme's-bone-hewing arrangement of verse."[3] The success of the lyrics in this anthology testifies to rap's lyrical possibilities and to the estimable body of contemporary poetry to be found in its rhythms and rhymes.

Rap as Music, Rap as Poetry

Like most music, rap appeals to the ear and to the human desire for song and celebration. By their very nature, lyrics rely on music to achieve their full effect. The synergy of driving beats and ingenious vocal cadences largely accounts for rap's popularity. When hip-hop was born in the early 1970s, the DJ, not the MC, dominated. DJs spun records and captured break beats, the funky drum sections the DJ isolated and repeated to motivate a dancing crowd. The MC's cadence developed in emulation of these flowing instrumentals, with the rapping voice eventually supplanting the

DJ's mix as the centerpiece of hip-hop performance. *Flow* is the word MCs use for synching their voice in rhythm to the beat—a fitting term given that *rhythm* comes from the Greek *rheo,* meaning flow. Certainly, the development of rap's musicality is a subject worthy of attention. This anthology, however, centers upon rap as lyrical craft.

Rap's identity as music reaffirms its connection to the ancestral traditions from which all poetry emerged. Two turntables and a digital sampler have simply taken the place of the lute and the lyre of the bardic past and the freestyle songs of West African griots. Rap's oral poetry expresses itself in sound through performance even as it retains its connection to the page. In hip-hop culture, lyrics are a form of currency, a means by which to exchange ideas about value and meaning in the music. Memorizing, reciting, analyzing, and being able to call upon a mental catalog of verses are the measures of one's knowledge of rap and dedication to hip-hop culture. Rap's lyrics, in other words, are already invested with value distinct from their place in the music; often, they are the most enduring part.

Rap songs almost always begin the same way: as lyrics written in an MC's book of rhymes—the journals many rappers keep for composing their verses. To read rap lyrics in print, therefore, is most often to restore them to their original form. Whether MCs are scribbling in a rhyme book, tapping out lyrics on a Blackberry or iPhone, or just composing in the mental journal in their heads, rap expresses itself as a fusion of the written and the oral. When Jay-Z boasts on his 2009 single "D.O.A. (Death of AutoTune)" that "my raps don't have melodies," he is celebrating rap's difference from most other musical genres—and, by implication, its added capacity for direct expression. The very qualities that leave rap open to criticism as music— heavy reliance on 4/4 beats, limited use of melody and harmony—are precisely what make it such an effective vehicle for poetry. Good rap lyrics are poetically interesting because they have to be; they have little in the way of melody or harmony to compensate for a poor lyrical line.

Certainly rap has its share of weak lyrics. Some even form part of popular and otherwise pleasurable songs. The difference is that when rap fails poetically, listeners cannot help but hear it because the rapping voice is so clearly in the foreground. Hip-hop's community of MCs and its discerning audience pass swift judgment on such lyrical failure; a predictable rhyme or an overused phrase can get an unwitting rapper booed off the stage or booted from a cipher, a collaborative and competitive circle of lyricists that often forms spontaneously wherever rap is heard. As Harvard scholar Marcyliena Morgan observes, hip-hop culture demands of its adherents "attention to the art and role of practice, critical evaluation, and performance in order to develop artistic and technical skills. Evaluation in the [hip-hop] underground is a thing of great value."4 Hip-hop's reliance on the word means that its terms of lyrical evaluation are often more rigorous than those of other musical genres.

The rhythm-driven beats of hip-hop are more than accommodating of poetic expression; they provide the perfect sonic climate for poetically sophisticated lyrics to flourish. The regularity of the beat, the limited melody and harmony, and a vocal delivery that falls closer to speech than to song mean that rap has the freedom to explore language in an infinite number of ways. Rap lyrics generally retain much of their resonance and meaning when isolated from their music. This is because so much of rap's meaning and even its sound are embedded in the language.

Reading rap lyrics, one comes to understand a rap song not simply as music, but also as a lyric poem, or what William Carlos Williams called a "small machine of words." Just as a mechanic might take apart an engine in order to understand how its constituent parts fit together before returning it to its functional form, this anthology encourages readers to focus upon the discrete elements of rap's poetic form in isolation before returning them to the whole performance. When a rap lyric appears on the page, aspects like rhyme schemes and enjambment suddenly become apparent; our attention is heightened to the point of awareness of similes and metaphors and other species of figurative language. It can be a remarkable aesthetic experience on its own, and one that carries over when the song is heard again in full. Cultivating knowledge of rap's poetic craft stimulates greater appreciation for rap music than one might otherwise gain from listening to the recordings alone.

This anthology treats rap as a literary form, albeit one primarily experienced as music. Langston Hughes made the same case for the blues, celebrating the poetry inherent in the music he would use as a model for his own verse. Far from denying rap's value as music, the comparison suggests that readers stand to gain a renewed appreciation for rap's music by considering the poetry of its lyrics. To study rap as poetry is to pause in contemplation before returning to the beats and rhymes of the music itself.

The Language of Rap

Rap's influence on the English language is palpable in the currents of contemporary, everyday speech. It is a vivid vocabulary, stylish and often explicit. Reading rap lyrics rather than simply hearing them underscores both their originality and, occasionally, their offensiveness. It calls attention to the fact that rap is often intended to confuse and even to affront many members of the listening public.

Readers of this anthology will undoubtedly come across lyrics with unclear meanings, whether in a slang term or an obscure reference. It is important to remember that such lack of comprehension is often by design. Slang is born of the desire to find new and compelling ways to speak about familiar things, but it also emerges out of the desire for coded communication. The young hope to confound the old; the poor, the rich; the black, the white; the people from one part of town want to distinguish themselves from the people in another. When confronted with uncertainty in rap lyrics, it is constructive to bear in mind the following: (1) not even hip-hop insiders are likely to understand everything in every song; (2) meaning changes over time, depending upon the particular circumstance of the language's use; and (3) obfuscation is often the point, suggesting coded meanings worth puzzling over.

Even the names rappers assume for themselves are a kind of coding, a way of transforming identity through language. A handful of MCs go by their given names—Kanye West, Keith Murray, Lauryn Hill—but the vast majority take on one or more rap aliases. Names in rap help define a persona, allowing for the necessary distance between person and performer and announcing certain defining qualities of the artist before he or she has said a word. They can suggest criminal personas: Capone (like Al) or Noreaga (like Manuel) or Rick Ross (like "Freeway Ricky" Ross, the drug dealer responsible for introducing crack cocaine to Los Angeles). They can suggest linguistic virtuosity and erudition: Punchline or Wordsworth or Saukrates. In short, they can suggest a range of meanings that help define an MC's style and persona.

MCs with multiple aliases often flow differently depending on the lyrical identity they choose to inhabit. The RZA rhymes one way, but as Bobby Digital he rhymes another. Kool Keith has a certain style, which changes when he becomes Dr. Octagon, Dr. Dooom, or Black Elvis. Eminem is a study in persona; he embodies three distinct poetic identities in his work: Slim Shady, Eminem, and Marshall Mathers, the latter his given name. "When does Slim Shady kick in, when does Eminem step in, where does Marshall begin?" Eminem asks.[5] His rhymes provide the answer. Rap aliases are a means of linguistic transformation; like slang, they fashion new expressive possibilities.

When rap first emerged, most of the slang that MCs employed could be puzzled out in context. When Biz Markie, on 1988's "Vapors," describes his friend TJ Swan's stylish attire as "fly Bally boots / Rough leather fashions and tough silk suits," we can glean that "fly," "rough," and "tough" are all superlatives. As rap spread across the United States in the 1990s, the varieties of slang often served as geographical markers, sometimes with quite specific relevance. Consider, for example, the different ways that rappers in the early-to-mid-1990s would refer to their friends: 2Pac's "homies," DMX's "dawgs," Mobb Deep's "duns," the Wu-Tang Clan's "gods," Mac Dre's "cuddies," E-40's "pardners." These differences in terminology reflect both regional and individual styles. They speak to the artists' identities and to their communities.

At the other extreme from these regional variations are those terms that have left hip-hop culture to become part of the general American lexicon, thereby undoing their value as coded speech. The word *dis* (for dismiss, disrespect, or insult) is now so prevalent that many are unaware that the term was popularized in rap. The source of such crossover words is often impossible to isolate, but occasionally it can be traced back to a specific point of origin. The term *bling bling*, or simply *bling* (to describe diamonds or any other form of jewelry that glints in the light), was popularized by the New Orleans rapper B.G. and a teenaged Lil Wayne on their 1999 hit "Bling Bling." Now suburban grandmothers use the term.

The lifespan of a given slang word is fleeting, as new ways of saying the same thing evolve and gain popularity. Thus certain words and phrases can become markers of particular historical moments. When Malice of The Clipse rhymes on "Zen" that "I'm from the old school when the gat was a jammy," he is calling attention not only to the shifting street terminology for firearms, but also to the power of words to define time and place. (This example is especially ironic since "gat" as used in hip-hop is itself a slang term more than a century old derived from the Gatling gun.) Using the term *def,* for instance, to say that something is great means that you are most likely somewhere in New York in the 1980s. *Def* waned in popularity as other terms (*phat, dope, fly, official*) took over, only to fade out as well; back in 1993, Rick Rubin, co-founder of Def Jam Records with Russell Simmons, even held a mock funeral for "def"—complete with casket. Just like "gat," it will probably be resurrected.

Slang is so prevalent in rap that it supports a cottage industry of online and even print lexicons, the most prominent of which is the Web-based "Urban Dictionary." The Web site Rap Genius offers line-by-line analysis of rap lyrics, interpreting slang and uncovering nuances of expression. We encourage readers who may be unfamiliar with some of the words in the lyrics to use such resources to explicate these poems of the present, just as one might use the *Oxford English Dictionary* to discern shades of meaning in poems of the past.

Most of rap's language, though, is quite plain and often explicit. Rap, after all, was the first musical genre to make cursing a customary practice. Because it emerged out of an underground scene, at first relatively heedless of commercial considerations, rap was free to stick more closely to the ways people actually speak. Ironically, this renegade attitude contributed to rap's commercial success. NWA went platinum in the early 1990s despite the fact that almost none of their songs were suitable for airplay. Music video viewers have often found themselves subjected to the farce of rap songs made incomprehensible by bleeped and edited lyrics. The Recording Industry Association of America essentially invented the parental advisory sticker in response to rap artists like 2 Live Crew and Ice-T.

But rap's explicit language and content is about more than simply causing a stir. Rap was born as a form of necessary speech. It provided young people, many of whom were from difficult and impoverished backgrounds, with a voice and a means of vivid expression. "When I was young," the pioneering rapper MC Lyte remembers, "I was like, how else can a young black girl of my age be heard all around the world? I gotta rap."[6] This new art form would be passionate, plainspoken, and at times profane. The young artists would take as their themes both the hardscrabble realities of everyday life as well as the aspirational imaginings of wealth, comfort, and success. In his memoir, *From Pieces to Weight* (2005), 50 Cent describes what rapping meant to him when he was just beginning: "I wrote about the things I had seen in my life and what was going on in the 'hood. I was able to express myself in rhyme better than I ever had in a regular conversation."[7] The fact that rap's rhymed expression is often blunt and confrontational, aggressive and offensive, makes profanity a necessary, even defining, element of its art.

This anthology is filled with explicit language, from garden-variety curse words to terms of more specific offense (the n-word and the b-word being most prominent). Rap's early years offer surprisingly little in the way of curse words; indeed, it wasn't until the early 1990s that explicit language and content became commonplace in the music. Set to a beat, such words endow rap with transgressive power rarely matched in popular music. But rap's most incendiary element may be its subject matter. Rap lyrics contain violence, misogyny, sexism, and homophobia. One must come to terms with these qualities when studying the formal elements of rap's poetry. As Tricia Rose observes in *The Hip Hop Wars* (2008), discussions of rap's content are increasingly reductive and politicized, with neither detractors nor defenders willing to engage in fruitful debate. "The hyperbolic and polarized public conversation about hip hop that has emerged over the past decade," she writes, "discourages progressive and nuanced consumption, participation, and critique, thereby contributing to the very crisis that is facing hip hop."[8] The purpose of this anthology is not to adjudicate such matters, but to present rap's lyrics in such a way that these discussions about content and value might be better grounded and contextualized.

Rap is a reflection of a broader culture that too often sanctions the same sexism, homophobia, and violence found in the music. By including lyrics with such content, we present occasions to challenge pernicious influences by confronting them directly rather than simply pretending they aren't there. At the same time, studying lyrics of targeted offense offers occasions to underscore the often-overlooked fact that hip-hop has formulated its own critiques of sexism, misogyny, and violence. "Most successful female MCs recognize that for them the only place where they can negotiate race, class, gender, and sexuality with relative freedom is the hiphop world," writes Marcyliena Morgan, describing one such homegrown response to hip-hop's own failings. "It is not an ideal space but rather one populated by those searching for discourse that confronts power."[9]

In addition to instances of sexism and misogyny, readers are urged to consider ways that rap's default tone of aggression might promote harmful attitudes toward women. Is hip-hop inherently unwelcoming to women, even when the lyrics are not specifically targeting them? Is there something in the very spirit or attitude of rap that can be identified as misogynist? These are important questions to ask as we seek to expand the discussion of gender in rap beyond the conventional critique of rap's overt sexism and use of derogatory language. In addition, we should explore how women artists have expanded rap to embody their own voices. Are artists like Lil' Kim and Foxy Brown, who flaunt their sexuality in a manner similar to their male counterparts, doing subversive and revolutionary work or are they simply succumbing to commercial pressures or adhering to the template established by many young men who've made rap their own? "It's up to female rappers to stand strong to create the yin and yang in this music," says Medusa, the Los Angeles–based underground MC. "There's a lack of connection with the male and female energy."[10]

Similarly, hip-hop culture is often hostile to the very idea of homosexuality. Though there are openly gay MCs in hip-hop's underground (e.g., Medusa, Deep Dickollective), to date there are no openly gay rappers who have made it into the mainstream. That said, rap lyrics offer rich ground for discussions of sexuality, particularly in its relation to masculinity. What are the broader implications of a hip-hop culture that sanctions, supports, and extends certain negative characteristics of young male behavior? What progressive futures suggest themselves that might redress rap's wrongs?

Such questions are crucial, but they are not the only ones to be asked; nor should the heated debates, deep concerns, and political posturing that often revolve around hip-hop culture obscure the music's other sides. The lyrics in this book were selected to demonstrate beyond a doubt that rap embodies the full range of human experience, not simply the brash and offensive content often associated with hip-hop in the public imagination. Rap is more than the sum of its offenses; it is a testament to human creativity at work.

Principles of Selection

The Anthology of Rap documents the tradition of rap written and performed in English, most often in the United States, over the course of four decades. Though it is not the first collection of rap lyrics, it is the first anthology of rap compiled with the specific intention of studying the lyrics as poetry. We have endeavored to include those indispensable lyrics that define the body of rap at the present time, lyrics whose formal virtuosity, thematic interest, or both merit preservation and sustained study.

The publication of an anthology is a potential moment of danger for any art form because it necessitates categorization and containment. For a tradition as dynamic as rap, this is a particular concern. Rap inherently resists such categorization; it denies our best efforts to define it and fix it under our critical gaze. As sociologist and cultural critic Oliver Wang observes, "So much of hip-hop's history has involved crushing canons."[11] We offer this anthology, therefore, fully aware of the limitations of any effort to render rap's lyrical legacy. Its publication is by no means the last word on rap's poetry but rather is the inauguration of a dialogue about what matters in rap lyrics.

Selecting lyrics for this anthology required a different set of criteria from, say, compiling the greatest mix tape in hip-hop history or naming the hundred most influential rap songs of all time. A collection of the greatest *songs* in rap history would differ substantially from the contents of an anthology that looks at rap *lyrics* as poetry and at rappers as poets. Great songs are more than just lyrics; indeed, sometimes great songs rely on the lyrics being unobtrusive and unremarkable.

Our lyrical selections aim to strike a balance among several competing interests. The most difficult challenge was in establishing the final table of contents. To do so, we began with a set of selection criteria. Each lyric included had to meet at least one of the following standards: (1) Does the song contribute to an accurate representation of hip-hop's lyrical history? (2) Does the song display lyrical excellence that is observable on the page? (3) Does the song help contribute to the fuller understanding of an individual artist's poetic range and development?

In terms of the first category, well-known and rightfully celebrated songs like Public Enemy's "Fight the Power" or Grandmaster Flash & the Furious Five's "The Message" have a place in this anthology both on their merits as poetry and for their wide-ranging influence on hip-hop culture. The anthology also includes songs whose historical import necessitates their inclusion even if their lyrical quality or explicit language and subject matter might render their selection controversial, such as Lil' Kim's "Queen Bitch" or Too $hort's "Cusswords." In addition, we have included lyrics to songs that are representative of particular historical moments, regional styles, themes, or elements of poetic form. The Sugarhill Gang's "Rapper's Delight" has playful and even rudimentary lyrics that might not distinguish it as cutting-edge poetry, but its broader cultural influence as rap's first mainstream hit makes it indispensable to the story of rap poetics.

Since this is an anthology that considers rap as poetry, it places heightened emphasis on those songs that distinguish themselves for their poetic interest. The second criterion, therefore, is observable excellence—granting, of course, that excellence in lyric poetry comes in a wide variety of forms as defined by a wide range of people. A song like Common's "I Used to Love H.E.R.," for instance, is notable for its ambitious extended metaphor. Lauryn Hill's "Lost Ones" stands out for the sharpness and innovation of her rhymes. Juvenile's "Ha" calls attention to itself in the incantatory nature of its repetition. The quality of these lyrics is apparent on the page alone, without even hearing their superb performances. This evaluative category also explains the inclusion of certain songs that never achieved widespread popularity, but that we believe merit close consideration.

The third category underscores the importance of encompassing the full range of a given artist's work. This means that certain songs might be included for their representative significance at the expense of other songs of perhaps greater aesthetic achievement. For example, one could make the argument for including every song from Nas's classic debut album, *Illmatic*. That said, the anthology has a more compelling interest in representing a comprehensive selection of Nas's lyrics from across his long career. So though we might wish to include "One Love" over, say, "Black President" on lyrical merit alone, the more recent song tells a fuller story of Nas's stylistic development.

Generally, artists with long careers garner more lyrics. Yet there are special cases in which the importance of an artist to the tradition demands what might be considered a disproportionate emphasis on that artist's work. For instance, though the Notorious B.I.G. recorded only two studio albums before his death, his impact on hip-hop and popular culture exceeds many artists who have enjoyed longer careers and greater total output; thus the number of his songs that are included is meant to be roughly commensurate with his contribution.

Though the majority of the MCs featured in this anthology are the authors of their own lyrics, in some instances the writer and performer are distinct. Grandmaster Flash & the Furious Five's "The Message," for instance, includes lyrics by the song's performer, Melle Mel, and by a songwriter, Duke Bootee. Big Daddy Kane began his rap career writing lyrics for his label mates Biz Markie and Roxanne Shanté. Run-DMC wrote some of the verses on the Beastie Boys' debut album. The importance of these artists to rap's history is undiminished by the fact that they did not author all of their rhymes.

Ghostwriting, the practice of one artist supplying lyrics for another to perform, has been around since rap's beginnings. However, given the audience's expectation that rappers' words should be their own, it has almost always been transacted behind the scenes. Rap lyrics are so closely associated with the identity of the artist that the idea of a distinction between writer and performer seems counterintuitive. Nonetheless, rap is in its essence a collaborative art form, from the tapestry of its densely layered samples to its borrowed lyrical riffs and references. For the purposes of this anthology, we have elected to include all lyrics under the names of their performers. We do this for both practical and aesthetic reasons. Practically, we recognize the impossibility of discerning with absolute certainty which artists wrote their own lyrics and which did not. Aesthetically, we believe that the act of performance constitutes a kind of composition; though the Beastie Boys, for instance, did not compose all the verses on "Paul Revere," their distinctive voices and deliveries shape the song and remain in our memory, even when the lyrics are brought back to the page.

As a rule, however, this anthology emphasizes poetry over performance. This is not, after all, a collection of lyrics from rap's greatest hits, but rather a collection of rap's best poetry. Some of the biggest hits in hip-hop history include lyrics that are undistinguished. MC Hammer's "U Can't Touch This" had one of the most infectious hooks of the 1990s; anyone listening to the radio at that time undoubtedly can recite the lyrics, no matter how much they might now distance themselves from the song. Hammer's album went platinum many times over and helped launch hip-hop into the realm of popular music, but considering "U Can't Touch This" for its poetic merits misses the point of the song. Many hit songs derive their appeal from performance rather than language; the substance and structure of the lyrics play a secondary role to the pop-ready hooks, catchy samples, and banging beats. To offer the lyrics alone in such cases would do an injustice to the songs themselves, to sap them of their vitality and value as popular entertainment. It would also do a disservice to the songs included in this anthology, whose lyrics better reward close attention.

For every song we include, there are likely a dozen others that we might also have selected. The purpose of this anthology, however, is not to be exhaustive, but rather to represent in a readable fashion the full depth and quality of rap from its roots to the present. We encourage readers to consider these selections as a starting point for further discussions of rap's poetry. And we hope that this anthology inspires others to compile their own collections of rap lyrics.

We regret that limitations of space and focus do not allow us to delve into the rich territory of rap outside the United States. Though we include a few lyrics by Canadian and British MCs, we have consciously chosen not to include artists from other parts of the world—continental Europe, Asia, Africa, the countries of the African diaspora, and South America among them. Only an anthology dedicated to global hip-hop could do justice to these rich traditions of innovation. Indeed, much of hip-hop culture today thrives outside the United States. We hope that such a collection will soon emerge.

One of the challenges in compiling an anthology of this scale is the practical matter of acquiring lyric permissions. Artists and labels maintain a financial interest in the song lyrics and command compensation. Acquiring permissions can become a costly, time-consuming, sometimes Kafkaesque process. A single song may have as many as a half dozen or more copyright holders, each of whom is owed some percentage of the total compensation. Often, these individuals are difficult if not impossible to contact. We have made every effort to reach all individual copyright holders for each of the songs we include. Some readers may bemoan the absence of certain classic songs, songs that logically should belong in this anthology. In such cases, there is a good chance that the reasons for not including the lyric have something to do with the practical matter of being denied the proper permissions. We are grateful to those artists and labels that facilitated our attempt to honor their impact on rap.

The Anthology's Structure

This anthology is structured to encourage a historical understanding of rap's development even as it underscores the importance of rap's distinguishing formal qualities and dominant themes. The book is divided into four historical sections, each with an introduction describing the major developments of that period. These four periods are simply a practical means of organizing the material; rap's artistic development is organic, defying attempts at periodization.

Within each section, lyrics are organized alphabetically by artist, with brief headnotes for each MC or group outlining stylistic characteristics and thematic concerns. Artists whose careers span multiple periods—such as LL Cool J, who has released music in all but the earliest period—are situated in the time period in which they were most visible and productive. The lyrics of MCs with careers both as part of a group and as solo artists are situated in the period in which most of the work appeared.

Part One contains lyrics dating from 1978 to 1984, rap's formative years, in which the art of MCing began taking shape and rap made its first appearance on radio. This is the period of rap's pioneers, particularly the founding triumvirate of DJ Kool Herc, Afrika Bambaataa, and Grandmaster Flash, the style shapers and taste makers who helped guide an organic cultural movement into an emerging popular form.

Part Two, spanning 1985 to 1992, is described by many as rap's "golden age," a term the anthology holds up to scrutiny even as it celebrates the unquestionable innovation and excellence of the artists of this period. This is the period when rap began spreading from East Coast to West Coast and also when it first pierced the consciousness of most of the country. Some of the best-known and most-respected artists in rap's history emerged in these years, from Run-DMC to Rakim, Public Enemy to De La Soul, Ice-T to NWA. This period ends with the emergence of what was popularly termed "gangsta rap," which sparked the first national controversies about rap's explicit content.

Part Three, from 1993 to 1999, encompasses rap's emergence as the dominant genre in American popular music and the rapid spread of rap music and hip-hop culture around the globe. It is punctuated by the rise and fall of two of rap's most important voices, 2Pac and the Notorious B.I.G. It also includes classic contributions from some of rap's distinctive figures, including Nas, Jay-Z, The Fugees, and The Roots.

The final section, Part Four, follows rap's development from 2000 to

2010. This period has witnessed the effects brought upon rap by rapid changes in the music industry, the influence of digital technology, and the cementing of rap as a multinational commercial force even as its domestic popularity seems to have reached a plateau. Together, these four periods serve as approximations of rap's historical course.

Editorial Procedures

Making an anthology is a collective effort. We began by putting together an advisory board of some of the leading figures in hip-hop culture and poetry—journalists, scholars, poets, and DJs (see page xxi). After assembling a provisional table of contents, we solicited suggestions from these advisers concerning the collection's form and content. They provided a rich array of suggestions, even down to particular lines in particular songs. We set to collating and digesting all of this feedback, ultimately arriving at a radically revised and expanded table of contents that we circulated again for final comment.

The most significant change that came directly as a result of the advisory board's suggestions was the conscious expansion of the coverage and commentary on the role of women in the rise of rap lyricism. This meant not simply giving due credit to the major female artists in hip-hop's history, but also considering more broadly the role of women in the culture, in both the introductory essays and the artist headnotes. The result, we believe, is a rendering of women in rap that doesn't distort their contribution, but rather acknowledges their fundamental influence in shaping the culture.

This anthology reflects hip-hop's gender imbalance inasmuch as the vast majority of the artists it includes are men. We highlight the vital contributions of key female MCs, but we believe it would be cynical to make a show of equity where none exists. The relative dearth of recognized women MCs is a troubling fact, particularly when one considers that, if anything, the place of female artists in the hip-hop mainstream may actually have diminished over the past decade. Hip-hop's future lies in the expansion rather than retraction of its voices; women must play a central role in this future development, not simply as consumers but as creators of the music.

Another significant change brought on by the advisory board was the decision to include as many full lyrical transcriptions as possible for the selected songs. The verse, more than the song, is rap's basic unit of poetic expression. That said, there is often significant value to the contextual understanding that a full transcription provides.

On Transcription

Studying rap's poetic form necessitates the existence of carefully transcribed lyrics from across hip-hop's tradition. Only with an accurate transcription, attentive to everything from deciphering individual words to establishing formal matters like line breaks and punctuation, is it possible to glean the poetic structure of a lyric.

The most significant effort to record rap lyrics to date is not in a book but online, in the numerous user-generated lyric databases launched in recent years. The OHHLA is the most comprehensive. One can find nearly every rap song imaginable with a few keystrokes. However, these transcriptions are often so flawed that they are of limited use for anything more than a casual perusal. This volume responds to an unmet need for accurate transcriptions, voiced so clearly by the thousands of people who care enough about rap to post lyrics, however imperfect, online. Of course, flawless transcriptions are nearly impossible to achieve; undoubtedly small errors remain in even the most scrupulous efforts, ours included. However, readers can rest assured that the lyrics included here have been meticulously vetted, sometimes by the artists themselves.

Though often starting as lyrics written in a book of rhymes, rap's final form as oral poetry makes for a number of challenges when it comes to presenting words on the page. Rap lyrics share with medieval ballads the pattern of first being performed before being presented for public consumption in written form. Those who wish to transcribe a song face the immediate challenge of comprehension: Can you decipher all the words? Particularly for rap, can you comprehend the slang? Next is the challenge of orthography: How do you represent the distinctive sound and accent of someone's speech? Do you resort to deliberate misspellings to capture, for instance, the difference between the artist saying "singin" rather than "singing"? The final matter for transcription is one of form: Where do you break the line? What are the basic structures upon which rap songs are forged?

Many of the transcriptions found online tend to follow a practice in which the line break signals a pause in the rapper's delivery. Whenever the flow stops, the line breaks. Another method involves transcribing as one would with musical notation—with the eighth note, quarter note, half note, and whole note. Both of these methods have a certain intuitive logic, but both go against the method most MCs employ when writing their lyrics to a beat.

Most MCs compose their lines with beat and song structure in mind.

This anthology follows a principle of transcription that takes its cue from rap's lyrical relationship in rhythm to the beat. Each measure (or bar) in a typical rap song consists of four beats, and a lyric line consists of the words one can deliver in the space of that bar. Therefore, one musical bar is equal to one line of verse. This description fits the way that rappers themselves most often talk about their lyrics. "I used to get the legal pad," the Long Beach MC Crooked I recalls, "and I used to write each bar as one line, so at the end, 16 lines, 16 bars."[12] When rappers say they're going to "spit sixteen," they mean that they are going to rap for sixteen bars, or sixteen written lines. Preserving this fundamental relationship makes it possible to discern a host of formal qualities in the verse. It allows us to distinguish between end rhymes and internal rhymes, to appreciate effective enjambment, to note the caesural pauses within lines, and to perceive a host of formal elements that might otherwise escape notice.

When MCs talk among themselves, they often talk about matters of poetic and musical craft—about syllables and bars, varieties of rhyme and rhythmic cadences, breath control and vocal intonation, metaphors and similes. As Mos Def rhymes on "Hip Hop," "I write a rhyme, sometimes won't finish for days / Scrutinize my literature from the large to the miniature / I mathematically add-minister, subtract the wack." This consciousness of craft is apparent in recent books such as Paul Edwards's *How to Rap*, with its rich array of interviews with old school and new school artists; stic.man of dead prez's *The Art of Emceeing*, in which the rapper breaks down the tools of his lyrical trade; and Brian Coleman's *Check the Technique*, in which rappers address their artistic process in creating particular albums. These and other books like them testify to the attention MCs direct to matters of language and sound, discussions that often get drowned out by the more controversial elements of hip-hop culture. Reading them reminds us that whatever else rap is, it is also poetic expression.

Reading rap will never be the same as listening to it, but it retains an essential value all its own. "Rap lyrics are important to analyze and dissect," Chuck D explains, "because they offer a way to look at society from a perspective rarely taken seriously. . . . Many Hip Hop lyricists have jewels woven deep down in the meanings of certain songs, but the whole duty of Hip Hop is firstly, writing, and secondly, to get the song across, and a lot of times artists are more focused on how to get it across so that the substance, reasoning, and metaphors that have been written into the rhymes get overlooked."[13] The goal of this anthology is to ensure that these lyrical jewels are not overlooked but instead are allowed to shine.

1978–1984

The Old School

The term *old school* has been applied to almost anything with a hint of history. For all of its applications, though, the term resonates most loudly in hip-hop. The old school is always audible when listening to rap. We hear it in direct references and recycled verses, or in glancing lyrical gestures and tendencies of rhyme.

No art is likely to survive without assimilating, critiquing, and transforming its past. It advances itself in time and in its range of aesthetic strategies with constant reference to what has come before. Rap has a particular genius for handling its own history. Even so, aging hip-hop heads sometimes decry just how little younger listeners know about the music's foundations. But since the current incarnation of rap music always contains those foundations, however submerged, it would be more accurate to say that rap's youngest listeners often don't *know* that they already know a lot about the old school.

To activate this knowledge, one need do only a little digging to discover the original recordings. Listen to Common's 2008 single "Universal Mind Control" and hear Afrika Bambaataa's 1983 old school classic "Looking for the Perfect Beat." Listen to Wale's 2009 single "Chillin" and hear the Audio Two's 1987 hit "Top Billin'." Whether or not we are aware of it, examples abound in which the old school lives on in the new.

Through overuse and nostalgia, the term *old school* can congeal into an abstraction that distances us from the immediacy of the actual music. Those artists who created the first rap recordings, of course, saw themselves as far from "old," either in age (most were in their teens or early twenties) or in art. Quite the contrary, the rap we now call "old school" was avant-garde. As Spoonie Gee and the Treacherous Three put it in the title of a 1980 song, what they were creating was the "New Rap Language."

When hip-hop culture as we know it was first stirring in the early 1970s, it was activated not by MCs, but by DJs spinning records and by dancers (later called b-boys and b-girls) responding to the music. The man most often mentioned as the sonic originator of hip-hop is DJ Kool Herc. In 1967, a twelve-year-old Herc immigrated to New York City from Jamaica. By 1973 he was spinning new sounds—most notably for the future of hip-hop, soulful tracks with powerful instrumental breaks—at 1520 Sedgwick Avenue in the Bronx. Because this first, humble venue was the recreation room at the community center in his apartment building, it wasn't long before the increasingly popular DJ found his chosen space too crowded. That's when Herc packed up and moved the gatherings outside to the block party. Around 1974–75 he began playing at a Bronx club called the Twilight Zone and continued his career by headlining shows and parties across the city as the burgeoning hip-hop underground took shape around him.

Kool Herc had a great impact on several of the figures who would make the first rap recordings, especially on such foundational DJs as Afrika Bambaataa and Grandmaster Flash. Unlike Bambaataa and Flash, however—both of whom, while cutting their chops as young DJs and group leaders, were associated with a crew of talented MCs—Kool Herc began before the MC had become a well-defined figure in the hip-hop sound. Herc himself would sometimes voice a few phrases, having been influenced both by the tradition of Jamaican toasting and by the on-air patter of New York radio DJs such as Cousin Brucie. But the main man on the microphone at a Kool Herc show was Coke La Rock. For many members of the first generation of hip-hop artists who went to a Kool Herc party, their initial exposure to the rudiments of the MC's art was hearing Coke La Rock's minimalist phrases and rhymes. Kool DJ Red Alert, who was a DJ in Bambaataa's Zulu Nation crew before becoming an important hip-hop radio DJ, remembers La Rock saying such phrases as "You rock and you don't stop" and "Rock on, my mellow."[1]

In addition to Coke La Rock, Herc's crew included Clark Kent and Timmy Tim. Kid Creole of the Furious Five recalls such phrases used by the so-called Herculoids as "On down to the last stop" and "More than what you paid at the door,"[2] while Creole's brother and fellow Furious Five member Melle Mel recalls two yet more extended verses by Timmy Tim, one incorporating an echo effect and the other matching the words to the music being mixed by his DJ:

The sounds that you hear-hear-hear

Def to your ear-ear-ear

'Cause you have no fear-fear-fear

'Cause Herc is here-here-here

We're going to give you a little taste of the bass

We're going to hit you with the highs

"They all rapped but not on the beat," Mel recalls.[3] Nevertheless, the impact of the Herculoids crew on future rappers was formative. When asked who was the first performer he saw who rapped in the sense that we now know the term, Kool Herc named Kid Creole and Melle Mel. Yet these pioneers acknowledge their early lyrical work as an extension of the Herculoid sound. "We used to listen to Kool Herc and them," Mel has said of himself and Creole. "They used to say things like 'And yes, y'all, the sound that you hear . . .' They were always saying 'and yes, y'all.' We really liked that, so we used it. So we would take that and lengthen it, and say it to the beat. So it would be, 'A yes, yes, y'all, to the beat, y'all, freak, freak, y'all.' We went to all of Herc's parties and studied their shit[.] We studied their format just like people would later study us; that's how we studied Herc."[4]

Along with their first partner in rhyme—Cowboy (the late Keith Wiggins), especially skilled at stoking crowd participation—Kid Creole and Melle Mel took the collective "y'all" and made it both more collective and more connective. That is, they brought the crowd into the proceedings even more by developing techniques of call and response; they initiated intrasong lyrical interplay among the group; and they shifted discrete phraseology into "flow," a virtually nonstop movement of responsive rhyming and syncopated lyricism. This latter innovation was an organic response to the music that both acknowledged the DJ's centrality and elevated the MC to an equal partner in sound.

Like any DJ, the hip-hop DJ mixed together a variety of sounds in a more or less continuous chain. However, for the most part he was playing instrumental sections of songs—and often instrumentally sparse sections at that, extending the part of the song called the "break" that was most rhythmically pronounced and least lyrically packed, by mixing together two copies of the same record. The MCs thus had ample space to fill and an impetus to fill it in a way that made musical sense in relation to the sonic environment. The MC's continuity of rhymes mimicked the continuous flow of the DJ, whose musical selections gave the MC an instrumental space to occupy. This fashioned a dual rhythmic relationship of beat and voice, the fundamental relationship in all rap music.

The block party, community center, and school gymnasium–based movement in the Bronx that spurred Cowboy, Kid Creole, Melle Mel, and, simultaneously or soon thereafter, dozens of others to start to rap had another genealogical line—namely, in twenty-one-and-over dance clubs that catered to a slightly older and more "upscale" black clientele. In the early to mid-1970s, several DJs who played disco primarily in parts of the city other than the Bronx developed elaborate spiels for their sets—indeed, they elevated the DJ's patter to the status of rap. Names such as Pete DJ Jones and Grandmaster Flowers were known throughout the boroughs, and there was much cross-pollination between the musical lines—Jones played in midtown Manhattan but also had a following in the Bronx; Flowers was from Brooklyn but was renowned for a sound system that often played Central Park.

Other DJs such as Lovebug Starski, Eddie Cheba, and DJ Hollywood began to mix into their disco and R & B sets the nascent hip-hop sound. None of these men went on to have a substantial recording career, accounting for about half a dozen singles among them, but they were popular as professional DJs. Cheba and Hollywood played for several years at Club 371, one of the most profitable Bronx dance clubs of the era, and Hollywood shared the marquee at the Apollo Theater with such acts as The Spinners and Harold Melvin and the Blue Notes.

Until fall 1979, when the first rap songs were released commercially on records, the only way to hear the music, aside from attending a live show, was to listen to a cassette tape recording of a live show. These tapes were passed around and even sold in a kind of underground art economy. In fact, several years after the release of rap records began in 1979, the live tape was still popular with listeners who wanted to experience the raw event of real-time music being made in front of a crowd. For some, the very idea of a rap record was inconceivable given the nature of the rap performance. "I'm like, a record?" recalls Eddie Cheba. "Fuck, how you gon' put hip-hop onto a record? 'Cause it was a whole gig, you know? How you gon' put *three hours* on a record?"[5] One tape that serves as a hinge between eras and that illustrates early style in rap is a recording of a performance late in 1979 at the Armory in Jamaica, Queens, that featured, among other performers, Cheba and DJ Hollywood. Such shows had multiple participants and the goal was to last for hours into the night. Although they were more than a half-decade into their careers at this stage, and thus the transcriptions included in this volume cannot be taken as representative of their earliest phases (which are unavailable on tape), Cheba and Hollywood in their lyrics still give us a strong sense of how the dance club DJ in a disco era handled the mic.

The first excerpt from the Armory tape (see "Live at the Armory 1979 [1]") transcribes four minutes of Cheba's performance. In the recording, his rap is backed by the break from Cheryl Lynn's "Got to Be Real." The reminder at the end of the excerpt, which pertains to Cheba's show the following night at the Manhattan club Harlem World, is a telling moment. At the time of the Armory performance, Sugarhill Gang's record "Rapper's Delight" had been out for only a few weeks yet it already had changed the landscape of rap. The Sugarhill Gang were not regarded by most practicing rappers as totally authentic, given that they had not honed their skills in public performance in the parks and the clubs. Yet their record, which contained rhymes that had been used in public by such MCs as Cheba, Hollywood, and especially Grandmaster Caz of the Cold Crush Brothers, was surprisingly popular with the record-buying public. A combination of artistic proprietary rights, skepticism about the technological shift to professional recording, and maybe even a touch of resentment over another artist's success can be read into the warning that "we got some unfinished business with Sugarhill"—which is also a reminder that art among artists is a competitive business.

Rap would take creative competition to elaborate and impressive levels. Cheba, however, is no battle rapper, and his performance is less about challenging another MC's name than it is about asserting his own; in under four minutes he repeats it fifteen times. There are also other forms of self-identification—such as his height (five feet nine and one-half inches) and the sexually inflected fact that he is "bowlegged"—as he tells us "who I am and what I do." There is little figurative language aside from the initial simile comparing the dancers to an eel and from Cheba's name itself, which (since "cheeba" is a synonym for marijuana) lets us know that the man means to get the crowd high. He employs several methods in trying to do so. For instance, he connects what he is saying to the music, announcing the record being played like the good DJ he also is. (The first four lines of the excerpt are a cappella and only after he says "It's time for you to be real" does his DJ begin playing "Got to Be Real.") He acknowledges the crowd in terms of location—the Armory was in Jamaica, Queens—and with a little bit of flattery: "Jamaica, y'all sound real good." He urges the crowd to do a new dance (the "Jack Benny") and peppers his patter with pedagogical pushes ("while I tell you how," "I'll tell you when") and the kinds of urging that would not be out of place from an aerobics instructor or drill sergeant ("Do it, do it, do-do-do it").

The rhyming that becomes synonymous with rap is here still rudimentary. Cheba has two ways to distribute his rhymes against the four-beat measures (or bars). One way is to have a rhyming couplet in which the two lines of the couplet correspond to two four-beat bars. Two such couplets that Cheba raps are familiar to any fan of hip-hop:

> You can dip, dive, or socialize
> Either way we gonna make your nature rise
>
> Raise your hands in the air
> Wave 'em like you just don't care

In one extended passage, Cheba connects his couplets not only by the final rhymes, but also by a repetitive structure at the beginning of the bars that further accentuates the couplets and links them in a rhetorical relationship of cause and effect:

> When the Cheba-Cheba's doing the do
> I'll work your body black and blue
> When the Cheba-Cheba's in the house
> I'll talk mo' shit than Mickey Mouse
> When the Cheba-Cheba decides to quit
> Everybody in the house would just say
> Awwwwww—
> Shiiiiiiiiit!

After setting up an expectation with the "When/I'll—When/I'll" pattern, he extends the anticipated two-bar couplet into four bars before closing the stanzaic unit (with the "shit" that rhymes with "quit"). Because Cheba begins with bar-filling lines that contain between eight and ten syllables in the initial couplets, the effect, when he fills the final two bars with only one syllable each, is to slow us down; for although the musical backing has not changed its tempo, the less propulsive (and thus variable) play of onrushing syllables at the end operates against the regularity of the musical beat. This change in *lyrical* tempo also marks a change in the total flow of the performance, before segueing into the next run of rhyming and call-and-response.

Cheba's other pattern is similar in its rhyme scheme to a standard ballad stanza—that is, a quatrain in which the second and fourth lines are rhymed and the first and third lines are unrhymed (designated *abcb* in prosodic terms). As opposed to his rhyming couplets, Cheba's *abcb* arrangement gives the listener a less dense sonic texture. Because most of the poetic work in this early rap is being done by the end rhymes, to distribute those rhymes at half the frequency as occurs in a string of couplets is also to alter the lyrical tempo. Thus, by alternating between the couplets and the ballad style, Cheba gives the crowd some formal and temporal variety despite the uniform simplicity of the content.

The next excerpt from the Armory show (see "Live at the Armory 1979 [2]") transcribes eight minutes of Hollywood's performance. In the recording, while Hollywood raps, Lovebug Starski serves as DJ and is mixing "Good Times," by Chic. Hollywood shares with Cheba several techniques: self-naming and self-description, the exhortation of the crowd, the introduction of a current dance, and the integration of his lyrics with the specific song being played by the DJ. This latter aspect of the MC's art reminds us of the close relationship between the MC and the DJ, as does Hollywood's first spoken interlude, which refers to the best known of the pre-hip-hop radio DJs whose patter was proto-rap: "If Wolfman Jack was here, he'd try to tell you to get one of those fine, foxy mamas, something like this, he might say: 'That's right, Clyde, got something good for your hide, something to keep you satisfied, talking about some heavy . . . medicine.'" Hollywood delivers these final lines in gravelly voiced and vowel-stretched imitation of the "Wolfman" (whose real name was Robert Smith), a rock and roll DJ who developed his hip-talking persona in the 1960s. Radio DJs with a wide listenership such as Jack, Cousin Brucie, and Frankie Crocker—a flamboyant and influential R & B DJ at New York's WBLS, whose nicknames included "Hollywood" and "Chief Rocker"—as well as numerous lesser known local on-air DJs, served as early examples for the hip-hop world of how to integrate music and words.

As in the Cheba excerpt, we find in the Hollywood excerpt a few different patterns of rhyme distribution. There are the couplets in the form of old standbys—"I said dippy-dippy-dive, so-socialize / Just-a come on and make my nature rise"; "Just throw your hands up in the air / Wave 'em around like you just don't care"—as well as the *abcb* pattern distributed over four bars:

> Said the disco lights and boogie nights
> Are really here to stay
> Sexy mamas and fancy papas
> Always want to play

Here is a variation on the ballad stanza as Hollywood, in addition to the
end rhymes in lines two and four, brings internal rhyme to lines one and
three: "lights/nights," "mamas/papas." The internal rhymes are balanced so
that the lines in which they occur are split into two parallel parts, with
"and" serving as a hinge. Hollywood at first seems to continue this pattern
of an internally rhymed line *a* that will lead to the *abcb* pattern; he then resists the expectation he has established in order to move with one variation
back into a series of couplets:

> With iron nerves I'm prepared to serve—
> A sugar-coated, red electric
> Super-freaky crumb off a disco cake
> To make you shake and bake

By leading us to expect a rhyme scheme that never develops, while string-
ing us along with a series of adjectives that move us across one line and into
the next, Hollywood gives us the sense of a run-on line, of enjambment,
meaning that a line-ending lacks any strong pause or clear stopping point.
This is especially interesting given that almost all the lines in early rap are
essentially "end-stopped" either by a rhyme or by the completion of a unit
of meaning; in rap's later stages, MCs are more adept at varying between
end-stopped and enjambed lines.

There is also in the Hollywood excerpt a fair amount of figurative language: the "disco cake" metaphor, the "battery" metaphor ("not a Duracell"
but "an alkaline"), the "bowl of soup" simile, and the comparison to "the
hot butter on your morning toast." This latter simile is a variation on another comparison that is ubiquitous in early rap in which the MC compares
himself to hot butter on popcorn. This comparison, which Cheba claims to
have invented, is doubtless derived from James Brown, who recorded a
number of songs—"The Popcorn," "Mother Popcorn," "Mashed Potato
Popcorn," "Popcorn with a Feeling," and "Let a Man Come In and Do the
Popcorn" among them—meant both to illustrate and to provide musical
backing for a once-popular dance called "The Popcorn" and variations
thereon. The popcorn/butter simile is so ubiquitous in early rap that it be-

came a tool for crowd participation, as everyone listening knew how the simile would end. When the MC would begin a couplet with a line like, "Rock on, to the break of dawn," and then start the next line with, "Like hot butter on the what?" the crowd would respond, "Popcorn!"

Another pronounced pattern in the nascent hip-hop scene was the growth of multimember groups centered around one or two DJs. We might call this not the radio or disco DJ model, but the DJ Kool Herc model. Initially the DJ was a bigger star than the MC and thus the MCs orbited around him. Some groups, like Cold Crush Brothers and the Funky Four + 1, had two DJs and a host of supporting MCs; some, like Afrika Bambaataa's various collectives, centered around one charismatic figure who also made space for younger DJs and a rotating crew of MCs. Another familiar model was groups consisting of one virtuoso DJ and a crew of MCs usually ranging in number from three to five, as in Grandmaster Flash and the Furious Five or Grand Wizard Theodore and the Fantastic Five.

This model of the rap group was both star-centered (the DJ) and collective (the MCs). That arrangement began to shift somewhat as standout MCs developed within the groups. For the most part, it is true, the various MCs within a group were not easily distinguishable in terms of lyrical content. Perhaps slightly different personas would be put on, such as that of the Fantastic Five's Kevie Kev, who also went by "Waterbed Kevie Kev" to signify his prowess as a lover; or perhaps a particular member would be considered especially good at a bedrock skill, such as Furious Five member Cowboy's strength at crowd exhortation. But a more significant development in terms of lyrical artistry in rap was the rise of certain virtuoso MCs within the group context—one thinks especially of Melle Mel of the Furious Five, Kool Moe Dee of the Treacherous Three, and Caz of the Cold Crush Brothers. The fact that Mel and Caz both took the honorific "grandmaster," the likes of which had previously been reserved only for DJs such as Flash and Theodore, is one sign of a subtle but significant shift in focus from the DJ to the MC in the late 1970s and early 1980s.

The biggest shift, however, was the advent of commercially recorded rap in 1979. Everything changed once rap made the move to studio recordings that could then be pressed onto vinyl and widely distributed. The first such release was Fatback's "King Tim III (Personality Jock)." When the funk band Fatback asked a radio DJ from Harlem, Tim Washington, whose handle was King Tim the Third, to rhyme over a track that in its nascent stages was called "Catch the Beat," the result was a song released late in the summer of 1979 and now credited as the first commercial, studio-recorded rap release. But it was the Sugarhill Gang's "Rapper's Delight," released a few weeks later, that truly marked rap's emergence as a commercially viable recorded art form. The song became so wildly successful that it was soon followed by a host of others.

The template of these songs only partially followed what had heretofore happened during a rap performance. For although many of the recorded rhymes were the same as their stage-show versions, the figure who before had been central—the DJ—was now relegated to a leader mainly in name. The DJ was not recorded in his element doing his mix-and-scratch thing. (The one major exception, "Grandmaster Flash on the Wheels of Steel" [1980], proves the rule.) Rather, in-house studio funk bands recreated the extension of a break. Whereas before a DJ would have mixed the break from between two copies of, say, Chic's "Good Times," now a band would lay down in the studio a ten-minute backing track consisting of an instrumental version approximating the extended break. Over this the rappers would rap, which, while hardly making the DJ obsolete, did shift attention to the MC.

The change also shifted attention to the commercial possibilities of rap. Established independent label owners began to release rap records, while many more new labels sprang up like mushrooms after a rain. Many lived only briefly, while some—like Sugar Hill Records, with its eye-catching candy-cane logo and ever-increasing stable of artists—thrived. Even major labels such as Mercury and Polydor got into the act. The story of production and distribution is an important one in understanding the eventual global reach of hip-hop. In a sense, rap ceased to be an "underground" phenomenon as soon as "Rapper's Delight" began selling hundreds of thousands of copies and as its immediate successors, if not always quite as successful, continued to disseminate the new sound.

And, despite its almost decade-long gestation period in the parks and clubs of New York, rap was a new sound indeed for the world at large. One way to measure the freshness of the music for the record-buying public is by the song titles of the first wave of record releases. Anything that is going to be sold needs to be categorized, and if the music is of a new genre, categorization is all the more imperative. The listener (and potential buyer) wants to know—or at least, initially, *name*—what he or she is listening to. The song titles helped the listener categorize what must have sounded like a mélange of disco, funk, poetry, and pop—something called "rap." The word had appeared sporadically in titles before, mostly to signify a soulful, spoken interlude in a song that was otherwise sung, but when rap music began to take commercially viable form on record, the word began its journey toward ubiquity. In the sixteen months between September 1979 and the end of 1980, dozens of songs were self-defined in their titles as "rap"—from admired tracks like Jimmy Spicer's "Adventures of Super Rhyme (Rap)" and Kurtis Blow's "Christmas Rappin'" to lesser-known recordings like Frederick Davies and Lewis Anton's "Astrology Rap" and Super Jay's "Santa's Rap Party."

This development follows patterns of popularization found in other kinds of music. The matter of whether to spell the new music's name "rap" or "rapp" in some titles reminds one of the occasional fluctuation early on between "jazz" and "jass," just as rock and roll was constantly naming itself as it began to get popular—"Jailhouse Rock," "Rock Around the Clock"—to categorize and attempt to distinguish it as a discrete musical entity.

As a new music comes into being, its status as "new" also leads to questions of whether songs in the new manner are essentially "novelty" songs. Anyone who was around to listen to rap in the early 1980s will remember the frequent claims that the music was a fad, a gimmick, a cheap trend destined to die a quick death. After more than thirty years of studio-recorded history, no reasonable person can hold this opinion; for while three decades is not so long in the great evolutionary scheme of things, it is a run of Methuselah-like persistence in the world of popular music. Still, something of the early anxiety over the seriousness and potential longevity of rap can be seen in the initial prevalence of rap novelty tracks. There were songs impersonating Jackie Gleason ("Honeymooner's Rap"), Sylvester Stallone ("Hambo—First Rap Part II"), and John Wayne ("Rappin' Duke"). There were songs about the National Basketball Association, ABC's *Monday Night Football,* the Los Angeles Lakers, and the Washington Redskins, as well as one performed in 1985 by the eventual Super Bowl champion Chicago Bears ("Super Bowl Shuffle"). There were songs that took their titles from puppets, video games, and cartoon characters such as Alf, E.T., Pac-Man, and the Smurfs. There was a "Haunted House of Rock" (in fact, a rap) and a "Groovy Ghost Party" rapped in the persona of Casper the Friendly Ghost. There were Fat Boys, Skinny Boys, and a ventriloquist rap duo called Wayne and Charlie (The Rapping Dummy). Even the comedian and director Mel Brooks recorded a rap called "It's Good to Be the King," which provoked a response record called "It's Good to Be the Queen" by Sugar Hill label owner Sylvia Robinson.

The epitome of the novelty trend in its most decadent phase remains the so-called Roxanne Wars of the mid-1980s, which began with a 12-inch

B-side called "Roxanne, Roxanne," by the group UTFO. That song spawned an answer from a teenager named Roxanne Shanté, after which the flood-gates opened and more answer songs appeared. There were songs about Roxanne's parents, her sister, her baby, her boyfriend, and her doctor. There were songs that described Roxanne as fat, as a cross-dresser, and as the inspiration for a dance. Some of these songs are fun and the whole saga is intriguing as a concept, but the only rapper involved to have a substantial career as a lyricist proved to be Roxanne Shanté.

The early 1980s also saw a profusion of space-based songs. Although a high percentage of these can be called novelty songs in a more or less pejorative sense, they were inspired by a song that certainly elevates itself above mere novelty—namely, "Planet Rock," by Afrika Bambaataa and the Soul Sonic Force. Bambaataa's song had a more computer-age sound than most of its rap predecessors and was evidence of the eclectic taste Bambaataa had been displaying live as a DJ for almost a decade. Influenced by the German electro-funk band Kraftwerk, "Planet Rock" was faster even than the brisk light funk that backed most early releases. Its edges were sharper and its underlying message was Utopian. (And to be genuinely Utopian, it took the sunlike presence of Afrika Bambaataa to keep the "planet rock" in orbit; most immediate attempts by others to follow the song's path were sonically apt but politically vacant.) The interstellar conceit also elevated the serious-ness of what is simultaneously one of the most perpetually playful songs in rap. Bambaataa was working with sonic and lyrical tropes that figured African Americans as alienated and thus as aliens, as people from another planet or galaxy—as had (among musicians) Sun-Ra before him, as would Outkast and many others after him. That this theme, and especially its electronic backdrop, spoke to people in a period of rapid technological, computer-based growth is not surprising. Its staying power perhaps has been surprising, as the sonic template Bambaataa crafted has made its mark on styles of music as diverse as house and Miami bass, and in more recent productions by producers such as Pharrell and Timbaland.

The interesting case of "Planet Rock" raises several more general questions about the status of the political in early rap. Is music made by a so-cially marginalized group necessarily political? Does popular music as a commercial medium tend to be inimical to political critique? Is all social critique political, and does description equal action? Certainly the reputation of rap's first years is that all of its songs were about dancing, parties, and having a good time, and there is much truth there. Whether this is good, bad, or something more ambiguous depends on one's perspective. A prosecutorial case is made in the lyrics of the most explicitly political of early rap songs, Brother D with Collective Effort's "How We Gonna Make the Black Nation Rise?" (1980), which critiqued the effects of the new music:

> Just move your body to the beat
> While it takes you on a disco ride
> Get high until you're pacified
> Now you're actin like the living dead
> Talkin 'bout the body, talkin 'bout the head
> Space out, y'all, to the disco rhyme
> You're movin to the rhythm but you're wastin time

Not all songs were without political content, although none at first were as definitive in their message as the words of Brother D. Songs such as Kurtis Blow's "Hard Times" or "The Breaks" did paint pictures in glimpses of the hardships of the urban poor, but their overtly didactic or corrective content was minimal. The best-known example of politicized early rap, "The Message," by Grandmaster Flash and the Furious Five, had a more powerful cumulative impact. The best-known verses in the song are these classic lines by Melle Mel:

> A child is born with no state of mind
> Blind to the ways of mankind
> God is smiling on you but he's frowning too
> Because only God knows what you'll go through
> You'll grow in the ghetto living second rate
> And your eyes will sing a song of deep hate
> The places you play and where you stay
> Looks like one great big alleyway

Melle Mel had been rapping these lines for years as a set piece in the Furious Five live show; they also appeared near the end of the group's first release, 1979's "Superrappin." Perhaps the sonic environment of that earlier track was not right for these bars to stick in the public's mind, and the replacement of a light funk with a harder, darker, more metallic sound on "The Message" buttressed the strength of the lines. Nevertheless, Melle Mel took a set of virtuoso verses and on "The Message" made them an organic part of a coherent and brilliant poem. There each set of verses paints a dif-

ferent but developing and related picture. The movement from inside a
ghetto apartment, to outside on the apartment's stoop, to vignettes involv-
ing the narrator's brother, mother, wife, and son, to a formally looser dramatic finale that portrays the arrest under false pretenses of the Furious
Five themselves—all this is cut through with the double refrain:

> Don't push me 'cause
> I'm close to the edge
> I'm trying not to
> Lose my head
> Uh-huh-huh-huh-huh
>
> It's like a jungle sometimes, it makes me wonder
> How I keep from going under

A warning, a description, a meditation—the art was growing in nuance and
implication as its poetic power grew and as its formal, rhetorical, and thematic possibilities became more strongly manifest. A new kind of music
was becoming the nesting ground for a new kind of poetry.

AFRIKA BAMBAATAA AND THE COSMIC FORCE, SOUL SONIC FORCE, AND ZULU NATION

Among hip-hop's pioneers, Afrika Bambaataa's only equals are his immediate progenitor Kool Herc and his contemporary Grandmaster Flash. Bambaataa, a resident of the South Bronx, is an artist of rich paradoxes: a onetime Black Spade gang member who inspired peace among fans who once were rivals; a bear of a man beloved among his collaborators for his caring ways; a devotee of African American culture and community who opened up that culture to other constituencies; a party-rocking DJ whose taste had pedagogical intent; a streetwise realist who through his eclectic music envisioned Utopia.

Bambaataa began to DJ in 1970, even before he had two turntables and a mixer. He would set up a record player on one side of a gymnasium and another DJ would do the same on the gym's other side. When his record was almost finished playing, one DJ would shine a flashlight across to the other, who would then begin to play his cued-up record, and back and forth it went.

Like many of his Bronx-based peers, Bambaataa ran with the Black Spades, a powerful gang in a gang-heavy era. Inspired by a trip to Africa and Europe, by the story of the Zulu warriors who fought the British, and by messages of black power that could be heard on record (James Brown, Sly Stone) and on the street (the Nation of Islam), Bambaataa essentially became a community organizer. In 1973 he founded the Mighty Zulu Nation as a conglomerate of friends, fans, and fellow travelers whose inclinations tended not toward intraborough violence but toward an appreciation for music and its thought-provoking, self-sustaining, community-based pleasures.

Bambaataa took younger DJs under his tutelage and founded crews like Soul Sonic Force and Cosmic Force that were chockfull of MCs. As Kool DJ Red Alert, one of those DJs who (along with his cousin Jazzy Jay) cut his chops under Bambaataa's mentorship, put it: "Bam was the type of person that if he liked you, he brought you in. He didn't care how many people there was. A lot of people don't know that at one time Bam had ten MCs!"[6] These included MCs like Hutch Hutch, Pow Wow, Mr. Biggs, G.L.O.B.E., and, fittingly for Bambaataa's message of inclusivity, one of the first female MCs, the self-proclaimed "Miss Lisa Lee, from the top of the key."

After almost a decade spent building up the beginnings of hip-hop culture and his Zulu Nation offshoot, Bambaataa was poised to carry his message of party-going and community-building to wax when the record phase of rap began. Early songs such as "Zulu Nation Throwdown" and "Zulu Nation Throwdown Pt. 2" (both from 1980) replicated to some degree what would happen at a Zulu Nation event. Bambaataa moved to Tommy Boy Records and in 1981 made "Jazzy Sensation" with another Zulu Nation group, the Jazzy Five.

As a DJ, Bambaataa's greatest strength was his eclectic taste and collector's mentality. Known as the "Master of Records," he dug for beats in the strangest of places, using his pulpit behind the tables to turn his congregation on to new sounds, without neglecting the popular breaks of the period. In 1982, having heard the German electro-funk band Kraftwerk, Bambaataa (working with producers Arthur Baker and John Robie) released "Planet Rock" with his group Soul Sonic Force. The song marked a sonic revolution in hip-hop. The studio funk band was gone, replaced on record by electronic keyboards and the bass-heavy sound of the Roland 808 drummachine. The tempo was fast, clocking in at 130 beats per minute. The theme was interstellar (the vocoder-ized, robotic-sounding voices could have come from another planet) and international, for this was a call to everyone around the globe, "all men, women, boys, and girls." That call would bear fruit in the eventual global reach of hip-hop, but at the time it was impressive enough that "Planet Rock" spawned dozens of songs on the space theme and began hip-hop's turn toward being a producer-influenced art.

Bambaataa's music was undeniably futuristic, but it also had a considerable respect for the past. His tendencies as an inventive DJ were part archeological and part alchemical; he would take bits of the past undiscovered by his peers and transform them into gold. While admitting the newness of the music he was making and facilitating, he also acknowledged that it hadn't come out of nowhere. Bambaataa's historical consciousness applied to the lyrics as well:

Rap always has been here in history. They say when God talked to the prophets, he was rappin' to them. You could go and pick up the old Shirley Ellis records, "The Name Game," "The Clapping Song," Moms Mabley, Pigmeat Markham, when he made "Here Comes the Judge." You could pick up Barry White with his love type of rap, or Isaac Hayes. You could get your poetry rap from Nikki Giovanni, Sonia Sanchez, the Last Poets, the Watts Prophets. You could get your militancy message rap coming from Malcolm X, Minister Louis Farrakhan, Muhammad Ali. A lot of the time, the black people used to play this game called The Dozens on each other, rappin' about your mama or your father, and stuff. And you could go back to the talks of Murray the K, Cousin Brucie, and all the other radio stations that was pushing the rap on the air or pushing the rock and roll. So rap was always here.[7]

ZULU NATION THROWDOWN

[All]
Say, what's the name of this nation?
Zulus, Zulus
And who's gonna get on down?
The Cosmic Force, the Cosmic Force

[Lisa Lee] Chitty-chitty-bang-bang, we are your main thing
[All three men] You listen to the song that she is gonna sing-sing
[Lisa Lee] We party all night to the people's delight
'Cause everybody knows that we rock out of sight
Say, we are the best in the creation
[All] We go by the name of the mighty Zulu Nation
We're the mighty Zulus, we're one of a crew
We're [Chubby Chub] coming by, [All] we're [Chubby Chub] coming through
[All] We're [Chubby Chub] worldwide and [All] we're [Chubby Chub]
   super divine
[All] 'Cause we [Chubby Chub] shock the house, [All] we [Chubby
   Chub] shock it right
[Chubby Chub] We'll say a little something to let you know
That my mellow Smitty D is on the echo
We do a routine and put on a show

And dedicate it to the people we know
We're one of a kind, we're easing the mind
The Zulu Nation, say time after time

. . . .

[All] She's [Lisa Lee] Lisa Lee and from the top of the key
You know I'm guaranteed to be the queen of MCs
[All] He's [Chubby Chub] MC Chubby Chub from the heavens above
No, I ain't never met a girl that I couldn't shook up
[All] And he's [Ice-Ice] MC Ice-Ice, the shocker-rocker on the mic
And doin it on, doin it high power, doin it right
[All] And he's [Ikey C] Little Ikey C and I'm the melody
Now all you young ladies get sexy—do it!

[Chubby Chub] This is a story from the yesteryear
[Ice-Ice] Said before it was the wack but now the ladies cheer
[Ikey C] Until we climb the ladder, say one by one
[Chubby Chub] And while we did it we spreaded some fun
[Ice-Ice] Say, we change the tempo so you can clap your hands
[Ikey C] And then we add a little music so y'all can dance
[Chubby Chub] And you like our style [Ice-Ice] which is just our voice
[Ikey C] So young ladies [All three men] come and pick your choice
Chubby Chub, Ice-Ice
I'm Little Ikey C, we are the three MCs
Lisa Lee, you're the queen—go girl!
Just get on the mic and do your own thing

[Lisa Lee]
So put your hands in the air and listen to me
'Cause you listen to the voice of MC Lisa Lee
Don't play no games, don't bite no style
When you came through the door we gave you a smile
We want you to get loose, get ready to rock
We're gonna paralyze your mind and put you in shock
We're gonna make you wanna yell, scream, and shout
We're gonna let you know without a doubt exactly what we be about

Rocking to the sounds that make you dance

Make the ants crawl in your pants, put you in a music trance

Listen to the beat and let yourself go

'Cause everybody knows this is nothing but a disco

Rock, shock the sure shot

This ain't a Broadway play or a high school plot

It's the real deal that makes you feel

Like, like you got sex appeal

Now party people in the place, you feel the bass

Can you check out the highs, check out the grace?

So wallflowers in the house, this is your chance

To show everybody that you can dance

Punk rock to the left and Patty Duke it to the right

Move your body now, you can do it all night

These are the devastating words that you never heard before

I'm Lisa Lee—ha!—I got rhymes galore

So young ladies out there, he's from the heavens above

[Chubby Chub]

That's right, never met a girl that I couldn't shook up

So won't you clap your hands and have some fun

It's the super dynamite—huh!—MC Chubby Chub

You don't stop—ha!—you don't stop—ha-ha!

Get it all together, girl, because we're starting to rock

And to all the young ladies, yes, his name is Chub

Say, I didn't come here to ask for your love

'Cause I'm a cool, cool kid with a healthy mind

And I figure that ballin will always take time

I'm looking for a girl that I can call mines

When she walk down the street, the sun will shine

And to all the young ladies, I'm talking 'bout me

'Cause I'm lookin for a girl that's so unique

I'm not lookin for a girl that drives a car

To me she'll always be my superstar

'Cause I'm a-lookin for a girl with a beautiful smile
And a young lady that's worth my while
Young ladies out there, don't you get uptight

[Ice-Ice]
'Cause it's me, baby doll, MC Ice-Ice
Just like a bike got wheels, sweet lemon peel
Now the MCs, they know the deal
That we always rock and we can't be stopped
Wherever we rock and hit the latest spot
I said the other MCs are standing tall
But the taller they are, the harder they fall
'Cause we the Funkadelic of the microphone
Because we are the MCs that's all alone
And when we get on the mic it's back to back
I said that we're the crew that leads the pack
And we'll teach you lessons that you'll never forget
Because we are the MCs that ever testify
We're on to the crack of dawn
We're on to the crack of dawn
And young ladies, he's from the top

[Ikey C]
He's Little Ikey C and I'm the master rock
You don't stop, you don't stop
Told you 'bout the ding-d'-d'-ding-d'-ding-dingy-ding
That thing that you call that body rock
Now let me tell you something that caught my eye
It was a real jazzy lady, she was so fly
She had long hair and clothes so fine
I said, "I'ma keep rappin until you're mine"
I said, "I'ma rap for just about an hour"
'Cause I knew the young lady was surely high power
And the way she moved was like a graceful swan
And we can make love to the break of dawn

And the way she move is like a graceful dove
Say, could it be I'm falling in love?
"Will you be mine?" is what I say
Why don't you chill out, just give me a play
You don't stop, you don't stop

[All]
Say, what's the name of this nation?
Zulus, Zulus
And who's gonna get on down?
Bambaataa, Bambaataa

. . . .

PLANET ROCK

*Party people—Party people—Can y'all get funky? Soul Sonic Force—can y'all get
funky? The Zulu Nation—can y'all get funky? Yeaaahhhh!—Just hit me. Just
taste the funk and hit me. Just get on down and hit me. Bambaataa's getting
so funky, now, hit me. Yeaaahhhh!—Just hit me . . .*

It's time to chase your dreams
Up out the seats, make your body sway
Socialize, get down, let your soul lead the way
Shake it now—go, ladies!—it's a living dream
Love—life—live
Come play the game, our world is free
Do what you want but scream
We know a place where the nights are hot
It is a house of funk
Females and males, both young and old
For the disco
The DJ plays your favorite blasts
Takes it back to the past, music's magic—poof
Hump-bump-bump, get bump with some class, people

Rock, rock to the Planet Rock, don't stop [2x]

The Soul Sonic Force—Mr. Biggs, Pow Wow, and MC G.L.O.B.E.
We emphasize to show we got ego
Make this your night, just slip it right in by day
As the people say, live it up, shucks
For work or play, our world is free
Be what you be—be

Rock, rock to the Planet Rock, don't stop [2x]

You're in a place where the nights are hot
Where nature's children dance and stand a chance
On this Mother Earth, which is our rock
The time has come and work for soul—to show you really got soul
Are you ready—hump-bump-bump—get bump—now let's go—house
Twist and turn, then you let your body slide
You got the body rock and pop, bounce and pounce
Everybody just rock and don't stop it
You gotta rock it, don't stop
You keep ticking and tocking, working all around the clock
Everybody keep rockin and clockin and shockin and rockin—go house
Everybody say, rock and don't stop it—"rock and don't stop it!"
Well, hit me, Mr. Biggs—"Mr. Biggs!"
Pow Wow—"Pow Wow!"
G-L-O-B-E—"G-L-O-B-E!"
The Soul Sonic Force

You gotta rock this poppin, 'cause in the century
There is such a place that creates such a melody
Our world is by the plan of a master jam, get up and dance
It's time to chase your dream
Up out your seats, make your body sway
Socialize, get down, let your soul lead the way
Shake it now—go ladies!—it's a living dream
Love—life—live

Everybody say, rock it, don't stop it—"rock it, don't stop it"

Everybody say, shockin and clockin—"shockin and clockin"

Everybody say, ichi ni san shi—"ichi ni san shi"

Say, Planet Rock—"Planet Rock"

It's the sure shot—"it's the sure shot"

Say, Planet Rock—"Planet Rock"

It's the sure shot—"it's the sure shot"

So twist and turn, then you let your

Body glide, you got the body

Rock and pop

Bounce and pounce—so hit me

Just taste the funk and hit me

Just get on down and hit me

Bambaataa's getting so funky, now hit me

Every piece of the world

Rate the message of our words

All men, women, boys, and girls

Hey, our Planet Rock is superb—Get on it

You got the groove, move

Feel the groove—feel it

Do what you want to but you know you got to be

Cool and boogie

Out on the floor, go down

Bring it low

Close to the ground

Everybody just rock and don't stop it

Gotta rock it, don't stop

Keep ticking and tocking

Workin all around the clock

Everybody just rock and don't stop it

Gotta rock it, don't stop

KURTIS BLOW

Kurtis Blow was one of the first rappers to make a career of the art and is often heralded as rap's first solo artist of note. Adaptable, personable, and good-looking, Blow had crossover appeal before rap really knew what crossover appeal was, paving the way for figures like LL Cool J and Will Smith. Most important, though, Kurtis Blow brought into the studio setting the bona fides of early hip-hop's prerecorded days—he began as "Son of Eddie Cheba"—while also advancing rap song-craft.

By most measures, Blow's rhymes are straightforward. More striking are his consistency and his range. Having honed his craft on rap's early stages, Blow—a native of Harlem who was managed at the start of his recording career by Russell Simmons and who was the first rapper signed to a major label—brings all of the old school crowd-pleasing tricks to bear on "Rappin Blow (Part 2)." The song is a classic exercise in crowd exhortation, as is "The Breaks," the second track on his first album.

"The Breaks" was a gold record for Blow and the song that led Kool Moe Dee to describe him as "the inventor of the hook for rap songs."[8] The song works through as many meanings of the title term as possible: "Brakes in a bus, brakes on a car / Breaks to make you a superstar / Breaks to win and breaks to lose / But these here breaks will rock your shoes." Blow's lyrics are in constant contact with the music, as the periodic call throughout the song to "break it up" or "break down" is punctuated by a percussive "break." If the hook serves not just a musical but a marketing purpose—since it usually drills into the listener's head the title of the song—"The Breaks" is a superlative self-advertisement, for even in extended series of verses every other line is an eponymous refrain that tells us what we are listening to.

The follow-up albums to Blow's self-titled debut, *Deuce* (1981) and *Tough* (1982), are less memorable than their predecessor, but *Ego Trip* (1984) remains a compelling collection on which Blow's versatility pays dividends. "I Can't Take It No More" gives us a Kurtis Blow on the edge of snapping (one hears echoes of "The Message") while the title track simply reminds us that, despite the in-your-face, first-person nature of rap, "You can't dance to my ego, you dance to my beat." A collaboration with Run-DMC, "8 Million Stories," continues the growing trend toward representing urban blight and the plight of big-city poor, while "Basketball" is more lighthearted and remains a favorite of hoops fans, re-creating as it does at the end the kinds of debates fans have among themselves. The most memorable track on *America* (1985) is "If I Ruled the World," which once again exhibits Blow's talent for the catchy hook, but also his skills as a storyteller, as he embarks on a fantasia in which, almost a quarter-century before Barack Obama, a black man leads the free world.

RAPPIN BLOW (PART 2)

"What did you say your name was?"

I see that it's not clear
For you, good buddy, so clean out your ears
Listen very close while I pop more game
'Cause my name's in the hall of fame
The K-U-R, the T-I-S
The first to the best I must confess
The B-L-O and the W
I make you wanna catch the boogaloo flu
Now if your name is Annie get up off your fanny
If your name is Clyde get off your backside
If your name is Pete you don't need a seat
'Cause I'm Kurtis Blow and I'm on the go
I'm rocking to the rhythms in ster-e-er-e-o

Now just throw your hands in the air
And wave 'em like you just don't care
If you're ready like Freddy to rock real steady
Somebody say, "Oh yeah"
Oh yeah—Young ladies
All the ladies in the house say, "Oww"
Oww—And you don't stop, come on
Come on, come on, let me see you rock
Get down, stop messing around
When Kurtis Blow is in your town
I'm Kurtis Blow on the microphone
A place called Harlem was my home
I was rockin one day, it started to shake

It sounded to me like a earthquake

I packed my bags, I said goodbye

I kissed my woman and I started to fly

I came to Earth by a meteorite

To rock you all on the mic

So just kick off your shoes, let your fingers pop

'Cause Kurtis Blow just about ready to rock

Now, the people in the back, if you're not the wack, say

Don't stop the body rock

The people in the front, if you want to bump, say

Don't stop the body rock

The people in the middle, if you wanna wiggle, say

Don't stop the body rock

And the people on the side, if you wanna slide, say

Don't stop the body rock

Not a preacher or a teacher or a electrician

A fighter or a writer or a politician

The man with the key to your ignition

Kurtis Blow is competition

Young ladies, shock the house, jazzy

Young ladies, shock the house

Now just throw your hands in the air

And wave 'em like you just don't care

If y'all really ready to rock the house this morning

Somebody say, "Oh yeah"

Oh yeah

Somebody scream . . .

. . . .

Keep on rockin on

Keep-keep on, rock the hip, the hop on

Like a little boy blue blowin on a horn

The needle on the record tryin to play a song

It's been that way since the day he was born

I like a twenty-five-cent bag of popcorn

Dip-dip-dab, so-socialize

Clean out your ears and open up your eyes

So you goin here can realize

That I'm here to tranquilize

Got the knack of Cool Jack, better than Baretta

Casanova Brown because I'm down

Get down, stop messing around

When Kurtis Blow is in your town

I'm a one of a kind, I'll wreck your mind

Put a wiggle-double-wiggle in your behind

Twice as nice, I'm skatin on ice

When my mama gave birth she named me the baddest

MC on Earth, y'all

To the beat that makes you freak

Get out of your seat and freak to the beat

The weather is cold so catch some heat

THE BREAKS

Clap your hands, everybody

If you got what it takes

'Cause I'm Kurtis Blow and I want you to know

That these are the breaks

Brakes in a bus, brakes on a car

Breaks to make you a superstar

Breaks to win and breaks to lose

But these here breaks will rock your shoes

And these are the breaks

Break it up, break it up, break it up

If your woman steps out with another man

That's the breaks, that's the breaks

And she runs off with him to Japan

That's the breaks, that's the breaks

And the IRS says they want to chat

That's the breaks, that's the breaks
And you can't explain why you claimed your cat
That's the breaks, that's the breaks
And Ma Bell sends you a whopping bill
That's the breaks, that's the breaks
With eighteen phone calls to Brazil
That's the breaks, that's the breaks
And you borrowed money from the Mob
That's the breaks, that's the breaks
And yesterday you lost your job
That's the breaks, that's the breaks
Well, these are the breaks
Break it up, break it up, break it up

Throw your hands up in the sky
And wave 'em round from side to side
And if you deserve a break tonight
Somebody say, "Alright"
Alright! Say, "Ho"
Ho! You don't stop
Keep on, somebody scream
Oh! Break down

Breaks on a stage, breaks on a screen
Breaks to make your wallet lean
Breaks run cold and breaks run hot
Some folks got 'em and some have not
But these are the breaks
Break it up, break it up, break it up, break down

To the girl in brown, stop messin around
Break it up, break it up
To the guy in blue, what you gon' do
Break it up, break it up
And to the girl in green, don't be so mean
Break it up, break it up

And the guy in red, say what I said
Break it up, break it up
Break down

Brakes on a plane, brakes on a train
Breaks to make you go insane
Breaks in love, breaks in war
But we got the breaks to get you on the floor
And these are the breaks
Break it up, break it up, break it up, break down

Just do it, just do it
Just do it, do it, do it [4x]

You say last week you met the perfect guy
That's the breaks, that's the breaks
And he promised you the stars in the sky
That's the breaks, that's the breaks
He said his Cadillac was gold
That's the breaks, that's the breaks
But he didn't say it was ten years old
That's the breaks, that's the breaks
He took you out to the Red Coach Grill
That's the breaks, that's the breaks
But he forgot the cash and you paid the bill
That's the breaks, that's the breaks
And he told you the story of his life
That's the breaks, that's the breaks
But he forgot the part about his wife
That's the breaks, that's the breaks
Well, these are the breaks
Break it up, break it up, break it up, break down

IF I RULED THE WORLD

If I ruled the world, was king on the throne
I'd make peace in every culture, build the homeless a home

I'm not running for Congress or the President

I'm just here to tell the world how my story went

You see, first it was a dream, I was living in Rome

And then I moved to London, bought a brand new home

And everywhere I went I drew lots of attention

Like a stretch limousine, one of those new inventions

It took a few years 'fore the day had come

But I was ruler of the world, ranked number one

So I headed toward Washington to claim the crown

Let the whole world know that the king was in town

As I arrived the crowd started to cheer

And then someone yelled out, "The king is here!"

So I headed toward a stage to make a speech

About the new style of living I was going to teach

[Chorus]

If I ruled the world

I'd love all the girls

Wear diamonds and pearls

If I ruled the world

People started flowing as they reached for my hand

I said, "Thank you for bringing me to the promised land

But now I must go, say goodbye to everybody

Tonight I'll see you all at my super dinner party"

And late that night at my super dinner party

I was dancing to the beat and entertaining, la-di-da-di

The music started ending, it was time for a speech

The crowd started sitting as I rose from my feet

"And this was once a dream," I explained to the crowd

"But now I rule the world and I feel so very proud

Excuse me, please, for stopping this show

I just had to thank you all for helpin me, so…"

My first day in office, the king on the throne

I spent my first three hours on the telephone

You know, with newsmen, reporters, and voters too
I had so many calls, I didn't know what to do
You know, out that office I continued to work
I signed so many papers my fingers started to hurt
Then I shook off the pain, say this ain't no thing
'Cause there's nothing in the world like being number one king!

[Chorus]

Now I rule the world and now I'm on top
And I'm rollin with folks that could never be stopped
And I'm here to let you know this is where I belong
And to you sucker MCs, this is my song
And it's a song that's strong about right and wrong
And I'ma rock it to your butt, baby, all night long
And it's a song about love and happiness
In a world of peace and you know that's fresh
Now I'm the king and I want you to know
That I'm the master blaster rapper who's running the show
And to all of you rappers in every country
You better stop what you're doing and listen to me
'Cause we gotta stop war and use unity
To fight crime and hunger and poverty
'Cause the African babies dying overseas
While you sucker metro-politicians busting out Z's
Twenty million people all unemployed
While the rich man try to play Pretty Boy Floyd
While the working class just struggles hard
Try to make ends meet against all odds
While the poor man can't even deal with life
You know he tried to escape and smoked the coke on the pipe
Well, it's time for a change to a better way
'Cause the sun has gotta shine through the cloudy day
So listen up, world, while I teach this class
And take heed to the message or we ain't gonna last

'Cause I know the solution is a contribution
Of woman and man to just join my revolution
That'll take your brain to a higher plane
And help you deal in a world that's gone insane
With the problems that I know we can stop
From the ruler of the world and the man on top
But the years went by and time was up
And then the ruler of the world had ran out of luck
And all the people at the time who said they were my friends
Didn't know me when my job had come to an end
They came up to my face as happy as can be
He was running his mouth like Muhammad Ali
So I shook his hand calmly as I headed to the door
On my way to the ghetto to treat once more

[Chorus]

BROTHER D WITH COLLECTIVE EFFORT

The first rap record to be explicitly political both in its lyrical content and in its methods of production and distribution, "How We Gonna Make the Black Nation Rise?," released in 1980 on Clappers Records, is an example of a song practicing what it preaches. Brother D, otherwise known as a teacher named Daryl Aamaa Nubyahn, "recorded a hip-hop tune to reflect the philosophy of a political and cultural organization called National Black Science."[9] On top of Cheryl Lynn's "Got to Be Real" rhythm, Brother D and his aptly named rhyming partners Collective Effort—a group of MCs not named individually in the song, but which includes both male and female members—urge their listeners to consider the disjunction between good time music and the actual times from which it derives. The lyrics, against their ironic sonic backdrop, diagnose the danger of becoming "pacified" to the point of living death and outline a litany of social problems.

Meant to serve as an antidote to pleasure addiction and as a call to arms against economic and racist oppression, "How We Gonna Make the Black Nation Rise?" is more aggressive, sustained, and specific in its politics than any rap songs that precede it. Much of this can be attributed not only to Brother D and Collective Effort but also to the fact that their independent label not only welcomed but initiated the project. "I got revved up and excited about the possibilities of forming a record company that had a Maoist approach instead of a capitalist approach," recalls label founder Lister Hewan-Lowe, "and I was obsessed with the fact that the shareholders should be the people who made the music." Deciding to make a "revolutionary hip-hop record," he put out the word, after which Brother D came knocking.[10] Follow-ups to that initial release included a solo 12-inch by Brother D called "Clappers Power/Mao Dub," as well as "Ms. DJ Rap It Up!" by She.

HOW WE GONNA MAKE THE BLACK NATION RISE?

If you want to know the truth and that's a fact
Let me hear you say, "And you know that"
And you know that

[Brother D]
You dippy-dippy-dive, you so-socialize
But how we gonna make the black nation rise?
While you party down yelling, shock the house
Get down, rock-shock the house
The Ku Klux Klan is on the loose
Training their kids in machine gun use
Obey everything has its place and time
We can rock the house, too, as we shock your mind

[Collective Effort]
We can brag and we can boast
Because you're neither bread nor butter for our breakfast toast

[Brother D]
Look at all the things that can prove the point
Sisters in the distance, brothers in the joint

[Collective Effort]
As you dippy-dippy-dive, you so-socialize
But how we gonna make the black nation rise?

[Brother D]
The people call me Brother D
And I'm here to shed some light
To bring the truth right on down to earth
From where it once was out of sight
But before I continue just let me say
This is not my ego soup
I sat down and thought and I wrote this verse
In the interest of the group—come on

[Collective Effort]
People, people, can't you see
What's really going on?
Unemployment's high, the housing's bad
And the schools are teaching wrong
Cancer from the water, pollution in the air
But you partyin hard like you just don't care
Wake up, y'all, you know that ain't right
'Cause that hurts everybody, black or white
Winter's cold, there is no heat
Just move your body to the beat
While it takes you on a disco ride
Get high until you're pacified
Now you actin like the livin dead
Talkin 'bout the body, talkin 'bout the head

[Brother D]
Space out, y'all, to the disco rhyme
You're movin to the rhythm but you're wastin time
Stop and think—do you know what's real?
Well, let me educate you to the real deal

The media is tellin lies
Devil takin off his disguise
They're killin us in the street
While we pay more for food that's cheap
And all you want to do is so-socialize

[Collective Effort]
How you gonna make the black nation rise?

[Brother D]
Remember the so-called Indian
Look what they did to him
Maybe they'll do that to us
Dare to struggle, dare to win
. . . .
The story might give you stomach cramps
Like America's got concentration camps

[Collective Effort]
People like that come, live, and die
Warning us about genocide

[Brother D]
While you're partying on-on-on-on and on
The ovens may be hot by the break of dawn
The party may end one day soon
When they round the niggers up in the afternoon

[Collective Effort]
And you're starting to wonder are the people dumb
Well, Martin Luther King said we'll overcome
How we gonna make the black nation rise?
All you wanna do is dippy-dippy-dippy dive
No, no, brothers, it's not like that
You gonna rap for the people, tell them where it's at

Elijah's told us how to build our wealth
Collectively we must do for ourselves

. . . .

Service for our people who we must redeem
Like Coltrane's horn blowing Love Supreme
You heard what Marcus Garvey said
And we can't stand still—He said
Up you mighty nation, you can
Accomplish what you will

Rising up, won't take no more
Rising up, won't take no more

[Brother D]
America was built, understand
By stolen labor on stolen land
Take a second thought as you clap and stamp
Can you rock the house from inside the camp?
As you movin to the beat to the early light
The country movin to, movin to the right
Prepare now, all, get high and wait
'Cause it ain't no party in a police state

[Collective Effort]
Blessed are we who dare to be free
We gotta change the way we behave
You gotta sacrifice for our righteous cause
Or remain a passive slave
We're not anti- any other racial group
Just understand we're pro-black
And we're against any one or thing
That tries to hold us back
So think but don't take too long
The time is getting late
And DJs if you got a mic
It's your job to educate

[Brother D]

Well, I know my voice is not rated X
We didn't talk about money or talk about sex
We didn't talk about clothes and cars and things
And you might be tired of my lecturing
So while you dance and while you sing
All we wanna do is ask just one thing
While you dippy-dippy dive and so-socialize
Are you gonna help the black nation rise?

[Collective Effort]

You dippy-dippy dive, you so-socialize
How we gonna make the black nation rise?

[Brother D]

How we gonna make the black nation rise?
Gotta agitate, educate, and organize
How we gonna make the black nation rise?
Agitate, educate, organize
[repeat to fade]

EDDIE CHEBA

A Harlem-based DJ who also rhymed, Eddie Cheba is the kind of often overlooked forefather whose actual contribution is under-remembered because his live sets never translated to record. Chuck D of Public Enemy remarks that "Eddie Cheba was as important to hip-hop/rap as Ike Turner was to rock and roll."[11] Kurtis Blow recalls that Cheba "was a master of the crowd response. He had routines, he had girls—the Cheba Girls—he had little routines, and he did it with a little rhythm, you know."[12] See the introduction to Part One for a discussion of Cheba's lyrical repertoire in relation to the verses below.

LIVE AT THE ARMORY 1979 (1)

Just keep your body, stay on the floor
We gonna do a little like an eel
We gonna continue on with the music, y'all
It's time for you to be real—you see
A while ago, but I want you to know
Just who you've been listening to
Just listen to me now while I tell you how
Who I am and what I do
Five-nine-and-a-half, bowlegged as
You ever want to see
Just look up on the stage, baby doll
Talking 'bout little old me
It's Cheba, girl, and I'm so glad
That you came on down
So we can spend some time together
Maybe even mess around—you see
You look so good, you look so fine
You make me shake and shiver
But in the end when it all goes down
You know Cheba's gonna be the winner
I'm mean, I'm mad, I'm cool and smooth
I know you do it with me
Guess that's why I ran my game
On WFUB
You've heard the rest who fail the test
So I guess now you know
Just who's the man with the master plan
That'll always steal your show
When the Cheba-Cheba's doing the do
I'll work your body black and blue
When the Cheba-Cheba's in the house
I'll talk mo' shit than Mickey Mouse
When the Cheba-Cheba decides to quit
Everybody in the house would just say

Awwwwww—

Shiiiiiiiit!

Once again, we gonna have a little fun, so let me hear everybody one time, come
on, say,

"Ooh ah, ooh-ooh ah"

Ooh ah, ooh-ooh ah

Somebody say, "oh la, oh la"

Oh la, oh la

Somebody say, "wake-a, wake-a"

Wake-a, wake-a

Everybody—well, how you feel?

How you feel?

Well, how you feel? Mighty real

With the Cheba, Cheba, Chee-chee-che-che-cheba

Cheba-cheba-cheba

You can dip, dive, or socialize

Either way we gonna make your nature rise

With the good music and funky vibe

It'll be Cheba keeping you satisfied

Raise your hands in the air

Wave 'em like you just don't care

If y'all think Jamaica is number one

Let me hear you say, "oh yeah"

Oh yeah

Jamaica, y'all sound real good, everybody

Come on—*let's go to work*

Come on—*let's go to work*

Don't stop, don't stop, don't stop, don't stop

Say what—I'll tell you when

Just kick off the shoes, relax the feet

Then you freak to the funky beat

On and on and on and on

If we can't get you up then we don't belong

Do it, do it, do-do-do do it, do it

Do it, do it, do it

But if yo' name is Kenny

Jack Benny—Jack . . .

How many people know about the Jack Benny?

Say, "oh yeah"—*oh yeah*

So if yo' name is Kenny

Jack Benny, Jack Benny

Say, "ho"—*ho*

Once again, get ready, girlfriend, we gonna have a little fun at the place to be. I
mean, if y'all really ready for a funky beat tonight, everybody put your hands
up real high. Come on, now, let me hear somebody scream. Come on, keep in
step. Once again, don't forget—we got some unfinished business with
Sugarhill in Harlem World tomorrow night. We gonna show 'em about the
bang-bang-the-boogie. Once again, if y'all having a good time I want y'all to
put your hands together, everybody clap your hands . . .

COLD CRUSH BROTHERS

The Cold Crush Brothers came from the Bronx. Consisting of six members—the DJs Charlie Chase and Tony Tone and the MCs JDL, Easy AD, "The Almighty" KG, and Grandmaster Caz—the group got together in 1978. Their live shows are legendary in the annals of hip-hop, and many of them were widely circulated on tape. They were not just popular, but also influential—for instance, Run-DMC credits the Cold Crush Brothers with inspiring them to shape their sound, which in turn shaped much rap that followed.

If the setting was a battle, as on the excerpt below from 1981 of a show that pitted the Cold Crush Brothers against the Fantastic Five, the four MCs would sometimes rap a series of verses alone, sometimes rap a series together, sometimes trade verses, sometimes rhyme by passing the baton from one to the next as in a relay; they also sang, or would rap in a sing-songy way to the melody of popular hits of the day. And all the while they told you who you were listening to, the better to earn your support in the contest.

Although remembered more for their work on the stage, they recorded some strong and representative records in the studio. "Weekend" marches us through the days of the workweek to bring us to the moment of release, which the song both describes and enacts. "Fresh Wild Fly and Bold" brings to the studio setting a sense of the group communication that characterized their tapes, as well as a sense of their combativeness.

The CC4 were one of the first groups to elaborate the trope of the "biter," or the rapper who stole rather than wrote his own rhymes. On the one hand, it is a mark of the group's strength and influence that they had to be concerned with being "robbed." On the other hand, it is a mark of the fact that the art form was growing enough that problems of lineage, imitation, originality, and influence were increasingly in play.

Maybe it is also a mark of the perception of actual theft. Anecdotal evidence suggests that many of the rhymes from the Sugarhill Gang's "Rapper's Delight," delightful as that song is, were purloined from Grandmaster Caz. If so, the Cold Crush Brothers in a sense went platinum and had their words heard early and often; in another, common sense, they didn't get credit for their contribution. One of their strengths is that there isn't a weak member in the group. That said, Grandmaster Caz (who was a DJ before he was an MC) is the acknowledged leader, the "captain." If Sugarhill's Big Bank Hank did pilfer Caz's rhymes, he at least put them to good use and, through a strange twist of fate, gave them maximum exposure— which might not be much consolation if you were the man who wrote the rhymes:

> I'm mad as hell 'cause it's bound to sell
> And you be biting what I'm writing and people can't tell
> You change it around, disguise the sound
> With no prior desire to write, that's why I frown

The subject matter is one thing here, the form another; the interlocking internal rhymes suggest why the group was attended to by fellow rappers back in the day:

hell		sell	a		a
biting	writing	tell	b	b	a
around		sound	c		c
prior	desire	frown	d	d	c

Arrangements such as these are more associated with lyricists from several years later, such as Rakim and Big Daddy Kane. It was advanced for the time and it still sounds fresh.

LIVE AT HARLEM WORLD 1981

What's up, fly guys? Hello, fly girls

It's the big throw-down at Harlem World

The Cold Crush Four versus Fantastic Five

They ain't no comp, we'll eat 'em alive

Because we're the best when it comes to rapping

And like the flier said, it was bound to happen

Well the time has come and let the battle begin

And let the crowd be the judge of who wins. . . .

Hey, y'all, yes it's true

The four got a brand new song for you

We got routines, rhymes, and dancing, too

So what you wanna do?

Chase, Tone, and the Four

You never heard a crew like this before

And the way we rock a crowd should be against the law

We got much more

Grandmaster Caz raising hell

And I'm the hut-maker called JDL

And I'm easy A, don't forget the D

And I'm KG—the Almighty

No doubt we're the best

With the CC4 you do not mess

And if there's a battle the four won't fess

So let's go west

Against the very best

So get it off your chest

And you'll be so impressed

Cold Crush

Cold-cold Crush

And it's like that, because we're never wack
We don't believe in that zodiac
Now throw your hands in the air
And wave 'em like you just don't care
Just throw your hands in the air
And wave 'em like you just don't care

. . . .

One for the bass, two for the treble
Come on Chase, yo, let's go level
Ah yeah, yeah, somebody
Somebody say, "Ho"—*Ho!*
Say, "Ho"—*Ho!*
Now it's thirteen, fourteen
No, it's fifteen—no, it's sixteen
It's seventeen, eight-eight eighteen
Say, nineteen-eighty-one
And the former year is done
Everybody's gonna know that we're on the go
Like Reggie Joe on the seven-oh
And when eighty-two rolls around
We'll still be getting down
With a funky dance that put you in a trance
You got to see it to believe it
We'll put on a show and you know
We can't be beaten
We proved that we could make you move
Our rhymes are bitten, chewed, and eaten
But we keep rocking on
And making up new songs
So here we go . . .

. . . .

Now how many of y'all know about other MCs? How many of y'all know about
other MCs? How many of y'all know other MCs? If y'all know about other
MCs, raise your hands in the air. Throw your hands in the air. How many of

y'all know other MCs? All right, you don't know about other MCs? Charlie Chase, Charlie Chase, keep the rocket in the pocket. We gonna let 'em know a little something about other MCs.

Now, first of all, we're not talking 'bout your sister—*your sister*
We're not talking 'bout your uncle—*your uncle*
We're not talking 'bout your father—*your father*
And not your mother or other or other-other-other-other

Other MCs can't deal with us
Because we are the four known as the Cold Crush
Putting fellas on the job, making girls blush
You know we got a funky song
So won't you come and sing and dance along
We got the two DJs on the wheels of steel
Charlie Chase and Tony Tone at the top of the field
Message to the competition, better be for real
We rock the party to the break of day
And this is how it sounds when we play
We are the four MCs with the most success
And if you wanna cold crush you better come correct
We might have to take you out and put your crew in check
Because the CC4's number one
And you got to walk before you run

LIVE AT THE DIXIE 1982

[Grandmaster Caz]
It was a long time ago but I'll never forget
I got caught in a bed with a girl named Yvette
Well, I was scared like hell but I got away
That's why I'm here telling you today
I was outside my school hooking up to rock
A crowd of people all around listening to my box
Just me and my fans and some guys from the crew
Chilling hard 'cause we had nothing better to do

It was me, the L, the A, and the All

And then I slipped away to make a phone call

To this very day it was a move I regret

But I didn't know then, so I called Yvette

I said, "Hello pretty mama, it's your lover man"

She said, "Baby, come on over as quick as you can"

I said, "I can't come now, someone's coming to get me"

Then she said, "I'm all alone, there's nobody with me"

I thought for a second, "Oh shit! She's alone"

Then I was knocking at her door before she hung up the phone

She let me in the house and gave me a kiss

And said, "Give me that thing that you know I miss"

So we went into her room and we got high

But she couldn't keep her hand from off my fly

So I made her lock the door and went to check it

When I came back in the girl was naked

That was my cue to do the do

I took my clothes off and started on the poo

Well, I was tearing shit up and 'bout a quarter to three

She said, "Caz, somebody's coming." I said, "Yeah, me"

Then the door bust open and there was her folks

I thought, "Damn, they coulda waited—say, damn—they coulda waited

Say, damn—they coulda waited 'til I finished my stroke"

Her mother was in shock, her father reached on the shelf

Pulled down the .45, I almost shit on myself

Said, "Please, don't shoot!" and pleaded my case

Said, "You'd have done the same thing if you was in my place

But if you spare my life, believe me, friend

You'll never see me round your daughter again"

Don't ask me why, but he let me leave

I ran twenty-six blocks then I stopped to breathe

Gave thanks to God he wasn't too upset

Went home and thought about poor Yvette

He must have beat her ass with everything, I assume

'Cause I could hear the girl screaming all the way in my room
Even though I don't see Yvette no more
Well, I know she ain't as fine—I know she ain't as fine
I know, ain't half as fine as she was before
So JDL—ha—you know my voice is sore
Therefore get on the mic and rock once more

[JDL]
Well, I'm here to be known and I'm known to be
As an electrified prince of poetry . . . [Fade]

WEEKEND

[All] Everybody listen to this
The weekend's coming so don't you dare miss
You're gonna regret if you're not on the scene
And then you get so mad it'll make you scream
[Grandmaster Caz] Everyone give us your attention please
[JDL] Especially those of you who like parties
[Easy AD] It's a message that we will like to extend
[Almighty KG] About why everybody love the what? [All] Weekend!
[Caz] 'Cause there's a time to work and a time to play
[JDL] But you can't do both effectively in one day
[AD] So without delay, without further ado
[KG] Let the four run down this week for you

[All] We're the Cold Crush Four, giving, giving you more
And we just came to say
Ooh-ah, what a relief it is
When the weekend comes your way
So grab a chair from anywhere
And listen while we speak
'Cause the Four's gonna start this record off
With the first day of the week—Monday
[Caz] The train was late and you hardly ate
Plus you wish you'd stayed in bed—[All] Tuesday
[JDL] You ran a game on your favorite dame

And then she messed up your head—[All] Wednesday

[AD] You try to be cool and stay out of school

Yeah, you fronted and showboated—[All] Thursday

[KG] Now your mind's in doubt, you can't figure out

Why you're not gonna get promoted—[All] Friday

[All] After work is through, you sleep for a few

Until you hear somebody say

[Caz] Wake up, wake up, now don't you know

[All] The weekend's when we play

This is Chase with the bass
Tone, leave the girl alone

[Caz] Friday and Saturday night, everybody's gonna show

[JDL] At the place where all the fly people go

[AD] You been working at school or your occupation

[KG] Now it's about time for some recreation

[Caz] Slip on your shirt and designer jeans

[JDL] Say the ones that are tight at the hip and the seams

[AD] Then you shoot out the door like you're running a race

[KG] And then you finally arrive at the Cold Crush place

[All] And...

[Caz] You can't [JDL] believe [AD] your eyes, [KG] 'cause

[Sung]
The party's packed and jumping
That funky bass is thumping
And the way the music rocks your mind
Ooh girl, it's really something
It's a place where you can dance
You can even find romance
And I know you can do it if you
Give yourself a chance

. . . .

[Caz] Now the lights are flashin, the people are dancin

[JDL] The guys are looking out for some serious action

[AD] It's richer than a diamond, finer than a pearl

[KG] And this is what happens when boy meets girl

[Caz] Introduce yourself as whoever you are

[JDL] Then you grab her by the hand and lead her to the bar

[AD] Offer her a drink, maybe a cigarette

[KG] 'Til she insists conversation is all you're gonna get

[Caz] Try another approach and ask her for a dance

[JDL] Your time is runnin out, this is your last chance

[AD] And then you sweep her off her feet with your prowess

[KG] And then you know you got it made—finally, success

[Caz] 'Cause we rock the best [All] and the Four is fresh

[Caz] When the jam is over you head for the stairs

[JDL] All the girls and the guys are leaving in pairs

[AD] You had such a good time, you wish you could stay

[KG] Now it's time to catch the bus, train, or OJ

[Caz] You get to your house and pull out your key

[JDL] You're tired as hell, you want to sleep 'til three

[AD] Wake up Sunday, wipe the sleep from your eyes

[KG] And go out in the sun for some exercise

[Caz] Play ball, [JDL] roller skate, [AD] or visit a friend

[KG] And go home and think about [All] the next weekend

FRESH WILD FLY AND BOLD

[Grandmaster Caz] Well, I'm fresh 'cause I'm the best

[JDL] And I get wild when I'm riled

[Easy AD] I never get passed by 'cause I'm fly

[Almighty KG] And I'ma put you on hold 'cause I'm bold

[All] And Charlie Chase will last 'cause he's fast

And Tony Tone got pull 'cause he's original

[Caz] The Cold Crush is on [JDL] 'cause we perform

[AD] And even in a storm [KG] we'll keep you warm

[Caz] Hey Crew! [All] Yeah, Cap!

[Caz] We gonna need a little scratch for the rap now

[All] Tone and Chase! [Tone and Chase] Yeah, Crew!
[All] You're the DJs, what ya gonna do?

[Caz] Guess what, y'all? I'm fresh
[All] What makes you think so, Cap?
[Caz] Because I look so good and I'm the Lord of Rap
[All] How fresh? [Caz] So fresh that when I was young
I learned to drive women crazy with my tongue
[All] Now that's fresh

[JDL] Well, I get wild. [All] What makes you say that, L?
[JDL] Because it don't take much to make me yell
[All] How wild? [JDL] So wild that when I start to break, hey
You better step back and let me flake
[All] Now that's wild

[AD] Well, I'm fly. [All] Who told you that, Easy?
[AD] Your girl, his mother, and my lady
[All] How fly? [AD] So fly sometimes it seems
All I got to do is smile and I get screams
[All] Now that's fly

[KG] I'm bold. [All] What gives you that impression, K?
[KG] Because I don't care what nobody say
[All] How bold? [KG] So bold I smack a man with his gun
And kiss his woman, dis his mother, and don't even run
[All] Now that's bold

[All]
Fresh, wild, fly, and bold
We'll be that way 'til we grow old
For the rest of our life as long as we live
We'll keep using those adjectives

[Caz] That do describe the heart-breaking tribe
[JDL] That do permit us to go with
[AD] A musical flow that makes you say, "Ho!"
[KG] With a fresh rap style to make you go wild

[Caz] Cold Crush—[JDL] us—[AD] good in the clutch
[KG] And if you don't believe we're real, [All] then touch
Us—The Cold Crush

[All] Fresh, wild, fly, and bold
Yes, we're what makes the Crush so Cold
Our rhymes'll freeze all fake MCs
That don't say please before they seize
[Caz] Rhymes and routines that we make up
[JDL] You can't pour juice in a fake cup
[AD] They cannot write [KG] so they just rob
[All] But a biter can't do a real rapper's job
[Caz] But if you're hard-headed and you still think so
Grab your rhymes and your mic [All] and go for what you know
Kick it, kick it, kick it, kick it
[KG] My name is KG, [All] better known as the Al-
[KG] Mighty and with the three [All] I'm sure you'll call
[KG] On us when your ear [All] is in need for a treat
[KG] And if you don't know the K [All] that's who you've got to meet
[KG] I'm fourth in line [All] and in due time
[KG] Every rapper in the business [All] will know that I'm
[KG] Serious about this [All] and I don't play
[KG] I told a sucker MC that [All] just the other day
[KG] 'Cause I learnt the ropes [All] and paid my dues
[KG] I'm going for the gold, [All] no way that I can lose

[AD]
It's Easy AD that you wanted to be
Ever since you saw me MC
You wanted to be fine and learn how to rhyme
Even wanted your braids as long as mine
But the rhymes I write are a real delight
If you're a true MC you would not bite
On me or them, just sit down and
Write a rhyme with your mind, paper, or pen

But you can't so you don't, you will and you won't
Take heed with speed and read what I wrote

[JDL]
When I'm on the stage I go a little berserk
Start breaking, flaking, you know I do work
I try to get you on mine when I deliver my line
'Cause it's about making rhymes like no one else can design
I do everything I can to make myself better
Live on a steady diet of stages and meda
Know all the celebs and when I'm in the crowd
They surround me like the press, scream my name out loud
[All] Say, yo! JDL! [Caz] What's happening?
[AD] Where have you been? [KG] When are you rocking again?
[JDL] And when I'm boppin away I hear a lot of them say
[KG] Goddamn, I wanna be like the L one day

[Grandmaster Caz]
So many biting MCs, you're all a pain in my neck, huh!
They should be sending me your royalty check
You just bit my rhyme, didn't pay no tax
Copied the music from someone else, put it on wax
I'm mad as hell 'cause it's bound to sell
And you be biting what I'm writing and people can't tell
You change it around, disguise the sound
With no prior desire to write, that's why I frown
On those of you that don't strive try to be
Original and write like the Captain do
So put your teeth away and try someday
And you can quote it 'cause I wrote it only yesterday

[All] Fresh, [Caz] and unless I missed my guess
I'm the best, oh yes, because I wrote the test
[All] Wild, [JDL] honey-child on the top of the pile
Once in a while I crack a smile
[All] Fly, [AD] know why? 'Cause 'til the day I die

I'll always be the guy you won't pass by

[All] Bold, [KG] so cold and so hard to hold

[All] And when they made the Cold Crush they broke the mold

DJ HOLLYWOOD

Like Eddie Cheba, DJ Hollywood was a disco-style DJ who played primarily at clubs with an older and more middle-class clientele than one would associate with early hip-hop. Nevertheless, his influence was extensive because of the rhymes he developed to supplement his sets. One artist who was greatly influenced by Hollywood, Kurtis Blow, sums up this pioneer's status: "His voice was golden like a god, almost— that's why I wanted to be an MC! . . . [He had] the first rhythmic rhymes I ever heard a cat say during the hip-hop days—we're talking about the 70s."[13] A discussion of his contribution and of the following verses can be found in the introduction to Part One.

LIVE AT THE ARMORY 1979 (2)

Clap your hands, everybody

Everybody, clap your hands

We want to hear you clap your hands, everybody

Everybody, clap your hands

Now I don't mean to brag or boast

I'm like the hot butter on your morning toast

I'm not a Duracell, I'm an alkaline

So let's have a . . . [good times]

That's right, y'all, and you don't stop, keep on

Now we want everybody to get somebody, come on, let's have a little fun out here. We gonna give you forty seconds to find you a fine young lady and bring her to the dance floor—everybody, come on! And you don't stop, keep on. Yes, it's Hollywood, turn out, because that is all I be about. We gonna see if we can't get everybody dancing—come on, fellas, don't stand around, get a fine, foxy

mama. Uh! If Wolfman Jack was here, he'd try to tell you to get one of those
fine, foxy mamas, something like this, he might say: "That's right, Clyde, got
something good for your hide, something to keep you satisfied, talking about
some heavy [good times] *. . . medicine."*

And you don't stop, keep on
Just hip-hip, you hop-a, don't stop
Everybody, come on, let's body rock
Now I rock the freak and I freak the rock
Now I'm playing the music and I just can't stop
Once again with a feeling that's so divine
Let's have a—Let's have a [good times]
That's right, yo, let's do it, let's do it

Alright, now, we got all the people in the house in the back, they ready to rock, all
you people in the front, just turn around and get somebody and kind of punk
rock, to the beat, come on down, let's punk rock a little bit . . . Oh shit . . . punk
rock! There's a few dances we do at the Kool, we change it up a little bit,
sometimes we might say . . . double up. Sometimes we get down, mama. . . .
Having a good time, we say, how many people out here know about the
Macho Man meeting the Patty Duke? Well, if you know anything about the
Macho Man meeting Patty Duke, somebody say,

"Macho"—*Macho*
Say, "mucho-macho"—*Mucho-macho*
Say, "ooh-ah, ooh-ooh-ah"—*Ooh-ah, ooh-ooh-ah*
Double up

Come on and let's go to work
Let's do it, let's do it
Said the disco lights and the boogie nights
Are really here to stay
Sexy mamas and fancy papas
Always want to play
With iron nerves I'm prepared to serve
A sugar-coated, red electric
Super-freaky crumb off a disco cake

To make you shake and bake
To enhance your mind and de-lighten your kind
To the feeling that's so divine
It's music, so use it
And don't you dare abuse it
Let's do it

*Right now, I know y'all didn't spend your money to come in tonight and stand
around and look. I want y'all to get on the floor and kind of cook. To all the
lovely ladies in the house—and we see some fine, foxy mamas out here this
morning—come on . . .*

I love the way you walk
I love the way you talk
Oh girl, the way you look
Like somethin out a picture book
Let's do it, let's do it
Do, do it, do it

The wheels of steel's being turned by my main man DJ Starski, girl
Just hip-hip-the-hop, but don't stop
Everybody, come on, let's body rock
Just throw your hands in the air
Wave 'em like you just don't care
And if you came out to work your body this morning
Somebody say, "Oh yeah"—*Oh yeah*
Alright, now we want all the good-feeling people in the house to feel good
Somebody say, "Sex"—*Sex*
"And more sex"—*And more sex*
Say, "Sex is good"—*Sex is good*
"Like Hollywood"—*Like Hollywood*
Then it's up my back, it's around my neck
Woo-hah! I got the girls in check

And you don't stop, a-keep on
Just clap your hands, everybody
I'ma tell you about Hollywood

Just clap your hands, everybody
As your feeling's got to be good

*Alright, we want Larry to come over by the door. Larry, you come over by the
    door. Everybody else, I wanna know, how many people out here in Jamaica
    know how to do the world-famous Patty Duke dance? If you can Patty Duke,
    let me hear you say,*

"Patty Duke"—*Patty Duke*
Say, "Patty Duke"—*Patty Duke*
Somebody say, "Yes, yes y'all"—*Yes, yes y'all*
"Yes, yes y'all"—*Yes, yes y'all*

*Alright now, for those of y'all who don't know how to Patty Duke, we gonna
    explain it to you, mama, come on . . .*

You just wiggle your hips and you rock your knees
And you Patty Duke any way you please
Now the best way to get into the swing
Is to act like you're doing the Shing-a-ling
Then, mama, let your body work
Then you wave your arms like you're doing the Jerk
Then you turn it on loose like a bowl of soup
Now you lookin real good doing the Patty Duke
Hey girl, don't you lose your stride
Just Patty Duke a little to the side
Then you give your partner a laugh and grin
And then you Patty Duke right back up to him
Come on—*Let's go to work*
Come on—*Let's go to work*
Get the bone out your back, boy
Get the bone out your back, girl
Just throw your hands up in the air
Wave 'em around like you just don't care
If you feelin the groove that makes you move
Somebody say, "Oh yeah"—*Oh yeah*

The music of Starski, we gonna get kinda mellow, we want everybody to put their
hands together right here. Everybody put your hands together, we want to
hear everybody right here, come on, y'all. Just a little bit—clap your hands.
Stomp your feet. Clap your hands. Stomp your feet—come on, Starski. That's
right, y'all, and you don't stop, you keep on. For all the lovely ladies in the
house, I'd just like to say,

[Sung]
I got a word for the wise
Just to tranquilize
Your mind, your body and soul
We got a brand new rhythm now
And we gonna let it take control
Come on, let's do it
Let's do it, let's do it, let's do it
We can do it, now
There's nothing to it, now
Come on, let me see you work it out to the music
Come on, let's do it
Let's do it, let's do it, uh-huh

That's right, y'all, and you don't stop, a-keep on
I said dippy-dippy-dive, so-socialize
Just-a come on and make my nature rise
When I come in the door, what did I see?
Too many people trying to freak with me
So I started to dance, I had a little fun
And all of a sudden it was four on one
So I started to freak, I did my best
And all of a sudden I had to grab my chest
Then my knees start to bend and I fall back
And to my surprise I caught a heart attack
Let's do it, let's do it
Starski, what you got for me?
What you say? Starski
That's right, y'all, and you don't stop now

Just hip-hip-the-hop, the hop, the hop

Dippy-dippy dip-dip-dop, but don't stop

From the coast of California to the shores of Maine

I said all the girls love the way I run my game

Because I got style and I got class

And I don't talk my shit too fast

Now your body's moving to the rhythm and the rhyme

And your feet keep stepping right on time

As you listen to the voice that's so divine

Just Hollywood in your mind

Said the bass is in your face

And the highs are in your eyes

It's the music of the Hollywood that'll

Definitely tranquilize

You see, I got the neck of gold, better than Baretta

I'm a Casanova Brown because I'm down

To the hip-hop, the hip-hip-hop, the hop

To the dippy-dippy dip-dip dop

To the hip-hop, you don't stop

Let's rock, y'all, to the beat

Right now, once again, to all the people out there dancing to the music, we want
you to put your hands together one more time. Come on—just clap your
hands, everybody; everybody, clap your hands . . .

FUNKY FOUR + 1

Like many of the groups that made their names as live performers before the advent of recorded rap, the Funky Four +1 has a tangled history. Originally known simply as the Funky Four, the group consisted of four MCs—KK Rockwell, Keith-Keith, Rahiem, and Sha-Rock —and two DJs, Breakout and Baron, who pumped their music through a sound system known as "Sasquatch." In a competitive realm where volume mattered, having a sound that couldn't be drowned out was as important for ensuring success as was skill in the finer points of moving a crowd.

The Funky Four was highly regarded but not every battle turned in the group's favor. After an unsuccessful contest versus Grandmaster Flash and (the then) Furious Four, the Funky Four lost Rahiem, who defected and joined Flash's crew. His move prompted Sha-Rock—one of the first and best female MCs—to leave the group. Since you can't have a Funky Four with only two MCs, two replacements—Jazzy Jeff and Lil' Rodney Cee—were recruited. After seeing the new incarnation of the group perform, Sha-Rock got back with the guys and The Funky Four + 1 was born.

Having honed their show in the gyms and the parks, the Funky Four + 1 found recording to be both a blessing and a curse. Their first single, released on Enjoy Records in 1979, was a fourteen-minute song called "Rappin and Rockin the House." As was the case for all rap records released in 1979 and 1980 (and for most records in the immediate years thereafter), the track featured not the group's DJs Breakout and Baron, but a backing band—in this case, one led by the percussionist and producer Pumpkin, who was the man in the studio behind many early rap recordings. The success of their Enjoy single led to an offer from Sugar Hill impresario Sylvia Robinson, who bought out the group's contract from Enjoy owner Bobby Robinson and took them on tour with other Sugar Hill groups. They released several singles for the label, including 1981's "That's the Joint," and also became—after Blondie's Debbie Harry saw them perform at a club in Greenwich Village—the first rap group to appear on national TV, coming on at the end of an episode of *Saturday Night Live*.

These positive developments were balanced by the unfortunate fact that the shift to studio work left their DJs in the lurch. The Funky Four + 1 now had the instrumental versions of their own records to rap to in performance, and Baron and Breakout no longer anchored the group. The change in emphasis led to fissures and the group disbanded. What remains on record, however, is a good representation of the nonstop, almost interminable flow of a multimember group, of interplay of verses among group members, and of the contribution to early rap of a dope female MC.

FROM **RAPPIN AND ROCKIN THE HOUSE**

[All]

This is the way we rock the house

Sure enough, everybody, gonna turn it out

[KK Rockwell]
Well, I'm KK Rockwell 'cause I rock so swell
Every time you hear my name it rings a bell

[Rodney Cee]
Well, I'm Lil Rodney Cee, making history
With all the fly girls yelling, "take me"

[Sha-Rock]
Well, I'm Sha-Rock and I can't be stopped
For all the fly guys, gonna hit the top

[Keith-Keith]
Well, I'm Keith-Keith but you can call me Keith Caesar
The reason why 'cause I'm the women pleaser

[Jazzy Jeff]
Well, I'm Jazzy Jeff with the most finesse
Now I do it to the rhythm 'til I do it the best

[All four guys] Now we're the Funky Four
                          [Sha-Rock] and I'm the plus one more
[All] And this is the way we go back and forth

[KK Rockwell]
We're the five MCs that are too much
And we rock the mics with the magical touch

[Rodney Cee]
We're on time, we're masterminds
We hypnotize when we run down the rhymes

[Sha-Rock]
They're four fly guys and the best female
I'm telling the truth, not a fairy tale

[Keith-Keith]
Now listen to the story that the five put down
And it's guaranteed, so let them travel around

[Jazzy Jeff]

We said it once, we said it twice

That we're proving to you that we're better than nice

. . . .

[Sha-Rock]

'Cause the sun won't shine, the rain won't stop

We got a style called punk rock

Just get up out your chair, start to have some fun

We're two DJs, Funky Four plus one

To the people out there, we want you to know

We are the ones with the magical show

We're two DJs and five MCs

Four of them fellas, plus one is me

We're here to please everybody out there

Forget about your problems, get 'em out your hair

So just get on the floor, don't you be shy

You can do it too, just give it a try

To the people out there, we want the best

Satisfaction guaranteed is what we possess

We can rock on the mic with a master plan

We do it for the girl, woman, boy, or man

Most people go around just thinking anyway

We want you to hear what we say

The things we say, the things we do

It's like runnin a race and along comes you

There's a lot of competition to beat

But we are the ones, they are the ones

I am the one with the most unique

Funky Four got rhymes galore, they got the

Best female, Sha-Rock—I'm down by law . . .

FROM **THAT'S THE JOINT**

. . . .

[All four guys] To the beat that makes you wanna rap

Come on, Sha-Rock, cut out the crap

Just turn on your mic and start to rap
And let everybody know you can never be the wack
[Sha-Rock] You know that. [All] And you know that
[Sha-Rock] And I know [All] and she knows and we know that
We know what, Sha-Rock? [Sha-Rock] When I rap Funky Four
I can never be the wack. [All] And we hear you, Sha-Rock
She's the joint

[Sha-Rock] Do it up, y'all—do, do it up
Sha-Rock is gonna show you how you get real rough
I'm Sha-Rock and I can't be stopped
For all the fly guys I will hit the top
Well, I can do it for the ones, for weak or strong
And I can do it for the ones that are right or wrong
Well, I'm listed in the column that's classified
I can be your nurse and I'm qualified
To talk about respect, I won't neglect
My strategy is for you to see
So don't turn away by what I say
'Cause I'm on, I'm bad when I'm talking to you
They're four fly brothers who can do it too
The party people in the place, it's just for you
So get down—get, get, get on down
I'm the plus one more and I'm throwin down
[All four guys] She's the best female in this here town
[Sha-Rock] And everybody know that I'm golden brown
And you know [All] she's the joint

[Jazzy Jeff] I can pull a young lady with nice fine thighs
I'm the kind of MC to make women just sigh
I'm Jazzy Jeff with the most finesse
I'm down with the five that rock the mic the best
'Cause I move the groove and I do it cool
Now rockin you and you I'm sure to prove
'Cause I want a young lady with a lot of finesse
And she's got to be on; [Sha-Rock] 'cause he's Jazzy Jeff

[Jazzy Jeff] She's got to be sweet, [All] yes, [Jazzy Jeff] fine and kind
And that's just the kind of woman I want to be mine
You know [All] he's the joint

[Keith-Keith] Now what you see is what you get
You say, I am bad and that you can bet
I have a quality for you and me
And to all the young ladies, this is what it be
[All] Say, his name is Keith-Keith, [Keith-Keith] as my rhymes go down
To all the young ladies, just gather around
With the rhymes I possess, the words I protest
And I can put together, I can call it finesse
Now listen up, young ladies, and listen up good
I'm gonna rock on the mic like I know I could
[All] Like you know he should. [Keith-Keith] Like I know I would
[All] He's Keith-Keith—[Keith-Keith] I rock the house
[All] He's Keith-Keith—[Keith-Keith] I rock, shock, rock, turn it out
And you know that [All] and he got [Keith-Keith] the finesse
To behold that [All] he's the joint

[Jazzy Jeff] Keepin on to, to the crack of dawn
Party people in the place, you got to keep on
If you like the beat and you want some more
Scream it out and say, "Funky Four"
[All] Funky Four! [Jazzy Jeff] "Plus one more"
[All] And the plus one more! [Jazzy Jeff] Now you don't stop
You said, the beat goes on [Keith-Keith] and it's high-powered stuff
[Rodney Cee] We won't stop rockin' [KK] 'til you all get enough
[Sha-Rock] Other—[All four guys] ooh, ah—ooh, ooh, [Sha-Rock] ah, ah
[All] Ooh, ah and don't stop—[Keith-Keith] hit it
[All] That's the joint

[Jazzy Jeff] We have an obligation that we must fulfill
[Keith-Keith] Like a .357 we are the kill
[Rodney Cee] We're like Machine Gun Kelly and Bonnie and Clyde

[KK] And when we shock the house we stand side by side
[Sha-Rock] We on top of the world, we're looking down
[All] We're going straight ahead, we never turning around
[Keith-Keith] Because we are so close but yet so far
[Rodney Cee] And to all the party people, [KK] you know who we are
[Sha-Rock] Get the point?
[Keith-Keith] And if you don't we want y'all to know
[Rodney Cee] We're down, [KK] we rock, [All guys] we're the Funky Four
[Sha-Rock] Plus one

[Rodney Cee] I was sitting in my house watching my TV
When all of a sudden it dawned on me
That I was all alone just wasting my time
So I grabbed the pen and paper and wrote down a rhyme
And I thought to myself how nice it would be
To be on top making cash money
To go on a tour all around the world
To tell little stories to all the fly girls
To sit on my throne, to command my own
To be number one on the microphone
Just telling a tale about how it's gonna be
For the Funky Four plus one MC
We'll be busting in and we'll be turning it out
While we rock to any beat without a doubt
Just chillin hard, livin in luxury
And being very proud to be an MC
[All] He's the joint

[KK] I'm KK Rockwell 'cause I raise a lot of hell
And I like to make love to the jazzy female
And I'm down with the crew from off the Hill
Now just walk through my door, you pose on my floor
First thing I touch is hips galore—[All] and then he—
[KK] Move her up—[All] and then he—[KK] kiss your lips—[All] and then
  he—

[KK] Hold on tight so I never slip—[All] and then he—

[KK] Tongue you down on to the ground

If any love is there it will be found

By the man you all can tell

Rockwell, to the depths of hell

And every time you hear my name, girl, it rings a bell

When the bell rings it goes, "Ding, dong"

Then I rock her and I shock her to the break of dawn

Like a hot butter on a bag of popcorn

Like Rockwell, just singing your song

And you know—[All] he's the joint

[Sha-Rock]

Come on, let's go to work (Go on, girl!)

Say, I got money and I can jerk

Let's go to work, let's go to work

We gave a lot of parties and we got jerked

But that's alright because we be good sports

'Cause we know some day we get the big

[All] Payoff

GRANDMASTER FLASH AND THE FURIOUS FIVE

Grandmaster Flash and the Furious Five are the best known of the groups of rap's first phase. Few groups can boast both one of the all-time greatest DJs (Grandmaster Flash) and one of the all-time greatest MCs (Melle Mel), as well as four other skilled MCs (Cowboy, Kid Creole, Mr. Ness/Scorpio, and Rahiem).

Grandmaster Flash was a DJ prodigy from the South Bronx whose claim to fame in the mid-1970s was being the fastest to mix from break to break, a skill he also helped refine by designing his own mixers. Realizing, as he puts it, that he "was not going to be an MC" since he was "totally wack on the mic," Flash endeavored "to find someone able to put a vocal enter-tainment on top of this rearrangement of music."[14] The first MC he enlisted was a gregarious and tough crowd-pleaser named Keith Wiggins, who went by the name Cowboy because of his bowed legs. He was soon followed by Kid Creole and Melle Mel, two brothers whose birth names were Nathaniel and Melvin Glover. Eventually to these three MCs were added Scorpio, a.k.a. Mr. Ness, and Rahiem (who came from the Funky Four)—thus bring-ing the total of the group to a furious five.

They played everywhere, amassing a major reputation as live perform-ers. The many tapes of their shows suggest how deserved that reputation was. Although they released a 12-inch under the name The Younger Gen-eration, under their own name their first release was "Superrappin" (1979). Given that the center of the group had always been Flash, the record re-vealed the kinds of changes that would quickly occur. Jeff Chang describes how Flash was relegated to the role of spectator, with a house band per-forming the instrumentals. "For the length of 'Superrappin,'" he writes, "the tension between what rap was—a live performance medium dominated by the DJ—and what it would become—a recorded medium dominated by the rappers—is suspended."[15]

Of the group's MCs, Melle Mel is the acknowledged master. His best ef-fort under Flash's name is undoubtedly "The Message," a dystopian series of urban vignettes that remains one of the most affecting raps ever recorded. Under his own name he also recorded widely, with perhaps his best track being "White Lines (Don't Don't Do It)," the double-negative subtitle of which suggests what an ambivalent antidrug song it is, if it can finally be called "antidrug" at all.

FROM **LIVE AT THE AUDUBON BALLROOM (12/23/78)**

Keep on
Keep on to the break of dawn
Like this, y'all, like that
Let the funk machine cause a heart attack

. . . .

Don't stop
Keep on to the heart drop
Fly girls, rock the house
Fly kids, rock the house

Let's rock, y'all, you don't stop
Keep on to the break of dawn
Grandmaster's in the house
Cooling out, turn the motherfucker out
Audubon, rock on
To the beat, y'all, freak freak
December twenty-third
Audubon, rock on
December twenty-third
Audubon, rock on
December twenty-third
Audubon, rock on
To the beat, y'all, freak freak
And you don't stop, you keep on
And then you rock to the rhythm of the rhythm of the rock
You can rock the hands right off the damn clock
You rock to the rhythm, you just don't quit
Because the music is on that be the serious shit

. . . .

He's the Jimmy Dean of the mean machine
Cutting a side with a gangster lean
Though his name is not found in the hall of fame
He'll shock and amaze and make you feel ashamed
Grandmaster's number one, Grandmaster's number one

. . . .

To the beat that makes you want to freak
To the highs that make your nature rise
To the sound that makes you want to get down
Is a song that makes you want to go on
Like hot butter on—say what? The popcorn
Females, what you want to do?
Go on, go on, because the beat don't stop 'til the break of dawn
Everybody, are you with me?
To the beat, y'all, freak freak

And I'm Melle Mel and I rock so well
From the World Trade to the depths of hell
I rock with the best with the most finesse
I took the top, I left the rest
So rock, y'all, and don't stop
Keep on to the break of dawn
You say Napoleon lost at Waterloo
And Custer lost and Lee did too
But Flash is a man that can't be beat
Because he never ever heard the word "defeat"

. . . .

You say unh, I like it
You say unh, I love it
So what the fuck of it?
To the beat, y'all, it don't stop
You say, sex is good, sex is on
If it wasn't for sex you wouldn't be born
Think about it

. . . .

One time, two time
Three times for your mind
Kick off your shoes and relax your feet
And dance to the rhythm of the sure shot beat

. . . .

He'll rock you high, he'll rock you low
He'll tell a sucker-nigger right where to go
Rock, rock, y'all, you don't stop
And then you dip dip dive, so-socialize
You clean out your ears, you open your eyes
You pay at the door as a donation
To hear the best sounds in creation

. . . .

Yes, yes, y'all—freak, freak, y'all
To the beat, y'all, it don't stop

We're bona fide, we're qualified
To hypnotize and tranquilize
And transact and double back
So we can keep the wack from off our track

. . . .

You go on and on and on-on and on
'Cause the beat won't stop 'til everybody's gone
Rock the spot to the crack of dawn
Like hot butter on the popcorn

. . . .

And when you rock the hip and when you rock the hop
Then you hip-hop and don't you dare stop

FROM **SUPERRAPPIN**

[All]
It was a party night, everybody was breakin
The highs was screamin and the bass was shakin
And it won't be long 'til everybody knowin that
Flash was on the beat box goin, that
Flash was on the beat box goin, that
Flash was on the beat box goin
And . . .
And . . .
And . . .
And . . . Sha-na-na

[Melle Mel] Italian, Caucasian, Japanese
Spanish, Indian, Negro, Vietnamese
MCs, disc jockeys
To all the fly kids and the young ladies
Introducing the crew you gotta see to believe
We're [All in succession] one, two, three, four, five [All] MCs
[Mel] I'm Melle Mel and I rock so well
[Mr. Ness] And I'm Mr. Ness because I rocks the best
[Rahiem] Rahiem, in all the ladies' dreams

[Cowboy] And I'm Cowboy to make you jump for joy

[Kid Creole] I'm Creole—[All] solid gold

The Kid Creole, [All] playing the role—[Mel] dig this—

[Mel] We're the Furious Five plus Grandmaster Flash

Giving you a blast and sho' nuf' class

So to prove to you all we're second to none

[All] We're gonna make five MCs sound like one

[Mel] You gotta dip-dip-dive, [Ness] so-so-socialize

[Rahiem] Clean out your ears [Cowboy] and then open your eyes

[Creole] And then pay at the door as a donation

[All] To hear the best sounds in creation

[Mel] He's a disco dream [Ness] of a mean machine

[Rahiem] And when he cuts the sides [Cowboy] you see what we mean

[Creole] You see his name is not found in the hall of fame

[All] But he'll shock and amaze and make you feel ashamed

[Mel] He'll mix a lime from a lemon [Ness] from a lemon to a lime

[Rahiem] He cuts the beat [Cowboy] in half the time

[Creole] And as sure as three times two is six

[All] You say Flash is the king of the quick mix

[Mel] We're five MCs [Ness] and we're on our own

[Rahiem] And we're the most well-known [Cowboy] on the microphone

[Creole] And we throw down hard and we aim to please

[All] With finesse to impress all the young ladies

[Mel] We got rhymes galore [Ness] and that's a fact

[Rahiem] And the satisfaction's guaranteed [Cowboy] to cause a heart
   attack

[Creole] We are the best as you can see

[All] So eliminate the possibility

[Mel] That to be an [All in succession] E-M-C-E-E

[All] Is not a threat to society

[Mel] Say, step by step, [All] stride by stride

[Mel] I know the fly young ladies would like to ride

[Mel] In my Mercedes, [All] young ladies

[Mel] In my Mercedes, [All] young ladies

[Mel] If my Mercedes break down and dull my grill

Well I [All] drive up in a new Seville

[Mel] If my Seville break down I take it all back

Well I [All] dull my grill in a new Cadillac

[Mel] If my Cadillac break down, it's just too much

Well I [All] shock your mind in a new Stutz-Stutz

[Mel] And if my Stutz break down I make another choice

Well I [All] dull my grill in a new Rolls-Royce

[Mel] And if my Royce break down I'll be out in the rain

[All in succession] And then forget it, forget it, forget it, forget it,
    forget it

Take the train, take the train, take the train

[All]

Can't, won't, don't stop rockin to the rhythm

'Cause I get down, 'cause I get down, 'cause I get down

[Kid Creole]

Ladies who don't know my name

And you fellas who don't know my game

Yes, I'm called the Prince of Soul

But others call me the Kid Creole

The MC delight, young ladies bite

When I'm on the mic I rock the house right

I'm the dedicated prince, heart of solid gold

Rockin to the rhythm while I'm playin the role

A cool calm customer, the master plan

It takes a sucker's man to try to jump my hand

And the things I do and what I say

Affect a lot of people in the strangest way

Makes them clap their hands and say "all right"

It's Creole to the broad daylight

Mister Ness, my mellow, what it look like

With you on the mic

[Mr. Ness]

Let's a-rock, y'all, let's a-rock the house

Because the Furious Five are gonna turn it out

So young ladies, if you think you heard

You heard the best rap, you heard the best word

Yes, it's true that we got the fuss

Because it can't be the best unless it came from us

There's five of us and we take no stuff

We comin through the city, we comin through rough

We number one—ain't nothing you can do

And if you wanna get down we'll rock you too

So freak for me, y'all, ya don't stop

Come on, come on, and let me see ya rock-rock

Cowboy, they say you're from the Bronx

So why don't you rock the beat and add a little spunk

[Cowboy]

Yes, yes, y'all, you don't stop

A-come on fly girls, I wanna hit the top

I am the C-O-W-B-O-Y

Why, the man so bad that you can't deny

You better watch your woman 'cause I'll tell you why

'Cause I'm Cowboy, I might give her a try

They call me Keith-Keith, the young ladies' relief

Known as the man of romance to make you dance

Can any of you ladies stand a chance?

I'm Cowboy and I'm shocking the house, you say

You say one, two, one more is three

And Melle Mel, come on, what you got for me?

[Melle Mel]

To the hip-hop, a hip-hop

A-don't stop, don't stop that body rock

Just get up out your seat, get ready to clap

Because Melle Mel is starting to rap

Ever since the top at my very first party
I felt I could make myself somebody
It was something in my heart from the very start
I could see myself at the top of the chart
Rapping on the mic, making cold, cold cash
With a jock spinnin for me called DJ Flash
Signin autographs for the young and old
Wearing big time silver and solid gold
My name on the radio and in the magazine
My picture on the TV screen
It ain't like that yet but—huh!—you'll see
I got potential and you will agree
I'm comin up and I gotta step above the rest
'Cause I'm using the ladder they call success
You say 1–2–3–4–5–6–7
Rap like hell and make it sound like heaven
7–6–4–5–3–2–1
A-come on, Rahiem, come and get some

[Rahiem]
Yes, yes, y'all, ya don't stop—come on
Come on—huh—I wanna hit the top
I'm a one of a kind, a man supreme
I know I'm in all of the ladies' dreams
I'm the R-A-H to the I-E-M
I put a wiggle in your butt if you tell me when
I'm the son of a gun with a hell of a fire
Fly girls can mess around and take you all higher
My clientele climb the great big boost
I'ma give it up and turn it loose—huh!
All you fly girls that don't know my game
Come up and talk to me and we'll tell you all the same
When you wake up in the night in a hell of a dream
You know you been possessed by the voice of
Rahiem, in all the ladies' dreams

[Melle Mel]

And making more currency than any MC

If your dream will turn to reality

. . . .

THE MESSAGE

[Chorus 2x]

It's like a jungle, sometimes it makes me wonder

How I keep from going under

[Melle Mel]

Broken glass everywhere

People pissing on the stairs, you know they just don't care

I can't take the smell, can't take the noise

Got no money to move out, I guess I got no choice

Rats in the front room, roaches in the back

Junkies in the alley with a baseball bat

I tried to get away but I couldn't get far

'Cause a man with a tow truck repossessed my car

Don't push me 'cause

I'm close to the edge

I'm trying not to

Lose my head

Uh-huh-huh-huh-huh

[Chorus]

Standing on the front stoop, hanging out the window

Watching all the cars go by, roaring as the breezes blow

Crazy lady, living in a bag

Eating out of garbage cans, used to be a fag hag

Says she danced the tango, skip the light fandango

A zircon princess seemed to lost her senses

Down at the peep show watching all the creeps

So she could tell the stories to the girls back home

She went to the city and got so-so-siditty
She had to get a pimp, she couldn't make it on her own

Don't push me 'cause
I'm close to the edge
I'm trying not to
Lose my head
Huh-huh-huh-huh

[Chorus 2x]

My brother's doing bad, stole my mother's TV
Says she watches too much, it's just not healthy
All My Children in the daytime, *Dallas* at night
Can't even see the game or the Sugar Ray fight
The bill collectors, they ring my phone
And scare my wife when I'm not home
Got a bum education, double-digit inflation
Can't take a train to the job, there's a strike at the station
Neon King Kong standing on my back
Can't stop to turn around, broke my sacroiliac
A mid-range migraine, cancered membrane
Sometimes I think I'm going insane, I swear, I might highjack a plane

Don't push me 'cause
I'm close to the edge
I'm trying not to
Lose my head

[Chorus 2x]

My son said, "Daddy, I don't wanna go to school
'Cause the teacher's a jerk, he must think I'm a fool
And all the kids smoke reefer, I think it'd be cheaper
If I just got a job, learned to be a street sweeper
Dance to the beat, shuffle my feet
Wear a shirt and tie and run with the creeps
'Cause it's all about money, ain't a damn thing funny

You got to have a con in this land of milk and honey"

They pushed that girl in front of the train

Took her to the doctor, sewed her arm on again

Stabbed that man right in his heart

Gave him a transplant for a brand new start

I can't walk through the park 'cause it's crazy after dark

Keep my hand on my gun 'cause they got me on the run

I feel like an outlaw, broke my last glass jaw

Hear them say, "You want some more?" Living on a seesaw

Don't push me 'cause

I'm close to the edge

I'm trying not to

Lose my head—say what?

[Chorus 4x]

A child is born with no state of mind

Blind to the ways of mankind

God is smiling on you but he's frowning too

Because only God knows what you'll go through

You'll grow in the ghetto living second rate

And your eyes will sing a song of deep hate

The places you play and where you stay

Looks like one great big alleyway

You'll admire all the number book-takers

Thugs, pimps, and pushers and the big money-makers

Driving big cars, spending twenties and tens

And you wanna grow up to be just like them—huh

Smugglers, scramblers, burglars, gamblers

Pickpockets, peddlers, even panhandlers

You say, "I'm cool, huh, I'm no fool"

But then you wind up dropping out of high school

Now you're unemployed, all non-void

Walking round like you're Pretty Boy Floyd

Turned stickup kid but look what you done did

Got sent up for a eight-year bid
Now your manhood is took and you're a Maytag
Spend the next two years as an undercover fag
Being used and abused, served like hell
'Til one day you was found hung dead in a cell
It was plain to see that your life was lost
You was cold and your body swung back and forth
But now your eyes sing the sad, sad song
Of how you lived so fast and died so young, so

Don't push me 'cause
I'm close to the edge
I'm trying not to
Lose my head
Huh-huh-huh-huh

[Chorus 2x]

[All]
Yo, Mel, you see that girl, man?
Yeah, man
—Cowboy!
Yo, that sound like Cowboy, man
That's cool
Yo, what's up, money
Yo
Hey, where's Creole and Rahiem at, man?
They upstairs cooling out
So, what's up for tonight, y'all?
Yo, we could go down to the Fever, man
Let's go check out Junebug, man
Hey, yo, you know that girl Betty?
Yeah, man
Her mom's got robbed, man
What?

Not again!

She got hurt bad

When this happen? When this happen?

[Screeching tires—Police enter scene]

Freeze! Don't nobody move nothing, y'all know what this is! Get 'em up!

What?

Get 'em up!

Man, we down with Grandmaster Flash and the Furious Five

What is that? A gang?

Naw, man!

Look, shut up! I don't want to hear your mouth

Excuse me, officer, officer, what's the problem?

Ain't no—you the problem! You the problem!

You ain't got to push me, man

Get in the car! Get in the car! Get in the godda—I said get in the car!

WHITE LINES (DON'T DON'T DO IT)

White lines

Vision dreams of passion

Blowin through my mind

And all the while I think of you

Pipe cries

A very strange reaction

For us to unwind

The more I see the more I do

Something like a phenomenon—Baby

Tellin your body to come along

But white lines . . .

Blow away . . .

Ticket to ride, white line highway

Tell all your friends they can go my way

Pay your toll, sell your soul

Pound for pound, costs more than gold

The longer you stay the more you pay
My white lines go a long way
Either up your nose or through your vein
With nothing to gain except killing your brain

[4x]
Freeze!
Rock!

Blow!

High—higher, baby
High—get higher, baby
High—get higher, baby
And don't ever come down—*Freebase!*

Pipe line
Pure as the driven snow
Connected to my mind
And now I'm having fun, baby
Pipe cries
It's getting kind of low
'Cause it makes you feel so nice
I need some one-on-one, baby
Don't let it blow your mind away—Baby
And go into your little hideaway
'Cause white lines
Blow away . . .

A million magic crystals
Painted pure and white
A multimillion dollars
Almost over night
Twice as sweet as sugar
Twice as bitter as salt
And if you get hooked, baby
It's nobody else's fault—so don't do it!

[4x]
Freeze!
Rock!

Blow!

High—higher, baby
High—get higher, baby
High—get higher, baby
And don't ever come down—*Freebase!*

Don't you get too high
Don't you get too high, baby
Turns you on
You really turn me on and on
'Cause you gotta come down
My temperature is rising
When the thrill is gone
No, I don't want you to go

A street kid gets arrested
Gonna do some time
He got out three years from now
Just to commit more crime
A businessman is caught
With twenty-four kilos
He's out on bail and out of jail
And that's the way it goes

Cane!
Sugar!
Cane!
Sugar!
Cane!

Athletes reject it
Governors correct it
Gangsters, thugs, and smugglers

Are thoroughly respected
The money gets divided
The women get excited
Now I'm broke and it's no joke
It's hard as hell to fight it—don't buy it

[4x]
Freeze!
Rock!

Blow!

High—get higher, baby
High—get higher, girl
High—get higher, baby
High—c'mon! Hu-rah!

White lines
Vision dreams of passion
Blowin through my mind
And all the while I think of you
Pipe cries
A very strange reaction
For us to unwind
The more I see the more I do
Something like a phenomenon—Baby
Tellin your body to come along
But white lines . . . blow away . . .

Little Jack Horner sittin on the corner
With no shoes and clothes
This ain't funny but he took his money
And sniffed it up his nose

[Spoken]
Hey, man, you wanna cop some blow?
Sure, whatcha got? Dust, flakes, or rocks?

I got China White, Mother of Pearl, Ivory Flake—what you need?
Well yeah, well, let me check it out, man, just let me get a freeze
Go ahead, man. The stuff I got should kill ya.
Yeah, man. That's ... that's raw ...

LADY B

Beginning her career as a DJ in Philadelphia, where she continues to spin on the radio, Lady B also wrote rhymes and was among the first handful of female rappers to record. She was also one of the earliest artists to break hip-hop outside of New York. In addition to showing that artists outside of the five boroughs had a stake in the burgeoning art, Lady B in her role as DJ apparently knew a sure-shot when she heard one: Mister Biggs of Soul Sonic Force claims that she was the first to play "Planet Rock" on the radio. In 2002 she received the Philly Urban Legend Award.

Known for her own "To the Beat, Y'all," the title of which is still a stock phrase of rap, Lady B is lyrically versatile, sliding from set pieces and stories ("From the age of one," "Jack and Jill went up a hill," "Me and Superman had a fight"), to propulsive crowd-moving, to self-aggrandizement. The final image of being buried with two turntables and a mixer could be updated from a Leadbelly blues tune. She even drops in a glancing interpolation of Bill Withers ("Put your foot on the rock and pat your foot / Don't stop—put your foot on the rock"). Her more direct references include Donald Duck, Mickey Mouse, John Travolta, Farrah Fawcett, Tony Dorsett, Alex Haley, Clark Gable, Reverend Ike, Perry Johnson, and Butterball. Her range of reference and various formal tactics suggest the versatility of the DJ, who must remember that the crowd is also a bunch of particular individuals.

TO THE BEAT, Y'ALL
I say clap your hands, everybody
Everybody, clap your hands

Just clap your hands, everybody

Everybody, clap your hands

Allow me to introduce myself

They call me Ms. DJ

I've got my name in the hall of fame

By the DJ rhymes I say

Now parental discretion is advised

We're gonna take this trip aloud

Say, the words I speak are very true

They're recommended by Triple Crown, you see

If you wanna know what moves my soul

Or shakes inside my brain

I got this beast I can't control

And it's driving me insane

I got eighteen years' experience

I'm the master of karate

Said don't nobody mess with me

And I don't mess with nobody

At the age of one, I was having fun

I was listening to the disco beat

At the age of two, I was doing to you

On turntables one and two

I've been number one all my life

And I've always played the dozens

Said I've got more rhymes in the back of my mind

Than Alex Haley's got cousins

To the mack, to the mack

To the front, to the back

Put your foot on the rock and pat your foot

Don't stop, put your foot on the rock

I've got a style that's all my own

You got Lady B on the microphone

I'm no Perry Johnson or Butterball

I just stopped by to freak out you all
I got a little black book with a thousand pages
With a listing of men that rank from all ages
To the beat, y'all, check it out, y'all
Don't stop

I said Jack and Jill went up the hill
To have a little fun
But stupid Jill forgot the pill
And now they have a son
The pot wasn't hot, the corn wasn't on
The butter didn't melt 'til the crack of dawn
I say, you bring the butter and I'll bring the salt
If you don't freak then it ain't my fault

. . . .

Said north, east, south, west
Said Lady B gonna rock the best
To the beat
To the DJ's funky beat
Lady B, as you know
Will rock you on your stereo
I'm no John Travolta, no Farrah Fawcett
I'll run more miles than Tony Dorsett
To the beat
To the DJ's funky beat
I said take out your ballpoint pen
And jot down these lines again
Said the beat's so fine it'll blow your mind
Way up your back and down your spine
Just do it
Just do it
I know a man with a golden voice
He has everything he needs

He's got two limousines and one Rolls-Royce
That travels at the fastest speed
Say Reverend Ike's on the mic
Clark Gable's on the turntable
Mickey Mouse gon' build a house
And Donald Duck don't give a—
Say what?
To the beat, y'all
I say hip hip-a-dop, oh-socialize
Come on, boy, and make my nature rise
Let's freak
Let's freak
Rock your body, rock it faster
I got a friend, he's the grand master
He'll rock your soul, control your mind
Said this is one of them master lines
Me and Superman had a fight
I hit him in the head with some kryptonite
I hit him so hard he went insane
Guess who's bustin out Lois Lane
It's him, y'all, yes yes, y'all
He's bustin out Lois Lane
I said hip-hop bop be bop be bop bop
I said uh-ah, I got it like that
To the beat, y'all, yes yes, y'all
Don't stop
I'm saying when I die, bury me deep
Plant two turntables at my feet
Put my mixer near my head
So when you close the casket I can rock the dead
To the beat, y'all, yes yes, y'all
Let's freak

SEQUENCE

When Sugar Hill Records owner Sylvia Robinson took the Sugar-hill Gang on tour in the fall of 1979 on the strength of their single "Rapper's Delight," a stop in Columbia, South Carolina, produced an unexpected discovery. Three young women—Angela Brown (Angie B), Gwendolyn Chisholm (Blondie), and Cheryl Cook (Cheryl the Pearl)—made their way backstage and asked to perform for the independent-label leader. Shortly thereafter Robinson had the group fly north to cut what would be the second-ever release on Sugar Hill, "Funk You Up," which went gold in three weeks.

This unlikely story yielded two firsts: Sequence became both the first all-female rap group signed to a label and the first group from the South to get attention. After the success of "Funk You Up," Sequence went on to record such songs as "And You Know That," "Monster Jam" (a collaboration with Spoonie Gee), and "Funky Jam (Tear the Roof Off)." In all, they recorded three full-length LPs. Unlike some of the Sugar Hill performers, the women from Sequence wrote their own rhymes; in fact, they often wrote rhymes for their label mates. Cheryl Cook was especially active as a ghostwriter, penning verses for "8th Wonder," "Apache," and "Livin in the Fast Lane" by the Sugarhill Gang. Angie B has since found success as a soul singer under the stage name Angie Stone.

In an interview with JayQuan on his Web site "The Foundation," Blondie recalls that "it took us a while to get with the pace and how things moved up North," but it didn't take long in musical terms.[16] Sequence not only "got with" but helped set the pace in rap's early days.

FROM **FUNK YOU UP**

[Blondie]

My name is Gwen, but they call me Blondie

I'm better known as the one and only

I'm five foot two, built so fine

36–26–36 down

I'm better known as freak and tan

A Sequence freak with all the fans

When I clap my hands and I stomp my feet

I jam to the sound of the Sequence beat

Wave your hands in the air

And wave 'em like you just don't care

Like Ginger Rogers and Fred Astaire

My main man Yogi Bear

I said I hip-ma-jazz and a raz-ma-jazz

And I jam to the disco beat

And if you can move your body like you move your hands

Then I'm sure you can move your feet

'Cause I'm supersonic, I'm a 3X tonic

When I'm not down, I'm up

When I get real hungry I run to the store

And get my Reese's Cup

I watch TV on my own

You gotta yabba-dabba-doo with Fred Flintstone

I'm sweeter than candy, I'm sweeter than honey

That's why they call me Blondie

I'm supercool and I'm superfine

And I'm one of a kind to shock your mind

And you can ring my bell all through the night

You can rock my body 'til the early light

Don't ring my bell, sayin please

If you cannot fulfill my needs

I don't mean to brag, I don't mean to boast

But they call my name from coast to coast

From the coast of California to the shore of Maine

Everybody loves the way I play my game

Say, I got more rhymes in the back of my mind

Than Billy Dee got lovers

I say I got style and I got class

I don't talk my stuff too fast

See, I'm cold as ice, I'm twice as nice

I get more sex than a cat chase mice

Blondie, hey, that's me
I'm rappin in the key of R-A-P

. . . .

[Cheryl the Pearl]

They call me Cheryl and I'll tell you why
'Cause I got such sexy bedroom eyes
When I pop 'em out and you look surprised
I got you and you're hypnotized
My love is strong if you can stand
To be within my sexy trance
But don't let this tell you all about me
I'm a jealous lady and that you'll see
If I don't get the things that I mention
That's when I start crying for attention
(Attention) That's what I say
And things just always go my way
Well, I talk a lot but I'm really shy
My loving ways just get me by
I write the baddest sounds around
I'm guaranteed to throw down
The only difference between you and me
And that is that I'm sexy
I'm an angel possessed with some devilish eyes
With the curvy hips to make your nature rise

. . . .

[Angie B]

I said Angie B is what they say
I got chocolate hips and a Milky Way
And I feel like a millionaire in space
Flying on a gold kite with the silver lace
Everybody calls me "never wrong"
'Cause I'm a freestyle freak with a funky song
Do you hear me talkin, do you hear me singin
On the microphone, won't you sing along

(You go do it, you go do it, you go do it, do it, do it)

I got two great partners standin by me

That's guaranteed to jam to the beat

One is Blondie and she's right on time

She calls herself Miss Super Fine

I said Cheryl the Pearl is the one with the eyes

She's guaranteed to hypnotize

Said Angie B, hey, that's me

I can rock you so dangerously

(You go do it, you go do it, you go do it, do it, do it)

At a quarter to six you got in a fix

And you called on Angie B

And you look surprised as I arrive

To see me dressed to a tee

(You go do it, you go do it, you go do it, do it, do it)

FROM **AND YOU KNOW THAT**

We rock you high and we rock you well

We rock you better than Southern Belles

When I say ring-ding-dong

Come on, Cheryl the Pearl, get on the microphone

[Ring-ding-dong]

[Cheryl the Pearl]

I'm Cheryl the Pearl and I'm ready to go

I'm gonna shock the house like Kurtis Blow

I came to earth to freak and make you groove

'Cause all I wanna do is see your body move

Like Magic Johnson, young Casanova Fly

Hitting forty-two points with tears in his eyes

MVP 'cause he rocked the game

And now his name'll go down in the hall of fame

I went back to heaven when I got the news

All the people on earth was hip to my groove

I came back down to shock the world

'Cause I'm better known as the wonder girl

Like a pow-pow shoot-'em-up, have you any guns?

I'm the deputy of love and they call me number one

Baa-baa black sheep, have you any lambs?

I'm Cheryl the Pearl, I rock Superman

Eeny meeny miny moe, which way you wanna go?

I'm going straight to the top, check it out, I can't be stopped

FROM **SIMON SAYS**

We're not like Jack or stupid Jill

Before we get punked we'll take the pill

The fellas wanna make love every day

But when you get punked they run away

You know it's something that you did

But he say, "Huh, it's not my kid"

You sit right there and you start to cry

And to your Moms you lie, lie, lie

But before you know it the kid is born

The man you love, check it out, he's gone

You sit there and you have to smile

You're wondering how you're gon' feed the child

But remember you're young, gifted, and black

And that your kid could never be the wack

SPOONIE GEE

Spoonie Gee is the smoothest-talking ladies' man from the early days of rap, a native of Harlem who dubbed himself the "metropolitician" and "Spoonie-Spoon, the medicine man." Befitting someone who grew up two blocks from the Apollo Theater, a soulful sophistication comes through in his delivery, which is characterized by a thick but silky timbre and an old school knack for keeping the rhymes coming, bar after bar. His lyrics are lightly lascivious, self-aggrandizing, and playful; the occasional flashes of humor find their lyrical flipside in serious moments such as those found on "Street Girl" (1984), where financial strains and psychosexual pressures mount. In addition to the singular strength of his player persona, he demonstrated an ability to give up solo status without diminishing rap returns in collaborations with Sequence ("Monster Jam") and the Treacherous Three ("The New Rap Language"). Whether with other artists or by himself, Spoonie has one of the most recognized voices from the early days of recorded rap.

Spoonie's first record, 1979's "Spoonin Rap," was produced by Peter Brown and released on his label Sound of New York—ironic, because Spoonie was raised by his uncle Bobby Robinson, owner of the label Enjoy Records. After hearing his nephew's song, Robinson released Spoonie's second, 1980's "Love Rap," which had "The New Rap Language" on the other side. These tracks alone would have cemented Spoonie's reputation as what Tuff City founder Aaron Fuchs calls "the first man, if man-child, in a world previously populated by boys . . . the first rapper whose content, style and character was R and X-rated."[17] Spoonie went on to record his only full-length album, *The Godfather* (1987), for Fuchs's label. His mid-1980s songs show no decrease in skill and formal sophistication, but it is for the songs of his earliest period that Spoonie is represented here, establishing as they did the basic template for the player persona in rap.

FROM **SPOONIN RAP**

You say one for the trouble, two for the time
Come on, y'all, let's rock the—

Yes, yes, y'all, freak, freak, y'all
Funky beat, y'all
Then you rock and roll, then you roll and rock
And then you rock to the beat that just don't want you to stop
'Cause I'm the S to the P, double O-N-Y
The one MC who you can't deny
'Cause I'm the baby maker, I'm the woman taker
I'm the cold-crushin lover, the heartbreaker
So come on, fly girls, and please don't stop

'Cause I'm MC Spoonie Gee, wanna hit the top
And young ladies, rock on

Say, I was driving down the street on a stormy night
Say, up ahead there was this terrible fright
There was a big fine lady, she was crossing the street
She had a box with the disco beat
So I hit my brakes, but they're not all there
I missed the young lady by only a hair
And then I took me a look, I said, "La-di-da-di"
A big fine girl, she had a hell of a body
Then she looked at me and then she started switchin
So I took my key out of the ignition
Got out the car and kept my mouth shut
'Cause my 20–20 vision was right on her butt
I caught up with her, I said, "You look so fine
I swear to God I wish you was mine"
She said, "Hey boy, you're Spoonie Gee"
"That's right, honey, how do you know me?"
She said, "Spoonie Gee, you're all the same
And everybody who disco know your name"
I said, "Come on, baby, it's not too far
We gonna take a little walk to my car"
As soon as we got to the car, then we sat in the seat
And then the box was rockin to the funky beat
And then I looked at her and pushed the seat back
Turned off her box and put on my 8-track
And then I started rappin without no pause
'Cause my mind was just gettin in those drawers
And then I got in the straw, we start to do it to the beat
And started doing like this, started doing the freak

Yes, yes, y'all, freak, freak, y'all
'Cause I'm MC Spoonie Gee, I wanna be known
As the metropolitician of the microphone
'Cause I'm a man's threat and I'm a woman's pet

And I'm known as the mademoiselle's joy
And I'm a man who fights on the microphone
And who all the people enjoy, y'all
Yes, yes, y'all, freak, freak, y'all
And don't stop, keep on

Say, I was cranking and a-freaking at a disco place
I met a fine girl, she had a pretty face
And then she took me home, you say, "The very same night?"
The girl was on and she was outta sight
And then I got the girl for three hours straight
But I had to go to work, so I couldn't be late
I said, "Where's your man?" She said, "He's in jail"
I said, "Come on baby, 'cause you're tellin a tale
'Cause if he comes at me and then he wants to fight
See, I'ma get the man good and I'ma get him right
See, I'ma roll my barrel and keep the bullets still
And when I shoot my shot, I'm gonna shoot to kill
'Cause I'm the Spoonie-Spoon, I don't mess around
I drop a man where he stand right into the ground
You say from Africa to France, say to Germany
Because you can't get a man tryin to mess with me
'Cause I'm a smooth talker, I'm the midnight stalker
I'm the image of the man they call the J. D. Walker
If you're gonna be my girl, just come along
And just-a clap your hands to my funky song
I don't drink, I don't smoke, I don't gamble neither
And most people call me a woman pleaser
'Cause I keep their phone numbers on the shelf
I go to make love and then I keep it to myself
So no one's gonna know what I'm doing to you
Not your sister, brother, niece, nor your mother, father too"

. . . .

And for you sucker-sucker dudes who commit the crime
You wanna do bad, but don't do the time

I say you wanna be this and then you wanna be a crook

You find a old lady, take her pocketbook

And then you steal your mother's, father's money on the sly

You can run, but you can't hide

When the cops crashed through, your face turned pale

I'ma tell you a little story about the jail

'Cause see, in jail there's a game and it's called survival

And they run it down to you on your first arrival

They tell you what you can and cannot do

But if you go to jail, watch yours for a crew

'Cause when you go in the shower, he's a-pulling his meat

And he's looking at you and say you look real sweet

And at first there was one, now ten walked in

Now how in the hell did you expect to win?

I said you better look alive, not like you take dope

And please, my brother, don't drop the soap

And if you get out the bathroom and you're alive

Just remember only a man can survive

. . . .

LOVE RAP

From the south to the west to the east to the north

Come on, Spoonie Gee, and go off and go off

Yes yes, y'all, freak freak, y'all

To the beat, y'all, so unique, y'all

Well, I was speedin down the street and then I pushed my brakes

Because I seen a fine girl make me shiver and shake

Then I blew my horn and she turned her head

And to the young lady this is what I said

I said, "Baby, baby, come on over to my car

And tell me your name so I can know who you are

And just give me your number, address and all

I might wanna see you, I might wanna call

Your friend's house, your house, wherever you be

But meanwhile, baby doll, just come with me"
So I opened my door, she got into my car
She looked into my face, said, "I know who you are"
She said, "I seen you once, I can't forget your face
You got style, got class, finesse and taste"
I said, "I'm glad you think so, I'm glad we met
'Cause I haven't met a girl nothing like you yet
Just lay on back and relax your head
Because my seats are soft just like a bed"
Then she looked at me and started to smile
She said, "Baby, let's have a little fun for a while
I know every move from A to Z
But if it's alright with you, it's alright with me
But if we do it in the car, that's no respect"
"So let's go to my house." She said, "It's a bet"
And when I got into my house it drove the female wild
The first thing she said is "let's have a child"
I said, "No, no, baby, I only got time
To make a lot of money and to say my rhyme
And if I had a baby I might go broke
And believe me, to me, girl, that ain't no joke"
People smile in your face and talk behind your back
And when you get the story it's never exact
Some say they're your friends but they really are not
Because they only out to try to get what you got
They wanna hang out all day, smoke cheeba, sniff coke
Then it's see you later, alligator, when you're broke
But you attract all the dudes and all the young ladies
With your diamond rings and your big Mercedes
Gold on your chest with your fine suit and clothes
'Cause that's the way the whole story goes
Now you got you a girl and you're doing the do
But every girl you see, you think she's made for you

She used to walk down the street and never did speak
Now she knows you got money at the tip of your feet
And you're a sucker-sucker dude for thinking you're slick
'Cause all you gonna do with the girl is trick
You can't lead yourself because you been led
The same young girl that messed up your head
Every time you look around she's asking for your money
She thinks it's cool and she thinks it's funny
If you're smart you leave her, if you're dumb you stay
But if you do you'll be a fool until your hair turns gray
'Cause when your money's gone, believe me, my friend
That those money-hawking girls are gonna get in the wind
'Cause when you ain't got a dime, that ain't no joke
And the girls you used to know will call you Mister Broke
So you better, better learn from the one mistake
And stop being a fool before it's too late
I gotta cure for all women and hope you understand
Why they call me Spoonie Gee, the medicine man
Because I do it with greed and not too much speed
So just take off your clothes, let me give you what you need
Make you feel like a woman from what I have to give
'Cause I'ma be a lover for as long as I live
'Cause I'm the S to the P, double O-N-Y-G
My purpose to service for you ladies to see
So fly guys, come drop, give the ladies a chance
To see the king of soul, the prince of romance
'Cause I'm sweet, not mean, every woman's supreme
I want all you fly girls to stay on the scene
See the microphone king while he's doing his thing
To the punk rock, disco, boogie, and swing
Let's rock, y'all, it don't stop
And before I rock and get you out your seat
I'm gonna give you a taste of the sure-shot beat

SUGARHILL GANG

Almost anyone who has even heard of rap has heard the Sugarhill Gang. Wonder Mike, Big Bank Hank, and Master Gee released two full-length albums, *Sugarhill Gang* (1980) and *8th Wonder* (1982), but their name is synonymous with one song: "Rapper's Delight."

Recorded in September 1979, "Rapper's Delight" became the first rap record to make a major impact on the listening public. After its release, Sylvia Robinson's Harlem-based independent label, Sugar Hill Records, became the major studio player of rap's early era; the nascent form began in earnest its transformation from an exclusively live (and underground, tape-based) medium to one that was pressed on vinyl; and the group became and remains a lightning rod attracting charges of plagiarism and lack of authenticity. Did Big Bank Hank, who was discovered by Robinson rapping while working in a pizzeria, steal his rhymes from the rhyme book of his acquaintance Grandmaster Caz? (Rahiem from the Furious Five has also said the song bit one of his rhymes.) Or did he and the other members merely take what was available at the time, the figures and forms that made up the lingua franca of rap, and with equal parts skill and luck deliver it artfully to a surprisingly eager public? (Says Wonder Mike: "I think there's no denying there's a lot of shout-outs and phrases that were just like the common vocabulary at the time.")[18]

Granted, the fact that the first big rap group did not hone its routines in the clubs and at park jams—though as individuals they had been members of groups—was striking. But "Rapper's Delight" had *something*. Part of that something was no doubt the Sugar Hill house band's re-creation of the bass line from Chic's disco hit "Good Times." But just as much or even more was the rhythmic ebullience of the delivery of the lyrics. At fifteen minutes' running time, the three rappers could trade riffs and stories with abandon, which gave the song a more flexible and human feel than could the disco dominating the era's airwaves.

Other performers, whatever their ambivalence about the song, knew that things were about to be different. Reggie Reg of the Crash Crew says, "Guys was going crazy over this 'Rapper's Delight' thing. It was a very good record, and seeing how good that record was doing, the attention that record got, we knew we had to make a record." Grandmaster Flash said, "The game of hip-hop changed. 'Rapper's Delight' just set the goal to a whole 'nother level. It wasn't rule the Bronx or rule Manhattan, or rule whatever. It was now how soon can you make a record."[19] And ultimately it was by making records that rap ruled not whatever but the world.

FROM **RAPPER'S DELIGHT**

[Wonder Mike]

I said a-hip-hop, the hibbie, the hibbie

To the hip-hip-hop and you don't stop the rockin

To the bang-bang boogie, say up jump the boogie

To the rhythm of the boogedy-beat

Now what you hear is not a test

I'm rapping to the beat

And me, the groove, and my friends

Are gonna try to move your feet

You see, I am Wonder Mike

And I'd like to say hello

To the black, to the white, the red and the brown

The purple and yellow—but first I gotta

Bang-bang, the boogie to the boogie, say

Up jump the boogie to the bang-bang boogie

Let's rock, you don't stop

Rock the rhythm that'll make your body rock

Well, so far you've heard my voice

But I've brought two friends along

And next on the mic is my man Hank

Come on, Hank, sing that song

[Big Bank Hank]

Check it out—I'm the C-A-S-N, the O-V-A and

The rest is F-L-Y

You see, I go by the code of the Doctor of the Mix

And these reasons I'll tell you why

You see, I'm six foot one and I'm tons of fun

And I dress to a tee

You see, I got more clothes than Muhammad Ali

And I dress so viciously

I got bodyguards, I got two big cars

I definitely ain't the wack

I got a Lincoln Continental and

A sun-roof Cadillac

So after school I take a dip in the pool

Which is really on the wall

I got a color TV so I can see

The Knicks play basketball—Hear me talking

'Bout checkbook, credit cards, mo' money

Than a sucker could ever spend

But I wouldn't give a sucker or a punk from the rocker

Not a dime 'til I made it again—everybody go

"Hotel, motel"

What you gonna do today—"Say what?!"

Is I'ma get a fly girl, gonna get some spank

And drive off in a def OJ—everybody go

"Hotel, motel

Holiday Inn"

You say, if your girl starts acting up

Then you take her friend

Master Gee, my mellow

It's on you, so what you gonna do?

[Master Gee]

Well it's on-'n-'n-on, 'n-on-on, 'n-on

The beat don't stop until the break of dawn

I said M-A-S-T-E-R, a G with a double E

I said I go by the unforgettable name

Of the man they call Master Gee—well

My name is known all over the world

By all the foxy ladies and the pretty girls

I'm going down in history

As the baddest rapper that ever could be

Now I'm feelin the highs and you're feelin the lows

The beat starts gettin into your toes

You start poppin your fingers and stompin your feet

And movin your body while you're sittin in your seat

And then damn!—you start doing the Freak

I said damn!—right out of your seat

Then you throw your hands high in the air

You're rockin to the rhythm, shake your derriere

You're rockin to the beat without a care

With the sure shot MCs for the affair

Now I'm not as tall as the rest of the Gang

But I rap to the beat just the same

I got a little face and a pair of brown eyes

All I'm here to do, ladies, is hypnotize

Singing on-'n-'n-on and on-on-'n-on

The beat don't stop until the break of dawn

Singing on-'n-'n-on and on-on-'n-on

Like a hot butter-'d-pop-'d-pop-'d-pop-dibbie-dibbie

Pop-d'-pop-pop, you don't dare stop

Come alive, y'all, give me what you got

I guess by now you can take a hunch

And find that I am the baby of the bunch

But that's okay, I still keep in stride

'Cause all I'm here to do is just a-wiggle your behind

Singing on-'n-'n-on and on-'n-on

The beat don't stop until the break of dawn

Singing on-'n-'n-on and on-on and on

Rock-rock, y'all, get on the floor

I'm gonna freak you here, I'm gonna freak you there

I'm gonna move you out of this atmosphere

'Cause I'm one of a kind and I'll shock your mind

I put the jig-jig-jiggles in your behind

I said a-one, two, three, four

Come on, girls, get on the floor

Come alive, y'all, give me what you got

'Cause I'm guaranteed to make you rock

I said one, two, three, four

Tell me, Wonder Mike, what are you waiting for?

[Wonder Mike]

To the hip-hop, the hibbie to the hibbie

The hip-hip-a-hop-a, you don't stop rockin

To the bang-bang boogie, say up jump the boogie

To the rhythm of the boogedy-beat

Skiddily-be-bop, we rock, Scooby-doo

And guess what, America? We love you

'Cause you rock and a-roll with-a so much soul

You can rock 'til you're a hundred and one years old

I don't mean to brag, I don't mean to boast

But we like hot butter on our breakfast toast

Rock it out, baby-bubba

Baby-bubba to the boogedy-bang-bang the boogie

To the beat, beat, it's so unique

Come on, everybody and dance to the beat

. . . .

[Big Bank Hank]

Well I'm Imp the Gimp, the ladies' pimp

The women fight for my delight

But I'm the grandmaster with the three MCs

That shock the house for the young ladies

And when you come inside, into the front

You do the freak, spank, and do the bump

And when the sucker MCs try to prove a point

We're a treacherous trio with a serious joint

From sun to sun and from day to day

I sit down and write a brand new rhyme

Because they say that miracles never cease

I've created a devastating masterpiece

I'm gonna rock the mic 'til you can't resist

Everybody, I say it goes like this

Well, I was coming home late one dark afternoon

Reporter stopped me for an interview

She said she's heard stories and she's heard fables

That I'm vicious on the mic and the turntables

This young reporter I did adore

So I rocked some vicious rhymes like I never did before

She said, "Damn, fly guy, I'm in love with you

The Casanova legend must've been true"

I said, "By the way, baby, what's your name?"

Said, "I go by the name Lois Lane

And you can be my boyfriend, you surely can

Just let me quit my boyfriend called Superman"

I said, "He's a fairy, I do suppose

Flying through the air in pantyhose

He may be very sexy or even cute

But he looks like a sucker in a blue and red suit"

I said, "You need a man who's got finesse

And his whole name across his chest

He may be able to fly all through the night

But can he rock a party 'til the early light?

He can't satisfy you with his little worm

But I can bust you out with my super sperm"

I go do it, I go do it

I go do it, do it, do it

And I'm here and I'm there

I'm Big Bank Hank, I'm everywhere

Just throw your hands up in the air

And party hearty like you just don't care

Let's do it, don't stop, y'all

A-tick-a-tock, y'all, you don't stop

Go, "Hotel, motel"

What you gonna do today? "Say what?!"

Say, I'm gonna get a fly girl, gonna get some spank

And drive off in a def OJ

Everybody go, "Hotel, motel

Holiday Inn"

You say, if your girl starts acting up

Then you take her friend

I say skip, dive, what can I say

I can't fit 'em all inside my OJ

So I just take half and bust them out

I give the rest to Master Gee so he can shock the house

. . . .

[Wonder Mike]

I say a can of beer that's sweeter than honey

Like a millionaire that has no money

Like a rainy day that is not wet

Like a gambling fiend that does not bet

Like Dracula without his fangs

Like the boogie to the boogie without the boogie-bang

Like collard greens that don't taste good

Like a tree that's not made out of wood

Like going up and not coming down

Is just like the beat without the sound, nonsound

To the beat-beat, you do the freak

Everybody just rock and dance to the beat

Have you ever went over a friend's house to eat

And the food just ain't no good?

I mean the macaroni's soggy, the peas are mushed

And the chicken tastes like wood

So you try to play it off like you think you can

By saying that you're full

And then your friend says, "Mama, he's just being polite

He ain't finished, huh-uh, that's bull"

So your heart starts pumping and you think of a lie

And you say that you already ate

And your friend says, "Man, there's plenty of food"

So you pile some more on your plate
While the stinky food's steamin your mind starts to dreamin
Of the moment it's time to leave
And then you look at your plate and your chicken's slowly rotting
Into something that looks like cheese
Oh, so you say, that's it, I got to leave this place
I don't care what these people think
I'm just sitting here making myself nauseous
With this ugly food that stinks
So you bust out the door while it's still close
Still sick from the food you ate
And then you run to the store for quick relief
From a bottle of Kaopectate
And then you call your friend two weeks later
To see how he has been
And he says, "I understand about the food
Baby-bubba, but we're still friends"
With a hip-hop, the hibbie to the hibbie
The hip-hip-a-hop-a, you don't stop the rockin
To the bang-bang boogie, say, up jump the boogie
To the rhythm of the boogedy-beat
I said, Hank, can you rock?
Can you rock to the rhythm that just don't stop?
Can you hip me to the shoobie doo?
I said, come on, make-the-make-the people move

[Big Bank Hank]
I go to the halls and then ring the bell
Because I am the man with the clientele
And if you ask me why I rock so well
I'm Big Bank, I got clientele
And from the time I was only six years old
I never forgot what I was told
It was the best advice that I ever had
It came from my wise, dear old dad

He said, "Sit down, punk, I wanna talk to you

And don't say a word until I'm through

Now there's a time to laugh, a time to cry

A time to live and a time to die

A time to break and a time to chill

To act civilized or act real ill

But whatever you do in your lifetime

You never let a MC steal your rhyme"

So from sixty six 'til this very day

I'll always remember what he had to say

So when the sucker MCs try to chump my style

I let them know that I'm versatile

I got style, finesse, and a little black book

That's filled with rhymes and I know you wanna look

But the thing that separates you from me

And that is called originality

Because my rhymes are on from what you heard

I didn't even bite, not a goddamn word

And I say a little more, later on tonight

So the sucker MCs can bite all night

A-tick-a-tock, y'all, a-beat-beat, y'all

A-let's rock, y'all, you don't stop

You go, "Hotel, motel"

What you gonna do today? "Say what?!"

You say, I'm gonna get a fly girl, gonna get some spank

And drive off in a def OJ

Everybody go, "Hotel, motel

Holiday Inn"

You say, if your girl starts acting up

Then you take her friends

A-like that, y'all, to the beat, y'all

Beat-beat, y'all, you don't stop

Master Gee, my mellow

It's on you, so what you gonna do?

[Master Gee]

Well, like Johnny Carson on the *Late Show*

A-like Frankie Crocker in stereo

Well, like the Bar-Kays singing "Holy Ghost"

The sounds to throw down, they're played the most

It's like my man Captain Sky

Whose name he earned with his "Super Sperm"

We rock and we don't stop

Get off, y'all, I'm here to give you what you got

To the beat that it makes you freak

And come alive, girl, get on your feet

A-like Perry Mason without a case

Like Farrah Fawcett without her face

Like the Bar-Kays on the mic

Like gettin right down for you tonight

Like movin your body so you don't know how

Right to the rhythm and throw down

Like comin alive to the Master Gee

The brother who rocks so viciously

I said the age of one, my life begun

At the age of two, I was doing the do

At the age of three, it was you and me

Rockin to the sounds of the Master Gee

At the age of four, I was on the floor

Givin all the freaks what they bargained for

At the age of five, I didn't take no jive

With the Master Gee, it's all the way live

At the age of six, I was a-pickin up sticks

Rappin to the beat, my thing was fixed

At the age of seven, I was rockin in heaven

Don't you know, I went off

I got right on down to the beat, you see

Gettin right on down, makin all the girls

Just take off, take off—to the beat, the beat

To the double beat-beat that makes you freak

At the age of eight, I was really great

'Cause every night, you see, I had a date

At the age of nine, I was right on time

'Cause every night I had a party rhyme

Going on-'n-'n-on, 'n-on-on-'n-on

The beat don't stop until the break of dawn

A-saying on-'n-'n'on, 'n-on-on-'n-on

Like a hot-buttered d'pop, d'pop, d'popcorn

TREACHEROUS THREE

At its inception, the Treacherous Three were Spoonie Gee, LA Sunshine, and Kool Moe Dee. But when Spoonie went solo on the success of "Spoonin Rap," Special K stepped in. For their first release, "The New Rap Language" (1980), the Treacherous Three—along with erstwhile member Spoonie Gee—came forth with a song that contains more syllables per line than any rap of its time. The "super-rhymin, fascinatin, faster rhyme originatin" style that Kool Moe Dee names late in the rather long song was in one sense virtuosic, though in another sense it sometimes didn't allow the rappers enough leisure to enunciate or elaborate on a theme at length. At any rate, the song is a kind of road-not-taken in early rap, for the speed-rapping style of the song was not taken up by other rappers and would emerge again only in the early 1990s with tongue-twisting groups such as the Fu-Schnickens. One road that was taken, however, was the path of the battle rap, laid down by Moe Dee in his infamous skirmish with the "Chief Rocker" Busy Bee in a way that was ahead of its time. The excerpt transcribed here finds the Treacherous Three phenom picking apart Busy's use of the phrase "in the place to be," as well as the "ba-diddy-ba" rap that Busy frequently used and that Kid Rock would later take to the top of the charts.

THE NEW RAP LANGUAGE

[All]

We rock … and don't stop

Well, it's the supercalifragilisticexpialidocious

With no strings attached, no bags of tricks, this is the way we get our
kicks

[Treacherous Three]

We're qualifyin, rectifyin, rock until the day we're dyin

Every time you're screamin, cryin, we'll be here with no denyin

[Spoonie Gee] We hold our honor and our pride

[Special K] Just take the step that kept in stride

[LA Sunshine] Set down rules you will abide

[Kool Moe Dee] We're gonna take you for a ride

[Spoonie Gee] Before we're rockin as a full, let's introduce us one by one

[Special K] I'm Special K, I'm on display, I rock across the USA

[LA Sunshine] LA Sunshine, I rock your mind, I do it to you every time

[Kool Moe Dee] Remember me, MC Moe Dee, the man that's at the t-o-p

[Spoonie Gee] I'm Spoonie Gee, as you can see, I rock the world society

And at the end, you will agree, nobody rock the mic like me

[Treacherous Three] But Special K, Sunshine, Moe Dee, you add us up,
we'll equal three

[Spoonie Gee] And on the mic we turn it out, young ladies bite without a doubt

[All] And if you don't believe it's true, just check out how we rock for you [3x]

Do it!

[Spoonie Gee] Moe Dee, you got a lotta class, so rock a rhyme and make
it fast

[Kool Moe Dee]

The super scooper, party pooper, man with all the super-duper

Disco breaks, have what it takes, a man who never makes mistakes

Can rap it low, I'm not a bore, the baddest man you ever saw

The money-makin, earth-quakin man who gets the party shakin

[Special K]

Undefeated, never beated, never cheated, but succeeded

If I need it, you believe it, rhymes on guarantee

Wheelin, dealin, women-stealin, Casanova booty-feelin

Understandin, reprimandin, rockin on it, that's demandin

[LA Sunshine]

No complication, stimulation, man who's gonna rock the nation

Rhyme, rhyme, battle time, my opponent, he's all mine

I'm not the baddest, not the maddest, when I win I am the gladdest

No beginner, not a sinner, on the mic I'm just a winner

[Spoonie Gee]

Well, I'm always clean, I'm not too mean, the baddest man you ever seen

The finger-poppin, nonstoppin man who gets the party rockin

I'm so vicious and ambitious to the young, 'cause I'm delicious

Good lovin I always make, I always do good, no mistake

[Kool Moe Dee]

And I'm very, very, very, very and my favorite flavor's cherry

Oh my God, it's fame and glory but I never tell a story

The only time I funk a mic because it's somethin that I like

To be assured the rhymes are low, I always keep some sex in store

[Special K]

The bad, bad, superbad, never sad, always glad

Not a day you find him mad, ain't nothin I never had

Sleek, sleek, so unique, guaranteed to move your feet

So every time I play the beat, ladies get up out their seat

[LA Sunshine]

The wheelin, stealin, double-dealin man who rock with all the feelin

Give you more of rhymes galore, I shoot my shot, I always score

Girls on my jock and all on lock, the man who rock around the clock

I never date, I never wait, the man who set the people straight

[Spoonie Gee]

Well, I'm Spoonie Gee, as you could see I rock the world society

I always rock, as you can tell, I rock with all the clientele

Finesse is do you know I will, I keep the people starin still

Eyes swollen, rhymes tollin, comin out this microphone

. . . .

[Special K]

For MCs who bite the fast-talkin rhymes

They're gonna feed ya, so get ready to eat

Moe Dee's the originator, so you might as well starve

'Cause you can't catch this fast beat (Hit it, Moe)

[Kool Moe Dee]

Hey, diddle-diddle on the fiddle, 'cause the cat is in the middle

Will he rhyme or will he riddle, does he want a tender vittle?

Have a lot, maybe a little, long as he can feel his middle

And an ocean full of lotion 'cause it's like his magic potion

But my notion's that the potion's workin some kind of commotion

With the cats and you don't seem to understand

Instead of high he's in the aisle, tip his hat at any town

Thought the cat was found missin somewhere on the line

The only thing he hears is me, you're desperate 'cause of Kool Moe Dee

You're walkin on a leash, whether talkin on the street

Whether north or south or east or whether human or a beast

I'm so full of disco (power), it ain't a MC that I can't (devour)

In a hour talkin fast and he goes sour, Moe Dee, the disco tower power

So take a deep breath, get a drink of water

Special K, you can say it, but make yours shorter

[Special K]

Well, I'm so sincere, just sincere, the baddest MC of the year

Say it low, say it loud, say it special, say it proud

Takin every year in hell, I weigh the highest on the scale

When I rock I take a bow, Sunshine, come on and show 'em how

[LA Sunshine]

The girl-teasin, woman-pleasin, take a girl, others freezin

Got the heart to play the part, I'm not too sweet, I'm not too tart

We're rockin to the funky beat, the kids all chowed us like a treat

So come on in and get a taste, believe me, girl, it's not a waste

[Kool Moe Dee]

The super-rhymin, fascinatin, faster rhyme originatin

Number one, we're rhyme creatin, number one with no debatin

If you look up on the rating, you will see that you've been waitin

And you're only commentatin and that gets to be frustratin

[Special K]

Yes, for real, we are the deal and on the mic we use our skill

The latest, greatest, no one hate us, take us home and gold-plate us

Rappin raw and never bore and always keep you on the floor

And rock and roll and take control and rock until we're gray and old

[LA Sunshine]

The law-abiding, never fighting, girls around us never hiding

Pain-enduring, love-ensuring, cool, calm, and most alluring

Constant on the jock, the man who make the party rock

I gratify and satisfy, girl, just say, just say good-bye

[Spoonie Gee]

Well, I'm lettin you know I am a pro, just give me a mic, I'm on the go

[Treacherous Three]

The three MCs that never freeze, that rock you on down to your knees

FROM **KOOL MOE DEE'S BATTLE WITH BUSY BEE (1981)**

*One two, one two, party people in the place to be. My name is MC Kool Moe
    Dee from the Treacherous Three. My man LA Sunshine in the place to be. We
    gon' get a little something straight here in the place to be. Don't worry about
    it, DJ Lee, in the place to be. We gonna get a little something straight in the
    place to be. My man Busy Bee Starski. How many people think Busy Bee
    Starski rocked the house? I hear that in the place to be. But if y'all noticed it or*

not, you know, I heard a lot of shit, you know, Busy Bee is popping shit, saying he'll take out any MC and all that. I give it to the man, he know how to rock the crowd. But when it come to having rhymes, no way he can fuck around. And I'ma prove that right now. In the place to be, MC Kool Moe Dee, the coolest of the cool. Can't nobody rock like me. Remember this. Cold Crush Four in the house. My man LA Sunshine in the place to be. We gonna have a little fun, have a little fun. DJ Lee, you think you got it together yet? One two . . .

One for the treble, two for the bass
Come on, Easy Lee, and let's rock the place
One-two, one-two, doing the do, now
Hold on, Busy Bee, I don't mean to be bold
But put that ba-diddy-ba bullshit on hold
We gonna get right down to the nitty-grit
Gonna tell you a little something why you ain't shit
It ain't an MC's jock that you don't hug
You even bit your name from the Lovebug
And now to bite a nigga's name is some low-down shit
If you was money, man, you'd be counterfeit
I got to give it to you, though, you can rock
But everybody know you on the Furious' jock
And I remember Busy from the olden times
When my man Spoonie Gee used to sell you rhymes
Remember that rhyme called diddy-ba-diddy?
Man, goddamn, that shit was a pity
Too hot to trot, here to rock the spot
Spoonie Gee rocked it whether you like it or not
He begged for the rhyme, asked for it twice
He said, "Spoonie Gee, I'll buy at any price"
Well, Spoonie finally sold it, oh, what a relief
Busy Bee stole it like a fuckin thief
Came out rockin the party hard
Got everybody thinkin that shit sound's yours
Every time I hear it, I throw a fit
Party after party, the same old shit

Record after record, rhyme after rhyme
Always want to know your Zodiac sign
He changed the shit to the favorite jeans
Come on, Busy Bee, tell me what that means
Hold on, brother man, don't you say nothing
I'm not finished yet, I gotta tell you something
Too hot to trot, I'm here to rock the spot
I'm gonna rock your ass whether you like it or not
He made up the title right on the spot
How can I take a title you ain't got?
You're not number one, you're not even the best
And you can't win no real MC contest
Celebrity clubs and bullshit like those
Those the kind of shows that everybody knows
Celebrity clubs, those the kind you can win
It's all set up before we come in
But in a battle like this you know you'll lose
Between me and you, who do you think they'll choose?
Well, if you think it's you, I got bad news
Because they hear your name, you're gonna hear some boos
'Cause you're faking the funk, 'cause you're faking the funk
And at the end of this rhyme you can call me uncle
Moe Dee—rock, shock the house—Call me uncle
Rock the house

TANYA ("SWEET TEE") WINLEY

Having become fans in its prerecorded stages, the sisters Paulette and Tanya Winley released a record in 1979 on the independent label run by their father, Paul Winley. With backing music by the Harlem Underground Band, "Rhymin and Rappin" contains a number of themes and tropes familiar to listeners of the first rap records: self-naming, claims of being the best, a genesis rhyme of the "age of one / I was having fun / at the age of two" type; however, more is different here than meets the ear. First broadcasting herself as "Sweet Tee on your radio dial," Tanya Winley fills her lines on "Rhymin and Rappin" with vibrant wordplay and worthy variations on the standard tropes and themes. Her finest extended moment is the solo "Vicious Rap," which hints at its vintage when Sweet Tee begins by introducing the house-band trio that is backing her. "Vicious Rap" contains some of recorded rap's first overtly political content in Sweet Tee's depiction of an unwarranted arrest. (Later such arrests in rap tend to have less-polite arresting officers.) The sisters also recorded together on the song "I Believe in the Wheel of Fortune."

The significance of these releases by the Winley sisters is enhanced by their being on Paul Winley Records. A respected Harlem doo-wop label started by the elder Winley in the 1960s, it changed to accommodate contemporary tastes. In addition to releasing records by his daughters Paulette and Tanya, Winley released some of the earliest break beat records (the "Super Disco Brakes" series), speeches by Malcolm X, both parts of "Zulu Nation Throwdown," as well as "Death Mix Live," a 12-inch lifted from a cassette tape recording of a performance by Afrika Bambaataa and his crew at James Monroe High School in the Bronx. The release was unauthorized by Bambaataa and its sound quality is just adequate, but original copies are among the most collectible records in hip-hop.

RHYMIN AND RAPPIN

This is Sweet Tee on your radio dial
And I'll be with you for just a little while
Or long enough to say my rhymes
I can't say them all 'cause there ain't enough time
I got rhymes ga-lot and rhymes galore
And when I finish with those I still got more
Because they're comin out my ears and out of my eyes
They are so devastating you will be surprised
MC Sweet Tee is my DJ name
I'm in the history books and the hall of fame
I rock so good and I rock so well
And my voice sounds better than Howard Cosell
'Cause I'm the crowd-pleaser, the Charmin-squeezer

A hell of a love bug
And you know when I'm rocking up in the sky
'Cause you always see an angel fly by
With a lovely smile up on their face
That tell you Sweet Tee's rocking the whole damn place
So you get on the elevator, press seven
When you walk out the door you will be in heaven
Take ten steps straight and turn to your right
Go down a flight of stairs and oh, what a sight
You're in a daze 'til the count of three
'Cause you can't believe what your eyes is seeing
When you get to earth, they won't believe your story
So you take out your book and you take inventory
On the def equipment that God has granted me
For rocking the heavens so viciously
You count fifteen speakers in the corner of the sky
A case of brew and some def get-high
A mic for every member of the gangster crew
Two turntables you can see right through
A serious mixer and I almost forgot
Three echo chambers and a def beat box
. . . .
I'm the best MC all across the land
And I got more rhymes than the beach got sand
Yes, I go by the name of MC Tee
I bite the sucker DJ's rhymes before they bite me
I say, when I came out my mama's womb
My doctor put me in a separate room
I was by myself and all alone
'Til my mama came and handed me a microphone
And at the age of one, it's just begun
I was beginning to have me a little bit of fun

At the age of two, I wasn't through
I was rocking all night and in the morning too
And at the age of three, I said to me
You're the finest MC that there could ever be
And at the age of four, I looked some more
I said, damn Tanya, you're beginning to score
And at the age of five, I made a man cry
Then I knew I was qualified
And at the age of six, I knew all the tricks
That got me into the disco mix
At the age of seven, I went to heaven
To rock a little, you know
They had to let me go, I was too good, you know
Because I gave those angels a hell of a blow
And at the age of eight, everything was straight
I was always on time and never late
And at the age of nine, I rocked my mind
I was known around the world as one of a kind
And at the age of ten, I had the urge again
But it ain't enough tape so this is the end

Bye-bye

VICIOUS RAP

I said before the Lord God made the sea and the land
He gave Sweet Tee the master plan
And the message to give all the other MCs
About the earth, sea, and sky, the birds and the bees
How to make money, take money, steal, cheat, and lie
The main definition of the word survive
I know you heard the philosophy about
You got to give a little to gain a lot
But these words don't pull

Take a good look, look at the government
How they sit back, relax, and don't give a damn
And every time you turn around they holdin out your hand
And when you think of it, I said you start to holler
About the eight cents tax that's on the dollar
So we all get mad and as hot as a fire
But soon you cool off and prices get higher
And before you know it you can't buy many
With a dollar because the value is a penny
For the money, huh, we're gonna scream and shout
And let the government know what we all about
So get in touch, huh, I'm too much, huh
And you don't stop, you keep on
See I was rocking a party, just a-doing my best
When a man told me I was under arrest
He said, "Follow me, ma'am, if you will
And when we get downtown, I'll tell you the deal"
So he read the rights and then he cuffed my hands
He drove me downtown to the big man
For a year or two they looked around and about
Want to know what Sweet Tee was all about
I said, "I don't know what or why I'm here
But without a doubt I have no fear"
He say, "Get in the cell and don't waste my time
Because you're under arrest for first degree rhymes"
The next day, huh, you see, I went to court
And I took the stand just like I was taught
They put the Bible in my hand and said, "Speak the truth"
And when they took it away, I said, "I do"
I said, "I'm just an MC, that's all I am
And I shock the house when there's a mic in my hand
I don't snort, I don't smoke, I just keep it clean
And I am not into the junkie scene

I'm just asking for a little sympathy
Because my crew, ha, my crew is waiting for me"
So they took the votes and they let me go
And here I am, I said, in stereo
In stereo, ha, and you don't stop . . .

1985-1992

The Golden Age

"It's all brand new, never ever old school," raps Run on Run-DMC's 1985 song "King of Rock," a hyperkinetic, electric-guitar-driven declaration of rap's independence from its own past. In the years between the mid-1980s and the early 1990s rap experienced a series of rapid transformations. The craft of MCing began settling into its maturity as artists started paying more attention to song structure with 4-bar choruses and 16-bar verses, with narratives and message raps. Stylistic trailblazers like Rakim, Big Daddy Kane, Kool G Rap, and KRS-One expanded the formal potentialities of rhythm, rhyme, and wordplay. Where end rhymes and, particularly, rhyming couplets were the norm, MCs began employing an array of techniques like internal rhyme and chain rhyme. The once-dominant effusive mode of rapping now shared space with a host of other flows. Hip-hop production moved from the break beat to intricate samples drawn from soul, funk, and jazz.

Thematically, hip-hop began pushing beyond the party rhymes and battle raps that had dominated its early life to include everything from Black Nationalist politics to Five-Percenter ideology to streetwise chronicles of the criminal underground. Women, while certainly a part of hip-hop in its early years, began to fashion distinct voices for themselves through the efforts of artists like Roxanne Shanté, Queen Latifah, MC Lyte, and Monie Love. Primarily a New York phenomenon in its early years, rap began to expand its regional parameters, most notably with the rise of the so-called gangsta rap of Ice-T and NWA. The hip-hop industry also expanded, as major labels began to see opportunities for profit in the music. And rap finally broke through to the pop charts and MTV, with artists as diverse as Run-DMC, the Beastie Boys, Salt-N-Pepa, and DJ Jazzy Jeff & the Fresh Prince leading the way.

With all of these advancements in the art, it should come as no surprise that this period is often referred to as the golden age of rap. The very concept of a golden age is, of course, a fiction—the product of nostalgia and wishful thinking combined with a healthy distrust of the music of the moment. Indeed, one generation's golden age is often another's era of decline or stagnation or worse. We should look upon such a designation with a degree of skepticism. That said, the years between the release of Run-DMC's 1985 platinum-selling *King of Rock* and the release of Dr. Dre's 1992 album *The Chronic* are inarguably a period of fertile creation, rapid expansion, and lasting importance in the history of rap. If hip-hop music can be said, like jazz, to have songs considered as "standards," then a disproportionate number of them can be credited to the artists who emerged in this period. The MCs of this era hover over hip-hop to this day, either by still putting out records (as do LL Cool J, Rakim, De La Soul, and KRS-One, for instance), or by lyrically influencing all other artists that followed.

One of the ways in which rap moved forward in this period was paradoxically by going back. By the mid-1980s the art had been around long enough to be marketed in certain ways that mainstreamed but diluted its power. A visual record of this transformation can be seen in the marked differences among the films *Wild Style* (1982), Charlie Ahearn's grimy hip-hop indie that was in essence a documentary; *Beat Street* (1984), a Hollywood version of Ahearn's film that nonetheless had a strong soundtrack that included several important early artists; and the widely distributed *Breakin'* and *Breakin' 2: Electric Boogaloo* (both 1984), a revelation to ten-year-olds in mall theaters far from the New York epicenter whose primary purpose seemed to be teaching outsiders what gear to wear and what slang to use in order to be hip—if not hip-hop. Rap artists themselves were less complicit but had still settled into the production of a particular image, often including elaborate costumes (a mélange of punk and new-wave paraphernalia filtered through a latter-day Funkadelic motif) that were heavy on leather, buttons, bracelets, and chains. Furthermore, despite a couple of crucial shifts in sound production, the perceived taint of disco lingered.

Those who were active in hip-hop at the time often mark a twofold shift that involved the rise of Run-DMC on the one hand and the advent of the Def Jam label on the other. Grandmaster Caz says, "Run-DMC was the cutoff point between us and hip-hop after that. That was the end of the era for Grandmaster Flash and the Furious Five, for the Cold Crush, for the Funky 4+1, for the Fearless 4s and for the Fantastic 5s and all that." Sal Abatiello, who ran the popular club called the Fever, noted that when the group first showed up there, "their outfits were so hysterical" for being so plain, given that "the whole scene was leather and fringes and sparkly and rhinestones—made outfits—and they came out with these plaid jackets."[1] DMC himself says that their decision to scale back the theatrics was derived from their heroes the Cold Crush Brothers:

> At a time when hip-hop was becoming really popular in all the five boroughs in New York, Bambaataa, Grandmaster Flash, everybody started dressin' up 'cause they had a little bit of money. The Cold Crush would just come to the parties as is and do their performance. And the performance became the attention-getter and not how good you looked, how many curls you had in your hair, how many braids you had in your hair. It was just about the beats and the rhyme. To Run-DMC, it was like, "Oh, you mean to tell me we don't gotta dress up?" They showed us what to rap about, how to rap, how to represent yourself with your title, to make it royal . . . but they also showed us come as you are, you know what I'm sayin'? And when Run-DMC first came out, that was the reason why people related to us—even the rock 'n' roll kids, the white kids. They could relate to us because we was just like the guys on the corner they saw, or the guys they went to school with, or the people they worked with. You know, we had on Lee jeans, shell-toe Adidas, Pro-Keds, Pumas, Kangol hats, sweatshirts, whatever was just common at the time. . . . The Cold Crush showed me that what my mother bought was cool. We don't have to go to the leather guy and get costumes made up to look like Superman or to look like the stars of the day 'cause we are the stars. We're normal guys, but we're good, and this is who we be. This is who we are.[2]

Of course, to make a worldwide mark, even such transparency needs a good hype man, and the promoter Russell Simmons, who was also Run's brother and later the founder of Def Jam Records, was up to the task. "The key to his success," remembers Bill Adler, is that Simmons said, "'I'm not going to water it down. I'm not going to whiten it up. This is going to be pure and uncut. This is what these young Black kids are bringing to the party. This is their ticket, okay?' . . . These rappers were much more everyday. And it was Russell's genius to broker them to the mainstream as they were. They didn't have to be white. They didn't have to have white mannerisms. They didn't have to speak standard English. None of that. And even so, they were going to get over. And more than that, Russell's point was that it was because they were authentic and true to themselves that they would get over. And he was right."[3]

It was not only the look that was scaled back and pared down. The sound of Run-DMC comes at you without excess. When they trade verses, it is more like a dialogue than a jumbled conversation. And while a master like Melle Mel could, in "The Message," paint a series of ghetto pictures that were effectively plaintive in their poetic decrepitude, most MCs who initially tried to follow that template merely dropped wooden platitudes. Run-DMC traveled the same road but did so in a way commensurate with their no-nonsense image:

> Unemployment at a record high
>
> People coming, people going, people born to die
>
> Don't ask me, because I don't know why
>
> But it's like that, and that's the way it is

The lack of a solution to such problems is less surprising than the absence of sentimentality. Their bluntness was also manifest in such songs as "Sucker MC's," a genesis song that quickly shifts into a battle rap:

> Two years ago, a friend of mine
>
> Asked me to say some MC rhymes
>
> So I said this rhyme I'm about to say
>
> The rhyme was def and then it went this way

Nor did the template change once the group had experienced some success, as on "My Adidas," where the eponymous sneakers are still good enough for now-popular entertainers:

> My Adidas
>
> Walk through concert doors
>
> And roam all over coliseum floors
>
> I stepped on stage at Live Aid
>
> All the people gave and the poor got paid

The music itself was stripped down, not disco derived and even without the rhythmic flourishes of funk. Its reliance on drum-machine patterns was much starker (and slower) than those found in post–"Planet Rock" electro-rap. What's more, their songs never ran any longer than typical radio or jukebox fare.

Another related shift was that this new style in rap incorporated a rock-and-roll aesthetic. If the kids could relate to wearing sweatshirts and sneakers, they could also relate to thrashing out a couple of bar chords on

an electric guitar. On their second LP Run-DMC even deemed themselves
the kings of rock, and their 1986 collaboration with Aerosmith on "Walk
This Way" was a huge hit. Rock guitar riffs had long been part of the rap
repertory; Billy Squier's "Big Beat" was a late 1970s DJ staple. The architect
of this sound as standardized in a studio setting was Rick Rubin, Simmons's
partner in Def Jam Records and the label's signature producer. His combination of drum-machine beats and recycled rock guitar helped make the
Beastie Boys album *Licensed to Ill* (1986) a number-one record. (Nor was
the group's race a deterrent to large-scale commercial success.)

At any rate, as Reggie Reg says, "When Def Jam came out, that was like
the nail in Sugarhill's coffin."[4] The look was changing, the sound was changing (even if the changes were sometimes old solutions deployed in new
contexts)—most of all, the rhymes were changing. The formal evolution of
MCing was brisk. Perhaps the change is best epitomized in Rakim, the
MC's MC. With his DJ Eric B., Rakim intensified the pace of the delivery of
rhymes without sacrificing enunciation or the sense of a solid presence. His
ability to break up his lines and to balance that fractured phrasemaking
with generous enjambment suggests how the rhythms of jazz were making
their way into the music. Since rapping at a formal level had always been
particularly associated with rhyme, it was the variety of Rakim's rhymes
that garnered special attention. As the MC Masta Ace said of Rakim's verses
on "Eric B. Is President": "Everybody's mind was blown because nobody
had ever put three words that rhyme together in a sentence, and that just
opened up so many doors. That just like really got the ball rolling in terms
of creativity as a lyricist. There was no limit to what you could do and figure out how to do it with words, and that's what got me really excited about
being an MC—the endless possibilities in terms of the cadences, the flows,
and how to make words rhyme."[5]

Perhaps because of that formal intensity, another aspect of Rakim's art
is sometimes overlooked, namely, the way he went from discrete metaphor
to developed conceit. Instead of just dropping in an isolated image of music
as a drug, for instance, Rakim in "Microphone Fiend" builds a complete
song around the metaphor, not just deepening but personalizing it, using
the initial comparison as the basis for a story of artistic development and
aesthetic value:

> I was a fiend before I became a teen
>
> I melted microphones instead of cones of ice cream
>
> . . . .
>
> So then I add all the rhymes I had

One after the other one, then I make another one
To dis the opposite then ask if the brother's done
I get a craving, like I fiend for nicotine
But I don't need a cigarette, know what I mean?

. . . .

But back to the problem, I got a habit
You can't solve it, silly rabbit
The prescription is a hyper-tone that's thorough when
I fiend for a microphone, like heroin
Soon as the bass kicks, I need a fix
Give me a stage and a mic and a mix

Nor was Rakim alone in making more of flow and figurative language than had been heard before in rap. Big Daddy Kane was also changing the scene. According to Masta Ace the two rappers were alike in advancing the art: "Up until [Rakim], everybody you heard rhyme, the last word in the sentence was the rhyming [word], the connection word. Then Rakim showed us that you could put rhymes within a rhyme, so you could put more than one word in a line that rhymed together, so it didn't have to be just the last word. Now here comes Big Daddy Kane—instead of going three words, he's going multiple, seven and eight words in a sentence."[6] And like Rakim, Kane was a master of metaphor and simile. When he developed a conceit it would usually be in service of slicing up other MCs:

You're just a butter knife, I'm a machete
That's made by Ginsu, wait until when you
Try to front, so I can chop into
Your body, just because you try to be basing
Friday the 13th, I'ma play Jason
No type of joke, gag, game, puzzle, or riddle
The name is Big Daddy, yes, big not little

Usually, however, rather than developing conceits, Kane was likelier to proliferate promiscuous strings of similes, as if he had so many options at his poetic disposal that restricting himself to one was miserly:

I relieve rappers just like Tylenol
And they know it, so I don't see why you all

Try to front, perpetrating a stunt

When you know that I'll smoke you up like a blunt

I'm genuine like Gucci, raw like sushi

Big Daddy Kane also exemplifies a trend toward rappers developing a more elaborate and sophisticated persona. The combative rapper had been around for a while, as had the occasional lover man. But Kane, like LL Cool J, attempted and largely achieved the creation of a more organic persona that brought verbal warfare and romantic love (or sexual conquest) together.

One way that a persona is successfully developed is through a convincing narrative. Thus it is no surprise that the increasing detail and range of the stories being told in rap provided a context in which a more interesting and complete persona could thrive. Slick Rick, for instance, was continuing the evolution of rap storytelling without ever letting the listener forget that just as important as the story was the teller who told it. That connection became especially strong in a rising genre that would become a powerful force—namely, gangsta rap.

Several songs are associated with the rise of gangsta rap: Schoolly D's "P.S.K. What Does It Mean," Ice-T's "6 'N the Mornin'," and Eazy-E's "Boyz-n-the-Hood," among others. But no song did more to establish the gangsta archetype and the genre of gangsta rap than the aptly titled "Gangsta Gangsta" by NWA. The song starts, "Here's a little somethin 'bout a nigga like me," while the chorus begins with Ice Cube claiming that he's "the type of nigga that's built to last." And what is the type? A young black man who is an anarchist, a hedonist, and a nihilist all rolled into one. Part of sustaining the gangsta character lies in formal decisions: Ice Cube's deliberately simple diction, the paucity of metaphor, the refusal to name himself as a rapper or to refer ostentatiously to his own rhetorical skills.

While rap was reaching a rhetorical height in the work of lyricists such as Big Daddy Kane and Rakim, both of whom never let it be forgotten that they were rapping, Ice Cube in "Gangsta Gangsta" exhibits another, concurrent trend toward what we might think of as the "plain style" of rap. Ice Cube's is an unadorned, propulsive diction that keeps coming and coming:

Boom boom boom, yeah I was gunnin

And then you look, all you see is niggaz runnin

And fallin and yellin and pushin and screamin

And cussin

The language fits the character. Such a perfect fit between a character and the language that character uses was once designated by the critical term *decorum*. This might be the last word under which anyone would class the explicit lyrics of NWA, which hardly strike most listeners as decorous. Yet in terms of constructing a character whose actions, setting, and speech all exist in a relationship of unobtrusive propriety, the lyrics of NWA may serve as a model of the term.

Decorum in this sense is an august literary value. The ancient Greeks prized it, if Aristotle's discussion of propriety of style is a proper indication. Latin critics elaborated on the topic, often arranging decorum into stylistic tiers. Of the plain style, Demetrius wrote that its "diction should be entirely ordinary and in everyday use." Cicero warned that "plainness of style may seem easily imitable in theory; in practice nothing could be more difficult." The plain speaker was deliberately "unpretentious, giving an appearance of using ordinary language, but in reality differing from the inexpert more than is commonly supposed."[7] This last description brings to mind the Renaissance term *sprezzatura*, which signifies minimizing the impression that a task is difficult, hiding the truth that its success is determined by tireless practice, insofar as it appears to be accomplished with ease.

In addition to this sense that simplicity itself is an elaborate performance—a kind of verbal puppeteering with the strings kept hidden—a common thread in descriptions of the plain speaker is the use of everyday words by everyday people to describe everyday actions and things. Such a notion was elaborated influentially in English-language poetry by William Wordsworth, who in the preface to *Lyrical Ballads* described his own attempt to write in the "language really used by men." The pub dwellers in T. S. Eliot's *The Waste Land*, the rustics of Robert Frost's New England poems, and the blues singers in the work of Langston Hughes all follow partially in this tradition.

In terms of diction, NWA adhere to the plain-style edict that less is more. Although there is an occasional specific reference ("Daytons," a brand of rims) and a scattering of slang ("eight bottle," "8-Ball," "whooride," "bum rush," "the bucket") that establishes local color, the song is otherwise devoid of neologisms and allusions. There is even a dearth of multisyllabic words, especially in rhyming positions where such words would draw particular attention. (The exception proving the rule is "penitentiary," which completes the opening couplet of "Gangsta Gangsta"; in fact, rhyming "penitentiary" with "a nigga like me" in the song's opening lines is a crafty way of linking the gangsta character to his antisocial role, a link developed through the rest of the song.) The starkness of the diction obtains not because Ice Cube doesn't know or couldn't choose different, bigger words but because the character he is creating is a gangsta figure whose modus operandi revolves more around action than talk.

Another factor in the successful creation of the gangsta archetype is the infrequent use of obtrusive poetic and rhetorical figures. For Cicero, the plain style demanded that "all obvious pearls of ornament" be removed; such writing should also be "modest and sparing in metaphor."[8] Certainly "Gangsta Gangsta" fits his two-thousand-year-old criteria. Unlike the lines of Rakim, those of NWA stay away from internal rhyme, sticking almost without exception to end rhyme. Unlike the delivery of Big Daddy Kane, that of Ice Cube resists bending words athletically to force them into a rhyming relation. (The one time he attempts it, rhyming "me to go" with "vehicle," is only slightly less convincing than Eazy-E rhyming "court" and "fart" in "Boyz-n-the-Hood.") There is a coherent characterization, but no running conceit as one finds in "Microphone Fiend" by Rakim; nor is there a cluster of motifs, as in Rakim's grouping of horror films, physical infirmity, and rap battles in his "Lyrics of Fury." In fact, "Gangsta Gangsta" is so "modest and sparing in metaphor" that metaphor hardly exists. The song's prime example is found in Ice Cube's introduction of Eazy-E, who is "built like a tank," which is a simile hackneyed enough to seem more natural than ornamental.

This paucity of elaborate poetry is matched by the simplicity of the storyline. "I got a shotgun and here's the plot," raps Ice Cube, "Taking niggaz out with a flurry of buck shots." Not much of a plot, perhaps, but "Gangsta Gangsta" has generic forebears; among other things, it is a circumscribed picaresque. (The term, designating a story that follows a character living by his wits through a series of adventures, comes from the Spanish word for "rogue"—in this case, a fitting etymology.) Instead of traveling across a whole country or continent, we merely move through the city of Compton. The limited range of motion—the characters seem to know only the violent streets of one city and to shuttle from there to prison and back—compounded by the limited range of action—they fight, they get fucked up, and they hunt for sex with futility—suggests a limited life. It is to the aesthetic credit of the song that the unrepentant aggression of its performance gives what could be a claustrophobic circumscription instead a feeling of audacity.

Another way in which NWA employ limited means to suggest the expansion of limits is in their use of expletives. "We knew the value of lan-

guage," Ice Cube has said, "especially profanity. We weren't that sophisticated"—he was only eighteen when he wrote "Gangsta Gangsta"—"but we
knew the power we had."[9] That power depended on not "breaking the
frame," on not referring to themselves as rappers in the song. As music
critic Kelefa Sanneh writes, "Time was, rappers were eager to tell you what
they did for a living, and how well they did it. In fact, that seemed to be the
only thing they wanted to talk about. Like generations of three-card monte
men before them, they rapped about rapping, explaining how the trick
worked even as they pulled it off. You can hear this on virtually any earlier
hip-hop record." However, as Sanneh points out, "Things changed with
NWA. They were riveting storytellers, and they realized, long before many
of their peers, that hip-hop storytelling was built on a paradox. How could
any rapper be convincing if he kept reminding his audience that he was
merely a rapper? How could he draw listeners into his narratives if he re-
fused to stay in character?"[10]

The template fleshed out by Ice Cube and company would continue to
be developed through the course of the 1990s. But the gangsta persona in
the later 1980s was matched by a different vision of the direction in which
rap should travel. If the West Coast was telling stories that were implicitly
sociopolitical, when one turned (to cite an X-Clan album) "To the East,
Blackwards," one heard voices that were explicitly political. Where Rakim
and Big Daddy Kane had made relatively subtle allusions to the Five-
Percent Nation ideology derived from the Black Muslim movement, X-
Clan and others came straight out with a pro-black message that was
steeped in arcane terminology. Chuck D of Public Enemy scattered his lyrics with references to Malcolm X, Louis Farrakhan, and other radical black
leaders, and his rhetorical style was that of the modern-day prophet crying
out against a racist and overly commercialized society.

There was a didactic impulse at work in these artists, as well as a sense
of rescuing rap from frivolity. One persona that developed as a result was
that of the teacher. Since rap had been around long enough to have an "old
school," there was felt to be a need to educate the newer generation of listeners. As only a teacher can, Kool Moe Dee even issued a "report card" on
the state of rap.

No one embodied the role of the teacher better than KRS-One of Boogie Down Productions. His example shows, however, that the teacher in rap
will often pitch his lesson far outside the conventional classroom. In fact,
KRS suggests how tricky these nascent categories were, since his pedagogical drive on tracks like "Poetry" met a more gangsta aesthetic on a song

such as "9mm Goes Bang." There was also a more subtle approach to instruction, as in the music of those groups associated under the rubric Native Tongues (among them Black Sheep, De La Soul, Jungle Brothers, and A Tribe Called Quest). Their lesson plan was an eclectic one, and what was being taught was creative engagement, not only with a range of external sources, but with the ultimate source of the self. Both the increased emphasis on self-realization and the widening of the tent under which one could rap are also manifest in the changing nature of women rappers. Whereas before, the best female lyricists crafted lyrics that were indistinguishable in essence from those of their distinguished male counterparts, figures such as MC Lyte, Roxanne Shanté, Salt-N-Pepa, and Queen Latifah began to speak on themes provoked by a sense of gender disparity and the untapped power of women. As Queen Latifah put it, they could be "ladies first" without giving up their status as rappers.

It was a rich time for rap. Whether it was a golden age depends on one's currency of choice. Maybe it was more of a barter economy, since so many wonderful verses were being traded. Or maybe an economic conceit is less appropriate than an environmental one. If the rise of Run-DMC and the sparse sounds of Def Jam equaled a kind of sonic slash-and-burn, a deliberate clearing of the old growth of the old school, then the landscape that remained was ripe for a burst of new and varied life that had been until then unimagined. And grow the new sounds did, proving that an art form that had only a few years before been dismissed by some skeptics as a fad was in fact real and self-sustainable.

BEASTIE BOYS

The career of the Beastie Boys now spans almost three decades. *Licensed to Ill* (1986), their debut LP, became rap's first certified platinum album. Crass in subject matter, rough in delivery, the Beasties' early style on that album also suggested adaptability and an independent streak that promised things to come.

Adrock (Adam Horovitz), Mike D (Mike Diamond), and MCA (Adam Yauch) were originally part of the indie punk rock scene, releasing the EP *Pollywog Stew* (1982). The move from punk to rap was more natural than it may appear; the two musics share a basic timeline, a rough-hewn aesthetic, and an irreverent view of authority. These characteristics meshed perfectly with the Rick Rubin–produced Def Jam template of drum-machine beats and heavy rock guitar samples.

In songs like "Brass Monkey" and "Fight for Your Right (to Party)," the Beasties develop personas that presaged the nihilism later perfected by gangsta rappers, as well as the "crazy white guy" position subsequently elaborated by Eminem. The description of a rapper as "beer drinking, breath stinking, sniffing glue" on "Hold It Now—Hit It" is not far from Eminem's Slim Shady.

After an acrimonious split from Def Jam, the group released *Paul's Boutique* (1989). Sonically, the music was marked by manic sampling and a wide-ranging repertoire of beats. Lyrically, their now familiar high jinks expanded to include a new penchant for pop cultural similes. On *Check Your Head* (1992), they continued to hone their skills while moving in yet another direction—this time back to their punk past, as many of the tracks featured the group playing their own instruments. Subsequent years brought such releases as *Ill Communication* (1994), *Hello Nasty!* (1998), and *To the Five Boroughs* (2004), each one another mark in a career of surprising vitality and duration.

PAUL REVERE

[Adrock] Now here's a little story I got to tell
About three bad brothers you know so well
It started way back in history
With Adrock, [MCA] MCA, [Mike D] and me, Mike D

[Adrock]
Been had a little horsy named Paul Revere
Just me and my horsy and a quart of beer
Riding across the land, kicking up sand
Sheriff's posse's on my tail 'cause I'm in demand
One lonely Beastie I be
All by myself without nobody
The sun is beating down on my baseball hat
The air is gettin hot, the beer is gettin flat
Lookin for a girl, I ran into a guy
His name is MCA, I said, "Howdy," he said, "Hi"

He told a little story that sounded well rehearsed
Four days on the run and that he's dying of thirst
The brew was in my hand and he was on my tip
His voice was hoarse, his throat was dry, he asked me for a sip
He said, "Can I get some?" I said, "You can't get none!"
Had a chance to run, pulled out his shotgun
Quick on the draw, I thought I'd be dead
He put the gun to my head and this is what he said

[MCA] "Now my name is MCA, I've got a license to kill
I think you know what time it is, it's time to get ill
Now what do we have here, an outlaw and his beer
I run this land, you understand, I made myself clear"
[Adrock] We stepped into the wind, he had a gun, I had a grin
You think this story's over but it's ready to begin. Now,
[MCA] "I got the gun, you got the brew
You got two choices of what you can do
It's not a tough decision as you can see
I can blow you away or you can ride with me"

[Adrock] I said, "I'll ride with you if you can get me to the border

The sheriff's after me for what I did to his daughter

I did it like this, I did it like that

I did it with a whiffleball bat—so

I'm on the run, the cop's got my gun

And right about now it's time to have some fun

The King Adrock, that is my name

And I know the fly spot where they got the champagne"

We rode for six hours then we hit the spot

The beat was a-bumping and the girlies was hot

This dude was staring like he knows who we are

We took the empty spot next to him at the bar

MCA said, [MCA] "Yippie yo, you know this kid?"

[Adrock] I said I didn't but I know he did

[MCA] The kid said, [Mike D] "Get ready 'cause this ain't funny

My name's Mike D and I'm about to get money"

Pulled out the jammy, aimed it at the sky

[Adrock] He yelled, [Mike D] "Stick 'em up!" [Adrock] and let two fly

Hands went up and people hit the floor

He wasted two kids that ran for the door

[Mike D] "I'm Mike D and I get respect

Your cash and your jewelry is what I expect"

[Adrock] MCA was with it and he's my ace

So I grabbed the piano player and I punched him in the face

Piano player's out, the music stopped

His boy had beef and he got dropped

[MCA] Mike D grabbed the money, [Mike D] MCA snatched the gold

[Adrock] I grabbed two girlies and a beer that's cold

SURE SHOT

Because you can't, you won't, and you don't stop [3x]

Mike D, come and rock the sure shot

[Mike D] I've got the brand new doo-doo guaranteed like Yoo-Hoo

I'm on like Dr. John—yeah, Mr. Zu Zu

I'm a newlywed, not a divorcé
And everything I do is funky like Lee Dorsey
[Adrock] Well, it's *The Taking of the Pelham One Two Three*
If you want a doo-doo rhyme then come see me
I've got the savoir faire with the unique rhymin
I keep it on and on, it's never quittin time and
[MCA] Strictly hand held is the style I go
Never rock the mic with the panty hose
I strap on my ear goggles and I'm ready to go
'Cause at the boards is the man they call the Mario
[Mike D] Pull up at the function and you know I Kojak
To all the party people that are on my Bozak
I've got more action than my man John Woo
And I've got mad hits like I was Rod Carew

Because you can't, you won't, and you don't stop [3x]
Adrock, come and rock the sure shot

[Adrock] Hurricane will cross fade on your ass and bust your ear drums
Listen everybody 'cause I'm shifting gears. I'm
Fresh like Dougie when I set my specs and
On the microphone I come correct
[MCA] Timing like a clock when I rock the hip-hop
Top notch is my stock on the soap box
I've got more rhymes than I've got gray hairs
And that's a lot because I've got my share
[Mike D] I've got a hole in my head and there's no one to fix it
Got to straighten my thoughts, I'm thinking too much sick shit
Everyone just takes and takes, takes, takes, takes
I've got to step back, I've got to contemplate
[Adrock] I'm like Lee Perry, I'm very
On—rock the microphone and then I'm gone
I'm like Vaughn Bodé, I'm a Cheech Wizard
Never quittin, so won't you listen

Ah yes indeed, it's fun time

Because you can't, you won't, and you don't stop [3x]

MCA, come and rock the sure shot

[MCA] I want to say a little something that's long overdue

The disrespect to women has got to be through

To all the mothers and the sisters and the wives and friends

I want to offer my love and respect to the end

[Mike D] Well, you say I'm twenty-something and should be slacking

But I'm working harder than ever and you could call it macking

So I'm supposed to sit upon the couch watching my TV

I'm still listening to wax, I'm not using the CD

[Adrock] Well, I'm that kid in the corner

All fucked up and I wanna so I'm gonna

Take a piece of the pie, why not, I'm not quittin

Think I'm gonna change up my style just to fit in?

[MCA] I keep my underwear up with a piece of elastic

I use a bullshit mic that's made out of plastic

To send my rhymes out to all the nations

Like Ma Bell, I've got the ill communication

SHADRACH

[MCA] Riddle me this, my brother, [Mike D] can you handle it?

[Adrock] Your style [Mike D] to my style, [Adrock] you can't hold a candle
   to it

[MCA] Equinox symmetry and the balance is right

[All] Smoking and drinking on a Tuesday night

[Adrock] It's not how you play the game, [Mike D] it's [Adrock] how you
   win it

[MCA] I cheat [Mike D] and steal [Adrock] and sin [MCA] and I'm a cynic

[Adrock] For those about to rock [All] we salute you

[Adrock] The dirty thoughts for dirty minds we contribute to

[Mike D] I once was lost [Adrock] but now I'm found

[MCA] The music washes over and you're one with the sound

[Adrock] Well, who shall inherit the earth? [All] The meek shall

[Adrock] And yo, I think I'm starting to peak now, Al

[Mike D] And the man upstairs, [MCA] well, I hope that he cares

[Adrock] If I had a penny for my thoughts I'd be a millionaire

[MCA] We're just [All] three MCs and we're on the go

[Adrock] Shadrach, [Mike D] Meshach, [MCA] Abednego

[Mike D] Only twenty-four [Adrock] hours in a day

[Mike D] Only [Adrock] twelve [Mike D] notes, [Adrock] well, a man can play

[All] Music for all and not just one people

[Adrock] And now we're gonna bust with the *Putney Swope* sequel

[Mike D] More Adidas sneakers than a plumber's got pliers

[MCA] Got more suits than Jacoby and Meyers

[Adrock] Well, [Mike D] if not for my vices [Adrock] and my bugged-out desires

[Mike D] My year would be good just like Goodyear's tires

[MCA] 'Cause I'm out picking pockets at the Atlantic Antic

[Adrock] And nobody wants to hear you 'cause your rhymes are damn frantic

[MCA] I mix business [Mike D] and pleasure [Adrock] way [MCA] too much

[Adrock] You know—[MCA] wine [Adrock] and women [Mike D] and song [Adrock] and such

[Adrock] I don't get blue, I got a mean red streak

[MCA] You don't pay the band, [Mike D] your friends—[Adrock] yo, that's weak

[MCA] Get even like Steven like pulling a Rambo

[Adrock] Shadrach, [Mike D] Meshach, [MCA] Abednego

[Mike D] Steal from the rich [Adrock] and I'm out robbing banks

[Mike D] Give it to the poor [MCA] and I always give thanks

[Adrock] Because I got more stories than J.D.'s got Salinger

[Mike D] I hold the title [MCA] and you are the challenger

[All] I've got money [Mike D] like Charles Dickens

[MCA] I got the girlies in the coupe like the Colonel's got the chicken

[Adrock] And I always go out dapper like the Harry S. Truman

[Mike D] I'm madder than Mad—[All] Alfred E. Newman

Never gonna let 'em say that I don't love you

[Adrock] Well, my [Mike D] noggin [Adrock] is [Mike D] high and [Adrock] all kinds of thoughts

[Mike D] And Adam [Adrock] Yoggin [Mike D] is [Adrock] Yauch [Mike D] and he's rocking of course

[MCA] Smoke the holy chalice, got my own religion

[All] Rally round the stage and check the funky dope musicians

[Mike D] Like Jerry Lee Swaggert [Adrock] or Jerry Lee Falwell

[Mike D] You like Mario Andretti 'cause he always drives the car well

[MCA] Vicious circle of reality since the day you were born

[Adrock] And we love the hot butter—[MCA] say what?—[All] the popcorn

[Mike D] Sipping on wine [All] and macking

[Mike D] Rocking on the stage with all the hands clapping

[MCA] Ride the wave of fate, [Adrock] it don't ride me, home

Being very proud to be an MC

[Adrock] And the man upstairs, [MCA] well, I hope that he cares

[Adrock] If I had a penny for my thoughts I'd be a millionaire

[Mike D] Amps and crossovers [MCA] under my rear hood

[All] The bass is bumping [MCA] from the back of my Fleetwood

[All] They tell us what to do? Hell, no!

[Adrock] Shadrach, [Mike D] Meshach, [MCA] Abednego

BIG DADDY KANE

Big Daddy Kane was an originator and a trendsetter. Eschewing old school reliance on rhymed couplets and simple similes, Kane expanded the terms of lyrical acceptability and innovation. His booming voice, rich with command, and his battle-anybody mentality have made him an enduring figure in hip-hop.

Kane was born in the Bedford-Stuyvesant section of Brooklyn. In 1984 he met Biz Markie, and both joined Marley Marl's Juice Crew. Even before Kane released his first single, he was already responsible for several hits as a ghostwriter for Biz and Roxanne Shanté. In 1988 Kane released "Raw," his first single and an underground hit. Over the next six years, he released four more albums and a slew of rap hits. He cultivated a personality that was at once gangster tough and lover-man smooth.

Like his contemporary Rakim, Kane focused closely on craft. Looking back on his career, he reflected on aspects that he has consciously honed over the years. "I believe that my vocabulary has broadened," Kane said. "I believe that I know how to deliver metaphors in ways that's not as typical as I used to. And, plus, I believe that I really tightened up my flow."[11] In the selection of lyrics that follows, one can see him expanding not only his own sense of lyrical possibility but that of rap as a whole.

RAW

Here I am . . . R-A-W
A terrorist, here to bring trouble to
Phony MCs, I move on and seize
I just conquer and stomp another rapper with ease
'Cause I'm at my apex when others are be-low
Nothing but a milliliter, I'm a kilo
Second to none, making MCs run
So don't try to step to me, 'cause I ain't the one
I relieve rappers just like Tylenol
And they know it, so I don't see why you all
Try to front, perpetrating a stunt
When you know that I'll smoke you up like a blunt
I'm genuine like Gucci, raw like sushi
The Sage of Rage is what rap did to me
To make me want to create chaos and mayhem
Cold rock a party until the A.M.
I'll make a muscle, grab the mic and hustle
While you stand dazed and amazed, I'll bust a little
Rhyme with authority, superiority
And captivate the whole crowd's majority

The rhymes I use definitely amuse
Better than *Dynasty* or *Hill Street Blues*
I'm sure to score, endure for more without a flaw
'Cause I get RAW!

I give a speech like a reverend, rappers start severin
And in my lifetime, believe I've never been
Beaten or eaten, and just tooken out
You know, come to think about, I keep MCs lookin out
And real nervous, when I'm at your service
So give me that title, boy, you don't deserve this
I work like a slave to become a master
And when I say a rhyme, you know that it has to
Be perfectly fitted, 'cause I'm committed
The entertainer and trainer and Kane'll get with it
I go and flow and grow to let you know
I'll damage ya, I'm not an amateur but a professional
Unquestionable, without doubt superb
So full of action, my name should be a verb
My voice will float on every note
When I clear my throat, that's all she wrote
The minute that the Kane starts to go on
Believe it's gonna be smooth sailing so on
As I put other rappers out of their misery
Get 'em in a battle and make them all history
Rulin and schoolin, MCs that I'm duelin
Watch 'em all take a fall as I sit back coolin
On my throne with a bronze microphone
Um, God bless the child that can hold his own
'Cause I get RAW!

Twenty-four seven chillin, killin like a villain
The meaning of raw is ready and willing
To do whatever is clever, take a loss never
And the rhymes I bust, comin off is a must
And I come off hard with rhymes that are odd

I rip the microphone and leave it scarred
Never smokin or hittin or takin a sniff
Only crushin MCs that be tryin to riff
I get strong and Titanic, do work like a mechanic
Make MCs panic, they all get frantic
And skeptic, like a girl on a contraceptive
As I rock, but hey, what you expected?
I'll get raw for ya, just like a warrior
Rather like a Samurai and I'll be damn if I
Ever let a Fisher-Price MC hang
Their rhymes are toy, nothing but yin-yang
So if we battle on the microphone
Bring your own casket and tombstone
And I'ma preach your funeral, tell me who in the world
Could ever come with more? I get RAW

WRATH OF KANE

The wrath of Kane, takin over your circumference
Destroyin negativity and suckers that come with
The weak, the wack, the worst, the poor
I trash, bash, clash, mash, and ten more
Blow up the scenery, I reign supremer, see
You need a savior to save ya, so lean on me
I prey on rappers like a haunted ghost
And stomp 'em out like a wanted roach
I slay my prey and they decay, I blow away
And throw away, so go away 'cause I don't play
Attackin like a psychopath, breakin rappers in half
So feel the wrath of Kane!

The name is Big Daddy
I'm here to bring trouble

The man at hand to rule and school and teach
And reach the blind to find their way from A to Z
And be the most and boast the loud and proud

Kane'll reign your domain (Yeah, Kane!)
The heat is on so feel the fire
Come off the empire on a more higher
Level than def, one step beyond dope
The suckers all scope and hope to cope, but nope
'Cause I can never let 'em on top of me
I play 'em out like a game of Monopoly
Let 'em speed around the board like an Astro
Then send 'em to jail for tryin to pass go
Shakin 'em up, breakin 'em up, takin no stuff
But it still ain't loud enough
So Mister Cee, let the volume grow
So I can flow. Now, yo . . .
Juice Crew's the family, Slick Rick's a friend of me
And Doug E. Fresh, Stet', KRS, and Public Enemy
Blasé-blah, you know who you are
The red, black, and green, the sun, moon, and star
Knowledge of self is bein taught hereon after
Peace in the name of I-Self Lord and Master
I come to teach and preach and reach in each
With the speech, every leech I'll impeach
Drop science and build with math
And the dumb, deaf, and blind'll feel the wrath of Kane!

The name is Big Daddy
I'm here to bring trouble

Marley Marl, break it down!

Bring it back, Cee

Line by line, chapter after chapter
Like a pimp on the street, I gotta rap to
Those who chose to oppose, friend or foes, I still dispose
And blow 'em out like Afros
So many rappers have fronted to get a name out

Yellin and screamin and dreamin but still came out

Off the wall and butter softer, y'all

'Til you waited for Kane to come forth to all

Competition, that bite and chew and crunch and munch

To play the opposition, you on a mission

So stop lyin and tryin to front adventures

Your rhymes are more false than dentures

Freeze as I get warm like a heater

You bite like a mosquito, but still can't complete a

Rhyme or find the time to design a line

Or phrase that pays, so you dine on mine

Instead of frontin and tryin to be a friend of

You might as well see *Guess Who's Coming to Dinner?*

So just quit, submit, forget

Huh—you must be on some new improved shit!

I get busy from sun to sun

I'm only twenty-one and untouched by anyone

No one throws bangs or blows

All foes, I keep 'em runnin like pantyhose

They get soft and tender, front and they'll surrender

I turned off more lights than Teddy Pender-

Grass, bring on your class, force be my staff

But when I'm in effect, they feel the wrath of Kane!

I'm here to bring trouble

AIN'T NO HALF STEPPIN'

Ah yeah, I'm with this. I'm just gonna sit here laid back to this nice mellow beat,
you know. And drop some smooth lyrics 'cause it's '88, time to set it straight,
know what I'm saying? And there ain't no half stepping, word, I'm ready.

Rappers stepping to me, they want to get some

But I'm the Kane, so, yo, you know the outcome

Another victory, they can't get with me

So pick a BC date 'cause you're history

I'm the authentic poet to get lyrical

For you to beat me, it's gonna take a miracle and

Stepping to me, yo, that's the wrong move

So what you on, Hobbes? Dope or dog food?

Competition I just devour

Like a pit bull against a Chihuahua

'Cause when it comes to being dope, hot damn

I got it good, now let me tell you who I am

The B-I-G-D-A double-D-Y-K-A-N-E

Dramatic, Asiatic, not like many

I'm different, so don't compare me to another

'Cause they can't hang, word to the mother

At least not with the principal in this pedigree

So when I roll on you rappers you better be

Ready to die because you're petty

You're just a butter knife, I'm a machete

That's made by Ginsu, wait until when you

Try to front, so I can chop into

Your body, just because you try to be basing

Friday the 13th, I'ma play Jason

No type of joke, gag, game, puzzle, or riddle

The name is Big Daddy, yes, big not little so

Define it, here's your walking papers, sign it

And take a walk as the Kane start to talk, 'cause

[Chorus 3x]

Ain't no half-steppin

I'm the Big Daddy Kane

My rhymes are so dope and the rappers be hopin

To sound like me, so soon I'll have to open

A school of MCin, for those who want to be in

My field and court, then again on second thought

To have MCs comin out sounding so similar

It's quite confusing for you to remember the

Originator and boy, do I hate a

Perpetrator, but I'm much greater

The best, oh yes, I guess suggest the rest should fess

Don't mess or test your highness

Unless you just address with best finesse

And bless the paragraphs I manifest

Rap prime minister, some say sinister

Nonstopping the groove until when it's the

Climax and I max, relax, and chill

Have a break from a take of me acting ill

Brain cells are lit, ideas start to hit

Next the formation of words that fit

At the table I sit, making it legit

And when my pen hits the paper? Aww, shit!

I stop and stand strong over MCs

And devour with the power of Hercules

Or Samson, but I go further the length

'Cause you could scalp my cameo and I'll still have strength

And no, that's not a myth, and if you try to riff

Or get with the man with the given gift

Of gab, your vocab, I'll only ignore

Be sleeping on your rhymes 'til I start to snore

You can't awake me, or even make me

Fear you, son, 'cause you can't do me none

So, think about it if you're trying to go

When you want to step to me, I think you should know that

[Chorus 3x]

I appear right here and scare and dare

A mere musketeer that would dare to compare

Put him in the rear, back there where he can't see clear

Get a beer, idea, or near stare, yeah

Sworn to be, want to be competition
Trying to step to me, must be on a mission
Up on the stage is where I'ma get you at
You think I'm losing? Pst, picture that!

[Chorus 3x]
Mister Cee, step to me

The name is Big Daddy, you know, as in your father
So when you hear a def rhyme, believe that I'm the author
I grab the mic and make MCs evaporate
The party people say, "Damn, that rapper's great"
The creator, conductor of poetry
Et cetera, et cetera, it ain't easy being me
I speak clearly so you can understand
Put words together like Letterman
Now that's dictation, proceeding to my innovation
Not like the other MCs that are an imitation
Or an animation, a cartoon to me
But when I'm finished, I'm sure that you are soon to see
Reality, my secret technique
Because I always speak with mentality
I put my title in your face, dare you to base
And if you try and come get it, yo, I'ma show you who's with it
So if you know like I know, instead of messing around
Play like Roy Rogers and slow down
Just give yourself a break, or someone else will take your title
Namely me, because I'm homicidal
That means murder, 'cause I'm out to hurt a-
Nother MC that try to get with me, I'll just
Break him and bake him and rake him and take him and mold him and
    make him
Hold up the peace sign, As-Salāmu Alaykum

BOOGIE DOWN PRODUCTIONS

Boogie Down Productions consisted of DJ Scott La Rock and KRS-One. The name *KRS-One* is an acronym for "Knowledge Reigns Supreme Over Nearly Everyone." He values the power that knowledge confers while he critiques the knowledge that we receive. His is a sound "with a cap and gown," as he puts it in "Ghetto Music." But BDP's purpose was not only pedagogical. KRS's lyrics move the crowd. He delivers his words like a lava flow—hot and unhurried, but faster than they seem.

BDP can be credited with helping to effect two important changes in rap. First, KRS-One brought West Indian rhythms and diction into his verses, which not only emphasized rap's historical link to reggae and dancehall but also expanded rap's sonic range. Second (and often passed over), BDP laid the foundation for gangsta rap. The first of their albums, *Criminal Minded* (1987), had the duo on its cover amid grenades and shotgun shells. *By All Means Necessary* (1988) also featured KRS on the cover with a gun, but the lyrics suggested a more conflicted persona. Songs like "Stop the Violence" show the gangsta archetype blended with radical politics, a revolutionary but gangsta sensibility later built upon by groups like dead prez.

It is finally as a teacher, however, that KRS has most made his mark. Never using "street knowledge" as a means to mystify or merely self-advertise, he makes it organic and substantial, specific and practical. He recommends vegetarianism; he outlines and categorizes hip-hop like a Linnaeus from the Bronx; he critiques "mental pictures, stereotypes, and fake history"; he urges curricular renewal at the secondary-school level; he teaches African American history. His lectures can take the form of disses, rhetorical question-and-answer sessions, self-catechisms, genealogies, and political broadsides. Most of all, though, KRS-One is giving poetry lessons.

POETRY
Well now you're forced to listen to the teacher and the lesson

Class is in session so you can stop guessing

If this is a tape or a written-down memo

See, I am a professional, this is not a demo

In fact, call it a lecture, a visual picture

Sort of a poetic and rhythm-like mixture
Listen—I'm not dissin but there's something that you're missin
Maybe you should touch reality, stop wishin
For beats with plenty bass and lyrics said in haste
If its meaning doesn't manifest, put it to rest
I am a poet, you try to show it yet blow it
It takes concentration for fresh communication
Observation, that is to see without speaking
Take off your coat, take notes, I am teachin
A class, or rather school, 'cause you need schooling
I am not a king or queen, I'm not ruling
This is an introduction to poetry
A small dedication to those that might know of me
They might know of you and maybe your gang
But one thing's for sure, neither one of y'all can hang
'Cause, yo, I'm like a arrow and Scott is the crossbow
Say something now—thought so
You seem to be the type that only understand
The annihilation and destruction of the next man
That's not poetry, that is insanity
It's simply fantasy, far from reality
Poetry is the language of imagination
Poetry is a form of positive creation
Difficult, isn't it? The point—you're missing it
Your face is in front of my hand so I'm dissing it

Scott La Rock
Innovating, decorating hip-hop
The beat may drop but not like all the others
They just cover while I just smother
Every single stupid mother—wait, wait, brother
KRS-One will have to show another
MC or self-proclaimed king or queen
Or gang or crew or solo or team that I mean

Business—so tell me, what is this?

See, I come from the Bronx, so just kiss this

Boogie Down Productions is somewhat an experiment

The antidote for sucker MCs and they're fearing it

It's self-explanatory, no one's writing for me

The poetry I'm rattling is really not for battling

But if you want I will simply change the program

So when I'm done you will simply say "Damn"

So this conversation is somewhat hypothetical

Boogie Down Productions attempts to prove somethin

I say "hypothetical" because it's only theory

My theory, so take a minute now to hear me

So what's your problem? It seems you want to be KRS-Two

From my point of view, backtrack, stop the attack

'Cause KRS-One means simply one KRS

That's it, that's all, solo, single, no more, no less

I've built up my credential financially and mental

Anytime I rhyme I request the instrumental

I speak clearly and that's merely

Or should I say a mere help to my career

I'm really not into fashion or craze

Just the one who pays and how soon I get a raise

You're probably in a daze, acting out of sympathy

Wrote a couple of rhymes and think that you can get with me

But what a pity, I'm rocking New York City

And everywhere else you put the jams on the shelf

You as an amateur is outspoken

I'm looking at your face, you seem to be hoping

That I might stutter, stop, or just mess up

But everything's live, that's why I don't dress up

Blastmaster KRS—a synonym for fresh

I'm the teacher of the class, I do not pass no test

Got DJ Scott La Rock by my side, not in back of me

'Cause we make up the Boogie Down Productions crew faculty
Get it right or train yourself not to bite
'Cause when you bite you have bitten, when I hear it, that's it
I do not contemplate a battle 'cause it really ain't worth it
I'd rather point a pistol at your head and try to burst it
I'm teaching poetry
I'm teaching poetry
Scott La Rock
We're teaching poetry

CRIMINAL MINDED
[First stanza sung to the tune of "Hey Jude"]
Boogie Down Productions
Will always get paid
We'll take the wackest song
And make it better
Remember to let us into your skin
'Cause then you'll begin
To master rhyming, rhyming, rhyming

Criminal minded, you've been blinded
Looking for a style like mine, you can't find it
They are the audience, I am the lyricist
Sometimes the suckers on the side gotta hear this
Page, a rage, and I'm not in a cage
Free as a bird to fly up out on stage
Ain't here for no fronting, just to say a little somethin
You suckers don't like me 'cause you're all about nothin
However, I'm really fascinating to the letter
My all-around performance gets better and better
My English grammar comes down like a hammer
You need a style, I need to pull your file
I don't beg favors, you're kissing other people's—
I write and produce myself just as fast

Keep my hair like this, got no time for Jheri curls
Attracting only women, got no time for little girls
'Cause girls look so good
But their brain is not ready, I don't know
I'd rather talk to a woman
'Cause her mind is so steady, so here we go

I'm not a musical maniac or b-boy fanatic
I simply made use of what was upstairs in the attic
I've listened to these MCs back when I was a kid
But I bust more shots than they ever did
I mean, this is not the best of KRS, it's just a section
But how many times must I point you in the right direction?
You need protection when I'm on the mic
Because my mouth is like a nine millimeter windpipe
You're a king, I'm a teacher—you're a b-boy, I'm a scholar
If this was a class, well, it would go right under drama
See, kings lose crowns but teachers stay intelligent
Talking big words on the mic, but still irrelevant
Especially when you're not college material
Wake up every morning to your Lucky Charms cereal
DJ Scott La Rock has a college degree
Blastmaster KRS writes poetry
I won't go deeper in the subject 'cause that gets me bored
It's a shame to know some MCs on the mic are frauds
Saying styles like this to create a dis
But if you listen, who you dissing? See, I am a musician
Rapping on the mic like this to me is fine
'Cause if I really want to battle I will pull out a nine
You can see that Scott La Rock and I are mentally binded
In other words we're both criminal minded

We're not promotin violence, we're just having some fun
He's Scott La Rock, I'm KRS-One
Never off beat 'cause it don't make sense

Grab the microphone, relaxed and not tense

You waited, debated, and now you activated

A musical genius that could not be duplicated

See, I have the formula for rockin the house

If you cannot rock a party do not open your mouth

It's that simple, no phony cosmetics for your pimple

Take another look because the gear is not wrinkled

The K, the R, the S, the O, the N, the E

Saying rhyme for '87, not from 1983

Well versed, to rehearse, in my rhymes I might curse

Originality comes first but the suckers get worse

Allow me to include I have a very stable mood

Poetic education of a high altitude

I'm not a MC, so listen—call me poet or musician

A genius when it comes to making music with ambition

I'm cool, collected with the rhyme I directed

Don't wanna be elected as the king of a record

Just respected by others as the man with the solution

An artist of the '80s came and left his contribution

On wax, relax, there's twenty-four tracks

After years of rocking parties now I picked up the knack

Because everything that flows from out my larynx

Takes years of experience and bottles of Becks

I cannot seem to recollect the time I didn't have sex

Is it real or is it Memorex?

I'm living in a city known as New York State

Sucker MCs gotta wait while I translate

I hang with real live dreads with knowledge in their heads

People with ambition and straight-up musicians

Although our lives have been so uprooted

I have it included, you all get zooted

So take each letter of the KRS-One

Means Knowledge Reigns Supreme Over Nearly Everyone

You look at me and laugh, but this is your class

It's an all-out discussion of the suckers I be crushin
So now you are awakened to the music I be makin
Never duplicated and also highly cultivated
Don't get frustrated 'cause nothing has been traded
Only activated, it came out very complicated
Not separated from my DJ
You see my voice is now faded, I'll see you folks around the way
Criminal minded

MY PHILOSOPHY

So you're a philosopher?
Yes, yes
I think very deeply
In about four seconds a teacher will begin to speak . . .

Let us begin—what, where, why, or when
Will all be explained like instructions to a game
See, I'm not insane, in fact I'm kinda rational
When I be asking you who is more dramatical
This one or that one, the white one or the black one?
Pick the punk and I'll jump up to attack one
KRS-One is just the guy to lead a crew
Right up to your face and dis you
Everyone saw me on the last album cover
Holding a pistol, something far from a lover
Beside my brother S-C-O-T-T
I just laughed 'cause no one can defeat me
This is lecture number two, "My Philosophy"
Number one was "Poetry," you know it's me
It's my philosophy, many artists gotta learn
I'm not flammable, I don't burn
So please stop burnin and learn to earn respect
'Cause that's just what KR collects
See, what do you expect when you rhyme like a soft punk?

You walk down the street and get jumped
You gotta have style and learn to be original
And everybody's gonna wanna dis you
Like me, we stood up for the South Bronx
And every sucker MC had a response
You think we care? I know that they are on the tip
My posse from the Bronx is thick
And we're real live, we roll correctly
A lot of suckers would like to forget me
But they can't 'cause like a champ I have got a record
Of knocking out the frauds in a second
On the mic I believe that you should get loose
I haven't come to tell you I've got juice
I just produce, create, innovate on a higher level
I'll be back but for now just seckle

In about four seconds a teacher will begin to speak . . .

I'll play the nine and you play the target
You all know my name so I guess I'll just start it
Or should I say, "Start this," I'm the artist
Styles and new concepts at their hardest
Yo, 'cause I'm a teacher and Scott is a scholar
It ain't about money 'cause we all make dollars
That's why I walk with my head up
When I hear wack rhymes I get fed up
Rap is like a setup, a lot of games
A lot of suckers with colorful names
"I'm so-and-so, I'm this, I'm that"
Huh, but they all just wick-wick-wack
I'm not white or red or black
I'm brown from the Boogie Down
Productions, of course our music be thumpin
Others say they're bad, but they're buggin
Let me show you something now about hip-hop

About D-Nice, Melodie, and Scott La Rock
I'll get a pen, a pencil, a marker
Mainly what I write is for the average New Yorker
Some MCs be talkin and talkin
Tryin to show how black people are walkin
But I don't walk this way to portray
Or reinforce stereotypes of today
Like all my brothers eat chicken and watermelon
Talk broken English and drug sellin
See, I'm tellin and teaching pure facts
The way some act in rap is kind of wack
And it lacks creativity and intelligence
But they don't care 'cause their company's sellin it
It's my philosophy on the industry
Don't bother dissin me or even wish that we'd
Soften, dilute, or commercialize all the lyrics
'Cause it's about time one of y'all hear it
And hear it firsthand from an intelligent brown man
A vegetarian, no goat or ham
Or chicken or turkey or hamburger
'Cause to me that's suicide, self-murder
Let us get back to what we call hip-hop
And what it meant to DJ Scott La Rock

In about four seconds a teacher will begin to speak . . .

How many MCs must get dissed
Before somebody says, "Don't fuck with Kris!"
This is just one style out of many
Like a piggy bank, this is one penny
My brother's name is Kenny, that's Kenny Parker
My other brother, ICU, is much darker
Boogie Down Productions is made up of teachers
The lecture is conducted from the mic into the speaker
Who gets weaker? The king or the teacher?

It's not about a salary, it's all about reality

Teachers teach and do the world good

Kings just rule and most are never understood

If you were to rule or govern a certain industry

All inside this room right now would be in misery

No one would get along nor sing a song

'Cause everyone'd be singing for the king—am I wrong?

S-C-O, what's up? It's me again

Scott La Rock, KRS, BDP again

Many people had the nerve to think that we would end the trend

When *Criminal Minded,* an album which is only ten

Funky, funky, funky, funky, funky hit records

No more than four minutes and some seconds

The competition checks and checks and keeps checkin

They take the album, take it home, and start sweatin

Why? Well, it's simple, to them it's kind of vital

To take KRS-One's title

To them I'm like an idol, some type of entity

In everybody's rhyme they wanna mention me?

Or rather mention us, me and Scott La Rock

But they can get bust, get robbed, get dropped

I don't play around, nor do I f' around

And you can tell by the bodies that are left around

When some clown jumps up to get beat down

Broken down to his very last compound

See how it sound? A little unrational

A lot of MCs like to use the word "dramatical"

Fresh for '88 . . . you suckers!

SOUTH BRONX

[Scott La Rock] *Yo, wassup, Blastmaster KRS-One? This jam is kickin.*

[KRS-One] *Word! Yo, what up, D-Nice?*

[D-Nice] *Yo, wassup, Scott La Rock?*

[Scott La Rock]

Yo man, we chillin this funky fresh jam. I wanna tell you a little somethin about us. We're the Boogie Down Productions crew, and due to the fact that no one else out there knew what time it was, we have to tell you a little story about where we come from.

South Bronx, the South-South Bronx [4x]

[KRS-One]
Many people tell me this style is terrific
It is kinda different but let's get specific
KRS-One specialize in music
I'll only use this type of style when I choose it
Party people in the place to be, KRS-One attacks
Ya got dropped off MCA 'cause the rhymes you wrote was wack
So you think that hip-hop had its start out in Queensbridge
If you pop that junk up in the Bronx you might not live
'Cause you're in

South Bronx, the South-South Bronx [4x]

I came with Scott La Rock to express one thing
I am a teacher and others are kings
If that's a title they earn, well, it's well deserved, but
Without a crown, see, I still burn
You settle for a pebble, not a stone like a rebel
KRS-One is the holder of a boulder, money folder
You want a fresh style, let me show ya
Now way back in the days when hip-hop began
With Coca La Rock, Kool Herc, and then Bam
B-boys ran to the latest jam
But when it got shot up they went home and said "Damn
There's got to be a better way to hear our music every day
B-boys gettin blown away but comin outside anyway"
They tried again outside in Cedar Park
Power from a street light made the place dark

But, yo, they didn't care, they turned it out
I know a few understand what I'm talkin about
Remember Bronx River rollin thick
With Kool DJ Red Alert and Chuck Chillout on the mix
When Afrika Islam was rockin the jams
And on the other side of town was a kid named Flash
Patterson and Millbrook projects
Casanova all over, ya couldn't stop it
The Nine Lives Crew, the Cypress Boys
The Real Rock Steady takin out these toys
As odd as it looked, as wild as it seemed
I didn't hear a peep from a place called Queens
It was '76 to 1980
The dreads in Brooklyn was crazy
You couldn't bring out your set with no hip-hop
Because the pistols would go
So why don't you wise up, show all the people
In the place that you are wack
Instead of tryna take out LL
You need to take your homeboys off the crack
'Cause if you don't, well, then their nerves will become shot
And that would leave the job up to my own Scott La Rock
And he's from

South Bronx, the South-South Bronx [8x]

BLACKMAN IN EFFECT

*Wake up! Take the pillow from your head and put a book in it. It's time for the
    massive BDP crew at the top of the pile.*

Yo. In the morning I'm yawning, at noon is when I wake up
Make up my bed, break up the bread, and said
Scratching my head, "Why am I so damn intimidating?"
Is it because of laws designed to keep us waiting and waiting
Thus hating all forms of a setback

Get back, if you can't understand a rap act

This is the language of the people ready to hear the truth

I've got no juice, 'cause I'm not getting juiced

To have juice means you kiss and lick a lot of booty

To have respect means you simply knew or knew me

Heard what I had to say and felt as though you'd say that too

I'm not down with a Juice Crew

But anyway, I say today the message I create is great

I don't preach hate, I simply get the record straight

It's not the fault of the black race that we are misplaced

We're robbin and killin, your own medicine you taste

You built up a race on the concept of violence

Now in '90 you want silence?

Well, I want science, not silence but science

Scientific fact about black

The board of education acts as if its only reality

Is talking about a Tom, Dick, and Harry

So now you learn your black history is questions and answers

Every question but the Black Panthers

Timbuktu existed when the caveman existed

Why then isn't this listed?

Is it because the black man is the original man?

Or does it mean humanity is African?

I don't know, but these sciences are hidden

For some strange reason, it's forbidden

To talk about or converse on a political outburst

I don't believe that I'm the first

Or should I say the first one or the first one that's done

Music like "I'm still #1"

But music like that or this is the incredible uplift

Those that oppose gets dissed

But who will oppose the Teacher when society's a wreck?

So check—the blackman in effect

Near the Tigris and Euphrates Valleys in Asia
Lies the Garden of Eden where Adam became a
Father to humanity, now don't get mad at me
But according to facts this seems as fantasy
'Cause man, the most ancient man
Was found thousands of years before Adam began
And where he was found, again, they can't laugh at ya
It's right dead-smack in Africa
But due to religious and political power
We must be denied the facts every hour
We run to school, tryin to get straight A's
Let's take a trip way back in the days
To the first civilization on Earth
The Egyptians, givin birth to
Science, mathematics, and music
Religion, the list goes on, you choose it
Egypt was the land of spiritual blessing
Egypt was the land of facts, not guessing
People from all over the world had come
To learn from Egypt, Egypt number one
So, people that believe in Greek philosophy
Know your facts, Egypt was the monopoly
Greeks had learned from Egyptian masters
You might say "Prove it," well here's the answers
640 to 322
BC originates Greek philosophy
But in that era Greece was at war
With themselves and Persia, what's more
Any philosopher at that time was a criminal
He'd be killed, very simple
This indicates that Greece had no respect
For science or intellect
So how the hell you created philosophy
When you kill philosophers constantly?
The point is that we descend from kings

Science, art, and beautiful things
African history is the world's history
This is the missing link and mystery
Once we realize they all are African
White will sit down with black and laugh again
So judge not lest ye might be judged
By the judgment ye judge, ye shall be judged
Matthew seven, first verse doesn't budge
No man should walk the Earth in sludge
If you don't believe, you can go and check
To see how and where the blackman's in effect

DE LA SOUL

Perhaps it was the Day-Glo cover of its debut album. Perhaps it was the surrealism of such titles as "Potholes in My Lawn." Perhaps it was the fact that even baby boomers could hear snatches of the Turtles and Steely Dan in the mix. It all added up to De La Soul being described at first as a group of hippies. Actually, De La Soul was—and remains—a necessary group of hip-hop eclectics.

De La Soul consists of three members who began performing as high-school students in Long Island: Posdnuos, Trugoy the Dove, and Pacemaster Mase. As part of the Native Tongues Posse—which also included groups like Black Sheep, the Jungle Brothers, and A Tribe Called Quest—they cultivated a shared aesthetic. Their first album, *Three Feet High and Rising* (1989)—produced by Prince Paul, a member of the rap group Stetsasonic—pulled in a wide range of sounds like some crazy magnet in the ear. What made it all function and not merely funny or frivolous was that the lyrics matched the sonic variety with their own wide range of themes, genres, and forms.

On the morbidly named *De La Soul Is Dead* (1991) the daisy on the cover is wilted. But despite the dark humor, the music was flourishing. The second album was more sonically subtle than the first, and the rhymes of

Posdnuos and Dove had gained in strength. Another thing that the album added to the group's repertoire was storytelling. "My Brother's a Basehead" and "Millie Pulled a Pistol on Santa" both use humor, dialogue, indirection, and fine detail to tell sad tales of misplaced trust and familial abuse.

On the subsequent albums *Buhlōōne Mindstate* (1993) and *Stakes Is High* (1996) the group exhibited artistic growth, consolidation, and transformation. And so De La Soul continues to this day, trailing with them a train of records and a deserved reputation for artistic integrity.

MY BROTHER'S A BASEHEAD

This song does not contain explicit lyrics, but what it does contain is an undesired element. This element is known as the basehead, the lowest of lowest of all elements that exist. And the sad thing is, this particular element . . . is me brudda!

[Posdnuos]
Brother, brother, oh, brother of mine
We used to be down and partners in crime
From our parents nickname was forged
I was the Beaver, you, Curious George
Wanted to be exposed to this and that
But curiosity had killed the cat
At this age no warning was read
But this was the fate that you were fed
Throughout high school our minds we'd waste
High off all the cheeba that we could taste
Soon you had converted to nasal sports
Every five minutes cocaine you'd snort
Told me that you needed a stronger fix
Stepped to the crack scene in '86
Unlike the other drugs where you had control
This substance had engulfed your body and soul
Now from me you lost dumb respect
Said you need to put the shit in check
Wanted me to believe that you had tried
But your mind and the craving didn't coincide

Said there was a voice inside you that talked
It said you shouldn't stop but continue to walk
Now the brother who could handle any drug
Had just found the one that could pull his plug

[Dove]
Yo, bro, got another rock for your hiking boots
Gonna make you scream and loop three loops
Gonna take you far on the freeway, okay?
Remember that day? Slipped me a smile for a twenty crack vial
Guess what? Time to collect, correct
Don't have a dime? It's payback time, payback time
Don't cry the blues 'cause I got bad news
Should I stab ya? Should I punch ya? Should I use my tools?
No, I got another way to earn my defeat, ah!
Slam the child on the hard concrete

Make the bass come out so clear

[Posdnuos]
Brother, brother, stupid brother of mine
Started getting high at the age of nine
Now at twenty-one you're lower than low
Nowhere to turn, nowhere to go
My dividends and wares started to disappear
Where it ended up, I had an idea
Bucking you with the quickness reversed intent
Instead went to Pop and gave him the print
Now Pop grew tired of being a mouse
Finally told you to get the hell out the house
From there mother figure came into play
Claimed for you she saw a better day
Now Mom was a product of Christ's rebirth
Thought the only chance was to go to church
Quitting this stuff you had tried before
This time you claimed you'd really score

Something I had to see to believe
Put on my suit and to church I weaved

My, my, my. What happened to the people? The people who used to care about
what took place in the world today? I've been summoned here today to reach
the people who still can be reached, to save the people who still can be saved.
Can I get an Amen? Can I get an Amen? Hit me! Forgive us. Said it's taking
over, all it's doin is taking over, takin over the world. Where them crackers at?
Them crackers that they serve, where they at?

[Posdnuos]
Bullshit, didn't believe a lick
Knew this fool too long for that to stick
Then they gave you benefit of the doubt
Wanted to see if you would work it out
First two weeks try frontin it calm
Walked round by readin verses of Psalms
Then you smiles with the funky frowns
What do you know, the voice is back in town
Mom was saying God would send it away
You and I knew it was here to stay
'Cause the man help you when you help yourself
That meant going to rehab for your health
Finally it went and blew your cork
Heard you moved to the comfortable streets of New York
And when my friends see me and come and ask
"Yo, where's your brother at?" I'll be the first to splash
"Yo, he's a basehead"

MILLIE PULLED A PISTOL ON SANTA

"If you will suck my soul, I will lick your funky emotions . . ."

[Posdnuos]
This is the stylin for a title that sounds silly
But nothing silly 'bout the triflin times of Millie
Millie—a Brooklyn queen originally from Philly

Complete with that accent that made her sound hillbilly
Around this time the slamming joint was "Milk is Chillin"
But even cooler was my social worker Dillon
Yeah, I had a social worker 'cause I had some troubles
Anyone who'd riff on me, I'd pop their dome like bubbles
He'd bring me to his crib to watch my favorite races
That's how his daughter Millie became one of my favorite faces
She had the curves that made you wanna take chances
I mean on her, man, I'd love to make advances
I guess her father must've got the same feeling
I mean, actually finding his own daughter Millie appealing
At the time no one knew, but it was a shame
That Millie became a victim of the touchy-touchy game

[Dove]
"Yo Millie, what's the problem? Lately you've been buggin
On your dookie earrings someone must be tuggin
You were a dancer who could always be found clubbin
Now you're world renowned with the frown you're luggin
Come to think, your face look stink when Dill's around you
He's your father—what done happen? Did he ground you?
You shouldn't flip on him 'cause Dill is really cool
Matter fact, the coolest elder in the school
He hooked up a trip to bring us all to Laces
He volunteered to play old Santa Claus at Macy's
Child, you got the best pops anyone could have
Dillon's cool, super-hip, you should be glad"

[Posdnuos]
Yeah, it seemed that Santa's ways was parallel with Dillon
But when Millie and him got home, he was more of a villain
While she slept in he crept inside her bedroom
And he would toss and then would force her to give him headroom
Millie tried real hard to let this hell not happen
But when she'd fuss, he would just commence to slappin

Yo, Dillon, man, Millie's been out of school for a week, man, what's the deal?
I guess he was giving Millie's bruises time to heal
Of course he told us she was sick and we believed him
And at the department store as Santa we would see him
And as he smiled, his own child was at home plottin
How off the face of this earth she was gonna knock him
When I got home I found she had tried to call me
My machine had kicked to her—"Hey, how ya doin—so-so-sorry"
I tried to call the honey but her line was busy
I guess I'll head to Macy's and bug out on Dillon

[Dove]
I received a call from Missus Sick herself
I asked her how was she recovering her health
She said that what she had to ask would make it seem minute
She wanted to talk serious—I said, "Go ahead, shoot"
She claimed I hit the combo dead upon the missile
Wanted to know if I could get a loaded pistol
That ain't a problem, but why would Millie need one?
She said she wanted her pops Dillon to heed one
Ran some style about him pushing on her privates
Look, honey, I don't care if you kick five fits
There's no way that you can prove to me that Dill's flip
He might breathe a blunt but your jeans he wouldn't rip
You're just mad, he's your overseer at school
No need to play him out like he's someone cruel
She kicked that she would go get it from somewhere else
Yeah, whatever you say, go for yourself

[Posdnuos]
Macy's department store, the scene for Santa's kisses
And all the little brats demanding all of their wishes
Time passes by as I wait for my younger brother
He has his wish, I waste no time to return him back to mother
As I'm jettin Millie floats in like a zombie

I ask her what's her problem, all she says is, "Where is he?"
I give a point, she pulls a pistol, people screamin
She shouts to Dill he's off to hell 'cause he's a demon
None of the kids could understand what was the cause
All they could see was a girl holding a pistol on Claus
Dillon pleaded mercy, said he didn't mean to
Do all the things that her mind could do nothing but cling to
Millie bucked him and with the quickness it was over

STAKES IS HIGH

[Posdnuos]

The instamatic focal point bringing damage to your borough
We some brothers from the East with them beats that be thorough
Got the solar gravitation so I'm bound to pull it
I gets down like brothers are found ducking from bullets
Gun control means using both hands in my land
Where it's all about the cautious livin
Migrating to a higher form of consequence, compliments
Of strugglin, that shouldn't be notable
Man, every word I say should be a hip-hop quotable

[Dove]

I'm sick of bitches shakin asses, I'm sick of talkin about blunts
Sick of Versace glasses, sick of slang, sick of
Half-ass awards shows, sick of name-brand clothes
Sick of R & B bitches over bullshit tracks
Cocaine and crack, which brings sickness to blacks
Sick of swoll' head rappers with their sicker-than raps
Claps and gats makin the whole sick world collapse
The facts are gettin sick, even sicker perhaps
I stick-a-bush to make a bundle to escape the synapse

[Posdnuos]

Man, life can get all up in your ass
Baby, you betta work it out. Let me tell you

What it's all about, a skin not considered equal
A meteor has more right than my people
Who be wastin time screaming who they've hated
That's why the Native Tongues has officially been reinstated

(Vibes . . . vibrations)
Stakes is high
(Higher than high)
You know them stakes is high
(Higher than high)
When we talkin 'bout the
(Vibes . . . vibrations)
Stakes is high, y'all know them stakes is high
When we dealin with the
(Vibes . . . vibrations)
Stakes is high
(Hey yo, what about that love?)

[Posdnuos]
Yo, it's about love for cars, love for funds
Loving to love mad sex, loving to love guns
Love for opposite, love for fame and wealth
Love for the fact of no longer lovin yourself, kid
We living in them days of the man-made ways
Where every aspect is vivid. These brothers
No longer talk shit; aiyo, these niggas live it
'Bout to give it to you twenty-four seven on the microphone
Plug One translating the zone
No offense to a player, but, yo, I don't play
And if you take offense, fuck it, got to be that way
Jay Dee, Dove show your love, what you got to say?

[Dove w/Jay Dee]
I say Gs are making figures at a high regard
And niggas dying for it nowadays ain't hard

Investing in fantasies and not God
Welcome to reality—see, times is hard
People try to snatch the credit, but can't claim the card
Showing out in videos, saying they costarred
See, shit like that'll make your mama cry
Better watch the way you spend it, 'cause the stakes is high

Y'all know them stakes is high
When we talkin 'bout the
(Vibes . . . vibrations)
Stakes is high

[Dove]
I think that smiling in public is against the law
'Cause love don't get you through life no more
It's who you know and "How you, son?" and how you gettin in?
And who the man holding heat? Hey, yo, and how was the skins?
And how high? Yo, what up, huh? I heard you caught a body
Seem like every man and woman share the life of John Gotti
(But they ain't organized!)
Mixing crimes with life enzymes
Taking the big scout route and niggas no doubt
Better than they know their daughters and their sons (Oh, boy)

[Posdnuos]
Yo, people go through pain and still don't gain
Positive contact just like my main man
Who got others cleaning up his physical influence
His mind got congested, he got the nine and blew it
Neighborhoods are now 'hoods 'cause nobody's neighbors
Just animals surviving with that animal behavior
Under I who be rhyming from dark to light sky
Experiments when needles and skin connect
No wonder where we live is called the projects
When them stakes is high you damn sure try to do
Anything to get the piece of the pie

Electrify, even die for the cash

But at last we be out even though you wantin more

This issue is closed like an elevator door

But soon reopened once we get to the next floor where the . . .

(Vibes . . . vibrations)

Stakes is high

You know them stakes is high

When we dealin with the

(Vibes . . . vibrations)

Stakes is high

Stakes is high, come on

ERIC B. & RAKIM

Rakim is among the most influential artists in the history of rap, with a style that is as relevant today as it was when he first emerged in the mid-1980s. Along with Eric B., he forged one of the most potent duos in hip-hop history, recording four classic albums between 1987 and 1992.

As a young man, Rakim played the saxophone, a skill to which he ascribes some of his rhythmic sensibility and timing as a rapper. He finds lyrical inspiration in his urban surroundings, in popular culture, and in the arcane lore of the Five-Percent Nation, or Nation of Gods and Earths, a derivative of the Nation of Islam that teaches a philosophy including knowledge of self, faith in the black man as God, and the division of the human population into categories of awareness. After joining the Nation of Gods and Earths in 1985, Rakim began liberally lacing his lyrics with its terminology.

Rakim's nickname, the GOD MC, is a nod not only to his Five-Percenter ideology but also to the high esteem in which he is held as a lyricist. Even before one considers his poetics, Rakim distinguishes himself with his delivery and his voice—a rich and resonant baritone. Inspired by the jazz instrumentalists he studied as a youth, he practices careful enunciation, mindful of giving rhythmic shape to his lines. At the same time, his delivery is not as highly stylized as Eminem or Lil Wayne but instead maintains a calm, controlled cadence that at times can even come across as deadpan.

Rakim's signal poetic achievements are in rhyme and its attendant aural effects like alliteration, assonance, and consonance. He brought scientific attention to the craft of MCing, employing a host of unusual compositional methods over the years that speak to his desire for lyrical distinction. Among them is his habit of writing the last line of a given verse first, then composing the preceding lines with that end in mind. Wishing to go beyond the old school strictures of end rhyme, Rakim developed a technique whereby he would split each individual line within a given verse in half, then conclude both the middle section and the end with rhymes. The result is a densely layered lyric, rich with internal rhymes and sonic echoes. Over time, Rakim has expanded his range of multisyllabic rhymes and slant rhymes. One can hear these techniques on such signature songs as "Paid in Full," "My Melody," and "Lyrics of Fury," as well as many more.

ERIC B. IS PRESIDENT

I came in the door, I said it before
I never let the mic magnetize me no more
But it's biting me, fighting me, inviting me to rhyme
I can't hold it back, I'm looking for the line
Taking off my coat, clearing my throat
The rhyme will be kickin until I hit my last note
My mind remains to find all kind of ideas
Self-esteem makes it seem like a thought took years to build
But still say a rhyme after the next one
Prepared, never scared, I'll just bless one
And you know that I'm the soloist
So Eric B., make 'em clap to this

I don't bug out or chill or be acting ill
No tricks in '86, it's time to build
Eric B., easy on the cut, no mistakes allowed
'Cause to me, MC means move the crowd

I made it easy to dance to this

But can you detect what's coming next from the flex of the wrist?

Say "indeed," then I proceed 'cause my man made a mix

If he bleed he won't need no Band-Aid to fix

His fingertips, so I rhyme until there's no rhymes left

I hurry up because the cut'll make him bleed to death

But he's kicking it, 'cause it ain't no half-steppin

The party is live, the rhyme can't be kept in-

Side of me, eruptin, just like a volcano

It ain't the everyday style or the same old rhyme

'Cause I'm better than the rest of them

Eric B. is on the cut and my name is Rakim

Go get a girl and get soft and warm

Don't get excited, you've been invited to a Quiet Storm

But now it's out of hand 'cause you told me you hate me

And then you ask what have I done lately

First you said all you want is love and affection

"Let me be your angel and I'll be your protection"

Take you out, buy you all kind of things

I must've got you too hot and burned off your wings

You caught an attitude, you need food to eat up

I'm scheming like I'm dreaming on a couch with my feet up

You scream I'm lazy. You must be crazy

Thought I was a doughnut, you tried to glaze me

PAID IN FULL

Thinkin of a master plan

'Cause ain't nothin but sweat inside my hand

So I dig into my pocket, all my money's spent

So I dig deeper but still comin up with lint

So I start my mission, leave my residence

Thinkin, "How could I get some dead presidents?"

I need money, I used to be a stick-up kid

So I think of all the devious things I did
I used to roll up: "This is a hold up, ain't nothin funny
Stop smiling, be still, don't nothin move but the money"
But now I learned to earn 'cause I'm righteous
I feel great, so maybe I might just
Search for a nine to five
If I strive, then maybe I'll stay alive
So I walk up the street whistlin this
Feelin out of place, 'cause, man, do I miss
A pen and a paper, a stereo, a tape of
Me and Eric B. and a nice big plate of
Fish, which is my favorite dish
But without no money it's still a wish
'Cause I don't like to dream about gettin paid
So I dig into the books of the rhymes that I made
So now's the test to see if I got pull
Hit the studio, 'cause I'm paid in full

MY MELODY

Turn up the bass, check out my melody, hand out a cigar
I'm lettin knowledge be born and my name's the R
A-K-I-M, not like the rest of them, I'm not on the list
That's what I'm sayin, I drop science like a scientist
My melody's in a code, the very next episode
Has the mic often distortin, ready to explode
I keep the mic at Fahrenheit, freeze MCs to make 'em colder
The listener's system is kickin like solar
As I memorize, advertise like a poet
Keep you goin when I'm flowin, smooth enough, you know it
But rough, that's why the moral of my story I tell'll be
Nobody beats the R, check out my melody

So what, I'm a microphone fiend, addicted soon as I seen
One of these, for MCs, so they don't have to scream

I couldn't wait to take the mic, flow into it to test it

Let my melody play, then a record suggested

I'm droppin bombs, but I stay peace and calm

Any MC that disagree with me, wave your arm

And I'll break, when I'm through breakin, I'll leave you broke

Drop the mic when I'm finished and watch it smoke

So stand back, you wanna rap? All of that can wait

I won't push, I won't beat around the bush

I wanna break upon those who are not supposed to

You might try but you can't get close to

Because I'm number one, competition is none

I'm measured with the heat that's made by sun

Whether playin ball or bobbin in the hall

Or just writin my name in graffiti on the wall

They shouldn't have told me you said you control me

So now a contest is what you owe me

Pull out your money, pull out your cut

Pull up a chair . . .

My name is Rakim Allah and R & A stands for Ra

Switch it around—it still comes out R

So easily will I E-M-C-E-E

My repetition of words is "check out my melody"

Some bass and treble is moist, scratchin and cuttin a voice

And when it's mine, that's when the rhyme is always choice

I wouldn't have came to say my name and run the same weak shit

Puttin blurbs and slurs and words that don't fit in a rhyme

Why waste time on the microphone?

I take this more serious than just a poem

Rockin party to party, backyard to yard

Now tear it up, y'all, and bless the mic for the gods

Check out my melody

The rhyme is rugged, at the same time sharp

I can swing off anything, even a string of a harp

Just turn it on and start rockin, mine, no introduction

'Til I finish droppin science, no interruption

When I approach, I exercise like a coach

Usin a melody and add numerous of notes

So when the mic and the R-A-K-I-M

Is attached, like a match I will strike again

Rhymes are poetically kept and alphabetically stepped

Put in an order to pursue with the momentum, except

I say one rhyme out of order, a longer rhyme shorter

Or pause … but don't stop the tape recorder

Check out my melody

I'm not a regular competitor, first-rhyme editor

Melody arranger, poet, et cetera

Extra events, the grand-finale-like bonus

I am the man they call the Microphonist

With wisdom, which means wise words bein spoken

Too many at one time, watch the mic start smokin

I came to express the rap I manifest

Stand in my way and I'll veto, in other words protest

MCs that wanna be dissed, they're gonna

Be dissed if they don't get from in front of

All they can go get is me a glass of Moët

A hard time: sip your juice and watch a smooth poet

I take seven MCs, put 'em in a line

And add seven more brothers who think they can rhyme

Well, it'll take seven more before I go for mine

Now that's twenty-one MCs ate up at the same time

Easy does it, do it easy, that's what I'm doin

No fessin, no messin around, no chewin

No robbin, no buyin, bitin, why bother?

This slob will stop tryin, fightin to follow

My unusual style will confuse you a while

If I was water, I'd flow in the Nile

So many rhymes, you won't have time to go for yours
Just because of applause I have to pause
Right after tonight is when I prepare
To catch another sucker-duck MC out there
'Cause my strategy has to be tragedy, catastrophe
And after this you'll call me "Your Majesty." My melody . . .

Check out my melody
Yes, my melody

Marley Marl synthesized it, I memorize it
Eric B. made a cut, then advertised it
My melody's created for MCs in the place
They try to listen 'cause I'm dissin them so pick up your face
Shook off your neck, 'cause you try to detect my pace
Now you're buggin, almost doggin off my rhyme-like bass
The melody that I'm stylin, smooth as a violin
Rough enough to break New York from Long Island
My wisdom is swift, no matter if
My momentum is slow, MCs still stand stiff
I'm genuine like leather, inclined to be clever
MCs, you'll beat the R, I say, "Oh, never"
So Eric B., cut it easily
And . . . check out my melody

I AIN'T NO JOKE
I ain't no joke, I used to let the mic smoke
Now I slam it when I'm done and make sure it's broke
When I'm gone, no one gets on, 'cause I won't let
Nobody press up and mess up the scene I set
I like to stand in a crowd and watch the people wonder, "Damn!"
But think about it, then you understand
I'm just an addict, addicted to music
Maybe it's a habit, I gotta use it
Even if it's jazz or the Quiet Storm

I hook a beat up, convert it into hip-hop form

Write a rhyme in graffiti in every show you see me in

Deep concentration, 'cause I'm no comedian

Jokers are wild, if you wanna be tame

I treat you like a child, then you're gonna be named

Another enemy, not even a friend of me

'Cause you'll get fried in the end when you pretend to be

Competing, 'cause I just put your mind on pause

And I complete when you compare my rhyme with yours

I wake you up and as I stare in your face you seem stunned, remember me

The one you got your idea from?

But soon you start to suffer, the tune'll get rougher

When you start to stutter, that's when you had enough of

Biting, it'll make you choke, you can't provoke

You can't cope, you should have broke because I ain't no joke

I got a question, as serious as cancer:

Who can keep the average dancer

Hyper as a heart attack, nobody's smiling

'Cause you're expressin the rhyme that I'm styling

This is what we all sit down to write

You can't make it so you take it home, break it and bite

Use pieces and bits of all my hip-hop hits

Get the style down pat then it's time to switch

Put my tape on pause and add some more to yours

Then you figured you're ready for the neighborhood tours

An E-M-C-E-E, don't even try to be

When you come up to speak, don't even lie to me

You like to exaggerate, dream and imaginate

Then change the rhyme around that can aggravate me

So when you see me come up, freeze

Or you'll be one of those seven MCs

They think that I'm a new jack, but only if they knew that

They who think wrong are they who can't do that

Style that I'm doing, they might ruin

Patterns of paragraphs based on you and

Your offbeat DJ, if anything he play

Sound familiar, I'll wait 'til E say

"Play 'em," so I'ma have to dis. You broke

You could get a smack for this—I ain't no joke

I hold the microphone like a grudge

B'll hold the record so the needle don't budge

I hold a conversation 'cause what I invent

I nominated my DJ the president

When I MC I'll keep a freestyle going steadily

So pucker up and whistle "My Melody"

But whatever you do, don't miss one

There'll be another rough rhyme after this one

Before you know it, you're following and fiendin

Waiting for the punch line to get the meanin

Like before, the moral of my story I'm tellin

Nobody beats the R, so stop yellin

Save it, put it in your pocket for later

'Cause I'm movin the crowd and B'll wreck the fader

No interruptions 'til the mic is broke

When I'm gone, then you can joke

'Cause everything is real on a serious tip

Keep playing and I get furious quick

And I take you for a walk through hell

Freeze your dome, then watch your eyeballs swell

Guide you out of triple-stage darkness

When it get dark again, then I'ma spark this

Microphone, 'cause the heat is on, you see smoke

And I'm finished when the beat is gone—I'm no joke

MICROPHONE FIEND

I was a fiend before I became a teen

I melted microphones instead of cones of ice cream

Music orientated, so when hip-hop was originated

Fitted like pieces of puzzles, complicated

'Cause I grab the mic and try to say, "Yes, y'all"

They try to take it, and say that I'm too small

Cool, 'cause I don't get upset

I kick a hole in the speaker, pull the plug, then I jet

Back to the lab—without a mic to grab

So then I add all the rhymes I had

One after the other one, then I make another one

To dis the opposite then ask if the brother's done

I get a craving like I fiend for nicotine

But I don't need a cigarette, know what I mean?

I'm raging, ripping up the stage and

Don't I sound amazing? 'Cause every rhyme is made and

Thought of, 'cause it's sort of an addiction

Magnetized by the mixing

Vocals, vocabulary, and verses, just stuck in

The mic is a Drano, volcano's eruptin

Rhymes overflowing, gradually growing

Everything is written in the cold so it can coin-

Cide, my thoughts to guide

Forty-eight tracks to slide

The invincible microphone fiend Rakim

Spread the word, 'cause I'm in

E-F-F-E-C-T

A smooth operator operating correctly

But back to the problem, I got a habit

You can't solve it, silly rabbit

The prescription is a hypertone that's thorough when

I fiend for a microphone, like heroin

Soon as the bass kicks, I need a fix

Give me a stage and a mic and a mix

And I'll put you in a mood or is it a state of

Unawareness? Beware, it's the reanimator

A menace to a microphone, a lethal weapon

Or assassinator, if the people ain't steppin
You'll see a part of me that you never seen
When I'm fiending for a microphone, I'm the microphone fiend
After twelve, I'm worse than a Gremlin
Feed me hip-hop and I start trembling
The thrill of suspense is intense, you're horrified
But this ain't the cinemas or *Tales from the Darkside*
By any means necessary, this is what has to be done
Make way, 'cause here I come
My DJ cuts material
Grand Imperial
It's a must that I bust any mic you hand to me
It's inherited, it runs in the family
I wrote the rhyme that broke the bull's back
If that don't slow 'em up, I carry a full pack
Now I don't want to have to let off, you should have kept off
You didn't keep the stage warm, step off
Ladies and gentlemen, you're about to see
A pastime hobby about to be
Taken to the maximum, I can't relax, see
I'm hype as a hyper-chondriac 'cause the rap be one
Hell of a antidote, something you can't smoke
More than dope, you try to move away but you can't, you're broke
More than cracked up, you should have backed up
For those that act up need to be more than smacked up
Any entertainer, I got a torture chamber
One on one and I'm the remainder
So close your eyes and hold your breath
And I'ma hit you with the blow of death
Before you go, you'll remember you seen
The fiend of a microphone, I'm the microphone fiend

LYRICS OF FURY

I'm rated R . . . this is a warning, ya better void
Poets are paranoid, DJs destroyed

'Cause I came back to attack others in spite
Strike like lightnin, it's quite frightenin
But don't be afraid in the dark, in a park
Not a scream or a cry, or a bark, more like a spark
Ya tremble like a alcoholic, muscles tighten up
What's that? Lighten up. You see a sight but
Suddenly you feel like you're in a horror flick
You grab your heart and wish for tomorrow quick
Music's the clue, when I come you're warned
Apocalypse Now, when I'm done, you're gone
Haven't you ever heard of a MC murderer?
This is a death penalty and I'm servin a
Death wish, so come on, step to this
Hysterical idea for a lyrical professionist
Friday the thirteenth, walking down Elm Street
You come in my realm, ya get beat
This is off limits, so your visions are blurry
All ya see is the meters of the volume, pumpin "Lyrics of Fury"

A furified freestyle . . .

Terror in the styles, never error-files
Indeed, I'm known to exile
For those that oppose to be level or next to this
I ain't a devil and this ain't *The Exorcist*
Worse than a nightmare, you don't have to sleep a wink
The pain's a migraine every time ya think
Flashbacks interfere, ya start to hear
The R-A-K-I-M in your ear
Then the beat's hysterical, that makes Eric go
Get a ax and chops the wack, soon the lyrical
Format is furier, faces of death remain
MCs decaying, 'cause they never stayed
The scene of a crime every night at the show
The fiend of a rhyme on the mic that you know
It's only one capable, breaks the unbreakable

Melodies unmakable, pattern unescapable
A horn if you want the style I possess
I bless the child, the Earth, the gods, and bomb the rest
For those that envy a MC it can be
Hazardous to your health so be friendly
A matter of life and death, just like a Etch-A-Sketch
Shake 'til you're clear, make it disappear, make the next
After the ceremony, let the rhyme rest in peace
If not, my soul'll release
The scene is re-created, reincarnated
Updated, I'm glad you made it
'Cause you're about to see a disastrous sight
A performance never again performed on a mic: "Lyrics of Fury"

A furified freestyle . . .

The R is in the house, too much tension
Make sure the system's loud when I mention
Phrases that's fearsome, you want to hear some
Sounds that not only pound but please your eardrum
I sit back and observe the whole scenery
Then nonchalantly tell you what it mean to me
Strictly business, I'm quickly in this mood
And I don't care if the whole crowd's a witness
I'ma tear you apart but I'ma spare you a heart
Program it to the speed of the rhyme, prepare to start
Rhythm's out of the radius, insane, it's the craziest
Musical madness MC ever made, see it's
Now an emergency, open-heart surgery
Open your mind, you will find every word'll be
Furier than ever, I remain the future
Battle's tempting, whatever suits ya
From words to sentence, there's no resemblance
You think you're rougher, then suffer the consequences
I'm never dying, terrifying results
I wake ya with hundreds of thousands of volts

Mic-to-mouth resuscitation, rhythm with radiation

Novocain ease the pain, it might save him

If not, Eric B.'s the judge, the crowd's the jury

How do I plead to homicide? Lyrics of Fury!

A furified freestyle ...

GANG STARR

Although he has produced beats for many of the biggest names in the game, DJ Premier's deepest and longest-lasting partnership was with the rapper Guru under the name Gang Starr. They debuted with *No More Mr. Nice Guy* (1989) and followed it with *Step in the Arena* (1990). The second album's title track elaborates on the concept of rap as a battle. Moving through a medieval British world to the Coliseum of ancient Rome, the song ends in an arena of another sort, a place we buy tickets to enter to hear rhymes styled as battle.

This historicizing expansion of a common metaphor into a conceit is joined on the album by "Just to Get a Rep," one of rap's best and most terrible stories. The terror there is Guru's plain reportage of how nonchalantly the desire to be known, respected, and feared by young men with little besides their reputations to bank on becomes another man's death.

Gang Starr's third album, *Daily Operation* (1992), continued the style of Guru's smoothly delivered yet sonically dense lyrics and Premier's impeccable beats. Three more Gang Starr releases followed in the 1990s. Throughout that time Premier was spreading around his gifts for the benefit of other rappers, while Guru was releasing his influential *Jazzmatazz* albums, which asserted the connection between rap and jazz, another rich African American contribution to the world's music.

STEP IN THE ARENA

Once you step in the arena, cheater, you're gonna be a-

Mazed when you gaze at the armor on this leader

Fully clad and glad to fight a cause, I won't pause

Fear is a joke, slowpoke, I'm like claws that'll rip
'Cause your gift is merely flesh
Superficial, and I wish you would give it a rest
But if you don't, I'll unsheath my Excalibur
Like a noble knight, so meet ya challenger
A true hero, while you're a true zero
Gettin beat to a pulp so that you can't run for help
I heard a gulp in your throat, 'cause you hope that I'll be merciful
But coo-cluck, I made you strut as I rehearse a few
Battle drills and watch your bladder spill
Yellow fluid, check how I mellowly do it
Face defeat to this beat, you can tell I'm into it
As I'm pullin out my lance to kill you and advance to
The winner's throne, 'cause I own you once you
Step in the arena

In the arena, or rather coliseum
There's people gatherin by multitudes to see one
Perpetrator fall to the dust after the other
Quickly disposed of at the hand of a known brother
Born with the art in his heart that is Spartacus
And one-to-one combat, Jack, just the thought of this
Matchup makes Gang Starr wanna snatch up
One or two phrases from the new book with new pages
Of rhymes that are built like a chariot
Dope vocals carry it to the battle set
If a beat was a princess, I would marry it
But now I must bow to the crowd as I stand proud
Victorious, glorious—understand now?
'Cause battles and wars and much fights I have been through
One MC got beheaded and you can, too
Forget it, 'cause you'd rather be just a spectator
An onlooker, afraid you may get slayed or
Struck by a blow from a mic gladiator

I bet you that later you might be sad that you played yourself

'Cause you stepped up, chest puffed out

And in just one lyric you got snuffed out

'Cause rhymin is serious, I'm strong, I'm like Hercules

You'll get hurt with these lines, close the curtains, please

The suckers can jet 'cause I wreck once you step

In the arena

In the arena or forum, weak MCs I will floor 'em

Causin mayhem, I'll slay them and the blood'll be pourin

Furthermore, I implore that as a soldier of war

I go in only to win and be the holder of more

Trophies, titles, and triumphs, 'cause I dump all the sly chumps

Never choosin to lose my spot, not once

For the mere idea of an opponent that I fear

Is foolish utterly, I mean but none'll be

Tryin to toy with a destroyer of many

You shitted your pants 'cause you can't think of any

Foe that can step to this concept so

You better sit again, citizen, weak MCs, I get rid of them

Watch the way they get distraught when they get caught

In the worst positions, 'cause they didn't listen and tried

Goin up against a hungry killer who's itchin

To maim and murder those who claimed that they were the

Toughest ones, they get done once they step

In the arena

JUST TO GET A REP

Brothers are amused by others brothers' reps

But the thing you know best is where the gun is kept

'Cause in the night you'll feel fright

And at the sight of a four-fifth I guess you just might

Wanna do a dance or two

'Cause he could maybe bust you for self or with a crew

No matter if you or your brother's a star

He could pop you in check without a getaway car

And some might say that he's a dummy

But he's sticking you and taking all of your money

It's a daily operation

He might be loose in the park or lurking at the train station

Mad brothers know his name

So he thinks he got a little fame from the stick-up game

And while we're blaming society

He's at a party with his man

They got their eye on the gold chain

That the next man's wearing

It looks big but they ain't staring

Just thinking of a way and when to get the brother

They'll be long gone before the kid recovers

And back around the way, he'll have the chain on his neck

Claimin respect, just to get a rep

Ten brothers in a circle had the kid trapped

The one with the hoodie said, "We'll hurt you

If you don't run out your dues and pay

Give up the Rolex watch or you won't see another day"

See, they were on the attack and one said

"Yo, you wanna make this to a homicide rap?

Make it fast so we can be on our way

Kick in the rings and everything, okay?"

The kid was nervous and flinchin

And little Shorty with the .38, yo, he was inchin

Closer and closer, put the gun to his head

Shorty was down to catch a body instead

Money was scared so he panicked

Took off his link and his rings and ran frantic

But Shorty said, "Nah," pulled the trigger and stepped

It was nothing, he did it just to get a rep

The rep grows bigger, now he's known for his trigger finger

Rollin with troops of his sons like a gangster figure

He's near the peak of his crazy career

His posse's a nightmare, mackin jewels and crazy gear

But as we know, the things we do come back

As Shorty's not peepin, others are schemin to counteract

Because the kid that got shot didn't perish, so

He pulls up in the Jeep with tinted windows

Too late—Shorty was caught in the mix

His time ran out, his number came up, and that's it

You know the rest, so don't front, the plan has been upset

Some brothers gotta go out just to get a rep

WORDS I MANIFEST (REMIX)

I profess and I don't jest, 'cause the words I manifest

They will take you, sedate you, and I will stress upon

You the need for you all to feed your

Minds and souls, so you can lead your-

Self to peace, I got a real objective here

I am effective here, 'cause I select a clear

Method for all—suckers I maul, they fall and crawl

Into the pit of purgatory

I go for glory, I'm takin inventory

Countin all the tough-luck ducks while I narrate

Relate and equate, dictate and debate

'Cause my fate is to be cold makin history

I use sincerity but I'll still bury the

Doubts and questions of all the skeptics

I'm kickin clout and I'll even bet this

Is true—there's nothing so-so 'cause I know

Right about this minute, I'm in it, admit it, I did it

For you, 'cause this is what I'm into

So chill while I instill that we all must fulfill

The proper mission for us, and yo, this is a must

Using lines of my rhymes I attest
These are the words that I manifest, I manifest

I suggest you take a rest for the words I manifest
They will scold you and mold you, while I impress upon
You the fact that I use my tact at
Rhymin, cold-climbin and chill while I attract that
Girl you're with, I got a sincere quality
I give her all of me, 'cause you're too small to be
Tryin to riff, so let me uplift and shift my gift
Let's go to the fullest capacity
I got tenacity because I have to be
The brother who must live and give with much insight
The foresight to ignite, excite, and delight
And you might gain from it or feel pain from it
Because I'm ultimate and I'm about to let off
Knowledge, wisdom, understanding
Truth—we cool, so won't you throw a hand in
The air, put up a peace sign and please find
That though we're feeling good, we should, we could, we would
Stop—think for a moment, okay?
And then sway while I convey that we must do away
With all the stress and the strife, so God bless your life
And use kindness and never blindness
And you will find that this perspective is best, check it out

These are the words that I manifest, I manifest

I convey that what I say will awaken you today
Have you jockin while I'm talkin, but anyway
That you put it, I give you lyrics to live to
Righteousness rules, so I forgive you this time
For you are being very ignorant
That's insignificant, I guess you figured and
Hoped you'd be dope as me, ID, you flee
Because the pressure's too much for you

I'm your professor, I got the touch to do

More than the rest who fess and can't compete

I'm elite, I'll defeat, delete and mistreat

Make mincemeat of other fools, 'cause I'm the brother who'll

Snatch up the funds and make lonely ones

I meant it, really, 'cause I'm clearly obsessed and I

These are the words that I manifest, I manifest

ICE-T

Taking his name from the pimp turned novelist Iceberg Slim, Ice-T cut a larger-than-life figure. In the spirit of his namesake, Ice-T early on developed a pimp persona in such songs as "Somebody Gotta Do It (Pimpin' Ain't Easy)." More pronounced, however, was his role in developing the persona of the West Coast gangsta. "6 'N the Mornin'" is a gangsta rap classic and displays Ice-T's success in exploiting a series of genres. The song is an aubade, as it begins at the crack of dawn, and partakes of the picaresque as it moves through its series of episodes. Each episode is contained in a discrete stanza, but each stanza advances the story. The song's chronology spans a couple of complete days and also encompasses a significant jail term.

In the years following *Rhyme Pays* (1987), Ice-T's work got more realistic (sometimes taking on a documentary-like feel, as in "Colors"), more political (as in 1989's *The Iceberg/Freedom of Speech . . . Just Watch What You Say*), and even more historical (1991's *O.G.: Original Gangster*). His rap-rock group Body Count released the deliberately provocative "Cop Killer" in 1992, and his performance with Jane's Addiction front man Perry Farrell of Sly Stone's "Don't Call Me Nigger, Whitey" on the first Lollapalooza tour was some of the most nerve-touching racial theater of the decade.

6 'N THE MORNIN'

6 'n the mornin, police at my door

Fresh Adidas squeak across the bathroom floor

Out my back window I make my escape
Didn't even get a chance to grab my old school tape
Mad with no music but happy 'cause free
And the streets to a player is the place to be
Got a knot in my pocket weighing at least a grand
Gold on my neck, my pistol's close at hand
I'm a self-made monster of the city streets
Remotely controlled by hard hip-hop beats
But just living in the city is a serious task
Didn't know what the cops wanted, didn't have time to ask

Word

Seen my homeboys cooling way, way out
Told 'em 'bout my morning, cold bugged 'em out
Shot a little dice 'til my knees got sore
Kicked around some stories 'bout the night before
Posse to the corner where the fly girls chill
Threw action at some freaks 'til one bitch got ill
She started acting silly, simply would not quit
Called us all punk pussies, said we all weren't shit
As we walked over to her, ho continued to speak
So we beat the bitch down in the goddamn street
But just living in the city is a serious task
Bitch didn't know what hit her, didn't have time to ask

Word

Continued clockin freaks with immense posteriors
Rolling in a Blazer with a Louis interior
Solid gold, the ride was raw
Bust a left turn, was on Crenshaw
Sean-E-Sean was the driver, known to give freaks hell
Had a beeper going off like a high-school bell
Looked in the mirror, what did we see?
Fucking blue lights, LAPD
Pigs searched our car, their day was made

Found a Uzi, .44, and a hand grenade
Threw us in the county, high power block
No freaks to see, no beats to rock
Didn't want trouble, but the shit must fly
Squabbled with this sucker, shanked him in the eye
But just living in the county is a serious task
Nigga didn't know what happened, didn't have time to ask

Back on the streets after five and a deuce
Seven years later, but still had the juice
My homeboy Hen Gee put me up on the track
Told me E's rolling villain, BJ's got the sack
Bruce is a giant, Nat C's clocking dough
Be-Bop's a pimp, my old freak's a ho
The Batterram's rolling, rocks are the thing
Life has no meaning and money is king
Then he looked at me slowly and Hen had the grin
He said, "Man, you out early, we thought you got ten"
Opened up his safe, kicked me down with cold cash
Knew I would get busy, he didn't waste time to ask

Word

I bought a Benz with the money, the rest went on clothes
Went to the strip, start pimpin the hoes
My hair had grew long on my seven-year stay
When I got it done, on my shoulders it lay
Hard from the joint but fly to my heart
I didn't want trouble but the shit had to start
Out with my crew, some punks got loud
Shotgun blasts echoed through the crowd
Six punks hit, two punks died
All casualties were applied to their side
Human lives had to pass just for talking much trash
We didn't know who they were, no one had time to ask

Word

SWAT team leader yelled, "Hit the floor!"
Reached in my pocket, pulled my .44
Dove across the room, peeped out the window
Twenty cops jumped behind a Pinto
Out the back door like some damn track stars
Broke down a alley, jumped into a car
Suckers didn't even see us, they musta been blind
Black wire touched red, the car was mine
We hadn't done nothin but some suckers got shot
Hit the first turn, goddamn roadblock
Broke through the block and we did it fast
Cops would've shot us on sight, they wouldn't of took time to ask

Word

The rollers gave chase at a serious speed
One more conviction was all I need
This shit was for real, it was no la-di-da-di
'Cause the boys had to pin the shit on somebody
And me and my crew, we were known to get ill
We carried heat for protection but not to kill
We bust a corner doing sixty, one police car spun
And all I was thinking was murder one
Bust a move into an alley and did it right
And me and my crew were gone into the night
Broke to my old lady's, who drew me a bath
She didn't even know what happened, didn't care, didn't ask

Word

We made love like crazy on top of the sheets
This girlie was my whirly, a natural freak
She ran her tongue over each and every part of me
Then she rocked my Amadeus while I watched TV
A technician with a mission, that's what she was
If there had been a crowd she would've gotten applause

This girl did everything on earth to me that could be done

The she backed off and teased me so I couldn't come

Then she cold got stupid, pushed me on the floor

Had me begging to stop while I was screaming for more

After she waxed my body, she let me crash

She knew her loving was def, she didn't waste time to ask

Word

Up the next morning feeling good as hell

Sleeping with the girlie sho' beats a cell

Hit the boulevard in my AMG

Hoes catching whiplash trying to glimpse the T

Ring on my mobile—yes, cellular

Got to have a phone when I'm in my car

With my homeboy Red, some say he's insane

Broke his bitch jaw for smokin 'caine

Told me to meet him at the airport

Said he's jumping bail, said he just left court

Caught the first thing smokin in a serious dash

We didn't know where we were going, didn't care, didn't ask

Fell asleep on the plane and so did he

Woke up chilling in NYC

Called up my posse when I got there

Hit the Latin Quarter and Union Square

Rooftop, Devil's Nest—the rest we passed

Back door at the Palladium just for class

About four A.M. we crashed the deuce

We never catch static 'cause my boy's got juice

Deuced it to the Bronx to rest our heads

Where a shoot-out jumped off, nine people lay dead

It sounded like it happened with a MAC-10 blast

But it was 6 'n the mornin', we didn't wake up to ask

Word

COLORS

[Chorus]
Colors, Colors, Colors [4x]

I am a nightmare walkin, psychopath talkin
King of my jungle, just a gangster stalkin
Living life like a firecracker, quick is my fuse
Vendettas of death back the colors I choose
Red or Blue, Cuz or Blood, it just don't matter
Sucker, die for your life when my shotgun scatters (Colors)
We gangs of LA will never die . . .
Just multiply—colors

[Chorus]

You don't know me, fool
You disown me? Cool
I don't need your assistance, social persistence
Any problem I got I just put my fist in
My life is violent, but violent is life
Peace is a dream, reality is a knife
My colors, my honor, my colors, my all
With my colors upon me, one soldier stands tall
Tell me, what have you left me? What have I got?
Last night in cold blood my young brother got shot
My homeboy got jacked, my mother's on crack
My sister can't work 'cause her arms show tracks
Madness, insanity, live in profanity
Then some punk claimin they understandin me?
Give me a break, what world do you live in?
Death is my sect—guess my religion

[Chorus]

My pants are saggin, braided hair
Suckers stare but I don't care
My game ain't knowledge, my game's fear

I've no remorse so squares beware
But my true mission is just revenge
You ain't in my set, you ain't my friend
Wear the wrong color, your life could end
Homicide's my favorite binge (Colors)

[Chorus]

So I'll just walk like a giant, police defyin
You'll say to stop but I'll say that I can't
My gang's my family, it's all that I have
I'm a star, on the wall's my autograph
You don't like it—so? You know where you can go
'Cause the streets are my stage and terror's my show
Psychoanalyze, try diagnosing me—why?
It wasn't your brother to brutally die
But it was mine, so let me define
My territory, don't cross the line
Don't try to act crazy 'cause that shit don't faze me
If you ran like a punk, it wouldn't amaze me
'Cause my color's death, though we all want peace
But our war won't end 'til all wars cease

[Chorus]

KOOL G RAP

Many rappers are described as cinematic, but the adjective is especially fitting in the case of Kool G Rap. "I'm not just a rapper, like, that try to get people to dance or to move and stuff like that," he explains. "I'll write that shit that's gonna have you sit there and you gonna see visuals of what I'm talking about. You're gonna see a short little movie—I'm gonna give somebody a visual of G Rap doing something."[12]

Kool G Rap's cinematic lyrics are often urban vignettes. Balancing short and long lines in "Streets of New York" and moving from scene to scene, he manages to evoke how the impact of these sad stories is cumulative, whereas at the day-to-day level it's like they never happened. He verbally paints the portrait of a prison cell on "Rikers Island" with such harsh brushstrokes that you can see the cellmate ready with the shank as you hear the bars lock shut. Not every tale is quite so morbid or fear inducing. G Rap also gives us new twists on the American success story in songs like "Road to the Riches."

Kool G Rap began his own upward trajectory as an artist alongside his partner DJ Polo on the single "It's a Demo / I'm Fly" (1986). His appearance on the Juice Crew cut "The Symphony," where he rapped alongside the likes of Masta Ace and Big Daddy Kane, garnered even more attention. Although it took some time for a full-length album to appear, the Marley Marl–produced *Road to the Riches* (1989) lived up to expectations. Kool G Rap continues to build on a body of work that has established his place among the most verbally dexterous MCs to emerge in the 1980s.

ROAD TO THE RICHES

When I was five years old I realized there was a road
At the end I will win lots of pots of gold
Never took a break, never made a mistake
Took time to create 'cause there's money to make
To be a billionaire takes hard work for years
Some nights I shedded tears while I said my prayers
Been through hard times, even worked part time
In a seafood store sweepin floors for dimes
I was sort of a porter, takin the next man's orders
Breakin my back with a shack for headquarters
All my manpower for four bucks an hour
Took the time and wrote rhymes in the shower
Shoes are scuffed 'cause the road gets rough
But I'ma rock it 'cause my pockets ain't stuffed enough
All the freaks wouldn't speak 'cause my checks were weak
They would turn the other cheek so I started to seek
A way to get a play and maybe one day

I'll be performin up a storm for a decent pay
No matter how it seems, I always kept the dream
All the girlies scream and suckers get creamed
Dreamed about it for five years straight
Finally I got a break and cut my first plate
The road ain't yellow and there ain't no witches
My name is Kool G Rap, I'm on the road to the riches

I used to stand on the block sellin cooked-up rock
Money bustin out my sock 'cause I really would clock
There were four kinda fiends bringin jackets and jeans
Magazines, anything, just to hustle a bean
The cash was comin fast, money grew like grass
People hungry for the blast that don't even last
Didn't want to be involved but the money will getcha
Gettin richer and richer, 'til police took my picture
But I still supplied, some people I knew who died
Murders and homicides for bottles of suicide
Money, jewelry, livin like a star
And I wasn't too far from a Jaguar car
In a small-time casino, the town's Al Pacino
For all of the girls, a pretty boy Valentino
I shot up the stores and I kicked down doors
Collected scars from little neighborhood wars
Many legs I broke, many necks I choked
And if provoked, I let the pistol smoke
Loyal members in a crew now down with the game
Sellin nickels and dimes in sunshine or rain
What I had was bad from my shoes to my pad
In the first time in my life loanin money to Dad
Now the table's turned and my lifestyle switches
My name is Kool G Rap, I'm on the road to the riches

A thug amongst the drugs, he eventually bugs
Lookin for crack on carpets and rugs

A squealer tells but the dealer still sells

Little spoiled kids inheritin oil wells

I was the type on the opposite side

Of smokin the pipe, in a beef I got hype

'Cause rags to riches switches men to witches

Become snitches, body bags in ditches

Bloodshed, I painted the town red

People fled as I put a dread's head to bed

That means dead, in other words deceased

Face got erased, bullets got released

Bombs were planted, the kids were kidnapped

In fact, this was a way to get back

At enemies who tried to clock Gs

On my block, now they forever knock Zs

Plans of rampages went for ages

Some got knocked and locked inside cages

Some bit the dust for crumbs and crusts

In God We Trust now rots to rust

Bust caps at cops, policeman drops

You blew off his top when the pistol went pop

Troopers, soldiers, rollin like boulders

Eyes of hate and their hearts get colder

Some young male put in jail

His lawyer so good his bail is on sale

Lookin at the hourglass, how long can the power last?

Longer than my song but he already fell

He likes to eat hearty, party

Be like John Gotti and drive a Maserati

Rough in the ghetto but in jail he's Jell-O

Mellow yellow fellow, tell or hell, hello

One court date can turn an outlaw to an inmate

The judge states "Ship him upstate" by the Great Lakes

And let him wait and wait and wait

Until he breaks, that's all it takes

So he fakes to be a man, but he can't stand

On his own two feet because now he's in a new land

Rules are different and so is life

When you think with a shank, talk with a knife

Not my lifestyle so I made a U-turn

The more money I earn, more money to burn

Pushin off buttons, pullin off switches

My name is G Rap, I'm on the road to the riches

STREETS OF NEW YORK

In the streets of New York

Dope fiends are leaning for morphine

The TV screens follow the homicide scenes

You live here, you're taking a chance

So look and I take one glance, there's a man inside an ambulance

The crowds are getting louder, I wonder how

The people want to go fight for the white powder

People hanging in spots, they waited 'til the blocks got hot

And got raided by the cops

I'll explain the man sleeping in the rain

His whole life remains inside a bottle of Night Train

Another man got his clothes in a sack

'Cause he spent every dime of his rent playing blackjack

And there's the poor little sister; she has a little baby daughter

Named Sonya, and Sonya has pneumonia

So why's her mother in a club unzipped though?

Yo, that's her job, Sonya's mommy is a bar stripper

Drug dealers drive around looking hard

Knowing they're sending their brothers and sisters to the graveyard

Every day is a main event, some old lady limps

The pushers and pimps eat shrimps

It gets tiring, the sight of a gun firing

They must desire for the sound of a siren

A bag lady dies in an alleyway

She's seen the last of her days inside the subways
More and more down the slope, the kid couldn't cope
So he stole somebody's dope and a gold rope
Now my son's on the run, he's a wanted one
Had fun then was done by a shotgun
Upstairs I cover my ears and tears
The man downstairs must have drank too many beers
'Cause every day of his life he beats his wife
'Til one night she decides to pull a butcher knife
Blind man plays the sax
A tune called "The Arms on My Moms Show Railroad Tracks"
…Many lives are cut short
That's when you're living…in the streets of New York

Baby needs new shoes
But his papa uses all the money for booze
A young girl is undressed in the back seat of a Caddy
Calling some man Daddy
Three men slain inside a apartment
All you could see is the sparks when it darkens
Daylight broke, cops roll on the scene
The drug war, daily routine
Gambling spots, just a poor man's jackpot
You winning a lot, you get shot
The drug-dealing fanatics
But you don't want no static 'cause they got crack addicts
With automatics, shoot-outs for a desire for territory
A kid got caught in the crossfire
A tired mother can't take no more
She grabbed the bottle full of sleeping pills and took about twenty-four
Human beings are laying on the pavement
'Cause they're a part of a mental enslavement
The cop snipers, little babies in dirty diapers
This type of life is making you hyper

People scouting a torched-out building
And got killed when the cold air filled in
Is hell really suggested?
No more persons arrested, a child molested
A little kid says, "Yo . . .
I got a color TV, CD player, and car stereo
And all I want is a castle
I also got a .38, don't give me no hassle"
One kid heads straight for the top
And gets stopped and popped by a crooked cop
Look behind you when you walk
That's how it is in the streets of New York

RIKERS ISLAND
Well, listen to me, you young hoods, this is some advice
You do the crime, you're payin the price
'Cause if you're in the drug spots, sellin crack on the block
Snatchin chains, bustin brains like a real hardrock
If you ever hear a cop say you're under arrest
Go out just like a trooper, stick out your chest
'Cause you might have been robbin, you might have been wildin
But you won't be smilin on Rikers Island

Just to hear the name, it makes your spine tingle
This is a jungle where the murderers mingle
This ain't a place that's crowded, but there's room for you
Whether you're white or you're black, you'll be black and blue
'Cause in every cellblock there is a hardrock
With a real nice device that's called a sock lock
Don't ever get caught in a crime, my friend
'Cause this bus trip is not to Adventure's Inn
They have a nice warm welcome for new inmates
Razors and shanks and sharp-edged plates
Posses will devour punks with power

After the shower it's rush hour
So watch your back before you get sacked
These a bunch of maniacs that's about to attack
If you're a hustlin pro, keep a low profilin
'Cause you won't be smilin on Rikers Island

C-74, adolescents at war
Put your ear to the floor, you can hear the roar
They take you out of BC, they now found you a cage
All eyes are glued to you like you're up on stage
If you're soft as a leaf don't get into a beef
And God be with you, chief, if you got gold teeth
Some try to be hard, front and say, "I'm God"
Don't know a lesson, say a blessin, you're gonna get scarred
"Yo, call the CO"—that won't be necessary
He'll watch him beat you down and take your commissary
Inside the lunchroom, you meet your doom
Someone is lookin at you sharpenin a tablespoon
Use your hands like a man, don't go out like a chump
Never fess, bench press so that you can be pumped
If you don't got a game, you get beaten as lame
And scared as a mouse in a house of pain
So to all the jailbirds that listen to hip-hop
Move your pelvis like Elvis, do the "Jailhouse Rock"
You might be coolin, you might be stylin
But you won't be smilin on Rikers Island

If you're on a drug tip don't be a Dumbo
Police investigate like Columbo if they think you're sellin jumbo
But don't get me wrong, it might be your thing
Whether smilin on the Island or singin in Sing-Sing
The way you're takin pictures and you're givin a smile
Cheerin the privilege for a long, long while
So keep your money pilin, keep profilin
'Cause, ahh, you won't be smilin on Rikers Island

KOOL MOE DEE

Having honed his skills and reputation in hip-hop's early years, onetime Treacherous Three member Kool Moe Dee found himself in limbo. The forefathers of rap were not yet classic, just old, and past success seemed more likely to predict irrelevance than longevity. But for a master lyricist who had helped develop "The New Rap Language" and whose park and club battles with the likes of Busy Bee shaped the combative nature of the art, longevity was a must.

Kool Moe Dee deftly made the jump out of the old school and made his mark in the late 1980s with several high-profile projects: his "Wild, Wild West" charted well for a rap song released in 1987, he joined in the KRS-One project "Stop the Violence," and he was one of four rappers (the others were Big Daddy Kane, Ice-T, and Melle Mel) to appear on Quincy Jones's Grammy-winning *Back on the Block* (1989). He also engaged in a long-running feud with LL Cool J, a win-win situation that helped establish the rhyme credentials of his younger opponent while further burnishing his own.

Kool Moe Dee's first solo song of note was "Go See the Doctor," which showcased a narrative side not evident in his work with the Treacherous Three. It was one of the first of many rap tales counseling watchfulness over STDs and seems quite tame compared to some that followed as AIDS became a scourge. "I Go to Work," in which Moe Dee calls himself a doctor, architect, boxer, and a "prophet for profit," is a hip-hop version of Walt Whitman's "A Song for Occupations," and like Whitman, he takes pleasure in the list. "How Ya Like Me Now" showcases a talent that shows up all the more when transcribed to the page—namely, Moe Dee's flow. The song's heavily enjambed lines culminate in the titular rhetorical question.

GO SEE THE DOCTOR

I was walking down the street, rocking my beat
Clapping my hands and stomping my feet
I saw a little lady so neat and petite
She was so sweet, yes, I wanted to meet her
So I asked this lady could I take her out
We could wine and dine and talk about
The birds and the bees and my waterbed

And you could treat me like a Buddha and bow your head
We continued to talk and before you knew it
We were at my house and it was time to do it
As soon as I finished, I lost my poise
Ran outside and told all my boys
I said, "Listen up, fellas, come over here, bust it"
They said, "Did you get it?" I said, "Yeah," they said, "How was it?"
The poontang was dope and you know that I rocked her
But three days later, go see the doctor

I rocked her to the left, rocked her to the right
She felt so good, hugged me so tight
I said, "Good night"
Three days later . . .
Woke up fussin, yellin, and cussin
Drip-drip-drippin and puss-puss-pussin
I went into the bathroom and said, "Mamma mia!"
I'ma kill that girl next time I see her
The madder I got, the more I reminisce
Why is my thing-thing burning like this?
Well, I remember the first day I saw that girl
I just couldn't wait to rock her world
I said, "Hey, good looking, what you got cooking?"
What have I done stuck my dick in?
Now I know why her ex-boyfriend Dave
Calls her Mrs. Microwave
'Cause she was hotter than an oven and I had to learn
The hard way—stay in the microwave too long, you get burned
But the poontang was dope and you know that I rocked her
But three days later, go see the doctor

I went to the doctor's office, I said, "What have I got?"
He said, "Turn around, boy, and take this shot"
I looked at him like he was crazy and I said, "What?
Ain't nobody sticking nothin in my butt"

He turned and said in a real deep voice
"Have it your way, if that's your choice
And I'll put it down if you want me to put it
But don't blame me if it turns into a foot ex-
Tending from the middle of your body
And the next time you see a cute hottie
You won't be able to screw, the only thing you can do
Is just kick her, so go take karate"
As I turned around to receive my injection
I said, "Next time I'll use some protection"
If I see another girl and I get an erection
I'm walking in the other direction
'Cause I don't wanna do the sick-sick dance
So I'm keeping my prick inside my pants
And if I see another girl and I know I can rock her
Before I push up, I'll make her go see the doctor

HOW YA LIKE ME NOW
I throw my tape on then I watch ya
Three seconds later I got ya
Shakin your head, dancin instead of sittin
The rhymes kick, the beats hittin you
Just like a home run, slammin like a slam dunk
Ride the wave James Brown gave funk
It happened to James like it happened to me
How you think I feel to see another MC
Get paid usin my rap style
And I'm playin the background meanwhile
I ain't with that, you can forget that
You took my style, I'm takin it back
Comin back like *Return of the Jedi*
Sucker MCs in the place that said I
Could only rock rhymes and only rock crowds
But never rock records—how ya like me now?

Now brothers are riding me like a pony

I'm no phony, I'm the only real mic-aroni

Playin the mic like it's supposed to be played

New jacks, you all shoulda stayed

Out of the business—what is this?

Amateur night at the Apollo? Get off this

Stage, I'm enraged, just like a lion

Trapped inside of a cage

I'm the real king, rap is a jungle

I never understood how could one go

To a party, watch me, stand around and jock me

Become a rapper, then try to rock me

Schemin like a demon, you're screamin and dreamin

I'm from the old school, I used to see men

Die for less, but I'm not livin that way

I'll let my mic do the talkin and let the music play

How ya like me now?

Rap is an art and I'm like Picasso

But of course why else would you try so

Hard to paint a picture and try to get your-

Self in my shoes but they won't fit ya—I'm

Bigger and better, forget about deffer

Every time I rocked the mic I left a

Stain in your brain that will remain

Stuck in the back of your brain until you see me again

Respect, I come correct

The rhymes I select are nothing short of perfect

Vernacular's pure and I can ensure

Life or death with my breath, my voice is a cure

I heal life from the words I spread

I'll make a sick man rock on his deathbed

Sucker MCs, I'll make your girl say "ow"

And she's jockin—now how ya like me now?

It irked my nerve when I heard
A sucker rapper that I know I'll serve
Run around town sayin he is the best
Is that a test? I'm not impressed, get real
You're nothin but a toy
Don't you know that I'll serve that boy
Just like a waiter, hit him with a plate of these
Fresh rhymes and make sure that he
Pay the, pay the, pay the bill and leave him standin still
And when he's had enough, hit him with a refill
And for dessert it won't be no ice cream, I'm just
Gonna shatter and splatter his pipe dreams
Make him feel the wrath, beat him down and laugh
And when I finish, then I'm gonna ask him
"Who is the best?" and if he don't say Moe Dee
I'll take my whip and make him call himself Toby
Whip him good, then I'll make him sweat
Always talkin about battles but he never had a battle yet
But if we ever did, how could he beat me?
He's so petrified, he's scared to even meet me
My word's the law, that's why you don't beef
You're nothing but a punk, track star, and a thief
So I'm puttin you on punishment, just like a child
Never touch another mic—how ya like me now?

I can continue, there's more on the menu
But I relax 'cause I'm so far in you
You had enough, I know you're overstuffed
And if I keep going you'll be throwin up old
Rhymes I used to say way back in the day
When you used to come to my parties and pay
Nobody's ever gonna rock me and this I vow
So all I wanna say is—how ya like me now?

I GO TO WORK

I go to work like a doctor
When I rock the mic you got to like
The way I operate, I make miracles happen
Just from rappin. I'm so lyrically potent
And I'm flowin and explodin
On the scene, mean, I got the potential
To make you go then chill, I got the credentials
That is so essential to make a rhyme send chills
Then you know I will fulfill
And make a couple of mil as I build a guild
For all the rappers of skill and kill the weak rappers with no frills
Hang 'em in effigy
If he's a sucker, hang him to the left of me
'Cause my right-hand man is my mic stand and
The microphone that I own and my game plan
Is keeping at a steady pace
Ain't no reason to rush, it ain't no race
I'ma hit the top just when I wanna
And it's a matter of time and I'm gonna
'Cause I know when to go 'head, enter
The classic Moe Dee rap that sent ya
Runnin around, holdin ya head, askin ya homeboy
"Yo, man, you heard what he said?"
Another funky rhythm, look at your man and give him
A high five 'cause I'm live runnin around with him
Telling everybody hanging out on the block
It's time to wake up and check the clock

Punch it
I go to work

I go to work like an architect
I build the rhymes, sometimes it climbs so erect

Skyscrapers look like atoms
Cars, electrons rollin in patterns
Writing out word after word
With each letter it becomes visibly better
'Cause my foundation built a nation
Of rappers and after I came off vacation
I came to roam the land I own and stand alone
On the microphone—Daddy's home
So open the door, playtime is over
Time to go to work, work and show the
Suckers in the place who run their face
A taste of the bass and who's the ace
Start the race, I'm coming in first
With each verse I build a curse
So rappers can't capture Moe Dee's rapture
And after I have ya I have to slap ya senseless
With endless rhymes, don't pretend this
Is anything short of stupendous and when this
Rhyme is done your mind will become
So trapped in the rap, you'll lust another one
But you gotta wait, it takes time
I don't write, I build a rhyme
Draw the plans, draft the diagrams
An architect in effect and it slams
And if it's weak when I'm done
Renovate and build another one

I go to work [2x]

I go to work like a boxer
Train the brain and aim to outfox ya
Like a punch my rhyme rocks ya, some-
Times it knocks ya so hard it stops ya
Dead in your tracks, so power packed

Before you can react you're flat on your back
Down for the count, get up and dismount
'Cause I'm coming with an endless amount
Of rhymes in a hurry like a flurry
A collage of camouflage, the power punch, but don't worry
Knowledge is an antidote, I got hands of smoke
Writing at the speed of light with insight I wrote
Rhymes on a level so you can't relate
Unless you're intelligent, so stay awake
Sleepwalkers, slick talkers
This time a native New Yorker's
Riding a crescendo wave to save the mental
State of the fan so he can understand—my pencil's
Writing a rhyme in its highest form
And I'ma drop it on ya like a bomb
And when it explodes, I'll blow up
A few casualties, but so what?
If you're slow, you blow, you know you go
I flow, I throw, all-pro, I go

To work

To say rap is not work is ludicrous
Whoever said it must be new to this
When you hear me you'll compare me
To a prophet for profit not merely
Putting words together for recreation
Each rhyme's a dissertation
You wanna know my occupation?
I get paid to rock the nation

I go to work [5x]

LL COOL J

I Need a Beat," "I Need Love," "I Can't Live Without My Radio," "I'm That Type of Guy," "I'm Bad"—as these song titles from early in his career suggest, LL Cool J has always been a supremely self-assured figure in an art form famous for first-person assertion. The young man who turned himself from James Todd Smith to Ladies Love Cool James was never short on confidence. On his first two albums, *Radio* (1985) and *Bigger and Deffer* (1987), his delivery was probably the most athletic of any rapper around. He directed this sonic vigor toward adversaries both abstract and concrete and, of course, toward hyping himself.

LL mixes aggression with likeability on early songs like "I Can't Live Without My Radio," where he posits himself as one of the mid-1980s archetypes of rebellious teenage behavior—the guy on the subway with the blaring boom box. He also shows a romantic side. "I Need Love" suggests the direction LL would explore in many subsequent releases, accounting in part both for the longevity of his career and for his crossover appeal.

Mama Said Knock You Out (1990) seems in retrospect like the album that gave LL the momentum necessary to catapult himself into a sort of perpetual orbit of the public's attention. As usual LL was backed by production that suited him (this time the tracks were Marley Marl's), and he showed more range than before: "Illegal Search" elaborated on the reality of "driving-while-black," "Cheesy Rat Blues" uncovered the duplicity of erstwhile friends, "Farmers Boulevard (Our Anthem)" was a vigorous walk down memory lane, and "The Power of God" describes itself. Hits from the album included "Boomin' System" and the remix of "Jingling Baby," but the title track remains the most memorable: "Don't call it a comeback, I been here for years / Rockin my peers, puttin suckers in fear." No comeback was necessary for a rapper who never left the scene.

ROCK THE BELLS

LL Cool J is hard as hell
Battle anybody, I don't care who you tell
I excel, they all fail
I'm gonna crack shells, Double-L must rock the bells

You've been waitin and debatin for oh so long
Just starvin like Marvin for a Cool J song
If you cried or thought I died, you definitely was wrong
It took a thought plus I brought Cut Creator along
Evened up, E-Love down with the Cool J force
Specializin in the rhymin for the record of course
I'm a tower full of power—wind, rain, and hail
Cut Creator scratch the record with his fingernail
Rock the bells

The king of crowd rockers finally is back
My voice is your choice as the hottest wax
You ask, "Who is it?" Just a wizard who ain't takin no crap
I'm rhymin and designin with your girl on my lap
The bass is kickin, always stickin 'cause you like it that way
You think it's fresher and it's deffer 'cause it's by Cool J
Cut Creator on the fader, my right-hand man
We rock the bells so very well 'cause that's the name of this jam
Rock the bells

Some girls will like this jam and some girls won't
'Cause I make a lot of money and your boyfriend don't
LL went to hell, gonna rock the bells
All you washed up rappers wanna do this well
Rock the bells

Now I'm worldwide known whether you like it or not
My one-man band is Cut Creator aka Philpot
He'll never skip it, only rip it when he's on the fader
What's my DJ's name? (Cut Creator!)
Now you know at my show who's on the wheels
He'll drive the cross fader like a cut mobile
So precise with a slice that you know he's greater
What's my DJ's name? (Cut Creator!)
Let you know, what do you know, Earl rolls the weed

I go to the store and get the Old Gold
So all you crabby-lookin nappy-head girls get back
'Cause there's a ten-to-one chance that you might get smacked
Rock the bells

The bells are circulatin the blood in your veins
Why are girlies on the tip? (LL's your name!)
Cut Creator's good, Cool J is good-good
You bring the woodpecker, I'll bring the wood
The bells are whippin and rippin at your body and soul
Why do you like Cool J? (It ain't rock and roll!)
'Cause it ain't the "Glory Days" with Bruce Springsteen
I'm not a virgin so I know I'll make Madonna scream
You hated Michael and Prince all the way ever since
If their beats were made of meat, then they would have to be mince
Rock the bells

So listen to the rhyme, the line, the rhyme on time
He'll cut the record in a second, make your DJ look blind
So all you Jheri-curl suckers wearin high-heel boots
Like ballerinas, what I mean is you're a fruit-loop troop
All you gonna-be, wannabes, when will you learn?
Wanna be like Cool J, you gotta wait your turn
Some suckers don't like me, but I'm not concerned
Six Gs for twenty minutes is the pay I earn
I'm growin and glowin like a forest blaze
Do you like Michael Jackson? (We like Cool J!)
That's right, I'm on the mic with the help of the bells
There's no delayin what I'm sayin 'cause I'm rockin you well
Rock the bells

I CAN'T LIVE WITHOUT MY RADIO

My radio, believe me, I like it loud
I'm the man with a box that can rock the crowd
Walkin down the street to the hardcore beat

While my JVC vibrates the concrete

I'm sorry if you can't understand

But I need a radio inside my hand

Don't mean to offend other citizens

But I kick my volume way past 10

My story is rough, my neighborhood is tough

But I still sport gold and I'm out to crush

My name is Cool J, I devastate the show

But I couldn't survive without my radio

Terrorizing my neighbors with the heavy bass

I keep the suckers in fear by the look on my face

My radio's bad from the Boulevard

I'm a hip-hop gangster and my name is Todd

Just stimulated by the beat, bust out the rhyme

Get fresh batteries if it won't rewind

'Cause I play every day, even on the subway

I woulda got a summons but I ran away

I'm the leader of the show, keepin you on the go

But I know I can't live without my radio

Suckers on my jock when I walk down the block

I really don't care if you're jealous or not

'Cause I make the songs, you sing along

And your radio's def when my record's on

So get off the wall, become involved

All your radio problems have now been solved

My treacherous beats make ya ears respond

And my radio's loud like a fire alarm

The floor vibrates, the walls cave in

The bass makes my eardrums seem thin

Def sounds in my ride, yes, the front and back

You would think it was a party, not a Cadillac

'Cause I drive up to the ave with the windows closed

And my bass is so loud, it could rip your clothes

My stereo's thumpin like a savage beast
The level on my power meter will not decrease
Suckers get mad 'cause the girlies scream
And I'm still gettin paid while you look at me mean
I'm the leader of the show, keepin you on the go
But I know I can't live without my radio
I'm the leader of the show, keepin you on the go
And I know I can't live without my radio

Don't touch that dial, I'll be upset
Might go into a fit and rip off your neck
'Cause the radio's thumpin when I'm down to play
I'm the royal chief rocker LL Cool J
Let your big butt bounce from right to left
'Cause it's a actual fact this jam is def
Most definitely created by me
Goin down in radio history
I'm good to go on your radio
And I'm cold gettin paid 'cause Rick said so
Make the woofers wallop and your tweeters twitch
Some jealous knuckleheads might try to dis
But it's nuthin, ya frontin, ya girl I am stuntin
And my radio's loud enough to keep you gruntin
My name is Cool J, I'm from the rock
Circulating through your radio nonstop
I'm lookin at the wires behind the cassette
And now I'm on the right, standing on the eject
Wearin light blue Pumas, a whole lotta gold
And jams like these keep me in control
I'm the leader of the show, keepin you on the go
And I know I can't live without my radio

Your energy level starts to increase
As my big beat is slowly released
I'm on the radio and at the jam

LL Cool J is who I am

I'ma make ya dance, boogie down and rock

And the scratch adds shade to my musical plot

And to expand my musical plan

Cut Creator, rock the beat with your hand

That's right, so don't try to front the move

As you become motivated by the funky groove

You can see me and Earl chillin on the block

With my box cold kickin with the gangster rock

See, people can't stop me, neither can the police

I'm a musical maniac to say the least

For you and your radio I made this for

Cool J's here to devastate once more

Pullin all the girls, takin out MCs

If ya try to disrespect me, I just say, "Please!"

Here to command the hip-hop land

Kick it live with a box inside my hand

I'm the leader of the show, keepin you on the go

But I know I can't live without my radio

Farmers Boulevard, yeah, you know that's where me and E hang out, cool out,
you know what I'm sayin? That's where the crib's at . . .

I'M BAD

"Calling all cars, calling all cars. . . . Be on the lookout for a tall light-skinned
brother with dimples wearing a black Kangol, sweat suit, gold chain, and
sneakers. Last seen on Farmers Boulevard headed east. Alias LL Cool J. He's
bad . . ."

Aaaahhhhhhhhhh . . .

No rapper can rap quite like I can

I'll take a muscle-bound man and put his face in the sand

Not the last mafioso, I'm a MC cop

Make you say "Go LL" and do the wop

If you think you can outrhyme me—yeah, boy, I bet

'Cause I ain't met a motherfucker who can do that yet
Trendsetter, I'm better, my rhymes are good
I got a gold nameplate that says "I wish you would"
And when rappers begin then I gotta join in and
Before my rhyme is over, you know I'ma win
Cool J has arrived so you better make way
Ask anybody in the crowd, they say the kid don't play
Slaughter competition, that's my hobby and job
I don't wear a disguise because I don't owe the mob
Got a pinpoint rap that makes you feel trapped
So many girls on my jock, I think my phone is tapped
I'm bad . . .

I'm like Tyson, icin, I'm a soldier at war
I'm makin sure you don't try to battle me no more
Got concrete rhymes, been rappin for ten years and
Even when I'm braggin, I'm bein sincere
MCs can't win, I make 'em rust like tin
They call me Jaws, my hat is like a shark's fin
Because I'm bad as can be, got my voice on wax
Some brothers think, "He's making records, now he must have relaxed"
I couldn't, I shouldn't, and it'll stay that way
The best rapper you've heard is LL Cool J
Kamikaze, take a look at what I've done
Used to rock in my basement, now I'm number one
And can happen on time, never standin on line
You wanna try me? First you better learn how to rhyme
I'm the pinnacle, that means I reign supreme
And I'm notorious—I'll crush you like a jelly bean
I'm bad . . .

I eliminate punks, cut 'em up in chunks
You were souped, you heard me, and your ego shrunk
I'm devastating, I'm so good it's a shame
'Cause I eat rappers like a cannibal, they call me insane
I'm as strong as a bull, of course you know I have pull

I enjoy what I'm doing plus I'm paid in full
Not Buckaroo Banzai, but bustin out as I
Say the kind of rhymes that make MCs wish that I'd die
Never retire or put my mic on the shelf
The baddest rapper in the history of rap itself
Not bitter or mad, just provin I'm bad
You want a hit? Give me a hour plus a pen and a pad
MCs retreat, 'cause they know I can beat 'em
And eat 'em in a battle and the ref won't cheat 'em
I'm the baddest! Takin out all rookies
So forget Oreos, eat Cool J cookies
I'm bad…

Never ever no never…

Never wearin no Levis, battle me why try?
I'll treat you like a stepchild, so tell Mommy bye-bye
Slaughterin MCs and I'ma never get whipped
When I retire I'll get worshipped like a old battleship
LL, I'm bad—other rappers know
When I enter the center they say, "Yo, yo, there he go!"
My paycheck's large, Mr. Bogart in charge
Not a puncher or hunter from a raccoon lodge
The original Todd, teachin how to be hard
Take the skin off a snake and split a pea from a pod
You're a novice, I'm noble, and I dissect with my tongue
Not Attila the Hun, [   ]
My vocals exact, like rack and pinion in a Jag
You try to brag, you get your rhymes from a grab bag
No good scavenger, catfish vulture
My tongue's a chisel and this composition's sculpture
I'm bad…

"Think I'm gonna need backup"
"Think I'm gonna need backup"

Gimme that walkie-talkie! Yo, this is LL Cool J and you'll never catch me so don't
even try it 'cause I'm too bad for ya. Understand? Aaaaaahhhh ...
I'm bad!

I NEED LOVE

When I'm alone in my room sometimes I stare at the wall
And in the back of my mind I hear my conscience call
Telling me I need a girl who's as sweet as a dove
For the first time in my life, I see I need love
There I was, giggling about the games
That I had played with many hearts, and I'm not saying no names
Then the thought occurred, teardrops made my eyes burn
'Cause I said to myself, "Look what you've done to her"
I can feel it inside, I can't explain how it feels
All I know is that I'll never dish another raw deal
Playing make believe, pretending that I'm true
Holding in my laugh as I say that I love you
Saying amour, kissing you on the ear
Whispering I love you and I'll always be here
Although I often reminisce, I can't believe that I found
A desire for true love floating around
Inside my soul because my soul is cold
One half of me deserves to be this way 'til I'm old
But the other half needs affection and joy
And the warmth that is created by a girl and a boy
I need love
I need love

Romance, sheer delight, how sweet
I gotta find me a girl to make my life complete
You can scratch my back, we'll get cozy and huddle
I'll lay down my jacket so you can walk over a puddle
I'll give you a rose, pull out your chair before we eat
Kiss you on the cheek and say, "Ooh girl, you're so sweet"

It's déjà vu whenever I'm with you

I could go on forever telling you what I do

But where you at? You're neither here nor there

I swear I can't find you anywhere

Damn sure you ain't in my closet or under my rug

This love search is really making me bug

And if you know who you are why don't you make yourself seen?

Take a chance with my love and you'll find out what I mean

Fantasies can run but they can't hide

And when I find you, I'ma pour all my love inside

I need love

I need love

I wanna kiss you, hold you, never scold you, just love you

Suck on your neck, caress you and rub you

Grind, moan, and never be alone

If you're not standing next to me, you're on the phone

Can't you hear it in my voice, I need love bad

I've got money, but love's something I've never had

I need your ruby-red lips, sweet face, and all

I love you more than a man who's ten feet tall

I'd watch the sunrise in your eyes

We're so in love, when we hug we become paralyzed

Our bodies explode in ecstasy unreal

You're as soft as a pillow and I'm as hard as steel

It's like a dreamland, I can't lie, I never been there

Maybe this is an experience that me and you can share

Clean and unsoiled yet sweaty and wet

I swear to you this is something I'll never forget

I need love

I need love

See what I mean? I've changed, I'm no longer

A playboy on the run, I need something that's stronger

Friendship, trust, honor, respect, admiration

This whole experience has been such a revelation
It's taught me love and how to be a real man
To always be considerate and do all I can
Protect you, you're my lady, and you mean so much
My body tingles all over from the slightest touch
Of your hand and understand I'll be frozen in time
'Til we meet face to face and you tell me you're mine
If I find you, girl, I swear I'll be a good man
I'm not gonna leave it in destiny's hands
I can't sit and wait for my princess to arrive
I gotta struggle and fight to keep my dream alive
I'll search the whole world for that special girl
When I finally find you, watch our love unfurl
I need love
I need love

Girl, listen to me. When I be sittin in my room all alone, staring at the wall,
fantasies, they go through my mind, and ... I've come to realize that I need
true love. And if you wanna give it to me, girl, make yourself seen. I'll be
waiting. I love you.

I'M THAT TYPE OF GUY
You're the type of guy
That can't control your girl
You try to buy her love
With diamonds and pearls
I'm the type of guy
That shows up on the scene
And gets the seven digits
You know the routine
You're the type of guy
That tells her, "Stay inside"
While you're steady frontin
In your homeboy's ride

I'm the type of guy
That comes when you leave
I'm doin your girlfriend
That's somethin you can't believe
'Cause . . .

[Chorus 4x]
I'm that type of guy

You're the type of guy
That gets suspicious
I'm the type of guy that says
"The puddin is delicious"
You're the type of guy that has
No idea that a
Sneaky, freaky brother's sneakin
In from the rear
I'm the type of guy
To eat it when he won't
And look in the places
That your boyfriend don't
You're the type of guy
To try to call me a punk
Not knowin that your main girl's
Bitin my chunk
I'm the type of guy
That loves a dedicated lady
Their boyfriends are boring
And I can drive 'em crazy
You're the type of guy
To give her money to shop
She gave me a sweater
[*kiss*] Thank you, sweetheart

[Chorus]

I'm the type of guy

That picks her up from work early

Takes her to breakfast, lunch

Dinner, and breakfast

You're the type of guy

Eatin a TV dinner

Talkin about . . .

"Goddamn it, I'ma kill her"

I'm the type of guy

To make her say, "Why you illin, B?"

. . . You're the type of guy to say

"My lower back is killin me"

. . . Catch my drift?

You're the type of guy

That likes to drink Olde English

I'm the type of guy

To cold put on a Pamper

You're the type of guy to say

"What you talkin 'bout?"

I'm the type of guy

To leave my drawers in your hamper

I'm that type of guy

[Chorus 4x]

T-Y-P-E-G-U-Y

I'm that type of guy

To give you a pound

And wink my eye

Like a bandit

Caught me red-handed

Took her for granted

But when I screwed her

You couldn't understand it

'Cause you're the type of guy

That don't know the time
Swearin up and down
"That girl's all mine"
I'm the type of guy
To let you keep believin it
Go 'head to work
While I defrost it and season it

[Chorus 4x]

"So ridiculous!"

So funny. I don't know. Come on down. Yeah. Like real cool, you know what I mean? I like just going to your front door ringin bells. And just like, ha, leave . . .

MAMA SAID KNOCK YOU OUT

C'mon, man

And with the local DBC News, LL Cool J with a triumphant comeback. But tonight . . .

Don't call it a comeback, I been here for years
I'm rockin my peers, puttin suckers in fear
Makin the tears rain down like a monsoon
Listen to the bass go boom
Explosion, overpowerin
Over the competition I'm towerin
Wreckin shop when I drop
These lyrics that'll make you call the cops
Don't you dare stare, you better move
Don't ever compare
Me to the rest that'll all get sliced and diced
Competition's payin the price

[Chorus 4x]
I'm gonna knock you out. (Huuuh!)

Mama said knock you out. (Huuuh!)

Don't you call this a regular jam
I'm gonna rock this land
I'm gonna take this itty-bitty world by storm
And I'm just gettin warm
Just like Muhummad Ali, they called him
Cassius. Watch me bash this
Beat like a skull that you know I had
Beef with. Why do you riff with me?
The maniac psycho
And when I pull out my jammy get ready 'cause it might go
Blaow! How ya like me now?
The Ripper will not allow
You to get with Mr. Smith, don't riff
Listen to my gear shift
I'm blastin, outlastin
Kinda like Shaft, so you could say I'm shaftin
Olde English fill my mind
And I came up with a funky rhyme

[Chorus 4x]

Breakdown!

Shadowboxin when I heard you on the radio
Huuuh! I just don't know
What made you forget that I was raw?
But now I got a new tour
I'm goin insane, startin the hurricane
Releasin pain
Lettin you know, you can't gain or maintain
Unless you say my name
Rippin, killin, diggin, and drillin a hole
Pass the Ol' Gold

[Chorus 4x]

Shotgun blasts are heard
When I rip and kill at will
The man of the hour, tower of power
I'll devour
I'm gonna tie you up and let you
Understand that I'm not your average
Man when I got a jammy in my hand
Damn!
Oooh! Listen to the way
I slaaay your crew
Damage (uuh!)—damage (uuh!)
Damage (uuh!)—damage
Destruction, terror, and mayhem
Pass me a sissy-soul sucker, I'll slay him
Farmers. (What?) Farmers (What?)
I'm ready. (We're ready!)
I think I'm gonna bomb a town
Get down!
Don't you never, ever pull my lever
'Cause I explode
And my nine is easy to load
I gotta thank God
'Cause he gave me the strength to rock
Hard—knock you out
Mama said knock you out

[Chorus 4x]

MC LYTE

MC Lyte is an especially versatile MC. This flexibility is measured by how she balances local poetic effects with the bedrock values of rap braggadocio, all while crafting a variety of compelling stories. As Kool Moe Dee observes, "She has an exceptional flow, a diverse body of work and subject matter, hit radio and hit street records, and an impeccable delivery on top of her battle skills. . . . Lyrically, she is a rap icon who sounds and feels as current today as she did fourteen years ago."[13]

"I Cram to Understand U," with its memorable simile serving as a chorus—"Just like a test / I cram to understand u"—has a twist at the end, where what seemed like a story of romantic disinterest opens up to reveal a bigger social problem. "Cappuccino" is an uneasy dream vision: neither Lyte nor we are ever totally sure what is real and what is dream; the song paints a picture of the randomness of much violence and the contingencies that shape our experience. Arbitrary choices have unintended consequences. To then shift us from this urban phantasmagoria into a straightforward description of the nature of the "cappuccino" is a funny, self-consciously "realistic" way to wake us from the dream.

10% DIS

Hot damn! Hot damn, ho, here we go again
Suckers steal a beat when you know they can't win
You stole the beat, are you havin fun? Now
Me and the Aud's gonna show you how it's done
You are what I label as a "nerve plucker"
You're pluckin my nerves, you MC sucker
I thought I oughta tell you, better yet warn
That I am like a stock and my word is bond
Like James, killin everybody in sight
The code's three-six, the name is Lyte
After this jam, I really don't give a damn
'Cause I'ma run and tell your whole damn clan that you're a

[Chorus 2x]

Beat-biter! Dope-style taker!
Tell you to your face you ain't nothin but a faker!

Hit me why dontcha, hit me why dontcha?
Milk's bodyguard is my bodyguard too
You wanna get hurt, well, this is what you do: you put your
Left foot up and then your right foot next
Follow instructions, don't lose the context
Thirty days a month your mood is rude
We know the cause of your bloody attitude

[Chorus]

Your style is smooth, even for a cheatin mic
You shoulda won a prize as a Rakim soundalike
Here's a Milk-Bone, a sign of recognition
Don't turn away, I think you should listen close
Don't boast, you said you wasn't braggin
You fuckin liar, you're chasin a Chuckwagon
The only way you learn, you have to be taught
That if a beat is not for sale then it can't be bought
When you leave the mic, you claim it's smokin
Unlike Rakim, you are a joke and I
Think you oughta stop before you get in too deep
'Cause with a sister like Lyte, yo, I don't sleep

[Chorus]

When I'm in a jam with my homegirl Jill
My cousin Trey across the room with a posse of girls
So I step in the middle, shake it just a little
Wait for some female to step up and pop junk
Give my cousin a cue, treat the girl like a punk
Now I'm not tryin to say that I'm into static
But yo, if you cause it, yup, we gotta have it
'Cause I ain't goin out like a sucker, no way

So I sit around and wait for you to make my day
We can go for the hands, better yet for the words
'Cause you'll be ignored and at the same time, I'll be heard
Throughout the city, the town, and the country
The beat is funky, my rhyme is spunky
There is no delayin in the rhyme I'm sayin
Neither are there flaws in what my DJ is playin, so
Sit back, Jack, and listen to this, it's 10% Dis
'Cause I'm just about ready to
Fly this fist against your lips!

But I'll wait for the day or night that you approach and I'm-
A serve and burn ya like a piece of toast
Pop you in the microwave and watch your head bubble
Your skin just crumble, a battle's no trouble
Get my homegirls Dohni and Kiki to get stupid
This thing called hip-hop, Lyte is rulin it
I hate to laugh in your face, but you're funny
Your beat, your rhymin, your timin—all crummy
On the topic of rappin, I should write a pamphlet
Better yet, a booklet
Your rap is weak, homegirl, and it's definitely crooked
Others write your rhymes, while I write my own
I don't create a character when I'm on the microphone
I am myself, no games to be played
No script to be written, no scene to be made
I am the director as far as you are concerned
You don't believe me then you'll have to learn
This ain't as hard as MC Lyte can get
And matter fact, you ain't seen nothin yet
So never let me step into a party-hearty
Talk to some people and then hear from somebody
"You wanna battle?" 'Cause you know where I am
You don't wanna come in the 90s and see me at a jam

When a mic is handy, ten feet away
I stretch my arm like elastic, hand like a magnet
Said assure, you know I don't play
When it comes down to it, the nitty-gritty
For a sucker like you I feel a whole lot of pity

I CRAM TO UNDERSTAND U

I used to be in love with this guy named Sam
I don't know why 'cause he had the head like that of a clam
But you couldn't tell me nothin 'cause Sam was number one
'Cause to me, oh my gosh, he was one in a million
I shoulda knew the consequences right from the start
That he'd use me for my money, and then break my heart
But like a fool in love, I fell for his game
But I got mine, so I show no shame. In Empire
Winked his eye, and then he kept walkin
All of those who live in Brooklyn know just what I'm talkin
The roller disco where we all used to go
Just to have some fun back in 1981
You know the place, Empire Boulevard
Is where I first saw the nigga, and he tried to play hard but
I knew the deal, 'cause I knew his brother Jerry
And Sam, he just broke up with his girlfriend Terry, so
Jerry introduced Sam and I that night. He said
"Hello, my name is Sam." I said, "Hi, my name is Lyte"
We yipped and we yapped and we chit 'n we chat about
This and that, from sneakers to hats. He said
"Look, I'm in the mood for love
Simply because you're near me"
(Let's go) To my house, lay back and get nice
Watch television, a Riunite on ice. I said
"Slow down, I know you wanna shake me down
But I'm not one of the girls that go rippin around"

[Chorus]
Just like a test
I cram to understand u

Next month, I finally went to his house. I walked
Into the door, there was a girl on the couch. I said
"Who's the frog, the bump on the log?
You chump, you punk, how could you do me wrong?
Singing sad songs about your love is so strong"
You said, "Wait Lyte, you're confused, the girl is my cousin"
Your brother agreed, but later said that she wasn't

[Chorus]

Forgotten, next month we went to the Deuce, well I
Thought it kinda strange 'cause you had lots of juice
You knew the dopes, the pushers, the addicts, everybody
Asked ya how you met 'em, said you met 'em at a party
Then these girls tried to tell me you were sellin the stuff
I said, "It's not your business, so shut the fuck up"
They said, "Oh, okay Lyte, think what you wanna think, but it's
Goin be some shit when your man becomes a fiend." I said
"Look, to bust a move, I don't even know you
To put it Lyte, I really don't care to"
They got kinda mad and sort of offended
They said, "We only lookin out for your best interest"
I said, "Thanks but no thanks" in an aggravated tone
"When I wanna find out, I find out on my own"

[Chorus]

Then my cousin said she saw you with this lady name of C
Well, I'm clawin my thoughts, I wonder who she could be
You're spending all your time with her and not a second with me
They say you spend your money on her and you're with her night and day
Her name starts with a C and it ends with a K

I strain my brain lookin for a name to fit this spellin
But I just couldn't do it 'cause my heart kept yellin
Burning, begging from affection from you, Sam
But just like a test I cram to understand u
Thought I knew you well enough to call you a man but

[Chorus]

Then it came a time you started looking kinda thin, I asked you
Why, you said, "Exercise, tryin to stay slim"
I bought it, even though I knew it was a lie, 'cause it
Really didn't matter, you were still lookin fly, but oh no
Oh no, you started askin me for money
Butter me up, beg me, and call me your honey, so I
Gave you two yards, and then I gave you one more
You picked up your jacket and you flew out the door
You came back an hour later and you asked me for a ten
I said, "I only got a twenty," you said, "Give me that, then"
I said, "Nope, I'll tell you now, you better stop slobbin
Find you a job, or you better start robbin"
So I stepped off—with a giant step
Picked up my belongings, and I just left
But now I see you in Empire every Sunday
Juicin the girls up for some money and a lay, but every
Time I see you doin it, I just ruin it
Tell 'em how ya on crack, smoke, sniff, and chewin it
As for this girl, Miss C, oh well
I was shocked as hell when I heard, Samuel
When your homeboys told me, I almost went wack
That the girl you was addicted to, her name was Crack

CAPPUCCINO
It was a cafe on the West Side, midtown
Said they had the best cap-a-cappuccino around
So I stepped in and I ordered a cup
Someone grabbed me by my throat and said, "Shut the fuck up!"

And I did—pronto, quick, fast

How much longer would the torture last?

In the wrong place, at the wrong time—it was

A drug sale. I could feel from behind

Death—it was gettin closer

Right behind my back, ready to attack

I got shot in a shoot-out and then I died

I could feel it, I was on the other side

In between lives, I'm so confused

What do I do, oh, what do I do?

Was it really time for me to go?

Why, oh why did I need cappuccino?

Why, oh why did I need cappuccino?

But then I calmed down, I spotted some friends

That I knew in a past life, way back when

A couple had died in the drug world

And this one guy died fightin over his girl

Another died drivin while intoxicated

Why do people make livin so complicated?

But then I saw a girl, her name was Mary

Introduced to drugs by her boyfriend Harry

He sold crack to the kids on the uptown corners

A social worker named Hannah Smith tried to warn her

But she wouldn't listen—no one listens

I saw the light, I awakened, it was a dream

Man, oh man, you shoulda heard me scream!

So glad to be given my life back

So good to be livin—or was dead better?

I didn't have to run from the bullets or drugs and I

Didn't have to run from the murderers or thugs

I didn't have to worry about fallin from a plane

But at this cafe was death still callin my name?

Or did this cafe even exist? There was

My name, just another on the death list

I knew it couldn't happen, even though
On the bottom of my shirt was a spot of cappuccino

Why, oh why did I need cappuccino?

Bust it, to some of you that really don't know
I break it down to you, the word "cappuccino"
It's somewhat like coffee, then again not quite
It's creamy and smooth and it goes down light
They charge you three dollars, you ask is it worth it?
But when you start drinkin, shit, it be workin
I'm hooked, well, I was, 'cause, yo, it's the best
But if every time I drink I voyage through death
I leave it alone and just stick to tea, Cappuc-
Cino was fly, but too fly for me

Why, oh why did I need cappuccino?

NWA

Any group whose name stands for "Niggaz With Attitude" is bound to garner attention, but for all of the tensions that NWA provoked, they were more important as innovators. They ushered in the rise of West Coast gangster rap. One of their members, Eazy-E, distributed their aesthetically, critically, and commercially successful album *Straight Outta Compton* (1988) on a label he owned. Two other members, Dr. Dre and Ice Cube, would go on to become hip-hop icons. And their music remains provocative and wildly playable.

The three aforementioned members, along with Yella and MC Ren, formed as a group in 1986 in Compton, California. Under his own name, Eazy-E (a former drug dealer who bankrolled Ruthless Records, on which NWA ultimately appeared) recorded the Ice Cube–penned "Boyz-n-the-Hood," a song that set the stage for the songs to follow with its credo "Ain't

nothing in life but to be legit." This and other songs were collected on
N.W.A. and the Posse (1987).

But it was *Straight Outta Compton* that had the greatest impact. The album was a virtual blueprint for the genre of gangster rap that would flourish in the 1990s. Almost every song felt archetypal. "Straight Outta Compton" established the importance of place to the genre, moving rap from East
to West; "Gangsta Gangsta" gave the genre a name and fleshed out its main
character, the young black male gangbanger; "Dopeman" described the
powerful figure who served as ghetto businessman and politician, a savvy
but sadistic street capitalist willing to destroy his people as long as his pockets got fat. "Fuck tha Police," the group's most controversial song (it raised
the ire of the FBI), was deathly anti-authoritarian, claiming that the Compton police "have the authority to kill a minority." Its shock value was that it
imagined scenarios in which brutality was not just coming from the police
but pointed back at them.

The ethos emanating from these songs was so against civic norms, the
"establishment," and its putative leaders that they likely would have offended many even had they delivered their message in nursery rhymes. As
it stood, the sentiments were appropriately conveyed in language more explicit than most rap fans had heard on record.

With a band this volatile, the center predictably could not hold. Ice
Cube left the group in an acrimonious split and took with him not only his
verbal virtuosity but also the sense of humor that lurked impishly beneath
his lines. *Niggaz4Life* (1991) still had Dr. Dre's production and thus
sounded as strong as ever, but on this album there was a sense, which had
been lacking on *Compton,* that the violence, misogyny, and incessant repetition of the n-word were merely gratuitous. They came, they saw, they
started a genre—and then NWA disbanded, a short-lived but high-impact
group.

DOPEMAN (REMIX)

Yo, Dre!

[Ice Cube]
It was once said by a man who couldn't quit
"Dopeman, please can I have another hit?"
The Dopeman said, "Cluck, I don't give a shit
If your girl kneel down and suck my dick"

It all happened and the guy tried to choke her

Nigga didn't care, she ain't nothin but a smoker

That's the way it goes, that's the name of the game

Young brother gettin over by slangin 'caine

Gold around his neck, in 14K heaven

Bitches clockin on his dick twenty-four seven

Plus he's makin money, keep the baseheads waitin

Rollin six-fo with the fresh ass Daytons

Livin in Compton, California C-A

His Uzi up yo' ass if he don't get paid

Nigga beggin for credit, he's knockin out teeth

Clockin much dollars on the first and fifteenth

Big wad of money, nothin less than a twenty

Yo, you want a five-oh, the Dopeman's got plenty

To be a Dopeman, boy, you must qualify

Don't get high off your own supply

From a key to a G, it's all about money

Ten piece for a ten, base pipe comes free

If people out there are not hip to the fact

If you see somebody gettin money for crack

He's the . . .

[Chorus]

Dopeman, Dopeman

Ay, man, give me a hit

Dopeman, Dopeman

Yo, man, fuck that shit

Dopeman, Dopeman

We just can't quit

Dopeman, Dopeman

Well, suck this, bitch

[Dr. Dre]

Wait a minute, wait a minute. Who the fuck are you talking to? Do you know who
the fuck I am? Man, I can't believe this shit. This bitch is tryin to gank me. Yo, I
oughta slap you upside yo' head with nine inches of limp dick.

[Ice Cube]

You need a nigga with money so you get a Dopeman

Juice that fool for as much as you can

She like his car and he get with her

Got a black eye 'cause the Dopeman hit her

Let that slide and you pay it no mind

Find that he's slappin you all the time

But that's okay, 'cause he's so rich

And you ain't nuttin but a Dopeman's bitch

Do what he say and you keep your mouth shut

Poppin that trash might get you fucked up

Will sit and cry if the Dopeman strike you

He don't give a fuck, he got two just like you

There's another girl in the Dopeman's life

Not quite a bitch but far from a wife

She's called the Strawberry and everybody know

Strawberry, Strawberry is the neighborhood ho

Do anything for a hit or two

Give the bitch a rock, she fuck the whole damn crew

It might be your wife and it might make you sick

Come home and see her mouth on the Dopeman's dick

Strawberry, just look and you'll see her

But don't fuck around, she'll give you gonorrhea

If people out there not hip to the fact

The Strawberry is a girl sellin pussy for crack

To the . . .

[Chorus]

[Ice Cube]

If you smoke 'caine, you a stupid motherfucker

Known around the 'hood as the schoolyard clucker

Doin that crack with all the money you got

On your hands and knees, searchin for a piece of rock

Jonesin for a hit and you're lookin for mo'

Done stole the Alpine out of Eazy's six-fo

You need your ass whooped 'cause it's out of this earth

To get a ten piece need a dollar fifty worth

Knucklehead nigga, yeah, you turned into a crook

But swear up and down, boy, that you ain't hooked

You beat your friend up and you whooped his ass long

'Cause he hit the pipe 'til the rock was all gone

You robbin and stealin, buggin and illin

While the Dopeman's dealin, what is healin yo' pain

Cocaine, this shit's insane

Yo, E, she's a berry, let's run a train

[Eazy-E] *Man, I wouldn't touch that bitch.* [Ice Cube] Me neither

Ho, go home and wash out your beaver

And niggaz out there messin up people's health

Yo, what the fuck you gotta say for yourself?

[Eazy-E] Well, I'm the Dopeman, yeah boy, wear corduroy

Money up to here but unemployed

You keep smokin that rock and my pockets gettin bigger

[Dr. Dre] Yo, got that five-oh, double up, nigga!

[Eazy-E] Yeah, high rollin, big money I'm foldin

Bitch on my tip for the dick I'm holdin

Sprung Strawberry jockin me so early

Ho, you wanna hit, you gotta get your knees dirty

Now that's my life, that's how it's cut

"Hey, Dopeman!" Bitch, shut the fuck up!

Gotta make a run, it's a big-money deal

Gankers got the fake but you can get the real

From the...

[Chorus]

Yo, Mr. Dopeman, you think you're slick

You sold crack to my sister and now she's sick

But if she happens to die because of your drug

I'm puttin in your culo a .38 slug

FUCK THA POLICE

[Dr. Dre]

Right about now NWA court is in full effect. Judge Dre presiding in the case of
NWA versus the police department. Prosecuting attorneys are MC Ren, Ice
Cube, and Eazy motherfuckin E. Order, order, order. Ice Cube, take the
motherfuckin stand. Do you swear to tell the truth, the whole truth, and nothin
but the truth, so help your black ass?

[Ice Cube]

You goddamn right.

[Dr. Dre]

Why don't you tell everybody what the fuck you gotta say?

[Ice Cube]

Fuck tha police, comin straight from the underground
A young nigga got it bad 'cause I'm brown
And not the other color, so police think
They have the authority to kill a minority
Fuck that shit 'cause I ain't the one
For a punk motherfucker with a badge and a gun
To be beatin on and thrown in jail
We can go toe to toe in the middle of a cell
Fuckin with me 'cause I'm a teenager
With a little bit of gold and a pager
Searchin my car, lookin for the product
Thinkin every nigga is selling narcotics
You'd rather see me in the pen
Than me and Lorenzo rollin in a Benzo
Beat a police outta shape
And when I'm finished bring the yellow tape
To tape off the scene of the slaughter
Still gettin swoll off bread and water
I don't know if they fags or what
Search a nigga down and grabbin his nuts
And on the other hand, without a gun they can't get none

But don't let it be a black and a white one
'Cause they'll slam ya down to the street top
Black police showin out for the white cop
Ice Cube will swarm
On any motherfucker in a blue uniform
Just 'cause I'm from the C-P-T
Punk police are afraid of me
A young nigga on the warpath
And when I'm finished, it's gonna be a bloodbath
Of cops dyin in LA
Yo, Dre, I got somethin to say

Fuck tha police [4x]

Pull your goddamn ass over right now.
Ah, shit. What the fuck you pull me over for?
'Cause I feel like it. Just sit your ass on the curb and shut the fuck up.
Man, fuck this shit.
All right, smart ass, I'm takin your black ass to jail.
MC Ren, will you please give your testimony to the jury about this fucked-up
    incident?

[MC Ren]
Fuck tha police and Ren said it with authority
Because the niggaz on the street is a majority
A gang is with whoever I'm steppin
And the motherfuckin weapon is kept in
A stash box, for the so-called law
Wishin Ren was a nigga that they never saw
Lights start flashin behind me
But they're scared of a nigga so they mace me to blind me
But that shit don't work, I just laugh
Because it gives 'em a hint not to step in my path
To the police I'm sayin, "Fuck you, punk"
Readin my rights and shit, it's all junk

Pullin out a silly club, so you stand

With a fake-ass badge and a gun in your hand

But take off the gun so you can see what's up

And we'll go at it, punk, and I'ma fuck you up

Make ya think I'ma kick your ass

But drop your gat and Ren's gonna blast

I'm sneaky as fuck when it comes to crime

But I'ma smoke 'em now and not next time

Smoke any motherfucker that sweats me

Or any asshole that threatens me

I'm a sniper with a hell of a scope

Takin out a cop or two, they can't cope with me

The motherfuckin villain that's mad

With potential to get bad as fuck

So I'ma turn it around

Put in my clip, yo, and this is the sound

Yeah, somethin like that

But it all depends on the size of the gat

Takin out a police would make my day

But a nigga like Ren don't give a fuck to say . . .

Fuck tha police [4x]

Yeah, man, what you need?

Police. Open up.

Oh, shit.

We have a warrant for Eazy-E's arrest. Get down and put your hands where I can
see 'em.

Man, what the fuck did I do? What did I do?

Just shut the fuck up and get your motherfuckin ass on the floor!

But I didn't even do shit!

Man, just shut the fuck up!

Eazy-E, why don't you step up to the stand and tell the jury how you feel about
this bullshit.

[Eazy-E]

I'm tired of the motherfuckin jackin

Sweatin my gang while I'm chillin in the shack and

Shining the light in my face, and for what

Maybe it's because I kick so much butt

I kick ass, or maybe 'cause I blast

On a stupid-ass nigga when I'm playin with the trigga

Of an Uzi or an AK

'Cause the police always got somethin stupid to say

They put out my picture with silence

'Cause my identity by itself causes violence

The E with the criminal behavior

Yeah, I'm a gangsta, but still I got flavor

Without a gun and a badge, what do ya got?

A sucker in a uniform waitin to get shot

By me or another nigga

And with a gat it don't matter if he's smaller or bigger

(Size ain't shit; he's from the old school, fool)

And as you all know, E's here to rule

Whenever I'm rollin, keep lookin in the mirror

And ears on cue, yo, so I can hear a

Dumb motherfucker with a gun

And if I'm rollin off the eight, he'll be the one

That I take out, and then get away

While I'm drivin off laughin this is what I'll say...

Fuck tha police [4x]

The verdict: The jury has found you guilty of bein a redneck, white bread,
    chicken-shit motherfucker.

Wait, that's a lie. That's a goddamn lie.

Get him out of here.

I want justice!

Get him the fuck out my face.

I want justice! Fuck you, you black motherfucker!

Fuck tha police [3x]

GANGSTA GANGSTA

[Ice Cube]
Here's a little somethin 'bout a nigga like me
Never shoulda been let out the penitentiary
Ice Cube would like to say
That I'm a crazy motherfucker from around the way
Since I was a youth, I smoked weed out
Now I'm the motherfucker that you read about
Takin a life or two, that's what the hell I do
You don't like how I'm livin? Well, fuck you
This is a gang and I'm in it
My man Dre'll fuck you up in a minute
With a right, left, right, left—you're toothless
And then you say, "Goddamn, they ruthless"
Everywhere we go they say, "Damn"
NWA's fuckin up the program
And then you realize we don't care
We don't just say no, we're too busy sayin "Yeah!"
About drinkin straight out the eight bottle
Do I look like a motherfuckin role model?
To a kid lookin up to me
Life ain't nothin but bitches and money
'Cause I'm the type of nigga that's built to last
If ya fuck with me I'll put my foot in ya ass
See, I don't give a fuck 'cause I keep bailin
Yo, what the fuck are they yellin?

Gangsta, Gangsta! That's what they're yellin
It's not about a salary, it's all about reality
Gangsta, Gangsta!
Hopin you sophisticated motherfuckers hear what I have to say

[Ice Cube]
When me and my posse stepped in the house
All the punk ass niggaz start breakin out

'Cause you know they know what's up
So we started lookin for the bitches with the big butt
Like her, but she keep cryin
"I got a boyfriend." Bitch, stop lyin!
Dumb-ass hooker ain't nothin but a dyke
Suddenly I see some niggaz that I don't like
Walked over to 'em, and said, "What's up?"
The first nigga that I saw, hit him in the jaw
Ren started stompin him, and so did E
By that time got rushed by security
Out the door, but we don't quit
Ren said, "Let's start some shit!"
I got a shotgun and here's the plot:
Takin niggaz out with a flurry of buckshots
Boom boom boom, yeah I was gunnin
And then you look, all you see is niggaz runnin
And fallin and yellin and pushin and screamin
And cussin, I stepped back, and I kept bustin
And then I realized it's time for me to go
So I stopped, jumped in the vehicle
It's like this because of that whoo-ride
NWA is wanted for a homicide
'Cause I'm the type of nigga that's built to last
Fuck with me, I'll put my foot in your ass
See, I don't give a fuck 'cause I keep bailin
Yo, what the fuck are they yellin?

Gangsta, Gangsta! That's what they're yellin
It's not about a salary, it's all about reality
Gangsta, Gangsta!
He'll tell you exactly how he feel, and don't hold a fuckin thing back

[Ice Cube]
Homies all standin around, just hangin
Some dope dealin, some gang bangin

We decide to roll and we deep
See a nigga on Daytons and we creep
Real slow and before you know
I had my shotgun pointed in the window
He got scared and hit the gas
Right then I knew I had to smoke his ass
He kept rollin, I jumped in the bucket
We couldn't catch him so I said, "Fuck it"
Then we headed right back to the fort
Sweatin all the bitches in the biker shorts
We didn't get no play from the ladies
With six niggaz in a car—are you crazy?
She was scared, and it was showin
We all said, "Fuck you, bitch!" and kept goin
To the 'hood and we was f'in to
Find somethin else to get into
Like some pussy or in fact
A bum rush, but we call it rat pack
On a nigga for nothin at all
Ice Cube'll go stupid when I'm full of 8-Ball
I might stumble but still won't lose
Now I'm dressed in the county blues
'Cause I'm the type of nigga that's built to last
If you fuck with me, I'll put my foot in your ass
I don't give a fuck 'cause I keep bailin
Yo, what the fuck are they yellin?

[Dr. Dre]
Wait a minute, wait a minute, cut this shit

Man, what you gonna do now?
What we're gonna do right here is go back
How far you goin back?
Way back
As we go a lil' somethin like this. Hit it!

[Ice Cube]
Here's a lil' gangsta, short in size
A T-shirt, Levis is his only disguise
Built like a tank yet hard to hit
Ice Cube and Eazy-E cold runnin shit

[Eazy-E]
Well I'm Eazy-E, the one they're talkin about
Nigga tried to roll the dice and just crapped out
Police tried to roll, so it's time to go
I creeped away real slow and jumped in the six-fo'
With the "Diamond in the back, sun-roof top"
Diggin the scene with the gangsta lean
'Cause I'm the E, I don't slang or bang
I just smoke motherfuckers like it ain't no thang
And all you bitches, you know I'm talkin to you
"We want to fuck you, Eazy!" I want to fuck you, too
Because you see, I don't really take no shit
("So let me tell you motherfuckers who you're fuckin with")
'Cause I'm the type of nigga that's built to last
If you fuck with me, I'll put a foot in your ass
I don't give a fuck, 'cause I keep bailin
Yo, what the fuck are they yellin?

Gangsta, Gangsta! That's what they're yellin
It's not about a salary, it's all about reality
Gangsta, Gangsta!
He'll fuck up you and yours and anything that gets in his way
Gangsta, Gangsta! That's what they're yellin
It's not about a salary, it's all about reality
Gangsta, Gangsta!
He'll just call you a low-life motherfucker and talk about your funky ways

STRAIGHT OUTTA COMPTON

You are now about to witness the strength of street knowledge

[Ice Cube]
Straight outta Compton, crazy motherfucker named Ice Cube
From the gang called Niggaz With Attitudes
When I'm called off, I got a sawed-off
Squeeze the trigger and bodies are hauled off
You too, boy, if ya fuck with me
The police are gonna hafta come and get me
Off yo' ass, that's how I'm goin out
For the punk motherfuckers that's showin out
Niggaz start to mumble, they wanna rumble
Mix 'em and cook 'em in a pot like gumbo
Goin off on the motherfucker like that
With a gat that's pointed at yo' ass
So give it up smooth
Ain't no tellin when I'm down for a jack move
Here's a murder rap to keep you dancin
With a crime record like Charles Manson
AK-47 is the tool
Don't make me act a motherfuckin fool
Me and you can go toe to toe, no maybe
I'm knockin niggaz out the box, daily
Yo, weekly, monthly, and yearly
Until them dumb motherfuckers see clearly
That I'm down with the capital C-P-T
Boy, you can't fuck with me
So when I'm in your neighborhood you better duck
'Cause Ice Cube is crazy as fuck
As I leave, believe I'm stompin
But when I come back, boy, I'm comin straight outta Compton

City of Compton, City of Compton

Yo, Ren
Whassup?
Tell 'em where you from!

[MC Ren]
Straight outta Compton, another crazy-ass nigga
More punks I smoke, yo, my rep gets bigger
I'm a bad motherfucker and you know this
But the pussy-ass niggaz won't show this
But I don't give a fuck, I'ma make my snaps
If not from the records, from jackin at craps
Just like burglary, the definition is "jackin"
And when illegally armed it's called "packin"
Shoot a motherfucker in a minute
I find a good piece of pussy and go up in it
So if you're at a show in the front row
I'ma call you a bitch or dirty-ass ho
You'll probably get mad like a bitch is supposed to
But that shows me, slut, you're composed to
A crazy motherfucker from the street
Attitude legit 'cause I'm tearin up shit
MC Ren controls the automatic
For any dumb motherfucker that starts static
Not a right hand 'cause I'm the hand itself
Every time I pull a AK off the shelf
The security is maximum and that's a law
R-E-N spells Ren but I'm raw
See, 'cause I'm the motherfuckin villain
The definition is clear, you're the witness of a killin
That's takin place without a clue
And once you're on the scope, your ass is through
Look, you might take it as a trip
But a nigga like Ren is on the gangsta tip
Straight outta Compton

City of Compton, City of Compton

Eazy is his name and the boy's comin . . .

[Eazy-E]
Straight outta Compton
Is a brother that'll smother yo' mother
And make yo' sister think I love her
Dangerous motherfucker raising hell
And if I ever get caught I make bail
See, I don't give a fuck, that's the problem
I see a motherfuckin cop, I don't dodge him
But I'm smart, lay low, creep a while
And when I see the punk pass, I smile
To me it's kinda funny, the attitude show a nigga drivin
But don't know where the fuck he going, just rollin
Lookin for the one they call Eazy
But here's a flash, they'll never seize me
Ruthless! Never seen like a shadow in the dark
Except when I unload
You see us flock and talk over our hesitation
And hear the scream of the ones who caught the lead's penetration
Feel a little gust of wind and know I'm jettin
But leave a memory no one'll be forgettin
So what about the bitch who got shot? Fuck her!
You think I give a damn about a bitch? I ain't a sucker!
This is a autobiography
Of the E, and if you ever fuck with me
You'll get taken by a stupid dope brother
Who will smother, word to the motherfucker
Straight outta Compton

City of Compton, City of Compton

Damn, that shit was dope!

PUBLIC ENEMY

O f all rap groups, Public Enemy mixed the most serious political engagement with many of the greatest innovations in sound and poetic form for the longest period of time. The group's leader, Chuck D, has been called by KRS-One "Hip Hop's authentic 'poet of protest.'"[14] The single-mindedness and range of that lyrical protest found a match in the group's sound.

The Long Island–based group—which in its most robust stage featured Chuck D as lead rapper, Flavor Flav as hype man and comic foil, Terminator X as DJ, Professor Griff as "Minister of Information," and a group of uniformed men called the S1Ws serving as "Security of the First World"—was founded in 1986.

PE's name came from a track called "Public Enemy #1," which Chuck made while working as a radio DJ. Although the song (as well as the track "Miuzi Weighs a Ton") was in fact a defense of Chuck's reputation as a rapper against the perceived slights of other local artists, such internecine feuds with fellow rappers were to be the exception rather than the rule in the group's oeuvre. As Kool Moe Dee has noted, "Chuck used none of the clichéd, familiar, conventional braggadocio emceeisms! He never talked about being the best, and he never criticized another emcee. He never even compared himself to another emcee."[15]

Public Enemy focused largely on public matters of political import. In doing so they injected hip-hop with a prophetic strain of politics reminiscent in content of the spoken-word tradition of artists such as Gil Scott-Heron and the Last Poets. The production that backed their lyrics—concocted by Hank and Keith Shocklee and Eric "Vietnam" Sadler under the name of the Bomb Squad—updated the overall sound, pushing it into public consciousness by means that included radically textured sampling from multiple sources and a propensity to demand attention by, if necessary, irritating eardrums with discomforting noises that emerged from a propulsive backbeat.

Chuck D often asserts a form-content connection in describing his lyrical strategy. For instance, discussing the song "Bring the Noise," he explains, "I was specifically talking about how people at the time considered all rap music 'noise.' It was common to hear, 'Cut that noise off, it's irritating, it has no melody.' We were like, 'If you're calling that noise, we have some noise for your ass.' . . . For those that didn't understand the music[,] the noise was not just a sonic thing, the noise that people considered irritating was hearing us talk about issues that rarely gets talked about; our history, our culture, our language, our God, and just coming out strong."[16]

MIUZI WEIGHS A TON

Step back, get away—give the brother some room
You got to all turn me up when the beat goes boom
Lyric to lyric, line to line
And then you'll all understand my reputation for rhyme
'Cause my rhyme reputation depends on what
Style of record my DJ cuts
His slice and dice—super mix so nice
So bad, you won't dispute the price
'Cause it's plain to see, it's a strain to be
Number one in the public-eye enemy
'Cause I'm wanted in fifty—almost fifty-one
States where the posse got me on the run
It's a big wonder why I haven't gone under
Dodgin all types of microphone thunder
A fugitive missin all types of hell
All this because I talk so well
When I—

[Chorus 4x]
Rock—get up—get down
Miuzi weighs a ton

The match-up title, the expression of thrill
For elite to compete and attempt to get ill
If looks could kill, I'd chill until
All the public catches on to my material
You know the ducks criticize my every phase of rapture
Can't wait to read the headlines of my capture
Accused of assault, a first-degree crime
'Cause I beat competitors with my rhymes

Tongue-whipped, pushed, shoved, and tripped
Choked from the hold of my kung-fu grip
And if you want my title, it would be suicidal
From my end, it would be homicidal
When I do work, you get destroyed
All the paranoid know to avoid
The Public Enemy seat I've enjoyed
This is no kid and I'm not no toy boy

[Chorus 4x]

I'm a Public Enemy but I don't rob banks
I don't shoot bullets and I don't shoot blanks
My style is supreme, number one is my rank
And I got more power than the New York Yanks
If miuzi wasn't heavy I would probably fire it
Make you walk the plank if I was a pirate
If they made me king I would be a tyrant
If you want to get me, go ahead and try it
Snatcher, dispatcher, biter never been a
Instead of takin me out take your girl to dinner
The level of comp has never been thinner
It's a runaway race where I'm the winner
It's unreal, they call the law
And claimed I had started a war
It was war they wanted and war they got
But they wilted in the heat when miuzi got hot

[Chorus 4x]

My style versatile, said without rhymes
Which is why they're after me and they're on my back
Lookin over my shoulder, seein what I write
Hearin what I say, then wonderin why
Why they can't ever compete on my level
Superstar status is my domain
Understand my rhythm, my pattern of lecture

And then you'll know why I'm on the run
This change of events results in a switch
It's the lateral movement of my vocal pitch
It eliminates pressure on the hunted
But the posse is around so I got to front it
Plus employ tactics so coy
And leave no choice but to destroy
Soloists, groups, and what they say
And all that try to cross my way

BLACK STEEL IN THE HOUR OF CHAOS

I got a letter from the government the other day
I opened and read it, it said they were suckers
They wanted me for their army or whatever
Picture me givin a damn, I said never
Here is a land that never gave a damn
About a brother like me and myself, because they never did
I wasn't wit' it, but just that very minute, it
Occurred to me the suckers had authority
Cold sweatin as I dwell in my cell
How long has it been? They got me sittin in the state pen
I gotta get out, but that thought was thought before
I contemplated a plan on the cell floor
I'm not a fugitive on the run
But a brother like me begun to be another one
Public Enemy servin time
They drew the line, y'all, they criticize me for some crime
Nevertheless, they could not understand
That I'm a black man and I could never be a veteran
On the strength, the situation's unreal
I got a raw deal, so I'm lookin for the steel

They got me rottin in the time that I'm servin
Tellin you what happened the same time they're throwin
Four of us packed in a cell like slaves—oh, well

The same motherfucker got us livin in his hell
You have to realize that it's a form of slavery
Organized under a swarm of devils
Straight up, word 'em up on the level
The reasons are several, most of them federal
Here is my plan anyway and I say
I got gusto, but only some I can trust, yo
Some do a bid from one to ten
But I never did, and plus I never been
I'm on a tier where no tears should ever fall
Cell block and locked—I never clock it, y'all
'Cause time and time again, time they got me servin
To those and to them, I'm not a citizen
But ever when I catch a CO
Sleepin on the job, my plan is on go-ahead
On the strength, I'ma tell you the deal
I got nothin to lose
'Cause I'm goin for the steel

Don't you know I caught a CO fallin asleep on death row
I grabbed his gun and he did what I said so
And everyman's the man got served
Along with the time they served, decency was deserved
To understand my demands I gave a warnin
I wanted the governor, y'all, and plus the warden to know
That I was innocent because I'm militant
Posing a threat, you bet it's fuckin up the government
My plan said I had to get out and break North
Just like Oliver's neck, I had to get off
My boys had the feds in check, they couldn't try
Nothin, we had a force to instigate a prison riot
This is what it takes for peace, so I just took the piece
Black for black inside, time to cut the leash
Freedom to get out to the ghetto, no sellout
Six COs we got, we ought to put their head out

But I'll give 'em a chance, 'cause I'm civilized

As for the rest of the world, they can't realize

A cell is hell, I'm a rebel so I rebel

Between bars, got me thinkin like an animal

Got a woman CO to call me a copter

She tried to get away, and I popped her

Twice, right—now who wanna get nice?

I had six COs, now it's five to go

And I'm serious; call me delirious

But I'm still a captive, I gotta rap this

Time to break as time grows intense

I got the steel in my right hand, now I'm lookin for the fence

As I ventured into the courtyard

Followed by fifty-two brothers, bruised, battered, and scarred but hard

Goin out with a bang, ready to bang out

But power from the sky and from the tower shots rang out

A high number in dose, yes, and some came close

I figure I trigger my steel, stand and hold my post

This is what I mean, an anti-nigger machine

If I come out alive, then they won't come clean

Then I threw up, my steel bullets flew up

And to my surprise, the water tower blew up

Who shot what, who, what, the bazooka was who

And to my rescue, it was the S1Ws

Secured my getaway, so I just got away

The joint broke from the black smoke

Then they saw it was rougher than the average bluffer

'Cause the steel was black, the attitude exact

Now the chase is on, tellin you to c'mon

Fifty-three brothers on the run, and we are gone

REBEL WITHOUT A PAUSE

Yes—the rhythm, the rebel

Without a pause, I'm lowering my level

The hard rhymer, where you never been I'm in
You want stylin? You know it's time again
D, the enemy—tellin you to hear it
They praised the music, this time they play the lyrics
Some say no to the album, the show
Bum rush the sound I made a year ago
I guess you know, you guess I'm just a radical
Not on sabbatical, yes, to make it critical
The only part of your body should be partying to
Panther power on the hour from the rebel to you

Radio: suckers never play me
On the mix, they just okay me now
Known and grown when they're clocking my zone
It's known, snakin and takin everything that a brother owns
(Hard): my calling card
Recorded and ordered, supporter of Chesimard
Loud and proud, kickin live, next poet supreme
Loop a troop, bazooka, the scheme
(Flavor): a rebel in his own mind
Supporter of my rhyme designed to
Scatter a line of suckers who claim I do crime
They're on my time—dig it?

Terminator X [4x]

From a rebel it's final on black vinyl
Soul, rock and roll comin like a rhino
Tables turn, suckers burn to learn
They can't disable the power of my label
Def Jam: tells you who I am
The Enemy's public, they really give a damn
Strong Island: where I got 'em wild and
That's the reason they're claimin that I'm violent
Never silent, no dope, gettin dumb

Nope, claimin where we get our rhythm from
Number one, we hit ya and we give ya some
No gun and still never on the run
You wanna be an S1, Griff will tell you when
And then you'll come again, you'll know what time it is
Impeach the president, pullin out my ray-gun
Zap the next one, I could be your Shogun
(Suckers) Don't last a minute
Soft and smooth, I ain't with it
(Hardcore) Rawbone like a razor
I'm like a laser, I just won't graze ya
Old enough to raise ya, so this will faze ya
Get it right, boy, maybe I will praise ya
Playin the role, I got soul, too
Voice my opinion with volume
(Smooth) Not what I am
(Rough) 'Cause I'm the man
No matter what the name, we're all the same
Pieces in one big chess game
(Yeah) The voice of power
Is in the house, go take a shower, boy
PE a group, a crew
Not singular, we wear black Wranglers
We're rap stranglers, you can't angle us
I know you're listenin, I caught you pissin in
Your pants, you're scared of dissin us
The crowd is missin us, we're on a mission, y'all

Terminator X [4x]

Attitude when I'm on fire
Juice on the loose, electric wire
Simple and plain, give me the lane
I'll throw it down your throat like Barkley
You see my car keys? You will never get these

They belong to the 98 Posse

You want some more, son? You wanna get some?

Bum rush the door of the store, pick up the album

You know the rhythm, the rhyme, plus the beat is designed

So I can enter your mind, boys

Bring the noise, my time

Step aside for the flex, Terminator X

FIGHT THE POWER

*Yet our best-trained, best-educated, best-equipped, best-prepared troops
refuse to fight. Matter of fact, it's safe to say that they would rather switch . . .
than fight.*

1989, the number, another summer

(Get down) Sound of the funky drummer

Music hittin your heart 'cause I know you got soul

(Brothers and sisters) Hey

Listen if you're missin, y'all, swingin while I'm singin

Givin what ya gettin

Knowin what I'm knowin while the black band's sweatin

In the rhythm rhyme rollin

Got to give us what we want

Got to give us what we need

Our freedom of speech is freedom or death

We got to fight the powers that be

(Lemme hear you say . . .)

Fight the power [8x]

As the rhythm's designed to bounce, what counts is that the rhyme's

Designed to fill your mind. Now that you

Realize the pride's arrived

We got to pump the stuff that make ya tough

From the heart, it's a start, a work of art to revolutionize

Make a change, nothin's strange

People, people, we all the same—no, we're not the same

'Cause we don't know the game

What we need is awareness, we can't get careless

You say, "What is this?"

My beloved, let's get down to business

Mental self-defensive fitness

(Yo) Bum rush the show

(You gotta go for what you know)

To make everybody see, in order to

Fight the powers that be

Fight the power [8x]

Elvis was a hero to most

But he never meant shit to me—you see

Straight-out racist, the sucker was simple and plain

(Motherfuck him and John Wayne) 'Cause I'm black

And I'm proud, I'm ready, I'm hyped, plus I'm amped

Most of my heroes don't appear on no stamp

Sample, a look back, you look and find

Nothing but rednecks for four hundred years if you check

("Don't Worry, Be Happy") was a number-one jam

Damn if I say it, you can slap me right here

Get it (Let's get this party started right)

Right on (C'mon)

What we got to say

Power to the people, no delay

Make everybody see, in order to

Fight the powers that be

Fight the power [8x]

WELCOME TO THE TERRORDOME

I got so much trouble on my mind

Refuse to lose

Here's your ticket
Hear the drummer get wicked
The crew to you to push the back-to-black attack
So I sat and japped then slapped the Mac
Now I'm ready to mike it
(You know I like it) Huh
Hear my favoritism roll, "Oh"
Never be a brother like me go solo
Laser, Anastasia, maze ya
Ways to blaze your brain and train ya
The way I'm livin, forgivin what I'm givin up
X on the flex, hit me now
I don't know about later
As for now I know how to avoid the paranoid
Man, I've had it up to here.
Gear I wear got 'em goin in fear
Rhetoric said read just a bit ago
Not quittin, though, signed the hard rhymer
Work to keep from gettin jerked
Changin some ways
To way back in the better days
Raw, metaphysically bold, never followed the code
Still dropped a load
Never question what I am, God knows
'Cause it's comin from the heart
What I got, better get some (Get on up)
Hustler of culture
Snakebitten, been spit in the face
But the rhymes keep fittin
Respect's been givin. How's ya livin?
Now I can't protect a paid-off defect
Check the record and reckon an intentional wreck
Played off as some intellect
Made the call, took the fall

Broke the laws
Not my fault that they're fallin off
Known as fair and square throughout my years
So I growl at the livin foul
Black to the bone, my home is your home
But welcome to the Terrordome

So long now, have a good trip. Yo, yo, who put this thing together, huh? Me. Me, that's who. Who I trust? Who I trust? Me. That's who. Now who you trust, man?

Subordinate terror, kickin off an era
Cold deliverin pain
My 98 was '87 on a record, yo
So now I go Bronco

Aw, Chuck, they out to get us, man. . . . Aw, aw, aw, aw, aw. . . . Aw, Chuck, they out to get us, man. Yo, we got to dust these boys off!

Crucifixion ain't no fiction
So-called chosen frozen
Apology made to whoever pleases
Still they got me like Jesus
I rather sing, bring, think, reminisce
'Bout a brother while I'm in synch
Every brother ain't a brother, 'cause a color
Just as well could be undercover
Backstabbed, grabbed a flag
From the back of the lab
Told a Rab get off the rag
Sad to say I got sold down the river
Still some quiver when I deliver
Never to say I never knew or had a clue
Word was heard, plus hard on the boulevard
Lies, scandalizin, basin
Traits of hate and celebratin wit' Satan

I rope a dope the evil with righteous bobbin and weavin
And let the good get even
C'mon down
But welcome to the Terrordome

Caught in the race against time, the pit and the pendulum
Check the rhythm and rhymes while I'm bendin 'em
Snakes blowin up the lines of design
Tryin to blind the science I'm sendin 'em
How to fight the power, cannot run and hide
Bullets shouldn't be suicide
In a game a fool without the rules
Got a hell of a nerve to just criticize
Every brother ain't a brother
'Cause a black hand squeezed on Malcom X the man
The shootin of Huey Newton
From a hand of a nigger pulled the trigger

It's weak to speak and blame somebody else
When you destroy yourself
First, nothing worse than a mother's pain
Of a son slain in Bensonhurst
Can't wait for the state to decide the fate
So this jam I dedicate
Places with the racist faces
Example of one of many places
The Greek weekend speech I speak
From a lesson learned in Virginia
I don't smile in the line of fire, I go wildin
But it's on bass and drums, even violins
Watcha do, getcha head ready
Instead of gettin physically sweaty
When I get mad I put it down on a pad
Give ya somethin thatcha never had

Controllin, fear of high rollin
God bless your soul and keep livin
Never allowed, kickin it loud
Droppin a bomb, brain game, intellectual Vietnam
Move as a team, never move alone
But welcome to the Terrordome

QUEEN LATIFAH

Queen Latifah's dignified demeanor and commanding presence earned her the regal name, but her rhymes maintain it. Latifah is adept at various styles, able to throw in a reggae flow, slow it down still further with a love song, deliver a message with the strength of her convictions, or slay a wack MC for daring to get in her way.

Latifah's debut single was the infectious "Wrath of My Madness," and the album that followed, *All Hail the Queen* (1989), contained "Evil That Men Do," a song that explores the gender disparity in structural poverty. Songs like "Princess of the Posse" and especially her duet with Monie Love, "Ladies First," asserted female priorities and called for women to stand together. These pieces constituted an important counterbalance in a rap world that at the time was becoming more brazenly misogynistic. That puerile but powerful trend raised Latifah's ire on "U.N.I.T.Y.," a classic song that would have appeared in this anthology had we not been denied permission to print it. This call to arms was her biggest single and appeared on her third album, *Black Reign* (1993), which, like her aptly named sophomore release, *Nature of a Sista* (1991), continued to develop a place for women in rap.

EVIL THAT MEN DO
You asked, I came, so behold the Queen
Let's add a little sense to the scene
I'm living positive, not out here knocked up

But the lines are so dangerous, I ought to be locked up
This rhyme doesn't require prime time
I'm just sharing thoughts of mine
Back again, because I knew you wanted it
From the Latifah with the Queen in front of it
Droppin bombs, you're up in arms and puzzled
The lines will flow like fluid while you guzzle
You slip, I drop you on a BDP-produced track
From KRS to be exact
It's a Flavor Unit quest that today has me speaking
'Cause it's knowledge I'm seeking
Enough about myself, I think it's time that I tell you
About the evil that men do

Situations, reality, what a concept!
Nothing ever seems to stay in step
So today, here is a message for my sisters and brothers
Here are some things I want to cover:
A woman strives for a better life, but who the hell cares?
Because she's living on welfare
The government can't come up with a decent housing plan
So she's in no man's land
It's a sucker who tells you you're equal
(You don't need him, Johannesburg's crying for freedom!)
"We the people hold these truths to be self-evident"
(But there's no response from the president)
Someone's living the good life, tax-free
'Cause some poor girl can't find a way to be crack-free
And that's just part of the message I thought I had to send you
About the evil that men do

Tell me, don't you think it's a shame
When someone could put a quarter in a video game
But when a homeless person approaches you on the street
You can't treat him the same?

It's time to teach the deaf, the dumb, the blind

That black-on-black crime only shackles and binds

You to a doom, a fate worse than death

But there's still time left

To stop puttin your conscience on cease

And bring about some type of peace

Not only in your heart

But also in your mind; it will benefit all mankind

Then there will be one thing that will never stop you

And it's the evil that men do

ELEMENTS I'M AMONG

Booty rappers posin as gun-clappers get bitch-smacked

Need to switch to bein actors, image is all ya after

Hold the laugher and the lip, the clappers and the clips

I flip a flow like Divine be turnin tricks, and my clique and I

Cut ya like [   ]

I leave darkness where there used to be your front teeth

I'm heartless when it comes to havin the back of my partners

Yeah, we artists, but testin us ain't the smartest

You can huff, puff, but blow me down—I doubt it, kid

Or get yo' ass whooped behind what ya mouth did

You need more Hail Marys than a Catholic

Your ass ain't slick, I'll mash yo' shit quick

I got connects, I get that ass stuck like glue

Stand to the F-U, I wag two and make your fans forget you

'Cause if I let you get over and then I pass you

Think you can do it on the reg, so I'ma wreck you

[Chorus 2x]

Elements that I'm among, these none

Fools gettin done, but over dumb reasons

You didn't know. Elements that I'm among, these none

Betta check it out before you become one

You said new tricks in '86, it's time to build

Here we go, we pushin '96 and niggas still love to kill

Tryin to keep it real ...

But is it really real?

If you could fly, is it? Get between my legs

You fuckin kid, you'd be the man but hold ya head

Because if a fifth was a fifth we'd all be drunk

Nigga, don't put no yayo in my blunt

I just wanna bring the funk like I pooted

Y'all wannabe niggas is fired or be the ill reputed

You throw shade, I throw it too, more than you can chew

I'll get back at you, lyrically hack at you

I keep the facts here. I keep it real, hell yeah

I keep the phat gear, don't make me hate you like a pap-

Smear, that's where I get ticked

Matter fact in the '96, almost a pistol grip

Pump on my lap at all times. Shit!

Niggas be on some black-on-black crime shit

And I can't let it slide 'cause I'm terrified

That I might be the next homicide, the pound is on my side

[Chorus 2x]

Niggas be all in my face like the government be in my check

Every time I pick up the mic and begin to wreck

But right now my job is more important than a nigga

I'm independent, so trickin just ain't the way I figure

And evident I wasn't raised that way

We chicks are quick to spray that way, and I'm tryin

To stay "Forever Free," like AZ, baskin in

The riches of this hip-hop M-U-S-I-C

'Cause when the East is in the house, "Oh My God!" is right

I know girls that's givin niggas fair fights, so you damn right

I'ma stick up for mine like a queen at a bee, and I'ma

Get my own rhythm without a "G." Hey!

If ya kiddie come-come, well, ya need to run-run

Like a bee you'll get stung by my diggy dum-dum

All because of ya tongue

And I'll be lampin in the sun when the day is done

[Chorus 2x]

RUN-DMC

un-DMC holds the distinction of being the second rap group (after Grandmaster Flash and the Furious Five) enshrined in the Rock and Roll Hall of Fame. They conquered the mainstream and changed rap by introducing it to a wider listening public, all without relinquishing their hip-hop credentials.

Run-DMC was born in Hollis, Queens, and consisted of Joseph "Run" Simmons and Darryl "DMC" McDaniels as the MCs and Jason Mizell, known as Jam Master Jay, as DJ and producer. Run's younger brother, Russell Simmons, helped conceive and promote the group before going on to found Def Jam Records and becoming hip-hop's first mogul.

Run-DMC brought both orchestrated rhymes and a new sense of style to rap. They quickly became known for their signature apparel: tracksuits, unlaced Adidas, and fedoras. They brought a similar sense of style to their rhymes. In 1983 they released their first single, "It's Like That," with the B-side "Sucker MC's." "Sucker MC's" was a bold alternative to the familiar rap sounds of the time. With no bass line, it placed the entire focus on the relationship between Jam Master Jay's hard-hitting beats and the lyrical duo's back-and-forth rhymes.

Run-DMC's self-titled first album sparked a sort of hip-hop revolution, breaking down conventions in lyricism by abandoning the melodic rhyming made popular by such artists as Melle Mel and Kurtis Blow. It seems only a small step from there to weaving in elements of rock music. Run-DMC's second album, *King of Rock* (1985), saw the group fully embrace their signature blend of rock and rap. This sound was only reinforced by their next album, *Raising Hell* (1986), which was a hallmark album in rap history and would change the state of the industry. Featuring the hit single "My Adidas," the album displayed the group's genius at branding themselves. Perhaps the most momentous single off the album, however, was "Walk This Way," a collaboration with the rock group Aerosmith that remade an earlier Aerosmith track. The song was a hit not just on radio but also on the newer video format of MTV, which had heretofore all but ignored rap.

In the years since, the group has explored a range of vocations and projects—both together and individually. Run went on to become an ordained minister and to star in a reality TV show. Jam Master Jay enjoyed a successful career as a producer for other acts until he was murdered in his studio on October 30, 2002, a case that has yet to be solved.

Run-DMC is not the most lyrically accomplished group in rap history, nor the longest running, but its members will be remembered as the innovators who took rap from the old school into its modern beginnings. As if this weren't enough, the group also became one of the first rap acts to achieve crossover success, propelling the genre from block parties to concert arenas.

SUCKER MC'S

[Run]
Two years ago, a friend of mine
Asked me to say some MC rhymes
So I said this rhyme I'm about to say
The rhyme was def and then it went this way
Took a test to become an MC
And Orange Krush became amazed at me
So Larry put me inside his Cadillac
The chauffeur drove off and we never came back
Dave cut the record down to the bone
And now they got me rocking on the microphone
And then we talking autographs and cheers and laughs
Champagne, caviar, and bubble baths
But see, that's the life that I lead
And you sucker MCs is who I feed
So take that and move back, catch a heart attack
Because there's nothing in the world that Run'll ever lack

I cold chill at a party in a b-boy stance
And rock on the mic and make the girls wanna dance
Fly like a dove that come from up above
I'm rocking on the mic and you can call me Run-Love

I got a big long Caddy not like a Seville
And written right on the side it reads "Dressed to Kill"
So if you see me cruising girls just a-move or step aside
There ain't enough room to fit you all in my ride
It's on a first-come, first-serve basis
Cooling out, girl, take you to the def places
One of a kind and for your people's delight
And for you sucker MC, you just ain't right
Because you're biting all your life, you're cheating on your wife
You're walking round town like a hoodlum with a knife
You're hanging on the ave, chilling with the crew
And everybody know what you've been through
Ah, with the one-two-three, three to two-one
My man, Larry Larr, my name DJ Run
We do it in the place with the highs and the bass
I'm rocking to the rhythm, won't you watch it on my face
Go uptown and come down to the ground
You sucker MC, you sad-face clown
You're a five-dollar boy and I'm a million-dollar man
You's a sucker MC and you're my fan
You try to bite lines, but rhymes are mine
You's a sucker MC in a pair of Calvin Kleins
Coming from the wackest part of town
Trying to rap but you can't get down
You don't even know your English, your verb or noun
You're just a sucker MC, you sad-face clown
So DMC and if you're ready
The people rocking steady
You're driving big cars, get your gas from Getty

[DMC]

I'm DMC in the place to be

I go to St. John's University

And since kindergarten I acquired the knowledge

And after twelfth grade I went straight to college

I'm light skinned, I live in Queens

And I love eating chicken and collard greens

I dress to kill, I love the style

I'm an MC you know who's versatile

Say, I got good credit in your regards

Got my name, not numbers, on my credit cards

I go uptown, I come back home

With who? Me, myself, and my microphone

All my rhymes are a sweet delight

So here's another one for y'all to bite

When I rhyme, I never quit

And if I got a new rhyme I'll just say it

'Cause it takes a lot to entertain

And sucker MCs can be a pain

You can't rock a party with the hip in hop

You gotta let 'em know you'll never stop

The rhymes have to make

[Run] a lot of sense

[DMC] You got to know when to start

[Run] when the beats come in

IT'S LIKE THAT

[Run] Unemployment at a record high

People coming, people going, people born to die

Don't ask me, because I don't know why

[Both] But it's like that, and that's the way it is

[DMC] People in the world tryin to make ends meet

You try to ride car, train, bus, or feet

I said you got to work hard, you want to compete

[Both] It's like that, and that's the way it is. Huh!

[Run] Money is the key to end all your woes

[DMC] Your ups, your downs, your highs, and your lows

[Run] Won't you tell me last time that love bought you clothes?

[Both] It's like that, and that's the way it is

[DMC] Bills rise higher every day

[Run] We receive much lower pay

[DMC] I'd rather stay young,

                        [Both] go out and play

It's like that, and that's the way it is. Huh!

[Run] Wars going on across the sea

[DMC] Street soldiers killing the elderly

[Run] Whatever happened to unity?

[Both] It's like that, and that's the way it is

[DMC] Disillusion

            [Run] is the word

[DMC] That's used by me

                 [Run] when I'm not heard

[DMC] I just go through life

                 [Both] with my glasses blurred

It's like that, and that's the way it is. Huh!

[Run] You can see a lot

               [DMC] in this lifespan

[Run] Like a bum eating out of

                 [DMC] a garbage can

[Run] You noticed one time

                 [DMC] he was your man

[Both] It's like that. What? And that's the way it is

[DMC] You should have gone to school

                      [Run] you could've learned a trade

[DMC] But you laid in the bed

                 [Run] where the bums have laid

[DMC] Now all the time you're crying

                    [Run] that you're underpaid

[Both] It's like that. What? And that's the way it is. Huh!

[Run] One thing I know is that life is short

[DMC] So listen up, homeboy, give this a thought

[Run] The next time someone's teaching, why don't you get taught?

[Both] It's like that. What? And that's the way it is

[DMC] If you really think about it, times aren't that bad

[Run] The one that blesses with successes will make you glad

[DMC] Stop playing, start praying,

[Both] you won't be sad

It's like that. What? And that's the way it is. Huh!

[DMC] When you feel your failure sometimes it hurts

[Run] For a meaning in life is why you search

[DMC] Take the bus or the train,

[Run] drive to school or the church

[Both] It's like that, and that's the way it is

[DMC] Here's another point in life you should not miss

[Run] Do not be a fool who's prejudiced

[DMC] Because we're

[Both] all written down on the same list

It's like that. What? And that's the way it is. Huh!

[DMC] You know it's like that,

[Run] and that's the way it is

[DMC] Because it's like that,

[Run] and that's the way it is

PETER PIPER

[Run (DMC)]

Now Peter (Piper) picked (peppers), but Run rocked (rhymes)

Humpty (Dumpty) fell (down), that's his hard (time)

Jack B. (Nimble) was (nimble) and he was (quick)

But Jam (Master) cut (faster), Jack's on Jay's dick

Now Little Bo Peep cold lost her sheep

And Rip van Winkle fell the hell asleep

And Alice chillin somewhere in Wonderland

Jack's servin Jill, bucket in his hand
And Jam Master Jay's making mad-ass sound
The turntables might wobble but they don't fall down

Now Dr. Seuss and Mother Goose both did their thing
But Jam Master's gettin loose and DMC's the king
'Cause he's adult entertainer, child educator
Jam Master Jay, king of the crossfader
(He's the better of the best, best believe he's the baddest)
Perfect timin when I'm climbin, I'm a rhymin apparatus
Lot of guts (When he cuts, girls move their butts)
His name is Jay (hear the play), he must be nuts
And on the mix (real quick) and I'd like (to say)
He's not (Flash) but he's (fast) and his name is Jay

It goes a one, two, three, and

[DMC]
Jay's like King Midas, as I was told
Everything that he touched turned to gold
He's the greatest of the greater—get it straight, he's great
Claim fame 'cause his name is known in every state
His name is Jay, to see him play will make you say
"Goddamn, that DJ made my day"
Like the butcher, the baker, the candlestick maker
He's a maker, a breaker, and a title taker
Like the little old lady who lived in a shoe
If cuts were kids he would be due
Not lyin, y'all, he's the best I know
And if I lie, my nose will grow
Like a little wooden boy named Pinocchio
And you all know how the story go

[Run (DMC)]
Trix are for kids, he plays much gigs
He's a big bad wolf and you're the three pigs

He's a big bad wolf in your neighborhood

Not (bad) meaning (bad) but (bad) meaning good

There it is

[DMC (Run)]

We're Run-DMC, got a beef to settle

(D's not Hansel), he's not Gretel

Jay's a winner, not a beginner

His pockets get fat, others get thinner

(J-J-J-J-Jump) on Jay like cows jump moons

People chase Jay like dish and spoon

And like all fairy tales end

You'll see Jay again, my friend

PROUD TO BE BLACK

You know I'm proud to be black, y'all, and that's a fact, y'all

And if you try to take what's mine, I take it back, y'all

It's like that

[Run]

Licki-licki-licki-licki-licki-licki-licki-licki

Listen, party people, here's a serious song

It's right, not wrong, I should say right on

I gotta tell you somethin that you all should know

It's not a mystery, it's history, and here's how it goes

Now Harriet Tubman was born a slave

She was a tiny black woman when she was raised

She was livin to be givin, there's a lot that she gave

There's not a slave in this day and age

I'm proud to be black

[DMC]

Goddamn, I'm tired, my man

Don't worry 'bout what color I am

Because I'll show you how ill this man can act

It could never be fiction 'cause it is all fact
And if you get in my way I will not turn back
I'm proud of my name, my name is Darryl Mack
I'm black and I'm proud and I'll say it out loud
I'll share my story with the whole crowd
Argh!

[Run] You know I'm proud to be black, y'all, [DMC] and that's a fact, y'all
[Run] And if you [DMC] try to take what's mine [Run] I take it [DMC] back,
    y'all
[Both] It's like that!

[Run]
DJ Run and I'm runnin things
You can hear it loud and clear like when the school bell rings
Like Martin Luther King, I will do my thing
I'll say it in a rap 'cause I do not sing

[DMC]
DMC, the man that's causin the grief
I got a message for the world so listen up, it's brief
Like Malcolm X said, I won't turn the right cheek
Got the strength to go the length if you wanna start beef
Start beef

[Run] You know I'm proud to be black, y'all, [DMC] and real brave, y'all
[Run] And motherfucker, I could never be a slave, y'all
[Both] So take that!

[Run] We're gonna tell ya something, put your mind in a swirl
God bless the next baby that comes in this world
The world's full of hate, discrimination, and sin
People judgin other people by the color of skin
I'll attack this matter in my own way
Man, I ain't no slave, I ain't balin no hay
We're in a tight position in any condition

Don't get in my way 'cause I'm full of ambition

I'm proud to be black [DMC] and I ain't takin no crap

[Run] I'm fresh out the pack [DMC] and I'm proud to be black

[Both] So take that!

[DMC] There was a man, [Run] an inventor, who invented so well

He invented a fortune for a man named Bell

[DMC] George Washington Carver made the peanut great

Showed any man with a mind could create

You read about Malcolm X in the history texts

Jesse Owens broke records, Ali broke necks

[Run] What's wrong with ya, man? [DMC] How can you be so dumb?

[Both] Like Dr. King said, "We Shall Overcome!"

SALT-N-PEPA

Salt-N-Pepa expanded the possibilities for women in rap by making their brash sexuality and assertiveness not simply stylish but marketable. As the first platinum-selling female rappers, they set the standard for an emerging hip-hop feminism. With major hits in both the 1980s and 1990s, they established the kind of popular longevity that few artists in rap's history can claim.

Salt-N-Pepa got their start in Queens in the mid-1980s. Beginning with their second album, Spinderella provided production. Together, they challenged the male-dominated industry as well as many of the established conventions for female artists. The title of their debut album, *Hot, Cool, and Vicious* (1986), speaks to their reconception of hip-hop gender roles. The album included several hits, such as "Tramp," "My Mike Sounds Nice," and "Chick on the Side," but it was "Push It," the B-side to "Tramp," that would score their biggest early hit, reaching number nineteen on the Billboard pop charts. The song was among the earliest hip-hop songs nominated for a Grammy.

Salt-N-Pepa returned in 1990 with *Blacks' Magic*. The lead single, "Let's Talk About Sex," reached number thirteen on the pop charts and earned the group heavy rotation on MTV; more than that, it opened up new lyrical terrain. With its frank attention to sex and relationships, it offered an alternative to the more exploitative language emerging from artists like 2 Live Crew, whose hit single from the year before, "Me So Horny," had generated much controversy. By advocating safe sex without denying sexual desire, Salt-N-Pepa responded to the new realities of the age of AIDS without being preachy or compromising their craft.

The group's commercial peak came with *Very Necessary* (1993), which spawned two smash hits, "Shoop" (which reached number four on the charts) and "Whatta Man" (which reached number three). These singles— alongside a host of fine album tracks that expand on the themes of sexuality, responsibility, and love—helped certify Salt-N-Pepa as essential voices in rap's enduring tradition of women on the mic.

TRAMP

Homegirls, attention you must pay
So listen close to what I say
Don't take this as a simple rhyme
'Cause this type of thing happens all the time
Now what would you do if a stranger said "Hi"?
Would you dis him, or would you reply?
If you answer, there is a chance
That you'll become a victim of circumstance
Am I right, fellas? Tell the truth!
Or else I'ma have to show and prove
You are what you are, I am what I am
It just so happens that most men are
—Tramps

Have you ever seen a dude who's stupid and rude?
Whenever he's around he dogs your mood
I know a guy like that, girl
He thinks he's God's gift to the world
You know the kind, excited all the time
With nothin but sex on the mind?
I'm no stunt, on me he can't front
I know the real deal, I know what they want

It's me (why?) because I'm so sexy
It's me (what?) don't touch my body
'Cause, you see, I ain't no skeezer
But on the real tip I think he's a
—Tramp

On the first date he thought I was a dummy
He had the nerve to tell me he loved me
But of course I knew it was a lie, y'all
He undressed me with his eyeballs
Trying to change the whole subject
'Cause everything he said pertained to sex
So I dissed him, I said, "You's a sucker
Get your dirty mind out the gutter
You ain't gettin paid, you ain't knockin boots
You ain't treatin me like no prostitute"
Then I walked away. He called me a teaser
You're on a mission, kid, yo, he's a
—Tramp

LET'S TALK ABOUT SEX
[Chorus]
Let's talk about sex, baby
Let's talk about you and me
Let's talk about all the good things
And the bad things that may be
Let's talk about sex

Let's talk about sex for now
To the people at home or in the crowd
It keeps coming up anyhow
Don't decoy, avoid, or make void the topic
'Cause that ain't gonna stop it
Now we talk about sex on the radio and video shows
Many will know anything goes

Let's tell it like it is and how it could be

How it was and of course how it should be

Those who think it's dirty have a choice

Pick up the needle, press pause

Or turn the radio off

Will that stop us, Pep? (I doubt it)

All right then, come on, Spin'

[Chorus]

Hot to trot, make any man's eyes pop

She use what she got to get whatever she don't got

Fellas drool like fools but then again they're only human

The chick was a hit because her body was boomin

Gold, pearls, rubies, crazy diamonds

Nothin she wore was ever common

Her dates: heads of state, men of taste

Lawyers, doctors, no one was too great for her

To get with or even mess with

The prez, she says, was next on her list

And believe me you, it's as good as true

There ain't a man alive that she couldn't get next to

She had it all in the bag

So she should have been glad

But she was mad and sad and feelin bad

Thinkin about the things that she never had

No love, just sex, followed next with a check and a note

That last night was dope

[Chorus]

Ladies, all the ladies, louder now, help me out

Come on, all the ladies (let's talk about sex) all right [2x]

Yo, Pep, I don't think they're gonna play this on the radio

And why not? Everybody have sex

I mean, everybody should be makin love
Come on, how many guys you know make love?

[Chorus]

SCHOOLLY D

Just as gangsta rap was springing up on the West Coast, from the streets of Philadelphia came an East Coast variation on the theme. Schoolly D's "P.S.K. What Does It Mean" (1986) not only spoke of a gang called the "Park Side Killers" but also drew a picture of the conflicted artist who was channeling violent urges into patterns of words.

As a rapper, Schoolly has the insouciance of a latter-day Spoonie Gee, cut through with more explicit language and darker stories. Schoolly collaborated with the director Abel Ferrara on the macabre gangster movie *King of New York*, providing a soundtrack that matched in its menace the scary cackling of the thuggish Laurence Fishburne and the ghost-faced stare of Christopher Walken in the title role. After selling tales of the street on albums such as *The Adventures of Schoolly D* (1987) and *Smoke Some Kill* (1988), the rapper turned in a different direction with an album, *Am I Black Enough for You?* (1989), that fit in with the Afrocentric artists beginning to emerge.

Fittingly, though, Schoolly D was less concerned with Five-Percenter ideology than with expressing the rage of someone perpetually put-upon by white society. The combative rhetorical question of *Am I Black Enough for You?* would give way to a consideration of *How a Black Man Feels* (1991), a topic that in essence Schoolly D had been trying to explain all along, at least if the black man in question was found on the streets of West Philadelphia.

P.S.K. WHAT DOES IT MEAN
The official adventures of . . . of . . . of

[Chorus 2x]
PSK, we're makin that green

People always say, "What the hell does that mean?"

P for the people who can't understand

How one homeboy became a man

S for the way we scream and shout

One by one I'm knockin you out

K for the way my DJ cuttin

Other MCs, man, you ain't sayin nothin

Rockin on to the break of dawn

I think, Code Money, your time is on

Drivin in my car down the avenue

Towin on a J, sippin on some brew

Turn around see the fly young lady

Pull to the curb and park my Mercedes

Sayin, "Fly lady, now you're lookin real nice

Sweeter than honey, sugar, and spice"

Told her my name was MC Schoolly D

All about makin that cash money

She said, "Schoolly D, I knows yo' game

Heard about you in the hall of fame"

I said, "Mama, mama, I tell you no lies

'Cause all I wanna do is to get you high

And, uh, lay you down and do the body rock

To the wall, to the corner," got into the car

Took a little trip to a fancy bar

Copped some brew, some J, some coke

Tell you now, brother, this ain't no joke

She got me to the crib, she laid me on the bed

I fucked her from my toes to the top of my head

I finally realized the girl was some whore

Gave her ten dollars, she asked me for some more

[Chorus]

Clinton Road one Saturday night

Towin on a cheeba, I was feelin all right

Then my homie-homie called me on the phone

His name is Chief Keith, but we call him Bone

Told me 'bout this party on the Southside

Copped my pistols, jumped into my ride

Got at the bar, copped some black

Copped some cheeba-cheeba, it wasn't the wack

Got to the place and who did I see

A sucker-ass nigga tryin to sound like me

Put my pistol up against his head

I said, "You sucker-ass nigga, I should shoot you dead"

A thought ran across my educated mind

Said, "Man, Schoolly D ain't doin no time"

Grabbed the microphone and I started to talk

Sucker-ass nigga, man, he started to walk

[Chorus]

SATURDAY NIGHT

It was Saturday night and I'm feelin kinda sporty

Went to the bar and copped me a forty

Got kinda high and a . . . kinda drunk

So I kicked the ass of this little punk

Forgot my key, had to ring my bell

My mama came first, she said, "Who the hell?"

"Wait Mama, wait, it's me, ya little son"

Before I knew it my mom pulled a gun

"I know who you are, but who the hell is that?"

I turned around, man, this bitch was fat

I really don't know how she got into the car

I musta picked her up when I left the bar

Ya know I'm horny, homie—man, I wanted to chill

But you know how mothers are, she wanted to ill

So I said, "Hey, baby, is you on the pill?

'Cause tonight I wanna be your lover

Just one thing: I forgot to buy a rubber"

Wait a little while then we snuck upstairs

Step by step with a hint of fear

We got into my room, bitch started to scream

Mama busted in, what a fucked-up scene

Shirt ripped off, drawers down to my knees

"Wait Mama, wait Mama, wait, wait, please!

Put back your gun, put down your broom"

My mom fucked up the room

The bitch jumped up with no respect

I had to put the big, big bitch in check

I said, "Ya come a little closer and ya will get shot".

"I'm sober anyway, I don't need no cock"

Oh yeah, them wild Saturday nights, man. You know what I mean, they wild as
shit, man. They wild, man, you know. Yeah, man, let me tell you about another
Saturday night experience I had...

It was Saturday night and I was feelin kinda funny

Gold around my neck, pockets full of money

Went to the corner, man, who did I see?

But the superbad bitch lookin back at me

I said, "Fly lady, man, you got a big butt"

This bitch turned around, all she said was, "What?"

I said, "My name is Schoolly, baby. Uh, what is yours?"

Before I knew it, up come my boys

Noisy as hell and drunk as shit

Sayin, "Yo, Schoolly School, what time is it?"

Looked a little closer and I knew it was gag

What I thought was a girl was nothin but a fag

Oh, man, you know what I mean. You know what I mean, M&M, man. Them wild
Saturday nights, man. You know I got somethin else to say, man. I got
somethin to say, man, to everybody. It's like this...

Everybody rappin but they don't know how

Shoulda seen the boy rappin to the cow

He rapped so hard that the nigga saw smoke

He lit up his cheeba and they both took a toke
The cow got high and the boy got by
Don't come in my face and ask me why
Cheeba, cheeba, y'all
Yeah, it's that cheeba cheeba makin 'em feel like that
Cheeba, cheeba, y'all
Um . . . some call it cheeba, some call it weed
It's the killer, it's a thriller, it's the thing that you need
Cheeba, cheeba, y'all
Little Miss Muffet sat on her tuffet
Smokin a J and scratchin the itch
Along came a spider and sat down beside her
And said, "Yo, what's up with that, bitch?"
But then down the road came Mary and her lambs
Smokin a Lacy in each and every hand
The poor little spider, he couldn't score any
They was two-dollar bitches and he only had a penny
Cheeba, cheeba, y'all
Yeah, cheeba, cheeba, y'all

Let me tell ya a little tale about Peter the Pimp
Sucker MC tryna cop a limp
Rode around town in a couple of cars
Got gagged by the man tryin to stick up a bar
The judge said, "Boy, what was on your mind?"
He said, "I had some cheeba cheeba, cocaine, and some wine"
The judge said, "Boy, relax and have a beer
You won't be doin shit for the next ten years"
Cheeba, cheeba, y'all
Yeah, it's that cheeba cheeba
Cheeba, cheeba, y'all
Some call it cheeba, some call it weed
It's the killer, it's a thriller, it's the thing that you need
So cheeba, cheeba, y'all

ROXANNE SHANTÉ

Hailing from the Queensbridge projects, Roxanne as a teenager first made her mark by responding to UTFO's "Roxanne, Roxanne" with "Roxanne's Revenge," the first and still the most serious sally in what quickly became a saga. A member of Mr. Magic and Marley Marl's Juice Crew, Roxanne followed her initial hit with such songs as "Queen of Rox," "Bite This," "Have a Nice Day," and "Def Fresh Crew," the last of which featured Biz Markie beatboxing. Her collaboration with Rick James, "Loosey's Rap," topped the Billboard black singles chart for a week in 1988.

The recorded output of Shanté is not large, but she is a fierce MC in bursts. Much of the pleasure of listening to her rap derives from something hardly extant before the likes of Foxy Brown and Lil' Kim—that is, a female MC as verbally combative and profane as her male counterparts. It has been said that those who rely on curse words are simply making up for a lack of vocabulary, but lovers of literary invective know otherwise. Shanté—especially in her freestyles—can drop an explicit bomb with the best, sometimes to dis the worst and sometimes just for fun. In fact, there is more than one side to Roxanne. Her song "Independent Woman," included here, is a clarion of tough-love feminism, by turns harsh and sympathetic.

ROXANNE'S REVENGE

Well, my name is Roxanne, a-don't ya know
I just a-cold rock a party and I do this show
I said I met these three guys and you know it's true
A-let me tell you and explain them all to you
I met this dude with the name of a hat
I didn't even walk away, I didn't give him no rap
But then he got real mad and he got a little tired
If he worked for me, you know he would be fired
His name is Kangol and that is cute
But he ain't got money and he ain't got the loot
And every time that I see him, he's always a-beggin
And all the other girls that he's always tryin to layin

Every time that I see him, he says a rhyme
But, see, compared to me, it's weak compared to mine
Every time I know that I am sayin somethin fresher
In any category I'm considered the best
And every time that I say it there ain't nothin less
And everybody knows I will win the contest
Then after that came the Educated Rapper
His fingers started snappin and his hands start to clappin
Every time-a that I see him, everything he say
He rock it to the beat-a and he come this way
He said-a, "Yeah, you know, your mother's name is Mary
And from what I heard, your father is a fairy"
But every time that I see him, he's sayin somethin new
But let me explain to him what he should do
He should be like me, a fly MC
Don't never have to bite, will always write
I have the freshest rhymes that I do recite
And after that and you know it's true
Well, let me tell you somethin else about the Doctor, too
He ain't really cute and he ain't great
He don't even know how to operate
He came up to me with some crabbish rap
But let me tell you something, don't you know it's wack
So when he came up to me, I told him to step back
He said, "You call yourself a MC?" I said, "This is true"
He said, "Explain to me really what MCs must do"
I said, "Listen very close 'cause I don't say this every day
My name is Roxanne and they call me Shanté"
But every time-a that I say a rhyme-a just-a like-a this-a
It ain't nothin you MCs want-a miss-a
Now, Kangol, if you think you cute, you think you so right
That's why you said it in a language so you wouldn't have to bite
You started talkin Pig Latin, didn't make no sense
You thought you was cute, yeah, you thought you was a prince

You're walkin down the block 'cause I'm the one you're gonna clock

And everybody knows that you're all on my yacht

I'm just a devastatin, always rockin, always have the fliest clockin

Everybody knows it's me, the R-O-X-A-N-N-E

Everyone knows I am fresh, in any category best

And every time I start to write, everyone insist to bite

Every time I do it, yeah, you know it is a me-a

Rockin on the beat-a, that you can see

So, the UTFO crew, you know what you can do

Lemme tell you one for me and then I'll tell you one for you

Every time you say a rhyme-a just-a like-a this-a

It ain't nothin that I don't wanna miss-a

And if you think you right and I'm bitin your beat

Well, then you just better know and a-listen to me

Because my name is Roxanne-a and I came to say

I rock it to the beat-a and I do it this way

I'm conceited, never beated, never heard of defeated

I rock it to the beat-a and you know it is-a me-a

The R-O-X-A-N-N-E-a

And if you wanna play a little game for me

Lemme show you what you can do, baby

'Cause with a twist of my cheek and a twist of my wrist

I have all the guys droppin down like this

Yeah, I am fly and you must admit

That everybody knows I don't go for it

So, if you're tryin to be cute and you're tryin to be fine

You need to cut it out 'cause it's all in your mind

Tryin to be like me, yeah, it is very hard

You think you are God, but you do eat lard

Tryin to be cute and you're tryin to be fly

Don't you know you wish you could be my guy?

So I can take you home, make you relax

And everybody knows that you're out there, tryin to tax

Like corn on the cob, you're always tryin to rob

You need to be out there lookin for a job
Yeah, you're tryin to meet and talk about Roxanne
But lemme let ya know—you're not a real man
'Cause a Roxanne needs a man, and yes
Someone fresh who always dress
Someone, yes, who will never fess
And then I'll say, yeah, forget the rest
You gotta be cute and you tryna be fly
But all you wanna be is Roxanne's guy
'Cause I turned you down without a frown
Embarrassed you in front of your friends, made you look like a clown
And all you do is get real mad
And you talk about me and make me look bad?
But everybody knows how the story goes
There's no ifs, no ands, no buts, or suppose
No coke up your nose, no dope in your vein
And then it won't cause no kind of pain
But yet and still, you're tryin to be fly
I ask you a question, I wanna know why
Why'd ya have to make a record 'bout me?
The R-O-X-A-N-N-E

INDEPENDENT WOMAN

Ladies, listen up, I really hope you're ready
'Cause what I've got to say is far from petty
We've come a long way, baby, so maybe
Shanté can help a sister that's way be-
Hind, lost in the mind and can't find
Her way to a better day, you know the kind
So wrapped up in fairy-tale dreams
So naive that every male seems
Honest and loyal, ready to spoil
Buyin him gifts as if the boy's loyal
But Shanté is here just to say a few things

Some you heard before, but some are new things
So lend me your ears, dry up your tears
And let's hear the cheers for the years
Of the independent woman

How many runny-nose kids can you have?
How many nights can you work on the ave?
Your so-called man has a car and a Visa
He's livin large while you're livin on pizza
Unemployed while you wait for the perfect mate
Let's get one thing straight 'cause it's gettin late
What you're waitin for is really never comin
No one hears the sorry tunes that you're hummin
I'm here to bring the news, that if you're singin the blues
Every day, it will not change the views
That people have of you, they say you're lost
Nobody forced you to quit, your future's tossed
You put your faith in the guys with the hazel eyes
You thought you would get a prize, all you got was lies
Now you're stuck in a room with a mop and a broom
Did you assume that one day you will find a groom?
Are you dizzy—who would ever marry you?
You're lookin for a man that will carry you
And buy you nice things, like diamond rings
You're amazed at the truth that my rhymin brings
But the truth is the only way you'll ever see
That the life that you're hopin for will never be
But the race isn't over, put down the rope
Shanté is here to say there's still hope
So lend me your ears, dry up your tears
And let's hear the cheers for the years
Of the independent woman

So much to live for, she wants to die
Life's full of pitfalls, maybe that's why

Her pops went to jail, her mother tapped her vein

City took custody and trapped her in pain

Feelin so alone in the room with a stranger

Hates her own blood and nothing's gonna change her

Angry at the world 'cause it doesn't play fair

So much despair does she feel, no one to care

Not a single family member will remember her

Smoke's in her eyes and the past is a blur

She's on her own now, livin with some other girls

With the same damn lives, but from a different world

These girls are lost, how the city is full of fools

So many years, no guidance, and no kinda rules

No love to give—yo, they need love to live

If not, instead, they'll ponder in a bed

Sex is the thing that makes her feel wanted

Love and care, for she's undaunted

Because whoever is laying there won't really matter

Such a sad song when young dreams shatter

I really don't think glue is gonna fix it

But homegirl can walk the right path if she picks it

So lend me your ears, dry up your tears

And let's hear the cheers for the years

Of the independent woman

The black woman's role grows larger each day

Nothing in the way so what we teach may

Somehow help those young sisters that doze

And sleepwalk through life with their eyes closed

You don't need a man, all you need is to know you can

Then you can stand on your own two feet and

Achieve anything that you want out of life

Do for yourself, then you can be a wife

And you'll feel so good that you wanna shout

Because you got to the top and got there without

Relying on Tom, Dick, or Billy Dee

You don't have to turn the lights on to really see

So lend me your ears, dry up your tears

And let's hear the cheers for the years

Of the independent woman

Independent woman

SLICK RICK

Slick Rick is the hip-hop Aesop. Employing a range of voices, moods, and narrative techniques, he defined the terms of rap storytelling. Dubbed "The Ruler," perhaps as much for his aristocratic English accent as for his command of the microphone, he also became known for his trademark attire of Kangol, gold rope chain, and eye patch (which covers an eye blinded in a childhood accident).

Slick Rick was born to Jamaican immigrant parents in South Wimbledon, London. After moving to the North Bronx as a teen, he befriended Dana Dane and formed the Kangol Crew. They began performing at local shows and hip-hop battles. At one such event Rick met Doug E. Fresh, an originator of the human beat box (that percussive technique that uses the human voice to fashion rhythm and sound effects), who invited him to join the Get Fresh Crew, which then consisted of Doug, Barry Bee, and Chill Will. In 1985 Rick made his debut as MC Ricky D alongside Doug E. Fresh on the classic single "The Show / La Di Da Di."

With his newfound exposure Ricky D, now named Slick Rick, signed a deal with Def Jam and released his platinum-selling solo debut, *The Great Adventures of Slick Rick* (1988). It stands as one of rap's indispensable albums for its commanding example of hip-hop storytelling and its raucous—often raunchy—sense of humor. Rick's rhymes, rich in detail and dialogue, are carefully crafted narratives of ghetto life. On songs like "Children's Story" and "Mona Lisa," he offers cautionary tales that are never preachy. The album is also marked by misogyny. Tracks such as "Treat Her like a Prostitute" and "Indian Girl (Adult Story)" show Rick employing his narrative prowess toward less-than-noble ends.

Slick Rick's influence is apparent among artists as divergent as Snoop Dogg, Black Star, Outkast, and Nas. Even into middle age, he remains relevant on the rap scene, as is made apparent by his warm and charming contribution to Ghostface's 2001 track "The Sun" and by his skillful verse on Mos Def's 2009 song "Auditorium," the latter of which is included in this anthology.

LA DI DA DI

(with Doug E. Fresh)

*Okay, party people in the house. You're about to witness something you've
never witnessed before. Yes, it's the original human beat box, Doug E. Fresh,
and his partner, the grand wizard, MC Ricky D, D. And that's me in the place
to be. We gonna show you how we do it for '85, kick it live, all right? Because,
um, I've got a funny feeling, um, you're all sick of all these crap-rappers bitin
their rhymes because, um, they're backstabbers. But when it comes to me
and my friend Doug Fresh here, there is no competition 'cause we are the
best, yeah. Finesse, impress, which we prove, and y'all will realize that we are
the move. So listen close, um, so you all don't miss as we go a little somethin
like this. Hit it!*

You know what? Yo, peep this
La di da di, we like to party
We don't cause trouble, we don't bother nobody, we're
Just some men that's on the mic
And when we rock upon the mic we rock the mic (right!)
For all of y'all, keepin y'all in health
Just to see you smile and enjoy yourself
'Cause it's cool when you cause a cozy condition and, uh
That we create 'cause that's our mission, so
Listen to what we say because
This type of shit, it happens every day—I
Woke up around ten o'clock in the mornin
I gave myself a stretch up, a mornin yawn and
Went to the bathroom to wash up, had some

Soap on my face and my hand upon a cup—I said, um

"Mirror, mirror on the wall

Who is the top choice of them all?"

There was a rumble dumble

Five minutes it lasted, the mirror said

"You are, you conceited bastard!"

But that's true, that's why we never have no beef

So then I washed off the soap and brushed the gold teeth

Used Oil of Olay 'cause my skin gets pale

And then I got the files for my fingernails

Chewed through the night and on my behalf

I put the bubbles in the tub so I could have a bubble bath

Clean, dry, was my body and hair

I threw on my brand-new Gucci underwear

For all the girls I might take home

I got the Johnson's Baby Powder and the Polo Cologne

Fresh dressed like a million bucks

Threw on the Bally shoes and the fly green socks

Stepped out my house, stopped short, "Oh no!"

I went back in, I forgot my Kangol

And then I dilly (dally), I ran through a (alley)

I bumped into my old girl (Sally) from the (Valley)

This is a girl plays hard to get so I said

"What's wrong?" 'cause she looked upset

She said, "It's all because of you

I'm feeling sad and blue. You went away

And now my life is filled with rainy days

And I love you so, how much you'll never know

'Cause you took your love away from me"

Now what was I to do? She's crying over me and she was

Feeling blue. I said, "Don't cry, dry your eye

Here comes your mother with those two little guys"

Her mean mother stepped up, said to me, "Hi!"

Looked Sally in the face and decked her in the eye

Punched her in the belly and stepped on her feet
Slammed the child on the hard concrete
The bitch was strong, the kids was gone
Something was wrong, I said, "What is going on?"
I tried to break it up, I said, "Stop it, leave her"
She said, "If I can't have you she can't either"
She grabbed me closely by my socks
So I broke the hell out like I had the chicken pox but
She gave chase, she caught up quick
She put a finger in the face of MC Rick
She said, "Why don't you give me a play
So we can go cruising in my OJ
And if you give me that OK
I'll give you all my love today
Ricky, Ricky, Ricky, can't you see
Somehow your words just hypnotize me
And I just love your jazzy ways
Oh, MC Rick, my love is here to stay"
And on and on and on she kept on
The bitch been around before my mother's born
I said, "Cheer up!" I gave her a kiss
I said, "You can't have me, I'm too young for you, Miss"
She said, "No, you're not," then she starts crying
I says, "I'm nineteen," she said ("Stop lying!")
I says, "I am, go ask my mother
And with your wrinkled pussy, I can't be your lover!"
To the tick tock, you don't stop
To the tick tick and you don't quit, hit it!

CHILDREN'S STORY

Once upon a time not long ago
When people wore pajamas and lived life slow
When laws were stern and justice stood
And people were behavin like they ought to: good

There lived a little boy who was misled
By another little boy and this is what he said
"Me and you, Ty, we're going to make some cash
Robbin old folks and makin the dash"
They did the job, money came with ease
But one couldn't stop, it's like he had a disease
He robbed another and another and a sister and her brother
Tried to rob a man who was a DT undercover
The cop grabbed his arm, he started acting erratic, he said
"Keep still, boy, no need for static"
Punched him in his belly and he gave him a slap
But little did he know the little boy was strapped
The kid pulled out a gun, he said, "Why'd you hit me?"
The barrel was set straight for the cop's kidney
The cop got scared, the kid, he starts to figure
"I'll do years if I pull this trigger"
So he cold dashed and ran around the block
Cop radios in to another lady cop
He ran by a tree, there he saw this sister
Shot for the head, he shot back but he missed her
Looked around good and from expectations
He decided he'd head for the subway stations
But she was coming and he made a left
He was runnin top speed 'til he was out of breath
Knocked an old man down and swore he killed him
Then he made his move to an abandoned building
Ran up the stairs, up to the top floor
Opened up a door there, guess who he saw?
(Who?) Dave the dope fiend shootin dope
Who don't know the meaning of water nor soap
He said, "I need bullets, hurry up, run!"
The dope fiend brought back a spanking shotgun
He went outside but there was cops all over
Then he dipped into a car, a stolen Nova

Raced up the block doing eighty-three
Crashed into a tree near University
Escaped alive though the car was battered
Rat-a-tat-tatted and all the cops scattered
Ran out of bullets and he still had static
Grabbed a pregnant lady and pulled out the automatic
Pointed at her head, he said the gun was full of lead
He told the cops, "Back off or honey here's dead"
Deep in his heart he knew he was wrong
So he let the lady go and he starts to run on
Sirens sounded, he seemed astounded, and
Before long the little boy got surrounded
He dropped his gun, so went the glory
And this is the way I have to end this story
He was only seventeen, in a madman's dream
The cops shot the kid, I still hear him scream
This ain't funny so don't you dare laugh
Just another case about the wrong path
Straight and narrow or your soul gets cast
Goodnight

I SHOULDN'T HAVE DONE IT
Well, I'ma tell you a story and I come out bluntly
Want a ugly child? Hey, nobody would want me
I used to walk around and get upset and upsetter
'Til I figured out ways to make myself look better
As I got older, my awareness expanded
I met this beautiful girl and my wish was commanded
Didn't hang with fellas, 'cause they started gettin shady
I'd always be with my girl and y'all could call her my lady
I loved her a lot, word up, not going to front, see?
The problem that arise is why on earth did she want me?
Couldn't figure it out and to make things worse
I was cursed to the torment of not being the first

And the first was this fly guy, made me very jealous
Always think she'd cheat on me and talk to other fellas
Two wrongs don't make a right, but any time we would fight
I would kindly pick up the phone and call a girl out of spite

[Chorus]
I shouldn't have done it, man
I'm feelin sad and blue
I'm feelin sad and blue
I'm feelin

I want to make this right, so directly was admiring
I tried to stop my love, but no, my love was not retiring
To catch her in a lie was near impossible and tricky
Didn't want her in certain clothes, getting really picky
We got into it again, this time she got too bright
So me, preventin a fight, I just stayed out for the night
I had to ease up off the pressure, all this heartache pain, so
I went up to the Parrot with Omega, Vance, and Dane
This girl came over, she was trucked down excessive
Started talkin to me and she was poppin quite aggressive
A pretty young thing, she didn't strike me as no ho
So weak-minded Rick the Ruler went on with the flow
My joint was gettin hard, word, without me even knowing
We stepped back to my van and I could feel it's for her growing
The girl took off her coat, her body was no joke
Well, a rub or two, unzip it, and I went for broke

[Chorus]

Well, now I've sinned and there's no one to blame
That night when I went home, I felt real guilty and ashamed
Snuck right into bed, I felt just like a shady fella
What made me so self-centered? How am I ever gonna tell her?
I shouldn't have cheated, just because we'd always doubt
Endurance, be a man, that's what I had to learn about

Now me, I guess I'm, like, "That's one of the secrets that I hid"

I figure, I'll patch things up and then I'll tell her what I did

Then after that night, she started actin heaven-sent

I found the house spotless and she'd help out with the rent

So, I bought the ring, it was a good twenty karat

Then word got back about me chillin at the Parrot

So when I got home, I thought she'd just be out to roast

Instead I found this letter and I found her overdosed

It said, "I do for you but I guess you didn't care"

All this went and happened 'cause of me and my affair

[Chorus]

TOO $HORT

Too $hort pioneered the westward expansion of rap with his raunchy tales of urban life. His slow-tempo flow and melodic, funk-inflected beats made him the indisputable father of Bay Area hip-hop. His career spans more than twenty years, nearly twenty albums, and scores of songs.

When Too $hort started rapping in East Oakland in the early 1980s, few major labels were signing West Coast artists, so he began recording and selling his own mix tapes. After a few successful independent releases, Too $hort formed his own record label, which was soon picked up by Jive Records. With major-label publicity behind him, his next two albums, *Born to Mack* (1987) and *Life Is . . . Too Short* (1989), had considerable commercial success, the second achieving platinum status. He retired after the release of his tenth studio album, in 1996, only to return three years later.

Too $hort helped inaugurate the West Coast gangsta style, not through gunplay and gangs but through the pimp persona. Though he helped start a tradition, he also marks the contemporary limit of another one that long precedes him: the toasts. Much is rightly made of the deep links between rap and the "toasting" tradition in African American oral poetry, those long narrative poems describing the exploits of outlaw and trickster figures. Too $hort's raps are modern-day toasts on wax, fitting comfortably alongside the tales of pimps and sexual freaks transcribed in Bruce Jackson's *Get Your Ass in the Water and Swim Like Me.*

The fact that such toasts tend to formalize misogyny makes them a perpetual problem, one that Too $hort doesn't disown but rather exacerbates. On songs like "Freaky Tales" he delights in the outrageous and explicit actions of his outsized persona. A coarse purveyor of the closed couplet, at the meeting point of two traditions, Too $hort brings a nonchalant vibrancy to his rhymes. That nonchalance does not extend to any reticence about placing himself in the history of rap, however. "When you talk about the earliest days of hip-hop and where it came from, I just wanna be right there," he has said. "There have been phases of pioneers. There have been the pioneers who pioneered hip-hop—Kool Herc, Afrika Bambaataa, that crew from the South Bronx. There have been the pioneers like Russell Simmons who brought it to the world. But you also have your West Coast pioneers, and that would be the Ice Cubes, Dr. Dres, Too $horts. And so on. We pioneered rap on the West Coast. It did not come from anybody but us."[17]

CUSSWORDS

So you motherfuckers thought I was gonna change my style?
—So what are you saying, Todd?

To all you bitches, hoes, and all that shit
Here's another rap that I'm ready to spit
It goes like this, my name is $hort
I'm tearin shit up like never before
Pimp slaps, makin snaps
Cold cash money and Too $hort raps
Oakland, California, that's where I'm from
The city where the boys say you don't want none
But if you do, I'm gonna tell you this
Trues and vogues ain't really shit
Wanna roll so hard, all the time
You and that bitch playin Too $hort rhymes

If you ask me what it's all about
I'll say it's about that money
But if you ask me could you have some
I'll say it doesn't concern me
Ronald Reagan came up to me
And said, "Do you have the answer
To the US economy
And a cure for cancer?"
I said, "What are you doin in the White House
If you're not sellin cocaine?
Ask your wife, Nancy Reagan
I know she'll spit that game
Like one night, she came to my house
And gave me a blow job
She licked my dick, up and down
Like it was corn on the cob"
What is life? Life is Too $hort
I play the bitches like it's a sport
Yeah, I'll play the bitches just like y'all
Like Dr. J played basketball
You can call me Too, don't say it twice
You get me real mad and I'll fuck your wife
See, I'm not proper, I'm rarely polite
Too $hort, Too $hort, don't say it tonight, beeatch
It started on a bright morning in 1987
I was in my drop-top Caddy, y'all
Gettin sucked by a bitch named Helen
Nasty bitches, around the world
I wrote this rhyme for you
You might not like my rap
But I'm tellin you, bitch, it's true
So much death in the Oakland streets
Am I gonna live 'til next week?
Will I get shot by a dope fiend

Tryin to get high, tryin to steal my ring?

I really can't say, 'cause I don't know why

People out here droppin dead like flies

I used to see a homeboy, give him five

Now I say, "Man, you still alive?"

Cold as hell, this town I'm from

Won't last too long when you're fakin the funk

I'm the master rapper, so unique

Clap my hand when I want my freak

You can't deny it, you know I'm right

I turn any rapper out when I'm on the mic

And I won't kick back or relax

'Til he knows I'm the best at the MC rap

'Til he knows Too $hort set the trap

They got him caught up in my serious cap

Motherfucker can't spit straight game on the mic

'Cause he's worse than a fag or a Frisco dyke

He's a sucker MC, I call him punk

You tryin to spit that rap, you can scratch that junk

You little punk-ass boy, wouldn't listen to me

Think I'm fakin but I'm takin all you sucker MCs

To the end of the world and push you over

Good luck couldn't find you in a four-leaf clover

If I ever said a rap, tryin to cap on you

I wouldn't even sweat it 'cause you'll be through

Lookin so far up, you might fall down

Gettin clowned by the hound from east Oaktown

And the look in your face when you're lookin at Too

Could make a grown man die, laughin at you

'Cause you're a no-rappin, no-rhymin

Played-out fake-ass simple simon

I never understood one word you said

But you're swearin up and down that you're killin me dead

There's only one thing I wanted to know

Sucker motherfucker, where's the joke?

I'm the player of players, just call me Pop

My name is Too $hort, no, I don't stop

I just don't stop mackin, don't stop cappin

Don't stop rappin, now you see what happens

Your mind is gone, your crew just cut

Sucker MC, I'll tell you what

Your rhymes are weak, your rap the same

And when it comes to game, you are lame

Never even heard of Too $hort, baby

Hit Oakland in 1980

Singin mo' raps than a rap could rhyme

Tellin sucker MCs don't waste my time

There's a girl I know, her name is Betty

Straight to the head, just rock it steady

She's so freaky she'll juice you up

All the homeboys just can't get enough

She's a PhD, don't even stop

In the back like that goin chop, chop, chop

I won't say white girl, won't say she's black

She's the kind of girl that make your knees go crack

Feel the beat, rock with me

Let me tell you what I be

I'm a MC rapper, a MC rapper

A big bank roller and a cold, cold capper

Hey, baby, I got this rhyme

It's not gonna stop 'til the end of time

Like rock and roll I'll play that song

To the beat all day and all night long

So listen up to what I'm sayin

I'm a Oaktown mack, bitch, I ain't playin

To all the homeboys doin time in the pen

Gonna rock this beat for you once again

If you can't get out and you're mad as hell

Say beeatch, now make it sound for real

I'ma tear shit up, if I get the chance

I could give a fuck less if your ho don't dance

See, I'm a big mack now, I'm so great

I was born and raised in the Golden State

Call me T-O-O, if you say $hort

I'ma rap my ass off 'til you give me some more

Big bank, now just make me rich

Bitch, bitch, bitch, bitch make me rich

Check out my style, baby, I don't quit

I heard this freak say, "That's the shit

He took the cake, fucked the rake

Too $hort, baby, damn sure ain't fake"

But the sucker MCs are screamin loud

Sayin, "Sir Too $hort, shut your mouth"

How can you talk about me and call me weak

When your father smokes coke and your mother's a freak?

So I keep on rappin, if nothin else

Keep your jealous-ass thoughts to yourself

(Beeatch) Picture this, he's a MC, right?

(Beeatch) Ain't sayin nothin but he's holdin the mic

(Beeatch) Fuck with me and boy you're doomed

I send a trick with a ho to the motel room

'Cause I'm the coldest MC on a microphone

Like a .357 pointed at your dome

I got cap for cap, you never heard

So fresh again with cusswords

Motherfuckin shit, fuckin with me

Fuck a stank bitch and a sucker MC

All you bastards got the claps

And fuck you, punk, 'cause you still can't rap

Cusswords, just let 'em know

Motherfuckin shit, goddamn asshole

Cusswords, just don't quit

Motherfuck you, damn shithead bitch
It's Too $hort, on the mic, and it don't stop
And it don't stop, and it won't stop, beeatch
Check out my style

THE GHETTO
[Chorus]
The ghetto
The ghetto
(Talking 'bout the ghetto)
The ghetto
The ghetto
(Funky funky ghetto)

Even though the streets are bumpy, lights burned out
Dope fiends die with a pipe in their mouths
Old school buddies not doing it right
Every day it's the same and it's the same every night
I wouldn't shoot you, bro, but I'd shoot that fool
If he played me close and tried to test my cool
Every day I wonder just how I'll die
Only thing I know is how to survive
There's only one rule in the real world
And that's to take care of you, only you and yours
Keep dealing with the hard times day after day
Might deal me some dope but then crime don't pay
Black man tryin to break into my house again
Thought he got off early doing time in the pen
Even though my brothers do me just like that
I get a lot of love so I'm giving it back to the . . .

[Chorus]

So just peep the game and don't call it crap
'Cause to me, life is one hard rap

Even though my sister smoked crack cocaine
She was nine months pregnant, ain't nothing changed
Six hundred million on a football team
And her baby died just like a dope fiend
The story I tell is so incomplete
Five kids in the house and no food to eat
Don't look at me and don't ask me why
Mama's next door getting high
Even though she's got five mouths to feed
She'd rather spend her money on a H-I-T
I always tell the truth about things like this
I wonder if the mayor overlooked that list
Instead of adding to the task force, send some help
Waiting on him, I'd better help myself
Housing Authority and the OPD
All these guns just to handle me in the . . .

[Chorus]

Even though they put us down and call us animals
We make real big banks and buy brand new clothes
Drive fancy cars, make love to stars
Never really saying just who we are
We use alias names like Too $hort
Sell you stuff you might kill for
Young kids grow up and that's all they know
Didn't teach him in school, now he's slangin dope
Only thing he knows is how to survive
But will he kill another brother before he dies?
In the ghetto, you keep one eye open
All day long, just hoping and hoping
You can pay your bills and not drink too much
Then the problems of life you'll be throwing up
Like me, but you don't see
Ten years from now, where will you be?

[Chorus]

So much game in a Too $hort rap

Blacks can't be white and whites can't be black

Why you wanna act like someone else?

All you gotta do is just be yourself

We're all the same color underneath

$hort Dog is in the house, you better listen to me

Never be ashamed of what you are

Proud to be black, stand tall and hard

Even though some people give you no respect

Be intelligent when you put 'em in check

'Cause when you're ignorant, you get treated that way

And when they throw you in jail you got nothing to say

So if you don't listen, it's not my fault

I'll be getting paid and you'll be paying the cost

Sitting in the jailhouse running your mouth

While me and my peoples try to get out

[Chorus]

A TRIBE CALLED QUEST

A Tribe Called Quest's two MCs, Q-Tip and Phife Dawg, present a stylistic contrast that reaches from the philosophical to the comic, from personal reflections to battle rhymes. As part of the Native Tongues collective, they cultivated a sense of musicality and a free-wheeling spirit of improvisation that charted new directions for rap in the early 1990s and beyond.

ATCQ formed in 1988 in Queens when childhood friends Q-Tip and Phife Dawg joined with DJ/producer Ali Shaheed Muhammad, a classmate of Q-Tip's, to form a group known simply as Tribe. (A fourth member of the crew, Jarobi, remained a behind-the-scenes influence, particularly on their debut album.) At the suggestion of Afrika from the Jungle Brothers, they expanded their name to A Tribe Called Quest.

After signing to Jive Records in 1989, ATCQ released their first album, *People's Instinctive Travels and the Paths of Rhythm* (1990). It was packed with jazz-inflected tracks on an eclectic range of subject matter: vegetarianism, safe sex, and road trips gone awry. *The Low End Theory* (1991) witnessed the successful fusion of opposites: the complex musical textures of jazz and the straightforward boom-bap of rap, Q-Tip's esoteric musings and Phife's sardonic battle rhymes. It saw Q-Tip emerge as the public face of the group, though Phife's contribution remained undeniable and essential. "Phife was always the battle rapper—he would take what was happenin' on the street and rhyme about it," Q-Tip would later explain. "And he was a great freestyler as well. My shit was always more cerebral, and the combo always worked really well. We'd always make up routines that would emulate Run-DMC."[18]

By the time they released *Midnight Marauders* (1993), ATCQ had become standard-bearers for a new rap aesthetic that had at its center a conscious mind-set, an informed eclecticism, and a jazz-based sound. *Marauders* challenged some of these assumptions, marking a shift away from the heavy jazz influence of the previous albums. Listeners were led through the tracks by the robotic voice of a tour guide advising us how to make our listening experience "precise, bass heavy, and just right." Including such standout songs as "Sucka Nigga," "Electric Relaxation," "Steve Biko (Stir It Up)," and "Award Tour," it remains the group's best-selling album. That A Tribe Called Quest became alternative hip-hop icons proved that intellectually stimulating hip-hop could gain mainstream success. With their beats and rhymes they infused rap with new life.

I LEFT MY WALLET IN EL SEGUNDO

I left my wallet in El Segundo
Left my wallet in El Segundo
Left my wallet in El Segundo
I gotta get it, I got-got to get it

My mother went away for a month-long trip
Her and some friends on an ocean-liner ship

She made a big mistake by leaving me home
I had to roam so I picked up the phone
Dialed Ali up to see what was goin down
Told him I'd pick him up so we could drive around
Took the Dodge Dart, a '74
My mother left a yard but I needed one more
Shaheed had me covered with a hundred greenbacks
So we left Brooklyn and we made big tracks
Drove down the Belt, got on the Conduit
Came to a toll, we paid and went through it
Had no destination, we was on a quest
Ali laid in the back so he can get rest
Drove down the road for two days and a half
The sun had just risen on a dusty path
Just then a figure had caught my eye
A man with a sombrero who was four feet high
I pulled over to ask where we was at
His index finger, he tipped up his hat
"El Segundo," he said. "My name is Pedro
If you need directions, I'll tell you pronto"
Needed civilization, some sort of reservation
He said, "A mile south, there's a fast-food station"
"Thanks, Señor," as I start up the motor
Ali said, "Damn, Tip, what did you drive so far for?"

"Well, describe to me what the wallet looks like."

Anyway, a gas station we passed
We got gas and went on to get grub
It was a nice little pub
In the middle of nowhere, anywhere would have been better
I ordered enchiladas and I ate 'em
Ali had the fruit punch
When we finished we thought for ways to get back

I had a hunch
Ali said, "Pay for lunch." So I did it
Pulled out the wallet and I saw this wicked
Beautiful lady. She was a waitress there
Put the wallet down and stared and stared
To put me back into reality, here's Shaheed:
"Yo, Tip, man, you got what you need?"
I checked for keys and started to step
What do you know, my wallet I forget

"Yo, it was a brown wallet, it had props numbers, had my jimmy hats. I got to get
   it, man."

Loooord, have mercy!
The heat got hotter, Ali starts to curse me
I feel bad but he makes me feel badder
Chit-chit-chatter, car starts, we scatter
Breaking on out, we was northeast bound
Jettin on down at the speed of sound
Three days coming and three more going
We get back and there was no slack
490 Madison, "We're here, Sha"
He said, "All right, Tip, see you tomorrow"
Thinking about the past week, the last week
Hands go in my pocket, I can't speak
Hopped in the car and torpe'ed to the shack
Of Shaheed. "We gotta go back"
When he said, "Why?" I said, "We gotta go
'Cause I left my wallet in El Segundo"

Yeah, I left my wallet in El Segundo
Left my wallet in El Segundo
Left my wallet in El Segundo
I gotta get it, I got-got to get it

CHECK THE RHIME

[Q-Tip] Back in the days on the boulevard of Linden
We used to kick routines and the presence was fittin
It was, I, the Abstract

       [Phife Dawg] and me the Five Footer
I kicks the mad style so step off the frankfurter
[Q-Tip] Yo, Phife, you remember that routine
That we used to make spiffy like Mr. Clean?
[Phife] Um, um, a tidbit, um, a smidgen
I don't get the message so you gots to run the picture
[Q-Tip] You on point, Phife?

           [Phife] All the time, Tip
[Q-Tip] You on point, Phife?

           [Phife] All the time, Tip
[Q-Tip] You on point, Phife?

           [Phife] All the time, Tip
[Q-Tip] Well, then grab the microphone and let your words rip

[Phife]
Now here's a funky introduction of how nice I am
Tell your mother, tell your father, send a telegram
I'm like an Energizer 'cause, you see, I last long
My crew is never ever wack because we stand strong
Now if you say my style is wack that's where you're dead wrong
I slayed that body in El Segundo then push it along
You'd be a fool to reply that Phife is not the man
'Cause you know and I know that you know who I am
A special shout of peace goes out to all my pals, you see
And a middle finger goes for all you punk MCs
'Cause I love it when you wack MCs despise me
They get vexed, I roll next, can't none contest me
I'm just a fly MC who's five foot three and very brave
On top remaining, no home training 'cause I'd misbehave
I come correct in full effect, have all my hoes in check
And before I get the butt the jim must be erect

You see, my aura's positive, I don't promote no junk
See, I'm far from a bully and I ain't a punk
Extremity in rhythm, yeah, that's what you heard
So just clean out your ears and just check the word

[Chorus 2x]
Check the rhyme, y'all [6x]
Check it out [2x]

[Phife] Back in days on the boulevard of Linden
We used to kick routines and the presence was fittin
It was I, the Phifer,
          [Q-Tip] and me, the Abstract
The rhymes were so rumpin that the brothers rode the 'zack
[Phife] Aiyo, Tip, do you recall when we used to rock
Those fly routines on your cousin's block?
[Q-Tip] Um, let me see.... Damn, I can't remember
I receive the message and you will play the sender
[Phife] You on point, Tip?
                    [Q-Tip] All the time, Phife
[Phife] You on point, Tip?
                    [Q-Tip] Yeah, all the time, Phife
[Phife] You on point Tip?
                    [Q-Tip] Yo, all the time, Phife
[Phife] So play the resurrector and give the dead some life

[Q-Tip]
Okay, if knowledge is the key then just show me the lock
Got the scrawny legs but I move just like Lou Brock
With speed. I'm agile, plus I'm worth your while
One hundred percent intelligent black child
My optic presentation sizzles the retina
How far must you go to gain respect? Ummm
Well, it's kind of simple, just remain your own
Or you'll be crazy sad and alone
Industry rule number four thousand and eighty:

Record company people are shady
So, kids, watch your back 'cause I think they smoke crack
I don't doubt it. Look at how they act
Off to better things like a hip-hop forum
Pass me the rock and I'll score 'em with decorum and
Proper. What you say, Hammer? Proper
Rap is not pop, if you call it that then stop

NC, y'all, check the rhyme, y'all
SC, y'all, check it out, y'all
Virginia, check the rhyme, y'all
Check it out, check it out
In London, check the rhyme, y'all

AWARD TOUR
We on Award Tour with Muhammad, my man
Goin each and every place with the mic in their hand
New York, NJ, NC, VA
We on Award Tour with Muhammad, my man
Goin each and every place with the mic in their hand
Oaktown, LA, San Fran, St. John

[Q-Tip]
People, give your ears so I be sublime
It's enjoyable to know you and the concubines
Niggas, take off your coats, ladies, act like gems
Sit down Indian style as we recite these hymns
See, lyrically I'm Mario Andretti on the mo-mo
Ludicrously speedy or infectious with the slo-mo
Heard me in the '80s, JBs on the promo
In my never-endin quest to get the paper on the caper
But now, let me take it to the Queens side
I'm takin it to Brooklyn side
All the residential Questers who invade the air
Hold up a second, son, 'cause we almost there
You can be a black man and lose all your soul

You can be white 'n' blue but don't crap the roll
See, my shit is universal if you got knowledge of dolo
Or of delf for self, see, there's no one else
Who can drop it on the angle, acute at that
So, do dat do dat do do dat dat dat (Come on)
Do dat do dat do do dat dat dat (Okay)
Do dat do dat do do dat dat dat
I'm buggin out but let me get back 'cause I'm wettin niggas
So run and tell the others 'cause we are the brothers
I learned how to build mics in my workshop class
So give me this award and let's not make it the last

We on Award Tour with Muhammad, my man
Goin each and every place with the mic in their hand
Chinatown, Spokane, London, Tokyo
We on Award Tour with Muhammad, my man
Goin each and every place with the mic in their hand
Houston, Delaware, DC, Dallas

[Phife]
Back in '89 I simply slid into place
Buddy, Buddy, Buddy all up in your face
A lot of kids was bustin rhymes but they had no taste
Some said Quest was wack, but now is that the case?
I have a quest to have a mic in my hand
Without that, it's like Kryptonite and Superman
So, Shaheed, come in with the sugar cuts
Phife Dawg's my name but on stage call me Dynomutt
When was the last time you heard the Phifer sloppy?
Lyrics anonymous, you'll never hear me copy
Top notch baby, never comin less
Sky's the limit, you gots to believe up in Quest
Sit back, relax, get up out the path
If not that, here's the dance floor, come move that ass
Nonbelievers, you can check the stats

I roll with Shaheed and the brother Abstract

Niggas know the time when Quest is in the jam

I never let a statue tell me how nice I am

Comin with more hits than the Braves and the Yankees

Livin mad phat like an oversized Bambi

The wackest crews try to dis, it makes me laugh

When my track record's longer than a DC-20 aircraft

So next time that you think you want somethin here

Make somethin different, take that garbage to St. Elsewhere

We on Award Tour with Muhammad, my man

Goin each and every place with the mic in their hand

SC, Maryland, New Orleans, Motown

We on Award Tour with Muhammad, my man

Goin each and every place with the mic in their hand

Chinatown, Spokane, London, Tokyo

We on Award Tour with Muhammad, my man

Goin each and every place with the mic in their hand

Houston, Delaware, DC, Dallas

We on Award Tour with Muhammad, my man

Goin each and every place with the mic in their hand

New York, NJ, NC, VA

ULTRAMAGNETIC MCS

Ultramagnetic MCs was an idiosyncratic Bronx-based trio consisting of DJ Moe Love and the rappers Ced-Gee and Kool Keith. There is something deliberately futuristic about their debut album, *Critical Beatdown* (1988), which is forward looking not only in its critique of "the simple back and forth, the same old rhythm / That a baby can pick up" (a jab at Run-DMC), but also in the use of pseudoscientific terminology: "Usin frequencies and data, I am approximate / Leaving revolutions turning, emerging chemistry / With the precise implications." Ced-Gee's lines in "Ego Trippin" point toward both exactness and approximation—an incoherent message, to be sure, but then it is not so much the message as the energy with which it is delivered that is the point of Ultramagnetic.

The battle rhymes of Ced-Gee's partner, Kool Keith, come at a staccato pace from a sadistic place. Although the "you" constantly being addressed is ostensibly another rapper, it is we—the listeners—who are attacked. On "Ego Trippin" we are "burned / By the flame of the lyrics which cooks the human brain." Listening to Keith's manic verses can be a masochistic experience.

As a solo artist, Keith developed this line of intrusive metaphor into something even more substantial, both by developing various personae— the sleazy medicine man of *Dr. Octagonecologyst* (1996); the science-fiction pompadoured rockabilly character of *Black Elvis / Lost in Space* (1999)— and by taking sexual tropes common in rap and pushing them past the parodic breaking point, as in *Sex Style* (1997), an album of Sadean excess that, for better or worse, belongs in rap's pornographic pantheon.

EGO TRIPPIN

Party peoples, in the place to be. Just for you, it's the Ultramagnetic MCs!

[Kool Keith] Say what, Peter Piper?

[Ced-Gee] To hell with childish rhymes!

[Kool Keith] 'Cause this jam is just movin,

[Ced-Gee] the crowd is steady groovin

[Kool Keith] To a supersonic pace

[Ced-Gee] with highs and stupid bass

[Kool Keith] With some pep

[Ced-Gee] in the step

[Both] 'Cause the beat is so funky the pace is well kept

'Cause we're . . .

"Ultra . . ." (magnetic, magnetic)

"MCs, Ultra . . ." (magnetic, magnetic)

"MCs, Ultra . . ." (magnetic, magnetic) "MCs"

Kool Keith!

[Kool Keith]

They use the simple back and forth, the same old rhythm
That a baby can pick up and join right with them
But their rhymes are pathetic, they think they copasetic
Using nursery terms, at least not poetic
On a educated base, intelligent, wise
As the record just turn, you learn, plus burned
By the flame of the lyrics which cooks the human brain
Providing overheating knowledge by means causing pain
Make a migraine, hated yourself, start to melt
While the Technics spin, the wax is on the belt
Motivating clockwise the more you realize
Moe Love's moving steady by most with Eveready
Like a battery, charged, I'm worth the alkaline
Yes, the mystery to solve, so seek and define
These words I've given, extreme and now driven
With a Datsun, a Maxima to glide
Yes, the wizard, Kool Keith and I'm sportin my ride
'Cause we're . . .

"Ultra . . ." (magnetic, magnetic)
"MCs, Ultra . . ." (magnetic, magnetic)
"MCs, Ultra . . ." (magnetic, magnetic) "MCs"

Ced-Gee!

[Ced-Gee]

Usin frequencies and data, I am approximate
Leaving revolutions turning, emerging chemistry
With the precise implications, achieved adversively
Explorating, demonstrating, ruling, dominating
Igniting, causing friction with nuclear alarms
Separates competing biters from me, the scientist
As I execute lyricists known as predators
When by strippin high potents and makin penicillin
I will surely sort out and stomp every pest

Oh, the rampaging paramedic, quoted is my title

To inform other worlds of such a hellacaust

Quick serve as a purpose, preparing first aid

With medical utensils, the wizard Ced-Gee

Is advanced with elevation, astonishing with rhythm

'Cause we're . . .

"Ultra . . ." (magnetic, magnetic)

"MCs, Ultra . . ." (magnetic, magnetic)

"MCs, Ultra . . ." (magnetic, magnetic) "MCs"

CRITICAL BEATDOWN

[Kool Keith]

Well, I'm the equalizer, known to be graphic

I clear static, breakin up traffic

Move, while I enter the groove

I'm on top and happy to prove

To wack MCs who claim to be better than

No way, I'm frankly more clever than

All of you, each and every one, my son

Pay close attention

I'll take your brain to another dimension

Hold it, mold it, shape it

You got a knife? Yes, I wanna scrape it

Up and down, sideways, anyway I can

Be rude to you

But I'll rap and be crude to you

And eat up, toy ducks I beat up

I am the oven, your brains I wanna heat up

Mega, supersonic degrees

I come around, roastin MCs

With fire, to burn the toy liar

Raw meat, turn the flame higher

Cook it, like a fish I'll hook it

For any beat, it's time that I took it

Right, correctly to the top

With the rhythm and add your head bop

I'm hype for the critical beatdown!

[Ced-Gee]

I'm attacking them, my job is stacking them

For every rapper, must I be smacking them

Once or twice in the face

With rough beats, producin the bass

That blow out, cause power to go out

Inner spark, I'm ready to blow out

Like this, altitude level

Reachin forth, stompin every devil

In sight, you might just wanna bite

My allusions, mental confusions

You're a mark, skulls I've been abusin

Losin, any rapper who follow me

Your girl loves me, now she wanna swallow me

Back up, move on to the rear

When I'm on the stage should be clear

Speakin, goin ear to ear

Places far, ducks would appear

For the countdown, so you wait to rhyme

And twist, stuttering, uttering

Parkay, margarine, everything butter and

Another thing, you shoulda been a Muppet

A toy boy, a fake string puppet

I'm takin titles and punks better up it

To me, Ced-Gee on the mic, and I'm hype

For the critical beatdown!

[Kool Keith]

Here's the K, combined the double-O

Swing in the L, I'm ready to go

As Keith, Rap General Chief Executive

Plus exquisitive

Mandatory, capital statements

I am the teacher, preaching what makes sense

Class, you wasn't able to pass

For any germ or lice who come last

I'm boric, high computing acid

Get off the mic and won't you please pass it

To me, for a one-two check

Give me a pound and lots of respect

No hands, you're disappointing my fans

You on reverb and talking through cans

Hello—how are you doing?

I come to wreck and parties I'll ruin

With rhymes, pumpin out smoke

Diesel advances makin them choke

And cough up, the hard-headed I'll soften

Spongee, then after that drink a dungee

Roll the sess, the buddha with the ganji

Puff up, while I make tough stuff up

I'm Kool Keith, cold rippin MCs

I'm hype—for the critical beatdown!

X-CLAN

Although they were not as prolific as their reputation might suggest, the X-Clan marks a rigorous extension of the Afrocentric direction that began in late 1980s hip-hop. They might even be said to epitomize rap's attempt to grow in racial self-understanding and to integrate larger self-histories into the mix. The group's two rappers, Brother J and the late Professor X, were attuned to contemporary problems. But they tackled such matters not by trying to paint pictures of the present so much as by insisting that their listeners go "back to Africa."

The journey implicit in their songs comes through even in the titles of their albums *To the East, Blackwards* (1990) and *Xodus* (1992). The journey was less geographical than temporal, however, as the group's lyrics developed the notion of Africa as the birthplace of humanity through imagery that recalls a distant past now suddenly relevant:

Living off the earth, eatin herbs and fruits

The children await me by the mountain and the river

And gather 'round the fire for the scrolls that I deliver

And speak of a house that's from the sand to the sky

The language akin to a religious text underscored the serious mien of the group. To a degree even greater than their more prolific political contemporaries, Public Enemy, the X-Clan referred to religious ideology in their lyrics. They are probably the most intense and concentrated, genuinely Afrocentric group of rappers of their era.

GRAND VERBALIZER

Grand Verbalizer, what time is it? [3x]

[Brother J]
African, very African
Come and step in Brother's temple, see what's happenin
Then taste the bass flow, comin from a zero
Tell me what a sissy know! Funkin lesson is a new flow
Stalkin, walkin in my big black boots
Living off the earth, eatin herbs and fruits
The children await me by the mountain and the river
And gather 'round the fire for the scrolls that I deliver
And speak of a house that's from the sand to the sky
And devils ever doubtin, want to measure how high
Your logic reveals you, your mind can't catch it
Dimensions of a God go far beyond brackets
Come into my oven, devils, come and you burn
I can always beat a vulture with the strength in black word
You're pissin me off because you swear you're higher level
Back to your cave, get yourself together

Chilly and Magilla, chocolate and vanilla

How can polar bears swing on vines with the gorillas? Please

Check your reasoning 'cause there's something amiss

My home is the void, you drown in abyss

I teach a funk code and don't preach a rap rhyme

Harambe to the sun as the mortals ask time

[Chorus]

(Grand Verbalizer, what time is it?)

The funkin lesson comes, the sundial speaks

(Grand Verbalizer, what time is it?)

The building of the strong or the lessons of the meek

(Grand Verbalizer, what time is it?)

My science is deep, my blackness is deep

[Brother J]

(HOW DEEP?) Deep, deeper than Atlantis

Deeper than the seafloor traveled by the mantis

You copycats'll never know

With you the funk'll never flow, but that's another blow

Make your move, beef apprentice, I never step

I'm a tribal move your master hasn't figured yet

Bring your weapons to my sword and shield

What's the higher level if your shit ain't real?

My mystic magic, whatcha gonna do?

Think before you step before the rebel, silly mortal you!

I tried to warn you but your mind won't catch it

You're just cookies in my oven

If I want to burn a batch, you just burn!

[Professor X]

VAINGLORIOUS! THIS IS PROTECTED BY THE RED, THE BLACK, AND THE
    GREEN WITH A KEY. SISSSSSY!

[Brother J]

Like this, like that, and like that, like this

How dark is the world, how strong is a fist?

Originals come from the sand and the sword

To the concrete, fightin wars in the street

The Day of Outrage, history, another page

You lack the word of this, but now there is a Brother J

The Prince of Warriors, leadin masses

Stomp a liverlip, punks playin asses

The damn sissies always stalk for the glory

Sissy bomb is comin, but that's another story

So many people forgot where they came

Disrespect religion, but their living is lame

Blackwatch, how you livin? (ZOOM!) Flow in the Nile (ZOOM!)

Teach the many mortals, the times of a sundial

To the East, teachin gods to be

What it was, what it is, and again shall be

What's my mind state if my state ain't black?

But Moses, Malcolm, and Huey are back

And the voice to a many goin verb to verb

Sit back and take heed, brother, YOU MUST LEARN!

Swimmin in the books and the books ain't givin

The scales of a black man, ways in the livin

[Chorus]

[Brother J]

Tick tock tick, we go sun to moon

Verbalizer speaks, it's a quarter to doom

Self-destruction is not a key function

Never mind the leaders 'cause the people keep frontin

When will they realize? The body needs head

It's more than what's said when a leader lies dead

Come into the darkness, past is light

Death meaning life as the pharaohs take flight

Too much degrees for a silly pale thief

You can't define what's direct from the East

God protect me, he selects me

God makes a path so the world respects me

Zero to nine, grandest creator
I pray for those on both sides of equator
Professor X, when will they learn?
Once life enters doors, death no return, no return

[Professor X]
This is an invitation to the crossroads if you dare, sisssssssy! With a key!

A.D.A.M.

Come diddy-dum! Welcome to this archeological find! At the road, witness me
before the coming of the sun; peeking at you from the Eastern side of
Plutonia. Dressed in armor of Order, to meet destiny with a strong black grip.
Teh-hun-zu, see you in from the zero, take 'em to the three. Stand firm at the
five; here's a star and a shield to support you at the nine!

[Brother J]
It's like A-D-A-M
Prepare your mind, run tell your children
Fire, air, water, let the earth make flesh
Now see from the Father, how funky can you get?
Now my activity is cosmitivity
Immortal is my soul, my God, my reality
I'm not measured by tradition, or any type of 'ligion, huh
Not even cosmic dimensions and such
But many fools, they try to post a duel
Try to post a front but they know it ain't cool, yeah
Boy, my mind goes back to things, just like the cosmic battle
When sword was my rattle
Shield was my bib and sarcophagi my crib
Not measured by my words, but the deeds that I did for God
A logical God, I was created and formed
Verbal shogun, yes, the cosmic storm
Whose scrolls to lyrics to bust
I roll 'em up with the papyrus, funk sealed, in God we trust
I laid it down from circumference to dry space
And now I'm back again, quite lyrical, to kick my bass

Energized by another plane

By logical fanatics, which try to examine my brain

They can't beat me, so they try to eat me

They can't keep me, so they try to freak me

Positive sin, again and again, degrees in a spin

Verbs are lockjaw, your silly mortal g-g-grin

Make you feel you could drown in some godly waters

Take control of your body like the farmer's daughter

And as you beg for control, what's the reason? What's the reason?

Yo, I am son of the Chaos so my brothers call me Cosmic

Teh-hun-zu for tribal, Brother J when trying to rock it

Six-foot black boot god in the suit of the warrior

So now I'm taller 'n ya, check'n me out

A-D-A-M

Prepare your mind, run, tell your children

Fire, air, water, let the Earth make flesh

Now see from the Father, now how funky can you

Get get get get get down, the rhythm must come to such

When it's time to bust and all the mortals lay crushed

Dark Son will get darker

'Cause I existed in the valley of the Father

I got whooped by my mate

'Cause the fruit had a taste

Of the curse that served as a marker

Now here we go, to deal with all the little "-isms"

To define me in simple "-ologies"? Hell no!

On with the flow, here we go, sickamo'

Let us slip on back into the blackwards row

Niggas didn't catch it anyway

They pat me on the back, talkin 'bout, "Yeah, J"

Well yeah, right

East I flow, East I go

Cover both your eyes, and what do you know?

What do you see? How does it be?

Is it circumference, or what's up, G?

It's like that on the break, with a verbal milkshake
And a godly vainglorious break

[Professor X]
You shall be moved, logical one! After a clear pouncing with energy from the
sun. At my beckoning—you and your landmark built without the zero pride
shall crumble, stumble my way to might to a pretender—your time has come!

[Brother J]
I once walked the heavens with Gabriel
Walked through the desert with Israel
Traveled onto Mecca with Ishmael
Crucified, resurrected—now ask how I feel
A-D that I AM, that I AM
From Father flesh to Father Solomon
From the pinky to the thumb 'pon my hand
Bring a other Caddy and a tribal j-j-j-j-jam
But yet I'm judged, leather prophet and all that
Still a pimp with a crown and a Yankee hat
And yet they ask me, "Brother, what's the time?
Is it African drum with some space-age rhymes, man?"
Yo, not at all, I say it's sexual, infectual, delectable
I'm not a masturbating intellectual
And couldn't read it from a book because that bores you all
So come to Umoja, Kujichagulia
Ujima, Ujamaa, and purpose stands for Nia
Kuumba, Imani, daughter named Simani
Came to the planet, Father Afer left his body
Leave the boy in the coffin within
Raise your head, let's the A to the D to the A to the M
This is the message from the cosmic storm
Let the doubters and the judges, disbelievers be warned!

[Professor X]
With a shield of David on the grill and the has-been proudly adorned with the
color pink. Bring on your Gs, your Qs, your Rs, and your Alphas. It is time—
Shalom! And ya don't stop—Sissssyyyyyyy!!!

1993-1999

Rap Goes Mainstream

Hip-hop in the 1990s was marked by tragedy: the slayings of two of rap's biggest stars, Tupac Shakur (2Pac) and Christopher Wallace (the Notorious B.I.G.). In September 1996, Shakur was killed in a drive-by shooting on the Las Vegas strip. Six months later, in March 1997, Wallace was killed in a drive-by shooting on Wilshire Boulevard in Los Angeles. These two acts of violence were fueled by an atmosphere that pitted East Coast against West Coast in a battle about style and substance. The West Coast's gangsta aesthetic clashed with the emerging "mo' money, mo' problems" ethos of East Coast flash. Some have dubbed the mid-1990s the Bling Era for its displays of conspicuous consumption and material excess. It is the era of champagne and shiny suits, of diamond chains and expensive cars. At the same time, it is the era that introduced some of rap's best poets and some of the most psychologically compelling, formally sophisticated lyrics in hip-hop history. In the 1990s hip-hop went mainstream, shaping American culture even as hip-hop was still shaping itself.

If the mid- to late 1980s marked the moment rap codified its formal elements and made its initial impression on the public at large, then the 1990s signaled rap's coming of age. Rap began the decade as a decidedly East Coast—even specifically New York—phenomenon and would end it as a national, and even an international, art. It began the decade as a niche genre, akin in audience share to bluegrass or Dixieland jazz in earlier eras, and would end the decade as far and away the dominant form of popular music, with a near hegemonic hold on the *Billboard* charts. It began the decade as an outsider idiom, with all the freedom and all the limitation that such status entails, and would end the decade with a significant share of its mainstream releases under the sway of corporate interests. Rap became big business, and, as a result, much of the music came to follow a new set of imperatives. Yes, some measure of the profit motive had always been present in rap—hence the "gotta get mine" perspective—but when the lust for funds shifted from the artist to the corporation, a serious transformation began to show in the music.

The risks that corporatized hip-hop presented were ones of homogenization and stagnation. With rap viewed as a commodity first, whatever else it might be, it became necessary to brand it to fit a particular image. That image was most often subsumed by extremes—the gangsta aesthetic, violence, sexual bravado. All of these have been part of rap since the beginning, but never were they the *only* images in hip-hop, nor were they ever so widely disseminated. "We made [hip-hop] into a stereotype when it's not," Common told CNN, looking back on the 1990s from the vantage point of 2007. "You have to remember that hip-hop had De La Soul. It had the Pharcyde. It had A Tribe Called Quest. It had Souls of Mischief, Kwamé, NWA, Compton's Most Wanted, the Geto Boys, Rakim, Slick Rick—it was never one thing. The stereotype came about when the corporations really started taking the artists who were producing one type of sound and said, 'Okay, this is what we're going to endorse.' But throughout the years, it's been much more than that."[1]

Any discussion of rap in the 1990s begins with 2Pac and Biggie. Shakur started as a backup dancer and sometime rapper with Digital Underground, a group known for its psychedelic, funk-inflected jams. His guest verse on the group's "Same Song" gave a glimpse of the prodigious talent still waiting to be expressed. In only eight bars, he delivers a playful but potent verse filled with sonic patterns of rhyme and assonance: "Now I clown around when I hang around with the Underground/Girls used to frown, say I'm down, when I come around." Tupac would soon refashion himself as 2Pac, crafting a "T.H.U.G. L.I.F.E." image that drew from the West Coast style of gangsta rap made famous by artists like Ice-T and NWA. Also transcending the genre, he penned rhymes about teen pregnancy, his mother's drug addiction, and life in poverty. In death, 2Pac became something that no one could become in life: an icon, a martyr, and a hip-hop existentialist hero. His reflections on his own mortality abound in lyrics such as "If I Die 2Nite" and "Death Around the Corner."

"I ain't never seen nobody that was just ghettofied and at the same time articulate and just able to maneuver them words and vocabulary and just expand to where you just be like, 'Damn!'" recalls frequent T.H.U.G. L.I.F.E. collaborator Big Syke, describing 2Pac's seeming contradictions. "See, Black Panthers was built on education. And streets are built on wildness. So when you mix them two together, oh, it's gunpowder. So that's what he was, he was an educated nut! You feel me?"[2] There wasn't an immediate alchemical reaction, however, in the melding of Pac's thoughtfulness and thuggishness; it took time for his multifaceted personality to express itself on record.

With more albums released posthumously than many artists release in their careers, 2Pac's influence on hip-hop and the broader culture remains active. The way his flow echoed both a country preacher and a city pimp, the way he endowed even simple rhymes like "black queen" and "crack fiend" with power and meaning, the way he stretched syllables as if an art unto itself—as on "California Love," when he says "Soon as I step on the sceeeene . . ."—the way he did all of these things would come to influence the lyrical style and posture of many MCs to follow. As much as his talents, his flaws too would come to stand for hip-hop's own conflicted identity. "Tupac keeps you searching, even now, for the line between how one rolls through life and how one rocks the microphone," writes Danyel Smith, former editor of *Vibe*. "Crazy motherfucker. Coward. Sucker. Sexist. Sex symbol. Superman. Provocateur. Hero."[3] Tupac is all that and then some.

And then there is Biggie. The Notorious B.I.G.'s career would usher in a host of pivotal developments in the music, many of which went on to shape rap today. In the early 1990s, Christopher Wallace left a life of petty crime and small-time drug dealing at the age of twenty for a new career in the rap game after meeting hip-hop impresario Sean "Puffy" Combs, who was soon to launch his record label, Bad Boy Entertainment. Biggie brought with him the slang, swagger, and street storytelling that went with his outlaw persona. His agile and infectious delivery, his booming but somehow still vulnerable voice, his menacing microphone presence always leavened by humor honed in street-corner battles and ciphers, would find an unlikely match in Puff Daddy's pop-oriented and hook-driven production. Few other rappers could invest a guttural "Uhh" with so much flavor. Few could deliver a hot line simply by spelling out their name: "B-I-G-P-O-P-P-A, no info for the DEA."

Biggie's debut album, *Ready to Die* (1994), included danceable pop tunes, such as "Big Poppa" and "One More Chance," laced with familiar R&B samples; alongside these were gritty stories of crime and self-reflective expressions of nihilism and despair. With only two albums recorded in his lifetime, Biggie would nonetheless have a major impact on hip-hop, ushering in the blend of rap and R&B that would come to dominate the music a few years later while also encouraging the development of lyrical craftsmanship among a generation of MCs to follow. "He had perhaps the greatest emotional range and straight-up literary skill of any rapper before or after him," writes Anthony DeCurtis. "He could seamlessly move from fury to vulnerability to sensuality to poignancy within a few lines."[4]

Perhaps the most dramatic development in rap during the 1990s was its emergence as a popular cultural form—not simply in music, but in style and image. Hip-hop expanded its audience from the metropolises on the East and West coasts to suburban outposts throughout the nation. Aided by the rise of music videos, hip-hop's version of urban cool would help shape youth fashion, slang, and, above all, musical tastes. With the growing influence of music videos, rap itself began to change. "Just as hip-hop reinvented the role of sampling, music videos altered hip-hop," observes pioneering hip-hop critic Nelson George. "Once an underground music based on beats and rhymes, in the '90s hip-hop became the most image-driven part of pop music."[5] Rap reached its apex of excess with MC Hammer's 1991 "Too Legit to Quit" video, a nine-minute mini-movie with a reported production budget of between $2 million and $3 million.

Rap's pop identity brought with it certain stylistic consequences. As with other genres of popular music before it, crossover rap settled into a recognizable form of hook/verse/hook/verse/hook/verse/hook. It put more emphasis on slick production and often involved singing, especially on the hook. Artists like Biggie, along with Diddy, ushered in the Bling Era. Jewels, cars, champagne, and women became the trappings—the last of these the most troubling—of hip-hop "success." The governing visual aesthetic of this era belonged to Hype Williams, a painter turned director whose penchant for fish-eye lenses, bold color palettes, cameos by other artists, and beautiful "video vixens" helped define not only rap's image but its musical sensibilities (to say nothing of its sexual and ethical sensibilities). All-video stations like the Box and finally MTV and BET abetted this transformation by playing the increasingly lavish videos in heavy rotation, saturating the consciousness of a new generation of rap listeners that stretched far beyond the music's original demographic.

This commercial expansion and the rise of video culture spawned a new phenomenon in hip-hop: the rap superstar. At the beginning of the decade, the biggest figures in rap were artists like LL Cool J, Run-DMC, and Public Enemy—respected artists who on their own could sell out a club or perhaps a midsized ballroom. By the end of the decade, artists like Eminem and Jay-Z were internationally known public figures selling out Madison Square Garden and other arenas and stadiums around the globe. The very nature of celebrity in rap had shifted.

Hip-hop's new white suburban audience had a great deal to do with the shift. A white teenager in Topeka, Kansas, or Eugene, Oregon, was for the first time constantly exposed to the energy and attitude, the swagger and style of rap without setting foot in New York or L.A. Judging by album sales, the particular variety of music that seemed to appeal most to this group was the brash, loud, and bombastic style of gangsta rap. Listening to Ice Cube or Snoop Dogg often brought with it not just entertainment but identity. "At its best," writes Jason Tanz in *Other People's Property: A Shadow History of Hip-Hop in White America,* "the desire of white teenagers to identify themselves with the African American struggle represents an urge to connect and to overcome the artificial separation of our past. At its worst, it is a fantasy that equates garden-variety suburban alienation with the struggle of ghetto life, and that defines the black experience by the cartoonish swagger of paid entertainers."[6] Rap's expanding audience carried with it much of the baggage that always accompanies cross-racial artistic exchange in America—in this case, anxieties about the "corruption of youth" on one side, fears of banalization and cooption on the other.

The only way to understand the multiplatinum success of such artists as NWA, Dr. Dre, Snoop Dogg, and others is in terms of a cross-racial audience dominated by young men. As a result, many of the other hip-hop voices were being excluded from major-label deals. With the growing influence of record labels and media conglomerates such as Clear Channel and Radio One, hip-hop became branded—paradoxically and profitably—as both mainstream and taboo. Rap record labels like Suge Knight's notorious Death Row Records were among the corporate beneficiaries of rap's newfound popularity. Between 1992 and 1996 alone, Death Row earned an estimated $125 million.[7]

Rap's expansion in the 1990s was not all about the money. One of the most significant developments of the decade was the broadening of rap's voices in spite of the constricting influence of commercial radio. Groups like the Fugees and the Roots extended an alternative hip-hop tradition initiated near the end of the 1980s with the likes of the Native Tongues collective of De La Soul, A Tribe Called Quest, and the Jungle Brothers. The Wu-Tang Clan, with its unconventional blend of gritty urban tales and Eastern mysticism, fashioned a new model for the rap supergroup. They recorded albums both as a collective and as individual solo artists, building a distinct aesthetic and philosophy. These groups set forth an alternative set of hip-hop values and a markedly different aesthetic from the artists in hip-hop's commercial mainstream—yet they were commercially successful and fully ensconced in many of the main streams through which cash and attention flowed. It could have been a precarious position, but it didn't damage the poetry. While acts like MC Hammer, Vanilla Ice, and Young MC were making platinum-selling albums, groups like Public Enemy, De La Soul, and Mobb Deep went gold at best. That said, their influence on the direction of hip-hop poetics went well beyond that of the commercial heavyweights of the genre.

Two years in particular, 1993 and 1994, marked a kind of second-wave hip-hop golden age. Nineteen-ninety-three saw the release of classic debuts like the Wu-Tang Clan's *Enter the Wu-Tang (36 Chambers)*, Snoop Doggy Dogg's *Doggystyle*, Souls of Mischief's *'93 'til Infinity*, Digable Planets' *Reachin' (A New Refutation of Time and Space)*, the Roots' *Organix*, and Black Moon's *Enter Da Stage*, as well as strong albums like A Tribe Called Quest's *Midnight Marauders*, De La Soul's *Buhlōōne Mind State*, and KRS-One's *Return of the Boom-Bap*. Nineteen-ninety-four saw such trailblazing releases as Nas's *Illmatic*, the Notorious B.I.G.'s *Ready to Die*, Outkast's *Southernplayalisticadillacmuzik*, Common's *Resurrection*, Method Man's *Tical*, and Scarface's *The Diary*. The years that followed would bring important debuts and important albums as well (Mobb Deep's 1995 *The Infamous*, Jay-Z's 1996 debut *Reasonable Doubt*, the Fugees' masterful 1996 album, *The Score*), but for sheer volume of classic hip-hop it is difficult to surpass 1993–94.

With this outpouring of excellence over such a short period of time, it would be easy to overlook any one of these releases. Together they speak to a kind of rap renaissance. Many of these MCs and groups would go on to enjoy long careers. One such group is the aforementioned Wu-Tang Clan. Hailing from Staten Island, the last of New York's five boroughs to gain rap recognition, the Wu consisted of a core group of nine members: RZA, GZA, Method Man, Raekwon, Ghostface Killah, Inspectah Deck, U-God, Masta Killa, and Ol' Dirty Bastard. With the RZA handling most of the production duties and tailoring the beats to the various vocal styles of the group's members, the Wu-Tang Clan built an impressive body of artistic work and a life philosophy to go along with it. "While the '90s saw no shortage of MTV rap stars, the Wu rewrote the rules on mass hip-hop success," explains Chris Norris. "They muscled in weird, edgy, and uncompromisingly hardcore hip-hop right next to the Spice Girls without one stupendously obvious pop loop. They blended ghetto street buzz with Madison Avenue pitchmanship, packaged densely intricate rhymes with love-line 900-numbers, wore Mecca instead of Versace. They recast the rap group as street gang, Mafia family, ninja corps, artistic collective, and multinational business conglomerate."[8] From their easily recognizable emblem to their indelible lyrical styles, the Wu helped define rap for the new era.

Rap's geographic expansion had important stylistic implications as well. Nowhere is this more apparent than in southern rap. The South was nearly invisible on the rap landscape in the 1980s, but by the late 1990s it would become arguably the dominant rap region, defying East Coast–West Coast hegemony. At the end of the decade, songs by southern MCs accounted for between 30 and 40 percent of hit singles on the hip-hop charts. By the early 2000s, that number was close to 60 percent.[9] The Dirty South, as it is often known because of its dank beats and raw rhymes, was supreme.

Yet defining rap from the South is challenging because it embodies such a diversity of style and place. "The South, truth be told, is full of contradictions, conundrums, and tautologies," writes Tony Green. "At once expansive and insular, cosmopolitan and not-around-here reactionary, the South offers infinite interpretations. It stands to reason that southern hip-hop would reflect all of that."[10] Rap's various southern scenes—from Atlanta to New Orleans, Houston to Miami—fashioned distinct sounds and linguistic innovations.

Atlanta's Outkast and Goodie Mob introduced southern slang, gutbucket soul, and rapid-fire flows with their debut albums *Southernplayalisticadillacmusik* and *Soul Food,* respectively. On "Dirty South," which featured members of both groups, you could hear Big Boi from Outkast recalling how he "wanted to live the life of Cadillacs, Impalas, and Regals," certainly not the cars rappers were dreaming about north of the Mason-Dixon line. You could hear them name-checking East Point Atlanta, Piedmont Park, and even public housing projects like Perry Homes and Herndon Homes. This was rap on the local level with a global audience.

In Houston it was the Geto Boys, DJ Screw, and later UGK (from nearby Port Arthur) delivering gritty street tales with a blues influence. In New Orleans, it was Master P's No Limit Records and Baby's Cash Money label building their own rap empires. In Miami, it was still Luke Campbell's Miami Bass sound along with emerging artists like Trick Daddy and Trina delivering songs for the clubs. Meanwhile, the Midwest was undergoing its own emergence. In Cleveland, Bone Thugs-N-Harmony developed their brand of rapid-fire rap harmonies. In Chicago, Common (formerly Common Sense) helped bring much-deserved exposure to that city's vital underground scene.

By the end of the decade, hip-hop had proved its staying power such that Nelson George could confidently assert that "while there are signs of weakness—its overwhelming dependence on major corporations for funding, its occasionally gleeful celebration of anti-social tendencies—hip-hop has outlived all its detractors and even surprised most ardent early supporters by always changing, and with each change, expanding its audience."[11] The 1990s now stand as perhaps the most important decade in hip-hop for the ways it made use of the past and predicted the future.

ARRESTED DEVELOPMENT

Arrested Development, founded in the late '80s by rapper Speech and DJ Headliner, crafted progressive Afrocentric lyrics set to funk- and soul-inflected rhythms. The group's debut album, *3 Years, 5 Months & 2 Days in the Life of . . .* (1992), drew its title from the time it took for them to secure a record contract. Part of the difficulty, no doubt, was convincing record labels that a rap group from outside of New York and Los Angeles—one from the South, no less—could sell records.

Their first album went quadruple platinum, producing melodically, spiritually, and narratively rich singles like the top ten hit "Tennessee," "People Everyday" (a reconception of Sly & the Family Stone's "Everyday People"), and "Mr. Wendal." They won Grammys for best rap album and best new artist in 1993, and were named *Rolling Stone*'s band of the year.

Speech's flow is melodic, coming close at times to singing. "I just wanted to come up with something unique, and I had just started to discover rhyming and putting it into more of a melodic style," he recalls. "I had never heard it in hip-hop, really, especially for the whole song. Afrika Bambaataa and the Soul Sonic Force would put melody in rhyme, but it would just be for one line of the rhyme. And for me, I saw a whole new opportunity to add more emotion to what I was saying when I started to put more melody to it, and so 'Tennessee' was one of the first songs that I did that."[12]

TENNESSEE

Lord, I've really been real stressed
Down and out, losing ground
Although I am black and proud
Problems got me pessimistic
Brothers and sisters keep messin up

Why does it have to be so damn tough?

I don't know where I can go

To let these ghosts out of my skull

My Grandma passed, my brother's gone

I never at once felt so alone

I know you're supposed to be my steering wheel

Not just my spare tire (Home)

But, Lord, I ask you (Home)

To be my guiding force and truth (Home)

For some strange reason it had to be (Home)

He guided me to Tennessee (Home)

[Chorus 2x]

Take me to another place

Take me to another land

Make me forget all that hurts me

Let me understand your plan

Lord, it's obvious we got a relationship

Talkin to each other every night and day

Although you're superior over me

We talk to each other in a friendship way

Then outta nowhere you tell me to break

Out of the country and into more country

Past Dyesburg into Ripley

Where the ghost of childhood haunts me

Walk the roads my forefathers walked

Climbed the trees my forefathers hung from

Ask those trees for all their wisdom

They tell me my ears are so young (Home)

Go back to from whence you came (Home)

My family tree, my family name (Home)

For some strange reason it had to be (Home)

He guided me to Tennessee (Home)

[Chorus 2x]

Eshe, she went down to Holly Springs. Rasa Don and Baba, they went down to Peach Tree. Headliner, I challenge you to a game of horseshoes. A game of horseshoes!

Now I see the importance of history
Why my people be in the mess that they be
Many journeys to freedom made in vain
By brothers on the corner playin ghetto games
I ask you, Lord, why you enlightened me
Without the enlightenment of all my folks
He said 'cause I set myself on a quest
For truth and he was there to quench my thirst
But I am still thirsty . . .
The Lord allowed me to drink some more
He said what I am searchin for
Are the answers to all which are in front of me
The ultimate truth started to get blurry
For some strange reason it had to be
It was all a dream about Tennessee

[Chorus]

BAHAMADIA

Bahamadia is a trailblazer for women in underground hip-hop. She began her career as a DJ before picking up the mic full time. She is a skilled lyricist with a decidedly laid-back delivery, and her intricate wordplay testifies to the intensity of her craft. Her skills are in evidence on her debut album, *Kollage* (1996), as well as on her numerous guest verses on songs by such artists as the Roots and Talib Kweli.

Bahamadia rose to prominence in underground hip-hop as the protégée of Gang Starr's Guru. Throughout the 1990s she lent her smooth-flowing raps to a variety of projects, including songs by electronica and acid jazz artists. Bahamadia is often associated with "conscious" hip-hop, a term that she wishes to complicate. "Well, we're all conscious of something," she says. "We're conscious of whatever we perceive. There are many people out there who are conscious of whatever type of reality they come in contact with. I'm conscious of being righteous, and that's just who I am, but I'm from the 'hood too. And telling my story through hip-hop is what I do, and that can change at any time, because I'm still growing and still learning."[13]

SPONTANEITY

Straight outta the metro, rhythm central

I'm innovative at the intro 'cause I go

Slow mo' but never slow poke

But never no joke, dope but never no toke

Spits the riddles like phlegm

Loose with my lyrics like a double-jointed limb

Twist and I bend, formin episodes past freak modes

The monstrous bass beneath my pace be like Morse code

Slash-beep, slash-beep scanners

Zero in to the systems in your Jeeps

I'm out there with Kool Keith and Ced-Gee

And De La, inventors of my third seeing eye

With futuristic vision I'm not among

Loony nut cakes upon no mission, I gets in where I fit in

'Cause life's too short, so you could

All label me weirdo but, yo, I know . . . it's talent

[Chorus]

Mad explosive spontaneity [8x]

At present I speak the new, beginning

When every other trend fell short, so who'll be

The shareholder of my kinda thoughts besides

The studious 'cause the gluteus maxi-

Mus lack ability . . .

To scoop all capabilities of spontaneity within

Depicted, kicked it true

Vibes past jazz but collaborated with the cool
Known flows but unfamiliar grooves
That soothe individuals' moods
Like soul food for thought . . .

[Chorus]

Rip here be dizz like everybody's on it
'Cause eternal verbal expansion keeps enhancing
Brainchild's ability to like
Surpass the swarm of booty ass. No grass roots-
Having ass MCs with lukewarm degrees
Trying to get hot like sun rays
But save your jazz for Sun Ra, ya na wanna spar
Our skills fill up the outer limits like Mars
And you's a little star, I jacked your twinkle
When I excelled well like Tinkerbelle
Of the higher level and
Hype cerebral flow takes flight on
Airborne time, I'm a prime candidate
Or specimen in your Walkman
As you're listenin I make things happen
'Cause I'm the cap-a-tain keepin this great . . .

[Chorus]

BIG L

Big L is part of the fated fraternity of talented MCs who died too young. He was shot and killed in 1999 at the age of twenty-four. At the time of his death he had released only one album, 1995's *Lifestylez ov da Poor & Dangerous,* but he had already established his reputation as a gifted lyricist who favored street tales drawn from his Harlem upbringing. His posthumously released second album, 2000's *The Big Picture*, burnished this reputation with a series of classic tracks including "Ebonics," "'98 Freestyle," "Flamboyant," and "Platinum Plus."

Big L was adept at both battle raps and more conceptually driven lyrics. "Ebonics (Criminal Slang)," for instance, perhaps his best-known song, is built upon the concept of a slang dictionary, explaining terms like "kicks" and "telly" to the uninitiated. "Platinum Plus" captures his distinctive flow—his use of idiosyncratic pauses in the midst of phrases and his doubling and tripling up of rhyme sounds. Big L's influence stretches well beyond what one might expect from such a modest body of work; echoes of his style are audible in the flows of such well-known artists as Jay-Z, Cam'ron, and Ludacris.

EBONICS (CRIMINAL SLANG)

Yo, pay attention . . . and listen real closely how I break this slang shit down.

Check it, my weed smoke is my lye, a ki of coke is a pie
When I'm lifted, I'm high, with new clothes on, I'm fly
Cars is whips and sneakers is kicks
Money is chips, movies is flicks
Also, cribs is homes, jacks is pay phones
Cocaine is nose candy, cigarettes is bones
A radio is a box, a razor blade is a ox
Fat diamonds is rocks and jakes is cops
And if you got robbed, you got stuck, you got shot
You got bucked and if you got double-crossed, you got fucked
Your bankroll is your poke, a choke hold is a yoke
A kite is a note, a con is a okey doke
And if you got punched that mean you got snuffed
To clean is to buff, a bull scare is a strong bluff
I know you like the way I'm freakin it
I talk with slang and I'ma never stop speakin it

[Chorus 2x]
(Speak with criminal slang)
That's just the way that I talk, yo
(Vocabulary spills, I'm ill)

Yo, yo, a burglary is a jook, a wolf's a crook

Mobb Deep already explained the meanin of shook

If you caught a felony, you caught a F

If you got killed, you got left

If you got the dragon, you got bad breath

If you 730, that mean you crazy

Hit me on the hip means page me

Angel dust is sherm, if you got AIDS, you got the germ

If a chick gave you a disease, then you got burned

Max mean to relax, guns and pistols is gats

Condoms is hats, critters is cracks

The food you eat is your grub, a victim's a mark

A sweat box is a small club, your tick is your heart

Your apartment is your pad, your old man is your dad

The studio is the lab and heated is mad

I know you like the way I'm freakin it

I talk with slang and I'ma never stop speakin it

[Chorus 2x]

The iron horse is the train and champagne is bubbly

A deuce is a honey that's ugly

If your girl is fine, she's a dime, a suit is a vine

Jewelry is shine, if you in love, that mean you blind

Genuine is real, a face card is a hundred dollar bill

A very hard, long stare is a grill

If you sneakin to go see a girl, that mean you creepin

Smilin is cheesin, bleedin is leakin

Beggin is bummin, if you nuttin you comin

Takin orders is sunnin, an ounce of coke is a onion

A hotel's a telly, a cell phone's a celly

Jealous is jelly, your food box is your belly

To guerrilla mean to use physical force

You took a L, you took a loss, to show off mean floss, uh

I know you like the way I'm freakin it

I talk with slang and I'ma never stop speakin it

[Chorus 2x]

Yeah, yeah. One love to my big brother Big Lee. Holdin it down. Yeah,
flamboyant for life. Yeah, yeah, flamboyant for life.

BIG PUNISHER

Big Punisher was the first solo Latino rapper to go platinum. He was also yet another member of the hip-hop community to fall victim to an early death, albeit from weight-related health complications rather than violence. At his death in 2000 he reportedly weighed close to seven hundred pounds. As an MC, however, he was light and agile, capable of tongue-twisting feats of lyrical dexterity.

Big Pun was a member of the Terror Squad, a Bronx-based hip-hop collective founded in the early 1990s by Fat Joe. Together, they cultivated a relentless rap style filled with street themes set to instrumentals often designed to appeal to a mainstream audience. Big Pun's solo debut, 1998's *Capital Punishment,* included the club-banger "Still Not a Player." On "Capital Punishment" he trades bars with fellow Terror Squad member Prospect. But it is "Twinz (Deep Cover '98)," his collaboration with Fat Joe, that is most often cited as his masterpiece, with its rapid-fire flow, ample use of assonance, and multilayered rhymes. Their freestyle from three years earlier, included here, captures much of the same spirit.

FROM **CAPITAL PUNISHMENT**

Yo, I've seen child blossom to man, some withered and turned to murderers

Led astray by the liars, death glorifiers observin us

Watching us close, marking our toast, 'cause he the perp, just

Purposely overtaxin the earnings, nervous, burning down the churches

They're scared of us, rather beware than dare to trust

Always in jail, million-dollar bail, left there to rust

Let's call in order, give ourselves a chance to enhance broader

Advance to where minorities are the majority voter

Holdin my own, I'm livin alone in this cold world

My sister just bought a home without a loan—you go, girl!

She's an exception, some people can leap to the impression

See, me myself, I start flippin and fall victim to deep depression

I'm stressin the issue here, so we can gross the fiscal year

Tired of gettin fired and hired as a pistol-eer

There's no longevity living off negativity

Fuck it, I'd rather sell reefer than do pizza delivery

That's how the city be, everybody gettin they hustle on

Judge singin death penalty like it's his favorite fuckin song

Word is bond, takin my life, you know they lovin it

God "F" the government and its fuckin capital punishment

Capital punishment, given by the government

System so organized they get to you and who you runnin with

Can't live alone, watch for the spies and tapped phones

Totin the yayo for life, the rightful heir to the throne

We come from Kings and Queens, people with dreams, Gods and Earths

For what it's worth, we benefit the Earth with infinite worth

First it's turnin tables, open our own labels

Disable the Republicans, then reverse capital punishment

I've seen it all up close, shit out the movies, you'd be buggin

My cousin JuJe, barely a juve', lost it and turned on the oven

He wasn't playin, blew out the flame and started inhalin

Bearin a secret too deep to keep, more discreet, for sharin

Wearin the virus, Acquired Immune Deficiency

Dishin his dick in every thick promiscuous fish in the sea

Listen to me, shit is rough in the ghetto

You bluff, blow your head off, fuck a snuff, we bust lead off

Get off your high horse or die off like an extinction

Boricuans are like Mohicans, the Last of the Po'Ricans

We need some unity, fuck all the Jeeps and jewelry

The maturity keeps me six feet above obscurity

The streets are deadly and everybody's a desperado

I guess the motto, we promise to let you homage in death your motto

Like Zorro, I mark my territory with a symbol

Not with a Z, but a P, 'cause punishment's what I resemble

I lend you this if it expands yours, for you and yours

A real man can't fall, he stands tall

The Man's claws is diggin in my back, I'm tryin to hit him back

Time to counteract, where my niggas at?

'95 FREESTYLE
(feat. Fat Joe)

[Fat Joe]
Power from the streetlights made the place dark

But, yo, they didn't care. They turned it out ...

Uh, you know who this is, South Bronx? Fat Joey Crack representin the realest. I got my man Big Dog Punisher in the house. Yo Punisher, let these niggas know ...

[Big Punisher]
Brothers are rappin like a rack of soldiers, actin like

They crackin boulders when they pack a cap but won't attack a blowfish

Always talkin shit, players that rather balk than pitch

And often counterfeit, Kings of New York on Mr. Walken's dick

You make me sick to my stomach; you don't really want it

Riffin like you sniffin coke to scare me but you barely blunted

You really done it; now you got me mad. Morenos be like

"Papi's bad," makin fakers stop me when I'm drivin back

[Fat Joe]
Many thought it couldn't happen: Joe is never rappin

He was always gettin loot off the crack and fuckin with

Them heavyweights, who had shit sewn in every state

The very sight'll make the average man defecate

Livin the life of stock, bonds, and cars—word bond

I be gone, I'll be worshipped like Nicky Barnes

It's on—you don't want no confrontation

Kill the communication or suffer from multiple lacerations

[Big Punisher]

I keep a Desert Eagle cocked back in my tuxedo

With my top hat, what you funny motherfuckers know about that?

Lookin Doug E. Fresh in my double breast

Like a pimp, eatin shrimp gumbo, bubble bathin

In the jumbo jet, set on auto-pilot

Gonna fly it to Puerto Vallarta, charter a chopper on top of the Hyatt

[Fat Joe]

Business chatter over shrimp and lobster platters

At Jimmy's Cafe, a glass of Perrier

Chick go for celly, booked a room at the Holiday

Inn, so I can get her and a friend

Ménage à trois, livin the life of a star

Overweight, overpaid, pockets bustin out the seams

While you niggas havin limousine dreams

I got you all sized up. Niggas, wise up

Or that meat truck'll be pickin all you guys up

[Big Punisher]

For you hilarious comedians, I'm at the Marriott with deviants

Arrangin chariots to carry us to various

Evening events, eating the best up in Jimmy's Caf'

Extortin wannabes for all they Gs—Fuck it, just gimme half

I make it last with the dough I got, if not

I'll blow your spot. If not, Joey Crack, please load the Glock

Let these niggas learn the hard way

The word to God way, the motherfuckin murder mob way

BONE THUGS-N-HARMONY

Bone Thugs-N-Harmony popularized a style of rapid, melodic flows that blurred the line between rap and song. Coming from Cleveland, they helped initiate a Midwest movement in hip-hop that would see rap's center of gravity shift from the coasts to the center of the country as the 1990s progressed.

It was a West Coast artist, Eazy-E, former member of the iconic gangsta rap group NWA, who signed the group—initially comprising Krayzie Bone, Wi$h Bone, Flesh-N-Bone, Layzie Bone, and Bizzy Bone—to Ruthless Records and released an EP and, a year later, a full-length debut album. *E 1999 Eternal* spawned a pair of hits, "1st of the Month" and "Tha Crossroads," the latter of which won a Grammy.

Krayzie Bone describes the origin of their rhyming style like this: "We always used to rap together, whether we were just sitting around the house or driving around in the car, we'd always just rap. We got so used to saying each other's ad-libs to the point that when we did it, it sounded like we were harmonizing. . . . We just kept doing it and doing it, till we eventually got real good at it like 'this is our style.'"[14] Of course, much of this style is lost on the page, though some suggestion of their rapid delivery is evident in the length of their lines—far longer than the average rap line. More so even than most rap groups, Bone Thugs-N-Harmony demands to be heard.

THA CROSSROADS

Bone, Bone, Bone, Bone, Bone, Bone, Bone, Bone, Bone

Now tell me whatcha gonna do

When there ain't nowhere to run (Tell me what)

When judgment comes for you (When judgment comes for you)

And whatcha gonna do

When there ain't nowhere to hide (Tell me what)

When judgment comes for you ('Cause it's gonna come for you)

[Bizzy]

Head South, let's all bring it in for Wally, Eazy sees Uncle Charlie

Little Boo, but God's got him and I'm gonna miss everybody

I only rolled and blows my gauge, looked at him while he lay

When playing with destiny, plays too deep for me to say

Lil' Layzie came to me, told me if he should decease, well, then please
Bury me by my grand-grand and when you can, come follow me

[Layzie]
God bless you, working on a plan to heaven, follow the Lord all twenty-four
    seven days
God is who we praise, even though the devil's all up in my face
But he keeping me safe and in my place, say grace
For the case to race with a chance to face the judge
And I betcha my soul won't budge, grudge, because there's no mercy for
    thugs
Oooh, what can I do? It's all about our family and how we roll
Can I get a witness? Let it unfold, we living our lives to eternal our soul,
    aye-oh-aye-oh

[Krayzie]
Prayyyyyyy, and we pray and we pray, and we pray, and we pray
Every day, every day, every day, every day
And we pray, and we pray, and we pray, and we pray
Still we laced . . .

Now follow me, roll, stroll, whether it's hell or it's heaven
Come, let's go take a visit of people that's long gone—Darris
Wally, Eazy, Terry, Boo. It's steadily creeping up on the family
Exactly how many days we got lasting?
While you laughing we're passing, passing away
So y'all go rest y'all souls, 'cause I know I'ma meet you up at the crossroads
Y'all know y'all forever got love from them Bone Thugs, baby

[Wi$h]
Lil Eazy's long gone. Really wish he would come home
But when it's time to die, gotta go bye bye
All a lil' thug could do is cry, cry
Why they kill my dog? And man, I miss my Uncle Charles, y'all
And he shouldn't be gone, in front of his home, what they did to Boo was
    wrong
Oh so wrong, oh so wrong, gotta hold on, gotta stay strong

When the day comes, better believe Bone got a shoulder you can lean on
  (Lean on)

Hey, and we pray, and we pray, and we pray, and we pray
Every day, every day, every day, every day
And we pray, and we pray, and we pray, and we pray
Every day, every day, every day, every day

[Chorus]
See you at the crossroads, crossroads, crossroads (So you won't be
  lonely) [2x]
See you at the crossroads, crossroads (So you won't be lonely)
See you at the crossroads, crossroads

[Bizzy]
And I'm gonna miss everybody [5x]

[Layzie]
Living in a hateful world (Sending me straight to heaven), that's how we
  roll [3x]
And I'm asking the good Lord "Why?" and sigh, it's I, He told me we live to die

[Krayzie]
What's up with murder, y'all? See, my little cousin was hung
Somebody was really wrong, everybody want to test us, dawg
Then Miss Sleazy set up Eazy to fall, you know why we sinning
And Krayzie intended on ending it when it ends
Wanna come again, again and again
Now tell me whatcha gonna do

[Wi$h]
Can somebody, anybody tell me why?
Hey, can somebody, anybody tell me why we die, we die?
I don't wanna die

Ohhh, so wrong [4x]

BUSTA RHYMES

When he debuted in the early 1990s as part of the rap group Leaders of the New School, Busta Rhymes had already cultivated his idiosyncratic delivery, growling voice, raucous humor, and halting, ragga-inspired cadence. His recognizable style is "animated," as Jay-Z once described it in a lyric. Far from a criticism, this quality accounts in large part for Busta's longevity.

Before launching his solo career—and even after—Busta Rhymes gained a considerable reputation for his guest verses. He delivered a feverish verse on A Tribe Called Quest's "Scenario," which included the memorable line "RRRRRROAW, RRRRRRROAW like a Dungeon Dragon." His solo debut, *The Coming* (1996), produced the hit single "Woo-Hah!! Got You All in Check," which is equally remembered for its video, which helped inaugurate a visual style to accompany Busta's signature performance.

Busta Rhymes is now a multidimensional artist capable of carrying an album and displaying a range of emotions in his lyrics. "I got my boom-bap shit for the street, I got big records for pop radio without compromising who I am, I got inspirational records and records that make you laugh, have fun and wanna enjoy your life," he told an interviewer upon the release of his most recent album.[15] The selections that follow show him in several of these lyrical modes.

FROM **SCENARIO**
(A Tribe Called Quest)
Watch, as I combine all the juice from the mind
Heel up, wheel up, bring it back, come rewind
Powerful impact—BOOM!—from the cannon
Not braggin, try to read my mind, just imagine
Vo-cab-u-lary's necessary
When diggin into my library
Oh my gosh! Oh my gosh!
Eating ital stew like the one Peter Tosh-a
Uh, uh, uhh, all over the track, man
Uh, pardon me, uhh, as I come back
As I did it ra' I had to beg your pardon

When I travel through the turn I roll with the squadron

RRRRRROAW, RRRRRRROAW like a Dungeon Dragon

Change your little drawers 'cause your pants are saggin

Try to step to this, I will twist you in a turban

And have you smellin rank like some old stale urine

Chockety-choco, the chocolate chicken

The rear cock diesel, buttcheeks they were kickin

Yo, bustin out before the Busta bust a nut the rhyme

The rhythm is in sync (UHH!), the rhymes are on time (TIME!)

Rippin up the sound just like Horatio

Observe the vibe and check out the scenario!

PUT YOUR HANDS WHERE MY EYES COULD SEE

Hit you with no delayin, so what you sayin, yo? (Uh)

Silly with my nine milli, what the deally, yo? (What?)

When I be on the mic, yes, I do my duty, yo

Wild up in the club like we wild in the studio (Uh)

You don't wanna violate, nigga, really and truly, yo (Uh)

My main thug nigga named Julio, he moody, yo (What?)

Type of nigga that'll slap you with the tool-io (Blaow!)

Bitch nigga scared to death, act fruity, yo (Uh)

Fuck that! Look at shorty, she a little cutie, yo (Yeah)

The way she shake it make me wanna get all in the booty, yo (Whoo)

Top miss, just hit the bangin bitches in videos (Huh?)

Wildin with my freak like we up in the freak shows (Damn)

Hit you with the shit make you feel it all in your toes (Yeah)

Hot shit, got all you niggas in wet clothes (Take it off)

Stylin my metaphors when I formulate my flows (Uh)

If you don't know, you fuckin with lyrical player pros, like that

[Chorus]

Do you really wanna party with me?

Let me see just what you got for me

Put all your hands where my eyes can see

Straight buckwhylin in the place to be
If you really wanna party with me
Let me see just what you got for me
Put all your hands where my eyes can see
Straight buckwhylin in the place to be

If you really wanna party with me . . .

. . . In God We Trust (What?)
Yo, it's a must that you heard of us, yo, we murderous (Uh)
A lot of niggas is wonderin and they curious (What?)
How me and my niggas do it, it's so mysterious (That's true)
Furious, all of my niggas is serious (Huh)
Shook niggas be walkin around fearin us (What?)
Front, nigga, like you don't wanna be hearin us (No)
Gotta listen to how radio be playin us (Ahh)
Thirty times a day, shit'll make you delirious (What?)
Damagin everything all up in your areas
Yo, it's funny how all the chickens be always servin us
All up in between they ass where they wanna carry us (What?)
Hit ya good then I hit 'em off with the alias (What?)
Various . . . chickens, they wanna marry us (Hah)
Yo, it's Flipmode, my nigga, you know we 'bout to bust (Uh)
Seven-figure money, the label preparin us
Bite the dust, instead of you makin a fuss (What?)
Niggas know better 'cause there ain't no comparin us (Nope)
Mad at us, niggas is never, we fabulous (Yup)
Hit my people off with the flow that be marvelous (Hah)
Oh shit, my whole clique victorious (Yup)
Takin no prisoners, niggas is straight up warriors (What?)
While you feelin that I know you be feelin so glorious (Uh)
Then I blitz and reminisce on my nigga Notorious

[Chorus]

CANIBUS

C anibus is, in the words of one publication, "one of the architects of post-modern hip-hop lyricism."[16] He laces his lyrics with arcane references and tightly stitched flows rich in figurative language. Though his lyrical style may be cutting edge, his content is traditional—a throwback to the socially and politically conscious lyrics of the 1980s. "I feel like poetry that was written in the earlier stages of rap music, like about '84, '85, anywhere up to '93 or '94, the rhymes and the lyrics were something that you could learn something from. You could listen to it and you could learn things about cultures and learn things about places that you've never been to before. It wasn't like it is now. Now it's just a bunch of people running around telling you about things that they have that you'll probably never be able to get. It's different now."[17]

Canibus's "Poet Laureate" series, the third installment of which is included here, extends over several hundred lines. "I feel like my lyricism and the dexterity of it has come from trying to re-create and recapture what was being done when I was coming up," Canibus explains. "I wanna say things that provoke emotion. Because emotion manifests thought and thought manifests words and words manifest action and action manifests reality."[18]

POET LAUREATE INFINITY 3

Cycles of time; it is ubiquitous, it goes all over. It's ancient, it's one of the most ancient symbols there are. And this is an interpretation of what that actually means.

This has never been done before with a rhyme
Outside the realm of time, it's the first of its kind
Poet laureate infinity
I will forever be the illest lyrically

Nobody do it better, there ain't a truer Ripper
I did this separate, imagine what we could do together
Inspired by God, inspired by the suffering
Was it done by a prophet? It must have been. Who was it then?
Rip the Jacker, hot but cold-blooded

Many utter the name, but very few love him

Other MCs be nervous or somethin

Rhymes in abundance, hip-hop justice, rappers are captured and punished

The Polar Manitoba's melted by lava

A team of ER doctors climb aboard the chopper

My skull is a submarine hull, I empty the ballast tanks

I could smell the shit from the seagulls

My mind dives deep beneath yours, Poseidon Trident

Seahorse bubbles form, I scream with extreme force

Mariana's Trench detour to Ultima Thule

Let me explain what my sonar saw

This is the greatest rhyme of all time, supposedly

Through a term I'd like to call "Pulse Detonation Poetry"

Industrialists, civilians, women and children directly

Military chiefs, aristocrats in buildings

Membership is based off your raw intelligence

Four hundred screen video editing with hard evidence

Imagine being fined over a rhyme for steppin over the line

When I inspired Hova and Nas

Recite thirty-three threes, thirty-three three times

For twenty-four hours, twenty-one thousand nautical miles, ah

Don't be upset with Can-I-Bus yet, the kids just want respect

You been a success, but what do he get?

Divine design, a miracle of metallurgy

Every clergy member from Mecca who heard of me worshipped me

I got away nervously, talked about it purposefully

Next time I see it, it's gonna have a word with me

The biological chemical emergency

I purchase the beat; I resumed PsyOps on the enemy

Mix the blood so it don't coagulate

The sex magic won't work if the bitch masturbates

Nobody can hold me back, my flow bloviates

Into a spiritual shape, a capsule in space

No MC could rhyme like this, there's no challenge

His poet laureateship pontificates balance

Telencephalon olfactory lobes I had to practice

When a woman has her period I smell it on the mattress

Advanced step in innovative mobility

Most MCs try to clone me lyrically

They can't battle me, so they rather embarrass me

But I need a volunteer, do I have any?

The NASA contractor with a satchel of answers

I passed up the Nobel Peace Prize for my passion

Most of you will never understand what I mean

My dreams are broken into storyboard scenes

Kill you with green lasers, evaporated weed vapor

Electromagnetic scalar, then somethin they call a maser

"That is not dead, which can eternally lie

And with strange eons, even death may die"

The leaders' lies got me reassigned, my loyalty was redefined

They will not be allowed to see the rhymes

In a town near Kadam and Kakrak Jalalabad

I pray in a hut constructed from Sago Palm

I'ma take you for a walk through a beautiful place called

Honey Swamp, we'll shoot hoops at Mosquito Lagoon Park

Emotion manifest thought, thought manifest words

Actions and reality, that's how it has to be

The overseer of poetic antiquity

The Victoria and Albert Museum kept them for me

Inject the gas into the centrifuge mass

The teleological dynamic will enhance

I remove the veil from in front of me suddenly

Truly, there is too much to see

The Law of Attraction is attracted to me

The Laws of Poetry in action is practiced quite actively

My body did not melt beyond the Van Allen Belt

I was transformed into a spirit with no shell

I'm modifying the weather from behind a weather shield

Writing with a feathered quill, gettin more ill

I hope I am not alone, that would be terrible

If I am celebrating, then that'd be a miracle

At least for my interconnected introspective perspective

The more pretentious, the more apprehensive the sentence

Hip-hop made me, hip-hop praise me

Ain't nothin changed me since 1980

Involuntary catalepsy, battle me, baby

One thousand bars, nigga, zero vector systems

Brain waves reveal high-yield E&D fields

Chew MCs like I'm eatin a meal

Normal life is not real, we are just cogs in a wheel

We work, we hurt, we search, we feel

The microphonist that utilizes the study of conics

Circular motion in both the para and the hyperbolas

Mad Max Beyond Thunderdome under Red Rock

It's no use if you can't use what you got

Do, Re, Mi, Fa, Sol, La, Si, Do

These are the tones that will activate your ohm

Who have lost their faith, who have lost their hope

Who have lost their point, who have lost their own

Are you food for the moon? The portion is you

Just in case you try to poison my food but I want you to

Rap music and those who listen to it don't owe me nothin

I don't want nothin from you, not even your judgment

I ride on a flatbed chariot, four ostriches carry it

I control their movements with lariats

Polygraphs flutter, the Lovecraft craft lover

I don't want it, that's why I'm rarely seen in public

If I were you I wouldn't waste my time readin rubbish

I don't care what you say, nigga, you a nigga lover

The relative radiance of the rhymes make it shine

Increase the star wattage with longer cycle time

How's my driving? Run you off the road smiling

1-800-Road Rage, start dialing

Don't care if I make history, I wanna be a part of infinity

Look at what your sun god did to me

I submit to the will of the creator willingly

The possibilities present a probable infinity

I climbed the slope shaped like a stop sign in record clock time

Hot lava rock rhymes, rock slide topside

At the observatory summit of Mount Graham

Lookin through the starlight scope in my hand

Creative writing and rhythm, grammar and composition

Don't ignore me, ignore the fools who tell you, "Don't listen"

Strivin my principal findings by designing a new style of rhyming

That you could take home and try out

A hundred bars per hour, sometimes I doubled the writing

Secret signature timing was the hardest part to figure out

Poetically paralyzing. "Where are you?" "Are you hiding?"

"No. I am sandbag diving." From the kinetic to the energetic

St. Germaine was made to explain the lesson with a thousand-bar message

Straight out the freak show, no preshow

Limited oxygen, when I rhyme fast you breathe slow

The pope shook, they ransacked Rome and burned books

I ran back home to hide mine in the woods

MOSES is a new weapon system, secret code

CONUS is the continent of the U.S., I suppose

I don't have all the answers; I am not in the know

I can only see what is above and only from below

Substratum of reality through the thick cloud canopy

"How can it be, Canibus? Answer me!"

My shelter is not far, you can borrow what you need

The bunker doors sequestered beneath the tall tumble trees

Gold chords from the organ cut down your swordsman

Tell everybody, "Shut the fuck up," when I'm talking

From a very cold place called Faraday Base

Right next to the South Pole's longest ice strait

My dream was identical seven nights in a row
I saw a sideways eight wrapped around a microphone
Extraterrestrial isotopic ratios
A broke scientist in his lab with no place to go
Fire and ash fallout, that's what it's all about
We must construct a shelter then build a wall around it
Geography is conducive to astronomy
And the study of celestial bodies, biopsy
My austere designs are so ahead of their time
Even when you press rewind, you're still left behind
I blasted through the limestone with water mixed with a dissolver
Then I signaled the remaining cave crawlers
Dig a hole for the collateral carnage, battle the hardest
Take out hip-hop trash and garbage
On the Sabbath, I write preplanning for the planet
Drawing mechanics, suspended in space as holographics
The quarantine isolation unit is where I house it
My team and I salvage the work of Dr. Fritz Albert
Hip-hop is the blackened pot placed next to a kettle
With my logo in it, a rigid rehomogenized metal
Greetings and salutations, my equations are inundated
With information, electrocranial stimulation
Password, please. Have patience, verification
I repeat, "What's your character string verification?"
Battle rap is just aimless entertainment
"Second Round Knockout" was one of they favorites, fuck all the haters
This shit was responsibility entrusted. There's only one way
For me to prove that I love it. That's why I'm bustin
I turned the page, wrote a turn of phrase
Verbal X-Rays, they say, "I don't burn, I blaze"
Attach the piezoelectric transducer to your computer
Poet laureate is the future
Next time we meet, this whole song'll be a new mix
For all the rippers out there who need a new fix

With these lyrics, I consecrate the spirit
Whenever I spit it, concentrate, you can hear it
I've almost perfected this, I'm one word away from
Excellence, Cyclotronic Resonance, patents are pending it
Can-I-Bus a.k.a. "The Spitzberg Beast"
Gave his bicentennial speech on Emerald Peak
What are you building, 'Bis? Is it a flyin silver disk?
GW—I'm positive it's him
I proofread my writtens, eat a chicken with the skin missin
In ten minutes. Now, that's some shit!
You think that's fast? Nah. That's faster than you think
By the time you blink, the whole Universe shrinks
We'll observe the Gods, my thoughts graduated
To the stars to infinity, listen to the bars
Thick rhymes compartmentalized, separatized to prevent
Bootleg pirates, gives me energy when I'm tired
I'm hooked on hip-hop, I can't live without it
You can mix this song a thousand ways, I don't doubt it
Several million years into the past, the primitive
Future, in a world without oil and gas
Gather the evidence then give it to the president
Don't reprimand him, ask him for help next
I hold hip-hop responsible, every magazine
Writer that wrote bullshit in his article
Always remember: I'll be gone forever
I made these bars so you all could remember
The rhyme's in my mind when I autograph sign
I can't wait to sign a autograph for the last time
The ungrateful dead recurring images playin
In my head, every color in America bled
Canibus grabbed the mic like a energized amulet
Then spit a rap that you can't forget
"With this sacred water, I consecrate this Talisman
So that it will make me poet laureate"
This is a no brainer, stop the complaining

If hip-hop was dead, I came here to save it

Classified payloads, no frequency safe modes

No safety, and I still made time for the ladies

No corruption, no disruption, no destruction, no budget

No nothin. It's never that easy, you just gotta trust it

The spin off from the press should be able to feed you

But I declined, 'cause I'm familiar with what greed can do

I sit down and think, when I write I can smell the ink

It's the dark-skinned Lizard King

Metronome man will never take commands from the drum

The beat is my slave and it will behave as I want

I heard hip-hop was dead, that's not fair

Who I talk to? "Go he there, Nasir"

Yeah, poet laureate infinity

I will forever be the illest lyrically

Poet laureate infinity

Poet laureate infinity

Poet laureate infinity

This never been done before in history

CHINO XL

C hino XL is a half–African American, half–Puerto Rican MC who forged his skills touring with Zulu Nation founder Afrika Bambaataa. Known for his expansive vocabulary and intricate wordplay, Chino has earned a loyal underground fan base. As a youth, Chino rode the momentum from performances in New Jersey neighborhood talent shows and began recording demos, which eventually caught the ear of Def Jam co-founder Rick Rubin. Since his first release, *Here to Save You All* (1996), Chino has worked with some of the biggest names in rap, including Common, J-Dilla, and the RZA.

On "What Am I?" Chino rhymes about the adversity he faced growing up as the child of Puerto Rican and African American parents. The lyrics highlight Chino's skill as a storyteller as the song moves in time from ages six to nineteen. Chino XL's *The Poison Pen* (2006), his third studio album, features "Wordsmith," a track on which his vocabulary pushes him to conceive unexpected rhymes.

WHAT AM I?

Yo, I don't even know what the vibe is, kid. All these different things separating us. It got me walking this fence, man, and I don't even know what side I'ma fall on, B. Can't see it.

Well, I'm a zebra, y'all
"Half Puerto Rican, half black, but you don't speak Spanish"
Don't call me zebra, y'all
"Half Puerto Rican, half black, but you don't speak Spanish"
(Now how old are you?)

About six, on my BMX, doin tricks
Back to Middlesex with a couple of poor white trashy brats
Everything was coochie crunch 'til it was time for lunch
They said to wait in the back, they said their Pops ain't like black
See, where I was the population's mostly white (Ain't it?)
They wanna see you jiggabooin with your (face painted)
Be brought home by one of their daughters and their fathers (fainted)
They want to see you a failure so I never (became it)
Light-skinned, showed them length, curly-headed
Called me names, I was different, I was gifted, they made me ashamed
Found out that I'm a different shade when I'm in the second grade
Abe Lincoln's play, they want me to portray a slave
My mama's face went pale; she looked like she wanted to puke
Now that I know the truth, I'd rather play John Wilkes Booth
Although my family came and bitched and in the play my role was switched
My grandma told me I was fixed, my problems wasn't fixed
My family seen my views of the world distort
Mom's last resort, she decided we would move to Newark
I took a deep breath leaving everything I knew behind

The country air, the green grass, and my peace of mind
Harassed by white cops, on our way were pulled out our car
Mistook my mom for Joanne Chesimard, now I'm really scarred

[Chorus]
What am I? I'm confused, can't decide
What am I? Who am I? What am I?
Black or white, I can't identify
What am I? Who am I? What am I?
I'm confused, can't decide
What am I? Who am I? What am I?
Black or white, I can't identify
What am I? Who am I? What am I?

Culture shock, Newark's a far cry from Middlesex
Bradley Court projects, black eyes, regrets
Torn lives, I've never seen so many people depressed
My mental gets molest, physical takes violent threats
Stress, walkin home from school's like a terrorist test
I learned blacks could be racist too, somehow still I felt I was blessed
Even my teachers called me half-breeds and all of that
I was scared of livin here but also scared of movin back
See, where I was before I was the darkest thing they ever saw
They figured that I'm black-white around
They kick me like a soccer ball
White people didn't accept me (Fuck you)
Black people didn't accept me (Fuck you)
Puerto Ricans didn't accept me (Fuck you)
Diggin, researchin my identity. It gots me goin cuckoo

*I'm the yellow nigga, right? I'm tired of that. I am not passing, I am black! I was
born black, I live black, and I'ma die probably because I'm black . . .*

So now I'm goin, "Hey, niggas," at niggas that say Chino's not black
Then come to my house and tell my African mother that
In fact, 'cause a cracker thinks no sister would attract to me

These same brothers got perms to get their hair like mine was naturally
Discrimination affects a brother's education
Hands up in black history class, they never called on my ass
But wait, growing at a rapid rate
I digest their hate, it's family, found out my daddy left me when I'm three
Dealt with, felt if I knew my Spanish family, they'd help
Every mixed person I met, they mostly just kept to themself
We moved to East Orange, I set it off, talent shows starring
A high-yellow nigga's progression, my flavor's foreign

[Chorus]

(Now how old are you?)

About nineteen, lettin off my steam
Used to be a punchin bag, but now I stomps in hip-hop fiend
Now I get the Goya jokes, Menudo jokes, Rico Suave jokes
But females rush me and the MCs steal up all my quotes
See, what I lacks in melanin I makes up with adrenaline
Your weak attempts at, blemishing my mixed heritage I'm treasurin
Don't need Caucasian acceptance, just that of a human being
Laughed and spit at, "I don't represent," 'cause I am not Spanish-speaking
Now, how many dues must I pay to win?
You're angry and you're stressin that oppression
But you judge me by the skin I'm in when
Adam Clayton Powell was light-skinneded
Farrakhan, the brother's light-skinneded
Elijah Muhammad's also light-skinned
Discrimination from my own peoples is making my temper go thin so
Stop playing me slight, saying my song's aight instead of hype
Don't call me red-boned, or light and bright and damn near white
I ain't no zebra, ain't no half an original either
Don't call me mulatto, I stab you with a broken bottle
Callin your brother Oreo, get off it, yo, now Tom, consider
He could be like Chino XL, that yellow-ass nigga

WORDSMITH

[Chorus]
Perfection, flawless masterpiece, no mistakes
Back in the 1800s, I was burned at the stake (I am the Wordsmith)
Metaphor Mephistopheles, degrees I've achieved
The brain fluid it takes to believe would equal the Seven Seas (I am the
   Wordsmith)
I could reveal the true name of God, you'd go insane upon hearing it
Release enough winds to blow down pyramids (I am the Wordsmith)
I'm the Michelangelo of syllables since I freestyle
Genesis been biblical. That's something you got to give in to

Since born in my mama vaginal sauna
As a sonogram, I've been fond of phonics
It's ironic, even as an embryonic
Fed through an umbilical, don't that sound biblical?
I've been a terror since I tear-eth out of that u-terus
Evil plans were made to defeat us as a fetus
Though now I walk in infamy, as a child they had it in for me
Was raised with guns and infantry in diapers and in infancy
The childhood of a hood that was raised in the 'hood
Cops said, "Put your hands in the hot sky," I put my hands down on the hot
   hood
I can't whine or drink wine, nine planets planned it
'Til it became apparent my parents shouldn't have been a parent
State to state we ran some, I wasn't worth no ransom
Money, won't you hand some? A nigga wasn't handsome
Raise the mind like Charles Manson's, knew I was some man's son
But, which one? That made me strong. Created my poison tongue . . .

[Chorus]

Why you cut school? 'Cause you ain't feel too good
I cut school 'cause my cuts ain't heal too good
Through all the physical abuse, my mind escaped through the gift of
   wordplay

I memorized encyclopedias and dictionaries

I wrote anthems from antonyms, harmonies from homonyms

Created cinema from synonyms, livid to eliminate that illustrious life you're
    livin in

Wrote rhetoricals in rhythms

I could paralyze with a parable, make rhymes out of religion

Crucify you with a prefix or suffocate you with a suffix

Wrote lectures so infectious they're known to infect the listeners

Who dissin us? Yo, punks, you wait, I punctuate

My karma's the comma that put you inside of a coma

Hyphen, dot, dot, semicolon, leave you semi-swollen

Question mark: You pregnant? Oh, you're not? I love you, period.

To sum it up, language is my essence

Fucked up in all my adolescence 'til my mom was out of lessons

Laws, I store convenient—still I robbed a convenience store

Love Mom? Fuck Mom. Shit, I ain't love me no more

Mentally it didn't register, "Bitch, empty the register, bitch

You just a cashier, bitch, give the cash here

Or I'll shoot you in your cabbage, hijack a getaway cab, bitch"

Words ain't makin me no loot, don't change no Dow Jones average

Regardless, we godless, they stole my innocence

In a sense, the judge sentenced me to three lifetime sentences

To write my life and times in sentences; art, my dark archnemesis

They want me off the premises. That's what the premise is

Locked on a tier where you can't shed a tear at

Studied more Shakespeare than any African shakes a spear at

And the whole world fear that and it hurts

I got caught killing time, but then I got a way with words

[Chorus]

People can say whatever they want about me

But agree that I am the Wordsmith (I am the Wordsmith)

They can try to ignore everything that I achieve

But agree that I am the Wordsmith (I am the Wordsmith)

The love of words is deep in my brain

Must be to silence my pain. I am the Wordsmith (I am the Wordsmith)
Even if I never move a million units
It's my blessin how I do it. I am the Wordsmith (I am the Wordsmith)

I'm in a game full of morons, they keep putting more on
I tutor the Torah, I'm in the core of the Qur'an
The mind's what I represent and MCs better re-present
I'm taking this rappin bullshit to the fullest extent
I have reservations why Indians are on reservations
Told the board of education: I was bored of education
As far as this go, I leave you deader than disco
Rocking sex and violence over sax and violins
Through your mind's camera lens you're in need of an ambulance
I'll knock you to the asphalt, it's your own ass fault
Your last thought, I'll never sell my self short to be famous
And taking it up the anus just ain't us
The world could get the penis of this classical trained pianist
My P.O. was p.o.'d, handed me a cup, told me to pee in this
The linguist musician, my college position is that my intuition
Told me I wouldn't be affordin tuition
My education's all on my own, so, I might have been born yesterday
But I rhyme like there's no tomorrow . . .

[Chorus]

COMMON

W hen Common emerged in the early 1990s, hip-hop was largely a bicoastal phenomenon in the public eye. Eschewing bling and gangsta trends for a more introspective style, Common wrote on such topics as abortion, the story of hip-hop, and the life of Assata Shakur. Many of his songs also described the people and places of his native Chicago.

Even in his early work, one can hear Common—then known as Common Sense—forging a lyrical identity as a socially conscious, emotionally engaged artist with the skills for battle rapping. *Resurrection* (1994), his second album, earned him critical praise. His allegory of hip-hop as a female lost love, "I Used to Love H.E.R.," is among the best-known hip-hop lyrics. "I wrote 'I Used to Love H.E.R.' . . . as a way of expressing how I felt about where hip-hop was at that point and where it might go," Common explains. "Because it was that serious for so many of us. We didn't just grow up with hip-hop; we grew up with hip-hop as hip-hop was also growing, and so that made for a very close and intimate relationship that was becoming more and more urgent—and we all felt it."[19]

Over the years, Common's style has gone through substantial evolution. He began his career primarily as a freestyler and battle rapper, relying on lines packed with syllables, delivered with speed. He had a penchant for chain rhyming and a fondness for playing games with words. In the years since, he seems consciously to have streamlined his flow, putting fewer syllables into individual lines. The result has been a shift toward songcraft over battle rapping, mirrored in his expanding range of themes.

I USED TO LOVE H.E.R.

I met this girl when I was ten years old
And what I loved most, she had so much soul
She was old school when I was just a shorty
Never knew throughout my life she would be there for me
On the regular, not a church girl, she was secular
Not about the money, no studs was mic checkin her
But I respected her, she hit me in the heart
A few New York niggas had did her in the park
But she was there for me and I was there for her
Pull out a chair for her, turn on the air for her
And just cool out, cool out and listen to her
Sittin on bone, wishin that I could do her
Eventually if it was meant to be, then it would be
'Cause we related, physically and mentally
And she was fun then, I'd be geeked when she'd come around
Slim was fresh, yo, when she was underground

Original, pure, untampered and down sister
Boy, I tell ya, I miss her

Now periodically I would see
Ol' girl at the clubs and at the house parties
She didn't have a body, but she started gettin thick quick
Did a couple of videos and became Afrocentric
Out goes the weave, in goes the braids, beads, medallions
She was on that tip about stoppin the violence
About my people she was teachin me
By not preachin to me, but speakin to me
In a method that was leisurely, so easily I approached
She dug my rap, that's how we got close
But then she broke to the West Coast and that was cool
'Cause around the same time, I went away to school
And I'm a man of expandin, so why should I stand in her way?
She probably get her money in L.A.
And she did, stud, she got big pub, but what was foul
She said that the pro-black was goin out of style
She said Afrocentricity was of the past
So she got into R&B, hip-house, bass, and jazz
Now black music is black music and it's all good
I wasn't salty she was with the boyz in the 'hood
'Cause that was new for her, she was becomin well rounded
I thought it was dope how she was on that freestyle shit
Just havin fun, not worried about anyone
And you could tell by how her titties hung

I might've failed to mention that this chick was creative
But once the man got to her he altered her native
Told her if she got an image and a gimmick
That she could make money and she did it like a dummy
Now I see her in commercials, she's universal
She used to only swing it with the inner-city circle
Now she be in the 'burbs lickin rock and dressin hippy
And on some dumb shit when she comes to the city

Talkin about poppin Glocks, servin rocks, and hittin switches

Now she's a gangsta rollin with gangsta bitches

Always smokin blunts and gettin drunk

Tellin me sad stories, now she only fucks with the funk

Stressin how hardcore and real she is

She was really the realest before she got into showbiz

I did her, not just to say I did it

But I'm committed, but so many niggas hit it

That she's just not the same, lettin all these goofies do her

I see niggas slammin her and takin her to the sewer

But I'ma take her back hopin that the shit stop

'Cause who I'm talking 'bout, y'all, is hip-hop

THE 6TH SENSE

*The revolution will not be televised. The revolution is here. Yeah, it's Common
    Sense with DJ Premier. We gonna help y'all see clear. It's real hip-hop music,
    from the soul, y'all. Yeah, check it, yo.*

The perseverance of a rebel, I drop heavier levels

It's unseen or heard, a king with words

Can't knock the hustle, but I've seen street dreams deferred

Dark spots in my mind where the scene occurred

Some say I'm too deep, I'm in too deep a sleep

Through me, Muhammad will forever speak

Greet brothers with handshakes on ghetto landscapes

Where a man is determined by how much a man make

Cop cognacs and spit old raps with young cats

With cigarettes in their ear, niggerish they appear

Under the FUBU is a guru that's untapped

Want to be in the rap race but ain't ran one lap

Ran so far from the streets that you can't come back

You tripping with nowhere to unpack, forgot that

[Chorus]

This is rap for real, something you should feel

And you know you should know [3x]

In front of two-inch glass from Arabs I order fries
Inspiration when I write, I see my daughter's eyes
I'm the truth, across the table from corporate lies
Immortalized by the realness I bring to it
If revolution had a movie I'd be theme music
My music, you either fight, fuck, or dream to it
My life is one big rhyme, I try to scheme through it
Through my shell, never knew what the divine would bring through it
I'd be lying if I said I didn't want millions
More than money saved, I wanna save children
Dealing with alcoholism and Afrocentricity
A complex man drawn off of simplicity
Reality is frisking me. This industry'll
Make you lose intensity. The Common Sense in me
Remembers the basement. I'm Morpheus
In this hip-hop Matrix, exposing fake shit

[Chorus]

Some days I take the L to jell with the real world
Got on at 87th, stopped by this little girl
She recited raps, I forgot where they was from
In 'em, she was saying how she made brothers come
I start thinking, how many souls hip-hop has affected
How many dead folks this art resurrected
How many nations this culture connected
Who am I to judge one's perspective?
Though some of that shit y'all pop to it, I ain't relating
If I don't like it, I don't like it, that don't mean that I'm hating
I just want to innovate and stimulate minds
Travel the world and penetrate the times
Escape through rhythms in search of peace and wisdom
Raps are smoke signals letting the streets know I'm with 'em
For now I appreciate this moment in time
Ballplayers and actors be knowing my rhymes, it's like

[Chorus]

THE LIGHT

I never knew a luh, luh-luh, a love like this

Gotta be somethin for me to write this

Queen, I ain't seen you in a minute

Wrote this letter and finally decide to send it

Signed sealed delivered for us to grow together

Love has no limit, let's spend it slow forever

I know your heart is weathered by what studs did to you

I ain't gon' salt 'em 'cause I probably did it, too

Because of you, feelings I handle with care

Some niggas recognize the light but they can't handle the glare

You know I ain't the type to walk around with matchin shirts

A relationship is effort; I will match your work

I wanna be the one to make you happiest and hurt you the most

They say the end is near, it's important that we close . . .

. . . To the Most High

Regardless of what happen, on Him let's rely

[Chorus]

There are times when you'll need someone

I will be by your side

There is a light that shines

Special for you and me . . .

Yo, yo, check it . . .

It's important we communicate

And tune the fate of this union to the right pitch

I never call you my bitch or even my boo

There's so much in a name and so much more in you

Few understand the union of woman and man

In sex and a tingle is where they assumin it land

But that's fly by night, for you in the sky I write

For in these cold Chi nights' moon, you my light

If heaven had a height, you would be that tall

Ghetto to coffee shop, through you I see that all

Let's stick to understanding and we won't fall

For better or worse times, I hope to me you call
So I pray every day more than anything
Friends will stay as we begin to lay this foundation
For a family; love ain't simple
Why can't it be anything worth having you work at annually?
Granted, we known each other for some time
It don't take a whole day to recognize sunshine

[Chorus]

Yeah . . . yo, yo, check it
It's kinda fresh you listen to more than hip-hop
And I can catch you in the mix from beauty to thrift shop
Plus you shit pop when it's time to, thinkin you fresh
Suggestin beats I should rhyme to. At times
When I'm lost I try to find you. You know
To give me space when it's time to. My heart's
Dictionary defines you as love and happiness
Truthfully, it's hard tryin to practice abstinence
The time we committed love it was real good
Had to be for me to arrive and it still feel good
I know the sex ain't gon' keep you, but as my equal
It's how I must treat you. As my reflection
In light I'ma lead you. And whatever's right
I'ma feed you digga-da, digga-da, digga-da, digga-digga-da-da
Yo, I tell you the rest when I see you

A SONG FOR ASSATA
(feat. Cee-Lo)
In the spirit of God, in the spirit of the ancestors, in the spirit of the Black
Panthers, in the spirit of Assata Shakur, we make this movement toward
freedom for all those who have been oppressed and all those in the struggle.
Yeah, yo, check it . . .

There were lights and sirens, gunshots firin
Cover your eyes as I describe a scene so violent
Seemed like a bad dream, she laid in a blood puddle

Blood bubbled in her chest
Cold air brushed against open flesh
No room to rest, pain consumed each breath
Shot twice with her hands up
Police questioned but shot before she answered
One Panther lost his life, the other ran for his
Scandalous the police were as they kicked and beat her
Comprehension she was beyond, tryna hold on
To life. She thought she'd live with no arm
That's what it felt like, got to the hospital, eyes held tight
They moved her room to room—she could tell by the light
Handcuffed tight to the bed, through her skin they bit
Put guns to her head, every word she got hit
"Who shot the trooper?" they asked her
Put mace in her eyes, threatened to blast her
Her mind raced 'til things got still
Opened her eyes, realized she's next to her best friend who got killed
She got chills, they told her that's where she would be next
Hurt mixed with anger, survival was a reflex
They lied and denied visits from her lawyer
But she was buildin as they tried to destroy her
If it wasn't for this German nurse they woulda served her worse
I read this sister's story, knew that it deserved a verse
I wonder what would happen if that woulda been me?
All of this shit so we could be free, so dig it, y'all

[Chorus: Cee-Lo]
I'm thinkin of Assata, yes
Listen to my love, Assata, yes
Your power and pride is beautiful
May God bless your soul

It seemed like the middle of the night when law awakened her
Walkie-talkies cracklin, not sayin where they takin her
Though she kinda knew. What made the ride peaceful
Was the trees and the sky was blue

Arrived to Middlesex Prison about six in the morning

Uneasy as they pushed her to the second floor in

A cell, one cot, no window, facing hell

Put in the basement of a prison with all males

And the smell of misery, seatless toilets and centipedes

She'd exercise, paint, and begin to read

Two years in a hole. Her soul grew weak

Away from people so long she forgot how to speak

She discovered freedom is a unspoken sound

And a wall is a wall and can be broken down

Found peace in the Panthers she went on trial with

One of the brothers . . . she had a child with

The foulness, they wouldn't feed her, hopin she'd lose her seed

Held tight, knowing the fight would live through this seed

In need of a doctor, from her stomach she'd bleed

Out of this situation a girl was conceived

Separated from her, left to mother the Revolution

And lactate to attack hate

'Cause federal and state was built for a black fate

Her emptiness was filled with beatings and court dates

They fabricated cases, hoping one would stick

And said she robbed places that didn't exist

In the midst of threats on her life and being caged with Aryan whites

Through dark halls of hate she carried the light

I wonder what would happen if that woulda been me?

All of this shit so we could be free

Yeah, I often wonder what would happen if that woulda been me?

All of this shit so we could be free, so dig it, people . . .

[Chorus]

From North Carolina her grandmother would bring

News that she had had a dream

Her dreams always meant what they needed them to mean

What made them real was the action in between

She dreamt that Assata was free in they old house in Queens

The fact that they always came true was the thing
Assata had been convicted of a murder she couldn't a done
Medical evidence shown she couldn't a shot the gun
It's time for her to see the sun from the other side
Time for her daughter to be by her mother's side
Time for this beautiful woman to become soft again
Time for her to breathe and not be told how or when
She untangled the chains and escaped the pain
How she broke out of prison I could never explain
And even to this day they try to get to her
But she's free with political asylum in Cuba

[Chorus]

Freedom! You askin me about freedom? Askin me about freedom? I'll be honest with you. I know a whole lot more about what freedom isn't than about what it is, 'cause I've never been free. I can only share my vision with you of the future, about what freedom is. The way I see it, freedom is—is the right to grow, is the right to blossom. Freedom is the right to be yourself, to be who you are, to be who you wanna be, to do what you wanna do.

DIGABLE PLANETS

Digable Planets were not the first to bring a jazz sensibility to hip-hop, but they were certainly among the most successful. The group's three MCs layered complex and politically conscious lyrics over laid-back tracks with live jazz instrumentation as well as with samples from jazz legends like Sonny Rollins, Miles Davis, and Herbie Hancock. They are also important in the story of hip-hop as one of a small number of mixed-gender groups.

Digable Planets consists of Butterfly, Doodlebug, and Ladybug Mecca. The insect aliases were political. "They work together for the good of the colony," Butterfly explains. "It was a socialist, communist thing that I was talking about."[20] Their first album, *Reachin' (A New Refutation of Time and Space)* (1993), was a critical success, driven by their jazz-inflected first single "Rebirth of Slick (Cool Like Dat)."

The three MCs share a wide-ranging allusive style that drops references to everyone from Karl Marx to bell hooks, Jimi Hendrix to Nikki Giovanni. In 1994 the group won the Grammy for Best Rap Performance by a Duo or Group. Digable Planets may have reached their peak of popularity in the early 1990s, but their effect on hip-hop is apparent in the work of later groups like the Fugees and the Roots.

REBIRTH OF SLICK (COOL LIKE DAT)

[Butterfly]
We like the breeze, flow straight out of our lids
Them, they got booed by these hard-rock Brooklyn kids
Us floor rush when the DJ's boomin classics
You dig the crew on the fattest hip-hop record
He touch the kinks and sinks into the sounds
She frequents the fatter joints called undergrounds
Our funk zooms like you hit the Mary Jane
They flock to booms, man, boogie had to change
Who freaks the clips with mad amount percussion?
Where kinky hair goes to unthought-of dimensions
Why's it so fly? 'Cause hip-hop kept some drama
When Butterfly rocked the light blue-suede Pumas
What by the cut we push it off the corner
How was the buzz entire hip-hop era?
Was fresh in fact since they started sayin "Audi"
'Cause funks made fat from right beneath my hoodie
The puba of the styles like Miles and shit
Like sixties funky worms with waves and perms
Just sendin chunky rhythms right down ya block
We be to rap what key be to lock
But...

I'm cool like dat [7x]
I'm cool . . . (I'm cool . . .)

[Ladybug]
We be the chocolates tap to my raps
She innovates after sweeter cat naps
He at the funk club with the vibrate
Them, they be crazy, down with the Five Nate
It can kick a plan then a crowd burst
Me, I be diggin it with the bug verse
Us, we be freakin 'til dawn blinks an eye
He gives the strangest smile so I say "Hi" (Wassup)
Who understood, yeah, understood the plans
Him heard a beat and put it to his hands
What I just flip let borders get loose
How to consume all the beats is like juice
If it's the shit we'll lift it off the plastic
The babes'll go spastic, hip-hop gains a classic
Pimp playin sharp, it don't matter, I'm phatter
Ask Butta how I zone (Man, Cleopatra Jones)
And . . .

I'm chill like dat [7x]
I'm chill . . . (I'm chill . . .)

Blink . . . blink . . . blink . . . blink . . . blink . . . blink . . . blink . . .
Think . . . think . . . think . . . think . . . think . . . think . . . think . . .

[Doodlebug]
We get ya free 'cause the clips be fat boss
Them dug the jams and commence to goin off
She sweats the beats and ask me could she puff it
Me? I got crew, kid, seven and a crescent
Us cause a buzz when the nickel bags are dealt
Him? That's my man with the asteroid belt
They catch a fizz from the Mr. Doodle-big

He rocks a tee from the Crooklyn non-pigs
The rebirth of slick like my gangsta stroll
The lyrics just like loot come in stacks and rolls
You used to find the bug in a box with fade
Now he boogies up your stage—plaits twists the braids
And . . .

I'm peace like dat [7x]
I'm peace . . . (I'm peace . . .)

[Butterfly]
Check it out, man, I groove like dat, I'm smooth like dat
I jive like dat, I roll like dat

[Ladybug]
Yeah, I'm thick like dat, I stack like dat
I'm down like dat, I'm black like dat

[Doodlebug]
Well, yo, I funk like dat, I'm fat like dat
I'm in like dat 'cause I swing like dat

[Butterfly]
We jazz like dat, we freak like dat
We zoom like dat, we out . . . we out

DMX

D MX is gifted with one of the most distinctive voices in all of rap—
a guttural baritone that favors the pit bulls he keeps as pets. His
flow often comes in bursts, punctuated by barks and growls. Beyond the signature ad-libs, his flow is swaggering, aggressive, even angry. "I
never saw any bright lights around me," DMX writes in his autobiography.

"Nothing about my Tims and hoodie was shiny. [I was] committed to taking hip-hop back to the streets where it belonged."[21]

DMX enjoyed one of the most successful runs of commercial success in hip-hop history. His first five albums, released between 1998 and 2003, debuted at number one on the Billboard 200 and all went platinum. His work is marked by confessional reflections ("Damien"), prayers (he has a series of numbered "Prayer" songs), personal family stories ("I Miss You"), street anthems ("Ruff Ryders Anthem"), and swagger-laden, come-hither jams ("Howz It Goin Down"). One of DMX's favorite tropes is to play multiple parts in his raps, as shown here on "Damien." Perhaps his most formally compelling song is "Who We Be," in which he matches his flow to the lurching beat, pushing together strings of short phrases before settling into fully expressed thoughts. The song is an exercise in control, containment, and release.

DMX's style is often strikingly introspective. As one reviewer noted on the release of his first album, "DMX is meaningful as well as symbolic. He professes an ideology that stresses the inner world—characterized by such qualities as survival, wisdom, strength, respect, and faith—rather than the material one that infatuates most rappers of his time."[22] X has made that inner turmoil—publicized through his many run-ins with law enforcement—the subject of his art.

DAMIEN

[Chorus 2x]
The snake, the rat, the cat, the dog
How you gon' see them if you livin in the fog?

Why is it every move I make turn out to be a bad one?
Where's my guardian angel? Need one, wish I had one
I'm right here, shorty, and I'ma hold you down
And tryin to fuck all these bitches? I'ma show you how
But who? *Name D like you, but my friends call me Damien*
And I'ma put you into somethin about this game we in
You and me could take it there and you'll be
The hottest nigga ever livin. That's a given? You'll see
Hmmm, that's what I've been wantin all my life
Thinkin 'bout my little man so I call my wife

Well your dada is about to make it happen

"What you mean, my nigga?" I'm about to make it rappin

Today I met this cat, he said his name was Damien

He thinks that we're a lot alike and wants to be my friend

"You mean like Chucky?" Haha, yeah, just like Chucky

"Dada, looks like we both lucky." Yeah

[Chorus 4x]

Hey yo, D? What up, D? You'se a smooth nigga

I seen you but nobody knew who pulled the trigger

Yeah, you know it's always over dough. *You sure?*

I could've swore it was over a ho. Na, na, that ain't my style

Nigga, you stay frontin but you still my man

And I ain't goin say nothin. Got yo' weed—

Go 'head smoke it, go 'head drink it

Go 'head and fuck shorty, you know I can keep a secret

I'm about to have you drivin, probably a Benz

But we gotta stay friends, blood out, blood in

Sounds good to me, fuck it, what I got to lose?

Hmmm. Nothin I can think of, any nigga would choose

Got me pushin the whips, takin trips across seas

Pockets stay laced, nigga, I flush G's

For that nigga I would bleed, give him my right hand

Now that I think about it—yo, that's my man

[Chorus 4x]

You like how everything is goin? You like what I did? Yeah

You know if you was goin down I'd be the one to save you. True

But, yo, I need a favor, these cats across town hate me. Uh-huh

Plus their behavior hasn't been too good lately. What!?

Anything for you, dog. Where them niggas at?

38th and Broadway. Let me get the gat

Run up on 'em strapped, bust off caps on four niggas

Laid low for 'bout a month and killed two more niggas

Now I'm ready to chill, but you still want me to kill
Look at what I did for you, dog, come on, keep it real
Aight, fuck it, I'm gonna do it, who is it this time?
Hey, yo, remember that kid Sean you used to be with in '89?
Nah, that's my man. *I thought I was your man?*
But, yo, that's my niggal *Hey, who's your biggest fan?*
Either do it or give me your right hand. That's what you said
I see now, ain't nothin but trouble ahead

[Chorus 4x]

WHO WE BE
[Chorus]
They don't knooow, who we beee
They don't knooow, who we beee

What they don't know is:
The bullshit, the drama (Uhh), the guns, the armor (What?)
The city, the farmer, the babies, the mama (What?!)
The projects, the drugs (Uhh!), the children, the thugs (Uhh!)
The tears, the hugs, the love, the slugs (C'mon!)
The funerals, the wakes, the churches, the coffins (Uhh!)
The heartbroken mothers, it happens too often (Why?!)
The problems, the things we use to solve 'em (What?!)
Yonkers, the Bronx (uhh!), Brooklyn, Harlem (C'mon!)
The hurt, the pain, the dirt, the rain (Uhh!)
The jerk, the fame, the work, the game (Uhh!)
The friends, the foes, the Benz, the hoes (What?!)
The studios, the shows, it comes and it goes (C'mon!)
The jealousy, the envy, the phony, the friendly (Uh-huh!)
The one that gave 'em the slugs, the one that put 'em in me (Whoo!)
The snakes, the grass, too long to see (Uhh, uhh!)
The lawnmower sittin right next to the tree (C'mon!)

[Chorus 2x]

What we seein is:

The streets, the cops, the system, harassment (Uh-huh)

The options: get shot, go to jail, or get ya ass kicked (Aight)

The lawyers, the part they are of the puzzle (Uh-huh)

The release, the warning, "Try not to get in trouble" (Damn!)

The snitches, the odds (uhh), probation, parole (What?!)

The new charge, the bail, the warrant, the hole (Damn!)

The cell, the bus, the ride up north (Uh-huh)

The greens, the boots, the yard, you caught (Uhh!)

The fightin, the stabbin, the pullin, the grabbin (What?!)

The riot squad with the captain, nobody knows what happened (What?!)

The two years in a box, revenge, the plots (Uhh!)

The twenty-three hours that's locked, the one hour that's not (Uhh!)

The silence, the dark, the mind so fragile (Aight!)

The wish that the streets would have took you when they had you (Damn)

The days, the months, the years, despair

One night on my knees, here it comes, the prayer

[Chorus 2x]

This here is all about:

My wife, my kids (Uh-huh), the life that I live (Uh-huh)

Through the night I was his (uh-huh), it was right what I did (Uh-huh)

My ups and downs (Uhh), my slips, my falls (Uhh)

My trials and tribulations (Uhh), my heart, my balls (What?!)

My mother, my father, I love 'em, I hate 'em (Uhh!)

Wish God I didn't have 'em, but I'm glad that he made 'em (Uhh!)

The roaches, the rats, the strays, the cats (What, what?!)

The guns, knives, and bats, every time we scrap

The hustlin, the dealin, the robbin, the stealin (Uhh!)

The shit hit the ceilin, little boy with no feelins (Damn)

The frustration, rage, trapped inside a cage

Got beatins 'til the age I carried a twelve gauge (Aight!)

Somebody stop me (please!), somebody come and get me (What?!)

Little did I know that the Lord was ridin with me

The dark, the light (Uhh), my heart (Uhh), the fight (Uhh)

The wrong (Uhh!), the right (Uhh!), it's gone (Uhh!), aight?

[Chorus 4x]

E-40

E-40 is the ambassador of Bay Area hip-hop. He has been in the industry for over two decades, producing a shelf's worth of albums and working with a range of artists, from 2Pac to Too $hort to Lil Jon. He is renowned for his verbal virtuosity, his knack for neologism. E-40 bends the rules of the English language in ways that sometimes go unnoticed but can challenge the comprehension of the uninitiated. He fashioned the "-izzle" technique (for example, turning "for sure" into "fo' shizzle"), though Snoop Dogg is more commonly associated with it. "Everybody wanna hear a little razzle-dazzle, they wanna hear something slick, they wanna hear new words," he explains. "The world revolves around slang, whether it's corny slang or hip slang from the 'hood. They just wanna hear it, and that's just how it goes. Some people have different ways of doing their slang, but I spit that 'hood slang."[23]

In recent years, E-40 has been an advocate of the hyphy movement, a kind of Bay Area equivalent of southern crunk. "Even though it was a drought on the West Coast, especially in the Bay, for a good 10 years, ever since Tupac passed away," he says, "I held on like a hubcap in the fast lane and kept carrying the Bay on my back."[24]

SPRINKLE ME
(feat. Suga T)

(Burrrp, burp) Yeah, hocus pocus, skiggedy skay. It ain't nuttin but me, that nigga E-40 finna sprinkle some of you fools with some of this. This G-A-M-E, man, some of this game. Understand, my sister. Finna sprinkle you fools with my sprinkle, sister. Understand this, doe. It don't stop 'til the motherfucking

Glock pop. (Don't stop) And fuck a Glock, I'm fuckin with a 6RP226 Diana
Ross cousin nina misdemeanor, that's what we do, understand it.

[E-40]
I be more hipper than a hippopotamus, get off in your head like a neurologist
Pushin more weight than Nautilus, got a partner by the name of 2Pacalypse
The seven-oh-seven, my roots go hella far back to Flor Terrace
I pull a forty out of my ballcap and then I flush it down my esopha-garus
The group that I'm with the Click: Suga, D-Shot, Legit
Family orientated, game related, it's the shit
Killing motherfuckers off crucial, sittin 'em down mutual
Running through these lyrics as if I was fibered like Metamucil

[Chorus]
Timah timah . . .
Forty wata, Forty wata
Sprinkle me, main. Sprinkle me, main
Sprinkle me, main. Sprinkle me, main
Big timah timah, big timah . . .
Forty wata-ahh
Sprinkle me, main. Sprinkle me, main
Sprinkle me, main . . . Kick that shit, Suga

[Suga T]
Here comes the top notch, ooh ooh ooh, here I be
Cliqued-out me, Suga T from the V
I'm quick to smob (Quick to smob), always down for the job
Ya gotta strut, that's a gang of shot (Gang of shot)
Ooh ooh ooh, I'm a fool
Slangin more mail as I smobs through yo' 'hood
Straight shakin all these bustas and busterettes
Tryin to claim fame off my sharp-ass rep (Sharp-ass rep)
Why, oh, why must I be so tight? (Why, oh, why)
Most folks tell me, Suga, you ain't right
(Why, oh, why, Suga, you ain't right)

It makes me wanna scream while I make ya holla
Pullin a gang of clout like that almighty dollar

[Chorus]

[Suga T] Check the flotation! [E-40] Niggas PHin on a playa-makin mega
Tryin to knock the hustle just because we way too major
[Suga T] E, they tryin to test your testicles, you know that shit ain't cool
[E-40] Suga, don't make me have to come up out the sound booth and act a
   fuckin fool
[Suga T] All these old hoe-cake ass niggas, they make me so damn sick
[Suga T and E-40] BOOM BOOM BOOM BOOM BOOM ON A TRICK!
[E-40] Playa play her for false and get rubbed off, ya don't want malse
Fuck around and get evaporated

[Chorus]

FOXY BROWN

Foxy Brown takes her name from the blaxploitation heroine made
famous in the 1970s by Pam Grier, but her style is hers alone. Before releasing an album, Foxy Brown appeared on several 1995–96
platinum singles from artists like Jay-Z, LL Cool J, and Toni Braxton.

Brown is most often compared to Lil' Kim. Both arrived on the music
scene at around the same time. Both were mentored by major rap stars
(Jay-Z for Foxy and Biggie for Kim). And both played upon their sexuality
while exuding an attitude of overwhelming confidence on the microphone.
Both also dealt with the rumor that their famous mentors wrote some of
their lyrics. What is undeniable, though, is that both women made major
impacts upon 1990s hip-hop, bringing female MCs a level of public recognition and commercial success rarely seen in years prior.

As Brown's career has evolved, her lyrics have become increasingly self-
reflective. While "I'll Be," her duet with Jay-Z from her first album, was all

glamour and flash, the later "My Life" and "BK Anthem" explore her Brooklyn upbringing and personal challenges. "I'm probably the most mysterious, misunderstood female rapper ever," she told MTV's Sway around the time of the release of 2001's *Broken Silence*. "And I think that I am sort of a voice of reason for the young teenagers, young adults that are struggling every day, that look up to me."[25]

MY LIFE

(Nigga, uh)
Yeah, huh (Nigga, uh)
Why don't y'all take a look into my life?
See what I see
(Nigga uh, nigga, nigga, nigga uh)

At the age of fourteen, introduced to coupes
Learnin how to seduce niggas, takin they loot
Quickly got involved with this money lifestyle
The finer things, all kind of things
Power, money, cars, and diamond rings
And nice braids, flaunt it, the Gucci boots with the G's on it
A high price for this high-price life
While I'm on tour, is my man cheatin just for spite?
And if you only knew, I hold my minks at night
We cheat, but no other hands can hold me right
My girls ain't the same, guess it's 'cause the fame
Bitches smile in my face then throw dirt on my name
Mad 'cause I made it, now friends intimidated
Hate it that I'm in the same game as them
With mo' fame than them, they know who they are
This life is no joke, I was happier broke
You was my sister, we used to dream together
How we could make it real big, do our thing together
Uhh, *Thelma & Louise* together
Remember them days? Them niggas we played?
Now we don't even speak, went our separate ways

Separate lives, lost friendship for pride

Playin the game, about to forfeit

High-price life, I can't afford it

[Chorus]

My life, do ya feel what I feel?

My life, a black girl's ordeal

My life, do ya see what I see?

Have you been where I've been? Can you go where I go?

My life, do y'all know what it feels like?

Do y'all know what it be like?

Do ya see what I see?

Have you been where I've been? Can you go where I go?

Daddy's girl, in his wildest dreams

Did he think that lil' Ing will be illest in this rap thing?

Age four in my mother's shoes, swore I could sing

And even as a little girl I was doin my thing

Uhh, confused, I ain't asked to be born

Nigga so dumb, shoulda used a condom

Ask Mommy every day, "When Daddy gon' come?"

But he never showed up, I would pimp for them

Became demented then. Men? Resented them

Just the scent of 'em made me 'url

'Specially the baller ones tryin to buy me with pearls

All I needed was love, all I wanted was love

Lack of love had me fallin for thugs

The niggas who ain't care, just like Daddy

If he ain't care, why should they?

For this high-price life, it's the price I pay

[Chorus]

All my girls 'cross the world that feel what I feel

Hearts bruised and been where I been? Keep it movin

Let him do his thing, I'm the one he's lovin

I'm here to show y'all, havin a kid ain't meanin nuthin
That ain't keepin him, 'specially if he in love
With another chick, then you stuck with the baby-mother shit
Don't be lovin niggas more than yourself
Let 'em roam, a dog always finds his way home
Think: y'all don't wanna take my place
Catchin cases, spittin in faces, I never seem
Falsely accused, while some say it's rude
But if I was a dude, they all be amused
But I'm a woman, so I'm a bitch, simple as that
Double-standards, call him a Mack, call me a ho
Say I'm in it for the dough, but tell me
What the fuck he in it for? Huh?
Wanted it all, now it's all mine
Loneliness, sorrow, confusion, and pain
Nightmares, headlines, "Rapper Found Slain"
If it wasn't for my moms I'd drown in this pain
Now y'all see what it's like, y'all don't wanna be me
'Cause it ain't always what it seem on TV
Shit, but this is my nine to five, y'all
Sometimes I wanna slit my wrist and end my life, y'all

[Chorus until fade]

BK ANTHEM
[Chorus]
Lemme tell you where I grew up at
Sip Mo', threw up at, flip coke, blew up at
Little fake thugs got they vests chewed up at
Brooklyn! Beef, who want that?

I grew up in the thoroughest borough: BK
Where Big had everybody rockin DK
Gav was the first dude with the CLK
And bricks was gettin shipped out of East L.A.

It's Brooklyn, where niggas lives is tooken
Rich cats got knocked and they wives was tooken
Fort Greene and Hemlock, the fifth been cocked
We cried when they killed Lenox and popped them rocks
(Aiyo, y'all ain't hear what the fuck I just said?)
BK—the home of Biggie and Jay
Where niggas got Will Smith chips, get jiggy all day
Bitches that boost in the City all day
Heckler & Koch, crack spots, federal watch
I grew up here, sip Mo', threw up here
Yo, the feds snatched two up here, in BK
Niggas in the 'hood in that all blue and gray
Gorillas got rich from stairwells in PA

[Chorus 2x]

Brooklyn! The livest borough
You come here frontin, you might die in this borough
The Eastern Field and Bed-Stuy's in this borough
It's full of projects, the wildest borough
Try to figure out which side is thorough
From C.I. to Saint Marks, it's carryin cons
Niggas rock Coogi and Dolce Gaban's
The women here make a livin just carryin bombs
We pop corks a little bit, we floss a little bit
In the club, buyin out Cris', pour us a little bit
I told y'all that my borough is thorough
I know niggas that'll clap you up and bury the metal
Same day, still in the 'hood, we so ghetto
Brook-non, holla back, get your crook on
Live from the seven-one-eight, we raised the eight
Every time Papi raise the rate of that weight

[Chorus 2x]

It's BK, nigga, get yo' vest ate up
Over them chips, you could get S-K'ed up

They find you in the back of the buildin, sprayed up

All for the love of this paper. We misled

By twenty-one some'll be dead

By twenty-two the rest of these dudes'll be in the feds

We got change but we still fucked up

Niggas is outta jail but they still locked up

The feds takin flicks when we pullin the drops up

BK open up, get popped up

You know it's the borough where cats drive wit' the box in they truck

Trey pound Glocked up, wrist be rocked up

Yellin out, "Get down, lay down!" when we pop up

Blocks so hot we drive the drops with tops up

Windows tinted, you can't see who's in it

It's Brown, nigga, I represent it, it's Brooklyn!

[Chorus 4x]

FREESTYLE FELLOWSHIP

Freestyle Fellowship is a group from Los Angeles consisting of rappers Aceyalone, Myka 9, P.E.A.C.E., Self Jupiter, and producer J Sumbi. They emerged out of the underground hip-hop workshop known as Project Blowed, which started at the Good Life Café in Compton. Together, they defined what photographer-writer Brian "B+" Cross has termed Los Angeles's "post-gangsta" era. Thematically, they offer a sharp contrast to the gangsta aesthetic that dominated Los Angeles rap in the 1990s. Instead, they favored Afrocentric messages and social commentary.

The group, as its name suggests, is known for its range of freestyle rhyming techniques. Their sound is heavily influenced by jazz music, not simply in their beats, but also in their use of scat. "That's what they say I helped do—I helped get the world to freestyle, me and the Freestyle Fellowship, by inventing the Freestyle Fellowship and by redefining what freestyle is," says Myka 9. "Back in the day freestyle was bust[ing] a rhyme about any random thing, and it was a written rhyme or something memorized. We have redefined what freestyle is by saying that it's improvisational rap like a jazz solo, so as a result we actually helped create another trend and culture, another pastime. So now kids can do something else other than just play basketball or whatever—they can sit on the staircase and exchange rhymes instead of going around getting into crimes. It's a good thing to not only MC but freestyle, because it kinda helps promote free thinking."[26]

CAN YOU FIND THE LEVEL OF DIFFICULTY IN THIS?

Can you find the level of difficulty in this? Hahahahaha [2x]

[Myka 9]
Every man for himself
Can be difficult, mythical, typical, critical, pitiful, beautiful, hypocritical, hypothetical
Alphanumerical in a Darwinian way, obstacle course, fittest survival
Unforgettable, unforgiveable, diabolical lies within the Bible
Unified field theory of love, ignoramus enlightened
To his path and purpose, creator, preserver, destroyer, curb server
Quantum mechanics converted from bowties to Mormon, also a paraplegic
Whirling dervish pledge of allegiance backwards rocket science nanotechnology
Awkward moments, caught between a rock and a hard place
You're in a sticky situation zero visibility late night radar emergency
Passenger planet typhoon hurricane broken components
Airstrip stormy rain military ship landing a plane in Malaysia amnesia
Indonesia with a squeegee, you were trying to make a dollar out of fifteen cents
For a ticket to Fiji with *Saturday Night Fever* without the Bee Gees
All the doohickies and thingamabobs of highly sensitive circuitry micro-engineering
A blind man behind the wheel steering energy equaling matter or mass
Times the speed of light squared foreplay with a Catholic nun
Making a ho into a housewife, making a crackhead drop the pipe
Lookin at Luke's peep show fully dressed with a number of angels dancing

On a nuclear warhead, everyone on earth chanting, "Aum"

Taking bong hits holding hands alone at the same time finding a truly righteous queen

In a strip club playing pattycake with heartless thugs

Smotherfuckin overdub

[Aceyalone]

What an elegant battle cry, young Pocahontas, you brought down a shower
of meteorites

Predicted well before Nostradamus described the fall, taking most of us
with it

Forever throwing the earth off of its axis, the autistic artistic art without the
practice

The parachute brainless aimless jump off the twenty-fifth floor

Onto a mattress on to Atlantis, we'll take the Milky Way

In a filthy way and try to dig a hole through China with a spoon handcuffed

To a thousand pounds of C4 we'll dip to the bottom of the sea floor

Then swim back up to the seashore then have a sharpshooting contest

I'll shoot a mango off your head from a mile away eyes shut

I ran a marathon barefooted on broken glass without a cut

Take my place in the stars, see my face on Mars

Hijack NASA for the shuttle with .38 snub nose and race the cars

Take the negative double gee out of man and then erase the wars

For the straightjacket and the crooked face and the broken stick shifter

Or a ceremony for the audio body of miracle spiritual uplifter

A Siamese twin Libra connected amoeba

A beautiful wonderful world, without Mrs. Moon Makeba

That's impossible like Ethan Hunt breathin a blunt, well, believe what you
want

A serial killer Gandhi, lovable Hitler, a fiddler on a burning roof

Learning the truth about the one arm, one leg, one peg, one hook

Rock climber to the top shock rhymer grandfather counterclockwise

Timer oldtimer rap rhyme designer purely indubitably excellent

Brilliantly intertwined her kinda off beat, off center

Odd, simple yet confusing, god, sun shiner with a twist now
Can you find-a the level of difficulty in this?

Can you find the level of difficulty in this? Hahahaha

[P.E.A.C.E.]
Time is running out, only thirty seconds to go
Keep marching in that madness but you must challenge the Final Four
Or the game, lock it up like a lo-lo, rock the cradle like a yo-yo
Bzzzz-uh-bzzzt. What is robo?
Another word for alright, so-so. Another word for chocolate cocoa
Stunt double Wesley Snipes, faster than yo' fo-fo
Now, that's velvet? How did you know? 'Cause I felt it
Your wack-ass albums, we'll shelve it. I hit a note like Harold Melvin
Earthquake every spots where wackness dwells in
They're melting. I can smell them
Stop. Sergio Tacchini, ma cherie amour Diador
In Fila, Reeboks, and Le Coque Sportif
Where's the beef? Barley malt in cereal grains
Choice hops with flip-flops, freshly fried pork chops
Eatin moon soup on a moon rock, collard greens boiled with the ham hocks
Sleep in a hammock and I flow on the shamrock
And I kill ya, kill ya with a overlocked Glock 9
Supply minds, plant landmines, can you find
The level of difficulty in this?

[Self Jupiter]
You'd rather jump off the Empire State building with
Explosive-tip helmet and copper-plated nuclear denture caps, perhaps
Maybe you'd rather dance through the streets of Iraq
Wearing American flag three-piece suit screamin at the top of your lungs,
    "Shoot
Fuck Saddam Hussein. There is no God," in Arabic
Truthfully, you got a better chance of hitting the lottery fifteen times in a row
    and winning

Now you tell me the odds on that. You'd rather get head from a wild bobcat
You'd rather slap the chief of police knowin you got two strikes
You'd rather run up on the White House with a bullseye T-shirt on
Blastin a starter pistol, yelling, "Revolution, revolution"
You'd rather skydive butt naked into a field of meat hooks
And bathe in a flammable solution, solution
Open a Philly overdose on the heron, you'd rather try to dope fiend
    Farrakhan
You'd rather walk through the lion's den wearing pork chop earrings
And cheap top sirloin and body oil cologne
You'd rather be fully awake while being operated on
You got a better chance of going back to the 1920s as a black transvestite
Running for president and winnin, you wanna go head up with a swinging
    wrecking ball
And drug at a hundred and twenty miles through a pavement of ten-inch
    titanium nails
You'd rather die for what you don't believe in . . .

Can you find the level of difficulty in this? Hahahahaha [2x]

THE GUIDELINES
(Aceyalone)
Let's begin . . . As-Salamu Alaykum, people of good will
I offer you the greeting of thought-manifested skill
To finally reveal the open-end chapter
As real as the flesh that you're embodied in
To the skull cavity your mind is rotting in, I'll be riding in
And there might have been a slight, rotation warp to curve
The course. Of course I'm cordial when I report
I won't distort, I don't contort
Connect, conduct, collect, console, or conceal
In full control of the roll of the wheel
My eyes are my appliance to decipher the science
Omitting defiance with the high-tech mic check
The buttons that flashed I pushed for absolute

Destruction, your structure is lifted from the ground

The foundation mound is broke, so you float around

I'm embedded in what is known as beat

Let it be shown every enzyme is complete

In time, you'll see the pace of the pulse pump

Rapidly, heart rate, happily marched

I happen to be the dark man who holds the charts

I arch my horizontal line to make a rainbow

But it ain't the same though, yo

The tried and true pros are chasing fool's gold

Sliding through holes like small rodents

It's obviously evident my embellishment

Peaks at two-ninety-two, I.Q.

'Cause Big Ace is the spinner in the center

Inventor, and I plan to be a winner, meaning

I'll be in the inner outer ovaries, overload, overboard

Overseas, hearing oversees more than the eye can

I stand, limited primitive, sentimentalist, escapist

The way I shape this landscape automatically makes this vivid

I give it a rivet, hold it, stand at the pivot

I love it, learn it, live it, then give you my exhibit

Not inhibited, not even a little bit, when I'm inclined

My attempts to redefine your hip-hop guidelines

And you can play the sideline; write rhymes in your spare time

My attempts to redefine your hip-hop guidelines

You can play the sideline; write rhymes in your spare time

'Cause I'd rather stimulate your mind than emulate your purpose

And we have only touched on the surface of the serpent

Consider me part of the dust, in the dusk

I must collect the samples from the rust

Penetrate the crust then trust no living

Driven by the sonic, language passion

Your ashes spark the flashes, of the neon

From be-yond, what kind of planet could I be on?

I don't know, but I'ma be on for eons and eons

While many think that they can never play out

Get trapped in a timeframe and never find their way out

I stay off the dramatization and I balance

Always seeking the challenge, to show the world

The incredible talents, I cut the corners, smooth out the surfaces

Worthlessness is just half of the problem

I read the grid, kid, I did every column

I note the animal kingdom and the phylum

Why-lum style 'em, until they get to hit the target

I mark it on the bullseye, of flies and the buffalo wing in the sky

My architectnique sparks the dark streets of your resting ground

I suggest that you warn your town

I inhabit the oxygen, mark off the memory

You will never forget to remember the lone wolverine

Marine biologist machine with the verbal

Internal mind fertile, foot over hurdle

Tight like girdle and my word'll be the last

I incubate every other millennium

I fast and I hibernate to pass any of 'em

I am potent, untraceable

No color, no odor, no taste, no replaceable parts

No heart, no head, just a carcass

The darkest days come right before the light

I watch my watch and stand right before the mic

By the powers vested in me, I digested MCs

Food for thought, caught on to the end of the rope and swung

Then stood stiff as if I was on a cliff

Not beneath sticks, my feet are made of bricks

When I walk my footprints indent cement

I am not practical, nor am I unusual

Nor am I oblivious to hideous crimes

Every city is captured and trapped in my mind

Given the spinal tap as the final rap climbs

My attempts to redefine your hip-hop guidelines

You can play the sidelines; write rhymes in your spare time

My attempts to redefine your hip-hop guidelines

You can play the sidelines; write rhymes in your spare time

'Cause I have become the night owl on the prowl

Master of the free pen pal style

'Cause I'm om-nipotent

I'm some government experiment that is out of control

I'm from some big black hole

I square up, select, and wrecked every tangle

I flare up and you can try any angle

Even Bermuda, but I bury the barracuda

Then I'm octa-gone in the wind with the pollen

THE FUGEES

The Fugees are among the most recognized groups in the history of rap, though they only released two albums. Consisting of Wyclef Jean and Pras Michel, both Haitian immigrants, and Lauryn Hill, from suburban New Jersey, they derived their name from the slang term for "refugee." The spirit of the African diaspora, most especially the Caribbean, suffuses their music. They crafted powerful, melodic hip-hop that was popular without compromise. Their Grammy-winning *The Score* (1996) is one of the bestselling rap albums in history, with over 18 million sold.

The trio was stylistically complementary. Jean's rhyming laced with Haitian patois and reggae-influenced singing matched well with Hill's commanding flows and cerebral content and Pras's resonant vocal tones. "They were definitely a group that didn't care what everyone else was doing," remarks Havoc of Mobb Deep. "They just were them, and you could tell they weren't trying to be different; they *were* different."[27]

VOCAB

Yo, this is the Fugees. Refugees. About to take you on a journey into the
dimensions of the Booga Basement, the Basements, word. Uhh

[Lauryn Hill]

Hey, yo, one two three! The crew is called Re-Fu-Ge-ee-es
An if you come fa' tes' the rap stylee
Stop the violence and just bring it on, wyo!

Hey, yo, I feel kind of melancholy people think they really know me
I keep my wrap about me while I'm driving Daddy's Audi
I pay the toll fighting for my own soul
'Cause the bourgeois type of mental sucks like a black hole
But I be raidin the rebel base to bass, distort the EQ
Them devils wishin they could send me back to Mogadishu
'Cause I've been wild since I was a juvenile
Afrocentric profile, back when righteous rap was still in style
Now kids are whylin so I ask the bad black
"Boogie bandit, what's the damage, gimme the estimate then
Pray tell me when the revolution will begin"
I turn on my TV, I check out Farrakhan on CNN, see
I'm like the phantom that's flying like the bird
Doing things you never heard, plus I come from the suburbs
Word to God, I heard you had it kind of hard
And you got your skin scarred when they was shootin on the boulevard

[Chorus]

(You got the vocab) I got the vocab
(On the real, got the vocab) You know we got the vocab
(All my peeps got the vocab) Yeah, we got the vocab
[Lauryn Hill] Aiyo, Pras, grab the mic and show that you got the gift
of gab

[Pras]

Then cast off from here to Mexico
You see my four-five-six a-be my cee-lo

And when I rest my head is on a pi-llow

Be-ba-dee-be, be-dee-be, be-dee-be-bo

You see the skills I manifest is very thorough

And if you don't believe me ask Frère Jacques-o

Mmmm, Frère Jacques-o, Frère Jacques-o

A dormez-vous? A dormez-vous?

WATCH OUT NOW! When I choose to speak

I'm forming the cipher fly, peace to the Five-Percenter

Knowledge is born to all beginners

Cast the first stone if you feel you ain't a sinner, ahh

Say, our Father who art in heaven

Forgive the foolish rapper for he not know how Fugee be steppin

Correct and, stopped and kept in, nuff respect to the

DJ that be selectin the type of record, ahhh

[Chorus]

[Wyclef Jean]

Check it out, here we go

Back in Eighty-TREE, no one wanted to be NAP-PY

I turn on my TV, it's a dreadlock for FREE

Kill the gimmick, it's nonsense, it's no sense or value

A rapper, disaster, nobody ever told me that

"Roxanne, you don't got to work for money no more!!"

And . . . Back in the days I used to listen to Kool G Rap

Way back when before guns became gats and

Run-DMC used to ask Mary was she buggin?

I loved P.E., they kept me conscious of what I was saying

Afrika Bambaataa, Poor Righteous Teachers

Got within myself so it made me a Five-Percenter

Say la-di-da-di, uhh, we like to party but

My jam was BDP, with "My Philosophy"

Say Grandmaster Flash, MC Melle Mel

Then LL Cool J came with "Rock the Bells"

See, I'm known for the crew, like a Jew is a Jew

Like Apollo got the moon, like the men who got the brew

Like the Fu got the Manchu, Shaka got the Zulu

Hawaii got the Honolulu

I got the rap blues, so skippedy-de-bop-bop, you don't stop

You do the rock-rock from hip-hop through be-bop

From be-bop to bee-bee

[Chorus 3x]

FU-GEE-LA

[Wyclef Jean]

We used to be number ten, now we permanent at one

In the battle lost my finger, mic became my arm

Pistol nozzle hits your nasal, blood becomes lukewarm

Tell the woman be easy, naah squeeze the Charmin

Test Wyclef, see death flesh get scorned

Beat you so bad make you feel like you ain't wanna be born, Jean

And tell your friends stay the hell out of my lawn

Chicken George became Dead George stealin chickens from my farm

Damn . . . another dead pigeon

If you're Mafiosos then I'm bringin on Haitian Sicilians

Nobody's shootin, my body's made of hand grenade

Girl bled to death while she was tongue-kissin a razor blade

That sound sick, maybe one day I'll write a horror

Blackula comes to the ghetto, jacks an Acura

Stevie Wonder sees crack babies becoming enemies

In they own families

Armageddon come, you know-a we soon done

Gun by my side just in case I gotta rum'

A boy on the side of Babylon

Trying to front like you're down with Mount Zion

[Chorus]

Oooh la la la

It's the way that we rock when we're doing our thing

Oooh la la la

It's the natural la that the Refugees bring

Oooh la la la la la la la

La-la-la la laaah, sweeeeet thing

She love me like she never before, hey

[Lauryn Hill]

Yeah, in saloons we drink Boone's and battle goons 'til high noon

Bust rap toons on flat spoons, take no shorts like poom-pooms

See, hoochies pop coochies for Guccis and loochie

Find me in my Mitsubishi, eatin sushi, bumpin Fugees

Hey, hey, hey, try to take the crew and we don't play play

"Say, Say, Say," like Paul McCartney, not hardly

Odd-ly enough, I can see right through your bluff

Niggas huff and they puff but they can't handle us, we

Bust! 'Cause we fortified, I could never hide

Seen *Cooley High,* cried when Cochise died

I'm twisted, blacklisted by some other Negroes

Don't remove my Polos on the first episode

(Ha ha ha ha) You shouldn't dis Refugees and

(Ha ha ha ha) Your whole sound set booty and

(Ha ha ha ha) You have to respect Jersey, 'cause I'm superfly

When I'm super-high on the Fu-Gee-La

[Chorus]

[Pras]

I sit ninety degrees underneath palm trees

Smokin bidis as I burn my calories

Brooklyn rooftops become Brooklyn teepees

Who that be? Enemy wanna see the death of me

From Hawaii to Hawthorne, I run marathons, like

Buju Banton, I'm a true champion, like

Farrakhan reads his daily Qur'an, it's a

Phenomenon, lyrics fast like Ramadan

[Wyclef Jean]

What's goin on? Armageddon come, you know-a we soon done

Gun by my side just in case I gotta rum'

A boy on the side of Babylon

Trying to front like you're down with Mount Zion [2x]

[Chorus 2x]

READY OR NOT

[Chorus]

Ready or not, here I come, you can't hide

Gonna find you and take it slowly

Ready or not, here I come, you can't hide

Gonna find you and make you want me

[Wyclef Jean]

Now that I escape, sleepwalk awake

Those who could relate know the world ain't cake

Jails bars ain't golden gates, those who fake, they break

When they meet their four-hundred-pound mate

If I could rule the world, everyone would have a gun

In the ghetto, of course, when giddy-uppin on their horse

I kick a rhyme drinking moonshine

I pour sip on the concrete for the deceased

But, no, don't weep, Wyclef's in a state of sleep

Thinkin 'bout the robbery that I did last week

Money in the bag, banker look like a drag

I wanna play with pelicans from here to Bagdad

Gun blast, think fast, I think I'm hit

My girl pinched my hips to see if I still exist

I think not, I'll send a letter to my friends

A born-again hooligan, only to be king again

[Chorus]

[Lauryn Hill]

I play my enemies like a game of chess

Where I rest, no stress if you don't smoke cess

Less, I must confess my destiny's manifest

In some Gore-Tex and sweats, I make tracks like I'm homeless

Rap orgies with Porgy and Bess

Capture your bounty like Eliot Ness (Yes)

Bless you if you represent the Fu'

But I hex you with some witches' brew if you do-do

Voodoo, I could do what you do easy (Easy)

Believe me, frontin niggas give me heebie-jeebies

So while you imitatin Al Capone

I be Nina Simone and defecating on your microphone

[Chorus]

You can't run away from these styles I got, oh baby

Hey, baby, 'cause I got a lot, oh yeah

And anywhere you go, my whole crew gonna know, oh, baby, hey, baby

You can't hide from the block, oh, no

[Pras]

Ready or not, Refugees taking over

"The buffalo soldier, dread-lock rasta"

On the twelfth hour, fly-by in my bomber

Crews run for cover, now they under pushin up flowers

Superfly, true lies, do or die, trust me I

Only puff lye with my crew from la caille

I refugee from Guantanamo Bay

Dance around the border like I'm Cassius Clay

[Chorus]

GOODIE MOB

G oodie Mob defined the Dirty South—quite literally, introducing the term on a song from their debut album. The Dirty South would come to embody a raw and uncompromising style of rap that stretched from Georgia to Texas. Goodie Mob consists of four MCs: Cee-Lo, Khujo, T-Mo, and Big Gipp. Along with fellow Atlanta rappers Outkast, they came to embody a southern rap aesthetic of soulful beats (both groups were produced by Organized Noize) and street-oriented and socially conscious lyrics. "Goodie Mob aimed to capture the entire existential struggle of the black man trying to get by on the land where his ancestors had been enslaved," writes Roni Sarig.[28]

Their debut album, *Soul Food* (1995), features everything from introspective rhymes concerning the South's legacy of slavery ("See, in the third grade this is what you told: / You was bought, you was sold") to odes honoring the wonders of southern cuisine ("a heaping helping of fried chicken, macaroni and cheese and collard greens / Too big for my jeans"). The group released two more albums in the 1990s before one of the key members, Cee-Lo, left the group for a solo career. Cee-Lo's dual talents of rhyming and singing are apparent on songs like "Cell Therapy" and "Soul Food."

CELL THERAPY

[Khujo]
When the scene unfolds, young girls
Thirteen years old, expose themselves
To any Tom, Dick, and Hank. Got mo'
Stretch marks than these hoes hollerin they got rank
See, Sega ain't in this New World Order, dem
Experimenting in Atlanta, Georgia
United Nations overseas, trained assassins
Do search and seize, ain't knocking or asking
Dem common folk, niggas like me, po' white trash like they
Tricks like her back in slavery
Concentration camps laced with gas pipelines
Infernos outdoors like they had back

When Adolf Hitler was living in 1945

Listen to me now, believe me later on

In the future. Look it up—Where they say it? In the Constitution

That in the event of a race war, places like

Operation Heartbreak Hotel, moments 'til

Until air-tight vents seal off despair

Dem say expect no mercy. Fool, you should be my least worries

Got to deal with W-2s

1099s, unmarked black helicopters

Swoop down and try to put missiles in my ass

[Chorus]

Who's that peeking in my window

Pow! Nobody now

Who's that peeking in my window

Pow! Nobody now

[Cee-Lo]

Me and my family moved in our apartment complex

A gate with the serial code was put up next

They claim that this community is so drug free

But it don't look that way to me 'cause I can see

The young bloods hanging out at the store twenty-four seven

Junkies looking fo' a hit of the blow, it's powerful

Oh, you know what else they tryin to do? Make a curfew

Especially for me and you, the traces of the New

World Order, time is getting shorter

If we don't get prepared, people, it's gon' be a slaughter

My mind won't allow me to not be curious

My folk don't understand so they don't take it serious

But every now and then, I wonder if the gate

Was put up to keep crime out or keep our ass in . . .

[Chorus]

[T-Mo]

Listen up, little nigga, I'm talking to you

About what yo' little ass need to be going through

I fall a victim, too, and I know I shouldn't

Smoke so much, but I do with the crew every day

On the average 'bout four or five, I'm lucky to be alive

At sunrise now I realize the cost after I lost

My best friend Ben I recognize as a kin

Who am I to tell you to stop smoking?

Now you're open to disease and colds and ain't sixteen years old

This shit has got to stop, let's take a walk through detox

I want outta this hole, I'm in a cell

Under attack. Loc' up, folks, they in the 'hood

Got an eye on every move I make

Open your face to info you ain't know 'cause it's kept low

How the New World plan reach the planet without the black man

[Big Gipp]

So what's your aim? Tryin to separate me from the blood

Is disrespect like coming in my home and not

Wiping your feet on the rug, the Citron Absolut

Has got me bucking, no hang with no phony

Look out for the man with the mask and the white pony

On my back are bills, staying off my toes, always on my heels

Insane plain, soldiers coming in the dark by plane

To enforce the new system by reign, tag my skin with your computer chip

Run your hand over the scanner, divide you dish now

No more fishing for your fish

Kiss the days of the old days past ways gone

Mind blown, conception, protection

My name on your selections but I caught you coming—Pow!

[Chorus 2x]

HIEROGLYPHICS

H ieroglyphics is an ever-expanding underground Oakland collective presently comprised of Del tha Funkee Homosapien, Casual,
Domino, Pep Love, DJ Touré, and the members of the group
Souls of Mischief (A-Plus, Opio, Tajai, and Phesto). The group formed in
the early 1990s, and though they have released only two studio albums—
3rd Eye Vision (1998) and *Full Circle* (2003)—the various members have
compiled an extensive discography through their outside efforts. The selections that follow include Hiero's "Classic" and lyrics from both Del and
Souls of Mischief.

Souls of Mischief cultivated a sound that helped broaden the accepted
range of West Coast rap and had a lasting effect on hip-hop from the Bay
Area and beyond. Their debut *93 'til Infinity* (1993) was a commercial success, due in large part to its distinctive sound, distinguished by hyperkinetic
flows. As Lefty Banks points out, on many of their songs "the verbal battery
is relentless, practically pummeling you into submission as the MCs finish
each other's sentences and hand off verses faster than a relay team does a
baton."[29] This back and forth lyrical style is evident on "Cab Fare," testifying
to the group aesthetic that Souls epitomizes. For his part, Del brings the
rich tones of his voice to lyrics that range from the offbeat (like rapping
about body odor on "If You Must") to the interplanetary (as on "Virus").

CAB FARE
(Souls of Mischief)

[Tajai]
Yo, the jam was fly. Oh my, now it's over
My batch of pals cut so Tajai must catch a
Taxicab. Dag nab, why'd they leave me?
Stuck in the late night alley. Cali's
Not so hype that everyone should be sweatin
Yet nobody's smilin, plus crews are pilin
Starin, thinkin what they'd look like wearin
My gear. A sigh when the Yellow Cab neared
He sped up, 'cause dreds made him think I'd vic him

Now I gotta dodge thugs like I'm playin chicken
An Englishman, an Irishman
Five or ten Caucasians passed me in their taxis
Oh, no such luck, I'm gonna get bucked
For my apparel as I seen a black gauge barrel
Just then a fat cab came to my rescue
Damn . . . I'm glad black men drive them cabs, too

[Opio]
It seems nowadays cab rides are rather pricely
Especially when the driver goes for self, in spite of the
Directions that are given, they are driven to cruise backstreets
That treats them to a pricely fair, exactly
What happened to myself when I chose to call a taxi
It pulled up to the curb and I hopped into the backseat
Gave him the destination—said he'd never heard of the place
And I'd have to tell him as we went along, and then placed it
In drive. When I said make a left he made a right
All right, I get it. You wanna make some slight
Detours so you can be sure that you get yours
And when I turn my head, you up the bill a little more
I told the cabbie to stop; he didn't think I watched it
Fake reached into my pocket and then jetted like I was Rocket
Ishmael. His taillight was broken as a token
Of appreciation. He started chasin but I smoked him

[Phesto]
What? You can't escape me, mop head
Drop dead, deceased, say your final summons
If I catch ya, bet ya regret ya ever ditched me
Drivin, connivin, guys been
Robbin me lately. He went up Blake Street, but I'm followin
Swallowin up steps. He ran to the left, I made a left
And crashed into a rose bush. My nose crushed
On impact. But, yo, I'll get him back . . .

[A-Plus]

I didn't have enough for a car; what a bummer

I had to get a job drivin taxis last summer

All the other drivers knew that my car was spectacular

'Cause I had a tight, very bright yellow Acura

Pilin in nine or ten skins at a time, G

Funny how the honeys with the money always find me

Payin their green to see what color my house is

Feelin like Del 'cause they would sleep on my couches

I'd charge senior citizens extra 'cause they never mention

I'd take all the money from they pension

And I'd drive a blind man around for a while

Even if he only had to travel just a mile

With a smile. And don't let your dog off the leash

'Cause if he stepped, then I would have to squash the beast

And if you didn't have the right change, don't even ask me

Or I woulda ran ya ass down with my taxi

CLASSIC

[Tajai]

It's the lynchpin, lynching, antsy inchin

Bit by bit, chompin at the bit

My shots hit accurate for profit, passionate

For profit, cashin in, that's the shit

Lyrical laxative runnin off afta'

Never relaxing, lashin different than the last one

So let's see, chocolate dipped nuts, I'm Nestle

Milk, World Wrestling Federation built

Y'all are complacent still? Display some skill!

My word placement, first place, and not a verse basic

My complex is complex, balance in check

No comment with comparable talents as yet

There's always a first, yet there's always a verse

And always a hearse, so they always disperse

Tails tucked, who, why, when, where, what?
And how? Sorry, but not with that style!
I'm fond of fondling these tactless tactile
Cats until they tapped out, put that down
'Cause I put that down. Yeah, I do that there
While you act scared, talkin 'bout "who that there"
I'll knock 'em out! If you ain't ship shape keep your shit shut
'Fore I shift shape, leave this shit shut
Closed up, sucker, get your flows up!
You hold down … what's the hold up, huh?

[Chorus: Del]
Uh, somethin ya do when you're fire resistant
An ion intrinsic instantaneous lenses
Diablo, domino effect, wobble
Stumble, tryin to follow? Ask Paulo
Dumbo! Need a model? Taj will
Assault silicone, reverberate with realer tone
Fill in holes 'til it hurt deep in your bones
I mean really drill it home to your inner zone

[Pep Love]
We put in the work to make your body jerk
We won't shirk the duty of makin you shake your glute-
Us maximus, yeah, that's what's up!
The music is movin, you need to be catchin up
Classical massacres occur in a flash, a blur
Smashin her iller than when we clash with words
Adrenaline rush shatter you fragile gentlemen
When I hit 'em up with agile style, venom
And change the game like two ways did pagers
And 2Pac did before the plagiarists came
Sword swing around, we not horsing
I'ma do mine, you do your thing
Hieroglyphics is monolithic, chronicle and I

Careen in on a collision course to contradiction

God is listenin, we collage

Analyze with the touch of a brush to paint this picture

I'm heartfelt with the texture of velvet

My art propellin, the wax start meltin

We makin the matrix break to this

And motivatin the shake complacentness

Mixed of many maneuvers, we get blitzed

And the groove is deep as it gets to reap benefits

From Oakland to Brooklyn, the language spoken

Broken and crooked, you know how we do it!

[Chorus]

VIRUS
(Del)
[Chorus]

I wanna devise a virus

To bring dire straits to your environment

Crush your corporations with a mild touch

Trash your whole computer system and revert you to papyrus

I want to make a super virus

Strong enough to cause blackouts in every single metropolis

'Cause they don't wanna unify us

So fuck it, total anarchy and can't nobody stop us

You see, late in the evening

Fucked up, on my computer and my mind starts roaming

I create like a heathen

The first cycles of this virus I can send through a modem

Infiltration hits your station

No Microsoft or enhanced DOS will impede

Society thinks they're safe when

Bingo! Hard drive crashes from the rending

A lot of hackers tried viruses before
Vaporize your text like so much whiteout
I want it where a file replication is a chore
Lights out, shut down entire White House
I don't want just a bug that could be corrected
I'm erecting immaculate design
Break the nation down section by section
Even to the greatest minds, it's impossible to find

[Chorus 2x]

I want to develop a super virus
Better by far than that old Y2K
This is 3030, the time of
Global unification, break right through they
Terminals, burn 'em all, slaves to silicon
Corrupt politicians with leaders and their keywords
FBI and spies stealin bombs
Decepticate their plans in their face and catch the fever
Everybody loot the stores, get your canned goods
Even space stations are having a hard time
Peacekeepers seek to take our manhood
Which results in the form of global apartheid
Ghettos are trash dumps with gas pumps
Exploded and burnt out since before the great union
The last punks walk around like masked monks
Ready to manipulate the database or break through 'em
Human rights come in a hundredth place
Mass production has always been number one
New Earth has become a repugnant place
So it's time to spread the fear and the thunder some

[Chorus 2x]

LAURYN HILL

L auryn Hill is one of the most beloved artists in hip-hop, though also one of the most enigmatic. Her production to date mostly came during the intensive period between the release of the Fugees' *Blunted on Reality* (1994) and her classic solo debut, *The Miseducation of Lauryn Hill* (1998). In between came another classic with the Fugees, *The Score* (1998). Hill, one of the most musical of rappers, has a style that comes at the listener in dense layers of melody, assonance, alliteration, and rhyme, both at the end and within the line. She brings a rich array of themes to her lyrics, delving into matters of politics, faith, and metaphysics. Many of her lyrics also deal with love—erotic, paternal, filial, divine.

Among the many inspirations heard in her music and lyrics is Bob Marley. "I grew up really appreciating Bob Marley's music until I realized that I had certain gifts that I had not exercised," she recalls. "I wasn't utilizing all of myself. Many people are artists, not because they decide to be artists. They stumble onto a talent, a favor from God, after He decided to anoint them, and give them a little more than others. But then they have to walk this fine line between being apologetic for their talent and being considered egotistical. The same thing people get celebrated for, that's the same they get hated for. A true artist has to understand humility, and be aware of how the world treats its prophets."[30] A singer, rapper, actress, and ambivalent sex symbol, Lauryn Hill was one of the biggest stars in hip-hop culture before receding from the limelight near the turn of the century.

DOO WOP (THAT THING)

It's been three weeks since you've been looking for your friend
The one you let hit it and never called you again
'Member when he told you he was 'bout the Benjamins?
You act like you ain't hear him then give him a little trim
To begin, how you think you really goin pretend
Like you wasn't down, then you called him again?
Plus, when you give it up so easy you ain't even foolin him
If you did it then, then you'd probably fuck again
Talking out your neck sayin you're a Christian

A Muslim sleeping with a djinn

Now that was the sin that did Jezebel in

Who you goin tell when the repercussions spin?

Showing off your ass 'cause you're thinking it's a trend

Girlfriend, let me break it down for you again

You know I only say it 'cause I'm truly genuine

Don't be a hard rock when you really are a gem

Baby girl, respect is just a minimum

Niggas fucked up and you still defending 'em

Now, Lauryn is only human

Don't think I haven't been through the same predicament

Let it sit inside your head like a million women

In Philly Penn; it's silly when girls sell they souls

Because it's in. Look at where you be in, hair weaves

Like Europeans, fake nails done by Koreans

Come again

Win, win, come again

Brethren, come again

My friend, come again

Guys, you know you better watch out

Some girls, some girls are only about

That thing, that thing, that thing

That thing, that thing, that thing

The second verse is dedicated to the men

More concerned with his rims and his Tims than his women

Him and his men come in the club like hooligans

Don't care who they offend popping yang (Like you got yen)

Let's not pretend, they wanna-pack-pistol-by-they-waist men

Cristal-by-the-case men, still-in-they-mother's-basement

The pretty-face-men, claiming that they did-a-bid men

Need to take care of their three and four kids then

They facing a court case when the child's support late

Money-taking, heartbreaking, now you wonder why women hate men

The sneaky-silent men, the punk-domestic-violence men

The quick-to-shoot-the-semen, stop acting like boys and be men

How you gon' win when you ain't right within?

How you gon' win when you ain't right within?

How you gon' win when you ain't right within?

Uh, uh, come again

Yo, yo, come again

Brethren come again

And sistren come again

Watch out, watch out, look out, look out

Watch out, watch out, look out, look out

Girls, you know you better watch out

Some guys, some guys are only about

That thing, that thing, that thing

That thing, that thing, that thing

LOST ONES

It's funny how money changes situations

Miscommunication lead to complication

My emancipation don't fit your equation

I was on the humble, you on every station

Some wan' play young Lauryn like she dumb

But remember not a game new under the sun

Everything you did has already been done

I know all the tricks from Brix to Kingston

My ting done made your kingdom wan' run

Now understand L. Boogie nonviolent

But if a thing test me, run for mi gun

Can't take a threat to mi newborn son

L been this way since creation

A groupie call, you fall from temptation

Now you wan' bawl over separation

Tarnish my image in your conversation
Who you goin scrimmage, like you the champion?
You might win some but you just lost one

You might win some but you just lost one [4x]

Now, now how come your talk turn cold?
Gained the whole world for the price of your soul
Tryin to grab hold of what you can't control
Now you all floss, what a sight to behold
Wisdom is better than silver and gold
I was hopeless, now I'm on Hope Road
Every man wanna act like he's exempt
Need to get down on his knees and repent
Can't slick-talk on the day of judgment
Your movement's similar to a serpent
Tried to play straight, how your whole style bent?
Consequence is no coincidence
Hypocrites always wanna play innocent
Always wanna take it to the full-out extent
Always wanna make it seem like good intent
Never wanna face it when it time for punishment
I know that you don't wanna hear my opinion
But there come many paths and you must choose one
And if you don't change then the rain soon come
See, you might win some but you just lost one

You might win some but you just lost one [4x]

[Chorus]
You might win some but you really lost one
You just lost one; it's so silly, how come?
When it's all done, did you really gain from
What you done, done? It's so silly, how come?
You just lost one

Now don't you understand, man, universal law?

What you throw out come back to you, star

Never underestimate those who you scar

'Cause karma, karma, karma come back to you hard

You can't hold God's people back that long

The chain of Shaitan wasn't made that strong

Trying to pretend like your word is your bond but

Until you do right, all you do will go wrong

Now, some might mistake this for just a simple song and

Some don't know what they have 'til it's gone

Now, even when you're gone you can still be reborn and

From the night can arrive the sweet dawn

Now, some might listen and some might shun and

Some may think that they've reached perfection; if you

Look closely you'll see what you've become

'Cause you might win some but you just lost one

You might win some but you just lost one [4x]

[Chorus]

FINAL HOUR

I treat this like my thesis

Well-written topic broken down into pieces

I introduce then produce words so profuse

It's abuse how I juice up this beat like I'm deuce

Two people both equal like I'm Gemini

Rather Simeon. If I jimmy on this lock

I could pop it, you can't stop it, drop it

Your whole crew microscopic like particles while I make international

Articles and on the cover

Don't discuss the baby mother business

I been in this—third LP, you can't tell me, I witness first-handed

I'm candid, you can't stand it, respect demanded

And get flown around the planet, rock-hard like granite

Or steel, people feel Lauryn Hill from New-Ark to Israel
And this is real, so I keep makin the street ballads
While you lookin for dressin to go with your tossed salad

[Chorus 2x]
You can get the money, you can get the power
But keep your eyes on the Final Hour

I'm about to change the focus from the richest to the brokest
I wrote this opus to reverse the hypnosis
Whoever closest to the line gon' win it
You gonna fall trying to ball while my team win the pennant
I'm about to begin it, for a minute, then run for Senate
Make a slum lord be the tenant, give his money to kids to spend it
And then amend it, every law that ever prevented
Our survival since our arrival documented in the Bible
Like Moses and Aaron, things gon' change, it's apparent
And all the transparent gon' be seen through
Let God redeem you, keep your deen true, you can get the green too
Watch out who you cling to, observe how a queen do
And I remain calm reading the 73rd Psalm
'Cause with all this going on, I got the world in my palm

[Chorus]

Now I be breaking bread, sipping Manischewitz wine
Pay no mind, party like it's 1999
But when it come down to ground beef like Palestine
Say your rhyme, let's see if that get you out your bind
Now I'ma get the mozzarella like a Rockefeller, still be
In the Church of Lalibela, singing hymns a cappella
Whether posed in *Mirabella* in couture—or
Collecting residuals from off *The Score*
I'm making sure I'm with the Hundred-Forty-Four
I been here before, this ain't a battle, this is war
Word to Boonie, I make Salah like a Sunni

Get diplomatic immunity in every ghetto community

Had opportunity, went from Hoodshock to 'hood-chic

But it ain't what you cop, it's about what you keep

And even if there are leaks, you can't capsize this ship

'Cause I baptize my lips every time I take sips

[Chorus]

ICE CUBE

Ice Cube was one of the big reasons that the West Coast earned legitimacy for its lyricism in the 1990s. As a founding member of NWA, along with Eazy-E, Dr. Dre, and DJ Yella, he honed his commanding lyrical style and helped give birth to gangsta rap.

With his solo debut, *AmeriKKKa's Most Wanted* (1990), Ice Cube took the unconventional step for a West Coast artist of recording with the East Coast production gurus the Bomb Squad, whose signature, post–Phil Spector "wall of noise" sound was made famous in rap by Public Enemy. This fusion of East and West Coast sounds was idiosyncratic and even controversial, but the result helped to launch Ice Cube's fame and further extend rap's reach. "The sound is what attracted me," Cube recalls, "because I knew I would be doin' what I do, but like I said, Public Enemy was a big influence on me, so I was waiting for Chuck D, to see what he brought to the table in terms of my style—the street knowledge and political hip-hop."[31] The album also occasioned a number of controversies, with Ice Cube being accused of racism and misogyny (the latter charge anticipated, exacerbated, and complicated by "It's a Man's World," a duet with Yo-Yo included below). Over the next three years he released three more hit albums, emerging along with Snoop Dogg as the leading figure in West Coast hip-hop.

Ice Cube's lyrical craft is sometimes overlooked because of his subject matter. "Greatest MC of all time to me?" Snoop Dogg once remarked. "I will say probably Ice Cube."[32] Cube has frequently stated in interviews, by way of explaining gangsta rap and his style in particular, that the violence and mayhem described in his lyrics require a sense of tone and context from the listener. "You take a little bit of Muhammad Ali, a little bit of Richard Pryor, you take a lot of the '80s and what was goin' on, and out comes gangsta rap," he says. "People gotta understand its ingredients, and if you don't have those ingredients of humor and command of the language and of course rhyming, bravado, you gotta bring a little ego wit' you, you know what I mean? The ingredients of bein' a great rapper. That is the key—these are the things you have to have to even be in the game, so that's a lot of people's startin' point."[33]

THE NIGGA YA LOVE TO HATE

I heard payback's a motherfucking nigga
That's why I'm sick of gettin treated like a goddamn stepchild
Fuck a punk 'cause I ain't him
You gotta deal with the nine-double-M
The damn scum that you all hate
Just think if niggas decide to retaliate
And try to keep me from runnin up
I never tell you to get down, it's all about comin up
So what they do? Go and ban the AK
My shit wasn't registered any fucking way
So you better duck away, run and hide out
When I'm rollin real slow and the light's out
'Cause I'm about to fuck up the program
Shootin out the window of a drop-top Brougham
While I'm shootin let's see who drop
The police, the media, and suckers that went pop
And motherfuckers that say they too black
Put 'em overseas, they be beggin to come back
They say keep 'em on gangs and drugs
You wanna sweep a nigga like me up under the rug
Kickin shit called street knowledge
Why more niggas in the pen than in college?

Because of that line, I might be your cellmate

That's from the nigga ya love to hate

[Chorus]

Fuck you, Ice Cube!

Yeah, ha-ha, it's the nigga you love to hate

Fuck you, Ice Cube!

Aiyo, baby, your mother warned you about me

It's the nigga you love to hate

"Yo, you ain't doing nothing pos'tive. Yo, you ain't doing nothing pos'tive for the brothers. What you got to say for yourself?" You don't like how I'm living? Well, fuck you!

Once again it's on, the motherfucking psycho

Ice Cube the bitch killa, cap peeler

Yo, runnin through the line like Bo

There's no pot to piss in, I put my fist in

Now who do ya love to hate?

'Cause I talk shit and down the eight-ball

'Cause I don't fake, you're begging I fall off

You crossed over, might as well cut them balls off

And get your ass ready for the lynching

The mob is droppin common sense and

We'll gank, in the pen we'll shank

Any Tom, Dick, and Hank or get the ass

Fake, it ain't about how right or wrong you live

But how long you live, I ain't with the bullshit

I meet cold bitches … mo' hoes

Don't wanna sleep so I keep poppin NoDoz

And tell the young people what they gotta know

'Cause I hate when niggas gotta live low

And if you're locked up, I dedicate my stylin

From San Quentin to Rikers Island

We got 'em afraid of the funky shit

I like to clown, so pump up the sound

In your Jeep, make the old ladies say
"Oh, my God." Wait, it's the nigga ya love to hate

[Chorus]

"Yo, who the fuck you think you are calling girls bitches? You ain't all that. That's all I hear, bitch, bitch. I ain't nobody's bitch." A bitch is a . . .

Soul Train done lost they soul
Just call it *Train* 'cause the bitches look like hoes
I see a lotta others, damn
It almost look like the *Bandstand*
You ask me, did I like *Arsenio?*
About as much as the bicentennial
I don't give a fuck about dissing these fools
'Cause they all scared of the Ice Cube
And what I say, what I portray and all that
And they ain't even seen the gat
I don't wanna see no dancing
I'm sick of that shit: listen to the hit
'Cause, yo, if I look and see another brother
On the video tryin to outdance each other
I'ma tell T-Bone to pass the bottle
And don't give me that shit about role model
It ain't wise to chastise and preach
Just open the eyes of each
'Cause laws are made to be broken up
What niggas need to do is start loc-ing up
And build, mold, and fold theyself into shape
Of the nigga ya love to hate

IT'S A MAN'S WORLD
(feat. Yo-Yo)

[Ice Cube]
Women, they good for no—

[DJ]

Wait, wait, wait, Cube. Trip this: We gonna dedicate this to the pretty young lady.
   You know them pretty young ladies that wouldn't give us the play before the
   album? This is for you . . .

Bitch . . . bitch on this gank move . . . bitches . . . no, bitch, I think you shit . . . ladies
   are beautiful . . . bitch on . . . bitches, bitch, bitch . . . a bitch is a . . . I'm not no . . .
   bitch is a . . . I'm not no . . . bitch is a . . . bitch! . . . I'm not no . . . bitch . . . I'm not no
   . . . bitch . . . ladies are beautiful . . . I'm not no . . . bitch, bitch . . . bitch . . . ladies
   are . . . no, bitch . . . bitch on . . . bitch, bitches, bitch, bitch, bitch . . . back up off
   my tip for the simple fact you on it like a gnat on a dog's dick . . . I'm not no . . .
   with me tonight I also have Mr. Anthony . . . what'd you say about my mother,
   man?

[Ice Cube]

Women, they good for nothing—nah, maybe one thing

To serve needs to my ding-a-ling

I'm a man who loves the one-night stand

'Cause after I do ya, huh, I never knew ya

'Cause to kick it, man, it gives me the fits

They wanna lay with they nose under your armpits

Ice Cube won't wait, so give it up, cow

After we do it, you can go home now

I'm a brother with a big long . . .

[Yo-Yo]

What the hell you think you talkin about?

First of all, let me tell you my name, it's Yo-Yo

When down on a girl, first the fist and that's a no-no

Yo-Yo thinks the kitchen sink should be thrown in

Niggas be schemin and fiendin to stick the bone in

No, Yo-Yo's not a ho or a whore

And if that's what you're here for, exit through the door

There's more to see of me, but you're blind so

Women like me are fading brothers in the 9–0

[Ice Cube]
Wait! First of all, how you gonna come on my record and talk—

[Yo-Yo]
I'm tryin to say all women are superior over men

[Ice Cube]
Yeah, yeah, yeah

[Yo-Yo]
No, wait. How you gonna rule the world when you broke as a joke?

[Ice Cube]
With your county check, baby

Ay, what up, buttercup or Miss Yo-Yo (That's me)
I know you like to rap and like to flow so (True)
But when it comes to hip-hop, this is a man's world
Stay down and play the playground, you little girl

[Yo-Yo]
What you're sayin, I don't consider is rapping
'Cause you're on rewind and I'm the new what's-happening
It never fails, I always get respect
And you lose, so take a rain check

[Ice Cube]
Hell no, 'cause you know that I'm first and you're second (Never)
If it wasn't for me, you'd probably be pregnant (What?)
And barefoot, complaining that your back is aching
Shaking and faking while I'm bringing home the bacon

[Yo-Yo]
Well, you're mistaken, it's not goin that far
I make brothers like you play the backyard (I doubt it)
You used to flow with the title but I took it
Bring home the bacon but find another ho to cook it

[Ice Cube] Damn it—look it, 'cause you're talking a lot of bull

[Yo-Yo] Well, I'm not your puppet, so don't even try to pull

[Ice Cube] This is a man's world, thank you very much

[Yo-Yo] But it wouldn't be a damn thing without a woman's touch

This is—this is—this is a man's world [4x]

[Ice Cube]

Ah, Miss Yo-Yo. (What's up?) So what gives?

I hear females always talkin about women's lib

Well, get your own crib and stay there

Instead of having more babies for the welfare (What?)

'Cause if you don't, I'll label you a gold-digger

The name is Ice Cube, you know that I ain't the nigga

For you to look at when your hair get nappy

So take a piece of the pole and be happy

[Yo-Yo]

Hell no, because to me you're not a thriller

You come in the room with your three-inch killer (What?)

Thinking you can do damage to my backbone (Yeah...)

Leave your child in the yard until it's full-grown

I'ma put it like this, my man (What's up?)

Without us, your hand would be your best friend

So give us credit like you know you should

If I don't look good, you don't look good

[Ice Cube] I doubt it, baby, 'cause we still most dominant

[Yo-Yo] But you don't know how funky that I can get

[Ice Cube] This is a man's world, thank you very much

[Yo-Yo] But it wouldn't be a damn thing without a woman's touch

This is—this is—this is a man's world [6x]

[Ice Cube]

Man, women, I put a lot of fear in 'em

'Cause I had it up to here with 'em

Drink a beer with 'em? No way
'Cause I can only deal with 'em about a hour every day
Yeah, if you know what I mean, baby

[Yo-Yo]
Well, I guess now that I think about it, I think maybe
If you was more of a man instead of faking it
Women deserve the credit when they're making it

[Ice Cube] Yeah, so what's the problem? [Yo-Yo] Well, I think we solved it
I know they know the best male from who's doggin it
[Ice Cube] Yeah, I admit you can flow. [Yo-Yo] Well, that's true
[Ice Cube] But you see I'm a pro with the bank too
[Yo-Yo] Yeah, I can see you got it good. [Ice Cube] Oh, that I know
[Yo-Yo] But you see you're not better than Yo-Yo
The brand-new intelligent black lady
[Ice Cube] You're kinda dope but you still can't fade me
[Yo-Yo] So what up then? [Ice Cube] Girl, what you tryin to do?
[Yo-Yo] To prove a black woman like me can bring the funk through
[Ice Cube] This is a man's world, thank you very much
[Yo-Yo] But it wouldn't be a damn thing without a woman's touch
[Ice Cube] Or a big butt... [Yo-Yo] See! You know what I mean?

This is—this is—this is a man's world [to fade]

A BIRD IN THE HAND
*Say, look at this! I've been cleaning out my nest and I found an old book of my
    poetry!*

Fresh out of school 'cause I was a high-school grad
Gots to get a job 'cause I was a high-school dad
Wish I got paid by rappin to the nation
But that's not likely, so here's my application
Pass it to the man at AT&T
'Cause when I was in school I got the AEE
But there's no S.E. for this youngsta

I didn't have no money, so now I gotta punch the

Clock at a slave and be half a man

But whitey says there's no room for the African

Always knew that I would clock g's

But "Welcome to McDonald's. May I take your order, please?"

Gotta serve ya food that might give you cancer

'Cause my son doesn't take no for an answer

Now I pay taxes that you never give me back

What about diapers, bottles, and Similac?

Do I have to sell me a whole lotta crack

For decent shelter and clothes on my back?

Or should I just wait for help from Bush

Or Jesse Jackson and Operation PUSH?

If you ask me the whole thing needs a douche

A Massengill. What the hell?

Crack'll sell in the neighborhood

To the corner-house bitches

Miss Parker, Little Joe, and Todd Bridges

Or anybody that he know

So I copped me a bird, better known as a kilo

Now everybody know I went from po'

To a nigga that got dough

So now you put the feds against me

'Cause I couldn't follow the plan of the presidency

I'm never gettin love again

But blacks are too fuckin broke to be Republican

Now I remember I used to be cool

'Til I stopped fillin out my W-2

Now senators are gettin high

And your plan against the ghetto backfired

So now you got a pep talk

But sorry, this is our only room to walk

'Cause we don't wanna drug push

But a bird in the hand is worth more than a Bush

IT WAS A GOOD DAY

Break 'em . . .

Just wakin up in the morning, gotta thank God

I don't know but today seems kinda odd

No barkin from the dog, no smog

And mama cooked a breakfast with no hog (Damn)

I got my grub on, but didn't pig out

Finally got a call from a girl I wanna dig out

(Whassup?) Hooked it up for later as I hit the do'

Thinkin will I live another twenty-fo'?

I gotta go 'cause I got me a drop top

And if I hit the switch, I can make the ass drop

Had to stop at a red light

Lookin in my mirror, not a jacker in sight

And everything is alright

I got a beep from Kim and she can fuck all night

Called up the homies and I'm askin y'all

Which park are y'all playin basketball?

Get me on the court and I'm trouble

Last week fucked around and got a triple double

Freakin niggas every way like M.J.

I can't believe today was a good day (Shit!)

Drove to the pad and hit the showers

Didn't even get no static from the cowards

'Cause just yesterday them fools tried to blast me

Saw the police and they rolled right past me

No flexin, didn't even look in a nigga's direction as I ran the intersection

Went to $hort Dog's house, they was watchin *Yo! MTV Raps*

What's the haps on the craps?

Shake 'em up, shake 'em up, shake 'em up, shake 'em

Roll 'em in a circle of niggas and watch me break 'em

With the seven, seven-eleven, seven-eleven

Seven even back do' Lil' Joe

I picked up the cash flow

Then we played bones and I'm yellin, "Domino"

Plus nobody I know got killed in South Central L.A.

Today was a good day (Shit!)

Left my nigga's house paid (Word)

Picked up a girl been tryin to fuck since the twelfth grade

It's ironic, I had the brew, she had the chronic

The Lakers beat the Supersonics

I felt on the big fat fanny

Pulled out the jammy and killed the punanny

And my dick runs deep, so deep

So deep put her ass to sleep

Woke her up around one, she didn't hesitate

To call Ice Cube the top gun

Drove her to the pad and I'm coastin

Took another sip of the potion, hit the three-wheel motion

I was glad everything had worked out

Dropped her ass off and then chirped out

Today was like one of those fly dreams

Didn't even see a berry flashin those high beams

No helicopter looking for murder

Two in the morning, got the Fatburger

Even saw the lights of the Goodyear Blimp

And it read, "Ice Cube's a pimp" (Yeah)

Drunk as hell but no throwin up

Halfway home and my pager still blowin up

Today I didn't even have to use my AK

I gotta say it was a good day (Shit!)

Hey wait, wait a minute, Pooh, stop this shit. What the fuck I'm thinkin about?

JAY-Z

If Jay-Z isn't the greatest MC of all time (as MTV ranked him in 2006), then he is certainly in the discussion. His reputation is built upon his longevity, ingenuity, and no small amount of business savvy. As Elizabeth Mendez Berry remarks, "Jay-Z raps like a kingpin: he's articulate, ruthless, in control."[34] Since his solo debut, *Reasonable Doubt* (1996), he has emerged as a crossover celebrity just as likely to be featured in the pages of *US Weekly* alongside his superstar wife, Beyoncé, or in the pages of *Forbes*, which once named him the most successful hip-hop entrepreneur alive, as in the pages of *The Source* or *XXL*. His career embodies many of hip-hop's enduring tensions: glamour and grime, celebrity and crime, craft and commercialism. Perhaps Jay-Z described himself best in rhyme: "I'm like Che Guevara with bling on, I'm complex."

Reasonable Doubt's sales were modest, but it soon gained acclaim as a classic. Originally intended to be his first and only album, it instead signaled the arrival of a prolific new voice; from 1996–2003, Jay-Z released an album a year.

The skilled veteran Kool G Rap offers the following assessment of Jay-Z's lyrical abilities: "That dude is a genius with his craft. He's got all the qualities that it takes for somebody to blow up to superstardom. He's got character, he's got lyrics, he knows how to put songs together. His wittiness . . . From the time he came out up 'til now, he grew musically—not so much lyrically. He was crazy lyrical on his first album. He grew musically as far as what plays on that radio and what bumps in that club. I think he just mastered that shit. Dude is in a class by himself. Dudes ain't even touching him as far as I'm concerned."[35]

Jay-Z is also known for his compositional practice; unlike most MCs, he does not write down his lyrics. "I can't explain it to y'all, man . . . It comes out the air for me. I start mumbling . . . They say you put the right artist with the right track in the studio, leave the door cracked and let God in."[36]

DEAD PRESIDENTS II

[Chorus]
Presidents to represent me
I'm out for presidents to represent me

I'm out for presidents to represent me
I'm out for dead fuckin presidents to represent me

Who wanna bet us that we don't touch lettuce?
Stack cheddars forever, live treacherous, all the et ceteras
To the death of us, me and my confidants
We shine, you feel the ambiance, y'all niggas just rhyme
By the ounce dough accumulates like snow. We don't just shine
We illuminate the whole show—you feel me?
Factions from the other side would love to kill me
Spill three quarts of my blood into the street, let alone the heat
Fuck 'em, they hate a nigga lovin his life
In all possible ways, know the feds is buggin my life
Hospital days, reflectin when my man laid up
On the Uptown hot block he got his side sprayed up
I saw his life slippin, this is a minor setback
Yo, still and all we livin, just dream about the get back
That made him smile though his eyes said, "Pray for me"
I'll do you one better and slay these niggas faithfully
Murder is a tough thing to digest, it's a slow process
And I ain't got nothin but time
I had near brushes, not to mention three shots
Close range, never touched me, divine intervention
Can't stop I from drinkin mai-tais with Ta-Ta
Down in Nevada, ha ha Poppa, word life
I dabbled in crazy weight without rap, I was crazy straight
Potna', I'm still spendin money from eighty-eight. What!

[Chorus]

I'll make you and your wack mans fold like bad hands
Roll like Monopoly, advance, you're coppin me
Like white crystal I gross the most
At the end of the fiscal year than these niggas can wish to
The dead presidential candidate with the sprinkles

And the presidential ice that'll offend you

In due time when crime flees my mind

All sneak thieves and playa haters can shine

But until then I keep the trillion cut

Diamonds shinin brilliant, I'll tell you half the story

The rest you fill it in, 'long as the villain win

I spend Japan yen, attend major events

Catch me in the joints, convinced my iguanas is bitin

J-A-Y hyphen, controllin

Manipulatin, I got a good life, man, pounds and pence

Nuff dollars make sense, while you ride the bench

Catch me swinging for the fence—Dead Presidents, ya know?

[Chorus]

So be it, the Soviet, the Unified Steady Flow

You already know, you light, I'm heavy roll, heavy dough

Mic machete'd your flow, your paper fall slow

Like confetti, mine's a steady grow, bet he glow

Pay five dead it from blow, better believe I have

Eleven-sixty to show, my dough flip like Tae-Kwon

Jay-Z the Icon, baby, you like Dom?

Maybe this Cristals'll change your life, huh? Roll with the winners

Heavy spenders like hit records: Roc-A-Fella. Don't get it corrected

This shit is perfected from chips to chicks that strip in the Lexus

Nekkid without your gun, we takin everything you brung

We cakin, you niggas is fakin, we gettin it done

Crime family, well connected Jay-Z

And you fake thugs is Unplugged like MTV

I empty three, take your treasure, my pleasure

Dead presiden-tials, politics as usu-al—baow!

Dead (fuckin) presidents to represent me (Whose . . .) [4x]

[Chorus 2x]

HARD KNOCK LIFE (GHETTO ANTHEM)

Take the bassline out, uh-huh. Jigga (Bounce with it), uh-huh uh-huh uh-huh,
   yeahh. Let it bump though.

[Chorus]
It's the hard knock life (Uh-huh) for us
It's the hard knock life for us!
'Stead a treated, we get tricked
'Stead a kisses, we get kicked
It's the hard knock life!

From standin on the corners boppin to drivin some
Of the hottest cars New York has ever seen, from droppin some
Of the hottest verses rap has ever heard, from the dope spot
With the smoke Glock fleein the murder scene, you know me well
From nightmares of a lonely cell, my only hell
But since when y'all niggas know me to fail? Fuck, naw
Where all my niggas with the rubber grips? Bust shots
And if you with me, Mama, rub on your tits, and whatnot
I'm from the school of the hard knocks, we must not
Let outsiders violate our blocks, and my plot
Let's stick up the world and split it fifty-fifty, uh-huh
Let's take the dough and stay real jiggy, uh-huh
Let's sip the Cris' and get pissy-pissy, flow infinitely
Like the memory of my nigga Biggie, baby!
You know it's hell when I come through, the life and times
Of Shawn Carter, nigga, Volume 2—y'all niggas get ready

[Chorus]

I flow for those dro'ed out, all my niggas
Locked down in the ten by fo' controllin the house
We live in hard knocks, we don't take over, we borrow blocks
Burn 'em down and you can have it back, Daddy, I'd rather that
I flow for chicks wishin they ain't have to strip to pay tuition
I see your vision, Mama, I put my money

On the long shots, all my ballers that's born to clock
Now I'ma be on top whether I perform or not
I went from lukewarm to hot, sleepin on futons
And cots to king size, dream machines, the green fives
I've seen pies, let the thing between my eyes analyze life's ills
Then I put it down type real
I'm tight grill with the phony rappers, y'all might feel we homies
I'm like still, y'all don't know me, shit
I'm type real when my situation ain't improvin
I'm tryin to murder everything movin—feel me?!

[Chorus 2x]

I don't know how to sleep, I gotta eat, stay on my toes
Got a lot of beef, so logically, I prey on my foes
Hustlin's still inside of me and as far as progress
You'd be hard-pressed to find another rapper hot as me
I gave you prophecy on my first joint and y'all all lamed out
Didn't really appreciate it 'til the second one came out
So I stretched the game out, X'ed your name out
Put Jigga on top and drop albums nonstop for ya, nigga

[Chorus 2x]

RENEGADE
(feat. Eminem)

[Jay-Z]
Motherfuckers say that I'm foolish, I only talk about jewels (Bling bling)
Do you fools listen to music or do you just skim through it?
See, I'm influenced by the ghetto you ruined
That same dude you gave nothin, I made somethin doin
What I do through and through and
I give you the news with a twist; it's just his ghetto point-of-view
The renegade, you been afraid, I penetrate
Pop culture, bring 'em a lot closer to the block where they

Pop toasters and they live with they moms

Got dropped roasters, from botched robberies, niggas crotched over

Mommy's knocked up 'cause she wasn't watched over

Knocked down by some clown, when child support knocked

No, he's not around. Now how that sound to ya? Jot it down

I bring it through the ghetto without ridin 'round

Hidin down, duckin strays from frustrated youths

Stuck in they ways. Just read a magazine that fucked up my day

How you rate music that thugs with nothin relate to it?

I help them see they way through it—not you

Can't step in my pants, can't walk in my shoes

Bet everything you worth you lose your tie and your shirt

[Eminem]

Since I'm in a position to talk to these kids and they listen

I ain't no politician but I'll kick it with 'em a minute

'Cause, see, they call me a menace and if the shoe fits, I'll wear it

But if it don't, then y'all'll swallow the truth, grin and bear it

Now who's the king of these rude ludicrous lucrative lyrics?

Who could inherit the title, put the youth in hysterics?

Usin his music to steer it, sharin his views and his merits

But there's a huge interference—they're sayin you shouldn't hear it

Maybe it's hatred I spew, maybe it's food for the spirit

Maybe it's beautiful music I made for you to just cherish

But I'm debated, disputed, hated, and viewed in America

As a motherfuckin drug addict—like you didn't experiment?

Now, now, that's when you start to stare at who's in the mirror

And see yourself as a kid again and you get embarrassed

And I got nothin to do but make you look stupid as parents

You fuckin do-gooders; too bad you couldn't do good at marriage (Ha ha!)

And do you have any clue what I had to do to get here

I don't think you do, so stay tuned and keep your ears glued to the stereo

'Cause here we go: he's Jigga joint Jigga-chk-Jigga

And I'm the sinister, Mr. Kiss-My-Ass, it's just the . . .

[Chorus 2x]

RENEGADE! Never been afraid to say

What's on my mind at any given time of day

'Cause I'm a RENEGADE! Never been afraid to talk

About anything (ANYTHING) anything (ANYTHING)

[Jay-Z]

I had to hustle, my back to the wall, ashy knuckles

Pockets filled with a lot of lint, not a cent

Gotta vent, lot of innocent lives lost on the project bench

Whatchu hollerin? Gotta pay rent, bring dollars in

By the bodega, iron under my coat, feelin braver

Doo-rag wrappin my waves up, pockets full of hope

Do not step to me; I'm awkward, I box leftier often

My pops left me an orphan, my mama wasn't home

Could not stress to me I wasn't grown, 'specially on nights

I brought somethin home to quiet the stomach rumblings

My demeanor, thirty years my senior

My childhood didn't mean much, only raising green up

Raising my fingers to critics, raising my head to the sky

B.I.G., I did it—multi before I die (Nigga)

No lie, just know I chose my own fate

I drove by the fork in the road and went straight

[Eminem]

See, I'm a poet to some, a regular modern-day Shakespeare

Jesus Christ, the King of these Latter-Day Saints here

To shatter the picture in which of that as they paint me is

A monger of hate and Satan, a scatterbrained atheist

But that ain't the case; see, it's a matter of taste

We as a people decide if Shady's as bad as they say he is

Or is he the ladder, a gateway to escape?

Media scapegoat, who they can be mad at today

See, it's as easy as cake, simple as whistlin "Dixie"

While I'm wavin the pistol at sixty Christians against me

Go to war with the Mormons, take a bath with the Catholics

In holy water—no wonder they try to hold me under longer

I'ma motherfuckin spiteful, DELIGHTFUL eyeful
The new Ice Cube, motherfuckers HATE to like you
What did I do? (Huh?) I'm just a kid from the gutter
Makin this butter off these bloodsuckers, 'cause I'm a muh'fuckin . . .

[Chorus]

DECEMBER 4TH

Shawn Carter was born December 4th. Weighing in at 10 pounds, 8 ounces, he
was the last of my four children, the only one who didn't give me any pain
when I gave birth to him. And that's how I knew that he was a special child.

They say they never really miss you 'til you dead or you gone
So on that note I'm leaving after this song
So you ain't gotta feel no way about Jay, so long
At least let me tell you why I'm this way, hold on
I was conceived by Gloria Carter and Adnes Reeves
Who made love under the sycamore tree, which makes me
A more sicker MC and my mama would claim
At ten pounds when I was born I didn't give her no pain
Although through the years I gave her her fair share
I gave her her first real scare, I made up for birth when I got here
She knows my purpose was on purpose, I ain't perfect, I care
But I feel worthless 'cause my shirts wasn't matchin my gear
Now I'm just scratchin the surface 'cause what's buried under there
Was a kid torn apart once his pop disappeared
I went to school, got good grades, could behave when I wanted
But I had demons deep inside that would raise when confronted. Hold on

Shawn was a very shy child growing up. He was into sports and a funny story is:
At four, he taught hisself how to ride a bike, a two-wheel at that. Isn't that
special? But, I noticed a change in him when me and my husband broke up.

Now all the teachers couldn't reach me and my mama couldn't beat me
Hard enough to match the pain of my pop not seeing me
So with that disdain in my membrane

Got on my pimp game, fuck the world, my defense came
Then DeHaven introduced me to the game
Spanish José introduced me to 'caine, I'm a hustler now
My gear is in and I'm in the in-crowd
And all the wavy light-skinned girls is loving me now
My self-esteem went through the roof, man, I got my swag
Got a vocal from this girl when her man got bagged
Plus I hit my mama with cash from a show that I had
Supposedly knowing nobody paid Jaz wack ass
I'm getting ahead of myself—by the way, I could rap
That came second to me moving this crack, give me a second
I swear I will say about my rap career
'Til '96 came, "Niggas, I'm here." Good-bye

*Shawn use to be in the kitchen, beating on the table and rapping and, um, until
the wee hours of the morning. And then I bought him a boom box and his
sisters and brothers said that he would drive them nuts. But that was my way
to keep him close to me and out of trouble.*

Goodbye to the game—all the spoils, the adrenaline rush
Your blood boils, you in a spot knowing cops could rush
And you in a drop, you're so easy to touch, no two
Days are alike except the first and fifteenth, pretty much
And trust is a word you seldom hear from us
Hustlers, we don't sleep, we rest one eye up
And a drought can define a man, when the well dries up
You learn to work the water, without work you thirst 'til you die—yup!
And niggas get tied up for product and little brothers'
Ring fingers get cut up to show mothers they really got 'em
And this was the stress I lived with, 'til I decided
To try this rap shit for a livin, I pray I'm forgiven
For every bad decision I made, every sister I played
'Cause I'm still paranoid to this day
And it's nobody fault, I made the decisions I made
This is the life I chose or rather the life that chose me

If you can't respect that your whole perspective is wack

Maybe you'll love me when I fade to black [4x]

99 PROBLEMS

If you're having girl problems I feel bad for you, son

I got 99 problems but a bitch ain't one

I got the rap patrol on the gat patrol

Foes that wanna make sure my casket's closed

Rap critics that say he's "Money, Cash, Hoes"

I'm from the 'hood, stupid, what type of facts are those?

If you grew up with holes in your zapatos

You'd celebrate the minute you was having dough

I'm like, fuck critics, you can kiss my whole asshole

If you don't like my lyrics you can press fast forward

Got beef with radio if I don't play they show

They don't play my hits, well, I don't give a shit. So?

Rap mags try and use my black ass

So advertisers can give 'em more cash for ads . . . fuckers

I don't know what you take me as

Or understand the intelligence that Jay-Z has

I'm from rags to riches, niggas, I ain't dumb

I got 99 problems but a bitch ain't one

Hit me

[Chorus]

99 problems but a bitch ain't one

If you having girl problems I feel bad for you, son

I got 99 problems but a bitch ain't one

Hit me

The year is '94 and in my trunk is raw

In my rearview mirror is the motherfucking law

I got two choices, y'all: pull over the car or

Bounce on the double, put the pedal to the floor

Now, I ain't trying to see no highway chase with Jake

Plus I got a few dollars, I can fight the case

So I pull over to the side of the road

I heard, "Son, do you know why I'm stopping you for?"

'Cause I'm young and I'm black and my hat's real low?

Do I look like a mind reader, sir? I don't know

Am I under arrest or should I guess some mo'?

"Well, you was doing fifty-five in a fifty-four

License and registration and step out of the car

Are you carrying a weapon on you? I know a lot of you are"

I ain't stepping out of shit, all my paper's legit

"Well, do you mind if I look round the car a little bit?"

Well, my glove compartment is locked, so is the trunk and the back

And I know my rights so you gon' need a warrant for that

"Aren't you sharp as a tack, you some type of

Lawyer or somethin? Somebody important or somethin?"

Nah, I ain't pass the bar but I know a little bit

Enough that you won't illegally search my shit

"Well, we'll see how smart you are when the K-9s come"

I got 99 problems but a bitch ain't one

Hit me

[Chorus 2x]

Now, once upon a time not too long ago

A nigga like myself had to strong-arm a ho

This is not a ho in the sense of having a pussy

But a pussy having no goddamn sense, try and push me

I tried to ignore him, talk to the Lord

Pray for him, 'cause some fools just love to perform

You know the type, loud as a motorbike

But wouldn't bust a grape in a fruit fight

The only thing that's gonna happen is I'ma get to clappin and

He and his boys gon' be yapping to the captain

And there I go trapped in the kit-kat again

Back through the system with the riffraff again
Fiends on the floor scratching again
Paparazzis with their cameras snapping them
D.A. tried to give a nigga shaft again
Half-a-mil for bail 'cause I'm African
All because the fool was harassin him
Trying to play the boy like he's saccharin
But ain't nothing sweet 'bout how I hold my gun
I got 99 problems, being a bitch ain't one
Hit me

[Chorus 3x]

You're crazy for this one, Rick. It's your boy!

MY PRESIDENT IS BLACK (D.C. MIX)
My president is black, my Maybach, too
And I'll be goddamn if my diamonds ain't blue
My money's dark green and my Porsche is light gray
And I'm headed for D.C.—anybody feel me?
[Repeat 2x]

My president is black, in fact, he's half white
So even in a racist's mind, he's half right
If you have a racist mind, you be aight
The president is black, but his house is all white
Rosa Parks sat so Martin Luther could walk
Martin Luther walked so Barack Obama could run
Barack Obama ran so all the children could fly
So I'ma spread my wings, you can meet me in the sky
I already got my own clothes, already got my own shoes
I was hot before Barack, imagine what I'm gon' do
Hello, Miss America, hey, pretty lady
Red, white, and blue flag, wave for me, baby!
Never thought I'd say this shit: "Baby, I'm good"
You can keep your puss, I don't want no more bush

No more war, no more Iraq
No more white lies, the president is black!

KRS-ONE

KRS-One is often referred to simply as the Teacher for his command of lyrical knowledge. He is among a handful of artists who can lay claim to being both old school and cutting edge. From 1987 to the present he has averaged nearly an album a year—first as the rapping half (alongside DJ Scott La Rock) of Boogie Down Productions, and then as a solo artist. He has also established himself as an authority on all things hip-hop through books, lectures, and interviews. He has written about the craft of MCing, the spiritual side of hip-hop culture, and a host of other topics.

KRS-One's style is defined by his vocal authority and flow. His rhymes are rarely adorned with complex figurative language, instead relying upon cadence and content to drive his message home. As a battle rapper, KRS has few peers. At the same time, he has fashioned didactic rhymes, charged with Afrocentric history and philosophy.

SOUND OF DA POLICE
[Chorus 4x]
Woop-woop! That's the sound of da police!
Woop-woop! That's the sound of the beast!

Stand clear! Don man a talk
You can't stand where I stand, you can't walk where I walk
Watch out! We run New York
Policeman come, we bust him out the park
I know this for a fact—you don't like how I act
You claim I'm sellin crack but you be doin that
I'd rather say "See ya" 'cause I would never be ya
Be a officer? You wicked overseer!

Ya hotshot, wanna get props and be a savior?

First show a little respect, change your behavior

Change your attitude, change your plan

There could never really be justice on stolen land

Are you really for peace and equality?

Or when my car is hooked up, you know you wanna follow me

Your laws are minimal

'Cause you won't even think about lookin at the real criminal

This has got to cease

'Cause we be getting hyped to the sound of da police!

[Chorus 2x]

Now here's a likkle truth, open up your eye

While you're checking out the boom-bap, check the exercise

Take the word "overseer" like a sample

Repeat it very quickly in a crew, for example

Overseer. Overseer. Overseer.

Overseer, officer, officer, officer, officer!

Yeah, officer from overseer

You need a little clarity? Check the similarity!

The overseer rode around the plantation

The officer is off patrolling all the nation

The overseer could stop you what you're doing

The officer will pull you over just when he's pursuing

The overseer had the right to get ill

And if you fought back, the overseer had the right to kill

The officer has the right to arrest

And if you fight back they put a hole in your chest!

Woop! They both ride horses

After four hundred years, I've got no choices

The police, them have a likkle gun

So when I'm on the streets, I walk around with a bigger one

(Woop-woop!) I hear it all day

Just so they can run the light and be upon their way

[Chorus 2x]

Check out the message in a rough stylee
The real criminal are the C-O-P
You check for undercover and the one PD
But just 'cause me a Black man, them wan' check me
Them check out me car for it shine like the Sun
But them jealous or them vexed 'cause them can't afford one
Black people still slaves up 'til today
But the Black police officer nah see it that way
Him want him salary, him want it
So he put on a badge and kill people for it
My grandfather had to deal with the cops
My great-grandfather dealt with the cops
My great-great-grandfather had to deal with the cops
And then my great, great, great, great … When it's gonna stop?

[Chorus 3x]

MCS ACT LIKE THEY DON'T KNOW

Clap your hands, everybody, if you got what it takes
'Cause I'm KRS and I'm on the mic and Premier's on the breaks

Goin out to the hardcore hip-hop
Goin out to the hardcore hip-hop
Of course, we don't flip-flop

If you don't know me by now, I doubt you'll ever know me
I never won a Grammy, I won't win a Tony
But I'm not the only MC keepin it real
When I grab the mic to smash a rapper, girls go, "IIIIII"
Check the time as I rhyme, it's 1995
Whenever I arrive, the party gets liver
Flow with the master rhymer
As I leave behind the video rapper
You know, the chart climber—clapper

Down goes another rapper, onto another matter

Punch up the data, Blastmaster

Knowledge Reigns Supreme Over Nearly Everybody

Call up KRS, I'm guaranteed to rip a party

Flat top, braids, bald heads, or natty dread

There once was a story about a man named Jed

But now Jed is dead, all his kids instead

Want to kick rhymes off the top of they head

Word, what go around come around I figure

Now we got white kids callin themselves "Niggas"

And tables turn as the crosses burn

Remember, "You must learn"

About the styles I flip and how wild I get

I go on like a space-age rocket ship

You could be a mack, a pimp, hustler or player

But make sure live you is a dope rhymesayer

"MCs act like they don't know" [4x]

This is what you waited all year for

The hardcore, that's what KRS is here for

Big up Grand Wizard Theodore, gettin ill

If you see then ya saw, I'm in your grill with mad skill

MCs can only battle with rhymes that got punchlines

Let's battle to see who headlines

Instead of flow for flow, let's go show for show

Toe for toe, yo, you better act like you know

Too many MCs take that word "MC" lightly

They can't Move a Crowd, not even slightly

It might be the fact that they express wackness

Let me show ya whose ass is the blackest

I flip a script a little bit, you ride the tip and shit

Too sick to get with it, admit you bit, your style

Is counterfeit, now tone it down a bit

My title you will never get, I'm too intelligent

I'll send your family my sentiments, my style is toxic

When I rock and shock and hip-hop it
Unlock your head, I knock it. It split quick from the lyric
Direct hit, perfect fit, you can't get with it ...

"MCs act like they don't know" [4x]

Some MCs don't like the KRS but they must respect him
'Cause they know this kid gets all up in they rectum
Slappin and selectin 'em, checkin 'em, disrespectin 'em
Just deckin 'em, deckin 'em, deckin 'em
Who in their right mind can mimic a style like mine?
I design rhyme and get mine all the time
MCs stand on the sidelines, always dissin
When I roll up and rush their crew they start bitchin
I don't burn, I don't freeze, yet some MCs
Believe they could tangle with the likes of these
Cross your t's and dot your i's whenever I arrive
Wide, magnified, live like the ocean tide
You dope, you lied, I reside like artifacts
On the wrong side of the tracks, electrified
Coming around the mountain, you run and hide
Hoping your defense mechanism can divert my heat-seeking lyricism
As I spark mad-ism
The 1996 lyrical style's what I give 'em

"MCs act like they don't know" [4x]

THE LADY OF RAGE

T he Lady of Rage's braggadocio and lyrical strength assume female empowerment without ever explicitly asserting it. Her appearances on Dr. Dre's *The Chronic* and Snoop Doggy Dogg's *Doggystyle* are song-stealing, but her career extends well beyond those memorable turns.

Rage first began composing lyrics in the sixth grade. "I used to write poetry a lot," she recalls, "so the transition from poetry to rap is not that hard. It's just music to poetry."[37] She received her moniker her senior year of high school after her best friend remarked on her temper. After high school she moved to Texas, where she developed her rhyming skills and gained a small following through local rap battles. Her style is commanding and effortless. Whether tackling common rap themes like self-aggrandizement ("Afro Puffs") or spitting vicious battle raps ("Unfucwitable"), she finds ways to refresh what might be overused material in the hands of a lesser MC.

AFRO PUFFS

[Chorus 2x]
I rock rough and stuff with my Afro puffs (Rage!)
"Rock on, witcha bad self"

I rock on with my bad self 'cause it's a must
It's the Lady of Rage still kickin up dust
So, um, let me loosen up my bra strap
And, um, let me boost you with my raw rap
'Cause I'ma break it down to the nitty-gritty one time
When it comes to the lyrics I gets busy with mine
Busy as a beaver, you best believe-a
This grand diva's runnin shit with the speed of a cheetah
Meet a lyrical murderer, I'm servin 'em
Like two scoops of chocolate, check out how I rock it
I'm the one that's throwin bolos, ya better
Roll a Rolo to find out I'm the number one solo, uh
The capital R-A, now take it to the G-E
I bring the things to light, but you still can't see me
I flow like the monthly, you can't cramp my style
For those that try to punk me here's a Pamprin, child
No need to say mo', check the flow
Rage in effect once mo', so now ya know

[Chorus]

Now I'm hitting MCs like, "Ha-dou-ken!"

Ain't no doubt about it, I'm the undisputed

So what you, uhh, wanna do is back on up

I'll tap that butt, wax the cuts, pass the bucks

So put your money on the breadwinner

I kick lyrics so dope that the brothers call 'em head spinners

I got the tongue that has outdone anyone

From the rising to the setting of the sun

Or the moon, I consume the room with doom

When I hear the kick of a 808 bass...BOOM

BOOM, BAM, GOD-DAYUMMM

I'm hittin so hard you could say it's a grand

Slam...dunk...punks...

Get broken off a chunk when they feel the funk

Of the rhythm (Fresh) that I give 'em

Let it hit 'em, split 'em, did it, now I'm rid of 'em

Yeah, I put that on my unborn kids

Rage in effect so you know how it is

[Chorus]

Now ever since my debut I've continued to lay you

Flat on your back from the raps that I spat

Spit, ohh shit, I'm the shit!

You can't get with the Rage then tough tit-ty

I pi-ty the fool that gets

With the lyrical murderer 'cause my shit is rude (Ooh!)

You wanna get with the wickedness?

With that big bot-ty girl that's kickin it

Rippin it apart like Jason, you'll be chasin a dream

Like Freddy, are you ready for the cream

De la crème? I'm steam-pressurin those who ain't

Measurin up, I keep competitors stuck

In the muck with they butt up. What? You wanna nut up

Like cashew, don't you know that I will mash you?

For real, that's the deal, I'm straight out of Farmville
VA (So what you gotta say?)

[Chorus 2x]

I am the roughest, roughest, roughest (Say what? Say what?)
I am the toughest, toughest, toughest (RAGE!) [Repeat 4x]

UNFUCWITABLE
You talkin smack, bitch? You wanna get at this? Think you need more practice
You way out your bracket, I rock the whole motherfuckin atlas
Save that racket for the tennis court and abort your mission
Resort to kissin these glutes or get played like flutes
'Cause, um, the agony that I inflict causes tragedy when I spit
And if you ain't the shit, you better dip, you better split
You better take off, before I break off, make off
Must be cupcakes that's soft, that's why I serve you like a bake-off
I'll rip your *Face/Off* like I'm Nicolas Cage
You wanna face off? That's ridiculous, I'm Rage
The mic brawler, the night crawler, I smoke 'em like I'm off that water
Clara Alice great-granddaughter
Would injure ya, your girl from Virginia (Uh, uh)
Make no bones about it, when it's on, I'm 'bout it
I got a niceness that remains raw, my iceless never thaws
Priceless, baby, ha, Rage, that's all …

I'm foldin MCs like towels with dirty consonants and vowels
When I'm creepin on the prowl and stay wide-eyed like an owl
Now who (Who) flows better than this rhyme writer?
You in a clique full of dicks and you still couldn't come tighter than
Robin Redbreast with a Afro puff headdress
Young and restless, naw, you nah wan' test this, ha
I break it down, baby, you best pray to the Lord
'Cause fuckin 'round with Rage is a wish you can't afford
I leave 'em standin on they tippy toes, dealin with a drippy nose

Bombard 'em with my fifty flows, I ain't fuckin with these silly hoes
Now, shit's about to get so retarded
I just got dumped and I got left brokenhearted
I ain't got shit to lose, the first bitch that move
They gon' catch it in the worst way, Rage blood thirsty
Attacks ready to throw down, that's how it goes down
I can't slow down, Judge Joe Brown convicted me of rhyme-slaughter
'Cause I spit killable syllables
Leave 'em pitiful, the cynical Rage unfucwitable

Now with my Timbos I could leave a bimbo in limbo
Make 'em tremble when I spit through the dental on these instrumentals
While I'm chewin on a Mento, flows wicked from the intro
I told y'all from the get-go I rock harder than Prudential
Save that shit for your colon, I strike 'em like I'm bowlin
You sweet cheeks can't compete with the heat that I'm holdin, ha
Dingbats better take they wings back and cash in
Lyrical murderer back up in this bitch to bashin
So, ante up and pull your panties up
And call your granny up, tell her that you got your fanny bust
Weak shit banged off the backboard
How about some hardcore? How about some rough, rugged, and raw?
With all sincereness I spit lyrics with raw severeness
Gladiator fearless, Tyson style, leave 'em earless
So which of you want me to snatch you by your britches, boo?
I hit you with my witches' stew, turn 'em into bitches' brew
Terror, when you up against Rage Hitchcock
From H block with a flow that make 'em scream, "Rage, stop!"
Now that's crazy—naw, that's the Lady of Rage (Rage . . .)

LIL' KIM

L il' Kim might be the anti–Lauryn Hill for the exuberant way she often seems to embrace the conventional trappings of misogyny. She dubbed herself the Queen B, or Queen Bitch, and made a career of reciting lyrics that would appear to support sexist fantasies of rampant materialism and hypersexuality. Many listeners, not to mention the artist herself, have instead understood Kim's explicit lyrics as radical acts of female empowerment. Her hardcore raps and overt eroticism challenge the presumed boundaries of hip-hop femininity.

Kimberly Jones was discovered by the Notorious B.I.G., and with Biggie's help, she would soon emerge as the larger-than-life Lil' Kim, a member of the Junior MAFIA, the collective of Biggie's Bedford-Stuyvesant associates. After success with Junior MAFIA, Kim released a double platinum–selling solo album, *Hard Core* (1996).

After a hiatus following Biggie's death, Kim returned with her sophomore album, *The Notorious Kim* (2000), which sold more than 1.4 million copies. Two notable singles, "No Matter What They Say" and "How Many Licks," revealed Kim's growing lyrical abilities.

Disagreement remains over whether Lil' Kim has been good or bad for the image of women in hip-hop; none can sensibly deny her impact on the industry. Her hypersexual language and image made her both revered and reviled. Her hardcore swagger and sharp delivery challenge the limitations often foisted upon female MCs.

QUEEN BITCH
(feat. The Notorious B.I.G.)
If Peter Piper pecked 'em, I betcha Biggie bust 'em
He probably tried to fuck 'em, I told him not to trust 'em
Lyrically, I dust 'em off like Pledge
Hit hard like sledgehammers, bitch with that platinum grammar
I am a diamond cluster hustler
Queen bitch, supreme bitch, kill a nigga for my nigga
By any means bitch, murder scene bitch
Clean bitch, disease free bitch
Check it, I write a rhyme, melt in your mouth like M&Ms

Roll with the M.A.F.I.A., remember them?

Tell 'em when I used to mess with gentlemen, straight up apostles

Now strictly niggas that jostle

Kill a nigga for the figure, how you figure?

Your cheddar would be better

Beretta inside of Beretta, nobody do it better

Bet I wet cha like hurricanes and typhoons

Got buffoons eatin my pussy while I watch cartoons

Sleep 'til noon, rap Pam Grier's here

Baby drinkers beware, mostly Dolce wear

Frank kill niggas' wives for one point five

While you struggle and strive we pick which Benz to drive

The M.A.F.I.A., you wanna be 'em

Most of y'all niggas can't eat without per diem

I'm rich, I'ma stay that bitch

Uh, who you lovin? Who you wanna be huggin?

Roll with the niggas that be thuggin, buggin in the Tunnel and Esso's

Sippin espresso, cappuccino with Nino

On a mission for the lucci creno

I used to wear Moschino, but every bitch got it

Now I rock colorful minks because my pockets stay knotted

C-note after C-note, Frank boat hold fifteen

Plus the caterer. You think you greater? Uh

[Notorious B.I.G.]

You niggas got some audacity

You sold a million, now you half of me. Get off my dick

Kick it, bitch . . .

          Check my pitch, or send it persona

And I'll still stick your moms for her stocks and bonds

I got that bomb-ass cock, a good ass shot

With hardcore flows to keep a nigga dick rock

Sippin Zinfandels up in Chippendales

Shop in Bloomingdale's for Prada bags

Female Don Dada has no problems splittin cream with my team
Shit's straight like nine fifteen, you nahmean?
Cruise the diamond district with my biscuit
Flossin my Rolex wrist—shit, I'm rich
I'ma stay that bitch

MIA X

Mia X was an important part of Master P's No Limit Records empire—the South's answer to Lil' Kim and Foxy Brown. Her sharp enunciation offered a nice contrast to Master P's southern drawl. As a hardcore southern rapper, she deals with all the themes one might expect. And while the No Limit instrumental production sometimes lacked originality, her lyrics were always delivered with energy and command. Her best songs, like "Hoodlum Poetry," put unusual spins on gangsta themes. In this instance, she raps from the perspective of crack cocaine, offering its life story in a style reminiscent of the jailhouse and street-corner toasts of previous eras.

HOODLUM POETRY
I came to this country with my mama
Everybody called her the white girl
But you all knew I had a lil' somethin somethin on me
'Cause my outer was slightly tanned
Southern folk called me a yella gal
I've been out here in this world for a while now
Bringing madness and mayhem to man, woman, and child
You see, my mother, the white girl, had several lovers
So my father's true identity has yet to be discovered
Some call it A-1 soda, others V-12
Doctor Tishner has been implicated
But all of their seeds are incriminating evidence

As far as my perception goes

My mother, she was indeed good, but I am most powerful

Just ask anybody in your 'hood

You can even ask those in corporate America about this mobstress

Most times, I, as little as a pea, though my weight fluctuates

Size ain't shit, 'cause I have enough game to make you steal from ya mama

And call her out her name

I can make her neglect her children, sell her body, perform dirty tricks

On her knees and be called the neighborhood hottie

Everybody's a thief and a liar once they make my acquaintance

They be anxious to buy my love, they lust for me

Want to hold me and test my purity, but it's only for a moment

You see the ecstasy that I give to you

It's only temporary but quite costly

I'm bossy from your very first encounter with me

I tell you you need me, gots to have me, can't live without me

The pea, my game extends, it gets deeper

You see my skills don't just pimp the weak-minded

The so-called big ballin brothers are obsessed with me

They kill, rob, plot, and rat on one another to possess me

They see me as a goddess

The financial path that will lead them out the ghetto

But don't they know, have a clue

That my mother and I were sent here to destroy them

To entice, baffle, and trap them

Conscious people call the conspiracy "genocide"

Well, what do you think?

I mean, you make money off me, while they pile evidence on you

Then get you to spend all the money you're stackin on lawyers and bail
    bondsmen

They seize your property and all your worldly items

That have you so caught up in this lifestyle

Material things that turn friend to foe

Woman to ho, and man to monster

Yeah, nigga, you've changed, but so what

'Cause I give you what you need, I give you power

Make you feel invincible—right, papi?

I make you feel like a big man, a timer

No matter how ugly, fat, or illiterate you are

I make the prettiest women love you

Fight over you and compete with others trying to give you plenty babies

I make your relatives want to kiss your ass

Treat you like a king and roll out the red carpet

All the while, they've got one hand out for money

And the other hand has a pen in it so you can sign your life policy

My existence makes you have that edge over the next man

'Cause it's all about me and the money, the root of all evil

The necessities that function in this society

I make all your gangsta dopeman stories interesting

'Cause you the man

I mean, we listen in awe while you speak of your murder tales

Ménage à trois, homosexual advances, and secret romances

I'm 'bout it and I make you feel 'bout it 'bout it

I split family, split friends, split lovers, and even business partners

So you nickname me crack, ain't that something?

I'm the reason why a lot of people are homeless, crazy, crippled

Why they're HIV positive and dead

But you still want me, feel the need for me to be in your possession

Fear to get high off my intoxicating little pieces

Or to spread my love for profit

You're even willing to kill and die for me

And even though my mother, the white girl

Engaged in several orgies for my creation

I still know my father, you know him too

You follow his lead to work with him

You claim you hate him but your actions are different from your tongue

Let's face it, you serve him faster than you do your God

We own you, nigga

And as far as the ones who send I and my mother here to destroy you
We own them, too
So after all my destruction, I must pat myself on the back, ummumm
I am crack, the devil's daughter
Human life, mind destroyer
And you need me, yeah ya do, for sho' ya do, you really do
So go head on, nigga, take a hit
I'ma keep putting you out on the streets
Freeze you now, help me to kill you
Hoodlum poetry, food for ya mind
Wake up deaf, dumb, and blind, it's time
I'm the masteress, I'm the mobstress
I'm the pimpstress and I own you
I'm the masteress, I'm the mobstress
And I own you, I'm trying to kill you
And I'm succeeding, yes, I'm succeeding
I'm trying to kill you and I'm gon' do it
I'm gon' kill you, I'm gon' kill you
I'm gon' kill you and it's bloody

MOBB DEEP

Mobb Deep are poet laureates of the streets. Havoc and Prodigy both hail from the Queensbridge projects, the largest public housing development in the United States, covering a six-block section of Queens. The QB gave birth to a host of hip-hop talents—from MC Shan and Nas to Capone and Noreaga. "We got our own language, style of dress out there, and attitude," Prodigy says. "You going to see some unique shit out there that you only going to see [in] the music, the language, how people tie their boots, the dress code."[38]

Their breakthrough album, *The Infamous* (1995), was dark with atmospheric beats, sinister piano loops, and cold, clever lyrics. The album encapsulated a profoundly nihilistic worldview. Most of the songs dealt with the "trife life," the drug trade and various other criminal enterprises. Led by the songs "Shook Ones, Pt. II" and "Survival of the Fittest," the album won a cult following. The group released three more albums in the 1990s and continued into the next decade. One of the highlights of their work late in the 1990s is "Quiet Storm (Remix)," which featured a blistering verse from Lil' Kim.

Because Mobb Deep produces most of its own music (Havoc does the majority of the production), one hears a striking correlation between beats and rhymes. "When we make an album it's different every time," Prodigy explains. "Sometimes we'll come at the lyrics first, but most of the time we'll have the beat first. We just go in and just have fun basically, you know, we don't think too hard on it and just let it be organic."[39]

SHOOK ONES, PT. II
Word up, son, word . . .
To all the killers and the hundred dollar billers
For real niggas who ain't got no feelins
Check it out now . . .

[Prodigy]
I got you stuck off the realness, we be the infamous
You heard of us, official Queensbridge murderers
The Mobb comes equipped for warfare, beware
Of my crime family who got nuff shots to share
For all those who wanna profile and pose
Rock you in your face, stab your brain with your nose bone
You all alone in these streets, cousin
Every man for theyself, in this land we be gunnin
And keep them shook crews runnin like they supposed to
They come around but they never come close to
I can see it inside your face
You're in the wrong place, cowards like you just get
They whole body laced up with bullet holes and such
Speak the wrong words, man, and you will get touched

You can put your whole army against my team and
I guarantee you it'll be your very last time breathin
Your simple words just don't move me, you're minor
We major, you all up in the game and don't deserve to be a player
Don't make me have to call your name out
Your crew is featherweight, my gunshots'll make you levitate
I'm only nineteen but my mind is old
And when the things get for real my warm heart turns cold
Another nigga deceased, another story gets told
It ain't nothin really, hey, yo, dun, spark the Phillie
So I can get my mind off these yellow-backed niggas
Why they still alive? I don't know, go figure
Meanwhile back in Queens, the realness, the foundation
If I die, I couldn't choose a better location
When the slugs penetrate you feel a burning sensation
Getting closer to God in a tight situation
Now, take these words home and think it through
Or the next rhyme I write might be about you

[Chorus 2x]
Son, they shook . . .
'Cause ain't no such things as halfway crooks
Scared to death, scared to look

Livin the life, that of diamonds and guns
There's numerous ways you can choose to earn funds (Earn funds)
Some brothas get shot, locked down, and turn nuns
Cowardly hearts end straight up shook ones (Shook ones)
He ain't a crook, son, he's just a shook one (Shook one)

[Havoc]
For every rhyme I write it's twenty-five to life
Yo, it's a must, in gats we trust, safeguardin my life
Ain't no time for hesitation, that only leads to incarceration
You don't know me, there's no relation

Queensbridge niggas don't play. I don't got time

For your petty thinking mind, son, I'm bigga than those

Claimin that you pack heat, but you're scared to hold

And once the smoke clears you'll be left with one in your dome

Thirteen years in the projects, my mentality is what, kid

You talk a good one but you don't want it

Sometimes I wonder: Do I deserve to live?

Am I going to burn in hell for all the things I did?

No time to dwell on that 'cause my brain reacts

Front if you want, kid, lay on your back

I don't fake jacks, kid, you know I bring it to you live

Stay in a child's place, kid, you outta line

Criminal mind thirsty for recognition

I'm sippin, E&J got my mind flippin

I'm buggin, dig a mind without a hope of hustlin

Get that loot, kid, you know my function

'Cause long as I'm alive I'ma live illegal

And once I get on I'ma put on all my peoples

React mix for lyrics, like MACs I hit

Your dome up. When I roll up, don't be caught sleepin 'cause I'm creepin

[Chorus]

QUIET STORM (REMIX)
(feat. Lil' Kim)

[Havoc]

*In broad daylight get right . . . Just been through it all, man. Blood sweat and
tears. Niggas is dead and shit. What the fuck else can happen, yo? I don't
think much more, son, word to mother, yo. We done seen it all, we done been
through it all, yo. Let y'all niggas know right now. Word to mother, for real,
for real.*

[Lil' Kim]
Queen Bee, baby

[Havoc]
That shit is the truth

[Lil' Kim]
Lil' Kim, B.I.G.

[Havoc]
I'm not lyin... Yo...
Blowin niggas with rusty-ass German things
Keepin it thorough is our motherfuckin claim to fame
Throw on your wetsuit, when it rains it pours and all
Hit 'em with the fall, don't even know him from a hole in the wall
Get at me, niggas wanna clap me, snitches wanna rat me?
Put it right where they back be
Keep my duns close to me, enemies even closer
Sendin kites with the Motorolas, yo
Give 'em the cold shoulder with a hollow-tip to match
Bad apple outta the batch, obsessed with gats
Since a little dude, eatin niggas' food, buck-fifty's
Niggas can kill me but they comin with me
How about that? Send the Queen Bee to attack
Only a fly bitch like that can leave 'em and laugh
Rock 'em to sleep, make 'em think the drama is dead
Yo, I smile up in your face though I'm plottin instead

[Chorus 2x]
Yo, it's the real shit, shit to make you feel shit
Thump 'em in the club shit, have you wildin out when you bump this
    (Hip-hop)
Drugs to your eardrum, the raw uncut
Have a nigga OD 'cause it's never enough

[Lil' Kim]
Hot damn, ho, here we go again
"Lyte as a Rock," bitch, hard as a cock, bitch

This shit knock for blocks through hardtops

In the parkin lots, where my nigga Rock like to spark-a-lot

My Brook-lyn style speak for itself

Like a wrestler, another notch under my belt

The embezzler, chrome treasurer, the U-N-O

Competitor, I'm ten steps ahead of ya

I'm a leader, y'all on some followin shit

Comin in this game on some modelin shit

Bitches suck cock just to get to the top

I put a hundred percent in every line I drop

It's the Q to the B, with the M-O, B-B

Queensbridge, Brooklyn and we D-double-E-P

What? Y'all wish I lived the life I live

Aiyo, Prodigy, tell 'em what this is, dun …

[Chorus 2x]

[Prodigy]

Yo, I could never get enough of it, yo, that's my shit

I need that shit to boost my adrenaline

Yo, rock that shit, that real-life shit

Makes bitches wanna thug it, makes the projects love it

We come through like, "Fuck it"

Y'all want problems? Pursue it, let's do it

Infamous Mobb bosses, check out the portrait

At the round table, my dun speakin with his twin ghost

It's gangsta how we rock, while you watch

Attracted to our style, this is how we get down

With big jewelry and big guns

We get busy, it get grizzly, beat niggas bloody

Twist niggas frontin, get to runnin

'Fore the mens get to dumpin, the fans get to thumpin

M-O-B-B, got the whole spot jumpin

When my niggas step in the place—Damn, you gotta love it

[Chorus 2x]

It's the real

Hah, it's the real baby, hip-hop, hip-hop, hip-hop

NAS

Raised in the Queensbridge Houses, Nas grew up in a street culture still palpable in his rhymes. With depth and delivery comparable to Rakim and a perspective that ranges from the anarchy of the corner to the penetrating consciousness of Eastern philosophy, Nas has built a body of work with few equals.

Even after two decades of recording, Nas's most notable achievement is still widely considered to be the album he began as a teenager, *Illmatic* (1994). On *Illmatic*, Nas rhymes with as much poetic sophistication as anyone in hip-hop at that time or since. "When Nas busted out with [*Illmatic*]," writes Matthew Diehl, "he was hailed as a neo-realist ghetto poet, a welcome return to rap's lyrical-invention roots."[40]

Nas's career reflects the many changes he has experienced during the transition from the project life of his youth to adulthood in the spotlight. This transition is a major theme in Nas's lyrics. From the ambition he expresses on *Illmatic* ("I dream I can sit back / And lamp like Capone with drug scripts sewn / Or the legal luxury life, rings flooded with stones, homes") to his reflective tone of arrival on "Nothing Lasts Forever" ("Nice cars, livin like a star, club hoppin / Poppin bottles at the bar, love shoppin / Gucci iceberg, coppin two, three nice furs") and finally to his ruminations on the limitations of wealth on *Hip Hop Is Dead* ("The way I flaunted it then would now embarrass me / It kinda make me wanna hate bling, it's a race thing"), we witness the evolution of an artist in rhyme.

FROM **LIVE AT THE BBQ (MAIN SOURCE)**

Street's disciple, my raps are trifle

I shoot slugs from my brain just like a rifle

Stampede the stage, I leave the microphone split

Play Mr. Tuffy while I'm on some Pretty Tone shit

Verbal assassin, my architect pleases

When I was twelve, I went to hell for snuffin Jesus
Nasty Nas is a rebel to America
Police murderer, I'm causin hysteria
My troops roll up with a strange force
I was trapped in a cage and let out by the Main Source
Swimmin in women like a lifeguard
Put on a bulletproof, nigga, I strike hard
Kidnap the president's wife without a plan
And hangin niggas like the Ku Klux Klan
I melt mics 'til the soundwave's over
Before steppin to me you'd rather step to Jehovah
Slammin MCs on cement
'Cause verbally, I'm iller than a AIDS patient
I move swift and uplift your mind
Shoot the gift when I riff in rhyme
Rappin sniper, speakin real words
My thoughts react like Steven Spielberg's
Poetry attacks, paragraphs punch hard
My brain is insane, I'm out to lunch, god
Science is dropped, my raps are toxic
My voicebox locks and excels like a rocket

N.Y. STATE OF MIND

Yeah, straight out the fuckin dungeons of rap
Where fake niggas don't make it back . . .
I don't know how to start this shit, yo . . .

Rappers, I monkey flip 'em with the funky rhythm
I be kickin, musician inflictin composition
Of pain, I'm like Scarface sniffin cocaine
Holdin a M-16, see, with the pen I'm extreme
Now, bullet holes left in my peepholes, I'm suited up
With street clothes, hand me a nine and I'll defeat foes
Y'all know my steelo: with or without the airplay
I keep some E&J, sittin bent up in the stairway

Or either on the corner bettin Grants with the cee-lo champs

Laughin at baseheads tryin to sell some broken amps

G-Packs get off quick, forever niggas talk shit

Reminiscing about the last time the Task Force flipped

Niggas be runnin through the block shootin

Time to start the revolution, catch a body, head for Houston

Once they caught us off guard, the MAC-10 was in the grass and

I ran like a cheetah with thoughts of an assassin

Pick the MAC up, told brothers, "Back up," the MAC spit

Lead was hittin niggas, one ran, I made him backflip

Heard a few chicks scream, my arm shook, couldn't look

Gave another squeeze, heard it click. Yo, my shit is stuck

Try to cock it, it wouldn't shoot, now I'm in danger

Finally pulled it back and saw three bullets caught up in the chamber

So now I'm jettin to the building lobby

And it was full of children, probably couldn't see as high as I be

(So whatchu sayin?) It's like the game ain't the same

Got younger niggas pullin the triggers bringing fame to they name

And claim some corners, crews without guns are goners

In broad daylight, stickup kids, they run up on us

Four-fives and gauges, MACs, in fact

Same niggas'll catch a back to back, snatchin yo' cracks in black

There was a snitch on the block gettin niggas knocked

So hold your stash 'til the coke price drop

I know this crackhead who said she gotta smoke nice rock

And if it's good she'll bring ya customers and measuring pots

But, yo, you gotta slide on a vacation

Inside information keeps large niggas erasin and they wives basin

It drops deep as it does in my breath

I never sleep, 'cause sleep is the cousin of death

Beyond the walls of intelligence, life is defined

I think of crime when I'm in a New York state of mind

New York state of mind [4x]

Be havin dreams that I'm a gangster

Drinkin Moëts, holdin TEKs

Makin sure the cash came correct, then I stepped

Investments in stocks, sewing up the blocks

To sell rocks, winnin gunfights with mega cops

But just a nigga walking with his finger on the trigger

Make enough figures until my pockets get bigger

I ain't the type of brother made for you to start testin

Give me a Smith & Wesson, I'll have niggas undressin

Thinkin of cash flow, Buddha, and shelter

Whenever frustrated I'ma hijack Delta

In the PJs, my blend tape plays, bullets are strays

Young bitches is grazed, each block is like a maze

Full of black rats trapped, plus the Island is packed

From what I hear in all the stories when my peoples come back, black

I'm livin where the nights is jet black, the fiends

Fight to get crack, I just max, I dream I can sit back

And lamp like Capone with drug scripts sewn

Or the legal luxury life, rings flooded with stones, homes

I got so many rhymes I don't think I'm too sane

Life is parallel to hell but I must maintain

And be prosperous, though we live dangerous

Cops could just arrest me, blamin us, we're held like hostages

It's only right that I was born to use mics

And the stuff that I write is even tougher than dice

I'm takin rappers to a new plateau, through rap slow

My rhymin is a vitamin, held without a capsule

The smooth criminal on beat breaks

Never put me in your box if your shit eats tapes

The city never sleeps, full of villains and creeps

That's where I learned to do my hustle, had to scuffle with freaks

I'm a addict for sneakers, twenties of Buddha, and bitches with beepers

In the streets I can greet ya, about blunts I teach ya

Inhale deep like the words of my breath

I never sleep, 'cause sleep is the cousin of death
I lay puzzle as I backtrack to earlier times
Nothing's equivalent to the New York state of mind

New York state of mind [4x]

LIFE'S A BITCH
(feat. AZ)

[AZ]
Visualizin the realism of life and actuality
Fuck who's the baddest, a person's status depends on salary
And my mentality is money orientated
I'm destined to live the dream for all my peeps who never made it
'Cause, yeah, we were beginners in the 'hood as Five-Percenters
But somethin must of got in us 'cause all of us turned to sinners
Now some restin in peace and some are sittin in San Quentin
Others such as myself are tryin to carry on tradition
Keepin the *Schweppervescence* street ghetto essence inside us
'Cause it provides us with the proper insight to guide us
Even though we know somehow we all gotta go
But as long as we leavin thievin we'll be leavin with some kind of dough
So and to that day we expire and turn to vapors
Me and my capers'll be somewhere stackin plenty papers
Keepin it real, packin steel, gettin high
'Cause life's a bitch and then you die

[Chorus 2x]
Life's a bitch and then you die; that's why we get high
'Cause you never know when you're gonna go
Life's a bitch and then you die; that's why we puff lye
'Cause you never know when you're gonna go

[Nas]
I woke up early on my born day, I'm twenty years of blessing
The essence of adolescent leaves my body, now I'm fresh in

My physical frame is celebrated 'cause I made it

One quarter through life, some godly-like thing created

Got rhymes 365 days annual, plus some

Load up the mic and bust one, cuss while I puffs from

My skull 'cause it's pain in my brain vein, money maintain

Don't go against the grain, simple and plain

When I was young at this I used to do my thing hard

Robbin foreigners, take they wallets, they jewels, and rip they green cards

Dipped to the projects flashin my quick cash

And got my first piece of ass smokin blunts with hash

Now it's all about cash in abundance, niggas I used to run with

Is rich or doin years in the hundreds

I switched my motto—instead of sayin fuck tomorrow

That buck that bought a bottle could've struck the lotto

Once I stood on the block, loose cracks produce stacks

I cooked up and cut small pieces to get my loot back

Time is illmatic, keep static like wool fabric

Pack a four-matic that crack your whole cabbage

FROM **THE WORLD IS YOURS**

I sip the Dom P watchin *Gandhi* 'til I'm charged

Then writin in my book of rhymes, all the words pass the margin

To hold the mic I'm throbbin, mechanical movement

Understandable smooth shit that murderers move with

The thief's theme—play me at night, they won't act right

The fiend of hip-hop has got me stuck like a crack pipe

The mind activation, react like I'm facin time

Like "Pappy" Mason with pens I'm embracin

Wipe the sweat off my dome, spit the phlegm on the streets

Suede Timb's on my feets, makes my cipher complete

Whether cruisin in a six cab or Montero Jeep

I can't call it, the beats make me fallin asleep

I keep fallin, but never fallin six feet deep

I'm out for presidents to represent me (Say what?)

I'm out for presidents to represent me (Say what?)

I'm out for dead presidents to represent me

. . . .

To my man Ill Will, God bless your life ("It's yours!")

To my peoples throughout Queens, God bless your life

I trip, we box up crazy bitches, aimin guns in all my baby pictures

Beef with housin police, release scriptures that's maybe Hitler's

Yet I'm the mild, money-gettin style, rollin foul

The versatile honey-stickin wild golden child

Dwellin in the Rotten Apple, you get tackled

Or caught by the devil's lasso, shit is a hassle

There's no days for broke days when sellin smoke pays

While all the old folks pray to Je-sus, soakin they sins in trays

Of holy water, odds against Nas's slaughter

Thinkin a word best describin my life, to name my daughter

My strength, my son, the star, will be my resurrection

Born in correction, all the wrong shit I did, he'll lead in right direction

How ya livin? Large or broke or charge cards or mediocre

You flippin coke or playin spit spades and strip poker?

. . . .

I'm the young city bandit, hold myself down singlehanded

For murder raps, I kick my thoughts alone, get remanded

Born alone, die alone, no crew to keep my crown or throne

I'm deep by sound alone, caved inside a thousand miles from home

I need a new nigga for this black cloud to follow

'Cause while it's over me it's too dark to see tomorrow

Trying to maintain, I flip, fill the clip to the tip

Picturin my peeps, now the income make my heartbeat skip

And I'm amped up, they locked the champ up, even my brain's in

    handcuffs

Headed for Indiana, stabbin women like the Phantom

The crew is lampin Big Willie style

Check the chip-toothed smile, plus I profile wild

Stash through the flock wools, burnin dollars to light my stove

Walk the blocks wit' a bop, checkin dames, plus the games
People play, bust the problems of the world today

ETHER
"Fuck Jay-Z." What's up, niggas? Aiyo, I know you ain't talkin about me, dog.
*   You? What? "Fuck Jay-Z." You been on my dick, nigga. You love my style,*
*   nigga. "Fuck Jay-Z."*

[Chorus]
(I) Fuck with your soul like ether
(Will) Teach you the king you know you
(Not) "GOD'S SON" across the belly
(Lose) I prove you lost already

Brace yourself for the main event
Y'all impatiently waitin
It's like a AIDS test, what's the results?
Not positive, who's the best? Pac, Nas, and B.I.G.
Ain't no best, East, West, North, South, flossed out, greedy
I embrace y'all with napalm
Blowed up, no guts left, chest, face gone
How could Nas be garbage?
Semiautos at your cartilage
Burner at the side of your dome, come outta my throne
I got this locked since 9-1
I am the truest, name a rapper that I ain't influenced
Gave y'all chapters, but now I keep my eyes on the Judas
With "Hawaiian Sophie" fame, kept my name in his music
Check it

[Chorus]

Aiyo, pass me the weed, put my ashes out on these niggas, man (No doubt). Ay,
*   y'all faggots, y'all kneel and kiss the motherfuckin ring.*

[Chorus]

I've been fucked over, left for dead, dissed, and forgotten

Luck ran out, they hoped that I'd be gone, stiff and rotten

Y'all just piss on me, shit on me, spit on my grave (Uh)

Talk about me, laugh behind my back, but in my face

Y'all some well-wishin (bitch niggas), friendly-actin, envy-hidin snakes

With your hands out for my money, man, how much can I take?

When these streets keep callin, heard it when I was sleep

That this Gay-Z and Cockafella Records wanted beef

Started cockin up my weapon, slowly loadin up this ammo

To explode it on a camel, and his soldiers, I can handle

This for dolo and his manuscript just sound stupid

When KRS already made a album called "Blueprint"

First Biggie's ya man, then you got the nerve to say that you better than Big

Dick-suckin lips, won't you let the late, great veteran live?

(I … will … not … lose …)

"GOD'S SON" across the belly, I prove you lost already

The king is back, where my crown at?

(Ill Will) Ill Will rest in peace, let's do it, niggas

[Chorus]

Y'all niggas deal with emotions like bitches

What's sad is I love you 'cause you're my brother

You traded your soul for riches

My child, I've watched you grow up to be famous

And now I smile like a proud dad, watchin his only son that made it

You seem to be only concerned with dissin women

Were you abused as a child, scared to smile, they called you ugly?

Well, life is harsh, hug me, don't reject me

Or make records to disrespect me, blatant or indirectly

In '88 you was gettin chased through your buildin

Callin my crib and I ain't even give you my numbers

All I did was give you a style for you to run with

Smilin in my face, glad to break bread with the god

Wearin Jaz' chains, no TEKs, no cash, no cars

No jail bars, Jigga, no pies, no case

Just Hawaiian shirts, hangin with little Chase

You a fan, a phony, a fake, a pussy, a Stan

I still whip your ass, you thirty-six in a karate class

You Tae-bo ho, tryin ta work it out, you tryin to get brolic?

Ask me if I'm tryin ta kick knowledge

Nah, I'm tryin to kick the shit you need to learn though

That ether, that shit that make your soul burn slow

Is he Dame Diddy, Dame Daddy, or Dame Dummy?

Oh, I get it, you Biggie and he's Puffy (III)

Rockefeller died of AIDS, that was the end of his chapter

And that's the guy y'all chose to name your company after?

Put it together: I rock hoes, y'all rock fellas

And now y'all tryin to take my spot, fellas?

Feel these hot rocks, fellas; put you in a dry spot, fellas

In a pine box with nine shots from my Glock, fellas

Foxy got you hot 'cause you kept your face in her puss

What you think, you gettin girls now 'cause of your looks? (Girls, girls, girls)

Ne-gro, please

You no mustache havin, with whiskers like a rat

Compared to Beans you wack

And your man stabbed Un and made you take the blame

You ass, went from Jaz to hangin with Kane, to Irv, to Big

And Eminem murdered you on your own shit

You a dick-riding faggot, you love the attention

Queens niggas run you niggas, ask Russell Simmons

Ha, R-O-C get gunned up and clapped quick

J. J. Evans get gunned up and clapped quick

Your whole damn record label gunned up and clapped quick

Shawn Carter to Jay-Z. Damn, you on Jaz' dick

So, little shorty's gettin gunned up and clapped quick?

How much of Biggie's rhymes is gonna come out your fat lips?

Wanted to be on every last one of my classics

You pop shit, apologize, nigga, just ask 'Kiss

BLACK PRESIDENT

[Barack Obama] *They said this day would never come.* [Crowd cheers]
   They said our sights were set too high. [Crowd cheers] *This country is too
   divided, too disillusioned, to ever come together around a common purpose.
   They said . . .*

[Chorus 2x]
And though it seems heaven-sent
We ain't ready to have a black president

Yes we can . . . change the world . . .

They forgot us on the block, got us in a box
Solitary confinement, how violent are these cops?
They need an early retirement
How many rallies will I watch? I ain't got it in me to march
I got a semi to spark, the game's in a drought
Public housing projects, cookin up in the Pyrex
My set, my clique, either gettin money
Or runnin from homicide trial, that's if they ain't died yet
Tryin to be rich, still I'm pledging allegiance
A predicate felon, a ghetto leader
Lendin my poetical genius to whoever may need it
I bleed this from Queensbridge, now living with my feet up
Never defeated, so a president's needed
You know these colored folks and Negros hate to see
One of they own succeeding
America, surprise us, and let a black man guide us

[Chorus]

What's the black prez thinking on election night?
Is it, "How can I protect my life? Protect my wife? Protect my rights?"
Every other president was nothing less than white
Except Thomas Jefferson and mixed Indian blood and Calvin Coolidge
KKK is like, "What the fuck?" Loadin they guns up
Loadin up mines, too, ready to ride

'Cause I'm ridin with my crew: he dies, we die, too

Yeah, but on the positive side

I think Obama provides hope and challenges minds

Of all races and colors to erase the hate

And try to love one another; so many political snakes

We in need of a break, I'm thinkin I can trust this brother

But will he keep it way real?

Every innocent nigga in jail gets out on appeal

When he wins, will he really care still?

I feel...

[Chorus]

Say a prayer for dude, we have to

You ain't right, Jeremiah, wrong pastor

In love with a slave master

Sincerely yours, USA's most brave rapper

Jesse carjacker, Uncle Tom kidnapper

Ask around, Bentley Coupe off the Richter

Bitch called Life, I pimped her, whaaaat?

Politics, politricks, Klan shooter

Deacon for defense, progress producer

Nothing on the stove, a survival booster

Gotta do what we gotta do

We ain't got no governors comin through to help

Anything we need done, we gotta do for self

New, improved JFK on the way

It ain't the '60s again, niggas ain't hippies again

We ain't fallin for the same traps

Standin on the balconies where they shot the King at

McCain got apologies, ain't nobody hearin that

People need honesty

[Chorus]

[Gov. Bill Richardson] *It is my distinct honor and privilege to introduce to you the next president of the United States: Barack Obama!*

THE NOTORIOUS B.I.G.

The Notorious B.I.G. died a homicide victim at the age of twenty-four. Despite his brief career, Biggie was an innovator who became an icon. Everything about him—his look, his voice, his flow, his cadence, his swagger, and even his ad-libs—have proved influential, and, like 2Pac, his friend turned rival, his memory lives on through his music.

After doing jail time for weapons and drug charges, Biggie began to see the potential of rap as a career. He landed a mention in *The Source*'s Unsigned Hype column and eventually wound up meeting Sean "Puffy" Combs, then record producer and A&R for Uptown Records. Biggie signed a deal with Uptown and immediately began working with other artists on the label, including Mary J. Blige. Biggie followed when Combs founded Bad Boy Records.

The hustler's work ethic and street morality that Biggie developed on the corner helped shape him as a lyricist and are reflected in his music. Perhaps the best example of this is "Juicy," a classic song that we were forced to cut from the anthology due to permissions issues. His sense of escape through hip-hop and his tragicomic sensibility, which no doubt carried him through his dangerous, cutthroat adolescence, are evident in his lyrics. Regarding the dark, hardcore street content of his music, Biggie (as he was known because of his six-foot-three-inch, more than three-hundred-pound frame) said, "My shit is just about me, yo. This is like an autobiography. . . . You can take it as you want to be like me or you want to take it as you want to stay away from what I was doin. Everybody got their own mind, you know what I'm sayin? Go to your parents for messages; come to me for good music."[41]

'95 FREESTYLE
(feat. Scoob, 2Pac, Shyheim, and Big Daddy Kane)
[Big Daddy Kane] *Where's 2Pac and Biggie Smalls?*
[Scoob] *Yeah. Aight? (Yeah!) Let's keep it goin . . .*
[Big Daddy Kane] *Mister Cee . . . Yo, Scoob, you set it off and let's get down for the crown . . .*
[Scoob] *Rock it. That ill shit . . .*
[Notorious B.I.G.] *One, two. One, two. One, two.*

[Scoob] *Brooklyn. JFK, all my niggas—Richie, Matt . . . Ready to get wreck.*
Aight? Uh! Awww, shit!

[Big Daddy Kane] *Go, Scoob!*

[Scoob]
Check it, check it, check it, check it
This here for the motherfuckin record
Here we, here we, here we go, here we, here we go
Can I, can I, can I kick a motherfuckin flow?
Chitty chitty bang bang, uh, chitty bang bang
Motherfuckin niggas can't hang
Well, oh no. Look at the cloud, it's gonna rain
But I don't give a fuck, I'm lettin niggas know they can't hang
Don't give me no lip, don't give me no backtalk, ya break North
Don't make me get my gun and blow your motherfuckin head off
Once again, niggas know my style, god damn it
Unless it's on the cut, so give me the mic and watch me slam it
Hard like Shaquille. Oh, you better kneel
When you see me comin, Big Scoob got 'em runnin
Sex when I flex, I catch wreck on the world tour
With dough in my pockets, big like the biscuits at CB4
Set up a contest, I'm comin, I'm takin the dough
They wouldn't pick you even if you had a Afro
So don't try me, you better walk by me
I'll do you like the first part in *Menace II Society*
Like Cypress Hill, yo, I'm insane
I'll shoot a hole in your toe; I'll make you jump like the House of Pain
Bang biggy, bang biggy, bang bang
Niggas can't hang, niggas can't hang
Bang biggy, bang biggy, bang bang
Motherfuckin niggas can't hang

[Big Daddy Kane] *Biggie Smalls, what you gonna do with it, baby?*

[Notorious B.I.G.]

One two, one two, gonna do it like this ... Where Brooklyn at? Where Brooklyn at? Where Brooklyn at? Where Brooklyn at? We gonna do it like this ... Any time you're ready, check it ...

I got seven MAC-11s, about eight .38s

Nine 9s, ten MAC-10s, the shits never ends

You can't touch my riches

Even if you had MC Hammer and them 357 bitches

Biggie Smalls, the millionaire, the mansion, the yacht

The two weed spots, the two hot Glocks

That's how I got the weed spot

I shot Dread in the head, took the bread and the lambsbread

Lil' Gotti got the shotty to your body

So don't resist or you might miss Christmas

I tote guns, I make number runs

I give MCs the runs drippin

When I throw my clip in the AK, I slay from far away

Everybody hit the D-E-C-K

My slow flow's remarkable

Peace to Mateo. Now we smoke weed

Like Tony Montana sniff the yayo

That's crazy blunts, mad Ls

My voice excels from the avenue to jail cells

Oh my God, I'm droppin shit like a pigeon

I hope you're listenin, smackin babies at they christening

[2Pac] *Motherfuckin Biggie Smalls!*

[Big Daddy Kane] *What you gonna do with it, 2Pac?*

[2Pac]

Yeah, where the motherfuckin thugs at? Throw your motherfuckin middle finger up. We gonna do this shit like this ...

I thank the Lord for my many blessings, know I'm stressin

Keep a vest for protection from the barrel of a Smith & Wesson

And all my niggas in the pen, here we go again

Ain't nuttin separatin us from a MAC-10

Born in the ghetto as a hustler—hold up

A straight soldier, buckin at the bustas

No matter how you try, niggas never die

We just retaliate with hate, then we multiply

You see me strikin down the block, hittin corners

Mobbin like a motherfucker, livin like I wanna

And ain't no stoppin at the red lights, I'm sideways

Thug Life, motherfucker, crime pays!

Let the cops put they lights on—chase me, nigga

Zig zaggin through the freeway—race me, nigga

In a high speed chase with the law

The realest motherfucker that you ever saw

[Big Daddy Kane] *Yeah! Come here, man. Now I wanna see what my man*
   Shyheim gonna do with it . . .

[Shyheim]
Yo, this goes out to everybody from Staten Island
(Ah, Mister Cee, and you don't stop)

Yo, times is gettin hard, word is bond, I swear to God

I even got caught tryin to steal from the junkyard

A born terror, a rebel without a pause

I never had a good Christmas, so who is Santa Claus?

I walk the streets at night with my head down

In this little town you see clowns that wanna be down

So they get a Glock and lick shots to get props

And when shit rocks all you can hear is the shells drop

An old man got shot in the parkin lot

In front of my building, I hang with his grandchildren

And for the nigga that pulled the trigga then tried to slide

And hide, but he got knocked by the homicide
And this happens everyday around my way
So I pray that I can live another day

[Big Daddy Kane] *This how we gonna do it. Hold up, Cee. Aiyo, let's try this*
    …

[Shyheim] *Staten Island in the motherfuckin house. What's up? Wu-Tang Clan*
    in here or what?

[Big Daddy Kane]
Hold up, Cee…

Now what's the bullshit niggas been sayin?
Don't try to act like Martin now with that "I was just playin!"
No need to grieve for more now that the beef is on
Uhh… Oh yeah, motherfucker, your teeth is gone
Just 'cause you rap don't meant that you're catchin wreck with me
Step to this, I'll give your mic a vasectomy
I only know one nigga that can come next to me
Yo, that's a tattle, 'cause I can't count my own shadow
A battle, I gots to have it, 'lest you're gonna rob me
Like they did Whittaker when he fought Chavez
'Cause when it comes to goin against Kane rappin
That's like a pimp trying to pull a nun, ain't nuttin happenin
Non-resistible, non-compatible
I'm not saying I'm the best, I'm just saying I'm fuckin incredible
And let's just make one more thing understood
If I fart on a record, trust me nigga, that shit gon' sound good

ONE MORE CHANCE (REMIX)
First things first, I Poppa, freaks all the honies
Dummies, Playboy bunnies, those wantin money
Those the ones I like 'cause they don't get nathan
But penetration, unless it smells like sanitation
Garbage, I turn like doorknobs

Heartthrob, never, black and ugly as ever
However, I stay Coogi down to the socks
Rings and watch filled with rocks
And my jam knock in your Mitsubishi
Girls pee-pee when they see me
Navajos creep me in they teepee
As I lay down laws like Allen Carpet
Stop it if you think they gonna make a profit
Don't see my ones, don't see my guns—get it?
Now tell ya friends Poppa hit it then split it
In two as I flow with the Junior M.A.F.I.A.
I don't know what the hell's stoppin ya
I'm clockin ya, Versace shade watchin ya
Once ya grin, I'm in, game begin
First I talk about how I dress, it's this
And diamond necklaces, stretch Lexuses
The sex is just immaculate from the back
I get deeper and deeper, help ya reach the
Climax that your man can't make
Call him, tell him you'll be home real late, then sing the break

[Chorus]
One more chance
Biggie, give me one more chance

She's sick of that song on how it's so long
Thought he worked his until I handled my biz
There I is, Major Payne like Damon Wayans
Low Down Dirty even like his brother Keenan
Schemin, don't leave your girl 'round me
True player for real, ask Puff Daddy
You ringin bells with bags from Chanel
Baby Benz, traded in your Hyundai Excel
Fully equipped, CD changer with the cell

She beeped me, meet me at twelve

Where you at? Flippin jobs, payin car notes?

While I'm swimmin in your women like the breaststroke

Right stroke, left stroke was the best stroke

Death stroke, tongue all down her throat

Nuttin left to do but send her home to you

I'm through—can you sing the song for me, boo?

[Chorus]

So, what's it gonna be? Him or me?

We can cruise the world with pearls, 'gator boots for girls

The envy of all women, crushed linen

Cartier wrist-wear with diamonds in 'em

The finest women I love with a passion

Your man's a wimp, I give that ass a good thrashin

High fashion—flyin into all states

Sexin me while ya man masturbates

Isn't this great? Your flight leaves at eight

Her flight lands at nine, my game just rewinds

Lyrically I'm supposed to represent

I'm not only a client, I'm the player president

[Chorus]

TEN CRACK COMMANDMENTS

"One, two, three, four, five, six, seven, eight, nine"

Uhh, it's the ten crack commandments. What? Uhh, uhh. Nigga can't tell me nothin 'bout this coke, uh-huh. Can't tell me nothin 'bout this crack, this weed. For my hustlin niggas. Niggas on the corner, I ain't forget you niggas. My triple-beam niggas, word up.

"One, two, three, four, five, six, seven, eight, nine"

"Ten"

I been in this game for years, it made me a animal

It's rules to this shit, I wrote me a manual

A step-by-step booklet for you to get

Your game on track, not your wig pushed back

Rule numbre uno: Never let no one know

How much dough you hold, 'cause you know

The cheddar breed jealousy especially

If that man fucked up, get your ass stuck up

Number two: Never let 'em know your next move

Don't you know Bad Boys move in silence and violence

Take it from your Highness (Uh-huh)

I done squeezed mad clips at these cats for they bricks and chips

Number three: Never trust no-bo-dy

Your moms'll set that ass up properly gassed up

Hoodie to mask up, shit, for that fast buck

She be layin in the bushes to light that ass up

Number four: Know you heard this before

Never get high on your own supply

Number five: Never sell no crack where you rest at

I don't care if they want a ounce, tell 'em bounce

Number six: That goddamn credit? Dead it

You think a crackhead payin you back, shit, forget it

Seven: This rule is so underrated

Keep your family and business completely separated

Money and blood don't mix like two dicks and no bitch

Find yourself in serious shit

Number eight: Never keep no weight on you

Them cats that squeeze your guns can hold jumps too

Number nine shoulda been number one to me:

If you ain't gettin bagged, stay the fuck from police (Uh-huh)

If niggas think you snitchin, they ain't tryna listen

They be sittin in your kitchen, waitin to start hittin

Number ten: A strong word called consignment

Strictly for live men, not for freshmen
If you ain't got the clientele say, "Hell, no!"
'Cause they gonna want they money rain, sleet, hail, snow
Follow these rules, you'll have mad bread to break up
If not, twenty-four years on the wake up
Slug hit your temple, watch your frame shake up
Caretaker did your makeup
When you pass, your girl fucked my man Jake up
Heard in three weeks she sniffed a whole half of cake up
Heard she suck a good dick and can hook a steak up
Gotta go, gotta go, more pies to bake up, word up, uhh

"One, two, three, four, five, six, seven, eight, nine"
"One, two, three, four, five, six, seven, eight, nine"
"Ten"

I GOT A STORY TO TELL

Who y'all talkin to, man? Uhh! Check it out, check it out. This here goes out to all the niggas that be fuckin mad bitches in other niggas' cribs. Thinkin shit is sweet . . . Nigga creep up on your ass, hahaha. Live niggas respect it, check it:

I kick flows for ya, kick down doors for ya
Even left all my motherfuckin hoes for ya
Niggas think Frankie pussywhipped—nigga, picture that
With a Kodak, Insta-ma-tic
We don't get down like that
Lay my game down, quite flat
Sweetness, where you parked at?
Petite-ness, but that ass fat
She got a body make a nigga wanna eat that
I'm fuckin with you
The bitch official though, dick harder than a missile, yo
Try to hit it and she trippin, disappearin like Arsenio
Yo, the bitch push a double-oh

With the Five in front, probably a conniving stunt

Y'all drive in front, I'ma peel with her

Find a deal with her, she fuck around and steal, huh?

Then we all get laced

Televisions, Versace heaven, when I'm up in 'em

The shit she kicked, all the shit's legit

She get dick from a player off the New York Knicks

Nigga tricked ridiculous, the shit was plush

She's stressing me to fuck like she was in a rush

We fucked in his bed, quite dangerous

I'm in his ass while he play against the Utah Jazz

My 112 CD blast, I was past

She came twice, I came last, roll the grass

She giggle, sayin, "I'm smokin on homegrown"

Then I heard her moan. "Honey, I'm home"

Yep, tote chrome for situations like this

I'm up in his broad, I know he won't like this

Now I'm like, "Bitch, you better talk to him"

Before this fist put a spark to him

Fuck around, shit get dark to him, put a part through him

Lose a major part to him: arm, leg

She beggin me to stop, but this cat gettin closer

Gettin hot like a toaster, I cocks the toast, uhh

Before my eyes could blink, she screams out

"Honey, bring me up somethin to drink!"

He go back downstairs, more time to think

Her brain racin, she's tellin me to stay patient

She don't know I'm cool as a fan

Gat in hand, I don't wanna blast her man

But I can and I will, though, I'm tryin to chill, though

Even though situation lookin kinda ill, yo

It came to me like a song I wrote

Told the bitch, "Give me a scarf, pillowcase, and rope"

Got dressed quick, tied the scarf around my face

Roped the bitch up, gagged her mouth with the pillowcase
Play the cut, nigga comin off some love potion shit
Flash the heat on 'em, he stood emotionless
Dropped the glass, screamin, "Don't blast, here's the stash
A hundred cash, just don't shoot my ass, please!"
Nigga pullin mad G's out the floor
Put stacks in a Prada knapsack, hit the door
Grab the keys to the Five, call my niggas on the cell
Bring some weed, I got a story to tell, uh, uh

Yo, man, y'all niggas ain't gonna believe what the fuck happened to me.
Remember that bitch I left the club with, man? (Yeah.) Yo, freaky, yo. I'm up in
this bitch, playa, this bitch fuckin one of them ol' Knick ass niggas and shit, I'm
up in the spot so . . . (Who, man? Who? Which one?) One of them six-five
niggas, I don't know. Anyway, I'm up in the motherfuckin spot, so boom, I'm
up in the pussy, whatever, whatever. I sparks up some lye, Pop Duke creeps in
up on some. (Get the fuck out of here!) Must have been rained out or
something because he comes up in the spot—Had me scared, had me scared.
I was shook, Daddy, but I forget I had my Roscoe on me. (He didn't know you
had ya heat.) Always. You know how we do. So anyway, the nigga comes up
the stairs, he creepin up the steps, the bitch all shook. She sends the nigga
back downstairs to get some drinks and shit. She getting mad nervous, I said,
"Fuck that, man!" I'm the nigga, you know how we do it, nigga, ransom note-
style. Put the scarf around my motherfuckin face, gagged that bitch up,
played the kizzock. Soon as this nigga comes up in the spot, flash the Desert
in his face, he drops the glass. Looked like the nigga pissed on hisself or
somethin, word to my mother! Ahh, fuck it, this nigga runs dead to the floor,
peels up the carpet, start givin me mad papers, mad papers. (I told you that
bitch was a sheisty bitch, cuz! Word to mother, I used to fuck with her cousin.
But you ain't know that! Hahaha. You ain't know that shit. Really, though.) I
threw all that motherfuckin money up in the Prada knapsack. Two words, "I'm
gone!" (No doubt, no doubt . . . no doubt!) Yo, nigga, got some lye, y'all got
some lye? (No doubt.)

OUTKAST

When Outkast appeared on the hip-hop scene with *Southernplay-alisticadillacmuzik* (1994), they laid the groundwork for one of the most diverse, genre-defying, and sustained careers in rap. From the outset, the Georgia natives André "3000" Benjamin and Antwan "Big Boi" Patton demonstrated a rare combination of skills behind the mic. In stark outline, André is the rebellious artist and romantic of the group; Big Boi is the streetwise, strip-club bottle-popper. Fill in the details and a more nuanced picture develops. Although his staccato flow may suggest a gangsta aggression, Big Boi often delivers astute social commentary and lays down personal stories that reveal a vulnerable side. André's rap eclecticism is given room to breathe by a deep-seated self-assuredness that sometimes manifests itself in tough talk that is initially hard to detect since it eschews all the thugged-out clichés.

Together the two artists make a potent if at times unlikely tandem. "Outkast is dope because they're two opposites and they come together to make cohesive-sounding music," remarked Q-Tip, half of another famous hip-hop tandem, A Tribe Called Quest. "That's amazing to me—they bumped it up and made it work for them."[42] On the track "Elevators (Me & You)," from Outkast's second album *ATLiens* (1996), they explain how their seemingly unlikely partnership came into being. The up-and-down motion of the elevators of the title also represents the trajectories of rap careers; that movement is balanced in the song by circular images of ceiling fans and MARTA routes, as the duo describe their early days of trying to break big in Atlanta and its surroundings. It is a spare and compelling genesis song, one which ends with André being accosted by an around-the-way fan who affects an old acquaintanceship.

The album that followed, *Aquemini* (1998), carried in its title another clue to the organic nature of Outkast's collaboration, combining as it did the Zodiac signs of André and Big Boi. "Rosa Parks," from the same album, was not the history lesson listeners might have expected from the name of the civil rights icon in the title, but rather a bumping, fast-paced track that lightened up and smartened up the normally heavier, blunter Southern sound of crunk. *Stankonia* (2000) also had a standout track whose title promised politics, "Bombs Over Baghdad (B.O.B.)," but which in fact made its arguments on aesthetic grounds.

Their biggest-selling album to date, *Speakerboxxx/The Love Below* (2003), was in essence two solo albums packaged together, but as with all of the group's releases, the final result was an organic concoction. They made singles such as "Hey Ya!" and "The Way You Move" that even casual listeners of pop radio came to love, but also kept producing bangers for the hip-hop heads. They spoke in the terms and forms most familiar to longtime fans of rap, but also stretched out in idiosyncratic songs such as "A Life in the Day of Benjamin André (Incomplete)," an unrelenting five-minute flow of raw rhymes without bridge or chorus. Big Boi and André remain those rarest of artists, in rap or otherwise—the kind you always have to attend to because their track records are marked by success without compromise.

(Note: The editors intended to include in this volume "Elevators [Me and You]," "Aquemini," "Rosa Parks," and "A Life in the Day of Benjamin André," but could not obtain permissions.)

RAS KASS

Ras Kass laces his lyrics with unexpected allusions to literature, history, and philosophy. Even before the release of his debut album, *Soul on Ice* (1996), he had won acclaim for his lyrics both in his native Los Angeles and nationwide.

Ras Kass's style is distinguished by his allusive breadth, his dense texture, and his swaggering delivery. His songs often contain ambitious conceits, as on "Interview with a Vampire," in which he conducts a lyrical conversation with God and Satan. Thematically, his subjects range from government conspiracy ("Ordo Abchao [Order Out of Chaos]") to more conventional hip-hop boasts taken to comic extremes. Ras Kass has never quite achieved the commercial success one would expect of such a skilled and inventive MC, but the quality of his lyrics only grows when they are seen on the page.

Like many MCs, Ras Kass usually writes his lyrics with a specific beat in mind. "Nowadays," he explains, "nine times out of ten, I write on the spot to the beat. That's something I picked up from Dre. The 10th time, usually a political song, or a personal song I write first then create the beat around it.

Sometimes the music is in my head and I just have to find the right producer to play what I hum, like [on] 'Interview with a Vampire.'"[43]

ORDO ABCHAO (ORDER OUT OF CHAOS)

The story begins like a Dickens novel, *David Copperfield*
"I am born," and naw, nigga, we can't all just get along
5996 A-L The Year of Light
Illuminati border on a New World Order
And a nigga fightin the struggle sorta kinda on some rappin shit
But real activists be on death watch like Mumia
Abu Jamal. Ain't this a bitch? Y'all figure
It only takes a trigger and $12.98 plus tax
To potentially murder fifty niggas
So motherfuckers better duck like Daffy
'Cause nowadays the average niggas think they Butch Cassidy
And the Sundance Kid, doin bids with no remorse
It's almost methodical, education is false assimilation
Building prisons is economical, so young niggas in gang modules
Be giving more head than hair follicles
And niggas like myself know the ledge and still jump like Geronimo
Huh, Supreme Mathematics and bad habits
'Cause chasing cabbage keeps a nigga savage (true)
Blame it on the disease, we all got the symptoms
Most of us niggas wanna be pimps, but Uncle Sam really pimpin them
What the fuck?

[Chorus]
Naw, they don't feel you, but what you don't know can kill you
They don't feel you, but what you don't know can kill you
They don't feel you, but what you don't know can kill you
Naw, they don't feel you, but what you don't know can kill you

The planet revolves, supposedly man evolves
But no problem is solved, 'cause man is the cause
For the sake of eugenics biochemists create ethno-specific

Epidemics, injecting the public in clinics

Then when the truth comes out ("You black people are so paranoid")

But who murdered Africa? The World Health Organization

Before 1978 there was no blood

With AIDS contamination. It ain't little green monkeys

It's little white honkies crossing bovine leukemia

With sheep Visna virus. (Whaat?) As Set tore out the iris

Of Horus and Isis loved Osiris, black men is blinded

While black women look for real men but can't find it

Sometimes I think to myself, "Why'd I even bring a

Child into this world?" I pay taxes so Bill Clinton

Can slang crack in Arkansas, buy gold

Imported from South Africa, but I don't eat swine

And beat the living shit out of skinheads. So where's my peace of mind, huh?

A Swiss watch, leasing a Lex on credit

All the liquor and pussy a nigga can get

Put together this puzzle but my pieces won't fit

What the fuck?

[Chorus]

Now shit gets no realer, reality dictates fate

Global Policy 2000, by then the planet depopulates

By about one billion men, women, and children

By whatever means necessary: wars, disease

Starvation, plagues, et cetera—set your watch and watch

Lord Maitreya's sin been in effect since

Before George Washington Monument, an obelisk

The thirty-three-hundred-pound capstone semi-conceals

The Masonic seal. I'm knowin, but it's like

Trying to stop the sun from shining, *Soul on Ice*

Damned if I do and fucked if I don't, dog eat dog

Like Jeff Dahmer. And most brothers ain't soldiers

'Cause you got no code, you got no honor. Wanna build

An empire, blood-sucking me to get richer? So, B

What's getting six figures when ya fuckin with bitch niggas?

I ask you. Don't make me gay bash you

So the longer I live the less love I have to give

And the tragedy is

It's a vicious cycle, everybody caught up the vortex

So we try to cash more checks and have more sex

The problem gets worse but a solution ain't clear

And we been sayin the same shit for 650 years

What the fuck?

[Chorus]

INTERVIEW WITH A VAMPIRE

[Ras Kass] You wanna talk to God? God never sleeps.

[Chorus]

[Ras Kass] Now what came first, the chicken or the egg?

[God] Armageddon. [Ras Kass] The arm, a leg, a leg, a arm, a head

Headin in your direction. The riddle was the answer to the question

Born of the flesh, what is perfection?

[Ras Kass]

Inside my mother's womb, doomed to return to the tomb

Or was it from the dead I was raised? All too soon to pay

On Judgment Day, is this beginning or the ending?

Died sinning, still winning, still grinning

Descending, verdict still pending, born pretending

Three hundred billion men, women, and children

Déjà vu, could be I'm dreaming

But we all ask for divine reason, while still breathing and until leaving

Who, what, when, where, how, but most of all why?

[God] Why what? [Ras Kass] Do we live just to die?

[God]

The Book was written way before the apple got bitten

There is no God but me, mathematically, in division

My decision was all inventions. I need not mention

Infinite dimensions, but the human mind's flaw

Was limited comprehension. So while you try to travel to Mars

And the stars, the God manifests through the entire universe

From the sun, moon, the earth

I created man in my image and the black man was first

The scientific explanation—yeah, I made man out of dirt

[Ras Kass] But how can a man be first when it's the woman that's giving
   birth?

[God] Listen, single-celled organisms. The homo sapiens, the albinen

[Ras Kass] What's that? [God] White people

[Ras Kass] They keep the world separate and unequal

[God] They teach you right is wrong, wrong is right, up is down (Shit)

Kick the king off his throne, is the planet flat or round?

[Ras Kass] Can we really time travel and is there life in outer space?

[God] Wait, you knew all this in the first place

You tryin to get to God. [Ras Kass] But I've fallen from your grace

A billion paths to take, but which one is truly straight?

[Chorus]

[Ras Kass]

Can you walk across water or rise from the dead?

I heard it's said he lived when the Son of Man bled

[God]

It's a process, shit don't just happen, I create it

Everything you see, and shit you don't, son, I made it

And waited. I'm the Big Bang Theory and evolution

Been there, done that, from revolution to prostitution

The first and final solution. The Qur'an, Bible

And Vedas is only tools, don't be confused when the medulla

Oblongata do. [Ras Kass] Oh, so Revelations is Genesis?

[God] Three-sixty degrees are limitless

[Satan] Shit, my motherfuckin nemesis [Ras Kass] Who's you?

[Satan]

Chump, I thought you knew. Who else?

Lucifer, the light-bearer, stupid, the Devil himself

He the creator, we all the creations, guess I'm eternal damnation

Got you bitches seeking your own salvation

Who taught you how to pray? 'Cause you read it in the book?

Look, you bear witness to Amon-Re

Every day when you say Amen, and turn around

And preach worshipin false gods is a unforgivable sin

Yeah, the Good Book is like comic books, you take 'em too literal

I tricked you into believin that the power to reason

Makes you able to live infinitely in the physical

Guess I'm the pawn con miracle

Basically I tell true lies in general, the yin and the yang

The player with a trillion years of game

[God]

He got you sellin your spiritual for power, money, and fame

I came out of triple-stage darkness, gave mortals my attributes

But even you made me the mystery God like the Loch Ness

And use science to prove or disprove my existence

Tryin to unlock this artificial intelligence

Cloned in a space station, tryin to build the Tower of Babylon

But you sadly mistaken, when I started raping homo sapiens

You lookin for an angel with wings

I'ma bring young niggas with a AK, fuck a alien

[Ras Kass] So what you sayin then? You the one that created sin

[God]

What you call Mother Nature was the nature of me (Oh)

What you call evil, ultimately, was the force inside of me

Matter can't be created or destroyed, it just changes shape

One God, many people and many faiths

And this is how I wanted it done. [Ras Kass] Wait, wait, hold up

Father, tell me, who is God's Son?

[Chorus 2x]

[God]

I be the Jesus to your Buddha, the Krishna at your Juma

The Big Kahuna, Jehovah Witnesses in suede Pumas

Zeus, Pharaoh, Elohim, Saturn, Yahweh, Jah

Rastafari, Allah, the Most High

A being, only that I'm not. I'm the oceans

The trees, a bumblebee, and a Glock

Earthquakes, how much money you ever take

The reason behind every mistake mankind continually makes

[Ras Kass] Did God create man or did man need to create God?

[Satan] The answer is both; that's how mortals look at God is odd

[God] You try to customize me to be comfortable

For what you want to do and how you choose to act

The Pope and Christians will tell you God ain't black

But to get something from nothing is physically impossible, that's a fact

[Satan] Black is the combination of all colors. [Ras Kass] White is the lack
  thereof

[God]

Darkness is beneath the ground and in the skies up above

The clue was that the true illumination is me

Not Illuminati, 'cause I alone discriminate

And eliminate any who be believing they can rationalize

Or out-reason He who created the creature

The student can never be greater than the teacher

Whether it's Adam and Eve, or atomic chemistry

I'm the one true source of all energy

Will eventually destroy every enemy when I see fit

I can't blaspheme my own name so when God damn it, so be it

[Satan]

That's called the wrath of God, but we got a deal, I can kill

Fuck up the whole world and in the end

He'll still fulfill his plan, to restore man to his original position

Nigga gave me some hooks and said I gets to go fishin

[God]

I gave man dominion over the earth, to master the wealth

But most of my children don't have dominion over theyself

[Satan]

That's where I come in. Call it original sin (Damn)

Who really gives a flying fuck?

I taught you how to blood suck and ultimately self-destruct

[God]

Know the ledge, wise the dome, do the data

I'm the alpha. [Satan] I'm the beta

[Ras Kass]

And I'm omega

To be or not to be was man's question since inception

"I think, therefore I am" was man's perception

But the birth is the resurrection. The son of God (Christ)

Or God's son, that lights our entire spectrum

You got everlasting life 'long as you got day and night

Illumination, not education, to bring the blind sight

And what you need to know is that you'll never know it all

I'm a lowercase g, son of the ever-living God

THE ROOTS

When Tariq Trotter, aka Black Thought, and drummer Ahmir "?uestlove" Thompson met at the Philadelphia High School for Creative Performing Arts around 1987, they fashioned one of the most enduring partnerships in hip-hop. ?uestlove brought a musical vocabulary of live beats and Black Thought brought his rapid-fire staccato lyricism. In those early years the two could be found on the Philly streets with Black Thought rapping over ?uestlove's beats. Their call-and-response style, the back and forth between voice and beat, is the soul of MCing laid bare; it has remained at the heart of the Roots' style for more than twenty years.

In their fourth year performing together, Black Thought and ?uestlove recruited other talented Philly musicians and created the Square Roots. In 1991, the group, now simply the Roots, released its first studio album, *Organix*. The album featured Black Thought as the primary MC with occasional appearances on the mic from ?uestlove and Malik B, another local Philly rapper.

Where *Organix* showcased the Roots' Philadelphia soul, their sophomore album, *Do You Want More!?!* (1995), featured Black Thought's lyricism. The album earned acclaim for its live instrumentation. The tracks "Proceed" and "Silent Treatment" had some success as singles, with the latter featuring Black Thought's storytelling and the former featuring him waxing philosophical and flexing his lyrical mental muscles with lines like "What if you could just think / just think yourself away."

The Roots' highest charting album to date is *Things Fall Apart* (1999), which featured the Grammy-winning romantic rap ballad "You Got Me." In the years since, they have kept up a rigorous schedule of recording and live performances. They continue to make music that defies critics and pushes rap music beyond its generic boundaries.

THE NEXT MOVEMENT

C'mon... Hey, yes, y'all. You are now in tune to the sounds... Of the legendary ... Foundation...

[Chorus]
Yeah, you go
Hey, you listeners, stop what you're doin and
Set it in motion, it's the next movement
You listeners, stop what you're doin and
Set it in motion, it's the next movement

Word up, we got the HOT-HOT music, the HOT MUSIC [1x]
The HOT-HOT music, the HOT music [3x]

Yo, one, two, one-two one-two

That's how we usually start, once again it's the Thought

The Dalai Lama of the mic, the prime minister Thought

This directed to whoever in listening range

Yo, the whole state of things in the world 'bout to change

Black rain fallin from the sky look strange

The ghetto is red hot, we steppin on flames

Yo, it's inflation on a price for fame

And it was all the same, but then the antidote came

The Black Thought, ill syllable-ist out the Fifth

This heavyweight rap shit I'm about to lift

LIKE a phylum lift up its seed to sunlight

I plug in the mic, draw like a gunfight

I never use a cordless or stand applaudless

Sippin chlorophyll out of ill silver goblets

I'm like a faucet, monopoly's the object

There ain't no way to cut this tap, you got ta get wet

Your head is throbbin and I ain't said shit yet

The Roots crew, the next movement, c'mon!

Hey, yes, y'all. You are now in tune to the sounds of the legendary Foundation.
   Check it out, uh . . .

[Chorus]

Word up, the formation of words to fit

That's what I usually disturb you with

A lot of rappers never heard of this, or know half the time it is

You doubt the Illa-Fifth, what could you accomplish?

Whether they skywriting your name or you anonymous

You be speechless with stinging sinuses

The Roots royal highnesses through your monitors

I tilt my crown then blow down a dime a kiss

You need to buy a CD and stop rewindin this

I'm the finalist, shinin like a rugged amethyst

And at your music conference I'm the panelist
Listen close to my poetry, I examine this
Like an analyst to see if you can handle this
(Check it out) You, got the groove, MCs
Freeze, stand still, nobody move
Unless you dealin with the Next Movement
The P-Phi-D, we be the mon-u-ment
I live my life nice, but I'm not too bent
You theatrical as a Broadway play, this ain't *Rent*
One hundred percent, straight out the basement
Spreading this across a planet on some next shit
How many people feelin this love music? (C'mon!)

[Chorus]

FROM *ACT TOO . . .* **THE LOVE OF MY LIFE**
(feat. Common)

. . . .

[Black Thought]
The anticipation arose as time froze
I stared off the stage with my eyes closed and dove
Into the deep cosmos, the impact pushed back
The first five rows, but before the raw live shows
I remember I'se a little snot-nosed
Rocking Gazelle goggles and Izod clothes
Learnin the ropes of ghetto survival
Peepin out the situation I had to slide through
Had to watch my back, my front, plus my sides, too
When it came to gettin mine I ain't tryin to argue
Sometimes I would'nta made it if it wasn't for you
Hip-hop, you the love of my life and that's true
When I was handlin the shit I had to do
It was all for you, from the door for you
Speak through you, gettin paper on tour for you

From the start, Thought was down by law for you
Used to hit up every corner store wall for you
We ripped shit and kept it hardcore for you
I remember late nights, steady rockin the mic
Hip-hop, you the love of my life

So tell the people like that, y'all (That, y'all)
And it sounds so nice
Hip-hop, you the love of my life
We 'bout to take it to the top . . .

[Common]
Yo, yo, I was speakin to my guy 'Riq and
How she was desperately seekin to Organize in a Konfusion
Usin no protection, told H.E.R. on *Resurrection*
Caught in the Hype Williams and lost H.E.R. direction
Gettin ate in sections where I wouldn't eat H.E.R.
An under-the-counter love, so silently I treat H.E.R.
Her daddy'll beat H.E.R., eyes all Puff
In the mix on tape niggas had her in the buck
When we touch, it was more than just ta fuck
The police, in her I found peace (Like who?)
Like Malcolm in the East
Seen H.E.R. on the streets of New York, trickin off
Tried to make a hit with H.E.R. but my dick went soft
Movin weight, losin weight, not picky with who she choose to date
Too confused to hate, with her struggle I relate
Close to thirty, most of the niggas she know is dirty
Havin more babies than Lauryn, she started showin early
As of late I realized that this is H.E.R. fate
Or destiny that brings the best of me
It's like God is testin me
In retrospect I see she brought life and death to me
Peace to us collectively, live and direct when we perform
It's just coffee shop chicks and white dudes

Over H.E.R. I got into it with that nigga Ice Cube
Now the fight move to in life makin the right moves
Besides God and family, you my life's jewel
Like that, y'all
Hip-hop ... [echoes]

. . . .

YOU GOT ME
(feat. Eve and Erykah Badu)
[Chorus: Erykah Badu]
If you were worried 'bout where
I been or who I saw or
What club I went to with my homies
Baby, don't worry, you know that you got me
If you were worried 'bout where
I been or who I saw or
What club I went to with my homies
Baby, don't worry, you know that you got me

[Black Thought]
Somebody told me that this planet was small, we used to live
In the same building on the same floor and never met before
Until I'm overseas on tour and peep this Ethiopian
Queen from Philly taking classes abroad
She studying film and photo flash focus record
Said she workin on a flick and could my clique do the score?
She said she loved my show in Paris at Elysée Montmartre
And that I stepped off the stage and took a piece of her heart
We knew from the start that things fall apart and tend to shatter
She like, "That shit don't matter," when I get home, get at her
Through letter, phone, whatever, let's link, let's get together
Shit, you think not? Think the Thought went home and forgot?
Time passed, we back in Philly, now she up in my spot
Tellin me the things I'm tellin her is makin her hot

Started buildin with her constantly round the clock
Now she in my world like hip-hop and keep tellin me

[Chorus]

[Black Thought]
Yo, I'm the type that's always catchin a flight
And sometimes I gotta be out at the height of the night
And that's when she flip and get on some 'ol…

[Eve]
Another lonely night?
Seem like I'm on the side, you only loving your mic
I know you gotta get that paper, Daddy, keep that shit tight
But, yo, I need some sort of love in my life, you dig me?
While politickin with my sister from New York City
She said she know this ballplayer and he think I'm pretty
Psych, I'm playin, boo. You know it's just with you I'm stayin, boo
And when cats be poppin game, I don't hear what they sayin, boo
When you out there in the world, I'm still your girl
With all my classes I don't have the time for life's thrills
So when you sweatin on stage, think of me when you rhyme
And don't be listenin to your homies, they be leavin you blind
[Black Thought] Yeah, so what you sayin? I can trust you?
[Eve] Is you crazy? You my king for real
[Both] But sometimes relationships get ill (No doubt)

[Chorus]

[Black Thought]
That snake could be that chick and that rat could be that cool cat
That's whispering, "She tryin to play you for the fool, Black"
If something's on your chest then let it be known
See, I'm not your every five minutes all on the phone
And on the topic of trust, it's just a matter of fact
That people bite back and fracture what's intact
And they'll forever be, I ain't on some "Oh, I'm a celebrity"

I deal with the real so if it's artificial let it be
I've seen people caught in love like whirlwinds
Listenin to they squads and listenin to girlfriends
That's exactly the point where they whole world ends
Lies come in, that's where that drama begins. She like...

[Chorus to fade]

WEB
Uh... and it weighs a ton
'Riq Geez, motherfuckers, I'm a son of a gun
Black master of any trade under the sun
Talk sharp like a razor blade under the tongue
Clear my path and come get your captain hung
Trying to breathe like Black'll collapse your lungs
Young chump, you could choke off the web I spun
I done cleared 'em out from the threat I brung
You done heard about what set I'm from
My nigga, word-a-mouth, lil' rule-a-thumb
Y'all better bow down when the ruler come
I'm a real 'hood nigga not a hood-a-lum
The way Thought put it down be confusin some of y'all
Cats can't walk while chewin your gum 'n all
What a keyboard gotta do with a drum 'n all?
School 'em on stage like I'm doin a seminar
Professional type, I'm adjusting my mic
Go to war, kid, I'll give you any weapon you like
Give you something to run from, bust off the dum-dum
Stop, kid, that hot shit, you know where it come from
It's Philly worldwide phenomenon
And reinforcin that shit is my nine-to-five
And when I finish making you recognize, I'm gettin at
A couple civilized women that's tryin to ride
You were waitin on the boy to come off the oil
You wanna get the bitches up off the wall

Just to see you smile and enjoy yourself
To keep you in health, this for all of y'all
I'm quick on the draw like Black McGraw
And I can't tell what y'all cats rappin for
My name 'Riq Geez and I'm back for more
To get more chips than the corner store
With a portrait of Malcolm X on the door
While I'm eatin MCs like a carnivore
Matter fact, ease back 'fore you get harmed
Ring the warning horn when I'm gon' perform
The first nigga that move or disturb the groove
I'ma have y'all flicks on the evening news
Play y'all part—get on y'all P's and Q's
And when y'all think Thought, be prepared to lose
Bring money to spend and somebody to lend
And some worthwhile money, not twenties and tens
Get took for your tuck right in front of your hens
Who coulda helped you, nigga? Not none of ya friends
Because I put a black fist under ya chin
Have your physical remains found under the pen
If I'm coming up in the place, I'm coming to win
Wasn't in it for a minute, now I'm dumbin again
'Riq Geez, ock, y'all can chat what y'all please
Receive what I'm gonna give back to y'all, please
'Cause y'all don't really wanna get clapped with all these
My man, you can take y'all strap when y'all leave
You see the squad come in the place, they all freeze
Ice cold, with his mellow cool breeze
MCs never showed loyalty yet
Kool Herc ain't never get a royalty check
I do work, no question, and bomb your set
I'm calm, collect, sharp like my name Gillette
RIP, my main Gillette, until I touch the mic
Y'all people ain't seen danger yet
I'm a decorated vet, I regulate and wreck

Never hesitated yet, I'm gettin heavyweighted checks

If you would dare ask if I'm dedicated—yes

I spit live rounds that'll penetrate a vest

Nigga, take ya seats, I'ma demonstrate a test

How to freak the beats, so gangsta fresh

And it thump from the East Coast to Bangladesh

Big Bank, Willy Gank smoke the thing to death

But hold tight, 'cause it's not over yet

I don't even feel like I'm not sober yet

And it ring like shots in the projects New Year's Eve

And it ain't even October yet

I'm a big bounty hunter like Boba Fett

Y'all more shell-shocked than a soldier get

If the prize in my sights then I'm goin for this

Whoo, whoo, 'Riq Geez be the ultimate

I'm the cul-pr-it, give me the bulk of this

'Riq set it on the magnetic ultra tip

Get down how you 'posed to get

I got nothing to lose, I'm a killer with no regrets

I'm like young LL 'cause I'm hard as hell

Makin niggas screw face like Gargamel

Now I'm all out on my own like Patti LaBelle

Put the pimp game down on your mademoiselle

SCARFACE

Scarface's influence is audible. Before there ever was such a thing as "crunk" or the Dirty South, Scarface was dishing out grimy rhymes, telling tales from the streets of Southside Houston, slanging stories ranging from crack deals to police shootings. Though Scarface often raps about the criminal life, he rejects the term "gangsta rapper." "I don't call my music 'gangsta rap,'" Scarface told the *Washington Post* in 1994. "I call my music reality.["44] Scarface kicks this reality flow slowly and deliberately, using a voice that is at once removed and observational yet still embedded in and encompassed by the raw power of the street life.

Scarface began his rap career as a teenager in the late 1980s as a member of the controversial Houston rap group the Geto Boys. After much publicity and media clamor over the explicitly violent lyrical content of their self-titled album (released 1990), their follow-up release, *We Can't Be Stopped* (1991), sold well enough to reach platinum. Scarface launched his solo career in the same year with his debut *Mr. Scarface Is Back*.

Scarface went on to release four more albums in the 1990s and another four in the first decade of the 2000s. But in 2008, the godfather of southern thuggery removed himself from the game, temporarily retiring after releasing *Emeritus*. In interviews, Scarface explained his exit by denouncing the state of current hip-hop, implicating the corporate machine in the forced commoditization of black cultural expression.

MIND PLAYING TRICKS ON ME
(Geto Boys)
I sit alone in my four-cornered room, staring at candles . . .
Oh, that shit is on? Let me drop some shit like this here. Real smooth.

[Scarface]
At night I can't sleep, I toss and turn
Candlesticks in the dark, visions of bodies being burned
Four walls just starin at a nigga
I'm paranoid, sleeping with my finger on the trigger
My mother's always stressing I ain't living right
But I ain't going out without a fight
See, every time my eyes close
I start sweatin and blood starts comin out my nose
It's somebody watching me act
But I don't know who it is, so I'm watching my back
I can see him when I'm deep in the covers
When I awake I don't see the motherfucker
He owns a black hat like I own
A black suit and a cane like my own

Some might say, "Take a chill, B"
But fuck that shit, there's a nigga trying to kill me
I'm poppin in the clip when the wind blows
Every twenty seconds got me peepin out my window
Investigating the joint for traps
Checking my telephone for taps
I'm staring at the woman on the corner
It's fucked up when your mind is playing tricks on ya

[Willie D]
I make big money, I drive big cars
Everybody know me, it's like I'm a movie star
But late at night, somethin ain't right
I feel I'm being tailed by the same sucker's headlights
Is it that fool that I ran off the block?
Or is it that nigga last week that I shot?
Or is it the one I beat for five thousand dollars?
Thought he had 'caine but it was Gold Medal flour
Reached under my seat, grabbed my popper for the suckers
Ain't no use to be lying, I was scareder than a motherfucker
Took a left into Popeye's and bailed out quick
If it's going down, let's get this shit over with
Here they come, just like I figured
I got my hand on the motherfuckin trigger
What I saw will make your ass start giggling
Three blind, crippled, and crazy senior citizens
I live by the sword
I take my boys everywhere I go because I'm paranoid
I keep looking over my shoulder and peeping around corners
My mind is playing tricks on me

[Scarface]
Day by day it's more impossible to cope
I feel like I'm the one that's doin dope
Can't keep a steady hand because I'm nervous

Every Sunday morning I'm in service
Praying for forgiveness
And trying to find an exit out the business
I know the Lord is looking at me
But yet and still it's hard for me to feel happy
I often drift when I drive
Havin fatal thoughts of suicide
Bang and get it over with
And then I'm worry-free, but that's bullshit
I got a little boy to look after
And if I died then my child would be a bastard
I had a woman down with me
But to me it seemed like she was down to get me
She helped me out in this shit
But to me she was just another bitch
Now she's back with her mother
Now I'm realizing that I love her
Now I'm feelin lonely
My mind is playing tricks on me

[Bushwick Bill]
This year Halloween fell on a weekend
Me and Geto Boys are trick-or-treatin
Robbing little kids for bags
'Til an old man got behind our ass
So we speeded up the pace
Took a look back and he was right before our face
He'd be in for a squabble no doubt
So I swung and hit the nigga in his mouth
He was going down, we figured
But this wasn't no ordinary nigga
He stood about six or seven feet
Now that's the nigga I be seein in my sleep
So we triple-teamed on him
Dropping them motherfuckin b's on him

The more I swung, the more blood flew

Then he disappeared and my boys disappeared, too

Then I felt just like a fiend

It wasn't even close to Halloween

It was dark as fuck on the streets

My hands were all bloody from punching on the concrete

Goddamn, homie

My mind is playing tricks on me

I SEEN A MAN DIE

He greets his father with his hands out

Rehabilitated slightly, glad to be the man's child

The world is different since he seen it last

Outta jail, been seven years, and he's happy that he's free at last

All he had was his mother's letters

Now he's mobile and he's gotta make a change and make it for the better

But he's black, so he's got one strike against him

And he's young, plus he came up in the system

But he's smart and he's finally making eighteen

And his goal's to get on top and try to stay clean

So he's calling up his homie who done came up

Living lavish, now they dealing with the same stuff

And had that attitude that who he was was worthless

And with that fucked-up attitude he killed his first man

Now it's different, he done did dirt

And realized killing men meant coming up, but it still hurt

And can't nobody change this

It's 1994 and we up against the same shit

I never understood why

I could never see a man cry 'til I seen a man die

Man cry

Imagine life at its full peak

Then imagine lying dead in the arms of your enemy

Imagine peace on this earth when there's no grief

Imagine grief on this earth when there's no peace
Everybody's got a different way of ending it
And when your number comes for souls, then they send it in
Now your time has arrived for your final test
I see the fear in your eyes and hear your final breath
How much longer will it be 'til it's all done?
Total darkness, at ease, be it all one
I watch him die and when he dies, let us celebrate
You took his life, but your memory you'll never take
You'll be headed to another place
And the life you used to live will reflect in your mother's face
I still gotta wonder why
I never seen a man cry 'til I seen a man die

I hear you breathing but your heart no longer sounds strong
But you kinda scared of dying so you hold on
And you keep on blacking out and your pulse is low
Stop trying to fight the reaper, just relax and let it go
Because there's no way you can fight it, though you'll still try
And you can try it 'til you fight it, but you'll still die
Your spirits leave your body and your mind clears
The rigor mortis starts to set, now you outta here
You start your journey into outer space
You see yourself in the light, but you're still feeling out of place
So you standing in the tunnel of eternal life
And you see the ones you never learned to love in life
Make the choice, let it go, but you can back it up
If you ain't at peace with God you need to patch it up
But if you're ready, close your eyes and we can set it free
Here lies a man not scared of dying, may he rest in peace
I still got to wonder why
I never seen a man cry 'til I seen that man die

SNOOP DOGG

T he gangsta-stoner-poet-pimp of rap, Snoop Dogg, with his smoothed-out, nearly southern drawl, brought a new vibe to West Coast hip-hop at a time when NWA and Ice-T were at the forefront of the game.

As a member of the Crips in high school, Snoop ran into legal trouble. When he got out of jail he recorded a demo with Warren G and Nate Dogg, titled "213," which got him noticed by Dr. Dre, who immediately got Snoop involved in his projects, particularly *The Chronic* (1991). Snoop was featured on most of the tracks on Dre's first solo album, which was a monstrous success. It went quadruple platinum and ushered in a new era of hip-hop through its smoked-out, soul-thickened beats that were meant to be bumped on the stoop as much as in the whip, and that were the perfect match for Snoop's laconic flow.

New York Times writer Jon Pareles commented that Snoop and Dre made the West Coast "gangsta life sound like a party occasionally interrupted by gunplay," which is another way of saying that Snoop and Dre took their thug-laden West Coast lifestyle and refashioned it lyrically to reach a mass audience.[45] The spirit of *The Chronic* was extended on Snoop's hotly anticipated solo debut, *Doggystyle* (1993).

In the years since, Snoop has emerged as a major figure not only in hip-hop but in popular culture at large. As MTV observed, "[Snoop's] laid-back flow has proven to be timeless, and his charisma transcends all categorization: How else can you explain his transformation from one of the most feared rappers into a beloved household name who can successfully peddle everything from cars to clothes—and still yell out his gang affiliation and proudly proclaim himself to be a pimp?"[46]

NUTHIN BUT A G THANG
(feat. Dr. Dre)

[Snoop Dogg (Dr. Dre)]
One, two, three and to the fo'
Snoop Doggy Dogg and Dr. Dre is at the do'
Ready to make an entrance, so back on up

('Cause you know we're 'bout to rip shit up)

Gimme the microphone first so I can bust like a bubble

Compton and Long Beach together, now you know you in trouble

Ain't nuttin but a G thang, baby!

Two loc'ed-out niggas, so we're crazy!

Death Row is the label that pays me!

Unfadeable, so please don't try to fade this (Hell, yeah!)

But, uh, back to the lecture at hand

Perfection is perfected, so I'ma let 'em understand

From a young G's perspective

And before me dig out a bitch I have to find a contraceptive

You never know, she could be earnin her man

And learnin her man (And at the same time burnin her man)

Now you know I ain't with that shit, Lieutenant

Ain't no pussy good enough to get burnt while I'm up in it

(Yeah!) And that's realer than Real-Deal Holyfield

And now you hookers and hoes know how I feel

Well, if it's good enough to get broke off a proper chunk

I'll take a small piece of some of that funky stuff

[Chorus]

It's like this and like that and like this and uh [3x]

[Snoop Dogg] Dre, creep to the mic like a phantom

[Dr. Dre]

Well, I'm peepin and I'm creepin and I'm creepin

But I damn near got caught 'cause my beeper kept beepin

Now it's time for me to make my impression felt

So sit back, relax, and strap on your seatbelt

You never been on a ride like this befo'

With a producer who can rap and control the maestro

At the same time with the dope rhyme that I kick

You know and I know, I flow some old funky shit

To add to my collection, this selection

Symbolizes dope, take a toke but don't choke

If you do you'll have no clue

Of what me and my homie Snoop Dogg came to do

[Chorus]

[Snoop Dogg]

Fallin back on that ass with a hellafied gangsta lean

Gettin funky on the mic like a old batch of collard greens

It's the capital S, oh, yes, I'm fresh, N double-O-P

D O double-G Y, D O double-G, ya see?

Showin much flex when it's time to wreck a mic

Pimpin hoes and clockin a grip like my name was Dolomite

Yeah, and it don't quit

I think they in the mood for some motherfuckin G shit

(Hell, yeah) So, Dre (What up, Dogg?)

Gotta give 'em what they want (What's that, G?)

We gotta break 'em off somethin (Hell, yeah)

And it's gotta be bumpin (City of Compton!)

[Dr. Dre]

Is where it takes place so when asked, show attention

Mobbin like a motherfucker, but I ain't lynchin

Droppin the funky shit that's makin the sucker niggas mumble

When I'm on the mic, it's like a cookie, they all crumble

Try to get close and your ass'll get smacked

My motherfuckin homie Doggy Dogg has got my back

Never let me slip, 'cause if I slip, then I'm slippin

But if I got my Nina, then you know I'm straight trippin

And I'ma continue to put the rap down, put the mack down

And if you bitches talk shit, I have to put the smack down

Yeah, and you don't stop

I told you I'm just like a clock when I tick and I tock

But I'm never off, always on, to the break of dawn

C-O-M-P-T-O-N and the city they call Long Beach
Puttin the shit together
Like my nigga DOC, "No one can do it better"

[Chorus]

GIN AND JUICE
With so much drama in the L-B-C
It's kinda hard bein Snoop D-O-double-G
But I, somehow, some way
Keep comin up with funky-ass shit like every single day
May I kick a little something for the G's? (Yeah)
And make a few ends as (Yeah) I breeze, through
Two in the mornin and the party's still jumpin
'Cause my mama ain't home
I got bitches in the living room gettin it on
And they ain't leavin 'til six in the mornin (Six in the mornin)
So what you wanna do? Shit
I got a pocket full of rubbers and my homeboys do too
So turn off the lights and close the doors
But (But what?) we don't love them hoes (Yeah)
So we gonna smoke a ounce to this
G's up, hoes down, while you motherfuckers bounce to this

[Chorus 2x]
Rollin down the street, smokin indo, sippin on gin and juice
Laid back (with my mind on my money and my money on my mind)

Now that I got me some Seagram's gin
Everybody got they cups, but they ain't chipped in
Now this type of shit happens all the time
You gotta get yours but, fool, I gotta get mine
Everything is fine when you listenin to the D-O-G
I got the cultivating music that be captivating he
Who listens, to the words that I speak

As I take me a drink to the middle of the street
And get to mackin to this bitch named Sadie (Sadie?)
She used to be the homeboy's lady (Oh, that bitch)
Eighty degrees, when I tell that bitch, please
Raise up off these N-U-T's, 'cause you gets none of these
At ease, as I mob with the Dogg Pound, feel the breeze
Be-otch, I'm just

[Chorus]

Later on that day, my homie Dr. Dre
Came through with a gang of Tanqueray
And a fat-ass J of some bubonic
Chronic that made me choke—shit, this ain't no joke
I had to back up off of it and set my cup down
Tanqueray and chronic, yeah, I'm fucked up now
But it ain't no stoppin, I'm still poppin
Dre got some bitches from the city of Compton
To serve me, not with a cherry on top
'Cause when I bust my nut, I'm raising up off the cot
Don't get upset, girl, that's just how it goes
I don't love you hoes, I'm out the do', and I'll be . . .

[Chorus 2x]

FROM **FREESTYLE CONVERSATION**

Anonymous: Ay, Dogg, let me holla at'cha, man.
Snoop: What's up homie?
Anonymous: Word is on the streets your beats gon' be delicate since Dre done shook the speezot, man.
Snoop: Delicate? Beats? So that's what makes me now? Nigga, I don't give a fuck about no beat.

I got more niggas tryin to get at me than the president do sometimes
Niggas be tryin to get at me 'cause I be droppin funky rhymes
What the fuck is goin on? This rap game is made to make money

You niggas is taking the shit outta hand, actin way too funny

Doin too much, y'know what I said from the get-go

What the fuck's goin on wit' you niggas? Y'all tryin to play low pro

And tryin ta be hard and tryin to be big willies or whatever they call it

And yet it's time for me to act just like a alcoholic

And step into the game. I'ma stumble in like I don't know

And if a nigga say somethin wrong, I'm takin off from the get-go

I ain't givin you no room to try to get me first

'Cause I done been bombed on before and I'ma tell you, man, that's the worst

Feelin in the world, but I'ma keep my thing together

'Cause I'ma keep makin money and hope everything is still together

Havin papers, man, now what y'all niggas doin?

Oh, y'all broke on the corner?

Drinkin y'all drink, wanna be doin what I'm doin

But don't get mad and don't be tryin to play-hate

'Cause, uhh, takin trips around state to state

Representin, uhh, what y'all wanna represent

But y'all can't represent it 'cause y'all ain't got no dollars nor cents

I'm movin on, groovin on, and I'm movin

Makin more moves than the average Cuban

Tryin ta get G's across the town, tryin ta make more hits

And tryin ta get my game tight and get at yo' bitch

Now, if she wants to get with this, she gon' come holla at a player, though

'Cause she know that Snoop Dogg is got that white Rolls-Royce

And she wants to jump in, bring a friend

'Cause everything is like alphabet, come on in

Come on in and bring a friend and you can come on back

'Cause when you do, we gon' be sippin on some cognac

It's on me, I'm feelin good tonight

'Cause I'ma do mines and I'ma keep everything tight

I ain't lettin nothin leak 'cause if thangs leak, then I'ma get caught

And I can't get caught 'cause you know how they do it about that child
support

Shit, bitches is cold on a nigga who ain't got his game tight
Gettin 18-point-5 percent, half your life
Shit, I love my baby boy and all
But I ain't gonna be payin no bitch, no, no, no way, dawg
I'm too slick on my toes, I'm too tight
I'm guaranteed to get away from some shit like that, ain't that right?
'Cause, uhh, when you play in this game you got to be the real player
You can't be no fake-ass nigga talkin about you wanna be the mayor
'Cause if you ain't with the game, the game ain't gonna be with you
And I can put that on everything, including you

One out of every five black males before the year 2000
Will be detained or deceased
No justice, no peace
Yeah, the truth hurts. If you're scared, go to church

. . . .

2PAC

Tupac Amaru Shakur, or 2Pac, is one of the most influential rappers of all time—a status he achieved as much in death as in life. He is one of the most prolific artists in the music's history, producing one gold and nine platinum records and selling more than 75 million albums. In the years since his death in 1996 at twenty-five, 2Pac has only grown in stature as one of hip-hop's most enigmatic, explosive, and thought-provoking figures.

2Pac delivered his rhymes with musicality and intensity; his flow was unmistakable. In subject matter, he gravitated toward gritty tales of thug life. Regarding his often violent, sometimes misogynistic, and usually profane lyrics, he once said, "I'm not saying I want to rule the world, but I know that if I keep talking about how dirty it is out here, somebody going to clean it up."[47] His lyrics also included more poignant subjects—reflections on love and loss, life and death.

Tupac's identity is rich in contradictions. Born in New York City to a single mother, Afeni Shakur, Pac would eventually grow up to become the standard-bearer of the West Coast rap scene. Afeni spent a large portion of her pregnancy defending herself before the New York Supreme Court, having been charged with 150 counts of conspiracy against the U.S. government, as part of the Panther 21, a group of Black Panthers.

After being acquitted on the conspiracy charges, Afeni moved with young Pac to Baltimore, where Pac enrolled in the Baltimore School for the Arts and studied poetry, philosophy, politics, jazz, ballet, and acting. In an interview with Tupac from high school he appears outgoing, bursting with optimism and positivity, speaking idealistically about his views of the world. Just a few years later, after moving to Oakland (Marin City), California, Tupac embraced what he called T.H.U.G. L.I.F.E. (The Hate U Give Little Infants Fucks Everybody), a nebulous worldview that he would advocate in his music and tattoo on his body.

Pac made his recording debut on Digital Underground's "Same Song," which he followed with his debut album, *2Pacalypse Now* (1991). Explosive, growling, and rhyming "from the pit of his stomach," as Digital's Shock G put it, Shakur developed his delivery and mic presence. The last three albums, released while Tupac was alive, represent the peak of his career: *Me Against the World* (1995), *All Eyez on Me* (1996), and *The Don Kiluminati: The 7 Day Theory* (1996) all went platinum. *Me Against the World* was recorded in just a few weeks after Shakur had been sentenced to serve an eight-month jail term. "It was like a blues record," Tupac said. "It was down-home. It was all my fears, all the things I just couldn't sleep about. Everybody thought I was living so well and doing so good that I wanted to explain it. And it took a whole album to get it all out. I get to tell my innermost, darkest secrets. I tell my own personal problems."[48]

Tupac's legacy is one of paradox: raucous in the limelight but introspective in private, a thug and a poet. His foresight concerning his own death, here displayed on "How Long Will They Mourn Me," as well as his insight into the emotional chasms of prejudice and inequality, helped his music achieve a resonance that reaches well beyond the span of a short life.

BRENDA'S GOT A BABY

I hear Brenda's got a baby, but Brenda's barely got a brain
A damn shame, the girl can hardly spell her name

(That's not our problem, that's up to Brenda's family)
Well, let me show you how it affects our whole community:
Now Brenda really never knew her moms
And her dad was a junkie putting death to his arms
It's sad, 'cause I bet Brenda doesn't even know
Just 'cause you're in the ghetto doesn't mean you can't grow
But, oh, that's a thought, my own revelation
Do whatever it takes to resist the temptation
Brenda got herself a boyfriend
Her boyfriend was her cousin. Now let's watch the joy end
She tried to hide her pregnancy from a family
Who really didn't care to see, or give a damn if she
Went out and had a church of kids
As long as when the check came they got first dibs
Now Brenda's belly's getting bigger
But no one seems to notice any change in her figure
She's twelve years old and she's havin a baby
In love with a molester who's sexin her crazy
And yet and all she thinks is that he'll be with her forever
And dreams of a world where the two of them are together
Whatever, he left her and she had the baby solo
She had it on the bathroom floor and didn't know so
She didn't know what to throw away and what to keep
She wrapped the baby up and threw him in a trash heap
I guess she thought she'd get away, wouldn't hear the cries
She didn't realize how much the little baby had her eyes
Now the baby's in the trash heap bawling
Mama can't help her, but it hurts to hear her calling
Brenda wants to run away, Mama say, "You making me lose pay"
And social workers here every day
Now Brenda's gotta make her own way
Can't go to her family, they won't let her stay
No money, no babysitter, she couldn't keep a job
She tried to sell crack but end up gettin robbed

So now what's next? It ain't nothing left to sell
So she sees sex as a way of leaving hell
It's paying the rent, so she really can't complain
Prostitute found slain and Brenda's her name
She's got a baby

DEAR MAMA

You are appreciated.

When I was young me and my mama had beef
Seventeen years old, kicked out on the streets
Though back at the time, I never thought I'd see her face
Ain't a woman alive that could take my mama's place
Suspended from school and scared to go home, I was a fool
With the big boys, breakin all the rules
I shed tears with my baby sister
Over the years we was poorer than the other little kids
And even though we had different daddies, the same drama
When things went wrong we blame Mama
I reminisce on the stress I caused, it was hell
Huggin on my mama from a jail cell
And who'd think in elementary?
Heeey, I'd see the penitentiary one day
Running from the police, that's right
Mama catch me, put a whoopin to my backside
And even as a crack fiend, Mama
You always was a black queen, Mama
I finally understand, for a woman it ain't easy
Tryin to raise a man
You always was committed. A poor
Single mother on welfare, tell me how ya did it
There's no way I can pay you back
But the plan is to show you that I understand
You are appreciated

[Chorus]
Lady … Don'tcha know we love ya? Sweet lady
Dear Mama
Place no one above ya, sweet lady
You are appreciated
Don'tcha know we love ya?

Now, ain't nobody tell us it was fair
No love from my daddy 'cause the coward wasn't there
He passed away and I didn't cry
'Cause my anger wouldn't let me feel for a stranger
They say I'm wrong and I'm heartless, but all along
I was looking for a father—he was gone
I hung around with the thugs and even though they sold drugs
They showed a young brother love
I moved out and started really hangin
I needed money of my own so I started slangin
I ain't guilty 'cause even though I sell rocks
It feels good puttin money in your mailbox
I love payin rent when the rent's due
I hope you got the diamond necklace that I sent to ya
'Cause when I was low you was there for me
And never left me alone because you cared for me
And I could see you coming home after work late
You're in the kitchen trying to fix us a hot plate
Ya just working with the scraps you was given
And Mama made miracles every Thanksgiving
But now the road got rough, you're alone
You're tryin to raise two bad kids on your own
And there's no way I can pay you back
But my plan is to show you that I understand
You are appreciated

[Chorus]

Pour out some liquor and I reminisce

'Cause through the drama

I can always depend on my mama

And when it seems that I'm hopeless

You say the words that can get me back in focus

When I was sick as a little kid

To keep me happy there's no limit to the things you did

And all my childhood memories

Are full of all the sweet things you did for me

And even though I act crazy

I gotta thank the Lord that you made me

There are no words that can express how I feel

You never kept a secret, always stayed real

And I appreciate how you raised me

And all the extra love that you gave me

I wish I could take the pain away

If you can make it through the night, there's a brighter day

Everything will be alright if you hold on

It's a struggle every day, gotta roll on

And there's no way I can pay you back

But my plan is to show you that I understand

You are appreciated

[Chorus 2x]

SO MANY TEARS

I shall not fear no man but God. Though I walk through the valley of death I shed
so many tears (If I should die before I wake). Please, God, walk with me (Grab
a nigga and take me to Heaven).

Back in elementary, I thrived on misery

Left me alone, I grew up amongst a dying breed

Inside my mind, couldn't find a place to rest

Until I got that T.H.U.G. L.I.F.E. tatted on my chest

Tell me, can you feel me? I'm not livin in the past

You wanna last? Be the first to blast
Remember Kato, no longer with us, he's deceased
Call on the sirens, seen him murdered in the streets
Now rest in peace. Is there heaven for a G? Remember me
So many homies in the cemetery, shed so many tears

Ahh, I suffered through the years and shed so many tears
Lord, I lost so many peers and shed so many tears

Now that I'm struggling in this business, by any means
Label me greedy, getting green but seldom seen
And fuck the world 'cause I'm cursed
I'm having visions of leaving here in a hearse
God, can you feel me? Take me away
From all the pressure and all the pain
Show me some happiness again, I'm goin blind
I spend my time in this cell, ain't living well
I know my destiny is hell. Where did I fail?
My life is in denial and when I die
Baptized in eternal fire, I'll shed so many tears

Lord, I suffered through the years and shed so many tears
Lord, I lost so many peers and shed so many tears

Now I'm lost and I'm weary, so many tears
I'm suicidal, so don't stand near me
My every move is a calculated step to bring me closer
To embracing early death, now there's nothing left
There was no mercy on the streets, I couldn't rest
I'm barely standing, 'bout to go to pieces, screaming peace
And though my soul was deleted, I couldn't see it
I had my mind full of demons trying to break free
They planted seeds and they hatched, sparking the flame
Inside my brain like a match, such a dirty game
No memories, just a misery
Paintin a picture of my enemies killing me in my sleep

Will I survive 'til the morning, to see the sun?
Please, Lord, forgive me for my sins, 'cause here I come

Lord, I suffered through the years (God) and shed so many tears
(God) I lost so many peers and . . .

Lord knows I tried, been a witness to homicides
And drive-bys taking lives, little kids die
Wonder why as I walk by
Brokenhearted as I glance at the chalk line, gettin high
This ain't the life for me, I wanna change
But ain't no future right for me, I'm stuck in the game
I'm trapped inside a maze
See, this Tanqueray influence me to getting crazy, disillusioned
Lately I've been really wanting babies
So I could see a part of me that wasn't always shady
Don't trust my lady, 'cause she's a product of this poison
I'm hearing noises, think she fuckin all my boys
Can't take no more
I'm falling to the floor
Begging for the Lord to let me into heaven's door
Shed so many tears

(Dear God, please let me in)
Lord, I've lost so many years and shed so many tears
I lost so many peers and shed so many tears
Lord, I suffered through the years and shed so many tears
God, I lost so many peers and shed so many tears

FROM **ALL EYEZ ON ME**
I bet you got it twisted, you don't know who to trust
So many playa-hating niggas trying to sound like us
Say they ready for the funk, but I don't think they knowin
Straight to the depths of hell is where those cowards goin
Well, are you still down, nigga? Holla when you see me

And let these devils be sorry for the day they finally free me
I got a caravan of niggas every time we ride
Hittin motherfuckers up when we pass by
Until I die, live the life of a boss playa
'Cause even when I'm high, fuck with me and get crossed later
The future's in my eyes, 'cause all I want is cash and things
A five-double-oh Benz, flaunting flashy rings, uh
Bitches pursue me like a dream, been known to disappear
Before your eyes just like a dope fiend. It seems
My main thing was to be major paid
The game sharper than a motherfuckin razor blade
Say money bring bitches, bitches bring lies
One nigga gettin jealous and motherfuckers died
Depend on me like the first and fifteenth
They might hold me for a second, but these punks won't get me
We got fo' niggas in lowriders and ski masks
Screamin "Thug life!" every time they pass
All eyes on me

CHANGES

I see no changes. Wake up in the morning and I ask myself
Is life worth living? Should I blast myself?
I'm tired of being poor, and even worse, I'm black
My stomach hurts, so I'm lookin for a purse to snatch
Cops give a damn about a Negro
Pull the trigger, kill a nigga, he's a hero
Give the crack to the kids, who the hell cares?
One less hungry mouth on the welfare
First ship 'em dope and let 'em deal to brothers
Give 'em guns, step back, watch 'em kill each other
It's time to fight back, that's what Huey said
Two shots in the dark, now Huey's dead
I got love for my brothers, but we can never go nowhere
Unless we share with each other

We gotta start makin changes
Learn to see me as a brother 'stead of two distant strangers
And that's how it's supposed to be
How can the devil take a brother if he's close to me?
I'd love to go back to when we played as kids
But things change, that's the way it is

[Chorus 2x]
That's just the way it is
Things'll never be the same
That's just the way it is
Aww, yeah

I see no changes, all I see is racist faces
Misplaced hate makes disgrace to races
We under, I wonder what it takes to make this
One better place, let's erase the wasted
Take the evil out the people, they'll be acting right
'Cause both black and white is smokin crack tonight
And the only time we chill is when we kill each other
It takes skill to be real, time to heal each other
And although it seems heaven-sent
We ain't ready to see a black president
It ain't a secret, don't conceal the fact
The penitentiary's packed and it's filled with blacks
But some things will never change
Try to show another way but you stayin in the dope game
Now tell me, what's a mother to do?
Bein real don't appeal to the brother in you
You gotta operate the easy way
("I made a G today") But you made it in a sleazy way
Sellin crack to the kids ("I gotta get paid")
Well, hey, well, that's the way it is

[Chorus 2x]

We gotta make a change. It's time for us as a people to start makin some
changes. Let's change the way we eat, let's change the way we live, and let's
change the way we treat each other. You see, the old way wasn't workin so it's
on us to do what we gotta do to survive.

And still I see no changes, can't a brother get a little peace?
It's war on the streets and the war in the Middle East
Instead of war on poverty, they got a war on drugs
So the police can bother me
And I ain't never did a crime I ain't have to do
But now I'm back with the facts givin it back to you
Don't let 'em jack you up, back you up
Crack you up and pimp smack you up
You gotta learn to hold ya own
They get jealous when they see ya with ya mobile phone
But tell the cops they can't touch this
I don't trust this, when they try to rush I bust this
That's the sound of my tool, you say it ain't cool
My mama didn't raise no fool
And as long as I stay black I gotta stay strapped
And I never get to lay back
'Cause I always got to worry about the payback
Some buck that I roughed up way back
Comin back after all these years
Rat-a-tat-tat-tat-tat—that's the way it is, uh

[Chorus 2x]

HOW LONG WILL THEY MOURN ME
(feat. Nate Dogg, Big Syke, Rated R, and Macadoshis)

[2Pac]
How long will they mourn me? Yeah! This for my nigga Kato. It's still on, nigga.
Believe that. Thug life, thugs for life, haha ... (How long will they mourn me?)
We handle this shit for you, boy. Yeah, nigga. 2Pac in this motherfucker ...

All my homies drinkin liquor, tears in everybody's eyes
Niggas cried to mourn a homie's homicide
But I can't cry, instead I'm just a shoulder
Damn, why they take another soldier?
I load my clip before my eyes blurry, don't worry
I'll get them suckers back before your buried (Shit)
Retaliate and pull a 1-8-7
Do real niggas get to go to heaven?
How long will they mourn me? Bury me a motherfuckin G
Bitch don't wanna die? Then don't fuck with me
It's kinda hard to be optimistic
When your homie's lying dead on the pavement twisted
Y'all don't hear me, though—I'm tryin hard to make amends
But I'm losin all my motherfuckin friends, damn!
They should've shot me when I was born
Now I'm trapped in the motherfuckin storm
How long will they mourn me?

[Chorus]

[Nate Dogg and 2Pac]
[Nate Dogg] I wish it would have been another
[2Pac] How long will they mourn me?
[Nate Dogg] How long will they mourn my brother?
(Half them niggas all dead and shit)
[2Pac] How long will they mourn me?
[Nate Dogg] I wish it would have been another
(Dedicated this to Kato, nigga, and every thug)
[2Pac] How long will they mourn me?
[Nate Dogg] How long will they mourn my brother?
(Yo, nigga, we gotta keep this shit goin on, yo, Syke)

[Big Syke]
How long will they mourn me?
Every motherfuckin day, homie

You stayed down when the other niggas didn't know me
From my heart to the trigger, you my fuckin nigga
And things won't be the same without you, nigga
I remember kickin back, you wanted a Lac
And goin half on a motherfuckin hundred sack
Smokin blunt after blunt and steady drinkin
Hung around so much, you knew what I was thinkin
Tell me, Lord, why you take big Kato?
So confused not knowing which way to go
I'm goin crazy and runnin out of fuckin time
I can't take it, I'm losin my fuckin mind
So day after day, ride after ride
We'll hook up on the other side
Watch over your family and your newborn
'Til we meet again, homie
How long will they mourn me?

[Chorus]

[Rated R]
Damn, a nigga tired of feelin sad, I'm tired of puttin in work
I'm tired of cryin watchin my homies leave the earth
I know soon one day I'll be in the dirt
And my peoples'll be mournin when they get a call from the coroner's
All niggas can say is, "That's fucked up"
And get tossed up, reminiscing how we grew up (My nigga)
Rest and love to my nigga Kato, see you in the crossroads real soon
For now let me pour out the brew
I'll be always thinkin of ya, homie
Rest in peace. How long will they mourn me?

[Macadoshis]
We know life's a fuckin trip, and everybody gotta go
But why the fuck it have to be my nigga Kato?
Another nigga fell victim to the chrome

It's enough to make you crazy, it's fuckin with my dome

You only live once on this earth

A nigga had it bad, since the day of my motherfuckin birth (Uh)

My niggas say they down and they always be my homie

But when a nigga gone, how long will ya mourn me? (Yeah)

[Chorus 2x]

TWISTA

Twista might be dismissed as a gimmick rapper. Having held the Guinness record as the world's fastest on the mic, and having begun his career with the moniker Tung Twista, he could have settled for a career founded entirely on his rapid-fire flows. Certainly, the clarity of his speedy delivery is astounding. "[I created my fast flow] by just trying to expand with the rap style," he explains. "It started with just tripling up the words with one sentence and then a whole four bars, and then it's like a whole verse. Probably around the time I wrote one complete verse like that was when I realized that this is a hot style for me."[49]

Twista tossed the "Tung" from his name and began to expand his expressive range and the varieties of his delivery. His flow is evident on the page as well. Notice that the lyrics follow just how long his lines are; they look like almost no other lines in the book. He somehow fits all of these words into a single musical measure. Whereas a line from most rappers might contain ten or twelve syllables, his lines routinely contain at least twice that many. More astounding still, he delivers his words without compromising the clarity of his speech. When speaking about a rapper as formally unique as Twista, it almost seems irrelevant to dwell on content. Most of his subject matter is straightforward: his mic skills, his luck with women, and the weakness of his opponents. When looking at Twista's lyrics, form is at the forefront.

EMOTIONS

"Well, a motherfucker could never control me, only squeeze me and
   hold me"

That's what the ho came up and told me. Now is she bold, G?

But in my mouth is where the gold be 'cause I be pimpin her like Goldie

Gotta get paid in this age, my fingers ain't made just to be choppin up
confetti with

If it's a ready dick you better steady lick—if you ain't with it you can git,
'cause I ain't even on that petty shit

So who the fuck you actin petty with? The rhythm I kick is like a rhythmly-
wicked arithmetic

Pick 'em up quick and then give 'em the dick, thinkin I'm innocent. They up
in the mall shoppin for me, pickin a fit

I got them heifers's nose red and when we get in the bed, I be leavin 'em with
rose legs

Stuff that'll make 'em wanna pose dead, but you ain't really got 'em until you
get 'em all up in them hoes's head

I don't mean to sound bogus or nothing, but it's the bomb when I be havin
them cuties thinkin I'm in love with 'em, when I'm rubbin 'em

Be gettin pub with 'em, in a club with 'em, smoke a dub with 'em, huggin 'em,
freakin in the tub with 'em

After gettin paid from her, she ain't trippin 'cause she know she got what
she paid for

She honor my name, I got her tame, here it go. Now we speakin with a game
of ways to make mo'

[Chorus 2x]

Let me play with your emotions, ho, to the rhythm of a hi-hat, take a puff and
lie back

Let me stimulate your mind, body, and soul, I know you want to try that.
Now, really, baby, can you buy that?

Tell me, baby, can you buy that?

I got you under my complete control, you know it's worth more than
diamonds and gold, now don't be bogus and deny that

Now how the fuck you gon' act, ho? I saw you creepin out the back do', what
you runnin from a mack fo'?

Lay you on your back slow 'cause you know I got you with my lasso. Blow
your mind like a Afro

Come and take a glimpse and a stare, it's the aroma of a pimp in the air, I bet
ya notice the smell

It's like a lotus when I flow this, 'cause my eyes be the lowest; if you didn't
notice then you bogus as hell

I'm puttin women under my spell, like I'm up in their brain pumpin their vein
with game for the anatomy that's feminine

Then fillin 'em up with adrenaline, got 'em geekin, we speaking, approachin
a po' pimp like a gentleman

Submission is surrendering, it ain't no endin if it's on with a blunt from a
bomb sack

In the right place, with the right mind and the right line, you can get a
lifetime contract

They be wise until they look into your eyes, a shorty freaked when she
spotted mine

Took her over to my crib, lay low, hit her off from behind then she signed on
the dotted-line, then she was like

("Oooh, Daddy, why you doin me like this?

I'd do anything to be with you, you got me gone in the head")

Ya mind, I don't mean to make a disaster of like my daddy, Master Love

But if a motherfucker breaking you for every penny you earn then how
could you still show the bastard love?

I guess it's 'cause I'm cold, shit. Thought you was gon' be spendin me? I bet
ya think, you sure did

But game recognize game, now you lame in the brain—stupid bitch, that's
what you get for tryin to gold dig, now

[Chorus 2x]

I know you think it's blasphemy, but won't you get my boys and ask for me? I
think he passed the beat

Since you said I was your majesty, I had to see, and when you get paid, then
bring some cash to me

Is it a tragedy that I can get her so gone the ho be trippin, talkin about love a
lot?

But the only love I got is when I grip a mic or I when I hug the Glock or when I rub the twat

Or pickin up a dub at spots, fuck the hoes, thugs, and clubs, and the phony perpetrators with dimes

The Speedknots, Match Voodoo or Die, Psycho Drama, Crucial Conflict be pimpin 'em with gators and dons

Collect the papers and dolls, player-haters' remarks will get smoked to a blunt dust

So keep walkin the next time you hear grown folks talking, motherfuckers betta shut the fuck up

'Cause we make the women suck up. You insist on bein trippin while we be gamin like Don Juan

What up? The filet mignon, the Grey Poupon, them hoes are slaves to charm, because we make the bomb?

Now I don't mean no harm, but either come on in or get on gone and let me pour my potion slow

In between your thighs, come take a pull and vibe and let your tongue go coastin low

[Chorus 2x]

UGK

UGK consisted of Pimp C and Bun B, both from Port Arthur, Texas. As the self-styled Underground Kingz of the South, they favored lyrics about women, money, cars, and hustling in the drug trade. As they continued to record through the 1990s and into the 2000s, they kept to their basic street template but expanded upon their themes and added elements to their style.

Bun B is regarded among his peers as a technically skilled lyricist, holding his own with the likes of Jay-Z and Outkast. "Well, the first thing I do is I try to listen to whatever rapping is already on the track," he told Jon

Caramanica in *The Believer* by way of describing how he writes. "I listen for cadence and melody to see how the track's already been written, and to make sure that whatever flow or flows I decide to run with, or patterns or melodies that I decide to put into the song, that they're not already in there. Then I try to see if there's a different part of the subject matter that I can talk about. If there isn't, I try to see if I can analogize it, break it down, flip it another way. If that can't be done, the best thing I can do is pretty much out-rap the guy. And when I say out-rap the guy—say, if he uses ten syllables in a line, I'm going to use fifteen. If he uses fifteen, I'm going to use twenty, twenty-five. If he's rhyming two or three words within two bars, I'm going to rhyme four or five words in two bars. I'm going to out-skill you."[50]

Unlike many MCs who govern their lyrics strictly to the beat, Bun B often intentionally raps off the beat, bulldozing through the bars. Though Pimp C died in 2007, Bun B carries on the group's work as a solo artist and frequent collaborator with a host of hip-hop luminaries.

MURDER

[Pimp C]
I'm still Pimp C, bitch, so what the fuck is up?
Puttin powder on the streets 'cause I got big fuckin nuts
Comin back from Louisiana in a Fleetwood Lac
I just served them niggas some shit to put they fiends on they back
Got the pound four by four 'cause you know I just pay two
Nigga bought thirty from me, so I fronted forty-two
He gon' pop to seven hundred times sixty-two
Twenty-four eight is what I do, so nigga, fuck what you do
If I told ya cocaine numbers, you would think I was lyin
Young-ass niggas twenty-two is talkin 'bout they retirin
In the game ain't a thang, comin foreign with Benz
Rick ass own two apartments where I entertain friends
More bounce to the ounce 'cause the Burm the shit
I done got me fifty ounces outta birds in this bitch
Tighten up, no slack, bitch checkin my stock
Got some birds I'm sellin, nigga, some I go rock for rock
Just got back from California, kicked it with B-Legit
Put me down with purple chronic and that hurricane shit

At the studio with Tone, man, I wish I could stay

I got to holla at Master P, 'cause we got money to make

We're the playas from the South, stack G's, man

Like Ball I got to stack big cheese, man

Bitch say he wanna show you got nine grand

I ain't rappin shit until my money in my hand

South Texas, motherfucker, that's where I stay

Gettin money from yo' bitches every goddamn day

Big paper I'm foldin. Hoes

Is on my motherfuckin jock for all this dick that I be holdin

I hate clone men, show it

Especially them fools take our style and act like my niggas don't know it

Kick it with the trill niggas so you best not trip

If ya keep on poppin shit, my niggas empty a clip

Ho-ass nigga

Murder, mur, murder [6x]

[Bun B]

Well, it's Bun B, bitch, and I'm the king of movin chickens

Got them finger-lickin stickin niggas that be trickin

You need a swift kickin, your ass is ripe for the pickin

Now as my pockets thicken, I be thinkin nigga's slippin

You sick when I be clickin. Now take a look at the bigger nigga

Malt liquor swigger, playa-hata, ditch-digger

Figure my hair-trigger give a hot one in your liver

You shiver, shake, and quiver, I'm frivolous if a nigga get wetter than a river

For what it's worth it's the birth of some niggas doin dirt

Fuck her first and take off her skirt

Make the pussy hurt, Mister Master hit the Swisha faster

Than you fever-blistered bastards. Fuck your sister, passed her

Fifty elbows for sale, yo, brother better have my mail, ho

Before I catch a murder case and go to jail—Oh

Hell no, time to bail, hit the trail so

We can sell mo' fuckin yayo, get the scale, no

Other bullet duckers could shove us out of this game. They better buck us

'Cause the cluckers, they love us. Make them glass-dick suckers
Shake they jelly like Smucker's, I hit like nunchuckers
'Cause Short Texas bring the ruckus, this for my motherfuckers
Cooking cheese, some crooked Gs, rockin up quarter ki's
Just to get the hook with ease, wannabes get on yo' knees
Feel the squeeze from them HK one-threes from here to overseas
We do what we please, don't trip 'cause we flip
Light up a dip, I'm breakin 'em off from they hip to yo' lip
Go ask that boy Skip, that nigga Bun rip
With one clip, soon as the gun slip, now I done whipped out my Berretta
Flyin through yo' Pelle Pelle and some smelly red jelly is drippin out of ya belly
Servin 'em up like a deli, jumped on my cellular tele'
Hoes sellin like it's goin out of style
You can't see me, Marcus, so have a motherfuckin Sweet and a smile

Murder, mur, mur, murder [6x]

DIRTY MONEY

[Bun B]
Say, look here, man, I'm a rapper—hold up, let me take that back
I make rap music, but that don't mean all a nigga do is rap
But that don't matter. I've been labeled, stigmatized, stereotyped
There's an entertainment disease worse than cancer, a venereal type
I spit imperial-type game like Digga from the Squad
But they act like they can't separate a real nigga from the fraud
Rule number one: Never send a boy to fuck a grown-ass lady
And respect the game 'cause the game is known to be gone fast, baby
Now that's a long pass, maybe you should try diving for it
Fools act like they striving for it, hit *Total Request Live* and blow it
No, it ain't a given and nothing is. See, all this candy-coatin
And bluffin is detrimental to our beautiful black southern kids
Enough of this, man, let's get this here straight like creases
It's a never-ending cycle and motion that never ceases
It compresses and releases, man, and for the love of Jesus
It breaks the soul, now we forever left to pick up the pieces, it's dirty money

[Chorus 2x]

Niggas laughing but ain't a damn thing funny

It's all about the paper in this land of milk and honey

Yeah, it's bright outside but not necessarily sunny

And no matter how you make it, it's all dirty money, baby

[Pimp C]

Every drug I sold was for the dirty money

Most of my niggas is dead because the game is funny

You can get your life took at the drop of the dime

But I'm a pimp 'til the end, I keep my money on my mind

Most of my life I've been broke, trying to save my bread

I never asked to be hustling, now I watch out for feds

'Cause niggas be talking and giving up game

About the cheese, the green, the pills, the coke D's

I marry my pockets, so now I chase my green

Keep a thang for them haters with the red beam

Ever since fifteen I've been a big money fiend

Sippin cold codeine and pulling up clean

Popping up at the spot and dropping the top

And keep a bad yellow box with my dick on rock, uh!

[Chorus 2x]

[Bun B]

You can't get no house, no car, no weed, no bar

No flash, no show, no class, no flow

No help, no love, no liquor, no drug

No clique, no crew, no tracks to flow to

No pager, no phone, no flavor, no zone

No fiend, no cut, no wife, no slut

No name, nowhere in the game to get me five

No nothing without dirty-ass M-O-N-E-Y

[Chorus 2x]

[Pimp C]

My mama taught me what the value of a dollar should be

But everybody I saw balling was rolling, selling ki's

In the late '80s niggas pulling up on D's

Putting dick up in these hoes and making 'em pay fees

Learn how to ride dirty 'cause ain't shit for free

Then all them niggas got popped, that's all I needed to see

For some the dope game cool 'cause that's all that they could be

I know God ain't put me down here just to be serving no fiends

I know God ain't put me down here just to be serving no fiends

[Chorus 2x]

THE WU-TANG CLAN

According to production guru and de facto group leader, the RZA, the Wu-Tang Clan is the first group ever to practice hip-hop as a martial art. By this he means a couple of things: that Wu-Tang rappers are masters of the battle rhyme and that they practice hip-hop with emotional content as a means of catharsis, spontaneity, self-defense, and the transformation of life into art.

On record the Wu-Tang Clan delivers an alternative, underground aesthetic—a world where griminess, hardness, danger, and criminality play against the sensitivity and self-consciousness of youth coming of age amid violence. The nine core Clan members include Ol' Dirty Bastard, Inspectah Deck, GZA, RZA, Method Man, U-God, Ghostface Killah, Raekwon, and Masta Killa. Whether rhyming about swinging swords or creating "poetry whirlpools" (as Wu associate Cappadonna once put it), the Wu MCs are lyrical martial artists.

Each MC's sound is distinctive, from Ol' Dirty Bastard's rowdy, free-associating, unmetered abstractions to Method Man's gravelly, steadily laid-back baritone to Raekwon's staccato strings of slang; together the Clan's lyricism is comprehensive and cinematic, with threatening storytelling and believable braggadocio. The abstraction and aphoristic quality of their dense, murky concrete wilderness of sound reveal an exceptional group of gifted poets.

The following selections from the extensive Wu-Tang library represent not only the collective strength of the group, which as a unit left its indelible mark on hip-hop, but also the development and achievements of the group as individuals. From the tragic rise and fall of Ol' Dirty Bastard to the spectrum traveled by the RZA—from rapper/producer to actor and soundtrack composer—to the mainstream success of Ghostface Killah, Raekwon, GZA, and the Method Man, much has happened in the decade and a half since the Clan began their reign as legendary denizens of the hip-hop arts.

PROTECT YA NECK

[RZA] Wu-Tang Clan comin at ya
Protect ya neck, kid, so set it off, the Inspectah Deck
[Method Man] Watch ya step, kid, watch ya step, kid [4x]

[Inspectah Deck]
I smoke on the mic like smokin Joe Frazier
The hell raiser, raisin hell with the flavor
Terrorize the jam like troops in Pakistan
Swinging through your town like your neighborhood Spiderman
So, uh, tick-tock and keep tickin
While I get ya flippin off the shit I'm kickin
The Lone Ranger, code red, danger!
Deep in the dark with the art to rip the charts apart
The vandal, too hot to handle
Ya battle, you're sayin "Goodbye" like Tevin Campbell
Roughneck, Inspectah Deck's on the set
The rebel, I make more noise than heavy metal

[Raekwon]
The way I make the crowd go wild, sit back, relax
Won't smile, Rae' got it goin on, pal

Call me the rap assassinator
Rhymes rugged and built like Schwarzenegger
And I'ma get mad deep like a threat
Blow up your project then take all your assets
'Cause I came to shake the frame in half
With the thoughts that bomb shit like math
So if ya wanna try to flip, go flip on the next man
'Cause I grab the clip and
Hit ya with sixteen shots and more, I got
Goin to war with the meltin pot, ock

[Method Man]
It's the Method Man, for short Mr. Meth
Movin on your left, ah!
And set it off, get it off, let it off like a gat
I wanna break, fool, cock me back
Small change, they puttin shame in the game
I take aim and blow that nigga out the frame
And like *Fame,* my style'll live forever
Niggas crossin over, but they don't know no better
But I do, true, can I get a "su"?
Nuff respect due to the one-six-ooh
I mean oh, yo, check out the flow
Like the Hudson or PCP when I'm dustin
Niggas off because I'm hot like sauce
The smoke from the lyrical blunt makes me cough

[U-God]
Ooh, what, grab my nut, get screwed
Ow, here comes my Shaolin style
True—B-A-ba-B-Y-U
To my crew with the "su"

[Method Man] Watch ya step, kid, watch ya step, kid [4x]

[Ol' Dirty Bastard] C'mon, baby, baby, c'mon [4x]

[RZA] Yo, ya best protect ya neck

[Ol' Dirty Bastard]
First thing's first, man, you're fuckin with the worst
I'll be stickin pins in your head like a fuckin nurse
I'll attack any nigga who's slack in his mack
Come fully packed with a fat rugged stack
Shame on you when you step through to
The Ol' Dirty Bastard straight from the Brooklyn Zoo
And I'll be damned if I let any man
Come to my center, you enter the winter
Straight up and down, that shit packed jam
You can't slam, don't let me get fool on him, man
The Ol' Dirty Bastard is dirty and stinkin
Ason-Unique rollin with the night of the creeps
Niggas be rollin with a stash
Ain't sayin gas, bite my style, I'll bite your motherfuckin ass!

[Ghostface Killah]
For cryin out loud, my style is wild, so book me
Not long is how long that this rhyme took me
Ejectin styles from my lethal weapon
My pen that rocks from here to Oregon
Here's more again, catch it like a psycho flashback
I love gats, if rap was a gun, you wouldn't bust back
I come with shit that's all types of shapes and sounds
And where I lounge is my stompin grounds
I give a order to my peeps across the water
To go and snatch up props all around the border
And get far like a shootin star
'Cause who I are is livin the life of Pablo Escobar
Point blank as I kick the square biz
There it is, you're fuckin with pros, and there it goes

[RZA]

Yo, chill with the feedback, black, we don't need that

It's ten o'clock, ho, where the fuck's your seed at?

Feelin mad hostile, ran the apostle

Flowin like Christ when I speaks the gospel

Stroll with the holy roll then attack the globe

With the buckus style, the ruckus

Ten times ten men committin mad sin

Turn the other cheek and I'll break your fuckin chin

Slang boom-bangs like African drums (we'll be)

Comin around the mountain when I come

Crazy flamboyant for the rap enjoyment

My Clan increase like black unemployment

Yeah, another one dare, G-Gka-Genius

Take us the fuck outta here

[GZA]

The Wu is too slammin for these Cold Killin' labels

Some ain't had hits since I seen Aunt Mabel

Be doin artists in like Cain did Abel

Now they money's gettin stuck to the gum under the table

That's what ya get when ya misuse what I invent

Your empire falls and ya lose every cent

For tryin to blow up a scrub

Now that thought is just as bright as a twenty-watt lightbulb

Should of pumped it when I rocked it

Niggas so stingy they got short arms and deep pockets

This goes on in some companies

With majors, they're scared to death to pump these

First of all, who's your A&R?

A mountain climber who plays an electric guitar?

But he don't know the meaning of dope when he's lookin for a suit–

And-tie rap that's cleaner than a bar of soap

And I'm the dirtiest thing in sight
Matter of fact, bring out the girls and let's have a mud fight

[RZA] You best protect ya neck

C.R.E.A.M.
[Raekwon]
I grew up on the crime side, the *New York Times* side
Staying alive was no jive
Had second hands, Moms bounced on old man
So then we moved to Shaolin land
A young youth, yo, rockin the gold tooth, lo' goose
Only way I begin to G off was drug loot
And let's start it like this, son, rollin with this one
And that one, pullin out gats for fun
But it was just a dream for the teen who was a fiend
Started smokin woolas at sixteen
And running up in gates and doing hits for high stakes
Making my way on fire escapes
No question, I would speed for cracks and weed
The combination made my eyes bleed
No question, I would flow off and try to get the dough all
Sticking up white boys on ball courts
My life got no better, same damn lo' sweater
Times is rough and tough like leather
Figured out I went the wrong route
So I got with a sick-ass clique and went all out
Catchin ki's from 'cross seas, rollin in MPVs
Every week we made forty G's
Yo, nigga, respect mine, or anger the TEC-9
Ch-chick-POW! Move from the gate now

[Chorus]
Cash Rules Everything Around Me

C.R.E.A.M., get the money
Dollar, dollar bill, y'all

[Inspectah Deck]
It's been twenty-two long, hard years, I'm still strugglin
Survival got me buggin, but I'm alive on arrival
I peep at the shape of the streets
And stay awake to the ways of the world, the shit is deep
A man with a dream with plans to make C.R.E.A.M.
Which failed; I went to jail at the age of fifteen
A young buck sellin drugs and such who never had much
Trying to get a clutch at what I could not touch
The court played me short, now I face incarceration
Pacin, knowin upstate's my destination
Handcuffed in back of a bus, forty of us
Life as a shorty shouldn't be so rough
But as the world turned I learned life is hell
Living in the world no different from a cell
Every day I escape from Jakes givin chase, sellin base
Smokin bones in the staircase
Though I don't know why I chose to smoke cess
I guess that's the time when I'm not depressed
But I'm still depressed, and I ask what's it worth?
Ready to give up, so I seek the Old Earth
Who explained working hard may help you maintain
To learn to overcome the heartaches and pain
We got stickup kids, corrupt cops, and crack rocks
And stray shots, all on the block that stays hot
Leave it up to me, while I be living proof
To kick the truth to the young black youth
But shorty's running wild, smokin cess, drinkin beer
And ain't trying to hear what I'm kickin in his ear
Neglect it for now, but yo, it gots to be accepted
That what? That life is hectic

[Chorus to fade]

FROM **BRING THE PAIN**

(Method Man)

I came to bring the pain, hardcore from the brain

Let's go inside my astral plane

Find out my mental's based on instrumental

Records, hey, so I can write monumental

Methods—I'm not the King, but niggas is decaf

I stick 'em for the C.R.E.A.M. Check it

Just how deep can shit get?

Deep as the abyss and brothers is mad fish, accept it

In your Cross Color clothes, you've crossed over

Then got totally crossed out and Kris Krossed

Who da boss? Niggas get tossed to the side

And I'm the dark side of the Force. Of course

It's the Method Man from the Wu-Tang Clan

I be hectic and comin for the head piece—protect it

Fuck it, two tears in a bucket, niggas want the ruckus

Bustin at me, bra', now bust it

Styles, I gets buckwild, Method Man on some shit

Pullin niggas' files, I'm sick

Insane, crazy, drivin Miss Daisy

Out her fuckin mind, now I got mine, I'm Swayze

Brothers want to hang with the Meth, bring the rope

The only way you hang is by the neck, nigga poke

Off the set, comin to your projects

Take it as a threat, better yet, it's a promise

Comin from a vet on some old Vietnam shit

Nigga, you can bet your bottom dollar, hey, I bomb shit

And it's gonna get even worse, word to God

It's the Wu comin through, stickin niggas for they garments

Movin on your left, southpaw, Mr. Meth

Came to represent and carve my name in your chest

You can come test, realize you're no contest

Son, I'm the gun that won that old Wild West

Quick on the draw with my hands on the four

Nine-three-eleven with the rugged rhymes galore

Check it, 'cause I think not when this hip-hop's like proper

Rhymes be the proof while I'm drinkin 90 proof

Huh, vodka, no OJ, no straw

When you give it to me, ay, give it to me raw

I've learned when you drink Absolut straight it burns

Enough to give my chest hairs a perm

I don't need a chemical blow to pull a ho

All I need is Chemical Bank to pay tha Mo'

DUEL OF THE IRON MIC
(GZA)

*Oh, mad one. We see your trap. You can never escape your fate. Submit with
honor to a duel with my son.*

I agree.

I see you using an old style. I wondered where you had learned it from.
You know very well. It's yours, too.
Yo, god, it's a duel, it's a duel.
Heh, by the gods, will you show me?
(Buck buck buck buck buck buck) And where do you come for?
(Duel of the Iron Mic) You come here, since you're so interested.
(Duel of the Iron Mic) Fight me.
(In the moonlight, niggas, lightning strike)
(What, what? Bring it!)

[GZA]

Yo, picture bloodbaths in elevator shafts

Like these murderous rhymes tight from genuine craft

Check the print, it's where veterans spark the letterings

Slow-moving MCs is waiting for the editing

The liquid soluble that made up the chemistry

A gaseous element that burned down your ministry

Herbal vapors in biblical papers

Smoking Exodus, every square yard is plush
Fuck the screw-faced photo sessions, facial expression
Leaves impressions, try to keep a shark nigga guessin
Give praise and shouts, son, here's the outcome
Cut across the semigloss rhymes you floss
Shit is outdated, just like neckloads of sterlings
Suede-fronts, bell bottoms, and tri-colored shearlings
I ain't particular, I bang like vehicular
Homicides on July 4th in Bed-Stuy
Where money don't grow on trees and there's thievin MCs
Who cutthroat to rake leaves
They can't breathe, blood splash, rushin fast
Like runnin rivers, I be that whiskey in your liver

[Ol' Dirty Bastard]
Duel of the Iron Mic!
It's the fifty-two fatal strikes!

[Masta Killa]
This is not a eighty-five affair, made clear
When the gods get on to perform, storms blew up
Wu's up, causin the crowd to self-destruct
Killer bees are stingin somethin while I reveal
Science that's heavily guarded by the culprit
Bombin your barracks with aerodynamic
Swordplay, poison darts by the doorway
Minds that's laced with explosive doses
Damaging lyrical launcher
Lunge at the youthful offender, then injure
Any contender, testin the murderous Master
Could lead to disaster, dynamite thoughts
Explode through your barrier, rips the retina
Who can withstand the astonishing punishing
Stings to the sternum? Shocked in the hip-hop
Livestock, seekin for a serum to cure 'em

[Inspectah Deck]
Thugs kill for drugs plus the young bucks bust
Duckin handcuffs, throats get cut when dough rush
Out-of-town foes look shook but still pose
We move like real pros, through the streets we stroll
Bullet holes lace the windows in one-six oh
So control the avenues, that's the dream that's sold
Building lobbies are graveyards for small-timers
Bitches caught in airports, ki's in they vaginas
No peace, yo, the police mad corrupt
You get bagged up, dependin if you're passin the cut
Plus shorty's not a shorty no more, he's livin heartless
Regardless of the charges, claims to be the hardest
Individual, critical thoughts, criminal minded
Blinded by illusion, findin it confusin

[Ol' Dirty Bastard]
Duel of the Iron Mics (*The master, he must be dreaming, heh*)
It's that fifty-two fatal strikes (*Well, if he is dreaming*)
Duel of the Iron Mics (*Then he must be asleep*)
It's that fifty-two fatal strikes, NUH (*But if he's asleep
Then I will wake him up!*)

*At the height of their fame and glory, they turned on one another, each
struggling in vain for ultimate supremacy. In the passion and depth of their
struggle, the very art that had raised them to such Olympian heights was lost.
Their techniques vanished.*

INCARCERATED SCARFACES
(Raekwon)
*He looks determined without being ruthless ... something heroic in his manner.
There's a courage about him ... doesn't look like a killer ... comes across so
calm ... acts like he has a dream ... full of passion ...
You don't trust me, huh?
Well, you know why.
I do. We're not supposed to trust anyone in our profession anyway ...*

[Chorus]

Now yo, yo, whattup, yo? Time is runnin out

It's for real though, let's connect politic, ditto

We could trade places, get lifted in the staircases

Word up, peace, incarcerated scarfaces

[Raekwon]

Thug-related style attract millions. Fans

They understand my plan. Who's the kid up in the green Land?

Me and the RZA connect, blow a fuse, you lose

Half-ass crews get demolished and bruised

Fake be frontin, hourglass heads niggas be wantin

Shuttin down your slot; time for pumpin

Poisonous sting which thumps up and act chumps

Raise a heavy generator, but, yo, guess who's the black Trump?

Dough be flowin by the hours. Wu, we got the collars

Scholars. Word life, peace to Power

And my whole unit. Word up! Quick to set it, don't wet it

Real niggas lick shots, peace, Connecticut

[Chorus]

Chef'll shine like marble, rhyme remarkable

Real niggas raise up, spend your money, argue

But this time is for the uninvited. Go head and rhyme to it

Big nigga mics is gettin fired

Morphine chicks be burnin like chlorine

Niggas recognize from here to Baltimore to Fort Greene

But hold up, Moët be tastin like throw-up

My mob roll up, dripped to death whips rolled up

Ya never had no wins, slidin in these dens

With Timbs wit' MAC-10s and broke friends

Ya got guns, got guns too—what up, son?

Do you wanna battle for cash and see who Sun Tzu?

I probably wax, tax, smack rap niggas who fax

Nigga's lyrics is wack, nigga can't stand unofficial

Wet tissue, blank bustin Scud missiles

You rollin like Trump, you get your meat lumped

For real, it's just slang rap democracy

Here's the policy, slide off the ring, plus the Wallabees

Check the status, soon to see me at Caesar's Palace

Eatin salads, we beatin mics and the keys to Dallas

I move rhymes like retail, make sure shit sell

From where we at to my man's cell

From staircase to stage, minimum wage

But soon to get a article in *Rap Page*

But all I need is my house, my gat, my Ac

Bank account fat, it's goin down like that

And pardon the French but let me speak Italian

Black Stallions whylin on Shaolin

That means the island of Staten and niggas carry gats

And mad police from Manhattan

[Chorus]

I do this for barbershop niggas in the Plaza

Catchin asthma, Rae is stickin gun-flashers

Well-dressed, skatin through the projects with big ones

Broke elevators, turn the lights out, stick one

Upstairs, switch like a chameleon, hip Brazilians

Pass the cash or leave your children, leave the buildin

Niggas, yo, they be foldin like envelopes

Under pressure, like Lou Ferrigno on coke

Yo, Africans denyin niggas up in yellow cabs

Musty like funk, wavin they arms, the Arabs

Sit back, coolin like Kahluas on rocks

On the crack spots, rubber band wrapped all my knots

Few bitches who fuck dreds on Sudafeds

Pussy's hurtin, they did it for a yard for the feds

Word up cousin, nigga, I seen it

Like a twenty-seven-inch Zenith—believe it!

[Chorus]

BROOKLYN ZOO

(Ol' Dirty Bastard)

I'm the one-man army, Ason

I've never been tooken out, I keep MCs lookin out

I drop science like girls be droppin babies

Enough to make a nigga go cra-a-azy

In the G building takin all types of medicines

Your ass thought you were better than

Ason, I keep planets in orbit

While I be comin with deeper and more shit

Enough to make ya break and shake ya ass

'Cause I create rhymes good as a Tastykake mix

This style I'm mastered in

Niggas catchin headaches, what? What? You need aspirin?

This type of pain you couldn't even kill with Midol

Fuck around, get sprayed with Lysol

In your face like a can of mace, baby

Is it burnin? Well, fuck it, now you're learnin

How? I don't even like your motherfuckin profile

Give me my fuckin shit, ch-ch-blaow!

Not seen and heard, no one knows

You forget, niggas be quiet as kept

Now you know nothing, before you knew a whole fuckin lot

Your ass don't wanna get shot!

A lot of MCs came to my showdown

And watch me put your fuckin ass lo-o-ow down

As you can go, below zero

Without a doubt, I never been tooken out

By a nigga who couldn't figure

Yo, by a nigga who couldn't figure

Yo, by a nigga who couldn't figure (Brooklyn Zoo)

How to pull a fuckin gun trigger

I said, "Get the fuck outta here!"

Nigga wanna get too close to the utmost

But I got stacks that'll attack any wack host

Introducin, yo, fuck that nigga's name!

My hip-hop drops on your head like ra-a-ain

And when it rains it pours, 'cause my rhymes' hardcore

That's why I give you more of the raw

Talent that I got will riz-ock the spot

MCs I'll be bur-r-rnin, bur-r-rnin hot

Whoa-hoa-hoa! Let me like slow up with the flow

If I move too quick, oh, you just won't know

I'm homicidal when you enter the target

Nigga, get up, act like a pig—try to hog shit!

That's why I take yo' ass out quick

The mics, I've had it my nigga, you can suck my dick

If you wanna step to my motherfuckin rep

Ch-ch-blaow! blaow! blaow! Blown to death

You got shot 'cause you knock knock knock

"Who's there?" Another motherfuckin hardrock

Slackin on your mackin 'cause raw's what you lack

You wanna react? Bring it on back . . .

Shame on you, when you step through to

The Ol' Dirty Bastard, Brooklyn Zoo! [Repeat to fade]

DAYTONA 500
(Ghostface Killah)

[Raekwon]

Say peace to cats who rock mack knowledge, knowledgists

Street astrologists, light up the mic, god, acknowledge this

Fly joints that carry two points, Corolla Motorola holder

Play it, god, he pack over the shoulder

Chrome tanks, player like Yanks, check the franchise

Front on my guys, my enterprise splash many lives

Rappel on fakes like reflectors

He had sugar in his ear in his last crack career

We can can him, manhandle him, if you wanna

Run in his crib-o, get ditto, skate like a limo

And jet to the flyest estate, relate, take a break

Break down the eighth and then wait, drop it like Drake

Thugs they be booing and screwing, we canoeing

Claim they doin the same shit we doin, fuck your union

It's the same style, RZA trainable, jump the turnstile

On the alley tried to challenge god for the new vials

Especially that aluminum bat in the Ac

Relax, lay back, sell a grenade a day, it pays, black

The MAC-10 flex white cats like Windex

Index finger be sore, bustin these fly scripts

The Wally kid count crazily grands with our plans

Layin with my bitches and my mans in Lex lands

We losin 'em, jet to the stash and now Jerusalem

Abusin 'em, rockin his jewels like we usin 'em

Low pro star, seven thick waves rock Polar

Roll with the older god, build with the Sun, Moon, Star

[Chorus]

All these MCs start realizing

That Ghost got that shit that'll keep you vibing

The Wu is here to bring you Shaolin's finest

But if your shields are weak, you better step behind us

[Ghostface Killah]

Mercury raps is roughed then god just shown like taps

Red and white Wallys that match, bend my baseball hat

Doin forever shit like pissin out the window on turnpikes

Robbin niggas for leathers, high swipin on dirt bikes

Voice be mellow like Vaughn Harper, Radio Barber

Murder sleep-away camp, the fly lady champ

The arsonist, who burn with his pen regardless

Slaying all these earthlings and fake foreigners

In the Philippines, pick herbal beans, bubbling strings

Body chemical cream, we burn kerosene

The conviction of my tape is rape, wicked like Nixon

Long-heads inscriptions with three sixes in

Kiss the pyramid experiment with high explosive

I slapbox with Jesus, lick shots at Joseph

Zoomin like binoculars, the rap blacksmith

Money's Rolex was rockless, Chef's ragtop is spotless

I'm Iron Man, no cheap cash metal, I'm steel alloy

True identity hidden inside secret tabloids

Breathe oxygen, both sides of my jaw carry oxes

The track hit like the bangers in hundred-watt boxes

Yo' jostling these cats while Little J be deli-ing

Sip Irish Moss out of Widelians

"Rhymes like retail, make sure shit sell"

[Chorus]

[Cappadonna]

Give me the fifty-thou small bills, my gold plate, my slang kills

My Benz spills, whattup Lils? Murder one dun

Killer bee stung, guess who back home, son?

My technique is slang camp one, third platoon soon

Cristal bottles, cages of boom, poppy wardrobe

The mad-hatter big dick style, beware goons

Smuggle balloons, Lorna Doones in fat pussy wombs

Let the gods build, pull up the grill, check out the mad skills

Top secret technique, too hard for you to peep it

And keep it, jiggy style of rap and watchin knuckle slang

Sweep it out of order, tape recorder can't record my slaughter

Spoil the rotten, Donna too good to be forgotten

High-top notch, borderline rhymes is handcocked

Ninety-six, my ill sound clash is still hot

Get yourself shot

[Chorus]

THE M.G.M.

(Ghostface Killah and Raekwon)

[Ghostface Killah and Raekwon] Yo, up in the M.G.M. coked up

[Ghostface Killah] Psyche! Six niggas walked in flashing they gems,
  peace. [Raekwon] Aight!

One dark skinned nigga, fifty-six-inch rope

Wrapped around twice. [Ghostface Killah] Smash the Gilligan boat
  with ice

[Raekwon] They threw sign language, [Ghostface Killah] ordered hot
  coffee [Both] wit' a danish

[Ghostface Killah] Relaxed, whispered they rap entertainers

[Raekwon] Had Lizzy on, two Japanese birds with furs look good, kid

[Ghostface Killah] Laid back handlin hors d'oeuvres

[Raekwon] It's like round three. [Ghostface Killah] We too black for BET

You memorize the one to forty? [Raekwon] I'm at the nineteenth degree

If a civilized person doesn't perform his duty

What shall be done? [Ghostface Killah] Pardon me, god, that nigga got a
  gun

Bulgin out his sweatpants, check out his stance

See the side of his grill? [Raekwon] Look like my cousin Lance

Left hand rock a Guess watch. [Ghostface Killah] Yo, I think I did his Clarks

He wanted crush bone leather with the strings dark

[Raekwon] Now I remember [Ghostface Killah] He from Bear Mountain

He and Mitch Greene shot the fair one [Raekwon] near the water fountain

[Ghostface Killah] Seventh round, Chavez bleedin from his right ear

Yo, keep ya eye on that same nigga from right here

[Raekwon] Popcorn spillin all on Liz Claiborne

Ghost had the fly Gucci mocs with no socks on

Seen Deion Sanders in the back with the fat fur on

[Ghostface Killah] Workin them hoes with the fly Wu shirts on

Mixed drink session, dun [Raekwon] Pour me some more

[Ghostface Killah] Chef leathered down, blinking at Chanté Moore

[Raekwon] Tenth round, Chavez tearin him down. [Ghostface Killah]
  Sweet Pea, get ya shit off!

[Raekwon] It's like blacks against the Germans. [Ghostface Killah]
    Gettin hit off

[Raekwon] Smooth and them walked in, [Ghostface Killah] Brownsville
    representin

[Raekwon] They sent a bottle over, autograph blessin

[Ghostface Killah] Chef pull out the doodle, twist the dank pink noodles

[Raekwon] Yo, I'm 'bout to roll one. [Ghostface Killah] Matter fact, twist
    two of those

[Raekwon] Yo, they wound up stoppin the fight. Steeles took a point away
    from Chavez

[Ghostface Killah] Rematch scheduled on October ninth

Rematch scheduled on October ninth

TRIUMPH

[Ol' Dirty Bastard]

What, y'all thought y'all wasn't gon' see me? I'm the Osiris of this shit. Wu-Tang is
    here forever, motherfucker. It's like this ninety-seven. Aight, my niggas and
    my niggarettes. Let's do it like this. I'ma rub your ass in the moonshine. Let's
    take it back to seventy-nine!

[Inspectah Deck]

I bomb atomically, Socrates philosophies

And hypotheses can't define how I be droppin these

Mockeries, lyrically perform armed robbery

Flee with the lottery, possibly they spotted me

Battle-scarred shogun, explosion when my pen hits

Tremendous, ultraviolet shine blind forensics

I inspect you, through the future see millennium

Killa B's sold fifty gold; sixty platinum

Shacklin the masses with drastic rap tactics

Graphic displays melt the steel like blacksmiths

Black Wu jackets, Queen B's ease the guns in

Rumble with patrolmen, tear gas laced the function

Heads by the score take flight, incite a war

Chicks hit the floor, diehard fans demand more
Behold the bold soldier, control the globe slowly
Proceeds to blow, swingin swords like Shinobi
Stomp grounds and pound footprints in solid rock
Wu got it locked, performin live on your hottest block

[Method Man]
As the world turns, I spread like germs, bless the globe
With the pestilence, the hard-headed never learn
It's my testament to those burned, play my position
In the game of life, standin firm on foreign land
Jump the gun out the fryin pan, into the fire
Transform into the Ghostrider, a six-pack
And *A Streetcar Named Desire,* who got my back?
In the line of fire holdin back, what?
My peoples, if you with me, where the fuck you at?
Niggas is strapped, and they tryin to twist my beer cap
It's court adjourned for the bad seed from bad sperm
Herb got my wig fried like a bad perm
What the blood . . . clot? We smoke pot
And blow spots. You wanna think twice? I think not
The Iron Lung ain't got ta tell you where it's coming from
Guns of Navarone, tearing up your battle zone
Rip through your slums

[Cappadonna]
I twist darts from the heart, tried and true
Loop my voice on the LP, martini on the slang rocks
Certified chatterbox, vocabulary Donna talking
Tell your story walkin
Take cover kid, what? Run for your brother, kid
Run for your team and your six camp rhyme groupies
So I can squeeze with the advantage
And get wasted. My deadly notes reign
Supreme, your fort is basic compared to mine

Domino effect, arts and crafts paragraphs
Contain cyanide, take a free ride
On my dart, I got the fashion catalogues for all y'all
To all praise to the gods

[Ol' Dirty Bastard]
The saga continues: Wu-Tang, Wu-Tang

[U-God]
Olympic torch flaming, we burn so sweet
The thrill of victory, the agony, defeat
We crush slow, flamin deluxe slow for
Judgment Day cometh, conquer, it's war
Allow us to escape hell glow spinning bomb
Pocket full of shells out the sky, Golden Arms
Tunes spit the shitty Mortal Kombat sound
The fateful step make the blood stain the ground
A jungle junkie, vigilante tantrum
A death kiss, catwalk, squeeze another anthem
Hold it for ransom, tranquilized with anesthesias
My orchestra, graceful, music ballerinas
My music Sicily, rich California smell
An ax-killer adventure, paint a picture well
I sing a song from Sing-Sing, sippin on ginseng
Righteous wax chaperone, rotating ring king

[RZA]
Watch for the wooden soldiers, C-Cypher-Punks couldn't hold us
A thousand men rushin in, not one nigga was sober
Perpendicular to the square, we stand and glow like flare
Escape from your Dragon's Lair, in particular
My beats travel like a vortex through your spine
To the top of your cerebrum cortex
Make you feel like you bust a nut from raw sex
Enter through your right ventricle, clog up your bloodstream

Now terminal, like Grand Central Station
Program fat basslines on Novation
Getting drunk like a fuck, I'm duckin five-year probation

[GZA]
War of the masses, the outcome, disastrous
Many of the victim family save they ashes
A million names on walls engraved in plaques
Those who went back received penalties for the ax
Another heart is torn as close ones mourn
Those who stray, niggas get slayed on the song

[Masta Killa]
The track renders helpless and suffers from multiple
Stab wounds and leaks sounds that's heard
Ninety-three million miles away from came one
To represent the Nation, this is a gathering
Of the masses that come to pay respects
To the Wu-Tang Clan as we engage in battle
The crowd now screams in rage
The high chief Jamel-I-Reef takes the stage
Light is provided through sparks of energy
From the mind that travels in rhyme form
Givin sight to the blind, the dumb are mostly
Intrigued by the drum, death only one
Can save self from this relentless attack
Of the track spares none

[Ghostface Killah]
Yo! Yo! Yo, fuck that, look at all these crab niggas laid back
Lampin like them gray and black Pumas on my man's rack
Codeine was forced in your drink, you had a navy green
Salamander fiend, bitches never heard you scream
You two-faces, scum of the slum, I got your whole body numb
Blowin like Shalamar in eighty-one

Sound convincin? Thousand-dollar cork pop convention
Hands like Sonny Liston, get fly permission
Hold the fuck up, I'll unfasten your wig, bad luck
I humiliate, separate the English from the Dutch
It's me, black Noble Drew Ali, came in threes
We like the Genovese, is that so? Seizin these degrees
It's earth ninety-three million miles from the first
Rough turbulence, the waveburst, split the megahertz

[Raekwon]
Aiyo, that's amazing, gun-in-your-mouth talk, verbal-foul hawk
Connect thoughts to make my manchild walk
Swift notarizer, Wu-Tang, all up in the high-riser
New York Yank visor, world tranquilizer
Just a dosage, delegate my Clan with explosives
While my pen blow lines ferocious
Mediterranean, see y'all, the number one draft pick
Tear down the beat, god, then delegate the god to see God
The swift chancellor, flex the white-gold tarantula
Track truck diesel, play the weed, god, substantiala
Max mostly, undivided, then slide in, sickenin
Guaranteed, made 'em jump like Rod Strickland

SHAKEY DOG
(Ghostface Killah)
Yo, making moves back and forth Uptown, sixty dollars
Plus toll is the cab fee, wintertime bubble goose
Goose, clouds of smoke, music blastin
In the A-rab V blunted, whip smelling like fish
From 125th, throwin ketchup on my fries
Hitting baseball spliffs, back seat with my leg all stiff
Push the fuckin seat up, tartar sauce
On my S Dot kicks, rocks is lit while I'm poppin the clips
I'm ready for war, got to call the Cuban guys
Got the Montana pulled in front of the store

Made my usual gun check, safety off, "Come on, Frank

The moment is here, take your fuckin hood off

And tell the driver to stay put. Fuck them niggas

On the block, they shook; most of 'em won't look

They frontin, they no crooks, they fuck up they own juks

Look out for Jackson 5–0 'cause they on foot"

Straight ahead is the doorway, see that lady with the shopping cart

She keep a shottie cocked in the hallway

"Damn, she look pretty old, Ghost." She work for Kevin

She 'bout seventy-seven. She paid her dues when she smoked his

Brother-in-law at his boss's wedding

Flew to Venezuela quickly when the big fed stepped in

Three o'clock, watch the kids, third floor, last door

"You look paranoid, that's why I can't juks with you"

Why? "Why you behind me leery? Shakey Dog stutterin

When you got the bigger cooker on you

You's a crazy motherfucker, small hoodie dude

Hilarious move, you on some Curly, Moe, Larry shit

Straight Perry shit, Krispy Kreme, cocaine

Dead bodies, jail time, you gon' carry it

Matter of fact, all the cash, I'ma carry it

Stash it in jelly and break it down at the Marriott

This is the spot. Yo, son—your burner cocked? These fuckin

Maricons on the couch watchin *Sanford and Son,* passin

They rum, fried plantains and rice, big round onions

On a T-bone steak. My stomach growling, yo, I want some

Hold on, somebody's comin, get behind me, knock at the door

Act like you stickin me up, put the joint to my face

Push me in quickly when the bitch open up

Remember you don't know me, blast him if he reach for his gun"

"Yo, who goes there?" "Tony." "Tony, one second, homie

No matter rain, sleet, or snow you know you 'posed to phone me"

Off came the latch, Frank pushed me into the door

The door flew open, dude had his mouth open

Frozen, stood still with his heat bulgin

Told him, "Freeze! Lay the fuck down and enjoy the moment"

Frank snatched his gat, slapped him, asked him

"Where's the cash, coke, and the crack? Get the smoke and you fast"

His wife stood up speakin in Spanish, big titty bitch

Holdin the cannon ran in the kitchen, threw a shot, then

Kick in the four fifth, broke a bone in her wrist and she dropped the heat

"Give up the coke!" But the bitch wouldn't listen

I'm on the floor like, holy shit! Watchin my man

Frank get busy, he zoned out, finished off my man's wizie

He let the pitbull out, big head Bruno

With the little shark's teeth, chargin, foamin out the mouth

I'm scared, Frank screamin, blowin shots in the air

Missin his target off the Frigidaire, it grazed my ear

Killed that bullshit pit, ran to the back room butt first

Frank put two holes in the doorman's Sassoon

"The coke's in the vacuum," got to the bathroom

Faced his bad moves, the big one had the centipede stab wound

Frank shot the skinny dude, laid him out

The bigger dude popped Frankie boy, played him out

To be continued …

2000–2010

New Millennium Rap

In 2006 Nas released the album *Hip Hop Is Dead* with its eponymous single, a sharp critique of present-day hip-hop from one of rap's most respected artists. The album cover shows Nas, clad in black, dropping a black rose into an open grave. "Everybody sound the same, commercialize the game / Reminiscin when it wasn't all business, it forgot where it started / So we all gather here for the dearly departed," he raps to a menacing beat driven by a psychedelic rock guitar riff from Iron Butterfly's "In-A-Gadda-Da-Vida."[1]

"Hip Hop Is Dead" inspired passionate responses from rappers, journalists, and fans, ranging from affront to agreement. Most of the discussions, however, failed to look beyond the bold title. Lyrically, the song is not an elegy but an exhortation. Rather than pronouncing hip-hop's demise, Nas voices a prophetic warning. In the words of the rapper Common, Nas was issuing "a call to arms, a battle cry almost."[2] Saving hip-hop, Nas insists, means shifting the course of the music away from commercial interests and toward the essence of what made rap great in the first place: beats and rhymes, love and lyrics.

Hip-hop began the 2000s as the undisputed face of mainstream music and popular culture; it closed the decade as a smaller, more segmented, though fiercely inventive part of a similarly transformed cultural landscape marked by the atomization of audience and popular taste. The Billboard Hot 100 charts from a typical week between 2000 and 2005 were dominated by rappers (50 Cent, Eminem, Jay-Z, Nelly, Missy Elliott) and by artists strongly influenced by the beats and rhymes of rap (Mary J. Blige, Usher, Beyoncé, Jennifer Lopez, Gwen Stefani, Mariah Carey).

By contrast, the rappers who earned significant critical and commercial attention in the waning years of the decade often did so with albums that few hip-hop traditionalists would recognize as rap at all—such as Gnarls Barkley's *St. Elsewhere* (2006), M.I.A.'s *Kala* (2007), Kanye West's *808s and Heartbreak* (2008), The Black Eyed Peas's *The E.N.D.* (2009), Kid Cudi's *Man on the Moon: The End of Day* (2009), and Lil Wayne's *Rebirth* (2010). Rap's ever-expanding soundscape, its genre-bending fusions of forms, means that many of the old definitions don't hold. Rhyming over beats is no longer the sole defining element of rap, though it remains essential to the art form.

In the past decade, hip-hop has undergone a handful of seismic shifts: rap's decreasing sales and its move from the pop music spotlight, its transformation through digital technology, and its rapid global expansion even as rap's growth seems to have slowed in the United States. In isolation, each of these could be read as a sign of decline, but taken together they suggest promising new directions for a culture in flux from the start.

We now live in a time, at least in the United States if not beyond, in which no one under the age of thirty has known a world without hip-hop. Its influence has stretched well beyond the music to such realms as sports, advertising, and fashion. *GQ*, for instance, observed in February 2010 that "hip-hop has been as influential on fashion as any other cultural force in the last thirty years."[3] The present generation of college students came of age when rap was the dominant form of popular music, ruling the radio and music video charts and defining youthful rebellion. But as the world has adjusted to hip-hop and hip-hop to the world, it has become increasingly difficult for anything related to hip-hop to be considered avant-garde. For an art form that was born in reaction to the establishment, that cobbled itself together out of the detritus of the mainstream (sampled records, spray-painted train cars, repurposed and refashioned parts put to new use), being at the seat of power is discombobulating and potentially stagnating.

Hip-hop is now institutionally grounded in a way that would have surprised—and maybe even slightly disturbed—its originators. Grandmaster Flash and the Furious Five and Run-DMC became the first hip-hop artists inducted into the Rock and Roll Hall of Fame, an honor for which groups don't become eligible until twenty-five years after the release of their debut album. In 2006 the Smithsonian's National Museum of American History launched "Hip-Hop Won't Stop: The Beat, The Rhymes, The Life," a major collecting initiative with the goal of establishing "an unprecedented permanent collection that will document the undeniable reach of hip-hop and commemorate it as one of the most influential cultural explosions in recent history." Harvard University's HipHop Archive, founded in 2002, has dedicated itself to fostering research and scholarship on hip-hop music and culture. Across the academic landscape, from grade school to graduate school, hip-hop is now part of the curriculum. This anthology, too, embodies these transformations.

Few artists better illustrate hip-hop's move to the mainstream than Eminem. By album sales and cultural impact, he was the most influential artist of the decade. In fact, *Billboard* magazine named him just that. Eminem sold more albums in the last ten years than did his closest competition—the Beatles and Britney Spears—over the same period of time. In 1999 he released his much-anticipated debut album, *The Slim Shady LP,* after spending years building his reputation on the freestyle battle scene, winning contests both in his native Detroit and throughout the country. Bolstered by production from Dr. Dre, the album and the two that followed in quick succession, *The Marshall Mathers LP* (2000) and *The Eminem Show* (2002), went multiplatinum and led the surge of hip-hop to its position of pop music dominance.

Many within the hip-hop community, however, felt uncomfortable that a white MC would gain for hip-hop even wider acceptance than it had already enjoyed. Some called Eminem the Elvis of Rap. What kept him from following in the path of another white rapper with trailblazing commercial appeal, Vanilla Ice, is that Eminem is a supremely gifted lyricist. His influence on hip-hop has been not only commercial but stylistic. Among his many formal innovations are his experiments in persona. His first three albums marked the introduction of three distinct lyrical identities—Slim Shady, the madcap, near-cartoonish alter ego whose high-pitched, nasally voice delivers comic and sinister lines with equal zeal; Eminem, the swaggering lyrical swordsman capable of dismantling any opponent with a phrase; and Marshall Mathers, his given name, a voice that produced more introspective lyrics such as those on "Mockingbird."

Eminem's innovations extend to nearly all of rap's formal elements. He introduced a host of compelling word pairs never heard before in hip-hop, or perhaps any other musical genre—rhyming "Britney Spears" with "switch me chairs," or "public housing systems" with "victim of Munchausen syndrome." He fashioned a signature flow that draws heavily on assonance and alliteration to capture a cadence that is both rhythmic and relentless, as he does on "Renegade" in lines like these: "Now who's the king of these rude ludicrous lucrative lyrics / Who could inherit the title, put the youth in hysterics." In his wordplay he expanded the potential of the hip-hop simile, sometimes stretching them across three or four lines, creating expressions that modulate in meaning as they develop in time: "I don't give a fuck if it's dark or not. I'm harder than me tryna park a Dodge / When I'm drunk as fuck right next to a humongous truck in a two car garage / Hoppin out with two broken legs tryna walk it off . . ."

Through all of this, Eminem emerged as a popular and a polarizing figure. By virtue of his confessional rhymes, the drama of his personal life is now public: his conflicted relationship with his mother and his ex-wife, his dedication to his daughter, and his battles with chemical dependence. He is one of those rare celebrities about whom we know far too much yet hardly anything at all.

Understanding rap in the 2000s requires paying close attention to another hip-hop icon: Jay-Z. After debuting in 1996 with *Reasonable Doubt,* he became a crossover cultural sensation late in the decade with such chart-topping songs as "Hard Knock Life (Ghetto Anthem)" and "Izzo (H.O.V.A.)." By the turn of the century, he was among rap's most visible figures, which made it all the more dramatic when he retired in 2003. His decision reflected a desire to pursue other interests, including his responsibilities as president of Def Jam Records and his business interests that would eventually include part ownership in an NBA franchise, a clothing label, and more. Rap called to him, however, and much like Michael Jordan's return to basketball, he came back reinvigorated and refocused.

Jay-Z's career has offered a model for the new hip-hop mogul and global celebrity. *Forbes* magazine cited him as the head of a new breed of "hip-hoprenuers," naming him the highest-earning hip-hop celebrity in its inaugural 2007 money list. Describing the group of hip-hop "Cash Kings" that also includes 50 Cent, Diddy, Kanye West, Ludacris, and others, the magazine noted that "these impresarios have mastered the arts of branding and cross-promotion, with licensing deals for everything from booze to books." In 2008 alone, the top twenty earners in hip-hop exceeded $500 million.[4]

Jay-Z's influence on the lyrical craft is equally significant. "With an acute eye for detail," writes David Bry, "an unparalleled ear for dialogue, and a sense of song structure rare among rap writers, Jay created compelling four-minute vignettes detailing topics long revered by the American public: Cool cars. Hot girls. Lotsa money. Jay-Z puts it all together in a dense, twisted mass of internal rhyme and cross-referential metaphor. And, of course, he flows like a faucet."[5]

Perhaps the most unlikely transformative figure in hip-hop over the past decade has been Kanye West. Kanye burst onto the scene as a rapper in 2004. By that time he had already gained a reputation as a masterful producer with hits like Jay-Z's "Izzo (H.O.V.A.)" and "This Can't Be Life." *The College Dropout* marked the debut of a fresh voice in rap—full of confident swagger but down-to-earth enough to rhyme about folding shirts at The Gap. On "All Falls Down" he reveals a vulnerability and self-doubt rarely heard in rap:

> I wanna act ballerific like it's all terrific
> I got a couple past due bills, I won't get specific
> I got a problem with spending before I get it
> We all self-conscious, I'm just the first to admit it

Thematically, the album ranged from reflections on organized religion ("Jesus Walks") to the excesses of consumerism ("All Falls Down") to the love of family ("Family Business"). Poetically, his greatest influence may be in rhyme, where he has taken the practice of slant rhyme and pushed it to the breaking point. This method—call it transformative rhyme—involves consciously altering the pronunciation of one word to forge a perfect rhyme with another. On "Gold Digger," for instance, he rhymes "Serena" with "Trina," a perfect rhyme, then makes both rhyme with "Jennifer" by pronouncing it "Ginafa." The result is a playful move that makes something new by flouting constraint.

Kanye's career trajectory has mirrored that of hip-hop as a whole. He has expanded his sound to embrace other genres, finally rejecting rapping entirely in favor of singing in Auto-Tune (a technological trick that alters the voice to endow it with a digitized quality) on his 2008 release, *808s and Heartbreak.* His energy, ego, and inventiveness put their mark on the 2000s in a way few other artists can claim.

For all the backlash Auto-Tune experienced by the close of the decade, rap has always developed, employed, and repurposed technological inventions in the making of its art. Kool Herc's sound system and Timbaland's arsenal of digital production tools represent a direct evolutionary line in innovation and artistry. Similarly, rap's audience has been quick to adopt technology that brings it closer to the music. Practices like peer-to-peer file sharing and services like iTunes have revolutionized the way people relate to music. They have both served consumer demand for more freedom of choice and shaped a new model for consuming music. As a result, songs have supplanted albums as the basic unit of musical measure. A whole sub-genre of so-called ring-tone rap has ensued, made with the specific purpose of sounding good through the tinny speakers of a cell phone. The rise of digital technology and the resulting web of interconnectivity that now binds nearly the entire planet enable new voices to make music and new ears to hear it.

Relatively inexpensive and high-quality music production software has allowed individuals to produce professional-sounding tracks in their homes. Once the track is finished, they can upload it to any number of Web sites like MySpace and YouTube and deliver their music directly to an audience without record labels and promoters. This new means of music production and dissemination not only challenges the corporate music business model, but also reshapes the aesthetics of rap. Fewer gatekeepers means that more artists than ever can find audiences for their music.

In 2007 a seventeen-year-old from Atlanta followed precisely this process, uploading his homemade single to SoundClick, YouTube, and My-Space. Commercial radio picked up Soulja Boy Tell 'Em's "Crank That (Soulja Boy)" and it became a nationwide craze, spending seven weeks at the number one spot on the Billboard Hot 100 chart. It sold millions of copies—both as a single and as a ring tone—and earned Soulja Boy a Grammy nomination for Best Rap Song. The song itself is a simple affair: beat- and hook-driven, with basic lyrics. Its massive popularity can be attributed to a number of factors: its stripped-down production translates well to a ring tone, its lyrics are easy to memorize, and it came complete with its own dance—which became a sensation as well.

For some, Soulja Boy's success was a sure sign of rap's decline. Ice-T accused the teenager of "killing hip-hop," leading to an unseemly beef between the venerable rapper and the young upstart. None would confuse Soulja Boy with Rakim, but his success suggests new possibilities for creating and consuming music. The potential now exists for a creative renaissance driven by a musical meritocracy, resisting the trend-chasing impulses of many record labels. At the same time, however, a gutted corporate infrastructure means that artist development is no longer as widespread. Could it be, then, that we will simply get more and more varieties of worse and worse music? The results of this dramatic transformation in the way rap music is made and consumed are still sorting themselves out.

Rap is paradoxically both more globally integrated and more fiercely regional than it has ever been. Rap's regionalism partakes of the energy of grassroots hip-hop scenes around the country. Local artists build local fan bases, touring within the region but rarely beyond. This is happening almost everywhere. Every now and then a regional scene becomes national and even global. Two large regions experienced rapid growth over the decade, shifting hip-hop's center of gravity away from the coasts and toward the South and the Midwest.

The rap industry in the South began building in the 1990s through the enterprising efforts of self-made moguls like Master P and his No Limit Records and Baby and his Cash Money Records. They offered a blueprint for commercial success—self-production, promotion, and distribution. The music coming from Atlanta and New Orleans, and from Memphis and Miami, was varied but shared a few dominant characteristics. Sonically, it tended toward slow, bass-heavy beats. Lyrically, it often relied on memorable hooks and chanted choruses. Thematically, the lyrics tended to center on clubbing, street life, and the drug trade. Sometimes the music was associated with—and advertised by—a particular dance, such as the "snap-music" trend of the later years of the decade.

Perhaps the greatest underground success story in southern style was crunk. Crunk, which takes its name from the wild response the music tends to elicit from the crowd on the dance floor, fused hip-hop and electro beats. With a slower tempo than that of New York–based hip-hop, it also tended to feature strong hooks rather than complex verses. Lyrics serve a complementary function, bolstering the energy of the music—hence the fact that shouts and screams, like Lil Jon's famous "Yeaaaah!" are often the most memorable part of the performance. Lil Jon & the Eastside Boyz were the most visible figures of this new movement, scoring a major hit with 2002's "Get Low."

The South also produced a new breed of hardcore lyricists, most notably Atlanta's T.I., the self-proclaimed "King of the South," and Young Jeezy. By the middle of the decade, T.I. was among only a handful of rap artists capable of charting major record sales. In the second half of the decade, Jeezy emerged as a commercial force in his own right. But the most transformative figure to emerge from the South over the past decade has been Lil Wayne. Wayne, or Weezy, was the youngest member of Baby's Cash Money Millionaires from New Orleans. He was recording by the age of eleven and before the age of twenty he already had gold records to his credit. He reached a new level of fame starting with 2004's *Tha Carter*, led by the hit "Go DJ."

Renowned for never writing down his lyrics, Lil Wayne has cultivated a style that draws on the strengths of this exclusive orality. He relies heavily on devices like homonyms and homophones, assonance, alliteration, and, of course, rhyme. His wordplay most often is grounded in puns, turns of phrase that make the most of the play of sound.

Wayne built a reputation as a relentless lyricist through a series of mix tapes. Traditionally, mix tapes formed part of a street economy with DJs blending the latest hits, punctuated by the occasional freestyle verse or unreleased track. In the past decade, however, mix tapes became far more polished, essentially functioning as ersatz albums, with high production values, sharp lyrics, and considerable listenership. Mix tapes allow the MC greater freedom—they can spit verses on other people's tracks, they can experiment with styles. For some artists, like The Clipse, their best work has arguably come out on mix tapes rather than on studio albums. Though some mix tapes are still offered for purchase (on CD as opposed to actual tape), many are available for free download. Lil Wayne became the master of the mix tape; *Vibe Magazine* even ran a feature entitled "The 77 Best Lil Wayne Songs of 2007." He did not release a studio album that year.

Conventional wisdom said that it was commercial suicide to give so much music away for free, yet when *Tha Carter III* was released in 2008, it sold over a million copies in its first week even though most of the songs had been previously available for download (both legally and illegally)—exceedingly rare in the new record industry economy. *Tha Carter III* earned eight Grammy nominations and cemented Lil Wayne's reputation as a prodigious lyrical talent. If not the greatest rapper alive, a title he sometimes claims for himself, then he is certainly one of the most ubiquitous and memorable.

Other regional scenes developed in unlikely places like Portland, Oregon, and the Twin Cities of Minnesota. From this latter locale the Rhymesayers label released its first album in 1996, shortly followed by Atmosphere's 1997 debut album. In the next several years, the label built one of the most respected rosters of MCs in the independent hip-hop world, including Atmosphere, Brother Ali, MF DOOM, Eyedea & Abilities, I Self Divine, Blueprint, and Soul Position. They brought international attention to the grassroots hip-hop in Minneapolis–St. Paul. Through relentless touring and word of mouth promotion, Rhymesayers fashioned a new model for independent hip-hop labels.

Hip-hop's trend in the first decade of the 2000s has been toward geographic expansion. Whereas the 1990s saw the reification of difference between East and West Coast, culminating in the violent deaths of two of hip-hop's biggest stars, the years since have seen a declining emphasis on the

dividing lines of place. This is not to say, however, that place has lost all significance—far from it. Rather, it suggests that rap has expanded to embrace
its multiregional and, indeed, multinational identity. Surely the Web, with
its aforementioned influence on the production and consumption of the
music, has led the way. Now that hip-hop resides largely beyond borders, its
beats and rhymes have become a kind of linguistic gumbo, with MCs bor-
rowing from other artists from other places.

Rap's global expansion is clearly audible in today's hip-hop. An influential rhyme style, like Nas's or Busta Rhymes's or André 3000's, quickly becomes a model for other rappers from Chicago to Kingston to Cairo and
back. Travel itself has become a popular theme in the lyrics as well, with
Jay-Z admonishing his adversaries on "30 Something" that "you ain't got
enough stamps in your passport." Hip-hop has always had its global vision—it was, after all, originated by a Jamaican (Kool Herc) and shaped by
a Bronxite (Bambaataa) heavily influenced by his formative experiences
traveling to Africa and Europe. What we are witnessing today, then, is a
turn back to hip-hop's global roots, a necessary embrace of the fact that
much of hip-hop now lives outside of America's shores. The present anthology has the space to gesture only broadly toward this rich global heritage;
the full wealth of lyrical excellence from abroad demands an anthology all
its own.

One international artist with considerable influence on American hip-
hop is M.I.A. London-born and Sri Lanka–raised, M.I.A. is an unlikely hip-
hop celebrity, not the least because hip-hop is only one of the influences behind the eccentric and energizing music she makes. Her 2005 debut, *Arular*,
was a daring blend of styles from East and West. Her lyrics complemented
the odd, ambient music, reflecting on a broad range of themes, from politics to poverty, self-reflection to revolution. Her next album, 2007's *Kala*,
extended her influence with its omnipresent hit "Paper Planes," a song that
lived an even more pervasive second life as a sample on the mega-hit
"Swagger Like Us" by Jay-Z, Kanye West, Lil Wayne, and T.I.

M.I.A.'s nearly unclassifiable music is one example of how hip-hop is
changing as it comes in contact with other cultures. As Mark Schwartz explains, "Across the globe, hip-hop has been customized, souped up, or ret-
rofitted into local relevance."[6] As a fungible commodity, hip-hop culture
easily adjusts to new environments and new aesthetic aims. The universal
sounds of rhythm—of both the voice and the beat—make hip-hop at home
almost anywhere. "I can go to Japan, not speak the language or communicate whatsoever," remarks Evidence from Dilated Peoples, "but a beat will

come on, and we'll all move our heads the same way. It lets me know that there's something bigger than just making rap songs."[7] Rhythm is universal, whether it comes from a kick drum and a snare or from an MC spitting flows to the beat.

One place rap seems to have least expanded in recent years is in gender equity. The first decade of the 2000s should have been the decade in which women took their rightful place in the music. Rap's second generation of female MCs blossomed in the 1990s. Lil' Kim, Foxy Brown, Eve, Rah Digga, Bahamadia, Lady of Rage, and a host of rappers from the South like Trina, Khia, Shawnna, and Mia X all made important records. But the most transformational figure of all was Lauryn Hill. Her supreme gifts as a lyricist and singer distinguished her as perhaps the most important artist, regardless of gender, in late 1990s hip-hop. Her retreat from music and fame in the 2000s has left a lyrical void.

Instead of continuing its expansion, the role of women in rap has seemingly contracted in the past ten years. While most other genres of popular music saw an expanding role for women in the decades after their inception, hip-hop appears to have inverted the model. The reasons for this are complex and also unclear. Many of the prominent female MCs of the 1990s and early 2000s ran into legal trouble (Lil' Kim, Foxy Brown, Rah Digga), slowing down their production of music. Perhaps, too, young women who might have gone into rap in generations past are now finding forms of expression in musical genres less seemingly hostile to women. However one interprets the recent troubled role of women in hip-hop, it is a crisis that deserves attention.

One of the few bright spots is the rise of women MCs in hip-hop's underground, both in the United States and around the globe. Several recent documentaries call attention to this expanding trend, such as Joshua Asen and Jennifer Needleman's *I Love Hip Hop in Morocco* (2007) and Maori Karmael Holmes's *Scene Not Heard* (2009). Young women are finding within hip-hop a means for self-expression and, at times, resistance.

At the end of the first decade of a new millennium, hip-hop is now just over thirty years old. As a cultural form, it is still in its adolescence—defining the forms of its art, establishing the terms of its aesthetics, settling upon its values and purpose. Rap is at the center of these changes, the voice for a culture born in both resistance and celebration, told in tones of both profundity and profanity. "Hip hop has so much power," Common says. "The government can't stop it. The devil can't stop it. It's music, it's art, it's the voice of the people. And it's being spoken all around the world and the world is appreciating it."[8] Hip-hop has finally proven itself in longevity; the next challenge is to establish its place in history.

Like jazz and rock and roll before it, hip-hop has gone from musical upstart to mainstream success only to face an identity crisis. Rap's mainstreaming in the early years of the decade and its declining sales in the waning years could be a story of demise, but it is more likely one of rebirth, as rap puzzles out its post-pop identity. What does rap do when faced with the threats of co-option and stagnation? In the words of André 3000, it "makes new shit."[9] This crass and creative injunction, echoing the modernist motto of Ezra Pound from nearly a century ago to "make it new," is an artistic call to action. Hip-hop's future lies in the ingenuity of its present-day artists as well as in its judicious use of its own past.

AESOP ROCK

Aesop Rock crafts jam-packed imagistic verses. His rhymes are characterized by their texture and abstraction. "It's kind of what comes naturally for me," he explains. "The way I write is how I like to write and how I prefer to write. It comes more naturally for me to be into an abstract idea, I guess. It takes a while to sit and hash it all out on paper, but it's what I want to write, so it's what gets me excited."[10]

Aesop Rock began rapping in the early 1990s. While studying painting at Boston University, he struck up a friendship with producer Blockhead, which evolved into a professional relationship that has spanned Aesop's career. In 2001 he signed to underground rapper/producer EL-P's Definitive Jux (Def Jux) label, which boasts a roster of talented MCs including Del, Dizzee Rascal, and Mr. Lif.

Some of Aesop's lyrics are plainspoken and powerful, such as the narrative-driven "No Regrets." Other rhymes can leave one grasping for meaning. Opacity through abstraction and allusion, however, is precisely what makes Aesop Rock's lyrics appeal to his fans. "Even if it's not laid out in perfect sentences—is any rap?—you'd have to be an idiot to not at least grasp a few things from these songs," Aesop says, "or have had no interest in pulling anything from them in the first place."[11]

9–5ERS ANTHEM

Zoom in to the fumin of an aggravated breed
Via the study of postadolescent agitated seeds
Half the patients wasted self prior to commencement
So I focus on the urban oxygen samples, the half that made it breathe
This old Pompeii impression sways infection in twelve steps or less
And cretins swiftly tippy-toe on hard to swallow barter concepts
The give-it/get-it never let itself past wrought iron stubbornness

Martyrs talk funny causes in a harvesting Spartacus

And so on . . . I throw long Hail Mary bombs

Toward cookie-cutter Mother Nature's bedazzled synthetic fabrics

Life treats the peasants like they tried to fuck his woman

While he slept inside, while they're merely chasing perfectionist emblems

When the clock strikes nine, I'll be wakin with the best of the

Routine caffeine team players for the cycle of it

Under a dusted angel harp-string, Big Brother is watching

My odometer like buzzard to fallen elk, hawkin stealth

We got babies, rubber stamps, and briefcase parts

We on some door-to-door now, order ten dollars or more

We'll shove it down your throat for free

I'll sacrifice my inborn tendencies for copper pennies

From one commander 'gimme that' so he can retain baby fat

Mega biter snake bedlam, Holocaust freak

Heckle shiesty brain headroom shake planet

Make a move, pause, make a move, break cannon

Bend barrel one-eight-zero U-turn, squeeze, end it

It's on like it's never been. It's bleeding well

It's bigger than a breadbox. It corrodes my leaky finance

I take my seat atop the Brooklyn Bridge with a Coke and a bag of chips

To watch a thousand lemmings plummet just because the first one slipped

Sometimes I laugh at victory, kissing these little question marks

I tend to underestimate my average

Just another bastard savage. Someday you'll all eat out of my cold hand

'Cause every dog has its day at which point, I'll pull it away

[Chorus]

Now, we the American working population

Hate the fact that eight hours a day

Is wasted on chasing the dream of someone that isn't us

And we may not hate our jobs

But we hate jobs in general

That don't have to do with fighting our own causes

We the American working population

Hate the nine-to-five day-in/day-out
When we'd rather be supporting ourselves
By being paid to perfect the pastimes
That we have harbored based solely on the fact
That it makes us smile if it sounds dope . . .

It's the Year of the Silkworm
Everything I built burned yesterday. Let's display the purpose
That these stilts serve. Elevate the spreading of the silk germ
Trying to weave a web but all I believe in is dead
Nah, brother, it's the Year of the Jackal
Saddle up on high horse. My torch forced Polaris embarrassed
Shackle up the hassle by the doom and legend marriage
I bought some new sneakers, I just hope my legacy matches
It's the Year of the Landshark
Dry as sand—parched—damn, get these men some water
They're out there being slaughtered in meaningless wars so you don't have
    to bother
And can sit and soak the idiot box, trying to fuck their daughters
Man, it's the Year of the Orphan
Seated adjacent to the fireflies circling the torches on your porches
Trying to guard the fortress of a king they've never seen or met
But all are trained to murder at the first sign of a threat
Maybe it's the Year of the Water Bug
Cockroach, utter thug specimen. Fury spawned from
Dreaming of your next of kin. I'm still dealing with this mess I'm in
I've been the object of your ridicule. You've been a bitch lieutenant
God, it's the Year of the Underpaid Employee
Spitting forty plus a week and trying to rape Earth in my off time
You bored dizzy, I can't keep myself busy enough
So you can run, run, run, and I'ma let you think you won
EVERYBODY!

[Chorus]

Fumble outta bed and stumble to the kitchen

Pour myself a cup of ambition

And yawn and stretch and my life is a mess

And if I never make it home today, God bless

Fumble outta bed and I stumble to the kitchen

Pour myself a cup of ambition

And yawn and stretch and my life is a mess

And if I never make it home today, God bless

NO REGRETS

Lucy was seven and wore a head of blue barrettes

City born into this world with no knowledge and no regrets

Had a piece of yellow chalk with which she'd draw upon the street

The many faces of the various locals that she would meet

There was Joshua, age ten, bully of the block

Who always took her milk money at the morning bus stop

There was Mrs. Crabtree, and her poodle, she always

Gave a wave and holler on her weekly trip down to the bingo parlor

And she drew: men, women, kids, sunsets, clouds

And she drew: skyscrapers, fruit stands, cities, towns

Always said hello to passersby, they'd ask her why she passed her time

Attachin lines to concrete, but she would only smile

Now all the other children living in or near her building

Ran around like tyrants, soaking up the open fire hydrants

They would say, "Hey, little Lucy, wanna come jump double dutch?"

Lucy would pause, look, grin, and say, "I'm busy, thank you much"

Well, well, one year passed and believe it or not

She covered every last inch of the entire sidewalk

And she stopped. "Lucy, after all this, you're just giving in today?"

She said, "I'm not giving in, I'm finished," and walked away

[Chorus 2x]

1-2-3, that's the speed of the seed

A-B-C, that's the speed of the need

You can dream a little dream or you can live a little dream
I'd rather live it 'cause dreamers always chase but never get it

Lucy was thirty-seven and introverted somewhat
Basement apartment in the same building she grew up in
She traded in her blue barrettes for long locks held up with a clip
Traded in her yellow chalk for charcoal sticks
And she drew: little Bobby who would come to sweep the porch
And she drew: the mailman, delivered everyday at four
Lucy had very little contact with the folks outside her cubicle day
But she found it suitable and she liked it that way
She had a man now: Rico, similar, hermit
They would only see each other once or twice a week on purpose
They appreciated space and Rico was an artist, too
So they'd connect on Saturdays to share the pictures that they drew (Look!)
Now every month or so, she'd get a knock upon the front door
Just one of the neighbors, actin nice, although
She was a strange girl, really, said, "Lucy, wanna join me for some lunch?"
Lucy would smile and say, "I'm busy, thank you much"
And they would make a weird face the second the door shut
And run and tell their friends how truly crazy Lucy was
And Lucy knew what people thought but didn't care, 'cause
While they spread their rumors through the street, she'd made another
    masterpiece

[Chorus 2x]

Lucy was eighty-seven, upon her deathbed
At the senior home, where she had previously checked in
Traded in the locks and clips for a headrest
Traded in the charcoal sticks for arthritis, it had to happen
And she drew no more, just sat and watched the dawn
Had a television in the room that she'd never turned on
Lucy pinned up a life's worth of pictures on the wall
And sat and smiled and looked each one over, just to laugh at it all
Now Rico, he had passed, 'bout five years back

So the visiting hours pulled in a big flock of nothin
She'd never spoken much throughout the spanning of her life
Until the day she leaned forward, grinned, and pulled the nurse aside
And she said: "Look, I've never had a dream in my life
Because a dream is what you wanna do, but still haven't pursued
I knew what I wanted and did it 'til it was done
So I've been the dream that I wanted to be since day one!"
Well! The nurse jumped back, she'd never heard
Lucy even talk, especially words like that
She walked over to the door and pulled it closed behind
Then Lucy blew a kiss to each one of her pictures and she died

[Chorus 2x]

ATMOSPHERE

Atmosphere is a Minneapolis-based rap duo comprised of the rapper Slug and the DJ/producer Ant. The group has existed in various iterations since 1993, one of the longest-lived and most successful independent acts in rap. Together with their Rhymesayers label mates, they have fashioned not only their own independent business model, but also a hip-hop aesthetic driven by varied storytelling, dense lyrical flows, and eclectic beats.

Both in beats and rhymes, Atmosphere's sound is often dark and emotional. The group is known for their series of songs about a woman named Lucy, who is, by turns, an actual woman or a poetic conceit used to talk about everything from politics to hip-hop. "Fuck You Lucy" is, as the title suggests, about a difficult breakup, but it is also a love lyric. The jumbled language of the sample that both opens and closes the song ("It leave never would you, you show could I if") reflects the speaker's confusion and his search for certitude. By contrast, "Sunshine" is both an aubade and a hip-hop pastoral. The speaker, hung over from a night of revelry, is initially reluctant to confront the light of day; the sun, Slug artfully rhymes, hits him "dead in the eye / Like it's mad that I gave half the day to last night." But once he goes outside, it inspires reveries of days past and present.

FUCK YOU LUCY

It leave never would you, you show could I if [6x]

She sayin that she still wants a friendship
She can't live her life without me as a friend
I can't figure out why I'd give a damn to what she wants
I don't understand the now before the then
Most of this garbage I write that these people seem to like
Is about you and how I let you infect my life
And if they got to know you, I doubt that they would see it
They'd wonder what I showed you, how you could leave it
A friend in Chicago said that I should stay persistent
If I stay around, I'm bound to break resistance
Fuck you, Lucy, for defining my existence
Fuck you and your differences . . .
Ever since I was a young lad with a part-time dad
It was hard to find happiness inside of what I had
I studied my mother, I digested her pain
And vowed no woman on my path would have to walk the same
Travel like sound across the fate ladder
I travel with spoon to mix this cake batter
And I travel with feel so I can deal with touch
It's like that. Thank you very much. Fuck you very much

[Chorus 2x]
Yes, yes it is
And everyone in his life would mistake it as love
Everyone in his life would mistake it as love
Everyone in his life would mistake it as love

Fuck the what happened, I got stuck
They can peel pieces of me off the grill of her truck
Used to walk with luck, used to hold her hand
Fell behind and played the role of a slower man

I wanna stand on top of this mountain and yell
I wanna wake up and break up this lake of hell
I feel like a bitch for letting the sheet twist me up
The last star fighter is wounded, time to give it up
On a pick it up mission, kept it bitter
Gettin in a million memories just to forget her
The difficulty in keeping emotions controlled
Cookies for the road took me by the soul
Hunger for the drama, hunger for the nurture
Gonna take it further, the hurt feels like murder
Interpret, the eyes read the lines on her face
The sunshine is fake, how much time did I waste?
Fuck you, Lucy, for leaving me
Fuck you, Lucy, for not needin me
I wanna say fuck you because I still love you
No, I'm not OK and I don't know what to do

[Chorus 2x]

Do I sound mad? Well, I guess I'm a little pissed
Every action has a point, five points make a fist
You close 'em, you swing 'em, it hurt when it hits
And the truth can be a bitch, but if the boot fits
I got an idea: You should get a tattoo
That says "warning." That's all, just a warning
So the potential victim can take a left and save breath
And avoid you, sober and upset in the morning
I wanna scream, "Fuck you, Lucy!"
But the problem is I love you, Lucy
So instead, I'ma finish my drink and have another
While you think about how you used to be my lover
(Fuck you)

[Chorus 2x]

It leave never would you, you show could I if . . . [repeat to fade]

SUNSHINE

Ain't no way to explain or say
How painful the hangover was today
In front of the toilet, hands and knees
Trying to breathe in between the dry heaves
My baby made me some coffee
Afraid that if I drink some it's probably coming right back out me
Couple a Advil, relax and chill
At a standstill with how bad I feel
I think I need to smell fresh air
So I stepped out the back door and fell down the stairs
The sunlight hit me dead in the eye
Like it's mad that I gave half the day to last night
My bad sight made me trip on my ass, right
Into that patch of grass like "That's life!"
All of a sudden, I realize something
The weather is amazing, even the birds are bumpin
Stood up and took a look and a breath
And there's that bike that I forgot that I possessed
Never really seen exercise as friendly
But I think something's telling me to ride that ten-speed
The brakes are broken, it's alright
The tires got air and the chain seems tight
Hopped on and felt the summertime
It reminds me of one of them Musab lines like

[Chorus 2x]
Sunshine, sunshine, it's fine
I feel it in my skin, warmin up my mind
Sometimes you gotta give in to win
I love the days when it shines. Whoa, let it shine

If I could I would keep this feeling in a plastic jar
Bust it out whenever someone's actin hard
Settle down, barbeque in the backyard
The kids get treats and old folks get classic cars

Every day that gets to pass is a success

And every woman looks better in a sundress

The sunshine's an excuse to shoot hoops

Get juice, show and prove them moves and let loose

I hear voices, I see smiles to match 'em

Good times and you can feel it in the fashion

Even though the heat cooks up the action

The streets still got butterflies, enough kids to catch 'em

Ridin my bike around these lakes, man

Feelin like I finally figured out my escape plan

Take it all in, the day started off all wrong

But somehow now that hangover is all gone

Ain't nothing like the sound of the leaves

When the breeze penetrates these southside trees

Leanin up against one, watchin the vibe

Forgettin all about the stress, thanking God I'm alive

It's so simple, I had to keep the song simple

And when I get home I'm gonna open all the windows

Feelin alright, stopped at a stop sign

A car pulled up, bumpin Fresh Prince's "Summertime"

[Chorus 2x]

BEANIE SIGEL

Beanie Sigel is part of a long tradition of streetwise Philadelphia rappers stretching back to the 1980s with Schoolly D. After delivering a guest verse on fellow Philadelphians The Roots's "Adrenaline!" Sigel was signed to Jay-Z's Roc-A-Fella Records label. He would appear on several Jay-Z tracks as well as release a series of hard-hitting solo albums, beginning with *The Truth* (2000).

Stylistically, Sigel is known for constructing long runs of chain rhymes, sometimes even repeating the same word in distinct contexts. While much of his subject matter concerns the life of crime, as in "Tales of a Hustler" and "The Truth," he also reveals a raw and confessional tone.

THE TRUTH

I hope you got a extra mic and a fireproof booth
'Cause you know I'm known to melt a wire, too
You need a fire engineer when I lay this blaze
I melt down tracks that's real since slaves
Hit the studio, jars of dro, bars to blow
B. Sigel with that arsenic flow
Fuck that, don't hold me back, I roll with crack
Y'all cats told Mac to rap
Y'all don't realize y'all released the beast untamed
Speech all flame, streets y'all blame
It should be a honor for y'all to speak my name
I could go before your honor, he couldn't peep my game
Gotta laugh, y'all act like ya spit it the same
Why you motherfuckers can't get in the game?
I come from high school and go straight to the league
Who you know who can spit it with Sig'?

[Chorus 2x]
Nigga, the truth, every time I step in the booth
I speak the truth, y'all know what I'm bringing to you
I bring the truth, you motherfuckers know who I be
I be the truth, what I speak shall set you free
Nigga, the truth

Ain't nothin changed with Sig', I'm still stuck in the kitchen
So what I'm signed? That's fine, still stuck in position
You motherfuckers know me well, couple court cases
From jail, couple .44 shells from hell
Stuck on this mission, go home, my girl fussin and bitchin

"Motherfucker, won't you change your life?" I'm thinkin
Motherfucker, won't I change my wife?
Ignorant bastard, laughin, like, "fuck the rap shit"
It's just another hustle, another way for niggas to touch you
Now they know the face of Beans
Now they see my face on screens and I ain't even
Chase this dream; I feel sorry for those who did
Y'all niggas can't stop the boar, whether rock or raw
I'm slingin coke in a Roc velour
You niggas know what block I'm on, Glock in palm
You wanna get shot, karate chopped, or stabbed—it's on
Motherfucker . . .

[Chorus]

Black Friday management and Roc's the label
And I still hit you niggas with shots that's fatal
That bullshit vest can't save you, I had a doc
Open you up from chest to navel
See my face on cable and have flashbacks
Of that cold-ass table and them holes I gave you
I'm that nigga that'll come and pour salt in your wound
At the hospital while the cops guardin your room
You got to see what I've seen, look where I've looked
Touch what I've reached and take what I've took
You got to go where I've gone, walk where I've walked
To get where I'm at to speak what I talk
You got to lay where I've laid, stay where I've stayed
Play where I've played to make what I've made
You got to move what I've moved, use what I used
Use tools how I use, use fools how I use

[Chorus 2x]

BLACKALICIOUS

Blackalicious is the partnership between MC Gift of Gab and producer Chief Xcel. Gift of Gab's flow is fast-paced and laced with multisyllabic rhymes, consciously crafted in relation to the beat. "I'm basically trying to be like another instrument on the track," he explains. "I want to ride it like the bass line is riding it, only with words. I wanna ride it just like the guitar or the violin or whatever instrument, just riding it."[12]

Blackalicious favors songs with clear formal and thematic structures. On "Alphabet Aerobics," for instance, Gab spits lyrics based upon each letter of the alphabet. From these kinds of self-imposed formal constraints, the group achieves a level of creative freedom within the structure.

ALPHABET AEROBICS

Now it's time for our wrap-up. Let's give it everything we've got. Ready? Begin

Artificial amateurs aren't at all amazing
Analytically, I assault, animate things
Broken barriers bounded by the bomb beat
Buildings are broken, basically I'm bombarding
Casually create catastrophes, casualties
Cancelling cats got their canopies collapsing
Detonate a dime of dank, daily do indulge
Demonstrations, Don Dada on the down low
Eatin other editors with each and every energetic
Epileptic episode, elevated etiquette
Furious, fat, fabulous, fantastic
Flurries of funk felt feeding the fanatics
Gift got great global goods gone glorious
Gettin godly in this game with the goriest
Hit 'em high, hella hype, historical
Hey, holocaust hymns, hear 'em, holler at your homeboy
Imitators idolize, I intimidate

In a instant, I'll rise in a irate state

Juiced on my jams like Jheri curls jockin joints

Justly, it's just me, writin my journals

Kindly I'm kindling all kinds of King Kong

Karate Kid type Brits in my kingdom

Let me live a long life, lyrically lessons is

Learned lame louses just lose to my liveries

My mind makes marvelous moves, masses

Marvel and move, many mock what I've mastered

Niggas nap knowin I'm nice naturally

Knack, never lack, make noise nationally

Operation, opposition, off, not optional

Out of sight, out of mind, wide beaming opticals

Perfected poem, powerful punch lines

Pummeling petty powder puffs in my prime

Quite quaint quotes keep quiet, it's Quannum

Quarrelers ain't got a quarter of what we got, uh

Really raw raps, risin up rapidly

Riding the rushing radioactivity

Super scientifical sound search sought

Silencing superfire saps that are soft

Tales ten times talented, too tough

Take that, challengers, get a tune up

Universal, unique, untouched

Unadulterated, the raw uncut

Verb vice lord victorious valid

Violate vibes that are vain, make 'em vanish

Why I'm all well what a wise wordsmith just

Weaving up words, weeded up on my work shift

Xerox, my X-ray-diation holes extra large

X-height letters and xylophone tones

Yellow back, yak mouth, young ones' yaws

Yesterday's lawn yards sell, I yawn

Zig-zag zombies, zoomin to the zenith
Zero in Zen thoughts, overzealous rhyme zealot!

Hahaha. Good. Can you say it faster?

MY PEN & PAD
Here we go [6x]

Back on the journey again, tool is a pad and a pen
Cool as the fan, as the wind soothing you after I send
True inner-vision risen and driven and givin you my
Isms of intuition while niggas is livin a lie
Syllables spill and I fly, high as the pinnacle rhyme
Not to belittle a fool, but try to get into you, my
Lyrics inherited from awareness somewhere in the sky
Clearly, you'll give them merit and cherish 'em better with time
There is none ever and on like rivers so clever I shine
Verbal ambassador travel in this endeavor of mine
Never a antigangster, the ghetto is still in the mind
If I was not rappin, a nigga might be up inside
All of your terraces, stealin wallets and necklaces, I
Give hella gratefulness for the blessing to share this and fly
Everywhere people outside the culture now try to divine
What it is, but it is mine, such it is, love it with blind-
Vision but no division is vivid, we livin inside
Vicious vindictive and mental prisons from within the mind
Sits and I find stillness, from minutes is written the rhyme
Gettin you smitten with it, particularly if you're a prime
Listener, listen up, twist it up like the lyrics was lime
Vintage is instant, so give it up when you hear it reci-ted
At attention, relieving tension and bending yo' spine
Sendin you signals to get yo' internal system aligned
Lyrical pinnacle situation is critical
Syllable after syllable, give it to you, deliver you my
Intervals, sendin you through dimensions you didn't know

Hidden in you, within you, when you get into the begin to intuit

Sentiments, internets, couldn't send you yet signals you get

Ripping through skin and through tissue, fix you elixirs that might

Lift your peripheral vision, the mystical wisdom that tends

To go into the infinite system of livin and this is the ending

As well as the beginning of the Gift in his prime

Mission the bliss is divine, christen it, isn't it fine?

Listen and dissin it, that's the incident innocent

Men and women hit lyrics is killin niggas, they shiverin

The predicament's thick and it splits the wig of the ignorant lyricist

Puttin fear in their spirit—Yo, that's my time! . . .

BROTHER ALI

Brother Ali is known for both his clever wordplay and his confessional subject matter. His lyrics embody a range of emotions—from insecurity to outrage, wry humor to reflection. He confronts difficult personal topics, including divorce, homelessness, and self-doubt. "I always want to make music that's really powerful and personal and real, and that when you hear it, you can feel that feeling that I'm going through. And so the only way that I really know to definitely ensure that is to [write] stuff about my life. Even if I'm writing things that aren't necessarily *my* story, it's somebody very close to me, or something that I've seen or that I've been involved in. So, it's all from real-life things, and then basically at that point the idea is to just tell you what you need to know to understand where this feeling is coming from."[13]

Born with albinism, a defect in melanin production that results in little or no pigment in the skin, hair, and eyes, he takes his physical appearance as a theme in ways both humorous ("Forest Whitaker") and poignant ("Picket Fence"). He is also known for "Uncle Sam Goddamn," a critique of U.S. government actions, both foreign and domestic. "My thing though is that I'm not a political rapper," he explains. "I had one political song ["Uncle Sam Goddamn"] that ended up being a video and a single. But that even isn't really a political song. I'm not talking about policies . . . I'm talking about the greed and the hatred that's written into the history of this country."[14]

ROOM WITH A VIEW

I guess it's nowhere different from anywhere else in the world, man. I look out my
window, I see the whole thing.

One side of the street is Malone's Funeral Home
And the other side's a library . . .

Try very hard to picture this shit, walk through where I live at
Where parents are embarrassed to tell you they raise their kids at
You need some half-and-half or an eight-ball, you can get that
Fuck with Little Rodney and you'll get all of your ribs cracked
In a location where slanging (crack rock) is not seen
As a fuckin recreation but a vocation
And the sellers and the smokers are both pacin
Got one eye on Minneapolis P.D., they both racin
Three for fifty is the supply and demand
And the Twin Cities, American heartland
And they been busy, masterminds tearing apart plans
And hoop dreamers ballin with blisters on they hands
With chains danglin from the rims
Pain strangles 'em from within
'Til a belt around the arm makes the veins stand at ATTENTION

I try to block it out with a bedsheet, the moonlight's as a curtain
'Cause I'm not comforted by red and blue lights when I'm hurtin
Mommy loves you. Yeah, I knew but I wasn't certain
'Cause the lenses through which she views life wasn't workin
As a boy she told me, "Wait 'til your father to come home"
I'm twenty-four, still waitin for my father to come home
And some parents only touch they children when the whip's brought
That's why bad kids do bad shit, just so they could get caught

And get touched, this growing up shit's rough

That's a big part of why we're so mixed up

Shit, we don't have Bar Mitzvahs, we become men

The first time our father hits us, and we don't open gifts up

Sister Regina from across the street is beautiful

But for fifty bucks ain't nothing she won't do to you

Used to be premium pussy, now she used up

For that same fifty bucks she got to do some new stuff

Whatever it takes to make you pull the dollars out

If you don't intervene then there's a day she'll turn her daughter out

Speaking of kids, I'm fixing lunch for my firstborn

I had the windows wide open 'cause the weather's warm

That's when the greatest hits of Donny Hathaway

Got interrupted by a drive-by shooting half a block away

Faheem was in the window, he didn't get hit, though

All praise due Allah

[Chorus 3x]

I see all this from the desk that I write my rhymes from

Pen starts to scribble on its own, my mind's numb

But you can call me modern urban Norman Rockwell

I paint a picture of the spot well

PICKET FENCE

I was up and out my mother's house at seventeen

Been a grown-ass married man ever since

Family reunions, I'm talked about but never seen

'Cause I learned that some of them can be your nemesis

Got a lot of scars on me and I'll tell you the stories

If you promise not to take offense

Homie, sit back, let Ant bring the beat in

I'll try to find a place that starts to make sense now

The first time I was pushed out blind

Cold and naked, spanked on the ass to breathe

An immigrant from heaven on Earth with a word piece
I announce myself with gasping screams
Before blight and white supremacy heisted my innocence
I was living out life behind the picket fence
Happy go lucky, scared of no one
With only the exception I'm allergic to the sun
Didn't know I had a image that a camera couldn't capture
One hundred percent Allah's manufacture
But then came the laughter and outside a battered
Picket fence shattered, I saw myself
As a bastard tag-along, harassed and spat upon
By the children of slave masters who passed it on
The saddest songs have been sung at the hands of
Who I call the race from hell, it's a disgrace from hell
Fell face first into self-hate
Burst into tears when I'd hear my own hellish name cursed
If I seem timid, it's only because every mirror
That I saw back then had the Earth's ugliest human being in it
And with that said
They would kick me 'til they got tired or I act dead
And I have to tell y'all that the obvious part
Is I always feel free when I'm talking to God
Alone on the playground, Friday afternoon
And the old sister who hums gospel tunes
I saw her, noticed her getting closer
She approached me and put a knowing hand on my shoulder
And booked my feelings 'cause she looked at me
In a way that adults very seldom look at children
And with the wisdom only earned by years
She read my thoughts and she welled up with tears and said:

"You look the way you do because you're special
Not the short bus way, I mean that God's gonna test you
And all of this pain is training for the day when you
Will have to lead with the gift God gave to you

Grown folks don't see it, but the babies do
And there's a chance that you can save a few"
And time would prove that, she started my movement
She didn't tell me to take it, she told me to use it

The second time Poppa ripped the womb open early
And exposed me to the coldness of life prematurely
Where Mom's love used to live now housed denial
And when that decayed, it made her bitter and spiteful
But me and my runaway, we share something special
Rode into the sunset, could barely touch the pedals
No strings attached, screaming, "Fuck Geppetto"
We may live in the gutter, but we cling to each other
A week before my son came, I caught a bad bounce
And had to step to Mom with my hands out
And Mama proved the two of us could not live in that house
She lied to the police so they would throw us in the streets
And separatin from you is something I feel I must do
It's not that I don't love you, it's more that I don't trust you
It's been a year since I've seen a living relative
And it's just now that I'm starting to live
But while I'm sitting here, choking on tears, wishing I didn't care
Feeling all alone in this hemisphere, I swear upon
Everything I hold dear and then my wife come near
And I hear a voice whisper in my ear:

"You're going through all of this because you're special
Not no superstar shit, I mean that God had to test you
And all of this pain has been training for the day when you
Would lead us with the gift God gave to you
Your parents might not see it, but your babies do
And there's a chance that you can save a few"
And time would prove that, she started my movement
She didn't tell me to take it, she told me to use it

So I use it

CAM'RON

Cam'ron was born and raised in Harlem amid poverty but also amid the atmosphere of creativity that has made Harlem synonymous with African American artistic achievement for generations. In the 1990s Cam formed part of the group Children of the Corn alongside his cousin Bloodshed, Digga, and two other MCs who would go on to have solo success, Ma$e and Big L. Cam'ron would ultimately found The Diplomats (also known as Dipset) and would help foster a roster of talented MCs that includes Jim Jones, Juelz Santana, JR Writer, and others.

Cam's solo career began in 1999 with *Confessions of Fire,* which featured the hit collaboration with Ma$e, "Horse & Carriage." It also introduced Cam's signature sound, which draws from hard-edged themes of crime and which includes the occasional R&B-inflected tracks. As *Pitchfork* notes, "Cam's flow is a thing of beauty. His bored, arrogant voice rolls syllables around until he's hit just about every possible permutation, transforming hard consonants into thrown rocks and idly toying with drug metaphors like they're Rubik's Cubes. In Cam's world, he's the king of Harlem, moving kilos, dispatching foes, and throwing around money with Machiavellian cool."[15]

GET IT IN OHIO

What up, Midwest? They forgot about the fourth coast—it ain't nuthin, though.
   What up, Arkansas, Minnesota, Kansas, Kentucky, Missouri? Everybody in
   the Lou . . . Holla!

Thinkin 'bout Guy Fisher
Never met him, but goddamn, that's my nigga
I figure real estate investor, pie flipper
Never snitch. Me, I'm in a bathrobe, fly slippers
Left Chicago with good money for five drops
West Side, did the South Side like the White Sox (What up, Stony Island?)
Vamboo and Pulaski, K-Town is Contra (Westside)
They'll dearly depart ya in front of MacArthur's (What up, Madison?)
I'm the author for gangstas, tough guys

Did the whole Ohio, but I started off a Buckeye
Columbus to 'Nati, them towns, I raped 'em
Few clowns was hatin, moved my pounds to Dayton
And in Akron, my niggas they would throw things
Not King James, these were coke kings
And he actin grown, doggy, you ain't back at home
The smack, it's on, wrapped in chrome, you better get a chaperone

[Chorus]
If you know like I know, you should lie low
Killa, I used to get it in Ohio
Don't forget the Chi though, guns are like a pyro
You keep playin you will look like a gyro

Yo, go 'head and hate me, hater, 'cause I'm flyer than a aviator
Well, you'll get smacked with the radiator
And I get catered, playa, wanna talk? Maybe later
Told her, her time was up, eighty-eight her, Flavor Flaved her
Need ya neck choked, rather your neck broke
Ya dead broke, yes folks, the jewels are like egg yolks
And you'll get yolked up, switchblade, poked up
Bitch-made since sixth grade, he need his rope cut
Cowboy roped up, y'all boys sold what?
Know what? Dope, crack, and coke is in the coat tucked
Roll up, hold up, family, this a holdup
Get close up, soaked up, I'm KG, post up
Ho, slut, no love, turn beef to cold cuts
Family gettin bread? Well, he about to get his loaf cut
Y'all doped up, this game is sewed up
Malcolm X, tell the white bitch: "Yo, I want my toes sucked"

[Chorus]

I'd rather be judged by twelve than carried by six
My twelve to twelve? Well, they carry my bricks
And them twelve-twelve fiends, they're married to sniff

And the V12? That's on various strips
Y'all make a brother laugh; me, I took another path
Come into my habitat, hovercrafts, bubble baths,
Duffle bags stuffed with cash, fell in love with math
I got the green Benz, red Range, mustard Jag
White coke, tan dope, black gun, Tre-Deuce
Silver bullets, purple piff, blue pills, Grey Goose
Pull out the rat-a-tat, duck-duck, say "Goose"
Beige Coupe, suede roofs, send him off to Jesus
H-deuce, yeah yeah, piss off the state troops
See me, then they don't, I disappear, say poof
Play Zeus. Homeboy, get a replaced tooth
Not 'Pac, mean dust when a nigga say "juice"
Killa, Killa

[Chorus]

CEE-LO

Cee-Lo, who made his name first as a member of Atlanta's Goodie
Mob and later as the lead singer of Gnarls Barkley, has built his
solo rap career on inventive and experimental sounds that fuse
hip-hop with soul, funk, blues, and electronica. His themes range from the
street to the spiritual. "There's a bit of Buddhism, a bit of that Baptist and
that Christianity, and Five Percent," he says by way of explaining the faith
expressed in his music. "My awareness is broad. To claim a religion is almost like to claim a gang or set, which would make you an adversary of another . . . and rightfully so, because you oppose their beliefs or question
their beliefs. I think that there's validity in all of the interpretations."[16]

As a member of hip-hop's southern fraternity, he is well aware of the
perception that southern artists lack lyrical complexity. Songs like "Big Ole
Words (Damn)" and "Childz Play" (the latter included here) demonstrate
beyond any doubt Cee-Lo's technical virtuosity and idiosyncratic style.

CHILDZ PLAY
(feat. Ludacris)

[Cee-Lo]
Well, hello, howdy do. How are you? That's good
Who me? I'm still hot. I still got. You got me?
I'm here, I'm there, 'cause I'm raw, 'cause I'm rare
I can spit on anything, got plenty game, authentic
My pen's sick, forensic, defends it, he wins it
Again and again and again and again and a
I'm the one, come see, lookey I, and come meet
The young Cee, the one treats everything the sun seek
I'm hollerin. Can you help? I'm hungry
I cake rap, bake rap, sack rap, trap rap
Same shoes, same shirt, the same work, the same jerk
Claim hurt, the game hurt, my name work, that ain't work?
I'm fast. How fast? I'm first, I'm last
Psychic, I knew you would like it like this
I write this, priceless, more than my right wrist
Cock back, block track, the beat bleed discretely
No need weed to feed seed, I speed-read, you need me
To give it to you like you want it, I own it when I'm on it
Maintain the same thing, nigga rap about the same game
None left, shame shame, plain game, insane
When I rap things change. Me and God? Same thing
Money jingle, money fold, I'm young, my money old
Maybe look, cross hanging down to my tummy toes
I know it, I'ma stop, I'm trying, it's like lyin

Yes, I can sing and I can rap
And I can act and I can dance
And I can dress and I'm the best
So is my guest—man, I'm impressed
Hurry, hurry, hurry, hurry, come and see
This is just like child's play to me, ah ha
Little melody and a little drum

All I really need to have a little fun
Hush, little one, let's get it done
Dress like a bum, bust like a gun
Hurry, hurry, hurry, hurry, come and see
This is just like child's play to me, ah ha

[Ludacris]
Who the only little nigga that you know with 'bout fifty flows
Do about fifty shows in a week but creep on the track with my tippy toes
Shhh, shut the fuck up, I'm tryin to work
Ah, forget it, I'm going berserk
'Cause I stack my change and I'm back to claim
My reign on top, so pack your thangs
I've racked your brain like crack cocaine
My fame won't stop or I'll jack your chain
Give it up, dad a ding ding ding, thanks, the price was right
That Grey Goose got me loose, but my eyes are tight
It's the truth, give me a light like I'm dyn-o-mite
Alright, alright, we gon' ride tonight
I'm so dangerous that I gotta bang with this
You could be famous or remain nameless
Better just drop down to your knees, call upon the Lord and pray
Better luck next time but you wanna open that door today
Your hair sorta gray, it's that sorta day
Flowing so hard over this track and I got more to say
I ain't new to this, I'm so true to this
See what you get fucking with Cee-Lo and Ludacris?

[Chorus 2x]

*Haha. Okay, there you have it, little kids. Wasn't that fun? Yeah. Saturday
morning, Cee-Lo Green and my man Ludacris. Doing this thing, ATL style.
This is child's play to us. Seriously though, I can rap better than you guys with
my tongue tied. Ha ha ha. Don't make me get serious on your ass. You
wouldn't like me when I'm serious. I could have said anything I wanted to . . .*

THE CLIPSE

The Clipse's brand of music is often derisively referred to as "crack rap" for its frequent references to the drug trade, but these lyricists are unconstrained by their subject matter. The group consists of Malice and Pusha T, a pair of brothers from Virginia Beach, Virginia. After connecting with Pharrell Williams of the Neptunes in the mid-1990s, they began working with the producer on crafting their distinctive sound. Though many of their songs tell tales of drug trafficking, their verses are rich and varied. As Pusha T explains, "It's one thing to say 'I sell bricks, I sell bricks.' But when you saying 'Trunk like Aspen / Looking like a million muthafuckin crushed aspirins,' dog, we getting back to the colors. A lot of dudes is working with the eight crayons in the box. They do not have the sixty-four box, yo. They don't got 'Burnt Sienna.' They got red, yellow, blue."[17]

Some of The Clipse's finest work can be found on their mix tapes, represented here by "Zen." With lyrical support from the other two members of the Re-Up Gang, Roscoe P. Coldchain and Ab Liva, they deliver hard-hitting rhymes, often over familiar beats from recent hip-hop hits.

GRINDIN

Yo, I go by the name . . . (I'm your pusher) of Pharrell from the Neptunes . . . and I
  just wanna let y'all know . . . (I'm your pusher) the world is about to feel . . .
  something . . . (I'm your pusher) that they never felt before. C'mon . . .

[Pusha T]
From ghetto to ghetto, to backyard to yard
I sell it whip on whip, it's off the hard
I'm the . . . neighborhood pusher
Call me subwoofer, 'cause I pump base like that, Jack
On or off the track, I'm heavy, Cuz
Ball 'til you fall 'cause you could duck to the Fedy govs
Sorry, my love, but I'm seeing through these eyes
Benz convoys with the wagon on the side
Only big boys keep deuces on the ride
Gucci Chuck Taylor with the dragon on the side

Man, I make a buck, why scram?
I'm trying to show y'all who the fuck I am
The jewels is flirtin, be damned if I'm hurtin
Legend in two games like I'm Pee Wee Kirkland
Platinum on the block with consistent hits
While Pharrell keep talking this music shit

[Chorus 5x]
Grindin! (Ahhh)

[Malice]
Patty cake, patty cake, I'm the baker's man
I bake them cakes as fast as I can
And you can tell by how my bread stack up
And disguise it as rap so the Feds back up
Watch it, like my whip like my chick: topless
Doing a buck-six with me in the cockpit
Grindin, cousin, I got holes for a dozen
Even eleven-five, if I see ya keep it comin
And my weight, that's just as heavy as my name
So much dough, I can't swear I won't change
Excuse me if my wealth got me full of myself
Cocky's something that I just can't help
'Specially when them twenties is spinning like windmills
And the ice thirty-two below minus the wind chill
Filthy the word that best defines me
I'm just grinding, man, y'all never mind me

[Chorus 5x]

Grindin, you know what I keep in a lining
Niggas better stay in line when
You see a nigga like me shinin (Grinding!)
Grindin, you know what I keep in a lining
Niggas better stay in line when
You see a nigga like me shinin (Grinding!)

[Malice]

My grind's 'bout family, never been about fame

Them days I wasn't able, there was always 'caine

Four and a half will get you in the game

Anything less is just a goddamn shame

Guess the weight, my watch got blue chips in the face

Glock with two tips whoever gets in the way

Not to mention the hideaway that rests by the lake

Consider my raw demeanor the icing on the cake

I'm grinding...

[Pusha T]

I move 'caine like a cripple

Balance weight through the 'hood, kids call me Mr. Sniffles

Other hand on my nickel-

Plated whistle, one eye closed I'll hit you

As if I was Slick Rick, my aim is still an issue

Lose your soul in... whichever palm I'm holdin

One'll leave you frozen, the other, noddin and dozin

I'm grindin, Jack...

[Chorus 5x]

Grindin, you know what I keep in a lining

Niggas better stay in line when

You see a nigga like me shinin (Grinding!)

Grindin, you know what I keep in a lining

Niggas better stay in line when

You see a nigga like me shinin (Grinding!)

ZEN
(feat. Roscoe P. Coldchain and Ab Liva)
[Chorus]

Is it them blings that make them watch us?

The awkward lean and the cars that's topless?

I got them things, I cut and chop it
I sell that ostrich, I'm so obnoxious
Gettin money, say . . .

[Pusha T]
Hands got the bubble touch, bike with the double clutch
Two diamond jump ropes, my neck do the double dutch
Give a fuck about such and such
On behalf of the Re-Up Gang I'm saying enough's enough
Turn it, turn it, fire burn it
Gram weight straight like a nigga just permed it
Pyrex and water, playa, how I earns it
Lame rap niggas, I'm so not concerned with
On another level, my third bezel, my fourth gas pedal
Fifty-five on the back, I'm a daredevil
The course is paved, the watch is Pave
You niggas gotta love me, I'm somethin the Lord made

[Roscoe P. Coldchain]
I got, gots to do it, do it
VVS my jewelry, don't need no jury
To find me guilty, I stay Goldie
Pockets bulky, how can y'all fault me?
Ghostrider driver, what that mean?
You small wheelin, nigga, fuck that Beam, us that team
Touch that C.R.E.A.M., digital scale, what's that scheme?
(It's all real) I won't touch that theme (Fake!)
Nigga's face gets spat in, then clacked in
Squad wants action, Re-Run, what's happenin?
Every episode, the TEC exposed, Gotti bodies
Tsunami homies, that's gotta be why they watch me

[Chorus]
Zen zen zen . . .

[Ab Liva]

Now, how that forearm glow on 'em, feelin so grown on 'em

I pitch work, sorta like Nomo on 'em

Snow on 'em, cover my tracks low on 'em

So on 'em streets I push blow on 'em

The car driver, the soft top like Bose on 'em

Rose on 'em, gold on 'em, I'm strikin the pose on 'em

No opponent can come close, match tone on it

Flow on it, hone on it, I'm feelin at home on it

That's Liva, the right of the man that hang clothes on 'em

With the belt matchin the shoes, the G soles on 'em

I'm classic, the plastique got olds on 'em

I rose on 'em, the self-murder doors close on 'em

[Malice]

Yeah … Good gosh almighty!

All we do is cook raw, push cars like whitey

Like a moth to a flame, it's so inviting

To opposite sexes, the stones so precious

Still in the resi', G-4, or Lear

No diamond in that bezie, I get growner every year

Pay me for that feature, that don't make it family

All I see is blackface and you singin "Mammy"

I'm from the old school when the gat was a jammy

Twin four-fifths, the resemblance is uncanny

I bust both in sync—Y'all niggas hear me

Now that's what I call the Big Bang Theory

[Chorus]

DEAD PREZ

Dead prez are hip-hop's self-styled political revolutionaries for the new millennium. Stic.man and M-1 have fashioned a body of work that goes beyond the music to describe an entire philosophy of living, down to dietary habits and exercise regimens. Beginning with their debut album, *Let's Get Free* (2000), the incendiary cover art of which included a photograph of a slave with a whip-mangled back on one side and a group of young, gun-toting revolutionaries with their hands in the air on the other, dead prez reignited a long-standing hip-hop tradition of radical political rhymes.

Their songs use an array of formal techniques to inculcate an eclectic political philosophy that draws equally from Marxist tracts, socialist manifestos, and spiritual books from the East like the I Ching. Although they sometimes rap allegorically (as on the Orwellian apocalyptic track "Animal in Man"), "Police State" and "Hip-Hop" opt for a more direct approach, with striking lyrics delivered in syncopated flows that draw from southern rhythms as well as New York styles.

POLICE STATE

[Chairman Omali Yeshitela]

You have the emergence in human society of this thing that's called the State.
  What is the State? The State is this organized bureaucracy. It is the po-lice
  department. It is the army, the navy. It is the prison system, the courts, and
  what have you. This is the State—it is a repressive organization. But the State—
  "And, gee, well, you know, you've got to have the police, 'cause . . . if there were
  no police, look at what you'd be doing to yourselves! You'd be killing each
  other if there were no police!" But the reality is . . . the police become
  necessary in human society only at that junction in human society where it is
  split between those who have and those who ain't got.

[stic.man]

I throw a Molotov cocktail at the precinct, you know how we think
Organize the 'hood under I Ching banners

Red, black, and green instead of gang bandanas

FBI spyin on us through the radio antennas

And them hidden cameras in the streetlight watchin society

With no respect for the people's right to privacy

I'll take a slug for the cause like Huey P.

While all you fake niggas (Unnngh!) try to copy Master P

I wanna be free to live, able to have what I need to live

Bring the power back to the street, where the people live

We sick of workin for crumbs and fillin up the prisons

Dyin over money and relyin on religion for help

We do for self like ants in a colony

Organize the wealth into a socialist economy

A way of life based off the common need

And all my comrades is ready, we just spreadin the seed

[Chorus]

The average black male

Live a third of his life in a jail cell

'Cause the world is controlled by the white male

And the people don't never get justice

And the women don't never get respected

And the problems don't never get solved

And the jobs don't never pay enough

So the rent always be late. Can you relate?

We livin in a police state

[M-1]

No more bondage, no more political monsters

No more secret space launches

Government departments started it in the projects

Material objects, thousands up in the closets

Could've been invested in the future for my comrades

Battle contacts, primitive weapons out in combat

Many never come back, pretty niggas be runnin with gats

Rather get shot in they back than fire back

We tired of that—corporations hirin blacks

Denyin the facts, exploitin us all over the map

That's why I write the shit I write in my raps; it's documented

I meant it, every day of the week, I live in it

Breathin it, it's more than just fuckin believin it

I'm holdin M1s, rollin up my sleeves and shit

It's cee-lo for push-ups, now many headed for one conclusion

Niggas ain't ready for revolution

[Chorus]

[Fred Hampton]

I am . . . a revolutionary. And you're gonna have to keep on sayin that . . . You're gonna have to say that I am a proletariat. I am the people, I'm not the pig.

[Unidentified Speaker]

Giuliani, you are full of shit! And anybody that's down with you! You could man-make things better for us and you cuttin the welfare, knowin damn well when you cut the welfare, a person gon' do crime.

HIP-HOP

Uh, uh, uh, 1, 2, 1, 2

Uh, uh, 1, 2, 1, 2, uh, uh

All my dogs

[Chorus]

It's bigger than hip-hop, hip-hop, hip-hop, hip

It's bigger than hip-hop, hip-hop, hip-hop, hip-hop

[M-1]

Uh, one thing 'bout music, when it hit you feel no pain

White folks say it controls your brain. I know better than that, that's game

And we ready for that, two soldiers head of the pack—matter of fact, who got the gat?

And where my army at? Rather attack and not react

Back the beats, it don't reflect on how many records get sold

On sex, drugs, and rock and roll, whether your project's put on hold

In the real world, these just people with ideas

They just like me and you when the smoke and cameras disappear

Again, the real world (world) is bigger than all these fake ass records

When po' folks got the millions and my woman's disrespected

If you check 1, 2, my word of advice to you is just relax

Just do what you got to do, if that don't work then kick the facts

If you a fighter, rider, biter, flame igniter, crowd exciter

Or you wanna just get high, then just say it. But then if you

A liar-liar, pants on fire, wolf-cry, agent with a wire

I'm gon' know it when I play it

[Chorus]

[stic.man]

Who shot Biggie Smalls? If we don't get them, they gonna get us all

I'm down for runnin up on them crackers in they city hall

We ride for y'all, all my dogs stay real

Nigga, don't think these record deals gonna feed your seeds and pay your
　　bills

Because they not. MCs get a little bit of love and think they hot

Talkin 'bout how much money they got, all y'all records sound the same

I'm sick of that fake thug, R&B, rap scenario all day on the radio

Same scenes in the video, monotonous material

Y'all don't hear me though, these record labels slang out tapes like dope

You can be next in line, and signed, and still be writing rhymes and broke

You would rather have a Lexus or justice, a dream or some substance?

A Beamer, a necklace, or freedom?

See, a nigga like me don't playa hate, I just stay awake

This real hip-hop and it don't stop

'Til we get the po-po off the block. They call it …

[Chorus]

Uh, DP's got that crazy shit, we keep it crunk up
John blazed and shit—what?

(Fake, fake, fake records)

DEVIN THE DUDE

D evin the Dude is a hip-hop comic—not a clown but a trickster, finding humor in unlikely places. In the 1990s Devin signed with Houston's Rap-A-Lot Records, which was best known for the raw street rhymes of Scarface and the Geto Boys. He forged an alternative persona: part stoner, part lady's man, all lyricist. Describing his writing, he observed that "60 percent is really just personal shit I went through; 20 percent is stuff I know about somebody who's close, or a story I heard. Ten percent is wishful thinking. And the other 10 percent is some high shit we just thought of [Laughs]."[18] His playfulness is on display on "Briarpatch," a modern-day reinvention of the Br'er Rabbit tale.

BRIARPATCH
[Chorus]
The briar patch
No, don't throw me in the briar patch
You can cut off all my toes, but not the briar patch
You can fill me full of holes, but not the briar patch
Don't throw me in the briar patch
Don't throw me in the briar patch
Please don't put me in the briar patch
You can season and cook me, but not the briar patch
For me, no one would ever look off in the briar patch
Don't throw me in the briar patch
Don't throw me in the briar patch

I hop, I jump, I skip through the rubble

Yo, me ain't lookin for trouble

I's just tryin to get to the other end, I never been

Maybe then I can tell my friends how it is, I been

Searching for someone to help me, maybe you can

But it's hard to tell you how I feel when you got a knife in ya hand

You can carve me, tie me up and starve me

Put me on the grill, still, nothing can harm me

Like the briar patch ... Don't chunk me in

What kind of luck would I have then?

Wait a minute, man, before you put me in it, use the gun

Bet you got a couple of bullets; I'll be finished, done

Or, hey, I can help you find a pot

Help you build a fire, help you get it good and hot

Well, unless you like to eat me cold

You can, but oh no, please don't throw me in

[Chorus]

You's an ugly motherfucker, dog, I just call it like I see it

And yo' breath is like death, if you don't like it so be it

I get mistreated by others if you cut for me or not

Slice off my toes if that's how it goes. I really don't give a fuck

If all this belongs to you, do what you do, go 'head

But throw me in the briar's patch and you'll never see so much red

I bled for less than just trespassing 'cause I'm just askin for a favor

Excuse my rude behavior, I'm just

Trying to savor the flavor of the fruit I just picked

And if you don't like it, you can suck my diiiiiiiiiiii-

-iiiick! But what you don't do

Is throw me in the briar patch and then I'm through

Come on, man. Can't we call a truce? Can't we do somethin about it

Before people end up crying and shoutin and poutin?

Man, come on, man
Now that would really hurt off in the church

[Chorus]

DOOM

D OOM (also known as MF DOOM) is among the most enigmatic figures in hip-hop—both for the trademark mask that he dons at
concerts and for the recondite nature of his lyrics. DOOM's raspy
baritone weaves an intricate web of allusions drawn from comic books and
metaphysics along with seeming nonsense and non sequiturs.

DOOM's career began in the early 1990s under the name Zev Love X as
a member of the group KMD along with his younger brother, DJ Subroc,
and another MC, Onyx the Birthstone Kid. They produced only two albums, *Mr. Hood* (1991) and *Black Bastards* (which was completed in 1994
but not released until 2000). The group disbanded shortly after Subroc died
in a 1993 car accident. Zev Love X retreated from the hip-hop scene for
several years before returning as MF DOOM in the late 1990s. His work includes album-length collaborations with producers Madlib (Madvillany)
and Danger Mouse (Danger Doom) as well as solo albums both as DOOM
and as his alter egos Viktor Vaughn, Metal Fingers, and King Geedorah.

To read DOOM's lyrics is to relinquish the need for certitude. His lines
often defy paraphrase. "Ever since third grade, I had a notebook and was
putting together words just for fun," he told Ta-Nehisi Coates in the *New
Yorker.* "I liked different etymologies, different slang that came out in different eras. Different languages. Different dialects. I liked being able to
speak to somebody and throw it back and forth, and they can't predict what
you're going to say next. But once you say it they're always like, 'Oh, shit!'"[19]

BENZI BOX
(feat. Cee-Lo)
[Chorus: Cee-Lo]
His name's DOOM

They wonder just who is he
But don't worry
Believe me, he'll get busy
When it comes to ...
Poetry he's got plenty la la la ...
La la la la la la

Jump 'em in like jump rope
Double dutch then turn on the mic with a thumb stroke
Subtle touch, cuddle clutch, is this thing on?
Like the fling with Mrs. King Kong, this spring gone
Sing a song of slap-happy crappiness
He came to flow like it was strapped to his nappy chest
Surely I jest, the best on a wireless
Mic not an eye test, yet I digress
But why stress, try and remember when
Maybe bit the tender-skinned babysitter Gwendolyn
The type to hit and run and go tell a friend
Word to El Muerto Cucaracha Exo-Skeleton
He know, flow like interstellar wind
Tow a rap djinn by his toe into hell again
Ahem! One, two, check me, too
Loose wreck, see through your goose-neck EQ

[Chorus]

Ay! If I may interject
Rap these days is like a pain up in the neck
Cornier and phonier than a play fight
Take two of these and don't phone me on the late night
The beat won't fail me
With more rhymes than times he wash his hands and feet daily
And all that kerosene ain't cheap
Villain been deep since a teenage creep, peep
He always was a gentleman

And kept a pen and a pencil in his mental den
Right there next to where the Rolodex was
Before it turned up all burnt by his solar plexus
He don't know his own strength
When he's on the bone it's like the microphone's length
And width . . . Ain't it funky like dingy socks
Feel the full effect off cassette in your Benzi Box

[Chorus]

SALIVA (AS VIKTOR VAUGHN)
Great balls of fire!
Guess who just crawled out the muck and mire
That could make you trust a motherfuckin liar?
A real shuck 'n' jiver, Vaughn never been a duck 'n' diver
He spit on the mic, yuck, saliva
Hold it like a drunk driver, hold a CB on a sharp turn
Still clutchin his chest from the heartburn
What's your handle? I need a Zantac, ack
And thanks before I blank into anaphylactic shock
Rock or disco? Chocolate or the Crisco ho?
Cock diesel, still tell a joke like Joe Piscopo
Tell 'em the basics: basically, break the Matrix
And just for kicks, make 'em gel like Asics
That's why they actin standoffish
Eat the beat by hand like canned raw crawfish
Can you please pass the cocktail sauce?
You might as well know, hell is hot as hell, boss
"Tell my horse" . . . He said, "Broads call me Vaughny"
I make sure I throws 'em back if they's too scrawny
Or boney, phony MCs use a stand-in
Leave him hangin like if I ain't know where his hand's been
Hussy, how 'bout we bloody up ya "just for me"
Bust a knee, then go finish study a plus degree

True victory, a new sick story

I never met a chick that was too thick for me

Holy Moses, my old Earth know me closest

And how I played the back and stayed bent like scoliosis

It's no puzzle, you can ask Doc Zizmor

The slow guzzle got your nizzle crooked like Biz jaw

Drink like a fishy, he wish she was a Pisces

Live since back when twenty-five cents Icees

Used to turn your tongue the color red

Now they want to fill ya full of lead. What the fuck that young fella said?

What, kid? It's Vaughn, the red-blooded

Do yourself a favor or come on, get head butted

Yoke him if he run, I'll be there in a jiffy, son

With the flame suppressor like off the 151

Quit your bitchin, or get *BLAOW* in your babble-box

Punishment for dry snitchin, now eat this Travel Fox

You'll be aight once it pass through your yellow belly

Only thing he said was, "Can you please pass the jelly?"

"Homosaywhat?" Like a promo play the cut on the late night

Before you touch the mic, get your weight right

A lot of crews like to act like a violent mob

They really need to just shut the fuck up like Silent Bob

Either that or get smoked like hickory

Should squash the beef and go wash they teeth quickly

Know the stee, write a rhyme like a mystery

And sign it at the bottom in calligraphy, "Your nigga, V"

FIGARO

The rest is empty with no brain, but the clever nerd

The best MC with no chain ya ever heard

Take it from the TEC-9 holder

They bit and don't know they neck shine from shineola

Everything that glitter ain't fishscale. Let me think

Don't let her faint, get Ishmael

A shot of Jack got her back, it's not a act, stack

Forgot about the cackalack, holla back, clack clack blocka

Villainy, feel him in ya heart chakra

Chart toppa, star, shit stoppa, be a smart shoppa

Shot a cop day around the way 'bout to stay

But who'd a know there's two mo' that wonder where the shooter go

'Bout to jet, get him, not a bet, dead 'em

Let 'em spit the venom, said 'em got a lot of shit with 'em

Let the rhythm hit 'em, it's stronger in the other voice

We makes the joints that make 'em spread 'em butta moist

Man, please. The stage is made of panties

From the age of baby hoochies on to the grannies

Ban me the dough rake, daddy, the flow make her

Fatty shake, patty cake, patty cake

For fake, if he was Anita Baker's man

He'd take her for her masters, hit it once an' shake her hand

On some ol' "Thank ya, ma'am" an' ghost her

She could mind the toaster if she sign the poster

A whole host of roller coaster riders

Not enough tracks (is it?) Hot enough, black? (for ya)

It's too hot to handle, you got blue sandals

Who shot ya? Ooh, got you new spots to vandal

Do not stand still, boast show-skills close

But no crills, toast for po' Lil's, post no bills

Coast to coast Joe Shmoe's flows ill, go chill

Not supposed to overdose, No-Doz pills

Off pride tykes talk wide through scar meat

Off sides like how Warf ride with Starfleet

Told ya, on some get-rich shit

As he gets older he gets colder than a witch tit

This is it, make no mistakes

Where my nigga go? Figaro, Figaro

O's beats and my rhymes attack

A scary act, all black like Miss Mary Mack

Wait 'til you see him live on the piano

When DOOM sings soprano like: "Uno dos y'ano"

My mama told me

Blast him and pass her glass of Ol' E

Not to be troublesome, but I could sure use

A quick shot of double rum, no stick of bubble gum

I like ice cream, we could skip the wedding

Have a nice dream, she only let him stick the head in

EMINEM

E minem is one of rap's most polarizing figures—a global celebrity whose personal struggles play themselves out for public view, an instigator in the culture wars, an exhibitionist at times but also a recluse, and above all, a gifted lyricist. "Air Jordan. Tiger Woods. You know how a person is made for something?" remarks 50 Cent. "Eminem is made for hip-hop. The best rapper is a white man."[20] That Eminem is one of the few white MCs to gain both popular success and respect among his peers has made him a pivotal figure in hip-hop's emergence in the mainstream.

He is the past decade's best-selling artist, outpacing the Beatles and Britney Spears, and two of his albums—*The Marshall Mathers LP* and *The Eminem Show*—have sold approximately ten million copies each. More than his considerable album sales, Eminem distinguishes himself by his lyrical skill. He's earned the attention of many outside of rap, including unlikely fans such as the Irish poet and Nobel laureate Seamus Heaney, who marvels at his "verbal energy."

Eminem plays with persona. He embodies three distinct poetic identities in his work: Slim Shady, his outrageous and antic voice, filled with pop cultural references and descriptions of absurd indulgence; Eminem, his hungry battle rapper voice; and Marshall Mathers, his given name and his more confessional voice. "When does Slim Shady kick in, when does Eminem step in, where does Marshall begin?" Eminem asks. "Let's say 'Just Don't Give a Fuck' is Slim Shady. Eminem is 'Lose Yourself,' and 'Mockingbird' is Marshall. I think those are the most blatant, extreme examples."[21] All three are included in the lyrics that follow.

JUST DON'T GIVE A FUCK

[Frogger]
Whoa! Ay, get your hands in the air, and get to clappin 'em and, like, back and forth because, ah, this is . . . what you thought it wasn't. It beez . . . the brothers representin the Dirty Dozen. I be the F-R-O-the-double-G and check out the man; he goes by the name of, er . . .

Slim Shady, brain-dead like Jim Brady
I'm a M80, you lil' like that Kim lady
I'm buzzin, Dirty Dozen, naughty rotten rhymer
Cursin at you players worse than Marty Schottenheimer
You wacker than the motherfucker you bit your style from
You ain't gon' sell two copies if you press a double album
Admit it, fuck it, while we coming out in the open
I'm doing acid, crack, smack, coke, and smokin dope then
My name is Marshall Mathers, I'm an alcoholic ("Hi, Marshall")
I have a disease and they don't know what to call it
Better hide your wallet 'cause I'm coming up quick to strip your cash
Bought a ticket to your concert just to come and whip your ass
Bitch, I'm coming out swinging, so fast it'll make your eyes spin
You gettin knocked the fuck out like Mike Tyson
The Proof is in the puddin, just ask DeShaun Holton
I'll slit your motherfucking throat worse than Ron Goldman

[Chorus]
So when you see me on your block with two Glocks
Screaming "Fuck the World" like Tupac
I just don't give a fuck!
Talkin that shit behind my back, dirty mackin
Tellin your boys that I'm on crack
I just don't give a fuck!
So put my tape back on the rack

Go run and tell your friends my shit is wack

I just don't give a fuck!

But see me on the street and duck

'Cause you gon' get stuck, stoned, and snuffed

'Cause I just don't give a fuck!

I'm Nicer than Pete, but I'm on a Serch to crush a Miilkbone

I'm Everlasting, I melt Vanilla Ice like silicone

I'm ill enough to just straight up dis you for no reason

I'm colder than snow season when it's twenty below freezing

Flavor with no seasoning, this is the sneak preview

I'll dis your magazine and still won't get a weak review

I'll make your freak leave you, smell the Folgers crystals

This is a lyrical combat—gentlemen, hold your pistols

But I form like Voltron and blast you with my shoulder missiles

Slim Shady, Eminem was the old initials (Bye-bye!)

Extortion, snortin, supportin abortion

Pathological liar, blowing shit out of proportion

The looniest, zaniest, spontaneous, sporadic

Impulsive thinker, compulsive drinker, addict

Half animal, half man

Dumping your dead body inside of a fucking trash can

With more holes than an afghan

[Chorus]

Somebody let me out this limousine (Hey, let me out!)

I'm a caged demon, on stage screaming like Rage Against the Machine

I'm convinced I'm a fiend, shootin up while this record is spinning

Clinically brain dead, I don't need a second opinion

Fuck droppin a jewel, I'm flippin the sacred treasure

I'll bite your motherfuckin style just to make it fresher

I can't take the pressure, I'm sick of bitches

Sick of naggin bosses bitchin while I'm washing dishes

In school I never said much, too busy having a head rush

Doing too much Rush had my face flushed like red blush

Then I went to Jim Beam, that's when my face grayed

Went to gym in eighth grade, raped the women's swim team

Don't take me for a joke, I'm no comedian

Too many mental problems got me snorting coke and smoking weed again

I'm going up over the curb, driving on the median

Finally made it home, but I don't got the key to get in

[Chorus]

Hey, fuck that! Outsidaz. Pace One. Young Zee

THE WAY I AM

Whatever . . . Dre, just let it run

Aiyo, turn the beat up a little bit

Aiyo . . . This song is for anyone—fuck it

Just shut up and listen, aiyo . . .

I sit back with this pack of Zig Zags and this bag

Of this weed, it gives me the shit needed to be

The most meanest MC on this—on this Earth

And since birth I've been cursed with this curse to just curse

And just blurt this berserk and bizarre shit that works

And it sells and it helps in itself to relieve

All this tension dispensin these sentences, gettin this

Stress that's been eatin me recently off of this chest

And I rest again peacefully (peacefully) . . .

But at least have the decency in you

To leave me alone when you freaks see me out

In the streets when I'm eatin or feedin my daughter

To not come and speak to me (speak to me) . . .

I don't know you and no, I don't owe you a motherfuckin thing

I'm not Mr. N'Sync, I'm not what your friends think

I'm not Mr. Friendly, I can be a prick if you tempt me

My tank is on empty (is on empty) . . .

No patience is in me and if you offend me

I'm liftin you ten feet (liftin you ten feet)...in the air
I don't care who is there and who saw me destroy you
Go call you a lawyer, file you a lawsuit
I'll smile in the courtroom and buy you a wardrobe
I'm tired of all you (of all you)...
I don't mean to be mean but that's all I can be, it's just me

[Chorus]
And I am whatever you say I am
If I wasn't, then why would I say I am?
In the paper, the news, every day I am
Radio won't even play my jam
'Cause I am whatever you say I am
If I wasn't, then why would I say I am?
In the paper, the news, every day I am
I don't know, it's just the way I am

Sometimes I just feel like my father, I hate to be bothered
With all of this nonsense—it's constant
And, "Oh, it's his lyrical content—
The song 'Guilty Conscience' has gotten such rotten responses"
And all of this controversy circles me
And it seems like the media immediately
Points a finger at me (finger at me)...
So I point one back at 'em, but not the index or pinkie
Or the ring or the thumb, it's the one you put up
When you don't give a fuck, when you won't just put up
With the bullshit they pull, 'cause they full of shit, too
When a dude's gettin bullied and shoots up his school
And they blame it on Marilyn (on Marilyn)...and the heroin
Where were the parents at? And look where it's at
Middle America, now it's a tragedy
Now it's so sad to see an upper class city
Havin this happenin (this happenin)...
Then attack Eminem 'cause I rap this way (rap this way)...

But I'm glad 'cause they feed me the fuel that I need for the fire

To burn and it's burnin and I have returned

[Chorus]

I'm so sick and tired of being admired

That I wish that I would just die or get fired

And dropped from my label, let's stop with the fables

I'm not gonna be able to top a "My Name is..."

And pigeon-holed into some poppy sensation

To cop me rotation at rock and roll stations

And I just do not got the patience (got the patience)...

To deal with these cocky Caucasians who think

I'm some wigger who just tries to be black 'cause I talk

With an accent and grab on my balls, so they always keep askin

The same fuckin questions (fuckin questions)...

What school did I go to, what 'hood I grew up in

The why, the who, what, when, the where and the how

'Til I'm grabbin my hair and I'm tearin it out

'Cause they drivin me crazy (drivin me crazy)...I can't take it

I'm racin, I'm pacin, I stand then I sit

And I'm thankful for every fan that I get

But I can't take a shit in the bathroom without someone

Standin by it...No, I won't sign your autograph

You can call me an asshole—I'm glad

[Chorus]

STAN

[Chorus 2x]

My tea's gone cold, I'm wondering why I

Got out of bed at all

The morning rain clouds up my window

And I can't see at all

And even if I could it'd all be gray

But your picture on my wall

It reminds me that it's not so bad

It's not so bad

"Dear Slim, I wrote you but you still ain't callin

I left my cell, my pager, and my home phone at the bottom

I sent two letters back in autumn, you must not-a got 'em

There probably was a problem at the post office or something

Sometimes I scribble addresses too sloppy when I jot 'em

But anyways, fuck it, what's been up man? How's your daughter?

My girlfriend's pregnant too, I'm 'bout to be a father

If I have a daughter, guess what I'ma call her? I'ma name her Bonnie

I read about your Uncle Ronnie too; I'm sorry

I had a friend kill himself over some bitch who didn't want him

I know you probably hear this every day, but I'm your biggest fan

I even got the underground shit that you did with Skam

I got a room full of your posters and your pictures, man

I like the shit you did with Ruckus, too, that shit was phat

Anyways, I hope you get this, man, hit me back

Just to chat, truly yours, your biggest fan. This is Stan"

[Chorus]

"Dear Slim, you still ain't called or wrote, I hope you have a chance

I ain't mad—I just think it's fucked up you don't answer fans

If you didn't wanna talk to me outside your concert

You didn't have to, but you coulda signed an autograph for Matthew

That's my little brother, man, he's only six years old

We waited in the blistering cold for you, four hours and you just said, "No"

That's pretty shitty, man, you're like his fuckin idol

He wants to be just like you, man, he likes you more than I do

I ain't that mad, though, I just don't like being lied to

Remember when we met in Denver? You said if I'd write you

You would write back—see, I'm just like you in a way

I never knew my father neither, he used to always cheat on my mom and

    beat her

I can relate to what you're saying in your songs

So when I have a shitty day I drift away and put 'em on
'Cause I don't really got shit else, so that shit helps when I'm depressed
I even got a tattoo of your name across the chest
Sometimes I even cut myself to see how much it bleeds
It's like adrenaline, the pain is such a sudden rush for me
See, everything you say is real and I respect you 'cause you tell it
My girlfriend's jealous 'cause I talk about you twenty-four seven
But she don't know you like I know you, Slim, no one does
She don't know what it was like for people like us growin up
You gotta call me, man, I'll be the biggest fan you'll ever lose
Sincerely yours, Stan—P.S. We should be together, too"

[Chorus]

"Dear Mister-I'm-Too-Good-To-Call-Or-Write-My-Fans
This'll be the last package I ever send your ass
It's been six months and still no word—I don't deserve it?
I know you got my last two letters, I wrote the addresses on 'em perfect
So this is my cassette I'm sending you; I hope you hear it
I'm in the car right now, I'm doing ninety on the freeway
Hey Slim, I drank a fifth of vodka—you dare me to drive?
You know the song by Phil Collins, "In the Air of the Night"
About that guy who coulda saved that other guy from drowning but didn't
Then Phil saw it all, then at a show he found him?
That's kinda how this is, you coulda rescued me from drowning
Now it's too late—I'm on a thousand downers now, I'm drowsy
And all I wanted was a lousy letter or a call
I hope you know I ripped ALL of your pictures off the wall
I love you, Slim, we coulda been together, think about it
You ruined it now, I hope you can't sleep and you dream about it
And when you dream I hope you can't sleep and you SCREAM about it
I hope your conscience EATS AT YOU and you can't BREATHE without me
See Slim—(screaming) Shut up, bitch! I'm trying to talk!
Hey Slim, that's my girlfriend screamin in the trunk
But I didn't slit her throat, I just tied her up—see, I ain't like you
'Cause if she suffocates she'll suffer more, and then she'll die, too

Well, gotta go, I'm almost at the bridge now

Oh shit, I forgot, how am I supposed to send this shit out?"

[Chorus]

Dear Stan, I meant to write you sooner but I just been busy

You said your girlfriend's pregnant now, how far along is she?

Look, I'm really flattered you would call your daughter that

And here's an autograph for your brother, I wrote it on a Starter cap

I'm sorry I didn't see you at the show, I musta missed you

Don't think I did that shit intentionally just to dis you

But what's this shit you said about you like to cut your wrists, too?

I say that shit just clowning, dog, c'mon—how fucked up is you?

You got some issues, Stan, I think you need some counseling

To help your ass from bouncing off the walls when you get down some

And what's this shit about us meant to be together?

That type of shit'll make me not want us to meet each other

I really think you and your girlfriend need each other

Or maybe you just need to treat her better

I hope you get to read this letter, I just hope it reaches you in time

Before you hurt yourself, I think that you'll be doin just fine

If you relax a little. I'm glad I inspire you but, Stan

Why are you so mad? Try to understand, that I do want you as a fan

I just don't want you to do some crazy shit

I seen this one shit on the news a couple weeks ago that made me sick

Some dude was drunk and drove his car over a bridge

And had his girlfriend in the trunk and she was pregnant with his kid

And in the car they found a tape, but they didn't say who it was to

Come to think about, his name was . . . it was you. Damn

LOSE YOURSELF

Look, if you had one shot . . . or one opportunity . . . to seize everything you ever
wanted . . . in one moment . . . would you capture it . . . or just let it slip?

His palms are sweaty, knees weak, arms are heavy

There's vomit on his sweater already, Mom's spaghetti

He's nervous, but on the surface he looks calm and ready

To drop bombs, but he keeps on forgetting

What he wrote down, the whole crowd goes so loud

He opens his mouth, but the words won't come out

He's choking, how? Everybody's joking now

The clock's run out, time's up, over, blaow!

Snap back to reality, oh, there goes gravity

Oh, there goes Rabbit, he choked, he's so mad

But he won't give up that easy, no, he won't have it

He knows his whole back's to these ropes, it don't matter

He's dope, he knows that, but he's broke, he's so stagnant

He knows when he goes back to this mobile home, that's when it's

Back to the lab again, yo, this whole rhapsody

He better go capture this moment and hope it don't pass him

[Chorus 2x]

You better lose yourself in the music, the moment

You own it, you better never let it go

You only get one shot, do not miss your chance to blow

This opportunity comes once in a lifetime, yo!

Soul's escaping through this hole that is gaping

This world is mine for the taking, make me king

As we move toward a New World Order

A normal life is boring, but superstardom's

Close to postmortem, it only grows harder

Homie grows hotter, he blows, it's all over

These hoes is all on him, coast to coast shows

He's known as the globetrotter, lonely roads, God only knows

He's grown farther from home, he's no father

He goes home and barely knows his own daughter

But hold your nose 'cause here goes the cold water

These hoes don't want him no mo', he's cold product

They moved on to the next schmoe who flows, he nose-

Dove and sold nada, so the soap opera

Is told, it unfolds, I suppose it's old, partner
But the beat goes on, da da dum da dum da da dum

[Chorus 2x]

No more games, I'ma change what you call rage
Tear this motherfuckin roof off like two dogs caged
I was playing in the beginning, the mood all changed
I been chewed up and spit out and booed off stage
But I kept rhyming and stepped right in the next cipher
Best believe somebody's paying the pied piper
All the pain inside amplified by the
Fact that I can't get by with my nine to
Five and I can't provide the right type of
Life for my family, 'cause man, these goddamn
Food stamps don't buy diapers and it's no movie
There's no Mekhi Phifer, this is my life
And these times is so hard and it's getting even harder
Trying to feed and water my seed, plus Teeter Totter
Caught up between being a father and a prima donna
Baby mama drama's screaming on and too much for me to wanna
Stay in one spot, another day of monotony
Has gotten me to the point I'm like a snail, I've got
To formulate a plot or I end up in jail or shot
Success is my only motherfucking option, failure's not
Mom, I love you, but this trailer's got
To go, I cannot grow old in Salem's lot
So here I go—it's my shot, feet fail me not
This may be the only opportunity that I got

[Chorus 2x]

MOCKINGBIRD

*Yeah. I know sometimes things may not always make sense to you right now. But,
hey, what Daddy always tell you? Straighten up, little soldier. Stiffen up that
upper lip. What you crying about? You got me.*

Hailie, I know you miss your Mom and I know you miss your Dad

Well, I'm gone but I'm trying to give you the life that I never had

I can see you're sad, even when you smile, even when you laugh

I can see it in your eyes, deep inside you want to cry

'Cause you're scared. I ain't there? Daddy's with you in your prayers

No more crying, wipe them tears, Daddy's here, no more nightmares

We gon' pull together through it, we gon' do it. Laney

Uncle's crazy, ain't he? Yeah, but he loves you, girl, and you better know it

We're all we got in this world, when it spins, when it swirls

When it whirls, when it twirls, two little beautiful girls

Lookin puzzled, in a daze, I know it's confusing you

Daddy's always on the move, Mama's always on the news

I try to keep you sheltered from it but somehow it seems

The harder that I try to do that, the more it backfires on me

All the things growing up as Daddy that he had to see

Daddy don't want you to see, but you see just as much as he did

We did not plan it to be this way, your mother and me

But things have got so bad between us I don't see us ever being

Together ever again like we used to be when we was teenagers

But then of course everything always happens for a reason

I guess it was never meant to be, but it's just something we

Have no control over and that's what destiny is

But no more worries, rest your head and go to sleep

Maybe one day we'll wake up and this'll all just be a dream

[Chorus]

Now hush little baby, don't you cry

Everything's gonna be alright

Stiffen that upper lip up, little lady, I told ya

Daddy's here to hold ya through the night

I know Mommy's not here right now and we don't know why

We feel how we feel inside

It may seem a little crazy, pretty baby

But I promise Mama's gon' be alright

It's funny … I remember back one year when Daddy had no money

Mommy wrapped the Christmas presents up and stuck 'em under the tree

And said some of 'em were from me 'cause Daddy couldn't buy 'em

I'll never forget that Christmas, I sat up the whole night crying

'Cause Daddy felt like a bum; see, Daddy had a job

But his job was to keep the food on the table for you and Mom

And at the time every house that we lived in either kept

Getting broken into and robbed or shot up on the block

And your Mom was saving money for you in a jar

Tryin to start a piggy bank for you so you could go to college

Almost had a thousand dollars 'til someone broke in and stole it

And I know it hurt so bad it broke your Mama's heart

And it seemed like everything was just startin to fall apart

Mom and Dad was arguin a lot so Mama moved back

Onto Chalmers in the flat one bedroom apartment

And Dad moved back to the other side of 8 Mile on Novara

And that's when Daddy went to California with his CD

And met Dr. Dre and flew you and Mama out to see me

But Daddy had to work, you and Mama had to leave me

Then you started seeing Daddy on the TV and Mama didn't

Like it and you and Laney were too young to understand it

Papa was a rollin stone, Mama developed a habit

And it all happened too fast for either one of us to grab it

I'm just sorry you were there and had to witness it firsthand

'Cause all I ever wanted to do was just make you proud

Now I'm sitting in this empty house, just reminiscin

Lookin at your baby pictures, it just trips me out

To see how much you both have grown, it's almost like you're sisters now

Wow, guess you pretty much are and Daddy's still here

Laney, I'm talkin to you too, Daddy's still here

I like the sound of that, yeah, it's got a ring to it, don't it?

Shh, Mama's only gone for the moment

[Chorus]

And if you ask me to
Daddy's gonna buy you a mockingbird
I'ma give you the world
I'ma buy a diamond ring for you
I'ma sing for you
I'll do anything for you to see you smile
And if that mockingbird don't sing and that ring don't shine
I'ma break that birdie's neck
I'll go back to the jeweler who sold it to ya
And make him eat every carat, don't fuck with Dad (ha-ha)

WHEN I'M GONE

Yeah. It's my life. But all in words, I guess . . .

Have you ever loved someone so much you'd give an arm for?
Not the expression, no, literally give an arm for
When they know they're your heart and you know you are their armor
And you will destroy anyone who would try to harm her
But what happens when karma turns right around and bites you
And everything you stand for turns on you to spite you?
What happens when you become the main source of her pain?
"Daddy, look what I made!" "Dad's gotta go catch a plane"
"Daddy, where's Mommy? I can't find Mommy, where is she?"
"I don't know, go play, Hailie, baby, your Daddy's busy
Daddy's writin this song, this song ain't gon' write itself
I'll give you one Underdog, then you gotta swing by yourself"
Then to write a rhyme in that song and tell her you love her
And put hands on her mother who's a spittin image of her
That's Slim Shady, yeah baby, Slim Shady's crazy
Shady made me, but tonight, Shady's rock-a-bye baby

[Chorus 2x]
And when I'm gone, just carry on, don't mourn
Rejoice every time you hear the sound of my voice
Just know that I'm lookin down on you smiling and I didn't
Feel a thing, so baby, don't feel no pain, just smile back

tinctive balance between voice and beat. Part of Minnesota's Rhymesayers label along with such acts as Aesop Rock, Atmosphere, Sage Francis, and Blueprint, E&A have helped define the Twin Cities hip-hop scene.

BOTTLE DREAMS (AS OLIVER HART)

Everyone knew she was a special young girl from her neighbors to her
     teachers
Some labeled her "prodigy," others called her a genius
It was amazing the way she could play the violin
It made it hard for people to believe that she was only ten
But behind every brilliant mind there lies a monster
This one just so happened to be her father
See, Daddy was sick, he'd get a rush by playin touchy touch
And tellin her to keep it hush. It was his secret way
Of loving, that he needed someone he could trust
Fucked her head up, sayin, "If Mama was alive she'd be so proud of us"
So she'd hide her desire to die
But if you paid close attention you could see the sorrow in her eyes
Walking around in the only real hell
No one would ever think she'd have such a story to tell
Afraid to go home, afraid to talk, afraid of cryin
She was too young to even know why

[Chorus]
And everyday she'd go to the river with a message in a bottle sayin
"Please, God help me, I don't wanna live to see tomorrow"
Each day she'd scrounge for a tiny shred of hope
Just to wish the bottle would stay afloat
But every single solitary day, the bottle seems to sink
I don't know why but the bottle always sinks
She never sees it happen, but the bottle always sinks
Now only the bottom of the river knows what she really thinks

She made that violin sing with so much pain
Could almost hear her scream through the strange vibrations

What was once sweet and innocent is now riding with the psychotic father
Chose to probe the flowers of the pure and sacred
Her instrument was a rolly tongue
To express the infinite abuse in its depths
At night the footsteps crept to her door and she'd begin to shake and weep
And with tears rolling down her cheeks she'd pretend she was asleep
When the nightmare was over and the sun dawn is light
She'd retreat to the same place she always did
Rip a page from her diary and write with all her might
Then send it off into the current, determined to find a way to live

[Chorus]

Being a victim of her daddy's hands for so long, she lost the will to move on
Sick of picking up her violin to hide from what's wrong
Exhausted but stayin strong, she tried to play the bright side
But couldn't bring herself to make nothing but sad songs
Sick of that sick feeling that stays in her stomach
Sick of waiting for a rescue by someone who found one of her bottles
Sick of keepin Daddy's little secret, she got up at
The crack of day and smashed her violin into pieces
Then proceeded to walk towards the river with a plan
Only this time the diary bottle was in her hand
Just walk with herself, away from the hell
Not knowin at the river bottom lied all the cries for help
It was weeks before they found her dead body. Some fisherman
Reeled it from the water like something from a detective novel
Diagnosis: suicide, stemmed from desperation
Was near where she drowned they found about five hundred messages in
    sunken bottles

NOW
[Chorus]
We're…here…to…
Bring the people and the music and the movement all together now

We...see...through...
Repetitive etiquette and the highly unoriginal
We're...here...to...
Bring the people and the music and the movement all together now
They...will...lose...

Check it out now, check it out now

This is a necessary change from the grim simple and plain
Gonna exercise that brain to break the chain, pain is a part of gain
No need to explain...
We innovate to generate an intricately interwoven tapestry of musical and
ethical epiphanies
The interest is minimal, I'm on my own mission to mess with an angel to take
it all the way to where the sun is
Just like a running leopard running around to turn it into a simple simile,
simple synonym adrenaline is coming back
I made it my own city, why's it gotta be a superstar, I'd rather be a galaxy, but
how you see is so dependent
On the medicine, the rhetoric, and how at any second you think you could
sit on the brink of
This world is all asleep and I have no apologies
I...breathe, keep my sight on what we ride on
Let bygones be bygones, the migraines don't sidetrack
My final destination, nothing rivals predetermination to exterminate the
germination
Of a nation that accepts anything that's thrown in its fat face
'Cause when there's nothing left, there's no more point to the rat race
We don't waste a minute of the day, don't be offended by what I'm saying,
trying to send it all the way to another stage
A creative alternative rated and greater, the crazy maniac melody take it
all up in your face
Wait...Success ain't only based on self-esteem
It takes a sense to differentiate between what's yours and someone else's
dreams

I felt the screams climbing up my cold spine
Saying now's the time, gotta give it all my energy to get rid of the enemy, I
    said it so . . .

[Chorus]

'Cause music ain't nothing if it ain't got style

Free us and touch what we can't see
Twist that knife and watch him bleed
Lost inside, it's way too deep
Someone choke me, help me breathe

Run from mistakes
Right in my face
Feels like I'm running in place

LUPE FIASCO

Lupe Fiasco represents the changing face of hip-hop, expanding the meaning of the culture and the music. He also represents a return to hip-hop's emphasis on lyrical content—skills over swagger and shine. His rhyme style is fluid and lyrical, rich with multisyllabic internal rhymes, assonance, and alliteration. One can hear on songs like "Dumb It Down" and "Go Go Gadget Flow" a near-incessant lyrical play with sound.

Lupe's records to date have all been concept albums in which he frequently adopts fictive personas. He understands this as a natural outgrowth of his desire to use rap for storytelling. "I come from a literary background," he explains, "and I loved to tell stories. I remember freestyling stories, not in rhyme, by just coming up with things when I was a kid on the bus. But I couldn't play an instrument, so I decided to take my storytelling mind and to apply it to rap, which seemed like a natural thing. So I practiced a lot and really tried to apply the techniques I'd learned from poetry—which, of course, is the predecessor of rap—and include new things. I'd add haikus and try all wild poetic things, and I knew I'd have something different and interesting to say."[23]

DUMB IT DOWN

I'm fearless, now hear this, I'm earless

And I'm peer-less, that means I'm eyeless

Which means I'm tearless, which means my iris

Resides where my ears is, which means I'm blinded

But I'ma find it, I can feel its nearness

But I'ma veer so I don't come near

Like a chicken or a deer . . . but I remember

I'm not a listener or a seer so my windshield smear

Here, you steer, I really shouldn't be behind this

Clearly 'cause my blindness, the windshield

Is menstrual, the whole grill is roadkill

So trill and so sincere. Yeah, I'm both them there

Took both pills when a bloke in a trench coat

And the locs in the chair had approached him here

And he clear as a ghost, so a biter of the throats

In the mirror, the writer of the quotes for the ghosts

Who supplier of the notes to the living, riveting

Is rosy, pockets full of posies, given to

The mother of the deceased. Awaken at war

'Til I'm restin in peace (peace, peace, peace)

[Chorus]

You goin over niggas' heads, Lu (Dumb it down)

They tellin me that they don't feel you (Dumb it down)

We ain't graduate from school, nigga (Dumb it down)

Them big words ain't cool, nigga (Dumb it down)

Yeah, I heard "Mean And Vicious," nigga (Dumb it down)

Make a song for the bitches, nigga (Dumb it down)

We don't care about the weather, nigga (Dumb it down)

You'll sell more records if you (Dumb it down)

And I'm mouthless, which means I'm soundless
Now as far as the hearing, I've found it
It was as far as the distance from an earring
To the ground is, but the doorknockers on the ear
Of a stewardess in a Lear. She fine
And she flyin, I feel I'm flying blind 'cause my mind's
On cloud nine and in her mind at the same time
Pimp C the wings on the Underground King
Who's also Klingon, to infinity and beyond
Something really stinks, but I Spinks like Leon
Or lying in the desert
I'm flying on Pegasus, you flying on a pheasant
Rider of the white powder, picker of the fire flowers
Spit hot fire like Dylon on Chappelle's skit
Yeah, smell it on my unicorn
Don't snort the white horse, but toot my own horn (sleep)

[Chorus]
You've been shedding too much light, Lu (Dumb it down)
You make 'em wanna do right, Lu (Dumb it down)
They're getting self-esteem, Lu (Dumb it down)
These girls are trying to be queens, Lu (Dumb it down)
They're trying to graduate from school, Lu (Dumb it down)
They're starting to think that smart is cool, Lu (Dumb it down)
They're trying to get up out the 'hood, Lu (Dumb it down)
I'll tell you what you should do (Dumb it down)

And I'm brainless, which means I'm headless
Like Ichabod Crane is
Or foreplay-less sex is, which makes me saneless
With no neck left to hang a chain with
Which makes me necklace-less
Like a necklace theft, and I ain't used my headrest yet
They said they need proof like a vestless chest
'Bout the best, fair F-F-jet in the nest
Who exudes confidence and excess depth

Even Scuba Steve will find it hard to breathe

Around these leagues

My snorkel is a tuba, Lu the ruler around these seas

Westside Poseidon, Westside beside 'em

Chest high and rising, almost touching the knees

Of stewardess and the pilot, lucky they make you fly with

Personal floating devices, tricks falling out of my sleeves

David Blaine, make it rain

You make a boat, I make a plane

Then, I pull the plug and I make it drain

Until I feel like flowing and filling it up again . . . (Westside)

[Chorus]

You putting me to sleep, nigga (Dumb it down)

That's why you ain't popping in the streets, nigga (Dumb it down)

You ain't winning no awards, nigga (Dumb it down)

Robots and skateboards, nigga? (Dumb it down)

GQ Man of the Year, G? (Dumb it down)

Shit ain't rocking over here, B (Dumb it down)

Won't you talk about your cars, nigga? (Dumb it down)

And what the fuck is Goyard, nigga? (Dumb it down)

Make it rain for the chicks (Dumb it down)

Pour champagne on a bitch (Dumb it down)

What the fuck is wrong with you? (Dumb it down)

How can I get on a song with you? (Dumb it down)

G, they told me I should come down, cousin

But I flatly refuse, I ain't dumb down nothin

HIP-HOP SAVED MY LIFE

Dedicate, dedicate . . . This one right here goes out to my homie with the dream,
nah mean?

He said, I write what I see

Write to make it right, don't like where I be

I'd like to make it like the sights on TV

Quite the great life, so nice and easy
See, now you can still die from that
But it's better than not being alive from straps
Agree, a Mead notebook and a Bic that click
When it's pushed and a wack ass beat
That's a track that's weak, that he got last week
'Cause everybody in the stu' is like that's that heat
A bass-heavy medley with a sample from the 70s
With a screwed-up hook that went, "Stack That Cheese"
Somethin, somethin, somethin, "Stack That Cheese"
Mother, sister, cousin, "Stack That Cheese"
He couldn't think of nothin, "Stack That Cheese"
He turns down the beat, writer's block impedes
Cryin from the next room, a baby in need
Of some Pampers and some food and a place to sleep
That, plus a black Cadillac on D's
Is what keep him on track to be a great MC, yeah

[Chorus]
One you never heard of, I push it hard to further the
Grind, I feel like murder but hip-hop, you saved me
One you never heard of, I push it hard to further the
Grind, I feel like murder but hip-hop, you saved my life

Reps Northside so he rocks them braids
Eleven-hundred friends on his MySpace page
"Stack That Cheese" got seven hundred plays
Producer made him take it down, said he had to pay
Open mic champ two weeks in a row
Ex-D-Boy with a B-Boy flow
Glow like Leroy, you should see boy go
Got a daddy servin life and a brother on the row
Best homie in the grave, tatted up while in the cage
Minute Maid, got his mama workin like a slave
Down baby mama who he really had to honor
'Cause she was his biggest fan, even let him use her Honda

To drive up to Dallas, went to open up for amateurs
Let him keep a debit card so he could put gas in it
Told her when he get on he gon' take her to the Galleria
Buy everythin but the mannequins, ya dig?

[Chorus]

His man called, said, "Ya time might be now
They played your freestyle over 'Wipe Me Down'
They played it two times, said it might be crowned
As the best thing out the H-Town in a while"
He picked up his son with a great big smile
Rapped every single word to the newborn child
Then he put him down and went back to the kitchen
And put on another beat and got back to the mission of
Get his mama out the 'hood, put her somewhere in the woods
Keep his lady lookin good, have her rollin like she should
Show his homies there's a way, other than that flippin yay
Bail his homie outta jail, put a lawyer on his case
Throw a concert for the school, show the shorties that it's cool
Throw some candy on the Caddy, chuck the deuce and act a fool
Man, it feels good when it happens like that
Two days from goin back to sellin crack—yes, sir

[Chorus 2x]

50 CENT

Few artists have been so shaped by personal catastrophe as 50 Cent. After several years toiling in relative obscurity as an underground artist, 50 Cent (often known simply as "50") burst onto the mainstream scene with his major label debut, *Get Rich or Die Tryin'* (2003). The hype surrounding it had as much to do with its infectious lead single, "In

Da Club," as it did with his celebrity label, Shady/Aftermath (the imprints of Eminem and Dr. Dre—each of whom produced tracks on the album). More than that, however, was the violence in 50's personal story. "Being shot defines how strong I am," he says. "It prepares you for the confusion of being an artist."[24]

In May 2000, 50 was ambushed outside his grandmother's house in South Jamaica, Queens. He was shot nine times at close range. He survived but suffered serious injuries, including gunshot wounds to his jaw. The resulting change in the timbre and texture of his voice would, ironically, help account for his distinctive sound—by turns vulnerable and menacing, plaintive and playful. One need only compare a track recorded before the shooting, like 1999's "How to Rob," with a postshooting song, such as "21 Questions" or "P.I.M.P."

Not only has 50's sound changed, but so has his style. The hungry, aggressive quality of the earlier songs is tempered in the later tracks by an assured tone and an almost bemused perspective on most every subject. "My music is a soundtrack," he says. "The film is my life. My music matches things I've experienced or felt. Even if the whole thing is made up."[25]

50 SHOT YA

That's the sound of the man cockin that thang—that thaaaang
That's the sound of the man clappin that thang—thaaang

Yo, in my 'hood we was taught not to say who shot ya
See the flash, you heard the shot, you feel the burnin, I got ya
Say a prayer for me if you care for me 'cause I'm on the edge
I'm finna put a shell in a nigga head
I rock a lot of ice, I dare you to scheme on it
The fifth got a rubber grip and a beam on it
Homie that took the hit on me couldn't shoot
They say I'm skinny now, but I look big in the coupe-dee
My cousin Uzi out in L.A. done tripped and do the sets again
Got shot the fuck up tryin to rob the wrong Mexicans
I write my lifestyle, y'all niggas is cheaters
Your lines come from feds, felons, and Don Diva
Oh, you the black hand of death? Why your name ain't Preacher?
If you a pimp like Kemp, why them hoes don't treat ya?

You wanna ball like Kirkland? Shorty, let me teach ya
This flow's God-sent, it's bound to reach ya

[Chorus]
Problem child, I'm familiar with problems
I know how to solve 'em
Semiautomatically or trey-eight revolve 'em
Shoot 'em up, rob 'em
In the 'hood we starvin, you don't want problems
Problem child

And why can't you be man enough
To tell me where you're comin from

They say you can never repay the price for takin a man's life
I'm in debt with Christ, I done did that twice
I'm nice, y'all niggas can't hang with 50
Blaaat, y'all niggas can't bang with 50
For every bar in a rhyme, there's a shell and a 9
For every stone in the cross, there's a bitch I tossed
See the wounds in my skin? They from a war, of course
You can check CNN for the "War Report"
See, the drama got me ridin with a sawed-off shottie
Catch you at the light, I blow ya ass off the Ducati
Man, niggas ain't gon' do me like Sammy did Gotti
I do it myself, I don't need no help
Give me a knife, I'll get rid of your neighborhood bully
Give me a minute, I'll take a fuckin car with a pully
See, the 'hood is the deepest, stole my innocence young
Niggas jumped me 'cause they couldn't beat me one-on-one

[Chorus]

I must've broke a mirror at three and had bad luck for seven
'Cause Pops slid and Mommy died before I turned eleven
They say it split—'posed to let black cats cross your path

The footprints in the sand is Satan carryin your ass

I got "God Understand Me" tattooed in my skin

When I die, come back, I'ma tattoo it again

I'm the young buck that let the gun buck

Roll the window down and say: "Wassup? Niggas, get ready to duck"

My heart is a house, homie, fear don't live here

Nigga, believe me when I say I don't care

Muslims mix a lot, gods studied they lessons

Even when my luck's hard I still count my blessings

See that look in my eye, ya betta keep on steppin

Spent time on my cell floor to sharpen my weapon

If you pussy I'ma smell you when you come around here

Them boys in Pelican Bay couldn't live on my tier

[Chorus]

GHETTO QUA'RAN

*Uh huh, uh huh, uh huh Southside, what y'all niggas know about the Dirty
    South? One time . . .*

[Chorus]
Lord forgive me, for I've sinned

Over and over again, just to stay on top

I recall memories filled with sin

Over and over, again and again

Yo, when you hear talk of the Southside, you hear talk of the Team

See, niggas feared Prince and respected Preme

For all you slow motherfuckers I'ma break it down iller

See, Preme was a businessman and Prince was the killer

Remember, he used to push the bulletproof BM, uh huh

This here get you seasick, I sat back and peeped shit

They roll with E-Z Wider and they ain't get blunted

Had the whole projects working for fifty on five-hundred

As a youth, all I ever did was sell crack

I used to idolize Cat. Hurt me in my heart to hear

That nigga snitched on Pap. How he go out like that?

Rumors in the 'hood was Gus was snitchin

I ain't believe that, pa, he helped me cop my first GSX-R

Had the four-runner, the Z, the 5, and the 3

Used to drive his truck through the 'hood draggin jet skis

From Gerald Wallace to Baby Wise, don't be surprised

Of how freely I throw out names of guys who dealt with pies

Like L-A-N-Y's, L got shot in the neck, then told us connect

Them niggas who shot him got him for ten bricks

Fucking Dominicans, turned around and gave 'em more bricks

[Chorus]

That first verse is just a dose of the shit that I'm on

Consider this the first chapter in the ghetto's Qua'ran

I know a lot of niggas that get dough like Remmy and Joe

And Prince and Righteous from Hillside with the mole on his nose

Throughout my struggles in the 'hood, I started learnin

Life's a bitch with a pretty face, but she burnin

Man, I'ma get cheese like Chaz then run through whips like Cigar

Gamble all the time like country-curly head Prince and Tah-Tah

Po-po under pressure too, they know what they facing

Go against crews like BeBos and killers like Pappy Mason

A lot of niggas I know been corrupted since birth

Enticed to rob nuns for fun, for everything they worth

I know some cats that hail out old complexes like Cooley Wall

Together niggas stand and divided they fall

Round here, shook niggas, they keep it in motion

Come around here with your Rollie you can get robbed like Ocean

Lord knows, Tommy had lost and sold

Helicopters, Rolls-Royces with Louis Vuitton interior

Might sound like I'm fantasizing, but, son, I'm dead serious

Montana was no dummy, brought Benice to watch the money

Had money out the ass, he politic like the Asian
Feds couldn't catch him dirty, so settled for tax evasion

[Chorus]

Yo, rest in peace to Rich and Ron, money what they was about, yo
The twins was from Queens but got crazy cream with Alpo
Throughout my time I heard tales of Hymie, Frenchy, Jamaican Pauly
Duckie Corley, Ronnie Bumps, and Chick, shit
A lot of niggas flow the way I flow
But ain't been in the game all their life so don't know who I know
Writing rhymes is the best way I express how I feel
If I ain't rich by twenty-six, I'll be dead or in jail
Coming up I heard sippin too much booze'll leave you confused
And if you watch the news, you see players in this game that lose
I'm forgettin Lefty and Jazz, Pretty Tony and Lance
Head Lou, Mel son, Troy and E Money Bags
In a conversation over shrimp and lobster at Benihana's
Heard Chico stopped boxing and started robbin diners
Shout out to Clarence and Clutch, Bob Dre, Black Will
If the flow don't kill you the MAC will

JEAN GRAE

J ean Grae is among the most admired and accomplished underground MCs. Now over a decade into her career, she is finally beginning to earn public attention to match her underground cred-
ibility. In the words of Talib Kweli, Jean Grae is "one of the last true MCs
left."26 Though her purposefully uninflected delivery has sometimes been
criticized as monotonous, Jean Grae responds to these critics with the same
force and directness she does with her rhyme adversaries. Her greatest contribution to rap poetics may be in storytelling, where she has found a way

of inserting varied female personas and narratives into hip-hop's hypermasculine world.

LOVESONG

She grew up believin in passion and love, whose folks divorced and
    remarried
Very naïve, seen life in commitments
That shoulda been dead and buried. Highly sentimental, sensitive
Gentle beyond the point she should be. What might be
Obvious to most, she says they too bitter
Can't see the world the way she does: clean lungs, undamaged liver
Sees thugs through her pink-tinted glasses. Occasionally
Weed does make her giggle, listen to some music closer
Dudes approach her lightly, wanna be her lover and she obliges
Likes to cuddle under the covers by candlelit fires
Oblivious to lying schemes to talk her out of clothes
Says she's just in love with love, cuts her classes, spends too much
Time entranced in romancing, things are changing quickly
She's asking, "Why aren't you spending more time with me?" Nigga's eyes
Are getting shifty, coming over later smelling of pussy
On his face, jeans, and sweaters; something's fishy, and it's not
What he tells her, man, it's what he don't. And she don't understand
And for some years, she probably won't. Just wants an honest man
For goodness sake, they backstabbin and cutting her throat
Restraining orders follow, but she's still optimistic about it
Like Annie, thinking tomorrow maybe will be a better day
I let her pray on bended knees, "Ask him to send Prince Charming, please"
She's never cheated, treats her man well, cooks, cleans
Dresses sexy for him—halter tops and tight jeans
Would break the law for him, go through a couple of these relationships
Still stays strong; she's too young and dumb to call it quits
Learns that she's carrying twice, scared and afraid the first time
The second, she don't even cry. Makes her wipe away his tears
And it hurts. They always leave, return crazy

So she doesn't flirt, spends time mourning the babies
Goes through a couple of these relationships and still stays strong
Too young and dumb to call it quits . . . It's still a love song

She's got a good man; she's nineteen, he's twenty-one and sweet and honest
Promised to love her, talk of marriage, she would never wanna be
Somebody's baby's mother. Use rubbers occasionally
When she's flowin, open off the affection and gifts
And all the good manners he's showing; he's trying to build a life for himself
Studies late, computer shit, and she's missing attention
That she's not getting, sex dwindles, crawling in the sheets
He say he tired and she say she feel neglect and defeat
Just doesn't see his ambition. She wanna be the Universe
And hold his center position. Starts hanging round her best friend more
Crazy attraction takes impulsive action, drop the drawers
And falls in love. The world explodes and she confesses, "Yeah I did it. So?"
They so tight it's like he move when she stretches
Over the couple years, too many stresses: girls who wanna fight her
Bitches writing letters, friendships disappearing
Plus he rhymes, so it's competitive. Pressure, miscarriage
They break up fifty times a week and make up just as much
He fuckin and I know, but pretending I'm out of touch
It's getting strained and gets physical. She cries until the river dries
And leaves her dead and cold, packs up her things and leaves behind
What I thought was gold was only gold-plated. Thinking of
All the other ones I coulda just left and up and dated
Single after four years, starting over's never easy
But it takes some time to realize your own worth
Come into your own, play your mental rebirth, she starts penning
Some better poems, straighten up her bank account
Likes to take herself out, I'm getting better at it
I've had a few relationships, but still too young and dumb enough
To call it quits . . . It's still a love song

Love
All I ever want is you

All I ever had, leading in my life was you
All that ever was, all I ever had [sung]

Maybe it's easier to talk about this shit in third person
Learning better, "Wookin' Pa Nub" in all the wrong places
Like I'm Eddie Murphy, curse me to repeat the same cycle
I'm breaking, no longer think relations make a better woman
Just for life, I'm pursuing, growing, but hopelessly romantic still
Tasted weather in the bitter climates, love the sunshine better
Dreaming of dream proposals, decent moral values
Placing higher on my chart, trying not to have a shallow heart
But battle scars are deep and reaching to the depth of Hell and back
Try to give up the grudges, think it's experience
And move from the clutches of sadness. It's difficult
Sometimes I wish I wasn't an adult, adolescent
Primetime sitcom star, I've been too far
And too much, too hard, for too long. It's still a love song

HATER'S ANTHEM

Liquid content may cause y'all faggots' frames to burst
Insane rhyme structure flame your brain, I'll blame birth
The game switched her, made her retain a greater picture
Of lame dames that couldn't be felt with Braille scripture
Even deaf kids are rockin earplugs
I'll rip you then stick you with sticks I dipped in arsenic-filled jugs
(Official, you bitches) I ignite under certain circumstances
Flip back and have your ass hit by backup dancers
Cancer-choker, the Mad Hatter, the Jabberwocky of rap
Been hibernatin, contemplatin, now I'm finally back
With rope chains so hopscotch yo' ass back
I play close like a thong huggin an ass crack
The verbs leave scabbed, riddled permanent scars
That scratch deep like a cheap box of CD-Rs
Spread heat like I'm Gia's drawers pleading the fourth
In court like he's the boss, then they'll carry you off (Fuck it)

I'm more necessary than violence on the Amistad (Oh, my God)

She's wrong like eating bacon in Ramadan

I'll piss on your shoes then make you clean it with your mouth

Then I'll tell all your friends to send Depends to your house

Must be crazy, put speed knots in your lady

Phallic DNA tests so it's not your baby

(Maybe we can be friends) Naw, just pretend

I'll slip razors in your charm bracelets, slit your skin, bitch

[Chorus 8x]

Fuck you. Fuck you. Fuck you. Fuck you.

Superenhanced survival shooter with a crucial plan

Infatuated with music and loops, no scruples, man

Phraseologist, nonapologetic mutilators

Stays on the list, defaming names so they can sue me later

Hater, yes! decatherm gas, the fate opposer

Philanthropist, misanthropist, underground soldier

Banana clips just start unloading in your supermarkets

Screaming 'til you're hoarse, bleeding, finding out that you're the target

Monotony flow, contradictory word placin

Like bringing Satan to a baptism in a flooded basement

(Jean's out to lunch) She ain't even punched in yet

You're a facsimile, I'm the original document

All shock and then—lights out—drop 'em in

Selections then very bury them proper things

I'm married to rap like J. Lo to scandals

Light up the room like J. Hov's birthday candles

I'm that bright, like Stephen Hawking's computer chair

Asked out a teacher on a Sadie Hawkins dare

Parallax view, see the future in my sleep

I'll battle-rap you until your gullet starts to leak

Gnash your teeth, smash you then bind your feet

Thrash holes in your dome, snatch your soul and retreat

Mad Maxish, the prose so dope it's fantastic

Now fold up your dough before you get yo' ass kicked

[Chorus 2x]

Rush the door like a Russian whore
Mail-order bitch sent to Dahmer's crib
It's an honor to split your armor, blood drip
Like *Pulp Fiction* when bits of bones get on ya
Shit, I just talk jargon, disregard margins
Liquidate any enemies, rap incarnate
I'm cynical, criminal actions excite me
My mic chord's an umbilical that radiates high beams
Humorous, filled with more flow than a cumulous cloud
Dentist mad, he said my words abuse my mouth
So I upchucked 'em, butt fuck 'em out
Chuckle loud, duck down screamin "Fuck the crowd"
Specialized stacker mixed malt liquor with Jolt cola
Start drinkin when the cops start lookin over they shoulder
Nastier than central booking samiches handled tough
Cranky in the morning when smokin that cannabis stuff
Can't see it like orphan Annie's pupils in cartoons
Can't be it like trannies who pay for implanted wombs
Nope—that's not it. Close, but no cigar
Dutch lit but I'm passin it right past you, parr
That's all. That's Jean. The definitive minister
The sarcastic wit, bar spit at competitor
The uncosmetic'd up shit on your pedestal
The sanatorium released, the most unforgettable
Moked off, dirt. Molotov your face
Then lock you in a box and watch you burn in a close space
Pig face, get your shit taken and replaced
With a tickin case that's strapped to your waist. (Duh!)
You move too slow, sloth, boost your movement
Your mind counts time like down South screw music
Who's it? The phoenix wings spread like the Ox said
I'll knock you out a window, make you literally drop dead

DON'T RUSH ME

Listen: There's nothing like knowing yourself like the way I know

That smoking's kinda broken my health like the way I know

My flow don't make appropriate wealth. I can't change that

But funny I'm sayin that when it's money I'm aimed at

I don't give a fuck if you frame that or quote it

I meant what I said 'cause I wrote it; point noted

I know I'm overly sensitive when it comes to, well . . .

Just about everything

And I'm so hardheaded, I don't need your help

Like, no advice for these records 'less it's me, myself

Like, I don't ever want to breathe if it requires assistance

Just . . . just shut down my system. I'm a victim of

Choosin bad love, Bad Luck Lucy

Every man's touch seems to be a doozy and plus

I'm attached to this loose leaf, stand on my two feet

So it's hard enough to even have to physically move me

Go ahead. Try

[Chorus]

I know I'm on the right path

To who I'm gonna be at last

But don't rush me, nigga

I know I'm wrong and right

At the same time both, I'm the dark and light

They say life needs everything to live

At the same time, I've got everything to give

So don't rush me

Don't rush me

I've got to be more disciplined, I'm listening

More to straight logic, blockin random shit that's driftin in

Age is a motherfucker, find myself starin

At the little kids, thinkin I could beat 'em like a stepmother

Creepin on a come-up of thirty soon, but lookin twenty, ooh

The food catches up to you now plenty

Attending christenings of my best friend's children

And they're asking who's next and I'm wishin for

Six more wishes for Christmas or kids on the wish list

Or time machines to be in existence

I'm a team player, not. The dry wit is similar

To Arizona weather—say it, nigga: hot

Patent-leather sole tappin at my goal

If the album's not platinum, then I'll have to rack a gold

'Cause rappin ain't for nothing, unless I hold plaques

So I can sit up on a boat like Colin, roll that

And you know that

[Chorus]

See, this here is the most serious

That I've ever been, the most clear-headed

My gear fetish clearly needs an account

So if I need, I'll smoke 'em all like Dennis Leary and I'm out

That's great, though. Thanks for adding more insecurities

Just as I was finding my level of maturity

Just as I was mindin my business, try to murder Jean's confidence

But lucky for me you're all incompetent

Road-blockin this guess, I see 'em tryin

To put a stop to my obnoxiousness, but

I stay long-winded like saying "George Papadopolis"

I know, but I write from the heart with this

So I've got some things to work on

My moodiness like masturbation gets its jerk on

My fascination with the fast pace—money's encapsulated

In my mind space like: "What a thrill"

Past-dated and I know I'm not in last place

But it's hard to work through it with this masked face

The masking tape up on the window keeps the cold out

And every time I'm layin down my back breaks 'cause it's old now

I yell too much, get stressed too quick

But the best thing about it, I can change that shit

And still remain who I came down to Earth to be

It's not Jean Grae, that's just a name, you'll see

[Chorus]

IMMORTAL TECHNIQUE

Immortal Technique is a defiantly political, stolidly independent artist known for clever wordplay and fearless commentary on a range of controversial subjects. "I've heard 'Revolutionary Rapper,' 'Street Politician,' 'Political Rapper,' 'Activist MC,' all that shit," he says. "I pay it no mind. I know what it is to be pigeonholed in the game, so I don't worry about what people say. The hardest albums, even the birth of gangsta rap, was all revolutionary: *AmeriKKKa's Most Wanted, The Chronic,* Ice-T's *O.G.* How can someone listen to these albums and not hear a revolutionary message encoded in them? I represent the streets here in America and I represent the people from other countries that come here as a result of what has been done to their homeland. Every aspect of this rap game is political, any veteran will tell you that."[27]

Immortal Technique is not defined by his politics alone. "Industrial Revolution" is a fierce battle rap, full of cutting punch lines. "Dance with the Devil" is an arresting narrative that tells the tale of a youth's decline into crime with a shocking ending. Unlike so many rap stories, the protagonist is not the "I" of the rapper, but another person entirely.

DANCE WITH THE DEVIL

I once knew a nigga whose real name was William

His primary concern was making a million

Being the illest hustler that the world ever seen

He used to fuck movie stars and sniff coke in his dreams

A corrupted young mind at the age of thirteen

Nigga never had a father and his mom was a fiend

She put the pipe down, but for every year she was sober

Her son's heart simultaneously grew colder

He started hanging out, selling bags in the projects

Checking the young chicks, looking for hit and run prospects

He was fascinated by material objects

But he understood money never bought respect

He built a reputation 'cause he could hustle and steal

But got locked once and didn't hesitate to squeal

So criminals he chilled with didn't think he was real

You see, me and niggas like this have never been equal

I don't project my insecurities on other people

He fiended for props like addicts with pipes and needles

So he felt he had to prove to everyone he was evil

A fever-minded young man with infinite potential

The product of a ghetto-bred capitalistic mental

Coincidentally, dropped out of school to sell weed

Dancing with the devil, smoked until his eyes would bleed

But he was sick of selling trees and gave in to his greed

[Chorus]

Everyone trying to be trife never face the consequences

You probably only did a month for minor offenses

Ask a nigga doing life if he had another chance

But then again there's always the wicked that knew in advance

Dance forever with the devil on a cold cell block

But that's what happens when you rape, murder, and sell rock

Devils used to be gods, angels that fell from the top

There's no diversity because we're burning in the melting pot

So Billy started robbing niggas, anything he could do

He'd get his respect back in the eyes of his crew

Starting fights over little shit up on the block

Stepped up to selling mothers and brothers the crack rock

Working overtime for making money for the crack spot

Hit the jackpot and wanted to move up to cocaine
Fulfilling the Scarface fantasy stuck in his brain
Tired of the block niggas treating him the same
He wanted to be major like the cutthroats and the thugs
But when he tried to step to 'em, niggas showed him no love
They told him any motherfucking coward can sell drugs
Any bitch nigga with a gun can bust slugs
Any nigga with a red shirt can front like a Blood
Even Puffy smoked a motherfucker up in the club
But only a real thug can stab someone 'til they die
Standing in front of them, staring straight into their eyes
Billy realized that these men were well guarded
And they wanted to test him before business started
Suggested raping a bitch to prove he was coldhearted
So now he had a choice between going back to his life
Or making money with made men, up in the ciph'
His dreams about cars and ice made him agree
A hardcore nigga is all he ever wanted to be
And so he met them Friday night at a quarter to three

[Chorus]

They drove around the projects slow while it was raining
Smoking blunts, drinking and joking for entertainment
Until they saw a woman on the street walking alone
Three in the morning, coming back from work, on her way home
And so they quietly got out the car and followed her
Walking through the projects, the darkness swallowed her
They wrapped her shirt around her head and knocked her onto the floor
"This is it, kid. Now you got your chance to be raw"
So Billy yoked her up and grabbed the chick by the hair
And dragged her into a lobby that had nobody there
She struggled hard but they forced her to go up the stairs
They got to the roof and then held her down on the ground
Screaming, "Shut the fuck up" and "Stop moving around"
The shirt covered her face, but she screamed and clawed

So Billy stomped on the bitch until he'd broken her jaw
The dirty bastards knew exactly what they were doing
They kicked her until they cracked her ribs and she stopped moving
Blood leaking through the cloth, she cried silently
And then they all proceeded to rape her violently
Billy was made to go first, but each of them took a turn
Ripping her up and choking her until her throat burned
A broken jaw mumbled for God but they weren't concerned
When they were done and she was lying bloody, broken, and bruised
One of them niggas pulled out a brand new twenty-two
They told him that she was a witness for what she'd gone through
And if he killed her he was guaranteed a spot in the crew
He thought about it for a minute, she was practically dead
And so he leaned over and put the gun right to her head

I'm falling and I can't turn back
I'm falling and I can't turn back

Right before he pulled the trigger and ended her life
He thought about the cocaine with the platinum and ice
And he felt strong standing along with his new brothers
Cocked the gat to her head and pulled back the shirt cover
But what he saw made him start to cringe and stutter
'Cause he was staring into the eyes of his own mother
She looked back at him and cried 'cause he had forsaken her
She cried more painfully than when they were raping her
His whole world stopped, he couldn't even contemplate
His corruption had successfully changed his fate
And he remembered how his mom used to come home late
Working hard for nothing, 'cause now what was he worth?
He turned away from the woman that had once given him birth
And crying out to the sky 'cause he was lonely and scared
But only the Devil responded, 'cause God wasn't there
And right then he knew what it was to be empty and cold
And so he jumped off the roof and died with no soul
They say death takes you to a better place but I doubt it

After that they killed his mother and never spoke about it
And listen, 'cause the story that I'm telling is true
'Cause I was there with Billy Jacobs and I raped his mom, too
And now the Devil follows me everywhere that I go
In fact, I'm sure he's standing among one of you at my shows
And every street cipher listening to little thugs flow
He could be standing right next to you and you wouldn't know
The Devil grows inside the hearts of the selfish and wicked
White, brown, yellow, and black—color is not restricted
You have a self-destructive destiny when you're inflicted
And you'll be one of God's children that fell from the top
There's no diversity because we're burning in the melting pot
So when the Devil wants to dance with you, you better say never
Because the dance with the Devil might last you forever

INDUSTRIAL REVOLUTION
"The day of the Geechie is gone, boy. And you goin with him"

Yeah, nigga, Immortal Technique, metaphysics

The bling-bling era was cute but it's about to be done
I leave you full of clips like the moon blocking the sun
My metaphors are dirty like herpes but harder to catch
Like an escape tunnel in prison, I started from scratch
And now these parasites want a percent of my ASCAP
Trying to control perspective like a acid flashback
But here's a quotable for every single record exec
Get your fucking hands out my pocket, nigga, like Malcolm X
But this ain't a movie, I'm not a fan or a groupie
And I'm not that type of cat you can afford to miss if you shoot me
Curse the heavens and laugh when the sky electrocutes me
Immortal Technique, stuck in your thoughts, darkening dreams
No one's as good as good as me, they just got better marketing schemes
I leave you to your own destruction like sparkin a fiend
'Cause you got jealousy in your voice like Starscream
And that's the primary reason that I hate y'all faggots

I've been nice since niggas got killed over eight-ball jackets

And Reebok Pumps that didn't do shit for the sneaker

I'm a heat seeker with features that'll reach through the speaker

And murder counterrevolutionaries personally

Break a thermometer and force-feed his kids mercury

A & R's try jerkin me, thinking they call shots

Offered me a deal and a blanket full of small pox

You're all getting shot, you little fucking treacherous bitches

[Chorus]

This is the business and y'all ain't getting nothing for free

And if you devils play broke, then I'm taking your company

You can call it reparations or restitution

Lock and load, nigga, industrial revolution

I want fifty-three million dollars for my collar stands

Like the Bush administration gave to the Taliban

And fuck packing grams, nigga, learn to speak and behave

You wanna spend twenty years as a government slave?

Two million people in prison keep the government paid

Stuck in a six-by-eight cell alive in the grave

I was made by revolution to speak to the masses

Deep in the club, toast the truth, reach for your glasses

I'll burn an orphanage just to bring heat to you bastards

Innocent deep in a casket, Columbian fashion

Intoxicated off the flow like thug's passion

You motherfuckers will never get me to stop blastin

You better off asking Ariel Sharon for compassion

You better off begging for twenty points from a label

You better off battling cancer under telephone cables

Technique, chemically unstable, set to explode

Foretold by the Dead Sea Scrolls, written in code

So if your message ain't shit, fuck the records you sold

'Cause if you go platinum, it's got nothing to do with luck

It just means that a million people are stupid as fuck

Stuck in the underground, a general that rose to the limit

Without distribution, managers, a deal, or a gimmick
Revolutionary Volume 2, murder the critics
And leave your fucking body rotten for the roaches and crickets

[Chorus]

K'NAAN

K'naan is a Somali-born, Toronto-based rapper who grew up amid the violence and refugee camps brought on by his native country's ongoing civil war. On his debut, *The Dusty Foot Philosopher* (2005), he raps in stark detail and emotion about the horrors he witnessed in Mogadishu. "What's Hardcore?" is a lyrical broadside against the gangsta rappers in America who glamorize the war going on in the streets of New York or Los Angeles or Atlanta when the real war of which K'naan speaks is far from glamorous. "My Old Home" is a rich and complicated portrait of his native land—the good, the bad, and the ambivalent.

With all of this weighty subject matter, one might assume that K'naan is one of the breed of conscious rappers that rely on their righteous content at the expense of their lyrical skill. This is far from the case. Rhyming over rich instrumental tracks that draw from the full range of the African diaspora, K'naan laces the beats with lyrics that are as attuned to the ear as they are to the mind. He considers himself a poet, but he does so with the understanding that his poetry is inextricably bound up with music. "At some point I started to think in terms of melody," he says, explaining why he is an MC and not a poet bound strictly by the page. "Words were like the same as writing like a poet writes, but I was still thinking of melody and something like the guitar sounds built up on its own. It's natural, rather than me trying to have a certain career plan."[28] In K'naan, consciousness and craft combine.

WHAT'S HARDCORE?

I put a pen to the paper, this time as visual as possible
Guns blast at the hospital

The walls are whitewashed with tin rooftops

To show love you lick two shots. It's dangerous, man

Journalists hire gunmen, there's violent women

Kids trust no one 'cause fire burned them

Refugees die in boats headed for peace

Is anyone scared of death here? Not in the least

I walk by the old lady selling coconuts under the tree

Life is cheap here but wisdom is free

The beach boys hang on the side, leaning with pride

Scam artists and gangsters fiendin to fight

I walk with three kids that can't wait to meet God lately

That's Bucktooth, Mohamed, and Crybaby

What they do everyday just to eat, Lord have mercy

Strapped with an AK and they blood thirsty

[Chorus 2x]

So what's hardcore? Really, are you hardcore? Hmm

We begin our day by the way of the gun

Rocket-propelled grenades blow you away if you front

We got no police, ambulance, or firefighters

We start riots by burning car tires

They lootin, and everybody start shootin

Bullshit politicians talking 'bout solutions

But it's all talk, you can't go half a block

Without a roadblock. You don't pay at the roadblock

You get your throat shot and each roadblock is set up by these gangsters

And different gangsters go by different standards

For example, the evening is a no-go

Unless you wanna wear a bullet like a logo

In the day you should never take the alleyway

The only thing that validates you is the AK

They chew on Khat, it's sorta like coca leaves

And there ain't no police

[Chorus 2x]

I'ma spit these verses 'cause I feel annoyed
And I'm not gonna quit 'til I fill the void
If I rhyme about home and got descriptive
I'd make 50 Cent look like Limp Bizkit
It's true, and don't make me rhyme about you
I'm from where the kids is addicted to glue
Get ready, he got a good grip on the machete
Make rappers say they do it for love like R. Kelly
It's hard, harder than Harlem and Compton intertwined
Harder than harboring Bin Laden and rewind
To that earlier part when I was kinda like
We begin our day by the way of the gun
Rocket-propelled grenades blow you away if you front
We got no police, ambulances, or firefighters
We start riots by burning car tires
They looting and everybody starting shooting

[Chorus 2x]

MY OLD HOME

So, yeah, basically a lot of people ask me how life was then. So here it is . . .

My old home smelled of good birth
Boiled red beans, kernel oil, and hand me down poetry
Its brick whitewashed walls widowed by first paint
The tin rooftop humming songs of promise while time is
Locked into demonic rhythm with the leaves
The trees had the wind hugging them
Lovin them a torturous love
Buggin when it was over and done
The round cemented pot kept the raindrops cool
Neighbors and dwellers spatter in the pool
Kid's playin football with his hand and sock
We had what we got and it wasn't a lot
No one knew they were poor

We were all innocent to greed's judgment

The country was combusting with life like a long hibernating volcano

With a long tale of success like J-Lo

Farmers, fishers, fighters, even fools had a place in production

The coastal line was the place of seduction

The coral reefs make you daze in reflection

The women walked with grace and perfection

And we just knew we were warriors, too

Nothing morbid, it's true, we were glorious BOOM!

Then one day it came, spoiled the parade like rain

Like oil in a flame, it pained

The heart attack sudden, odder than eleven

Harder than a punch in the womb

Harder than the lunch you consume

For us, it had a cancerous fume, or a lust

Men who made killing holy

Selling powerfully like healthy livestock

It made tides rock with a diligent mock

Confused are the people, infused in the evil

Professed to eject like Jews in the sequel, so when

It came in the morning, with a warning and without

The hurting was a burden, only certain was doubt

A mythical tale, no soul knows well

Liberty went to hell, freedom called for shells

Fierce was the blow, keep your ears to the show

It appears Orwell was right in '84

Had big brother kill Mother in her store

With all of us watching, we didn't love her anymore

Peep my poem, Mother was my old home

Good will is looted in my old home

Religion is burned down in my old home

Kindness is shackled in my old home

Justice has been raped in my old home

Murderers hold post in my old home
The land vomits ghosts in my old home

We got pistols with eyes, corruption and lies
Trusting snakes, and death without breaks
Suspicious newborns live in our horn
Used to the pain, rack bodies not grain
Chopped limbs not trees, spend lives not wealth
Seek vengeance not truth, the craziest youth
Hoist pain not plans, nigga, fuck your plans

Bandits will beat us down in my old home
Rumors are law now in my old home
Sedatives of faith in my old home
Rapers are praised in my old home
Demons dress well in my old home
Infants are nailed in my old home
Spirits are jailed in my old home
Grudges grow tails in my old home

Our roads have seen electric hate and
Our women labor beneath stubborn faith and
Our farms produce guilty grub and
Our kids depend on shifty luck, see
Our news is life for death is old, so
Don't blame me for truth I've told, say

Good will is looted in my old home
Religion is burned down in my old home
Kindness is shackled in my old home
Justice has been raped in my old home
Murderers hold post in my old home
The land vomits ghosts in my old home

TALIB KWELI

In rap, Talib Kweli's name is synonymous with depth and excellence. Even Jay-Z, considered by many to be the greatest rapper ever, famously named-checked Kweli on "Moment of Clarity": "If skills sold, truth be told / I'd probably be lyrically Talib Kweli." Though some consider Talib Kweli a "conscious" rapper rather than a commercial one, he rejects the designation, preferring to understand hip-hop as a culture without divisions. "I'm a fan of demolishing those terms because I think those terms divide our music," he told hip-hop journalist Davey D.[29]

Talib Kweli is a technically sophisticated rhymer who makes ample use of a range of poetic techniques, all while delivering provocation for thought. His vocal tone is high-pitched and nasal, which he uses to his advantage, even bending his voice toward song at times. His style employs a dense tapestry of syllables, delivered at whim and consciously off the beat, and he makes ample use of wordplay, particularly of similes. "When you are honest with your craft," he says, "it comes out fly-er than anything you try to write for radio."[30]

RE:DEFINITION
(Black Star w/ Mos Def)
What what what, what what, what what, what what
Whyohh!

[Chorus]
One two three, Mos Def and Talib Kweli
We came to rock it on to the tip-top
Best alliance in hip-hop, whyohh
I said, one, two, three, Black Star shine eternally
We came to rock it on to the tip-top
And Hi-Tek make the beat drop, whyohh

[Talib Kweli]
RE:DEFinition, turning your play into a tragedy
Exhibit level degree on the mic passionately
Niggas is sweet, so I bet if I bit I'd get a cavity
Livin to get high, you ain't flyer than gravity

We Die Hard like the battery done in the back of me by the mad MC

Who think imitation is the highest form of flattery, actually

Don't be mad at me, I had to be the one to break it to you

You get kicked into obscurity like judo—no, Menudo

'Cause you pseudo, tryin to compete with reality like Xerox

Towards destruction you spiraling like hairlocks, wipe them teardrops

Chasing stars in your eyes, playing games with your lives

Now the wives is widows soakin up pillows, weepin like willows

Still mo' blacks is dyin, kids ain't livin, they tryin

"How to Make a Slave" by Willie Lynch is still applyin

Regardless, the Mos is one of my closest partners

Rockin ever since before Prince was called The Artist

Rockin before Funkmaster Flex was rockin Starter

When 'Pac and Biggie was still cool, before they was martyrs

Life or death, if I'm choosin, with every breath I'm enhancin

Stop, there comes a time when you can't run

[Mos Def]

What, lyrically handsome, call collect, a king's ransom

Jams I write soon become the ghetto anthem

Way out like Bruce Wayne's mansion, move like a phantom

You'll talk about me to your grandsons

Cats who claimin they hard be mad fag

So I run through 'em like flood water through sandbags

Competition is mad, what I got, they can't have

Sinkin they ship like Moby Dick did Ahab

Son, I'm way past the minimum, enter a millennium

Where rap stars hold a gat to your back like Palestinians

Ancient Abyssinia, shorn a horn of Gideon

Official b-boy gentlemen won't turn off at the interim

Born inside the winter wind, day after December 10

These simpletons, they mentionin the synonym for feminine

Sweeter than some cinnamon in Danish rings by Entenmann's

Rush up on adrenaline, they get they asses sent to them

(Gentlemen) you got a tenement, well then assemble it
Leave your unit tremblin like herds of movin elephant
Intelligent embellishment, follow for your element
From Flatbush settlement, skin possesses melanin
Hotter than tales of crack peddlin, makin 'em WOOP
Like blue gelatin, swing like Duke Ellington
Broader than Barrington Levy, believe me
The hot Apache red who burnt down your chief teepee
You see me?

One two three, Mos Def and Talib Kweli
We came to rock it on to the tip-top
Best alliance in hip-hop, wayohh
I said, one, two, three, Black Star shine eternally
We came to rock it on to the tip-top
Because we rulin hip-hop, yes, we is rulin hip-hop
Talib Kweli is rulin hip-hop
Say we Black Star, we rule hip-hop-ah-ahh-ah-ahh-ahh
Whoahhhh!

FOR WOMEN

*Yeah, so we got this tune called "For Women," right? Originally, it was by Nina
    Simone. She said it was inspired by, you know, down South. In the South, they
    used to call her Mother "Auntie." She said, "No Mrs., you know, just Auntie,"
    you know what I'm saying? She said if anybody ever called her "Auntie" she'd
    burn the whole goddamn place down. Know what I'm sayin? But, you know,
    we're movin past that, you know what I'm sayin, coming into the new
    millennium, we can't forget our elders . . .*

I got off the 2 train in Brooklyn on my way to a session
Said let me help this woman up the stairs before I get to steppin
We got in a conversation, she said she a 107
Just her presence was a blessing and her essence was a lesson
She had her head wrapped and long dreads that peeked out the back
Like antenna to help her get a sense of where she was at

Imagine that, livin a century, the strength of her memories
Felt like an angel had been sent to me
She lived from nigger to colored to Negro to Black
To Afro then African-American and right back to nigger
You'd figure she'd be bitter in her twilight
But she aight, 'cause she done seen the circle of life
Yo, her skin was black like it's packed with melanin
Back in the days of slaves, she packin like Harriet Tubman
And her arms are long and she moves like song
Feet with corns, hand with calluses, but the heart is warm
And her hair is wooly and attract a lot of energy
Even negative, she gotta dead that, the head wrap is her remedy
Her back is strong and she's far from a vagabond
This is the back the master's whip used to crack upon
Strong enough to take all the pain that's been inflicted
Again and again and again and again and flip it
To the love for her children, nothing else matters
What do they call her? They call her Aunt Sarah

I know a girl with a name as beautiful as the rain
Her face is the same but she suffers an unusual pain
Seems she only deal with losers who be usin them games
Chasin the real brothers away like she confused in the brain
She try to get in where she fit in on that American Dream mission
Paid tuition for that receipt to find out her history was missing
And started flippin, seeing the world through very different eyes
People askin her what she'll do when it come time to choose sides
Yo, her skin is yellow, it's like her face is blond, word is bond
And her hair is long and straight just like Sleeping Beauty
See, she truly feel like she belong in two worlds
And that she can't relate to other girls
Her father was rich and white, still livin with his wife
But he forced himself on her mother late one night—they call it rape
That's right, and now she take flight through life with hate and spite

Inside her mind that keep her up to the break of light a lot of times

(I gotta find myself) (I gotta find myself)

(I gotta find myself) She had to remind herself

They called her Safronia, the unwanted seed

Blood still blue in her vein and still red when she bleeds

(Don't, don't, don't hurt me again) [8x]

Teenage lovers sit on the stoops up in Harlem

Holdin hands under the Apollo marquee dreamin of stardom

Since they was born the streets is watchin and schemin, and now it got them

Generations facin diseases that don't kill you, they just got problems

And complications that get you first. Yo, it's getting worse

When children hide the fact that they pregnant 'cause they scared of givin
   birth

"How will I feed this baby? How will I survive? How will this baby shine?"

Daddy dead from crack in '85, Mommy dead from AIDS in '89

At fourteen the baby hit the same streets, they became a master

The children of the enslaved, they grow a little faster

They bodies become adult while they keep the thoughts of a child

Her arrival into womanhood was hemmed up by her survival

Now she twenty-five, barely grown, out her own

Doin whatever it takes—strippin, workin out on the block, up on the phone

Talkin about, "My skin is tan like the front of your hand

And my hair? Well, my hair's alright whatever way I want to fix it

It's alright; it's fine. But my hips, these sweet hips of mine

Invite you, Daddy. And when I fix my lips my mouth is like wine

Take a sip; don't be shy. Tonight I wanna be your lady

I ain't too good for your Mercedes, but first you got to pay me

Quit with all them questions, sugar—whose little girl am I?

Why? I'm yours if you got enough money to buy

You better stop with the compliments, we running out of time

You wanna talk? Whatever. We could do that; it's your dime

From Harlem is where I came, don't worry about my name

Up on one-two-five they call me Sweet Thang"

A daughter come up in Georgia, ripe and ready to plant seeds

Left the plantation when she saw a sign even though she can't read

It came from God, when life get hard she always speak to him

She'd rather kill her babies than let the master get to 'em

She on the run up North to get across the Mason-Dixon

In church she learned how to be patient and keep wishin

The promise of eternal life after death for those that God bless

She swears the next baby she'll have will breathe a free breath

And get milk from a free breast, and love being alive

Otherwise they'll have to give up being themselves to survive

Being maids, cleaning ladies, maybe teachers or college graduates

Nurses or housewives, prostitutes and drug addicts

Some will grow to be old women, some will die before they born

They'll be mothers and lovers who inspire and make songs

"But me, my skin is brown and my manner is tough

Like the love I give my babies when the rainbow's enuff

I'll kill the first motherfucker that mess with me, I never bluff

I ain't got time to lie; my life has been much too rough

Still running with bare feet, I ain't got nothin but my soul

Freedom is the ultimate goal, life and death is small on the whole

In many ways. I'm awfully bitter these days

'Cause the only parents God gave me, they were slaves

And it crippled me, I got the destiny of a casualty

But I live through my babies and I change my reality

Maybe one day I'll ride back to Georgia on a train

Folks round there call me Peaches—I guess that's my name"

GIVE 'EM HELL

*Okay. This what it is nowadays, right? Little noises and whatnot. I got one
   though. Ready or not.*

[Sung]
We know that what we reap we sow
But we forget how low we can go

We think it's bad here on earth
But if we don't get to Heaven it's Hell

[Chorus]
It's all going to (Hell)
It's all going to (Hell)
Yup, we living in (Hell)
Yup, they giving us (Hell)
It's all going to (Hell)
It's all going to (Hell)
Yup, we living in (Hell)
Word

Every Sunday dressing up, catching gossip at its worst
Couldn't see the difference in the Baptist and the Catholic Church
Caught up in the Rapture of the first chapter and second verse
If we all God's children then what's the word of the Reverend worth?
Taught early that faith is blind like justice when you facing time
If we all made in God's image then that means his face is mine
Wait—or is that blasphemy? It's logical, it has to be
If I don't look like my father then the way I live is bastardly
Naturally that's confusion to a young'un trying to follow Christ
Taught that if you don't know Jesus then you lead a hollow life
Never question the fact that Jesus was Jewish, not a Christian
Or that Christianity was law according to politicians
Who was King James? And why did he think that it was so vital
To remove chapters and make his own version of the Bible?
They say Hell is underground and Heaven is in the sky
And they say that's where you go when you die—but how they know?

[Chorus]

I've been to many churches; I've quoted many verses
I've dealt with my base self; I control my many urges
I used to study my lessons, it was a blessing not a curse
I learned that Heaven and Hell exist right here on Earth, word

I've studied with Rastafarians and learned from the dreads
That Hell is called Babylon and that's where them crazy baldheads dwell
They got us thinking that Muslims like to make bombs
But real Muslims believe in paradise and resist the Shaitan
So it all sound the same to me, that's why when they say
One's right and the other's wrong it just sound like game to me
It's like God skipped past the church and came to me. No, that ain't vain
To me, it's just a particular way that I came to see
The difference between those who claim to be religious
And those that say they spiritual and recognize that life is full of miracles
You could see my glow in a rhyme, the poem divine 'cause it coincide
With the growin tide of those who lookin for God and know to go inside

[Chorus]

Living in mass confusion, looking for absolution
The gas-seducer psychopath produced the last solution
Based on his interpretation of what the words were saying
Trying to get to God but ended up doing the work of Satan
Religion create division, make the Muslim hate the Christian
Make the Christian hate the Jew, make up rules of faith that you
Conditioned to and gotta follow and God forbid you go to Hell
But if you ever walked through any ghetto then you know it well

[Chorus]

"The Lord is my shepherd; I shall not want." Just because the Lord is my shepherd
don't mean I gotta be no sheep, feel me? More blood is spilled over religion
than anything in world history. We saying the same thing.

LIL WAYNE

Lil Wayne divides people into sides, with some—including himself—calling him the greatest rapper alive, and others dismissing him as a gimmick rapper or a victim of his own vices. Much of what surrounds him carries the weight of myth: He never writes down a single line of lyrics. He records almost every waking hour. He is—again in his own words—a Martian.

Whatever one might think of him, he is a lyrical craftsman in the oral tradition, using the fact that he does not write down his lyrics to his advantage. Wayne relies heavily on aural devices like homonyms and homophones, assonance, alliteration, and, of course, rhyme. He grounds his wordplay in puns, turns of phrase that make the most of the play of sound.

When Lil Wayne released his first solo album, *Tha Block Is Hot* (1999), he was already a rap veteran, having recorded alongside his Cash Money label mates since he was eleven years old. Between 1999 and 2008 he released six studio albums, a respectable output. But it is through mix tapes that Wayne built his considerable fame. In that same span, dozens of official and unofficial mix tapes have appeared featuring hundreds of songs.

The lyrics that follow chart the trajectory of Lil Wayne's career to this point, with his early solo effort "Tha Block Is Hot" all the way to his 2008 multiplatinum album *Tha Carter III*. But it may be on his mix tape lyrics that we get the clearest glimpse into Wayne's mind and mad artistry. "I Feel Like Dying" is an ambivalent and abstract paean to chemical dependency in which Wayne fragments his words, reciting them with deliberate attention to each broken syllable.

FROM **THA BLOCK IS HOT**

Straight off the block thang, nuts in my hand, trustin no man
Got my Glock cocked, runnin this thing, ya understand?
We be steamin, blazin, nines pumped in caves and
Hollygrove Seventeenth, the 'hood where I was raised in
Niggas bustin heads in, runnin, duckin Feds and
Rocks under they tongues and ki's under they beds and
Do it for the real niggas, twenty-four seven hustlers
Ehhh, until we shove a barrel down ya pipe, suckers
Ain't no love for no busta, no pimp for no coward

No respect for no stunt and no money without power

We keepin niggas hotter, ewwww, nasty and sour

Pile up in the Eddie Bauer and blakka at every hour

Some niggas like that powder, fold it up with that drain

Some like that weed or that dope and some shoot it up in they veins

From the home of the game, jackin and crackin brains

Broadcastin live from Tha Block it's Lil Wayne

I FEEL LIKE DYING

Only once the drugs are done that I feel like dying . . . I feel like dying [3x]

Yeah, hello . . .
Get lifted . . .
Yeah, I get lifted
Yeah, yeah, so get lifted . . . yup! Haha . . .

I am sittin on the clouds, I got smoke comin from my seat

I can play basketball with the moon, I got the whole world at my feet

Playin touch football on Marijuana Street

Or in a marijuana field, you are so beneath my cleats

Get high, so high that I feel like lying

Down in a cigar, roll me up and smoke me 'cause . . .

(I feel like dying)

Only once the drugs are done that I feel like dying . . . I feel like dying [2x]

Swimming laps around a bottle of Louis the XIII

Jumpin off of a mountain into a sea of Codeine

I'm at the top of the top, but still I climb

And if I should ever fall, the ground would then turn to wine

Pop-pop, pop-pop, I feel like flying . . .

Then I feel like frying, then . . .

(I feel like dying)

Only once the drugs are done that I feel like dying . . . I feel like dying [2x]

I can mingle with the stars and throw a party on Mars

I am a prisoner locked up behind Xanax bars

I have just boarded a plane without a pilot

And violets are blue, roses are red

Daisies are yellow, the flowers are dead

Wish I can give you this feeling I feel like buying

And if my dealer don't have no more, then . . .

(I feel like dying)

Only once the drugs are done that I feel like dying . . . I feel like dying [2x]

LIVE FROM THE 504

Live from the five hundred and fo'

It's Mr. Crazy Flow jumpin like a bungee, no rope

Even in the dungeon I glow, even if it ain't sunny I glow

If it ain't about money I go . . . nowhere, I'm nailed to the flo'

Money controls where I go; it is the sail to my boat

And it's goin down, it's goin down like there's a whale in the boat

See, you can smell that I smoke, and, yeah, I sip that Lean

You hit me with that combination that make my eyes bleed

I'm a shark in the water, yep, I swim with the bigs

So I don't have time to deal with Willie the Squid

Li-li-lilipad niggas, I-I-look at the monsta

You-you-you don't wanna crash like La-La-La Bamba

See, it's me, Ronnie, and Terry and my new drop is berry

Watermelon plum, just call it fruit punch

I'm a old rapper gettin new bucks

And all ya new rappers, ya just new lunch

Flow sick, so sick need a doc, yes

A creature monster like the Loch Ness

I gets hotter by tha tock before I sizzle to death

I just tell the clock, "Gimme a sec"

In the middle of the war, where my enemy at?

I'm runnin this bitch like Eric Bieniemy back

'Cause every time I hear the track I'm like a energy pack

The instruments are cryin out, "Where the sympathy at?"

Yeah, if you bettin money, baby, him'll be back

Whatever legends look like, bitch, I'm fin ta be dat

I walk right in hip-hop like, "Where my dinna be at?"

I ate that and I was like, "Where my dinner be at?"

I hate that women lie, so I lie to them back

Got two bitches in my pants, quiet, nada dem that

Lotta bitches want dick, I give a lot of them that

Let's do a pill, I could fuck ya for a hour with that

To the kids, drugs kill—I'm acknowledgin that

But when I'm on the drugs, I don't have a problem with that

And my niggas got guns the size of toddlers, biatch

And we aimin right at ya fuckin collar, biatch

DR. CARTER

Where's my coffee?

Good morning, Dr. Carter

Hey, Sweetie

Looks like it's going to be a long day

Ahh, another one ... What we got?

Your first patient ...

Yeah

... is suffering from a lack of concepts

Uh-huh

originality

Ugh

his flow is weak

Another one ...

and he has no style

Ugh

Whatcha got for him?

Okay, let me put my gloves on and my scrubs on

Dr. Carter to the rescue. Excuse

Me if I'm late, but like a thief it takes

Time to be this great. Uh, so just wait

Your style is a disgrace, your rhymes are fifth place

And I'm just grace. One, uno, ace

And I'm tryin to make your heart beat like bass

...But you're sweet like cake

And I come to fix whatever you shall break

Where is your originality? You are so fake

So picture me like a gallery, capture what I say

All I need is one mic. All I need is one take

Like hey, brighter than the sun ray

Got a pistol on the playground, watch the gun play

Like, no kidding, no kids in the way

But the kids do watch, gotta watch what we say

Gotta work everyday, gotta not be cliché

Gotta stand out like André Three-K

Gotta...kick it, kick it like the sensei

You gotta have faith, you gotta gotta—...wait wait

(I think I...think I lost him...)

Good afternoon, Dr. Carter

Nurse

I don't know about this one. His confidence is down, vocab and metaphors needs
*   work, and he lacks respect for the game.*

Ahhh. Let me see

You think you can save him?

Okay, respect is in the heart. So that's where I'ma start

And a lot of heart patients don't make it

Now hey, kid—plural, I graduated

"'Cause you could get through anything if Magic made it"

And that was called recycling, RE: reciting

Something 'cause you just like it so you say it just like it

Some say it's biting but I say it's enlightening

Besides, Dr. Kanye West is one of the brightest

And Dr. Swizz can stitch your track up the tightest

And Dr. Jeezy can fix you back up the nicest

Arthritis in my hand from writin

But I'm a doctor, they don't understand my writin

So I stop writin. Now I'm like lightnin

And you ain't Vince Young so don't clash with the Titan

Fast and excitin, my passion is frightening

Now let me put some more vocab in your I.V.

Here, take this Vicodin, like it and love it

And confidence has no budget

So pay me no mind, I don't walk it

Like I talk it 'cause I run it, I don't do it 'cause I done it

And I'm in the emergency on it

God darnit, I've lost another one . . .

Good evening, Dr. Carter. It's been a long day, but this one looks much better

than the others. His respect is back up, concepts sound good, his style is

showing strong signs of improvement. All he needs now is his swagger.

Okay, let me take my gloves off then . . .

Swagger tighter than a yeast infection

Fly, go hard like geese erection

Fashion patrol, police detection

Eyes stay tight like Chinese connection

I stay tight like pussy at night

Baby, don't get me wrong, I could do that pussy right

But I'm too wrong to write, too fresh to fight

Too paid to freestyle, too paid to freestyle

Had to say it twice, swagger so nice

And don't ask me shit unless it concern a price

And I don't rap fast, I rap slow

'Cause I mean every letter in the words in the sentence of my quotes

Swagger just flow sweeter than honey oats

That swagger, I got it, I wear it like a coat

Wait, as I put the light down his throat

I can only see flow. His blood starting to flow

His lungs starting to grow. This one starting to show

Strong signs of life. Where's the stitches? Here's the knife

Smack his face, his eyes open. I reply with a nice
"Welcome back, Hip-Hop. I saved your life"

He looks good. His vitals are up. He's looking good. He's looking good. I think we
got one. Dr. Carter, I think we got one. Yup. Yup, we got one. We saved him.
He's good. He's good. We got one. He's good.

LITTLE BROTHER

Little Brother is a rap duo from Durham, North Carolina, comprised of two MCs, Phonte and Rapper Big Pooh; the producer 9th Wonder was a founding member but left the group in 2007. Their debut, *The Listening* (2003), was laced with 9th Wonder's soulful, booming beats and Phonte and Pooh's often comic tales of everyday life. "All for You," transcribed below, appeared on *The Minstrel Show* (2005), a loosely conceptual album that critiques potentially nefarious trends in commercialized rap.

Both MCs approach their craft with analytical focus. Reflecting on his writing style, Big Pooh notes: "I write everything like one big run-on sentence, no slashes, no nothing, like one big block of words."[31] Phonte sees significant development in his writing style across their albums: "For me personally as a writer I used to be scared to go into a studio without something pre-written already. But now, for the past couple of years, I been pretty much doin my stuff on the spot. All my concepts have been worked on in the studio instead of writing at home, writing at work, writing in the car. I actually use the studio as my workplace. I've also been more into editing. We used to go and do a song in one night, but now I listen to a song and go back and redo the harmony."[32]

ALL FOR YOU

[Rapper Big Pooh]
Uh, Dear Pops. It's your boy. I got some things I want to say to you, man. Just a
couple of words. Bear with me. Gimme a minute

Time to face it
Sitting in the middle of the basement holding a jack
How I'm anticipating he gon' call me back
Got so much on my mind, ain't no holding it back
In fact, I give a fuck how he gon' react
For my first nineteen, asking, "Where Lee at?"
Never seen him in the spots where we be at
For the next couple hours I sat 'til the phone rang
No luck or no cigar
So I said to myself I'll try tomorrow
Me and Vincent left out, went to shoot some ball
Came back, had a message like, "This your pa"
Then I took to the phone, conversation was raw
Shit, I had to let him know that his child was scarred
And right now we working through our mess
But I had to get some shit off my chest, so bear with me, y'all

[Chorus]
Just want to take the time to let you know
Sometimes it's hard to let my feelings show
The possibilities are really so...
This is all for you, you

[Phonte]
I was looking at your photograph, amazed how I favored you
I remember being young, wanting to play with you
'Cause you was a wild and crazy dude and now I understand
Why my mama couldn't never stay with you
From the roots to the branch to the leaves
They say apples don't fall far from the trees
Used to find it hard to believe and I swore that I would
Always hold my family as long as I could
But damn, our memories can be so misleading
It's misery, I hate to see history repeating
Thought you were the bad guy, but I guess that's why

Me and my girl split and my son is leaving

I did chores, did bills, and did dirt

But I swear to God I tried to make that shit work

'Til I came off tour to a empty house

With all the dressers and the cabinets emptied out

I think I must've went insane, thinking I was in love

But really in chains, trapped to this girl

Through the two-year-old who carried my name

I tried to stop tripping, but, yo, I couldn't and the plot thickened

That shit affected me, largely

Because I know a lot of people want me to fail as a father

And the thought of that haunts me, especially when I check

My rearview mirror and don't see him in his car seat

So the next time it's late at night

And I'm laid up with the woman I'ma make my wife

Talking 'bout how we gon' make a life

I'm thinking about child support, alimony, visitation rights

'Cause that's the only outcome, if you can't make it right

Pissed off with your children feeling the same pain

So, Pop, how could I blame 'cause you couldn't maintain?

I did the same thing, the same thing . . .

[Chorus 2x]

LUDACRIS

L udacris is a wild card, capable of comedic performances, head-
bobbing club bangers, menacing dis tracks, and songs of emotional reflection. In each instance, his personality and charisma
are at the forefront. "Just as my name implies—Ludacris—that's how my
music is," he says in explaining his style, "as long as they understand that

Ludacris means crazy and wild and ridiculous, that is exactly how I would explain it . . . It's looking for a little fun in [people's] lives."[33]

Though born and raised in Illinois, Ludacris has long called Atlanta home. After a successful career as a radio personality, he broke into rap in 2000 with his major-label debut, *Back for the First Time*. It boasted the hits "What's Your Fantasy" and "Southern Hospitality," the latter of which was driven by an infectious Neptunes-produced beat.

The hallmark of his style may be the idiosyncratic way that he emphasizes unexpected syllables, creating a kind of music to the line. At least in this regard, his flow bears some resemblance to the effusive deliveries popularized by old school artists like Kurtis Blow and Kool Moe Dee. But where those artists fell into regular rhythm patterns within the pocket of the beat, Ludacris bobs and weaves in relation to the music.

In 2000 Ludacris formed his own label, Disturbing tha Peace, and has gone on to amass a minor media empire that *Forbes* magazine estimated to be worth tens of millions of dollars. For all the wealth that the business of rap has brought him, Ludacris considers himself above all an artist. On "I Do It for Hip Hop" Luda, alongside Nas and Jay-Z, rhymes about his love of the culture: "I don't do it for the money, I do it from the heart / The van Gogh flow, Luda do it 'cause it's art."[34]

SOUTHERN HOSPITALITY

Cadillac grills, Cadillac mills
Check out the oil my Cadillac spills
Matter fact, candy paint Cadillacs kill
So check out the holes my Cadillac fills
Twenty inch wide, twenty inch high
Ho, don't you like my twenty-inch ride?
Twenty-inch thighs make twenty-inch eyes
Hoping for American twenty inch pies
Pretty-ass clothes, pretty-ass toes
Oh, how I love these pretty-ass hoes
Pretty-ass, high-class, anything goes
Catch 'em in the club throwin pretty-ass 'bows
Long-john drawers, long john stalls
Any stank puss' make my long john pause

Women on they cell makin long john calls
And if they like to juggle, get long John's balls

[Chorus]
All my players in the house that can buy the bar
And the ballin-ass niggas with the candy cars
If you a pimp and you know you don't love them hoes
When you get on the flo'—nigga, throw dem 'bows
All my women in the house if you chasin cash
And you got some big titties with a matchin ass
Witcha fly-ass boots or ya open toes
When ya get on the flo'—nigga, throw dem 'bows

Dirty South mind blowin Dirty South bread
Catfish fried up, Dirty South fed
Sleep in a cot pickin Dirty South bed
Dirty South guls gimme Dirty South head
Hand-me-down flip-flops, hand-me-down socks
Hand-me-down drug dealers hand-me-down rocks
Hand-me-down a fifty-pack Swisher Sweets box
And goodfella rich niggas hand-me-down stocks
Mouth full of platinum, mouth full of gold
Forty Glock cal' keep your mouth on hold
Lie through your teeth, you could find your mouth cold
And rip out ya tongue 'cause of what ya mouth told
Sweat for the lemonade, sweat for the tea
Sweat from the hot sauce, sweat from the D
And you can sweat from a burn in the third degree
And if you sweat in your sleep then you sweat from me

[Chorus]

Hit by stars, hit by cars
Drunk off the liquor, gettin hit by bars
Keep yo' gul close 'cause she's hit by far
Hit by the Neptunes, hit by guitars

Afro picks, Afro chicks

I let my Soul Glow from my Afro dick

Rabbit out the hat pullin Afro tricks

Afro-American, Afro thick

Overall country, overall jeans

Overall Georgia, we overall clean

"Southern Hospitality" or overall mean

Overall triple, overall beams

Thugged out niggas wear thugged out chains

Thugged out blocks playin thugged out games

All black tinted up thugged out Range

DTP stay doing thugged out thangs

[Chorus 2x]

HIP HOP QUOTABLES

Hi, my name's Ludacris and I'm high as giraffe butts (yeah)

And I'm close to the edge so your parents can come push me

I curse so much just to get on they nerves

I got kids acting a fool from the traps to the 'burbs

My filthy mouth, it won't fight cavities or beat plaque

So I shot the Tooth Fairy (aahhh) and took my old teeth back

I'll take a shit on the equator the size of a crater

And make government officials breathe harder than Darth Vader

It's the chicken and the beer that makes Luda keep rapping

But no pork on my fork, I don't even speak pig Latin

I go fishing on my lake with your bitch as the bait

Plus I eat many MCs but I don't gain no weight

The number one chief rocker, clean out your rap lockers

I'm as stiff as a board, y'all more shook than maracas

But my tricks ain't for kids, if you dig 'em you'll get smacked

I'll clock ya—I'll spring forward, you fall back (whoo)

Every album that I drop has got more than ten bangers (yeah)

That's 'cause I'm a shot caller, y'all fools is Crank Yankers

Ain't a damn thing changed but the ice on my chain

I get chicks from Portland, Oregon, to Portland, Maine

Now I roll up torpedoes, get blunted with Rastas

For a hefty fee I'm on your record like Bob Costas (yeah)

I own so many jerseys, I'm a throwback mess

I hit the cleaners and tell 'em I want a full court press (ohh)

So, mama, toast ya glass while I'm counting my cash

'Cause every single is a smash, I'm hot as a camel's ass (ha)

The competition never just wanna admit that they lost

And that they last about as long as my part in *The Wash*

From your car to crap game, no one rolls with you

One of Mini-Me's shoes got more soul than you (okay)

So by the time you figure out why your record ain't spinning

I'm in the strip club smokin with President Clinton (cough cough cough)

So stand clear of the long sideburns and goatee (tee)

They make the mold of the penis enlarger off me (me)

I'll be in another when I hit from the back (back)

Not to mention my refrigerator's taller than Shaq (yeah)

So yippie ka ye yippie ya ya yo (yo)

If you can't swim don't smoke my hydro (dro)

I've been looking for a woman just to put my stamp on

But a lotta y'all are more stuck up than tampons (whoo)

So wash all your sins away and stop playing (yeah)

If God's line is busy you might have to two-way him (uh hmm)

Then catch me in your backyard playing croquet

And when I'm drunk, tellin kids, "Drugs are bad, umm-kay"

Or watch me swing my chains at the Roscoe's off Pico

Got seven cars, get all my rims at Chrome Depot

And people think I'm bad, they say, "Ooh, he's so evil"

'Cause I go on blind dates with actual blind people (ohh)

But my album's out the store, yours be on the shelf (uh-hmm)

I heard you masturbate a lot, so y'all keep to yourself

'Cause these women want a man to stay up and stay strong

Like the NBA, you gotta play hard or go home

All that shit that y'all talking, y'all can pop it to them

'Cause Ludacris will beat you down with a prosthetic limb
I'll put my foot so deep in your ass that you can smell it
And your breath'll turn to Foot Locker water repellent
I'm the man, I got money far as the eyes can see
And I'm in a group—I split dough wit' me, me, and me
So much money in my jewelry that I'm damn near sorry
So I'ma trade my earrings in and get a Ferrari (whoo)
I buy cars with straight cash, have meetings with Donald Trump
Y'all meet with Honda, no payments for twelve months (uh huh)
Take a look at your life and no wonder you so sad
Y'all put up with more shit than a colostomy bag
Fool! Ha ha ha...

M.I.A.

M.I.A.'s music collects sounds from all around the world and blends them in a musical genre she playfully identifies as "other." For those familiar with her dynamic vocals and eclectic soundscapes, her style is something less ambiguous: a polyphonic and political music for a new hip-hop era.

Maya Arulpragasam was born in London but raised in Sri Lanka, where she witnessed civil war firsthand. When her father left to found a Tamil revolutionary party, she relocated to London with the rest of her family. Her family history shapes her music—her first two albums, *Arular* (2005) and *Kala* (2007), are named after her father and mother, respectively. M.I.A. ties her political lyrics to pounding beats, and her unique but spare mélange of diction finds a fitting environment in a thicket of sounds both familiar and fresh to rap.

SUNSHOWERS

I bongo with my lingo
And beat it like a wing, yo

To Congo, to Colombo
Can't stereotype my thing, yo
I salt and pepper my mango
Shoot spit out the window
Bingo, I got him in the thing, yo
Now what? I'm doing my thing, yo
Quit bending all my fingo
Quit beating me like you're Ringo
You wanna go? You wanna win a war?
Like P.L.O., I don't surrendo

[Chorus]
'Cause sunshowers that fall on my troubles
Are over you, oh, baby
And some showers I'll be aiming at you
'Cause I'm watching you, my baby

I bongo with my lingo
And beat it like a wing, yo
To Congo, to Colombo
Can't stereotype my thing, yo
I checked that mouth on him
Fucking checked my gas on him
I had him, cornered him
Fucking shut that gate on him
Why would you listen to him?
He had his way, I'm bored of him
I'm tired of him
I don't wanna be as bad as him
It's a bomb, yo, so run, yo
Put away your stupid gun, yo
'Cause see through, like, protocol
This is why we blow it up 'fore we go

[Chorus 2x]

Semi-nine and snipered him
On my wall they posted him
They cornered him
And then just murdered him
And he told them he didn't know them
He wasn't there, they didn't know him
They showed him a picture then:
"Ain't that you with the Muslims?"
He got Colgate on his teeth
And Reebok Classics on his feet
At a factory he does Nike
And then helps a family
Beat heart, beat, he's
Made it to the *Newsweek*
Sweetheart, seen it, he's
Doing it for the peeps, peace

[Chorus 3x]

PAPER PLANES
I fly like paper, get high like planes
If you catch me at the border I got visas in my name
If you come around here, I make 'em all day
I get one done in a second if you wait
I fly like paper, get high like planes
If you catch me at the border I got visas in my name
If you come around here, I make 'em all day
I get one done in a second if you wait
Sometimes I think sitting on trains
Every stop I get to I'm clocking that game
Everyone's a winner, we're making our fame
Bona fide hustler, making my name
Sometimes I think sitting on trains
Every stop I get to I'm clocking that game

Everyone's a winner, we're making our fame
Bona fide hustler making my name

[Chorus 4x]
All I wanna do is (BANG BANG BANG BANG!)
And (KKKAAAA CHING!) and take your money

Pirate skulls and bones
Sticks and stones and weed and bombs
Running when we hit 'em
Lethal poison for the system
Pirate skulls and bones
Sticks and stones and weed and bombs
Running when we hit 'em
Lethal poison for their system

No one on the corner has swagger like us
Hit me on my burner, prepaid wireless
We pack and deliver like UPS trucks
Already going to hell just pumping that gas
No one on the corner has swagger like us
Hit me on my burner, prepaid wireless
We pack and deliver like UPS trucks
Already going to hell just pumping that gas

[Chorus 4x]

*M.I.A. Third world democracy. Yeah, I got more records than the K.G.B. So, uh,
no funny business …*

Some some some I some I murder
Some I some I let go
Some some some I some I murder
Some I some I let go

[Chorus 4x]

PHAROAHE MONCH

Pharoahe Monch is known for multisyllabic rhymes and intricate flows that use idiosyncratic rests to lend rhythmic variety. He released three albums in the 1990s as part of the duo Organized Konfusion along with Prince Poetry. Later, he signed a solo deal with the independent label Rawkus, releasing *Internal Affairs* (1999), an indie classic led by the anthem "Simon Says."

Pharoahe Monch's lyrical complexity has led some to criticize him for being too technical. "With me a lot of times, it is a concerted effort to do a dense piece of work—and I guess that's not for everybody," he explains. "Everybody doesn't go into a gallery and look at art the same way, and over the years I have painted more simple portraits. I just enjoy not being boxed in as a portrait painter or an abstract artist. You have works like 'Who Stole My Last Piece of Chicken?' and 'Fudge Pudge' and 'My Life' and 'Oh No,' and you also have works like 'Agent Orange' and '[Releasing] Hypnotical Gases' and 'Rape' and 'Trilogy,' which are a little more complicated and take more time for the listener to retrieve. But the beauty about that is that you listen to the album for a month and put it down, and [then you] pick it up again and you hear something new."[35]

RELEASING HYPNOTICAL GASES
(Organized Konfusion w/ Prince Poetry)

[Pharoahe Monch]
As you look from whenceforth I come
Riding the wind, thus eliminating
Competition from bird's-eye view, I'm
Descending in helicopters in a village raid
Flesh will burn when exposed to the poetical germ
Grenade, I'm highly intoxicating your mind
When I'm operating on cell walls to membranes
Cytoplasms and protoplasms, disintegrate 'em
Eliminate 'em, now no one has 'em in battle
I display a nuclear ray that'll
Destroy bone marrow in cattle

Thereby destroying the entire food supply

That's crawling with AIDS, maggots, flies

It's ironic when a demonic government

Utilizes bionics in a six million dollar man

To capture me. Clever. However

You could never ever begin to apprehend a hologram

Who's determined to fight solely

To defend in wars a land of the holy

I threw a rock and I ran

'Cause I couldn't stand anymore within the depths of the sand

So don't ask me who sane

'Cause the hypnotical gases are eating my brain

Oxygen levels? Check. Hydrogen levels? Check. Nitrogen levels? Check

[Prince Poetry]

Twenty-thousand leagues down below

Minus one hundred and forty-three degrees

Seize the info, gather the archeologists

The aftermath needs to follow this 'cause it's

Deep, equivalent to the esophagus

Spreads to scientists, a.k.a. Optimus Prime

Time, television is dead

On this issue and very much irrelevant to this intuition

Deleting any alias info and descriptive

Mortal calm, partition with infrared light

Vision, precision, beams

Colors, reds, fuchsias, lime-greens

Black, don't you know my formulas form dope lyrics

Uplift spirits? And, yo, I hear it's fatal

To walk the path of Konfusion

Where it's torture, some cherish while most

Humanlike beings perish, subjected to death

Their bodies don't agree with the hypnotical intellect

Poetical acid is burning up flesh

At the end of the corridor you see me sitting there
Jotting more grotesque literature somewhat equivalent
To concentrated sodium hypochlorite
Insight, foresight, more sight
The clock on the wall reads a quarter past midnight
You feel nauseous, forever you will
Avoid my royal presence as I step into darkness

Now is the time . . . to stretch your brain to its maximum

[Pharoahe Monch]
I am one who is one with all things
Thus the unorthodox I am
The paradox I am, the equinox extending my hand
Into dimensions to unlock new doorways
And so the light has revealed to me
That there must be more ways
And so I play with rhythms, for something more
Than a mere game enabling me to advance in wisdom
Words will exist like vampires
No need for sunlight, from concentration
Camps I escape with my sanity—
In 2010 every man will be
Subject to global warming, formless oval
Millions of locusts swarming
Seek and you shall find the deliverer of a rhyme
The intelligent one, utilizing the mind
Third vision surrounded by a three-sided figure
Containing the brain, the triggering mechanism
From which I strike sight beyond sight
Sound beyond sound, which comes from below
The magma, the granite, the ground
The surface will separate, dispersing harmful ashes
Your optics will not be able to detect
The deadly hypnotical gases

Damn, it's hard to breathe
But if I got one breath left
I'll suck wind from the valley of death
Here I come from the slums of Earth to center
I reveal myself as a beast within a
Unbreakable shell, walking through
The doorways of Heaven . . . or is this Hell?

The time is now. Right now. This is the hour, this is the new dawn! This is the
*   new day . . .*

[Prince Poetry]
As I step into the Thunderdome
With flows as the wind blows
Visualize the intros
Releasing hypnotical gases
Chemicals mixed, fixed
Takin it to the sixth round of poetical warfare
Energetically I walk with the flare
Rampaging like a rocklike figure
Throughout the night's atmosphere I swear
My wrist holds mind-trigger, darkness can't overshadow me
'Cause I have radar smashin you, then trashin you
After I'm bashin you with my hammer
Pitchfork passed to me by Odin
Occasionally my profile is low-key. Gamma
Rays brainwashed to transforms me
But I still withhold my hammer, to lift me up
For God still is my uplifter
I use this knowledge just to crush the cluster of grifter
Night approaches so I proceed in flight
Back to the Hall of Justice as I continue to disintegrate 'em
Translating the codes in hypnotical language
Then a Theta assault steppin up
Frontin to be blunt but I'm a radical creator

Of a poetical hypothetical mathematical slay slur
Punch that stuns and amazes and dazes
And phases and stages with pages of the
Lost chapters, unfound factors
So I stretch like Reed Richards across the land
Continue with reading your equilibrium
With concepts that confuse ya, metabolism's fallin off
Data can fit in a prism
Now as I walk through the valley of death ignorin
The battle lashes and gashes and rashes, the atom smashes
'Cause I released the last hypnotical gases!

SIMON SAYS
[Chorus]
Get the fuck up
Simon says get the fuck up
Throw your hands in the sky
Queens is in the back sippin yak, y'all, what's up?
Girls, rub on your titties (yeahhhhhh)
Yeah, I said it—rub on your titties
New York City gritty committee pity the fool that
Act shitty in the midst of the calm, the witty

Y'all know the name …
Pharoahe-fuckin-Monch, ain't a damn thang changed
You all up in the Range and shit, inebriated
Strayed from your original plan, you deviated
I alleviated the pain with the long-term goals
Took my underground loot without the gold
You sold platinum round the world, I sold wood in the 'hood
But when I'm in the street, then shit, it's all good
I'm soon to motivate a room, control the game like Tomb
Raider Roc-clock dollars flip, tips like a waiter
Block shots, style's greater, let my lyrics anoint
If you holdin up the wall, then you missin the point

[Chorus]

Yo, where you at? Uptown, let me see 'em

Notorious for the six-fives and the BMs

Heads give you beef, you put 'em in the mausoleum

And the shit don't start pumpin 'til after 12 P.M.

Ugnh, ignorant minds, I free 'em

If you tired of the same old everyday you will agree I'm

The most obligated, hard, and R-Rated

Stated to be the best, I must confess the star made it

Some might even say this song is sexist-eses

'Cause I asked the girls to rub on their breast-eses

Whether you're ridin the train or in Lexus-es

This is for either/or Rollies or Timex-eses

Wicked like *Exorcist,* this is the joint

You holdin up the wall, then you missin the point

[Chorus]

DESIRE

[Chorus]

Said it's my desire, yes it is, yeah

Yes it is, yes it is, oh yes it is, uhhh

Comprehend the guidelines

My chest out, chinchilla on, relaxed on the sidelines

I'm so famous, understand

New York City respect my game like Joe Namath

And I protect my name like your anus

In prison, y'all don't hear me, y'all don't listen

Y'all just wanna shine, y'all just wanna glisten

Floss, knowin that the soul is still missing

Who am I? I am the poetical pastor

Slave to a label but I own my masters

Still get it poppin without artist and repertoire

'Cause Monch is a monarch only minus the A&R

When my brain excels, your train derails

Pop shit, make you feel The Clipse like Pharrell

You will feel me, you will admire

(My) Struggle, (My) Hustle, (My) Soul, Desire

[Chorus]

My book is a ovary, the pages I lust to turn

My pen's the penis, when I write the ink's the sperm

Desire, the fire that ignites the torch that burns

This is not rocket science, this is easy to learn

My mic's a gavel; when I talk, court's adjourned

Respect, even if you were assets you couldn't earn

I embody antibiotics; you are infected with germs

Rap's fatally ill, please get concerned

Players, pick turns to play, get burned

I color-commentate the game like Chick Hearn

This is the moment of truth for my opponents and liars

Vocals alone invoke the emotion of black choirs

Fire, you don't wanna get burned like Rich Pryor

Move back. Who's that there? The live wire

You will feel me, you will admire

(My) Struggle, (My) Hustle, (My) Soul, Desire

[Chorus]

MOS DEF

Mos Def helped take the underground aboveground, gaining popular acclaim and record sales without making simple songs. He is a multitalented performer, known for his singing and acting as well as for his rhyming. As a singer, Mos has recorded in the dulcet tones of a song like "Umi Says" or in the hard-rock sounds of his

Black Jack Johnson project. As an actor on both the stage and the screen, Mos has elevated the reputation of the much-maligned rapper/actor hybrid.

Mos Def also stands out for the force of his political voice and vision, on display in the scathing lyrics to "Dollar Day," his response to the government's failures to respond to the ravages of Hurricane Katrina. Some of Mos Def's finest work came in his collaboration with Talib Kweli as Black Star. Mos's solo debut, *Black on Both Sides* (1999), announced the arrival of a powerful voice in contemporary hip-hop. "Hip hop is a beautiful culture," Mos told the *Los Angeles Times* in 2004. "It's inspirational, because it's a culture of survivors. You can create beauty out of nothingness."[36]

HIP HOP

You say one for the treble, two for the time
Come on, y'all, let's rock this!
You say one for the treble, two for the time
Come on!

Speech is my hammer, bang the world into shape, now let it fall . . . (Hungh!!)

My restlessness is my nemesis, it's hard
To really chill and sit still, committed to page
I write a rhyme, sometimes won't finish for days
Scrutinize my literature from the large to the miniature
I mathematically add-minister, subtract the wack
Selector, wheel it back, I'm feelin that
(Ha ha ha) From the core to the perimeter, Black
You know the motto: stay fluid even in staccato (Mos Def)
Full blooded, full throttle, breathe deep inside the drum hollow
. . . There's the hum
Young man, where you from? Brooklyn, number one
Native Son, speaking in the native tongue
I got my eyes on tomorrow (there it is), while you still tryna
Find where it is, I'm on the ave' where it lives and dies
Violently but silently . . . Shine
So vibrantly that eyes squint to catch a glimpse
Embrace the bass with my dark ink fingertips
Used to speak the King's English, but caught a rash on my lips

See, now my chat just like this

Long range from the baseline (swish). Move like a apparition

Go to the ground with ammunition (chi-chi-POW)

Move from the gate, voice cued on your tape

Putting food on your plate, many crews can relate

Who choosing your fate, yo

We went from picking cotton, to chain-gang line chopping

To be-bopping, to hip-hopping

Blues people got the blue-chip stock option

Invisible Man, got the whole world watching

(Where ya at?) I'm high, low, east, west, all over your map

I'm getting big props with this thing called hip hop

Where you can either get paid or get shot, when your product in stock

The fair-weather friends flock, when your chart position drop

Then the phone calls . . .

Chill for a minute, let's see who else hot

Snatch your shelf spot. Don't gas yourself, ock

The industry just a better-built cell block

A long way from the shell tops

And the bells that L rocked (rock, rock, rock, rock . . .)

Hip hop is prosecution evidence

A out of court settlement, ad space for liquor

Sick without benefits (hungh!), luxury tenements

Choking the skyline, it's low life getting tree-top high

It is a backwater remedy

Bitter intent to memory, a class C felony

Facing the death penalty (hungh!), stimulant and sedative

Original repetitive, violently competitive

A school unaccredited (there it is)

The break beats you get broken with on time and inappropriate

Hip hop went from selling crack to smoking it

Medicine for loneliness, remind me of Thelonious and Dizzy

Propers to b-boys getting busy

The wartime snapshot, the working man's jackpot

A two dollar snack box sold beneath the crack spot

Olympic sponsor of the black Glock

Gold medalist in the back shot from the sovereign state

Of the have-nots where farmers have trouble with cash crops

It's all-city like Phase 2, hip hop will simply amaze you

Praise you, pay you

Do whatever you say do, but Black, it can't save you

MATHEMATICS

*Booka-booka-booka-booka-booka-booka. Ha hah. You know the deal. It's just
me, yo. Beats by Su-Primo for all of my peoples, Negroes and Latinos. And
even the Gringos.*

Yo, check it, one for Charlie Hustle, two for Steady Rock

Three for the fourth comin live, future shock

It's five dimensions, six senses

Seven firmaments of heaven to hell, eight million stories to tell

Nine planets faithfully keep in orbit

With the probable tenth, the universe expands length

The body of my text possess extra strength

Power-liftin powerless up out of this towerin inferno

My ink so hot it burn through the journal

I'm blacker than midnight on Broadway and Myrtle

Hip-hop passed all your tall social hurdles

Like the nationwide projects, prison-industry complex

Workin class poor, better keep your alarm set

Streets too loud to ever hear freedom ring

Say evacuate your sleep, it's dangerous to dream

For cha-ching cats get they CHA-POW, who dead now?

Killin fields need blood to graze the cash cow

It's a number game, but shit don't add up somehow

Like I got sixteen to thirty-two bars to rock it

But only fifteen percent of profits ever see my pockets, like

Sixty-nine billion in the last twenty years
Spent on national defense but folks still live in fear, like
Nearly half of America's largest cities is one quarter black
That's why they gave Ricky Ross all the crack
Sixteen ounces to a pound, twenty more to a ki
A five minute sentence hearing and you no longer free
Forty-percent of Americans own a cell phone
So they can hear everything that you say when you ain't home
I guess Michael Jackson was right, "You Are Not Alone"
Rock your hardhat, Black, 'cause you in the Terrordome
Full of hard niggas, large niggas, dice tumblers
Young teens in prison greens facin life numbers
Crack mothers, crack babies, and AIDS patients
Young bloods can't spell but they could rock you in PlayStation
This new math is whippin motherfuckers' ass
You wanna know how to rhyme you better learn how to add
It's mathematics . . .

[Chorus 2x]

Yo, there's one universal law, but two sides to every story
Three strikes and you be in for life, mandatory
Four MCs murdered in the last four years
I ain't tryin to be the fifth one, the millennium is here
Yo, it's six million ways to die from the seven deadly thrills
Eight-year-olds getting found with nine mils
It's 10 P.M., where your seeds at? What's the deal?
They on the hill pumpin krill to keep they belly filled
Light in the ass with heavy steel, sights on the pretty shit in life
Young soldiers tryin to earn they next stripe
When the average minimum wage is $5.15
You best believe you gotta find a new grind to get cream
The white unemployment rate is nearly more than triple for black
So frontliners got they gun in your back
Bubblin crack, jewel theft, and robbery to combat poverty
And end up in the global jail economy

Stiffer stipulations attached to each sentence
Budget cutbacks but increased police presence
And even if you get out of prison still livin
Join the other five million under state supervision
This is business, no faces, just lines and statistics
From your phone, your zip code, to S-S-I digits
The system break man, child, and women into figures
Two columns for who is and who ain't niggas
Numbers is hardly real and they never have feelings
But you push too hard, even numbers got limits
Why did one straw break the camel's back? Here's the secret
The million other straws underneath it—it's all mathematics

[Chorus]

DOLLAR DAY FOR NEW ORLEANS (KATRINA KLAP)

*So there's a story about the lady in Louisiana. She's a flood survivor and the
rescue teams, they come through, and they, I guess tryna recover people.
And they see this woman, she's wadin through the streets. I guess it'd been
some time after the storm and I guess they were shocked that, you know, she
was alive. And rescue worker said, "So, oh my God, h-how did you survive?
How did you do it? Where've you been?" And she said, "Where I been?
Where you been?" Hah, where you been? You understand? That's about the
size of it.*

This for the streets, the streets everywhere
The streets affected by the storm called . . . America
I'm doin this for y'all, and for me, for the Creator

God save these streets
One dollar per every human being
Feel that Katrina clap
See that Katrina clap

Listen, homie, it's Dollar Day in New Orleans
It's water, water everywhere and people dead in the streets
And Mr. President, he 'bout that cash

He got a policy for handlin the niggas and trash
And if you poor, you black
I laugh a laugh, they won't give when you ask
You better off on crack
Dead or in jail, or with a gun in Iraq
And it's as simple as that
No opinion, my man, it's mathematical fact
Listen, a million poor since 2004
And they got -illions and killions to waste on the war
And make you question what the taxes is for
Or the cost to reinforce the broke levee wall
Tell the boss he shouldn't be the boss anymore
Y'all pray, amin?

[Chorus]
God save these streets
One dollar per every human being
Feel that Katrina clap
See that Katrina clap
God save these streets
Quit bein cheap, nigga, freedom ain't free
Feel that Katrina clap
See that Katrina clap

Lord have mercy
Lord God God save our soul
A-God save our soul, a-God
A-God save our souls
Lord God God save our soul
A-God save our soul soul soul
Soul survivor

It's Dollar Day in New Orleans
It's water, water everywhere and babies dead in the streets
It's enough to make you holler out
Like where the fuck is Sir Bono and his famous friends now?

Don't get it twisted, man, I dig U2

But if you ain't about the ghetto then fuck you, too

Who care 'bout rock and roll when babies can't eat food

Listen, homie—man, this shit ain't cool

It's like Dollar Day for New Orleans

It's water water everywhere and homies dead in the streets

And Mr. President's a natural ass

He out treatin niggas worse than they treat the trash

[Chorus]

Lord did not intend for the wicked to rule the world

Say, God did not intend for the wicked to rule the world

God did not intend for the wicked to rule the world

And even when they knew it's a matter of truth

Before they wicked ruling is through

God save these streets

A Dollar Day for New Orleans

God save these streets

Quit bein cheap, homie, freedom ain't free

[Chorus]

Don't talk about it, be about it

Peace

AUDITORIUM

(feat. Slick Rick)

[Mos Def]

The way I feel sometimes it's too hard to sit still

Things are so passionate, times are so real

Sometimes I try to chill, mellow down, blow a smoke

Smile on my face, but it's really no joke

You feel it in the street, the people breathe without hope

They goin through the motion, they dimmin down the focus

The focus get cleared then the light turn sharp

Then the eyes go teary, the mind grow weary

I speak it so clearly sometimes y'all don't hear me

I push it past the bass, no nations gotta feel me

I feel it in my bones, Black, I'm so wide awake

That I'm hardly ever sleep, my flow forever deep

And it's volumes of scriptures when I breathe on a beat

My presence speak volumes before I say a word

I'm everywhere: penthouse, pavement, and curb

Cradle to the grave, tall cathedral or a cell

Universal ghetto life—holla, Black, you know it well

Quiet storm, vital form, pen pushed it right across

Mind is a vital force, high level right across

Soul is the lion's roar, voice is the siren

I swing 'round, ring out, and bring down the tyrant

Chop a small axe and knock a giant lopsided

The world is so dangerous there's no need for fightin

Somethin's tryna hide like the struggle won't find 'em

And the sun bust through the clouds to clearly remind him, it's

Everywhere: penthouse, pavement, and curb

Cradle to the grave, tall cathedral or a cell

Universal ghetto life holla, Black, you know it well

[Chorus 2x]

What it is

You know, they know

What it is

We know y'all know

What it is

Ecstatic, there it is

Huh

What it is

You know, we know

What it is

They know y'all know

What it is

You don't know? Here it is

[Slick Rick]

Sit and come relax, riddle of The Mack

It's The Patch, I'm a soldier in the middle of Iraq

Well, say about noonish, comin out the whip

And lookin at me curious, a young Iraqi kid (awww)

Carrying laundry, what's wrong, G? Hungry?

"No, gimme my oil. Get the fuck out my country!"

And in Arabian barkin other stuff

'Til his moms come grab him and they walk off in a rush

Distrust, bitter like I's pissed upon wound

I'm like, "Shorty, hope that we can fix our differences soon. Bye!"

Buying apples, hung breakin on

"Brooklyn take everything, why not just take the damn food, black bastard!"

I don't understand it, on another planet?

Fifty-one of this stuff, how I'm gonna manage?

And increasing the sentiment, gentlemen

Gettin down on their Middle Eastern instruments

Realized trapped in this crowd

Walk over, kicked one of my fabulous raps (La Di Da Di . . .)

Arab jaws dropped, they well-wished, they glad-wrapped

Now the Kid considered like an Elvis of Baghdad

T.I.

O n his first album, T.I. dubbed himself the "King of the South," a title that he seems to have grown into, having released nearly an album a year between 2001 and 2008. His rhymes frequently concern hustling, partying, and women. However, as his public profile
increased, for good and for ill—through pop-friendly collaborations with
Rihanna, Justin Timberlake, and Usher; a budding film career; and federal
conviction on weapons charges—his songs began to show a greater the-

matic and emotional range. Always a lyricist with tight command of his flow and frequent use of chain rhyming, he puts those skills to work on lyrics that range from the braggadocio of "U Don't Know Me" to the mournful introspection of "Dead and Gone."

T.I. VS. T.I.P.

I wanna talk to you, shawty. *(Why?)* 'Cause you be trippin sometimes

Man, I'm just trying to stay true to what I say in my rhymes

It ain't a doubt in my mind, but you got a lot on the line

You need to think 'bout yo' actions. *(Why?)* You be overreactin. *(Maaaan...)*

Look at Cap and K.T., listen to K.P.

What about 'em? Where the fuck this shit come from?

Or to a J.G., to your mama or D.P.

Or somebody, shawty, shit, you be makin me sick. *(Nigga, fuck you!)*

You'd be a motherfuckin fool if you blow this lick. *(Alright, alright)*

This the chance of a lifetime, you know this shit

Remember what Jarmel told us: "Stay focused, Tip." *(I remember, nigga)*

Man, but they be tryin me, shawty. Niggas be tryin you how?

Aye, let them tell it, you was just another guy in the crowd

Naw, but they be talkin too loud. Man, you be listenin too hard

Just pay these niggas no attention and keep fuckin they broads. *(Alright)*

I know you harder than these niggas and smarter than these niggas *(Yeah)*

More heart than these niggas *(Yeah),* quit worryin 'bout these niggas

Aye, man, fuck these niggas. I'm from Bankhead and I don't know where you
*   stayed at*

But talkin sideways behind my back, I never played that

Since you become a paid cat, T.I., you been so laid back

I wonder where lil' bad ass Tip from back in the day at

Man, that nigga had to stay back there so we could be that

Nigga on TV and F.Y.I. we got the P back

Hold up, shawty, freeze Jack. *(What?)* Lame, I'll never be that. *(Yeah, okay)*

Changed my name a thousand times and still a G, believe that

Oh, yeah? Good, we got ki's. That nigga from overseas back

You see what I be sayin 'bout this nigga. *(What, man? Shit)* I don't believe that

You ain't listenin, is you? You got issues, I got kids

Two boys, a lil' girl—*Man, I know, nigga, they my kids, too*

You know it's one false move and it's back to the big house

The judge told our ass one more time and we ain't gettin out. *(I wouldn't*
say that)

Be thinkin 'bout standin outside in the sunshine *(Ho)*

Watchin niggas' heads get buck for cuttin the lunch line

Aye, shawty, you ain't 'posed to make the same mistake more than one time

And I ain't made the same mistake twice since, uh, '99

Please, boy, stop—don't get me started, folk, it's not the time

And let's just do this shit my way, get paid and have a lot of time

Plenty fine bitches, who gon' pull 'em, Shawty? You is

Man, you know Tip got the hoes . . . and Tip hoes got gold teeth

What that mean? What you tryna say, nigga?

Mine got jobs, good credit, and they own features

And mine boost clothes, sell 'dro, got the blow cheap

I guess it's just depend on what ya like, folk. That's right, folk

And I was just kiddin 'bout them kites, folk. Heh, alright, folk

I'm really glad we had a chance to sit it down and rap a tad

I admit you had a couple points, sometimes I act a ass

Aye, but it is so important to keep it real, though, just like ya said

No record deal, no amount of mil' shall go to my head

And with that said can't nobody tell us shit, so fuck the hatin

How many niggas real enough to stand and give theyself a straightenin?

U DON'T KNOW ME

I'm gonna tell y'all sucker-ass niggas something. Who wants to follow me? Look
here, dawg . . .

[Chorus]

You might see me in the street, but nigga, you don't know me

When you holla when you speak, remember you don't know me

Save all the hating and the popping, nigga, you don't know me

Quit telling niggas you my partner, nigga, you don't know me

Don't be a groupie, keep it moving, nigga, you don't know me
Hey, I ain't tripping but the truth is really you don't know me
Yeah, you know they call me T.I., but you don't know me
You be hating and I see why 'cause you don't know me

I think it's time I made a song for niggas who don't know me
I graduated out the streets, I'm a real OG
I've been trapping, shooting pistols since I stood four feet
So while you niggas acting bad, you're gonna have to show me
You gon make me bring the Chevy to a real slow creep
My nigga's hanging out the window, mouth full of gold teeth
When the guns start popping, wonder when it's gonna cease
Cap'll hit you in the side and create a slow leak
We can end in the speculation, 'cause today we're gonna see
What's the future of a pussy nigga hating on me
I give a fuck about the feds' investigation on me
I don't care that they at my shows and they waiting on me
I'ma keep on flossin, poppin 'long as Toop is on the beat
Tell polices I ain't stoppin, I'ma keep it in the streets
Contrary to your beliefs, I'm as real as you can be
Fuck your thoughts and your feelings, nigga, you don't know me

[Chorus]

Hey, once again let me remind you, nigga, you don't know me
So don't be walking up and asking, "What's the deal on a ki?"
I don't know if you wearing wires, you could be the police
If I was slangin blow you couldn't get a o-z
See me in the PAC, follow through at a show deep
Police holding up the door 'cause they know we tote heat
I just wanna ride with C, blowin dro in the Fleet'
Only playing 'bout a dozen different bitches in a week
I just wanna chill with Country and his daddy, Freddy G
Balling out at anytime, get in a store and spill a G
Wanna ball in the Bahamas courtesy of KT

Mac Boney got a mil' as well as Dollar DP

AK house on the hill right next to JG

Every week meet at Philant's Restaurant and eat free

Get Inda paid, Lil Craig, and B

That's the only shot we got at getting Cap back on the streets

[Chorus]

You see a nigga hating on a G, ask him what's it gonna be

What are you looking at, pussy nigga? You don't know me

At the club, in the streets or wherever we should meet

It's chopper chopping, pistols popping, nigga, you don't know me

You see a nigga hating on a G, ask him what's it gonna be

What are you looking at, pussy nigga? You don't know me

At the club, in the streets or wherever we should meet

It's chopper chopping, pistols popping, nigga, you don't know me

[Chorus]

KANYE WEST

Kanye West has quickly emerged as one of the leading figures in hip-hop—a tastemaker in beats, rhymes, and fashion. His lyrical content spans everything from traditional themes like his own ego to subjects rarely if ever discussed in rap, like folding shirts at The Gap.

Born in Atlanta to a Black Panther father and an academic mother, West moved to the South Side of Chicago at the age of three. West's breakout moment came when he produced a number of songs on Jay-Z's multiplatinum-selling *The Blueprint* (2001), including the lead single "Izzo (H.O.V.A.)." The following year West suffered a near-fatal car accident that left him with a metal plate in his jaw and an unbreakable resolve to become an MC. The result was *The College Dropout* (2004), with its vivid singles "Through the Wire," "All Falls Down," and "Jesus Walks."

On *The College Dropout*, Kanye forged the constitutive elements of his style: sampling, fresh content, inventive wordplay, and transformative and slant rhyme–laden lyricism. For example, in "All Falls Down," he rhymes "The concept of school seems so secure / Sophomore three years, ain't picked a career," altering his pronunciations of "secure," "years," and "career," so that they all rhyme with an "-ur" sound.

In subsequent years West's strong personality and experimental style have helped define the cutting edge of hip-hop, both musically and lyrically. Infusing his rhymes with wit and lyrical density, and employing his skill as a producer to craft songs with complex beats and catchy samples, he has set himself apart with swagger but also with substance.

ALL FALLS DOWN

[Chorus 4x]
Oh when it all, it all falls down
I'm telling you, ohh, it all falls down

Man, I promise, she's so self-conscious
She has no idea what she doing in college
That major that she majored in don't make no money
But she won't drop out, her parents'll look at her funny
Now, tell me that ain't insecurrre
The concept of school seems so securrre
Sophomore three yearrrs, ain't picked a carurrr
She like: "Fuck it, I'll just stay down herre and do hair"
'Cause that's enough money to buy her a few pairs of new Airs
'Cause her baby daddy don't really care
She's so precious with the peer pressure
Couldn't afford a car so she named her daughter Alexis
She had hair so long that it looked like weave
Then she cut it all off, now she look like Eve
And she be dealing with some issues that you can't believe
Single black female addicted to retail and well . . .

[Chorus 2x]

Man, I promise, I'm so self-conscious
That's why you always see me with at least one of my watches

Rollies and Pashas done drove me crazy

I can't even pronounce nothing, pass that Versay-see!

Then I spent four hundred bucks on this

Just to be like, "Nigga, you ain't up on this!"

And I can't even go to the grocery store

Without some Ones that's clean and a shirt with a team

It seem we living the American Dream

But the people highest up got the lowest self-esteem

The prettiest people do the ugliest things

For the road to riches and diamond rings

We shine because they hate us, floss 'cause they degrade us

We trying to buy back our forty acres

And for that paper, look how low we'll stoop

Even if you in a Benz, you still a nigga in a coupe

[Chorus 2x]

I say "fuck the police," that's how I treat 'em

We buy our way out of jail, but we can't buy freedom

We'll buy a lot of clothes, but we don't really need 'em

Things we buy to cover up what's inside

'Cause they made us hate ourself and love they wealth

That's why shorties holler: "Where the ballas at?"

Drug dealer buy Jordans, crackhead buy crack

And the white man get paid off of all of that

But I ain't even gon' act holier than thou

'Cause, fuck it, I went to Jacob with twenty-five thou'

Before I had a house and I'd do it again

'Cause I wanna be on "106 & Park" pushing a Benz

I wanna act ballerific like it's all terrific

I got a couple past due bills, I won't get specific

I got a problem with spending before I get it

We all self-conscious, I'm just the first to admit it

[Chorus to fade]

JESUS WALKS

Yo, we at war
We at war with terrorism, racism, and most of all we at war with ourselves
(Jesus walks)
God show me the way because the Devil's trying to break me down
(Jesus walks with me) with me, with me, with me

You know what the Midwest is? Young and restless
Where restless (Niggas) might snatch your necklace
And next these (Niggas) might jack your Lexus
Somebody tell these (Niggas) who Kanye West is
I walk through the valley of the Chi where death is
Top floor, the view alone'll leave you breathless. Uhhhh!
Try to catch it. Uhhhh! It's kinda hard
Getting choked by the detectives—Yeah, yeah, now check the method
They be asking us questions, harass and arrest us
Saying, "We eat pieces of shit like you for breakfast"
Huh? Y'all eat pieces of shit? What's the basis?
We ain't going nowhere but got suits and cases
A trunk full of coke, rental car from Avis
My mama used to say only Jesus can save us
Well, mama, I know I act a fool
But I'll be gone 'til November, I got packs to move. I hope…

(Jesus walks)
God show me the way because the Devil's trying to break me down
(Jesus walks with me)
The only thing that I pray is that my feet don't fail me now
(Jesus walks)
And I don't think there's nothing I can do now to right my wrongs
(Jesus walks with me)
I want to talk to God but I'm afraid 'cause we ain't spoke in so long

To the hustlers, killers, murderers, drug dealers, even the skrippers
(Jesus walks with them)

To the victims of Welfare feel we living in hell here, hell yeah

(Jesus walks with them)

Now hear ye, hear ye, want to see Thee more clearly

I know He hear me when my feet get weary

'Cause we're the almost nearly extinct

We rappers is role models, we rap, we don't think

I ain't here to argue about His facial features

Or here to convert atheists into believers

I'm just trying to say the way school need teachers

The way Kathie Lee needed Regis, that's the way I need Jesus

So here go my single, dawg, radio needs this

They say you can rap about anything except for Jesus

That means guns, sex, lies, videotape

But if I talk about God my record won't get played, huh?

Well, if this take away from my spins

Which'll probably take away from my ends, then I hope

It take away from my sins and bring the day that I'm dreaming about

Next time I'm in the club, everybody screaming out . . .

(Jesus walks)

God show me the way because the Devil's trying to break me down

(Jesus walks with me)

The only thing that I pray is that my feet don't fail me now

HOMECOMING

Yeah. And you say Chi city . . . Chi city . . . Chi city

I'm coming home again

Do you think about me now and then?

Do you think about me now and then?

'Cause I'm coming home again

Coming home again

I met this girl when I was three years old

And what I love most, she had so much soul

She said, "Excuse me little homie, I know you don't know me, but

My name is Windy and I like to blow trees"

And from that point I never blow her off

Niggas come from outta town, I like to show her off

They like to act tough, she like to to' 'em off

And make 'em straighten up they hat, 'cause she know they soft

And when I grew up she showed me how to go downtown

And at nighttime her face lit up, so astounding

And I told her in my heart is where she always be

She never mess with entertainers 'cause they always leave

She said, "It felt like they walked and drove on me

Knew I was gang affiliated, got on TV and told on me"

I guess it's why last winter she got so cold on me

She said, "'Ye, keep making that, keep making that platinum and gold

   for me"

Do you think about me now and then?

Do you think about me now and then?

'Cause I'm coming home again

Coming home again

Do you think about me now and then?

Do you think about me now and then?

Oh, now I'm coming home again

Maybe we can start again

But if you really cared for her, then you wouldn't a

Never hit the airport to follow your dream

Sometimes I still talk to her, but when I talk to her

It always seems like she talking 'bout me

She said, "You left your kids and they just like you

They wanna rap and make soul beats just like you

But they just not you and I just got through

Talking 'bout what niggas trying to do, just not new"

Now everybody got the game figured out all wrong

I guess you never know what you got 'til it's gone

I guess that's why I'm here and I can't come back home
And guess when I heard that? When I was back home
Every interview I'm representing you, making you proud
Reach for the stars so if you fall you land on a cloud
Jump in the crowd, spark your lighters, wave 'em around
If you don't know by now, I'm talking about Chi Town

Do you think about me now and then?
Do you think about me now and then?
'Cause I'm coming home again
Coming home again
Baby, do you remember when fireworks at Lake Michigan
Oh, now I'm coming home again
Coming home again
Baby, do you remember when fireworks at Lake Michigan
Oh, now I'm coming home again
Maybe we can start again

Loyee oyeee oh, loyee oyeee oh
Coming home again
Loyee oyeee oh, loyee oyeee oh
Coming home again

Maybe we can start again

CAN'T TELL ME NOTHING
I had a dream I could buy my way to heaven
When I awoke, I spent that on a necklace
I told God I'd be back in a second
Man, it's so hard not to act reckless
To whom much is given, much is tested
Get arrested, guess until he get the message
I feel the pressure, under more scrutiny
And what I do? Act more stupidly
Bought more jewelry

More Louis V, my mama couldn't get through to me

The drama, people suing me

I'm on TV talking like it's just you and me

I'm just saying how I feel, man

I ain't one of the Cosbys, I ain't go to Hillman

I guess the money should've changed him

I guess I should've forgot where I came from

[Chorus]

La, la, la, la—wait 'til I get my money right

La, la, la, la—then you can't tell me nothin, right?

Excuse me, was you saying something?

Uh, uh, you can't tell me nothin

(Ha ha) you can't tell me nothin

Uh, uh, you can't tell me nothin

Let up the suicide doors

This is my life, homie, you decide yours

I know that Jesus died for us

But I couldn't tell you who decide wars

So I parallel double-park that motherfucker sideways

Old folks talking about "Back in my day"

But, homie, this is my day

Class started two hours ago—oh, am I late?

No, I already graduated

And you can live through anything if Magic made it

They say I talk with so much emphasis

Ooh, they so sensitive

Don't ever fix your lips like collagen

To say something where you gon' end up apology-in

Let me know if it's a problem then

Aight, man, holla then

[Chorus]

…Let the champagne splash

Let that man get cash, let that man get passed

You don't need to stop to get gas

If he can move through the rumors, he can drive offa fumes 'cause

How he move in a room full of no's?

How he stay faithful in a room full of hoes?

Must be the pharaohs, he in tune with his soul

So when he buried in a tomb full of gold

Treasure. What's your pleasure?

Life is a, uh, dependin how you dress her

So if the Devil wear Prada, Adam Eve wear nada

I'm in between, but way more fresher

… With way less effort

'Cause when you try hard, that's when you die hard

Ya homies looking like "Why, God?"

When they reminisce over you, my god

[Chorus]

YOUNG JEEZY

Young Jeezy is part of a new wave of southern rappers that swept through hip-hop in the middle of the decade. Drawing inspiration from the first rise of the South with artists like The Geto Boys, 8Ball & MJG, Master P, and others, this new generation of regional rhymers spits lyrics about crime and urban blight, but also about the strength of friendship and community.

Young Jeezy draws inspiration from his upbringing in Atlanta. His solo debut, *Thug Motivation 101* (2005), put his street credentials on display with rhymes about hustling in the drug game. "I always had a way with words," Jeezy says, explaining how he got into rapping. "I was always motivational so even if I didn't make it into rap . . . I was speaking to cats as a motivationalist. That's what I do."[37] Jeezy was embroiled in controversy after his Snowman logo, which depicts a sinister, scowling face on a traditional snowman's body, said to symbolize the drug trade, became popular among schoolchildren. He made news of another kind during the 2008 presidential election when his song "My President" became a de facto anthem among many young supporters of Barack Obama.

FROM **PUT ON**

I put on ... [3x]

I put on for my city, on, on for my city [4x]

When they see me off in traffic they say Jeezy on some other shit
Send them pussy niggas runnin straight back to the dealership
Me, I'm in my spaceship, that's right, I work for NASA
This 7-H is not a fraud, call that bitch my bodyguard
Call that bitch a bodyguard? Yeah, that's my bodyguard
Wear a lot of jewelry, Young don't do security
It was whiter than a napkin, harder than a dinner plate
If you want it come and get it, you know I stay super straight
Ran up in my spots and now I'm workin out the Super 8
Know you niggas hungry, come and get a super plate
Y'all sing happy birthday, yeah, I got that super cake
Hundred carat bracelet, I use it like some super bait

[Chorus 2x]
I put on for my city, on on for my city
I put on for my city, on on for my city
Put on ... (Eastside)
Put on ... (Southside)
Put on ... (Westside)
Put on ...
Let's go

Half bag, top back, ain't nothin but a young thug
HKs, AKs, I need to join a gun club
Big wheels, big straps, you know I like it supersized
Passenger's a redbone, her weave look like some curly fries
Inside fish sticks, outside tartar sauce
Pocket full of celery, imagine what she tellin me

Blowin on asparagus, the realest shit I ever smoked

Ridin to that *Trap or Die,* the realest shit I ever wrote

They know I got that broccoli, so I keep that Glock on me

Don't get caught without one comin from where I'm from

Call me Jeezy Hamilton, flyin down Campbellton

So fresh, so clean, on my way to Charlene's

MY PRESIDENT

(feat. Nas)

Yeah, be the realest shit I never wrote. I ain't write this shit by the way, nigga.

   Some real shit right here, nigga. This'll be the realest shit you ever quote.

   Let's go!

[Chorus]

My president is black, my Lambo's blue

And I'll be goddamn if my rims ain't, too

My mama ain't at home and Daddy's still in jail

Tryna make a plate, anybody seen the scale?

My president is black, my Lambo's blue

And I'll be goddamn if my rims ain't, too

My money's light green and my Jordans light gray

And they love to see white, now how much you tryna pay?

Let's go!

[Young Jeezy]

Today was a good day, hope I have me a great night

I don't know what you fishin for, catch you a great white

Me, I see great white, heavy as killer whales

I cannot believe this, who knew it came in bales?

Who knew it came with jail? Who knew it came with prison?

Just 'cause you got opinions doesn't make you a politician

Bush robbed all us, would that make him a criminal?

And then he cheated in Florida, would that make him a Seminole?

I say and I quote, "We need a miracle"

And I say a miracle 'cause this shit is hysterical

By my nephews and nieces, I will e-mail Jesus
Tell him forward to Moses and cc: Allah
Mr. Soul Survivor, guess that make me a Konvict
Be all you can be, now don't that sound like some dumb shit?
When they die over crude oil as black as my nigga Boo
It's really a Desert Storm, that's word to my nigga Clue
Catch me in Las Vegas, A.R. Arizona
Rep for them real niggas, I'm winnin in California
Winnin in Tennessee, hands down Atlanta
Landslide Alabama, on my way to Savannah

[Chorus]

[Young Jeezy]
I said I woke up this morning, headache this big
Pay all these damn bills, feed all these damn kids
Buy all these school shoes, buy all these school clothes
For some strange reason my son addicted to Polos
Love me some spinach dip, I'm addicted to Houston's
And if the numbers is right I take a trip out to Houston
An earthquake out in China, a hurricane in New Orleans
Street Dreams Tour, I showed my ass in New Orleans
Did it for Soulja Slim, brought out B.G.
It's all love, Bun, I'm forgivin you, Pimp C
You know how the Pimp be, that nigga gon' speak his mind
If he could speak down from heaven, he'd tell me stay on my grind
Tell him I'm doin fine, Obama for mankind
We ready for damn change, so y'all let the man shine
Stuntin on Martin Luther, feelin just like a King
Guess this is what he meant when he said that he had a dream

[Chorus]

[Nas]
Yeah, our history, black history, no president ever did shit for me
Had to hit the streets, had to flip some keys so a nigga won't go broke

Then they put us in jail, now a nigga can't go vote, so I spend dough on these
   hoes is strippin
She ain't a politician, honey's a pole-itician
My president is black, rose golden charms
Twenty-two-inch rims like Hulk Hogan's arms
When thousands of peoples is riled up to see you
That can arouse your ego, we got mouths to feed so
Gotta stay true to who you are and where you came from
'Cause at the top'll be the same place you hang from
No matter how big you could ever be
For whatever fee or publicity, never lose your integrity
For years there's been surprise horses in this stable
Just two albums in, I'm the realest nigga on this label
Mr. Black President, yo, Obama for real
They gotta put your face on the five-thousand-dollar bill

[Chorus]

*So I'm sittin right here now, man. It's June 3rd, ha-ha, 2:08 A.M. Nigga, I wanna
   say win, lose, or draw, man, we congratulate you already, homie. See, I
   motivate the thugs, right? You motivate us, homie, that's what it is. This a
   hands-on policy, y'all touchin me right, nigga. Yeah, first black president, win,
   lose, or draw, nigga. Ha-ha, matter of fact, you know what it is, man? Shouts
   out to Jackie Robinson, Booker T. Washington, homie. Oh, you ain't think I
   knew that shit? Sidney Poitier, what dey do? Ha-ha, my president is black. I'm
   important, too, though, my Lambo's blue. I was, I was the first nigga to ride
   through my 'hood in a Lamborghini. Yeah. Ha-ha! Naw, for real though, we
   ready for change . . .*

LYRICS
for Further Study

What follows is a varied selection of lyrics, most of which are from artists not otherwise found in the anthology. Given the constraints of space, we can only gesture toward these artists' bodies of work with a song. The selections are drawn from three decades of hip-hop history and represent a diversity of regions, genres, styles, and themes. They include recognized gems like EPMD's "Strictly Business" and Pete Rock & C. L. Smooth's "They Reminisce over You (T.R.O.Y.)" as well as lesser-known but still memorable lyrics like Crooked I's "Grindin Freestyle" and Binary Star's "Reality Check." This representative selection simply begins to suggest the rich variety and complex interconnections that characterize rap poetics.

CADILLAC ON 22'S
DAVID BANNER

[Chorus 2x]
Cadillacs on twenty-twos
I ain't did nothin in my life but stay true
Pimp my voice and mack these beats
And pray to the Lord for these Mississippi streets, hey!

God, I know that we pimp; God, I know that we wrong
God, I know I should talk about more in all my songs
I know these kids are listening, I know I'm here for a mission
But it's so hard to get 'em with twenty-two rims all glisten
I know these walls are talking. Lord, I wanna do right
I try to fight, but these demons they come at me at night

Like my mama, my daddy, my girl, and all my boys

I lost Michelle, but I guess I still got Dwayne and Roy

My cousin Sweets, Mamalita, and Jason

Lord, I'm praying for Swack and my heart is steadily pacin

Keep 'em off them drugs, far away from thugs

He still my hero, but just a shell man of what he was

Yeah, I smoke and get a buzz, but God, I hear you calling

Ain't shit wrong wit' ballin, but my soul is just steadily falling

Into sex, into debt, in the earthly jail

God, I'm stacking my mail, but will I end up in hell?

[Chorus 2x]

Lord, they hung Andre Jones, Lord, they hung Renard Johnson

Lord, I wanna fight back but I'm just so sick of bouncing

Lord, I'm sick of jumping, Lord, please just tell me something

My folks still dumping, my music bumping, but I feel nothing

My heart is steadily pumping, my heart is steadily breaking

Sometimes I feel like I'm faking, man, I'm so sick of takin

Maybe hell ain't a place meant for us to burn

Maybe Earth is hell and just a place for us to learn

'Bout yo' love, yo' will and grace

Sometimes I wish I wasn't born in the first place

Maybe this first base, God knocked the ball up out the park

So we can come home, this world right here is feeling so dark

Feeling so cold, Lord, I'm getting so old

I don't know if I can take this world right here no more

Twenty-two-inch rims on the 'Lac

I guess that was yo' footprint in the sand carrying us on yo' back

[Chorus to fade]

REALITY CHECK
BINARY STAR

I have a request tonight. When you hear this, that is the introduction . . .

[One Be Lo]

This is how I represent, I rock the mic 110 percent

It's intimate, I keeps the party moving like a immigrant

Binary Star, superstar, it's no coincidence

Every verse is intricate, this ain't a circus in a tent

We don't get down like them clowns and the kids

I'm used to being indigent, who said it's all about the Benjamins?

I want a fortune, I want to make music and hit the lottery

Fortunately, my music is never watery

That's how it got to be, as far as I can see

Maybe you should grab a telescope to see my view is like astronomy

It ain't all about economy, so the fact

That all these wack MCs is making G's don't bother me

Honestly, my number-one policy is quality

Never sell my soul is my philosophy, high velocity

Lyrics like Nostradamus make a prophecy

I told you cats a long time ago it ain't no stopping me

I bomb your set; that's not a threat, it's a promise

Got everybody ridin on my wagon like the Amish

But still I never claim to be a big rap star

'Cause no matter who you are it's still Allahu Akbar

Better believe this, most rappers can't achieve this

I'm bad to the bone but X-rays can't even see this

See, I'm strategic, I let your money talk, bullshit walk

While I keep it rolling like paraplegics

Whoever's on the microphone let it be known

You in danger, I got next like the Boston Strangler

You ain't never heard a MC speak like this

And Rodney King ain't never felt a beat like this

That is the main theme. I want to do something else...

[Senim Silla]

Get a grip on yourself 'cause you ain't gripping mine's

Life and times idolize rap guys, out of line careers I finalize

Collide with this serenade cyanide

You've applied for Silla-cide

The thing that makes killas hide

Hang 'em high by they gold link necktie

And drain 'em dry, enter temper sty

Now you ain't Ki so you ain't that high

Wanna be aeronautic then get swatted for acting fly

Masterminds, crafty rhymes, ill wind from drafty lines

They chill spines like the Alpines

Running up on Senim turbine's a close encounter

Of the worst kind. Go ask them cats that heard I'm

Lyrical turpentine. Who wanna taste mine?

I carry hell on the waistline, God's gift to bass line

So let the phlegm fly, I semi seven-five through the

MI when I forcefully Jedi

In a bull's eye—red-eye, heads fly, bet I

Sharp-shoot, deadeye, snooze crews bed bye

Mary Lou flipping, I paper punk rippin

I stomping, I Semper Fi represent, temper high

Signified, walking rhyme, ain't nothing similar

Like a Gemini, or in this perimeter 'cept him and I

Cats be cut dry, I'm a wild wet guy

I be raining precipitation 'til it's one inch from neck high

Arrest fly kids mid-sky without an alibi

Who said you rap tight? You come unraveled by

A slice of this rap scalpel guy as quick as apple pie

I'm learned in all schools of thought and shit you baffled by

Conceptual intellectual fox-sly

Silla-oxide rhymes flow like a rock slide

You must have forgot I'd slap yo' ass knock-kneed and cockeyed

Bruised, battered, broken up, open cut

Dipped in peroxide, death to the pop fly . . .

Usually don't do request numbers, unless, of course, I have been asked to do so . . .

VAPORS

BIZ MARKIE

Radio, TV, and even the press

Say what's the meaning of the V-A-P-O-R-S

The meanin of this word without no doubt

Means nobody want to be down when you're down and out

Now once you're established and got a lot of money

Everybody wanna be your buddy and honey

Like tall buildings they call skyscrapers

Can you feel it? Nothin can save ya

For this is the season of catchin the vapors

And since I got time, what I'm gonna do

Is tell ya how they spreaded throughout my crew

Well, you all know TJ Swan who sang on my records

"Make the Music," "Nobody Beats the Biz," well, check it

Back in the day before this began

He used to try to talk to this girl named Fran

The type of female with fly Gucci wear

With big truck jewelry and extensions in her hair

When Swan tried to kick it, she always fessed

Talkin about, "Baby, please, you work for UPS"

Since he wasn't no type of big drug dealer

My man TJ Swan didn't appeal to her

But now he trucks gold and wears fly Bally boots

Rough leather fashions and tough silk suits

Now she stop frontin an' wants to speak and be

Comin to all the shows every single weekend

To get his beeper number, she be beggin "Please!"

Dyin for the day to get skeezed

She caught the vapors [4x]

I got another partner that's calm and plain

He goes by the name of the Big Daddy Kane

The mellow type of fellow that's laid back

Back in the days, he was nothin like that
I remember when he used to fight every day
What grown-ups would tell him he would never obey
He wore his pants hangin down and his sneakers untied
And a Rasta-type Kangol tilted to the side
Around his neighborhood, people treated him bad
Said he was the worst thing his moms ever had
They said that he will grow up to be nothin but a hoodlum
Or either in jail or someone would shoot him
But now he's grown up, to their surprise
Big Daddy got a hit record sellin worldwide
Now the same people that didn't like him as a child be sayin
"Can I borrow a dollar? Ooh, you're a star now!"

They caught the vapors [4x]

Now I got a cousin by the name of Vaughn Lee
Better known to y'all as Cutmaster Cool V
He cuts, scratch, transforms with finesse . . .
And all that mess
I remember when he first started to rock
And tried to get this job at a record shop
He was in it to win it but the boss fronted, said
"Sorry, Mr. Lee, but there's no help wanted"
Now my cousin Vaughn still tried on and on and on
'Til the, like, break of dawn
To get this J-O-B in effect
Then they'd look right past him and be like, "Next!"
Now for the year of '88
Cool V is makin dollars so my cousin's like straight
He walks into the same record shop as before
And the boss'll be like, "Vaughn, welcome to my store"
Offerin him a job, but, naw, he don't want it
Damn, it feels good to see people up on it
'Cause I remember when at first they wasn't
Now guess what they caught from my cousin?

They caught the vapors [4x]

Last subject of the story is about Biz Mark
I had to work for mine to put your body in park
When I was a teenager, I wanted to be down
With a lot of MC-DJ in crews in town
Saw a crew on Noble Street, I say, "Can I be down, champ?"
They said no and treated me like a wet food stamp
After gettin rejected, I was very depressed
Sat and wrote some def doo-doo rhymes at my rest
When I used to come to parties they'd make me pay
Would have to beg to get on the mic and rap that day
I was never into girls, I was just into my music
They acted like I wanted to keep it instead of tryin to use it
But now things switched, without belief
"Yo, Biz, do you remember me from Noble Street, Chief?
We used to be down back in the days"
It happens all the time and never cease to amaze

They caught the vapors [4x]

THE CHOICE IS YOURS (REVISITED)
BLACK SHEEP
Here they come, yo, here they come [3x]
This (or that), this (or that) [4x]

Yo, who's a Black Sheep? What's a Black Sheep?
Know not who I am or when I'm coming, so you sleep
Wasn't in my realm or wasn't in your sphere
Knew not who I was, but listen here
Drés, D-R-E-S, yes, I guess I could start
If it's all right with you, I'll rip this here joint apart
Back, middle, to the front, don't front
Want a good time, wanna give you what you want
Can I hear a "hey"? (Hey!) Now get a "yo" (Yo!)
You got a "hay"? (Huh!) It's for the hoes (Oh!)

The styling is creative, Black Sheep of the Native
Can't be violated or even decepticated
I got Brothers in the Jungle, cousins on a Quest
Dead retarded uncles and departed may they rest
Guess: which way, what, when, how?
Mista Lawnge, Drés, Black Sheep slam now
Know you've heard the others, phonies to the lovers
Then of course, the choice is yours

[Chorus 2x]
You can get with this, or you can get with that
You can get with this, or you can get with that
You can get with this, or you can get with that
I think you'll get with this, for this is where it's at

Where's the Black Sheep? Here's the Black Sheep
Even if we wanted to, the flock could not be weak
Watch me swing like this, why should I swing it like that?
Because in fact, on me it might not attract
Therefore I ignore, do as I feel inside
I live with me, I've got my back tonight
Ya know what I'm sayin? Yo, black, I'm not playin
Need to go with this and go with this with no delay and
See, in actuality, one day can it be
I made it look easy, because it is to me
Any time capacity was filled, tried to rock it
Any time a honey gave us play, tried to knock it
Never was a fool so we finished school
Never see us sweat and you'll never see us drool
Out to rock the globe while it's still here to rock
Don't punch girls and we don't punch a clock
Gotta go, gotta go, see you later by the cat
And you can't beat that with a bat

[Chorus 2x]

Engine, engine, number nine

On the New York transit line

If my train goes off the track

Pick it up! Pick it up! Pick it up!

Back on the scene, crispy and clean

You can try, but then why, 'cause you can't intervene

We be the outcast, down for the settle

Won't play rock, won't play the pebble

Open the door, you best believe we're slidin through it

Swiftly ...

Niftily, we can make it hip to be

What we are 'cause what we be

Be the epitome, doo-dah-dippity

So now I dwell just to say you're plainer

Hold your cup 'cause I got the container

Pass a plate across the fader

Black Sheep get played like the Sony Innovator

Never the traitor, party inflater

And you can get a scoop, later

[Chorus 2x]

Here they come, yo, here they come [8x]

LUCHINI
CAMP LO
[Chorus]
This is it (What?!), Luchini pourin from the sky

Let's get rich (What?!), the cheeky vines and sugar dimes

Can't quit (What?!), now pop the cork and steam the Vega

And get lit (What?! What?! What?!)

[Geechi Suede]
Introducin phantom of the dark, walk through my heaven

With levitation from reefers, drenching divas in these sevens

Showboatin with Rugers, flash vines, Belafonte jigga
Landscape for what it's worth as we confiscate your figures

[Sonny Cheeba]
Casanova Brown levitatin jiggy in dashikis
De la hotter a Car 54, chasin diamond runners
Headed ice bound, reppin killer diamond convention
Harlem buck strut, freezin world heist Hollywood
Madame Butterfly, let me in your house of pleasure
From the knuckle swat shadow boxers catching black-eye blues

[Geechi Suede]
I play the thief—what?!, sensations at the Monte Barbie
Screamin "Cheeba!" fulfillin pleasures at my castles
Blow the smoke out, the Garcia Vega substitutes
When the Dutch is gone, the Lo don't stop, give me shouts
It's the season sauté-ers, soufflé-ers for swervin on corners
We magnets to moolah, livin with Charlie's Angels hornets
No smilin, we're slidin, that gets you caught up in the Octa'
Or deaded for movin, it's just like that as we proceed

[Sonny Cheeba]
Saturday night special, better take it light, you JahJah
A capi-tan, quest to the coast of Key Largo, wire
The chain gang keep your ears out for our air
Sippin Fontainebleau, house of bamboo, paradise

[Chorus 2x]

[Sonny Cheeba]
For these pharaohs, courtesies of Black Caesar, the convincer
Silky Days, satin nights, takin flight, Donald Goines
Sweet sensation, Spanish flyin with the lady Scarface
Bottoms up, sunshine, love potion number nine

[Geechi Suede]

And we headed from the magic city, transcendin sweeter on your aura

Fly-chini in London, relaxation in Bora Bora

Got notion to bring it, sing it, never been my function

Stonin, robbin, we heisting merchandise and gunnin

Love it, leave it, but bless the war chief for his pricin

Get it, got it, the Lo will forever be nice and

[Sonny Cheeba]

Yeah, the Sonny Cheeba, he be sippin Armaretta

The Geechi Gracious, he be sippin Armaretta

We float the tristate draped in the satin vines

This Cooley High jack pack from the Sugar Shack

Then what we do after we sip the Armaretta

We start the Harlem River quiver, dig it sweet daddy

Sharpen the crimson blade, high sierra serenade

Anatomy for seduction beat his ebony chest in

[Geechi Suede]

As we exit the place with grace, drizzly Armaretta

That bursts into clouds and pours, everything seems better

On flax, with love, we move, only in the mist

It's Lo, it's life, and we can't get enough of this

[Chorus 2x]

GRINDIN (FREESTYLE)
CROOKED I

[Crooked I]

Yo, this nigga never goin broke again: picture me poor

I walk in the jewelry shop, draw Glocks, empty the store

Crooked's a man-eating lion, please don't tempt me to roar

Ghetto enough to put hydraulics on a Bentley Azure

Pimp me a whore, tough talk I simply ignore

Thousand-dollar automatic weapons defend me in war
I rock the stocking cap in case I gotta pull it right
Over my well-known face and lay down the whole place
It's killa Cal, this hour where criminals prowl
My residual prizzowl my lyrical style
Make them niggas sound bourgie. It's like you're tellin
A statue to flinch, my nigga: your words don't move me
They make me want to trip with this gauge and you suckers'll
Be *Gone in 60 Seconds,* quicker than Nicolas Cage
You get no action, I beats more ass than Joe Jackson
I tote Magnums even if I got four platinums
I blast that Enyce shirt, I make your bitch drop her DK skirt
'Cause that's how niggas in Southern CA work
I stay swift, walk with my chest out
Like an ese on May 5th, I tell you you ain't shit
Plus gangsta rap ain't dead, it never died
It took steroids to the head and became Crooked I
On the roof place by the gift, we could feud
Like Cowboys and Indians or Israelis and Palestinians
I didn't want to resort to this, but my cerebral cortex
Is a fortress where metaphors exist, hit you with the force of
Morpheus after I transform my fist into a hammer
Too heavy for Thor to lift through a course of metamorphosis
The U-Gang is more than sick, sicker than newborn porn
Swingin on some George Foreman shit. Warn your clique
I'm comin, nobody fucks with Mr. Icon
A natural-born time bomb. You know I gotta drop cowards
With nine millimeters of Glock power
Drop trousers, do your girl in a hot shower
For a hot hour, drop her off at the Watts Towers
The block's ours, you seein me not now
Or never, I never let these snake niggas take me
I blow out brains to entertain me when I'm angry
Don't tangle, I choke, strangle, break both ankles

Dangle you from a rope, clothes hang you from a coat hanger

The mangler, so anxious to kill, able to spill

Ancient languages, dangerous as eighty painkillin pills

Young jacker, Gucci hat tilted gun clapper

I'm every artist Suge ever signed in one rapper

Chrome ending your life, I'm strong enough

To stab you with the wrong end of a knife, gangsta type

And the lyrics that I quote poke through my clothin

My father didn't want me here but I broke through a Trojan

It's on, Wake Up Show

It never stops on the Wake Up Show

Wake Up Show

It can't stop, it's the ruh-oh, uh-oh

[Sway] *Damn, I almost cursed. Damn.*

[Crooked I] *And we grinding and I keep a four-five in my lining*

[King Tech] *We're about to have a funeral for the microphone . . .*

THEY WANT EFX
DAS EFX

[Dre]

Bum stiggedy bum stiggedy bum, hon

I got the old pa-rum-pum-pum-pum

But I can fe-fi-uh-fo, diddly-fum, here I come

So Peter Piper, I'm hyper than Pinocchio's nose

'Cause I'm a supercalifragilistic tic-tac-toe

I gave a oopsy daisy, now you've got the crazy

Crazy with the books, googly-goo, where's the gravy

So one, two, unbuckle my, um, shoe

Yabba doo, hippity-hoo, crack a brew

So trick or treat, smell my feet, yup, I drippedy-dropped a hit

So, Books, get on your mark and spark that old censorship

[Books]

Drats and double drats, I smiggedy-smacked some whiz kids

The boogedy-woogedly Brooklyn boy's about to get his, dig

My waist bone's connected to my hip bone

My hip bone's connected to my thigh bone

My thigh bone's connected to my knee bone

My knee bone's connected to my—hardy-har-har-har

The jibbedy-jabber jaw ja-jabbing at your funny bone, um

Skip the Ovaltine, I'd rather have my Honeycomb

Or preferably the sesame, let's spiggedy-spark the blunts, um

Dun dun dun dun dun, dun dun

[Chorus]

They want EFX, some live EFX [3x]

Snap a neck for some live EFX

[Dre]

Well I'll be darned, shiver me timbers yo, head for the hills!

I picked a weeping willow and a daffodil

So back up, bucko, or I'll pulverize McGruff

'Cause this little piggy gets busy and stuff

Arrivederci, heavens to mercy, honky-tonk, I get swift

I caught a Snuffleupagus and smoked a boogaloo spliff

I got the nooks, the crannies, the nitty-gritty forty doe

So all aboard, castaway, hey, where's my boogaloo?

Oh-h-h-h-h-h-hhh I'm steamin, a-go-ny!

Why's everybody always pickin on me?

[Books]

They call me Puddin Tane and rap's my game

You ask me again and I'll t-tell you the same

Since I'm the vocal vegemintarian, stick 'em up, freeze, so

No pork sausages, mom, please?

A-Blitz shoots the breeze, Twiddly-dee shoots his lip

Crazy Drayzie shot the sheriff, yup, and I shot the gift

And that's PRET-TY SNEA-KY SIS, oh yo

I got my socks off, my rocks off, my Nestle's cup of cocoa

Holly Hobbie tried to slob me, tried to rob me, silly stunt

Diggedy-dun dun dun dun dun, DUN DUN!

[Chorus 2x]

[Dre] Yahoo, hidee-ho, yup, I'm coming around the stretch

So here, Fido boy, fetch, boy, fetch

I got the rope-a-dope, a slippery choker, look at me get raw

[Books] And I'm the hickory-dickory top of morning boogaloo big jaw

[Dre] With the yippedy zippedy Winnie the Pooh bad boy blue

[Books] Aiyo, crazy, you got the gusto?

[Dre] What up, I swing that too

So nincompoop, I give a hoot and stomp a troop without a strain

Like Rosco P.-P. Coltrane

I spiggedy-spark a spliff and give a twist like Chubby Checker

[Books] I takes my Fruit Loops with two scoops and make it double-decker

Oh Vince, the baby come to Papa Duke

A babaloo, ooh, a babaloo boogedy boo

I went from Coogi to Stussy, to fliggedy-flam a groupie

To Zsa Zsa, to yibbedy-yabba dabba hoochie koochie

Tallyho, I-I'll take my Stove Top instead of potatoes, so

Maybe I'll shoot 'em now (Nope), maybe I'll shoot 'em later (Yep)

I used to have a dog and Bingo was his name-oh, so uh

B-I-N-G-O-oh

You do the hokeypokey and you turn yourself around, hon, so uh

Dun dun dun dun dun dun, dun dun

[Chorus]

FOR COLORED BOYS
DEEP DICKOLLECTIVE

[Marcus René Van]

This is a song made for colored boys

Whose rainbows forgot how to bloom

Whose moons forgot how to change into suns

To illuminate the gray days

This is a song made for colored boys

Whose heroes forgot how to fly

Whose wings were clipped with rage

And cages waited to take them with no reasons why

This is a song made for colored boys

Whose up-ins that never come up

Whose mothers and fathers

Became the sons and the daughters

Of revolution's eternal corrupt

[Solas B. Lalgee]

So this is for the colored boys

Colored boys like me

Brother, fence walker, fringe society

Pressure rising exponentially

[Tim'm West]

This is for the colored boys like me

Dirty-dirty, the city streets

Literary geeks that control, alternate, and delete

To reboot, we be the strange fruit

Blackberry sweet juice

We be rigging your reel telling our truth

We got moods like Langston Hughes

We the Countee Cullen blues

Be the soul of his shoes

Marvin White's blackbirds

Taking flight with words

With our pens and manifestos

We bourgie and ghetto

Thug and crud

The "nigga please!" and "nigga what?!"

The Essex of the mic check

We the boys suspect

When they fail to love themselves well

We Ntozake's warriors, homo revolutionary males

Following our hearts we spark

Sunshine in the dark, DDC

Famous Outlaw MCs, we get free

[Jeree "JB Rap" Brown]

We on some other shit

Spit so sick, choke on it

Hear me on MySpace, JBRap sick with it

Call me Gaylord, feel the face and fire grace

Of those who expired

Rickey, Kaya, Alizé, and Tanya

We miss you bad, love—won't retire

Ready to blow like Golden State, puff

White girl, we done had enough

Moist and sticky on the same brain

Like cotton field's pain in yesterday's rain

How you gon' make it through

All the pain and all the anguish?

Ball to the death and stand tall

Ball to the death and stand tall

[Chorus]

So this is for the colored boys

Colored boys like me

Brother, fence walker, fringe society

Pressure rising exponentially

And yet, we traverse on

Well, I was born inside of a pot of gold

At the end of a rainbow that no one knows

So the answer is clear if you recognize

If you're looking for truth, look into my eyes

[Juba Kalamka]

The point is this colored noise

This joint is for colored boys

This is for Essex, Assoto, Donald, and Marlon Troy

This is for Aimé, for Melvin, Claude, and for Countee C.

This is for Larry Duckette, for Joseph and Jimmy B.

For cousins and lovers

Who couldn't be because you would laugh

This is for Luther, Poetic, Eazy, and Sugar Shaft

For brothers whose names we will never know

I'ma get it right

Labeija, Infiniti, Ninjas twistin it through the night

In spite of the pressures and expectations to hide desire

Like Bayard, who paved it

Through slings and arrows while walking fire

We pomo, our Afros so homo stories will see the light

The slights had me frightened

But now I'm ready to fuck and fight

Chocolate-colored rainbows, black boys get on down

Chocolate-colored rainbows, love to hear that sound

[Solas B. Lalgee]

I like to see your shade of brown

I like to see you get on down

Down, down, down, down, down

Love to see them boys get down

I like that UK-Irish brown

I like that Tamil-Trini brown

Brown, brown, brown, brown, brown

Love to, love to see the sound

I love to see the sound

I love to see the brown

Love to see that sound (I like to ...)

[Chorus]

Chocolate-colored rainbows, black boys get on down

Chocolate-colored rainbows, love to hear that sound

SUMMERTIME
DJ JAZZY JEFF & THE FRESH PRINCE

Here it is, a groove slightly transformed

Just a bit of a break from the norm

Just a little somethin to break the monotony

Of all that hardcore dance that has gotten to be

A little bit out of control. It's cool to dance

But what about a groove that soothes and moves romance?

Give me a soft, subtle mix

And if it ain't broke then don't try to fix it

And think of the summers of the past

Adjust the bass and let the Alpine blast

Pop in my CD and let me run a rhyme

And put your car on cruise and lay back

'Cause this is summertime

School is out and there's a sort of a buzz

But back then I didn't really know what it was

But now I see what habit is

The way that people respond to summer madness

The weather is hot and girls are dressing less

And checkin out the fellas to tell 'em who's best

Riding around in your Jeep or your Benzos

Or in your Nissan sitting on Lorenzos

Back in Philly we'd be out in the park

A place called the Plateau is where everybody go

Guys out hunting and girls doing likewise

Honking at the honey in front of you with the light eyes

She turn around to see what you beepin at

It's like the summer's a natural aphrodisiac

And with a pen and pad I compose this rhyme

To hip you and to get you equipped for the summertime

It's late in the day and I ain't been on the court yet

Hustle to the mall to get me a short set

Yeah, I got on sneaks but I need a new pair

'Cause basketball courts in the summer got girls there

The temperature's about eighty-eight

Hop in the water plug, just for old time's sake

Break to your crib, change your clothes once more

'Cause you're invited to a barbecue that's startin at four

Sittin with your friends as y'all reminisce

About the days growing up and the first person you kissed

And as I think back, makes me wonder how

The smell from a grill could spark up nostalgia

All the kids playing out front

Little boys messin 'round with the girls playing double dutch

While the DJ's spinning a tune

As the old folks dance at your family reunion

Then six o'clock rolls around

You just finished wiping your car down

It's time to cruise so you go

To the summertime hangout, it looks like a car show

Everybody come lookin real fine

Fresh from the barbershop or fly from the beauty salon

Every moment frontin and maxin

Chillin in the car they spent all day waxin

Leanin to the side, but you can't speed through

Two miles an hour, so everybody sees you

There's an air of love and of happiness

And this is the Fresh Prince's new definition of summer madness

SAY WHAT'S REAL

DRAKE

Why do I feel so alone like everybody passing through the studio

Is in character as if he's acting out a movie role

Talking bullshit as if it was for you to know

And I don't have the heart to give these bitch niggas the cue to go

So they stick around kicking out feedback

And I entertain it as if I need that

I had a talk with my uncle and he agreed that

My privacy about the only thing I need back

But it's hard to think of them polite flows

When Stefano Polato suits are your night clothes

And Jordan sweat suits are your flight clothes

And you still make it even when they say your flight closed

Eyes hurt in front of camera phone light shows

Life was so full, now this shit just being lipo'd

Always said I'd say it all on the right track

But in this game you only lose when you fight back

Black diamond bracelets showing you the basics

I can't live and hold the camera, someone gotta tape this

I make hits, unlike a bitch that's married I ain't miss

Twenty-four hours from greatness, I'm that close

Don't ever forget the moment you began to doubt

Transitioning from fitting in to standing out

Los Angeles cabanas or Atlanta south

Watchin Hov's show, embarrassed to pull my camera out

And my mother embarrassed to pull my Phantom out

So I park about five houses down

She say I shouldn't have it until I have the crown

But I don't wanna feel the need to wear disguises around

So she wonder where my mind is, accounts in the minus

But yet I'm rolling round the fuckin city like your highness

Got niggas reactin without a sinus

'Cause what I'm working with is timeless

And promoters tryna get me out to they club

And say I had fun, but I can't imagine how

'Cause I just seen my ex-girl standing with my next girl

Standing with the girl that I'm fuckin right now

And shit could get weird unless they all down

And so I stay clear, we from a small town

Everybody talks and everybody listen

But somehow the truth just always comes up missing
I've always been something that these labels can't buy
Especially if they tryin to take a piece of my soul
And Sylvia be tellin Tez, "Damn, Drake fly"
And he just be like, "Silly motherfucker, I know"
"That was your bad, how could you pass up on 'em?
He just take them records and he gas up on 'em
Wayne will probably put a million cash up on 'em
Surprised no one ever put your ass up on 'em"
Oh, they did, Po, at least they tried to
And that's what happens when you spitting what's inside you
But slip up and shoot the wrong fucking video
And they think they can market you however they decide to
Nah, but Forty told me to do me
And don't listen to anybody that knew me
'Cause to have known me would mean that there's a new me
And if you think I changed in the slightest, could have fooled me
Boy, and to my city I'm the 2–3
Drug dealers live vicariously through me
I quit school and it's not because I'm lazy
I'm just not the social type and campus life is crazy
Understand, I could get money with my eyes closed
Lost some of my hottest verses down in Cabo
So if you find a BlackBerry with the side scroll
Sell that motherfucka to any rapper that I know
'Cause they need it much more than I ever will
I got new shit, I'm gettin better still
Little niggas put my name in they verses
'Cause they girlfriend put my ass on a pedestal
Future said 'cause this 'Ye shit, you better kill
And I think this got that making of a legend feel
Problem with these other niggas, they ain't never real
Yeah. That's all I can say . . .

FUMBLING OVER WORDS THAT RHYME
EDAN

Pure rap music ain't made under pressure
Expose a jewel, teach school at my leisure
Fumble over words that rhyme with a verse divine
I backtrack and think of the greatest of all time
Class is in session, master this lesson
Teacher was a student, study like a Buddhist
Reviewing on the best to do it so let's do this
(Do it) Nothing to it

Considered the first MC to blow the spot and do work
Was Coke La Rock spittin for Kool Herc
Following the influence of Herculord parties
Brothers like Cowboy made you move your body
Cowboy would toast for the GM Flash
And the skills elevated as crews started to clash
Flash and Bam, they both sought clientele
So Flash formed the Four with the father Melle Mel
Four became Five, law became live
Routines over breaks, true kings motivate
Out the L Brothers came the Five Fantastic
With Theodore they battled with the Cold Crush Four
Few had the confidence of GMC
Without the CCBs, there'd be no Run-DMC
The Funky and the Fearless Four, Force MC's, the suave Spoonie Gee
And I can't forget the Treacherous Three MCs

Praise to the Kool Moe Dee, he elevated
And changed it with records like "The New Rap Language"
Before the first full-length LPs
There was abstract brothers like the one Rammellzee
Run-DMC broke through in '83 outta Queens
And started rappin hard over drum machines
808s started shaking up floors ("It's Yours")

With T La Rock's complex metaphors

(T-L-A-R-O-C-K)

A primary influence on LL Cool J

T La Rock's futurism must've been respectable

'Cause Tragedy from Queens was young but very technical

Shan was eloquent, Kris was intelligent

The R was all of the above with added elements

Slick Rick the Ruler was a screenplay producer

Ultramagnetic had the vision for the future

Big Daddy Kane gettin raw at the Apollo and

Kool G Rap was probably the sickest of all of 'em

Jaz from the BK, Percee and Finesse from the BX

Prince Po and Pharaohe came next

Wu with the G-Z-A, G-F-K

N-A-S, one of the best out today

Any MC that's addin on to the list

Pump your fist, but first give praise to true scientists

THE RAIN (SUPA DUPA FLY)
MISSY ELLIOTT

Me, I'm supa fly, supa dupa fly, supa dupa fly [4x]

When the rain hits my window

I take in (puff) me some Indo

Me and Timbaland, oooh, we sang-a-dango

We so tight that you get our styles tangled

Sway your do-si-do like you loco

Can we get kinky tonight? Like Coko, so-so

You wanna play with my yo-yo?

I smoke my hydro on the d-low

I can't stand the rain against my window [4x]

Beep, beep, who got the keys to the Jeep?

Vroom . . . I'm drivin to the beach

Top down, loud sounds, see my peeps

Give them pound, now look who it be

It be me, me, me and Timothy

Look like it 'bout to rain, what a shame

I got the Armor All to shine up the stain

Oh, Missy, try to maintain

Freaky, freaky, freaky, freaky, freaky, freaky, freaky

I can't stand the rain against my window

I feel the wind

Five, six, seven, eight, nine, ten

Begin, I sit on hills like Lauryn

Until the rain starts comin down, pourin

Chill—I got my umbrella

My finger waves these days, they fall like Humpty

Chunky, I break up with him before he dump me

To have me: yes, you lucky

I can't stand the rain against my window [repeat to fade]

STRICTLY BUSINESS
EPMD

[Erick Sermon]

Try to answer to the master or the MC rap artist

No joke on the lyric, it's hard to be modest

I knew I was the man with the master plan

To make you wiggle and jiggle like gelatin

Just think while I sink into the brain structure

(Yo, don't sleep on the E) Ya see, somethin might rupture

It don't take time for me to blow your mind

It take a second to wreck it because you're dumb and blind

So just lounge, 'cause you a MC clown

Go join the circus, EPMD is in town

[PMD]

Total chaos, no, mass confusion

Rhymes so hypnotizin known to cause an illusion

Like a magician, he draws a rabbit out a hat, son

I pull 'em all like a .44 Magnum

MCs, freeze, stop, look, and listen and try to imagine

It's travelin the speed of light, but everything's motionless

Frightening, plus the thought you alone

You now enter dimension called the Twilight Zone

You're terrified, plus you can't bear the thought

You and I one-on-one in the Land of the Lost

You start to shiver, but then you scream, my friend

Yo, wake up, Muttley, because you're dreamin again

But next time I'm on the scene, do not try to dis us

Just keep your mouth shut, suckaduck, because I'm strictly business

I'm strictly business . . .

[Erick Sermon]

This is the rap season, where the E starts pleasin

Girls around the world, no need to be skeezin

When I roll I stroll, cool, always pack a tool

Just in case (just in case) a brother acts a fool

I've got the energy to put the girls in a frenzy

Put 'em in shock, when I rock, give enough, I'm not stingy

Make sure I don't bore when I'm on the dance floor

(Get busy, boy) like you never saw before

Rhyme flow, good to go

After the show, I pull your ho, boy

(Yo, you sniff blow?) Hell, no

Have my whole life ahead of me, no time to be sniffin

My parents find out, then they start riffin

So I stay A-OK

'Cause I'm the E—the R-I-C-K

[PMD]

MCs look me in my face, then their eyes get weak

Pulse rate descends, heart rate increase

It's like "Beam me up, Scotty," I control your body

I'm as deadly as AIDS when it's time to rock a party

In all due respect, when I say "mic check"

Let a sucker slide once, then I break his neck

So when I say "Jump," you'll reply, "How high?"

Because I'm takin no prisoners, so don't play hero and die

You're just a soldier and I'm a Green Beret

I do not think twice about the MCs I slay

So if you want to battle, I highly recommend this

Bring your dog, mom, and dad, because I'm strictly business

I'm strictly business . . .

[Erick Sermon]

Yo yo, you're still pickin on that four-leaf clover?

Bring in the Sandman, sucker, because it's over

My name is Erick Sermon and I'm back again

I see the heads still turnin, and my so-called friends

They smile in my face, behind my back they talk trash

Mad and stuff, because they don't have cash

Like the E-Double, or the PMD

He drives a Corvette, I drive a Samurai Suzuki

I'm the locksmith with the key to fame

Never high on myself, always stay the same

Play a lot because I'm hot, like a horse I trot

Around the track and back. (Fatigued?) No, I'm not

[PMD]

Well, I'm the mellow, the fellow, the one that likes to say "hello"

To a fly girl that is good to go

With the slow tempo and the offbeat rhyme flow

'Cause when I am in action, there is no time for maxin

Or relaxin, just subtractin and reactin
On a sucker MC who mouth keep on yappin
And flappin. I lose my cool, then I'll start slappin
And smackin. You on a roll? Then I'll be start jabbin
And cappin. No time to lounge, I'm packin a strap
And at my point of attack, I soar at you like a eagle
I'm the sheriff and bitin is illegal
So when I'm in town, I highly recommend this
You gots to chill, because I'm strictly business

KING TIM III (PERSONALITY JOCK)
THE FATBACK BAND (FEAT. KING TIM III)

All right, y'all
Here we go

You just clap your hands and you stomp your feet
'Cause you're listening to the sound of the sure-shot beat
I'm the K-I-N-G, the T-I-M
King Tim the Third, and I am him
Just me, Fatback, and the crew
We're doing it all just for you
We're strong as an ox and tall as a tree
We can rock you so viciously
We throw the highs in your eyes, the bass in your face
We're the funk machines that rock the human race
Skate down, boogie shot
Come on girl, let's do the Rock
Slam dunk, do the Jerk
Let me see your body work

To the break, everybody
To the break, everybody
2, 4, 6, 8
Fatback, don't you hesitate

. . . .

To the break

Just keep the same old beat

About a while ago and I want you to know

Just who you been listening to

I am the voice of King Tim the Third

Tell you what I want you to do

A little left hand, right hand in the air

And you sway 'em like you just don't care

You put your left leg out, your right leg in

Say the Hustle is out and the Rock is in

About a quarter to four somebody was at your door

And you wondered who it was

You started to shake and shiver so I said

It's me, your little ol' cuz

I said open the door and let me in

I'll rock you so good you'll want it again

I rocked you so good you heard bells ring

They went ring-ding-dang-a-ding-a-ding-ding

Ring-ding-dang-a-ding-a-ding-ding

To the break, everybody

Do it to me and I'll do it to you

Stomp your feet and clap your hands

'Cause you're listening to the sounds of the Fatback Band

It ain't nothing new in what I do

'Cause I'm doing it all just for you

I'm hotter than tea, I'm sweeter than honey

I'm not doing it for the money

I'm sugar-coated, double-dunk

Chocolate-MC man

I'm sweeter than the Almond Joy

And grandma's sweet old jam

I'm the modified, the rectified

Ka-zink-di-fied, ka-jook-di-fied

Caput-a-fied, ca-dook-a-fied

To rock your mind, say all the time

To the break, everybody
To the break, everybody
It's on and on and on and on
Like hot butter on—say what?—the popcorn

Do it to me and I'll do it to you

To the beat, everybody
You keep the pep in the step, the hip in your hop
You don't stop 'til you get on the mountain top
Once you reach the top you won't be alone
You got King Tim on the microphone
Just grab your partner, you start to swing
'Cause I'm well-known just like Burger King
I don't sell burgers or French fries
I'm only here to make your nature rise
Just grab your partners around and round
And grab her by the butt and boogie down
Just open up her jacket and open her bra
And then just lay at the Mardi Gras
I'm the man of action, the main attraction
The girls call me the satisfaction
I'm the Romeo, the Casanova
Here tonight, I'm gonna get over
To the beat, everybody
To the beat, everybody
To the beat, everybody
To the beat, everybody

HATE IT OR LOVE IT
THE GAME (FEAT. 50 CENT)

[50 Cent]
Coming up I was confused, my mama kissing a girl
Confusion occurs coming up in a cold world

Daddy ain't around, probably out committing felonies

My favorite rapper used to sing, "Check, check out my melody"

I wanna live good, so, shit, I sell dope

For a four-finger ring, one of them gold ropes

Nana told me if I passed, I'd get a sheepskin coat

If I could move a few packs, I'd get that hat, now that'll be dope

Tossed and turn in my sleep that night

Woke up the next morning, niggas done stole my bike

Different day, same shit, ain't nothing good in the 'hood

I run away from this bitch and never come back if I could

[Chorus 2x]

Hate it or love it, the underdog's on top

And I'm gon' shine, homie, until my heart stop

Go 'head and envy me, I'm rap's MVP

And I ain't going nowhere, so you can get to know me

G-G-G-G-G-G-G-Unit!

[Game]

On the grill of my low rider

Guns on both sides, right above the gold wires

I four-five 'em, kill a nigga on my song

And really do it; that's the true meaning of a ghostwriter

Ten G's will take your daughter outta Air Forces

Believe you me, homie, I know all about losses

I'm from Compton, wear the wrong colors, be cautious

One phone call'll have your body dumped in Marcy

I stay strapped like car seats, been banging

Since my little nigga Rob got killed for his Barkleys

That's ten years, I told Pooh in '95

I'll kill you if you try me for my Air Max 95s

Told Banks when I met him, I'ma ride

And if I gotta die, rather homicide

I ain't had 50 Cent when my grandmama died

Now I'm going back to Cali with my Jacob on
See how time fly?

[Chorus 2x]

[50 Cent]
From the beginning to the end, losers lose, winners win
This is real, we ain't got to pretend
The cold world that we in, it's full of pressure and pain
Enough of me, nigga, now listen to Game

[Game]
Used to see 5-0, throw the crack by the bench
Now I'm fucking with 5-0, it's all starting to make sense
My ma's happy, she ain't gotta pay the rent
And she got a red bow on that brand new Benz
Waiting on Sha Money to land, sitting in the Range
Thinking how they spend thirty million dollars on airplanes
When there's kids starving, Pac is gone
And Brenda's still throwing babies in the garbage
I wanna know what's going on like I hear Marvin
No school books, they use that wood to build coffins
Whenever I'm in a booth and I get exhausted
I think, What if Marie Baker got that abortion?
I love you, Ma

[Chorus 2x]

WHY
JADAKISS
Yo, why is Jadakiss as hard as it gets?
Why is the industry designed to keep the artist in debt?
And why them dudes ain't ridin if they're part of your set?
And why they never get it poppin but they party to death?
Yeah, and why they gon' give you life for a murder, turn around
Only give you eight months for a burner? It's goin down

Why they sellin niggas' CDs for under a dime?

And if it's all love, daddy, why you come wit' your nine?

Why my niggas ain't get that cake?

Why is a brother up North better than Jordan that ain't get that break?

Why you ain't stackin instead of tryin to be fly?

Why is rattin at an all-time high? Why are you even alive?

Why they kill Tupac 'n' Chris?

Why at the bar you ain't take straight shots instead of poppin Crist'?

Why them bullets have to hit that door?

Why did Kobe have to hit that raw? Why he kiss that whore?

Why?

[Chorus]

All that I been given

Is this thing that I've been living

They got me in the system

Why they gotta do me like that?

Tried to make it my way

But got sent up on the highway

Why, oh, why

Why they gotta do me like that?

Why would niggas push pounds and powder? Why did Bush

Knock down the towers? Why you around them cowards?

Why Aaliyah have to take that flight? Why my nigga D

Ain't pull out his Ferrari? Why he take that bike?

Why they gotta open your package and read your mail?

Why they stop lettin niggas get degrees in jail?

Why you gotta do 85 percent of your time?

And why do niggas lie in 85 percent of they rhymes?

Why a nigga always want what he can't have?

Why I can't come through in the pecan Jag?

Why did crack have to hit so hard, even though it's almost over?

Why niggas can't get no jobs?

Why they come up with the witness protection? Why they let

The Terminator win the election? Come on, pay attention
Why sell in the stores what you can sell in the streets?
Why I say the hottest shit but we sellin the least?

[Chorus]

Why Halle have to let a white man pop her to get a Oscar?
Why Denzel have to be crooked before he took it?
Why they didn't make the CL6 wit' a clutch?
And if you don't smoke, then why the hell you reachin for my Dutch?
Why rap? 'Cause I need air time
Why be on the curb wit' a "Why lie; I need a beer" sign?
Why all the young niggas is dyin 'cause they moms at work
They pops is gone, they livin wit' iron
Why they ain't give us a cure for AIDS?
Why my diesel have fiends in the spot on the floor for days?
Why you screamin like it's a slug, it's only the hawk?
Why my buzz in LA ain't like it is in New York?
Why they forcin you to be hard? Why ain't you a thug by choice?
Why the whole world love my voice?
Why, try to tell 'em that it's the flow, son
And you know why they made the new twenties? 'Cause I got all the old ones
That's why...

[Chorus]

EXHIBIT C
JAY ELECTRONICA

It's coming. Ladies and gentlemen, this time around the revolution will not be televised. Woo.... As we proceed... to give you what you need. '09 muf—, get live muf—. Ladies and gentlemen of the court, in the hearing against the state of hip-hop versus Jay Electronica, I present Exhibit C...

When I was sleepin on the train, sleepin on Meserole
Ave out in the rain, without even a single slice of pizza

To my name, too proud to beg for change

Mastering the pain, when New York niggas

Was calling Southern rappers lame, but then jacking our slang

I used to get dizzy spells, hear a little ring

The voice of a angel tellin me my name

Tellin me that one day I'ma be a great man

Transforming with the Megatron Don, spitting out flames

Eatin wack rappers alive, shittin out chains

I ain't believe it then, nigga, I was homeless

Fighting, shooting dice, smokin weed on the corners

Trying to find the meaning of life in a Corona

'Til the Five-Percenters rolled up on a nigga and informed him

"You either build or destroy. Where you come from?"

"The Magnolia projects and the Third Ward slum"

"Hmm . . . it's quite amazing that you rhyme how you do

And that you shine like you grew up in a shrine in Peru"

Question fourteen, Muslim lesson two:

Dip-diver, civilize a eighty-fiver

I make the devil hit his knees and say the Our Father

Abracadabra, you rocking with the true and livin

Shout out to Lights Out, Joseph I, and Chewy Bivens

Shout out to Baltimore, Baton Rouge, my crew in Richmond

While y'all debated who the truth was like Jews and Christians

I was on Cecil B, Broad Street, Master

North Philly, South Philly, Twenty-Third, Tasker

Six Mile, Seven Mile, Heartwell, Gratiot

Where niggas really would pack a U-Haul truck up

Put the high beams on, drive up on the curb

At a barbeque and hop up out the back like: "What's up?"

Kill a nigga, rob a nigga, take a nigga, bust up

That's why when you talk that tough talk I never feel ya

You sound real good and you play the part well

But the energy you givin off is so unfamiliar

I don't feel ya. (We need something realer)
Nas hit me up on the phone, said, "What you waiting on?"
Tip hit me up with a twit, said, "What you waitin on?"
Diddy's sending texts every hour on the dot sayin
"When you gonna drop that verse? Nigga, you takin long"
So now I'm back spitting that He Could Pass a Polygraph
That Reverend Run rockin Adidas out on Hollis Ave
The FOI, Marcus Garvey, Nikki Tesla
I shock you like the ill electric field, Jay Electra
(Oh my God, keep going)

They call me Jay Electronica—fuck that
Call me Jay Elec-Hanukkah, Jay Elec-Yarmulke
Jay Elec-Ramadan Mohammed Asalaamica
Rasoul Allah Supana Watallah through your monitor
My Uzi still weigh a ton, check the barometer
I'm hotter than the motherfuckin sun, check the thermometer
I'm bringin ancient mathematics back to modern man
My mama told me never throw a stone and hide your hand
I got a lot of family, you got a lot of fans
That's why the people got my back like the Verizon man
I play the back and fade to black and then devise a plan
Out in London smokin, vibin while I ride the tram
Giving out that raw food to lions disguised as lambs
And by the time they get they seats hot
And deploy all they henchmen to come at me from the treetops
I'm chilling out at Tweetstock, buildin by the millions
My light is brilliant

*I rest my case. '09, act three, first chapter of the end, the last chapter of the new
beginning. Ain't this so, the things we do without even trying be better than a
lot of y'all's records, don't get mad. Morning after, world premiere. Man, for
real though, I ain't even gonna say nothing. Matter fact, I ain't saying—I don't
even know why I'm saying this. Jay, you should get Puff to do this over. We
moving out, on to the next record. And, um, I'ma let this just ride. Ride . . .*

UNCOMMON VALOR: A VIETNAM STORY
JEDI MIND TRICKS (FEAT. R.A. THE RUGGED MAN)

[Vinnie Paz]
I don't know why I'm over here, this job is evil
They send me here to Vietnam to kill innocent people
My mother wrote me, said the president, he doesn't care
He trying to leave the footprints of America here
They say we're trying to stop Chinese expansion
But I ain't seen no Chinese since we landed
Sent my whole entire unit thinking we can win
Against the Vietcong guerrillas there in Gia Dinh
I didn't sign up to kill women or any children
For every enemy soldier, we killin six civilians
Yeah, and that ain't right to me
I ain't got enough of motherfuckin fight in me
It frightens me, and I just want to see my son and moms
But over here they dropping seven million tons of bombs
I spend my days dodging all these booby traps and mines
And at night, praying to God that I get back alive
And I'm forced to sit back and wonder
Why I was a part of Operation Rolling Thunder
In a foxhole with nine months left here
Jungle like the fuckin harbinger of death here

[Interlude]
[soldier] *I don't want to be here. I'm scared, I just want to go home.*
[officer] *You fucking kidding me? Don't be a pussy. Don't you love your*
country?
[soldier] *I like being here. I'm ready.*

[R.A. the Rugged Man]
True story...
Call me Thorburn, John A. Staff Sergeant
Marksman, skilled in killing, illing, I'm able and willing

Kill the village elephant, rapin and pillage your village

Illegitimate killers, US Military guerrillas

This ain't no real war, Vietnam shit, World War II

That's a war, this is just a military conflict

Soothing, drug-abusing, Vietnamese women screwin

Sex, gambling, and boozin, all this shit is amusin

Bitches and guns, this is every man's dream

I don't want to go home, where I'm just a ordinary human being

Special OP, Huey chopper gun ship, run shit

Gook run when the mini-gun spit, won't miss

Kill shit, spit four thousand bullets a minute

Victor Charlie, hit trigger, hit it, I'm in it to win it

Get it, the lieutenant hinted the villain, I've been in

The killin, I did it, crippled, did it, pictures I painted is vivid

Live it, a wizard with weapons, a secret mission, we about to begin it

Government funded, behind enemy lines

Bullets is spraying, it's heating up, a hundred degrees

The enemy's the North Vietnamese—bitch, please

Ain't no sweat, I'm totally at ease until I see

The pilot got hit and we 'bout to hit some trees

Tail of the rotor broke, crash land, American man

Cambodia, right in the enemy hand

Take a swig of the whiskey to calm us, them yellow men

Wearing black pyjamas, they want to harm us, they all up on us

Bang, bang, bullet hit my chest, feel no pain

To my left, the captain caught a bullet right in his brain

Body parts flying, loss of limbs, explosions

Bad intentions, I see my best friend's intestines

Pray to the one above, it's raining and I'm covered in mud

I think I'm dying, I feel dizzy, I'm losing blood

I see my childhood, I'm back in the arms of my mother

I see my whole life, I see Christ, I see bright lights

I see Israelites, Muslims, and Christians at peace, no fights

Blacks, whites, Asians, people of all types

I must have died, then I woke up, surprised I'm alive

I'm in a hospital bed, they rescued me, I survived

I escaped the war, came back, but ain't escape Agent Orange

Two of my kids born handicapped

Spastic, quadriplegia, microcephalic

Cerebral palsy, cortical blindness—name it, they had it

My son died, he ain't live, but I still try to think positive

'Cause in life, God take, God give

COME CLEAN
JERU THE DAMAJA

You wanna front, what? Jump up and get bucked

If you're feeling lucky duck, then press your luck

I snatch fake gangsta MCs and make 'em faggot flambé

Your nine spray, my mind spray

Malignant mist that'll leave con defunked

The results: your remains stuffed in a car trunk

You couldn't come to the jungles of the East poppin that game

You won't survive, get live, catchin wreck is our thing

I don't gangbang or shoot out "bang-bang"

The relentless lyrics the only dope I slang

I'm a true master, you can check my credentials

'Cause I choose to use my infinite potential

Got a freaky, freaky, freaky-freaky flow

Control the mic like Fidel Castro

Locked Cuba, so deep that you can scuba

Dive, my jive's origin is unknown like the Jubas

I've accumulated honeys all across the map

'Cause I'd rather bust a nut than bust a cap

In ya back, in fact my rap snaps ya sacroiliac

I'm the mack so I don't need to tote a MAC

My attack is purely mental and its nature's not hate

It's meant to wake ya up out of ya brainwashed state

Stagnate nonsense but if you persist

You'll get ya snot box bust, you press up on this
I flip, hoes dip, none of the real niggas skip
You don't know enough math to count the mics that I ripped
Keep the dirty rotten scamp as his verbal weapons spit

[Chorus 5x]
Uh oh, heads up, 'cause we droppin some shit

Real rough and rugged, shine like a gold nugget
Every time I pick up the microphone I drug it
Unplug it on chumps with the gangsta babble
Leave your nines at home and bring your skills to the battle
You're rattlin on and on and ain't sayin nothin
That's why you got snuffed when you bumped heads with dirty rotten
Have you forgotten? I'll tap your jaw
I also kick like kung-fu flicks by Run Run Shaw
Made frauds bleed every time I G'd
'Cause I've perfected my drunk good style like Sam Seed
Pseudopsychos, I play like Michael
Jackson when I'm bustin ass and breakin backs
Inhale the putrefied aroma
Breathe too deep and you'll wind up coma
Toast the king, I'm hard like a fifth of vodka
And bring your clique 'cause I'm a hard rock knocka
I gotcha, out on a limb, about to push you off the brink
Let you draw your craw but your burner shot blanks
When the East is in the house you should come equipped

[Chorus 9x]

Fly like a jet, sting like a hornet
Knuckleheads get live and set it off if you want it
Dirty rotten scoundrels is crushin fools, no joke
With styles more fatal than secondhand smoke
Don't provoke the wrath of this rhyme inventor
'Cause I blow up spots like the World Trade Center

Come with the super-trooper on his assault mission

The TEK's technique, 'cause he's a technician

Wishin he'll go away won't help the weapons stop

Your skills are shot 'cause any idiot can let off a Glock

Hard rocks melt in the clutch of the sun toucha

You claim you got beef on the streets, so whatcha

Gonna do when real niggas roll up on you

And you don't got your crew?

Pull your Glock but you don't got the heart

You was webbed straight from the start

Bought a tool and didn't learn how to use it

Got lost in Brooklyn so you had to lose it

Just for frontin you got that ass waxed

[Chorus 10x]

LETTER TO OBAMA
JOELL ORTIZ

YAOWA! What's up, future president. My name is Joell Ortiz and I'm the voice of the underdogs in the 'hood, so I wanted to write this letter to you to see what you thought . . .

Dear future president, I grew up with no brothers and sisters

And my moms was on public assistance, and her husband

Was missing. She developed this disgusting addiction

That had her on some of the ugliest missions. So she missed

Some appointments. She was supposed to keep my coverage consistent

I was a chronic asthmatic: huffin, puffin, and whistlin

Can't get a breath, I wished for death, it hurt my chest when I coughed

Oh yeah, I'm from the projects of New York. We love basketball

But last summer my boy got left on the court

Some kid reached next to his shorts and put some lead in his thoughts

And the murder's moms, she jetted from court. Her only son

Had eighteen years in the street, he livin the rest up north

My other homie sellin crack, he always tell me it's wack

Every day he filling out apps but they don't call him back
Background check spotted his felony, but that ain't fair
You make a mistake, you can't fix it, man, this world don't care
That's how he feelin; he got bills, so he movin them krills
Livin life over his shoulder, boys in blue on his heels
His little sister, man, she grown; she done threw on them heels
Exotic dancing on the pole; look what she do for a bill
Took one of them young boys backstage, pursuing a thrill
Caught that thing, now every day she wake up doin them pills
I get mad when I see what other artists do with a mil
With a couple Gs I gave my Ps a few computers, for real
Y'all done forgot where y'all came from. Have you no honor?
Only thing that chain doin is causing you more drama
Here's a couple wise words from the dude that goes "YAOWA"
It's time for a change and that change is Obama
So dear future president, I hope you heard this letter
And do some things to make sure the next one I'm writing is better
Peace!

HA
JUVENILE

That's you with that badass Benz, ha?
That's you that can't keep yo' old lady 'cause you keep fuckin her friends, ha?
You gotta go to court, ha? You got served a subpoena for child support, ha?
That was that nerve, ha?
You ain't even much get a chance to say a word, ha?
I know I ain't trippin; don't your brother got them birds, ha?
You want to bust one of them niggas' heads, ha?
You ain't scared, ha? You know how to play it, ha?
I know you just ain't gonna let a nigga come and punk you, ha?
Stunt and front you, ha? Straight up run you, ha?
You know who got that fire green, ha?
You know how to use a triple beam, ha? Shit ain't hard as it seems, ha?
You keep your body clean, ha? You got a lot of Girbaud jeans, ha?
Some of your partners dope fiends, ha?

You don't really want to fuck with them niggas, ha?

You come up with them niggas, ha? You stuck with them niggas, ha?

[Chorus 2x]

You a paper chaser, you got your block on fire

Remaining a G until the moment you expire

You know what it is to make nothing out of something

You handle your biz and don't be cryin and suffering

You can't do nothing but love fresh, ha?

You want to know what we gonna do next, ha? You bought my tape with your
   check, ha?

You wearing a vest, ha? You tryin to protect your chest, ha?

You spent seventy on your Benz, ha?

That ain't yours, that's for your friends, ha? You wanna stop

These niggas from playing wit' you, ha? You wanna run the block, ha?

You wanna be the only nigga with rocks, ha? You keep your gun cocked, ha?

You count the money at the end of the night, ha?

You on a three-day flight, ha? You full of that diesel, ha?

You duckin them people, ha? Your face was on the news last night, ha?

You the one that robbed them little dudes out they shoes last night, ha?

You don't go in the projects when it's dark, ha?

You claim you a thug and you ain't got no heart, ha?

You came in the Nola on New Year's Eve, ha?

You got stuck in that bitch and you couldn't leave, ha?

It was hard for you to breathe, ha?

[Chorus 2x]

You got a trespassing charge, ha?

Your dick got hard, ha? When you was looking at them little broads, ha?

You don't know when to quit, ha? That's you with that shot-calling shit, ha?

That's you with that balling shit, ha?

That's you that's taking them hits, ha?

That ho don't know when to shut up her mouth, ha? You gonna knock that ho
   teeth out, ha?

You done switched from Nikes to Reeboks, ha?

You twinkle yo' golds every time you leave your house, ha?

Them income tax checks out, ha? You 'bout to flip that, ha?

You 'bout to go score you a gram, ha?

You gonna treat your nose, ha? You 'bout to go

Put the dope dick on one of these hoes, ha?

When you broke you drove, ha?

When you paid you got beaucoup places to go, ha?

You on top, ha? You rob a nigga's shop, ha?

You don't even think you can be stopped, ha?

You ridin in the Benz on twenty-inch rims, ha?

[Chorus 2x]

BAKARDI SLANG
KARDINAL OFFISHALL

We don't say, "you know what I'm sayin," T-dot says, "ya dun know"

We don't say, "hey, that's the breaks," we say, "yo, a so it go"

We don't say, "you get one chance," we say, "you better rip the show"

Before bottles start flyin and you runnin for the door

Y'all talkin about "cuttin and hittin skins," we talkin about "beat dat face"

T-dot niggas'll eat your food before y'all cats say grace

Your cats is steady saying "word," my niggas is steady yellin "zeen"

Half the time we talking about "more times" and don't even know what
    "more times" mean

More times we rock fresher, more times we come correct

More times y'all think it's the hot shh . . . y'all haven't heard nothin yet

Differently, still ya know, the circle gettin ill, ya know

Step on the wrong Bally boot, you might get kill, ya know

So every time you walk through the dance, tell a youth "'scuse me"

Tellin your jubie "I like her style," she's talkin about "abuse me"

"Use me," "Show me how the T-dot rolls"

My style's off the thermostat plus I'm comin from the cold, yo

[Chorus]
(What the . . . chill)
My niggas in the street, throwin dot slang

Each and every single time we meet

(What the ... chill)

My ladies lookin hot, screw face

Kissin teet, representin the T-dot

Kardinal rock the party in T-dot drinking Bacardi and

Kardi drinkin Bacardi in T-dot rocking the party and

Niggas jumpin and wildin and ladies showin a smile and

Everybody knows it's the T-dot

So when we singin about the girls, we singin about the gyal dem

Y'all talkin about "say that one more time," we talkin about "yo, come again"

Y'all talkin about "that nigga's a punk," we talkin about "that yout's a fassy"

For the kids that think I'm comin wit' it, brother, just watch me

A shoe is called a "crep," a big party is a "fete"

Y'all talkin about "watch where you goin," we talkin about "mind where
  you step"

We backin a 2–4 of Guinness, we ain't messin with Moët

And if you runnin out of liquor the bar might get wet

You're talkin about "yo, that girl's hype," we like, "she's the bundown"

Y'all say "a DJ battle," we say "a clash with two sounds"

We rock the hottest things no matter how much it cost

You talkin about "yeah, son," we talkin about "yo, lock it off"

Wheel that and tek it from de top and just

Flash up lighta and watch the dance rock

Kardinal's gonna show you how the T-dot rolls

My style's off the thermostat plus I'm comin from the cold, yo

[Chorus]

Yo, instead of "your boys," we talkin about "de man dem"

When we talkin about your "breddren," yo, we talkin about your friend

When you say "the club's over," yo, we say "the jam done"

When you're thinkin about the west, you're thinkin about Red-1

Big ups and salutations to the Figure IV crew

When you sayin "she's a chicken," she a "skettlebam," too

When you talkin about a "thug nigga," we talkin about a "shotta"

When you think you got it locked, T-dot comin much hotta

Y'all think we all Jamaican, when enough man are Trinis

Bajans, Grenadians, and a whole heap of Haitians

Guyanese and all of the West Indies combined

To make a T-dot, O-dot, one of a kind

IRS said "we burn corn," that means they puff la

When we say "hell no," that means "yo, that nuh mek it"

Look me in the eye and tell me y'all ain't sold

My style's off the thermostat plus I'm comin from the cold, yo

[Chorus 2x]

FROM **THIS PUSSY'S A GANGSTA**
MEDUSA

This pussy's a gangsta

But I don't want her to be, so I gotta cut her

Cut her right out of your game

When I say she's a big gangsta, she's a G

You 'bout to feel the depth of the G-spot inside of me

I got nine months of energy that you can't even touch, let alone fuck

By the time you finish fuckin with a G like this, you gonna need a crutch

And it's guaranteed to drop you to your knees

And a little further down so you'll be a dick in the dirt motherfucker

I try to be courteous, but you know, if you can say "ho," I can say "dick in the
    dirt," dumb shit

But I'ma uplift and prove by the end because the sister just got that goddess
    glow

And that's a part of what I'm talkin 'bout to be a gangsta

Tired of these niggas grabbin the mic and becoming wacktors

And pretendin they got to get with ...

This pussy's a gangsta

But I don't want her to be, so I gotta cut her

Cut her right out of your game

Now, when I say we fittin to cut her up out yo' game

I don't mean you gonna give me a hysterectomy and remove my thang

I don't want you to scrape out the box it came in

I want you to spend about a year tryin to get in

See, 'cause you got to support me, it's most important, see

A G don't like you rushin up on this gangsta

You'll hear a couple of click clicks and get a cat scratch on your back and it
   won't leave you . . .

And do you know what a real gangsta is?

See, a real gangsta don't give a fuck if you stand up or sit down to piss

'Cause it's all love and tears with it

See, while you out gangbangin, I got time on my hands so I'm finger bangin

EVERYTHING'S GONNA BE ALRIGHT (GHETTO BASTARD)
NAUGHTY BY NATURE

Nurse Johnson, is the mother still in the recovery room?

Yes, Dr. Blair

Okay, I'll go to the waiting room and inform the father it's a boy

I'm afraid there is no father, sir

Another ghetto bastard, huh?

I'm afraid so

Well, put him with the rest of the born losers

All right, Doctor. A shame, isn't it?

Not a shame—a problem

(Paging Dr. Blair, Dr. Blair, Dr. James Hamilton, Dr. James Hamilton)

*Smooth it out. . . . This is a story about the drifter who waited for the worst 'cause
   the best live 'cross town, who never planned on having someday. Why me?*

Some get a little and some get none

Some catch a bad one and some leave the job half done

I was one who never had and always mad

Never knew my dad, motherfuck the fag

Well anyway, I did pickups, lifts, and click ups

See many stickups, 'cause niggas had the trigger hiccups

I couldn't get a job, nappy hair was not allowed

My mother couldn't afford us all, she had to throw me out

I walked the strip with just a clip. Who want a hit?

Thank God I'm quick, I had to eat, this money's good as spent

I threw in braids, I wasn't paid enough

I kept 'em on 'cause I couldn't afford a haircut

I got laughed at, I got chumped, I got dissed

I got upset, I got a TEC and a banana clip

Was down in dope, don't let any dealer tack in

I sealed 'em in rope, so a lot of good it woulda did

Or done, if not bad luck I would have none

Why did I have to live the life of such a bad one?

Why when I was a kid and played I was a sad one

And always wanted to live like this or that one?

[Chorus 4x]

Everything's gonna be all right (all right)

A ghetto bastard, born next to the projects

Livin in the slums with bums, I said, "Now why, Treach

Do I have to be like this?" Mama said I'm priceless

So I am, I'm worthless, starvin, that's just what being nice gets

Sometimes I wish I could afford a pistol, then though

To stop the hell, I woulda ended things a while ago

I ain't have jack, but a black hat and knapsack

War scars, stolen cars, and a blackjack

Drop that, and now you want me to rap and give

Say something positive; well, positive ain't where I live

I live right around the corner from West Hell

Two blocks from South Shit and once in a jail cell

The sun never shined on my side of the street, see

And only once or twice a week, I would speak

I walked alone, my state of mind was home sweet home

I couldn't keep a girl, they wanted kids and cars with chrome

Some life, if you ain't wear gold, your style was old
And you got more juice and dope for every bottle sold
Hell, no, I say there's gotta be a better way
But hey, never gamble in a game that you can't play
I'm gonna flaunt it, gonna know when, know when and not now
How will I do it? How will I make it? I won't, that's how
Why me, huh?

[Chorus]

My third year to adulthood and still a knucklehead
I'm better off dead, huh, that's what my neighbor said
I don't do jack but fightin, lightin up the street at night
Playing hide-and-seek with a machete, set to Freddy's spike
Some say I'm all in all, nothing but a dog now
I answer that with a "fuck you" and a "bowwow"
'Cause I done been through more shit within the last week
Than the fly flowin in doo-doo on the concrete
I've been a dead beat, dead to the world and dead wrong
Since I was born, that's my life—oh, you don't know this song?
So don't say jack and please don't say you understand
All that man-to-man talk can walk, damn
If you ain't live it, you couldn't feel it, so kill it, skillet
And all that talkin 'bout it won't help it out, now will it?
In Illtown, "Good luck" got stuck up, "Props" got shot
"Don't worry" got hit by a flurry and this punk ass dropped
But I'm the one who has been labeled as an outcast
They teach in schools, I'm the misfit that will outlast
But that's cool with the fool, smack 'em backwards
That's what you get for fuckin with a ghetto bastard

If you ain't never been to the ghetto, don't ever come to the ghetto. 'Cause you
  wouldn't understand the ghetto, so stay the fuck out of the ghetto. Why me?
  Why me?

COUNTRY GRAMMAR (HOT SHIT)
NELLY

Hot shit!

[Chorus 2x]
Mmmmm, I'm going down, down, baby, North Street in a Range Rover
Street sweeper, baby. Cocked, ready to let it go
Shimmy shimmy cocoa, what? Listen to it now
Light it up and take a puff, pass it to me now

Mmmmm. . . . You can find me in St. Louis rolling on dubs
Smoking on dubs in clubs, blowing up like cocoa puffs
Sippin bub, getting perved and getting rubbed
Daps and hugs, mean mugs and shoulder shrugs
And it's all because accumulated enough scratch
Just to Navigate it, wood decorated on chrome
And it's candy painted, fans fainted while I'm entertaining
Wild, ain't it? How me and money end up hanging
I hang with Hannibal Lecter (Hot shit!) so feel me when I bring it
Sing it loud (What?) I'm from the Lou and I'm proud
Run a mile for the cause, I'm righteous above the law
Player, my style's raw, I'm "Born to Mack" like Todd Shaw
Forget the fame and the glamour, give me D's with a rubber hammer
My grammar be's Ebonics, gin, tonic, and chronic
Fuck bionic, it's ironic, slamming niggas like Onyx
Lunatics 'til the day I die, I run more game than the Bulls and Sonics

[Chorus 2x]

Who say pretty boys can't be wild niggas?
Loud niggas, O.K. Corral niggas, foul niggas
Run in the club and bust in the crowd nigga
How, nigga? Ask me again and it's going down, nigga
Now nigga, come to the circus and watch me clown, nigga
Pound niggas, what you be giving when I'm around, nigga

Frown niggas, talking that shit when I leave the town, nigga

Say now, can you hoes come out to play now?

Hey, I'm ready to cut you up any day now

Play by my rules, boo, and you gon' stay high

May I answer yo' third question like AI?

Say hi to my niggas left in the slamma

From St. Louis to Memphis, from Texas back up to Indiana

Chi-Town, KC, Motown to Alabama

LA, New York Yankee niggas to Hotlanta

Louisiana, all my niggas with country grammar

Smoking blunts in Savannah, blow thirty mil like I'm Hammer

[Chorus 2x]

Let's show these cats how to make these millions, so you niggas quit actin
    silly, mon

Kid quicker than Billy, mon, talking really not needed, mon

Flows I kick 'em freely, mon, especially off Remy, mon

Keys to my Beemer, mon, holler at Beenie Man

See me, mon? Chiefin rollin deeper than any mon

Through Jennings, mon, through U-City back up to Kingsland

With nice niggas, sheist niggas who snatch yo' life, niggas

Trife niggas who produce and sell the same beat twice, nigga (Hot shit!)

Ice niggas all over, close to never sober

From broke to havin brokers, my price range is Rover

Now I'm knocking like Jehovah. Let me in now, let me in now

Bill Gates, Donald Trump, let me in now

Spin now, I got money to lend my friends now

We in a candy Benz, Kenwood and 10s now

A winner (Whoo!) fuckin lesbian twins now

Seeing how through the pen I make my ends now

[Chorus]

SOMETIMES I RHYME SLOW
NICE & SMOOTH

Sometimes I rhyme slow, sometimes I rhyme quick [2x]

[Greg Nice]
Sometimes I rhyme slow and sometimes I rhyme quick
I'm sweeter and thicker than a Chick-O-Stick
Here's an ice-cream cone, honey, take a lick
Or go to Bay Plaza and catch a flick
Wore my Timberland boots so I can stomp the ticks
Scandalous, get a whiff of this mist
Just left the Yardboy, now I'm blissed
I feel good, per se, good state of mind
Drive a red Sterling and the seats recline
I love it when a lady treats me kind
Go to Tavern on the Green and have a glass of wine
He say, she say, I heard it through the grapevine
No static, got an automatic
Too much of anything makes you an addict
Teasin, skeezin, also pleasin
Don't ask why, I got my own reasons
Smooth B, Greg Nice, Slick Nick clique
Sometimes I rhyme slow, sometimes I rhyme quick

Sometimes I rhyme slow, sometimes I rhyme quick [2x]

[Smooth B]
Sometimes I rhyme slow, sometimes I rhyme quick
I was on 125 and Saint Nick
Waitin on a cab, standin in the rain
Under my heart, three clouds of pain
She got the best of me. What was her destiny?
Maybe I should lick her with my nine millime-
Ter.... My mind is in a blur
'Cause you could never pay me to think this would occur

Me and this girl Jane Doe was living together

We were inseparable, no one could sever

At least that's what I thought, but later I fought

With her substance and almost ended up in Supreme Court

When I was on the road doing shows, getting ends

She was in my Benz getting sniffy with her friends

And even when she crashed my whip I didn't flip

My man Slick Nick said, "Smooth, you're starting to slip"

Time went on, I started noticing weight loss

Then I had to ask her was she riding the white horse

At first she said no, then she said, "Yo

Smooth, I'm sorry, but I keep having visions of snow

I need blow." And I said, "Whoa, little hottie

I'm not DeLorean, Gambino, or Gotti

I don't deal coke, and furthermore you're making me broke

I'll put you in a rehab and I won't tell your folks"

...And what do you know

In eighteen months she came home and I let her back in

And now she's sniffing again...

Sometimes I rhyme slow, sometimes I rhyme quick [repeat to fade]

TIME'S UP
O.C.

Time's up

You lack the minerals and vitamins, irons and the niacin

Fuck who that I offend, rappers sit back, I'm 'bout to begin

'Bout foul talk you squawk, never even walked the walk

More or less destined to get tested, never been arrested

My album will manifest many things that I saw, did, or heard about

All told firsthand, never word of mouth

What's in the future for the fusion in the changer?

Rappers are in danger, who will use wits to be a remainder?

When the missile is aimed to blow you out of the frame

Some will keep their limbs and some will be maimed
The same suckers with the gab about killer instincts
But turned bitch and knowin damn well they lack
In this division the connoisseur, crackin your head with a four-by-four
Realize, sucker, I be the comin like Noah
Always sendin you down, perpetrating, facadin what you consider
A image, to me this is just a scrimmage
I feel I'm stone, not 'cause I bop or wear my cap cocked
The more emotion I put into it, the harder I rock
Those who pose lyrical but really ain't true, I feel
"Their time's limited, hard rocks too" [2x]

Speakin in tongues about what you did but you never done it
Admit it, you bit it 'cause the next man gained platinum behind it
I find it ironic, so I researched and analyzed
Most write about stuff they fantasized
I'm fed up with the bull, on this focus of weed and clips
And Glocks gettin cocked and wax not bein flipped
It's the same-old same-old, just strain it from the anal
The contact is not complexed or vexed
So why you pushing it? Why you lying for? I know where you live
I know your folks, you was a sucker as a kid
Your persona's drama that you acquired in high school in actin class
Your whole aura is plexiglass
What's-her-face told me you shot this kid last week in the park
That's a lie, you was in church with your moms
See, I know, yo, slow your roll, give a good to go
Guys be lacking in this thing called rapping just for dough
Of course, we gotta pay rent so money connects, but, uh
I'd rather be broke and have a whole lot of respect
It's the principle of it, I get a rush when I bust
Some dope lines I wrote that maybe somebody'll quote
That's what I consider real in this field of music

Instead of putting brain cells to work, they abuse it

Nonconceptual, nonexceptional

Everybody's either crime related or sexual

I'm here to make a difference, besides all the riffing

The traps are not sticking, rappers stop flipping

For those who pose lyrical but really ain't true, I feel . . .

"Their time's limited, hard rocks too" [2x]

THEY REMINISCE OVER YOU (T.R.O.Y.)
PETE ROCK & C. L. SMOOTH

I reminisce, I reminisce [9x]

I reminisce for a spell, or shall I say think back

Twenty-two years ago to keep it on track

The birth of a child on the 8th of October

A toast, but my granddaddy came sober

Countin all the fingers and the toes

Now I suppose you hope the little black boy grows

Huh (yeah) eighteen years younger than my mama

But I rarely got beatings 'cause the girl loved drama

In single parenthood there I stood

By the time she was twenty-one, had another one

This one's a girl, let's name her Pam

Same father as the first but you don't give a damn

Irresponsible, plain not thinkin

Papa said "chill" but the brother keep winkin

Still he won't down you or tear out your hide

On your side while the baby maker slide

But mama got wise to the game

The youngest of five kids, hon, here it is

After ten years without no spouse

Mama's getting married in the house

Listen: positive over negative, for the woman, a master

Mother queen's rising a chapter
Déjà vu, tell you what I'm gonna do
When they reminisce over you, my God

When I date back I recall a man off the family tree
My right-hand Papa Doc I see
Took me from a boy to a man, so I always had a father
When my biological didn't bother
Taking care of this so who am I to bicker?
Not a bad ticker but I'm clocking pop's liver
But you can never say that his life is through
Five kids at twenty-one, believe he got a right to
Here we go while I check the scene
With the Portuguese lover at the age of fourteen
The same age, front page, no fuss
But I bet you all your dough they live longer than us
Never been senile, that's where you're wrong
But give the man a taste and he's gone
Nodding off, sleep to a jazz tune
I can hear his head banging on the wall in the next room
I get the pillow and hope I don't wake him
For this man to cuss, hear it all in verbatim
Telling me how to raise my boy unless he's taking over
I said, "Pop, maybe when you're older"
We laughed all night about the hookers at the party
My old man standing, yelling, "Good God Almighty"
Use your condom, take sips of the brew
When they reminisce over you, for real

I reminisce so you never forget this
The days of way back, so many bear witness, the fitness
Take the first letter, add up each word in this joint
Listen close as I prove my point
T to the R, a O, Y, how did you and I meet?
In front of Big Lou's, fighting in the street

But only you saw what took many time to see

I dedicate this to you for believing in me

Rain or shine, yes, in any weather

My grandma Pam holds the family together

My Uncle Doc's the greatest, better yet the latest

If we're talking about a car, Uncle Sterling got the latest

I strive to be live 'cause I got no choice

And run my own business like my Aunt Joyce

So, Pete Rock, hit me, 'nuff respect due

When they reminisce over you, listen

PASSIN ME BY
THE PHARCYDE

[Imani]

Now in my younger days I used to sport a shag

When I went to school I carried lunch in a bag

With an apple for my teacher 'cause I knew I'd get a kiss

Always got mad when the class was dismissed

But when it was in session, I always had a question

I would raise my hand to make her stagger to my desk

"Can you help me with my problem?" It was never much

Just a trick to smell her scent, I'd try to sneak a touch

Oh, how I wish I could hold her hand and give her a hug

She was married to the man, he was a thug

His name was Lee, he drove a Z, he'd pick her up from school

Promptly at three o'clock, I was on her jock

Yes indeedy, I wrote graffiti on the bus

First I'd write her name then carve a plus

With my name last on the looking glass

I seen her yesterday but still I had to let her pass

[Chorus 4x]

She keeps on passing me by . . .

[Bootie Brown]

When I dream of fairy tales I think of me and Shelly

See, she's my type of hype and I can't stand when brothers tell me

That I should quit chasin and look for something better

But the smile that she shows makes me a go-getter

I haven't gone as far as asking if I could get with her

I just play her by ear and hope she gets the picture

I'm shooting for her heart, got my finger on the trigger

She could be my broad and I could be her nigga

But all I can do is stare . . .

Back as kids we used to kiss when we played truth or dare

Now she's more sophisticated, highly edu-ma-cated

Not at all overrated, I think I need a prayer

To get in her boots and it looks rather dry

I guess a twinkle in her eye is just a twinkle in her eye

Although she's crazy stepping, I'll try to stop her stride

'Cause I won't have no more of this passing me by

[Slim Kid Tre]

It's time for me to voice my opinion, can't be pretending she didn't have me

Sprung like a chicken, chasin my tail like a doggy

She was kind of like a star, thinkin I was like a fan

Damn, she looked good, down side: she had a man

He was a rooty-toot, a nincompoop

She told me, "Soon your little birdie's gonna fly the coop"

She was a flake like corn and I was born not to understand

By lettin her pass I proved to be a better man

[Chorus 4x]

[Fatlip]

Now there she goes again, the dopest Ethiopian, and now

The world around me, B, gets moving in slow motion when-

Ever she happens to walk by, why does the apple of my eye

Overlook and disregard my feelings no matter how much I try?

Wait, no, I did not really pursue my little princess

With persistence, and I was so low-key that she was unaware

Of my existence, from a distance I desired her, secretly admired her

Wired her a letter to get her, and it went:

"My dear, my dear, my dear, you do not know me but I know you very well

Now let me tell you about the feelings. Does it bore you when I try

Or make some sort of attempt? I simp

Damn, I wish I wasn't such a wimp!

'Cause then I would let you know that I love you so

And if I was your man then I would be true

The only lying I would do is in the bed with you"

Then I signed: "Sincerely, the one who loves you dearly. P.S., Love me
     tender"

The letter came back three days later: return to sender

Damn!

[Chorus 4x]

ROCK DIS FUNKY JOINT
POOR RIGHTEOUS TEACHERS

Time to get funky-nomatical hip as I get to the point

(Rock dis funky joint)

Wait a sec, the teacher's gotta check the intellect

My stummer stepped in, then give you it, but . . .

But give you what? The P, the R, the T, fire often comes

To twist your top, but my style be just enough

To manifest the fabric mathematics black be that of Asiatic

Rock the bass, subtract the static, then let you rock into

My concept, like I should stand for this

For this, why, civilized, it hip-hop rhyme

From a black mind, to kickin it to you all the time

As-salaam alaikum or a peace sign

Rap is just my way of life and this be that of Islam

I'll take my time just before I manifest the rhyme

Sharp and accurate, to stop the music on a dime

Knowledge—me a cappella, wisdom, G, I'm manifestin
Understanding, understood, so there's no need fa keep you guessin
Follow me now, see? See, I be rockin
The second hand is tickin, still the posse don't be clockin
Controllers of the block be tickin closer to the point
(Rock dis funky joint)

The stummer step, the style that I use when folks would rather rap at me
PRT posse backin me
Easy now, star, you know exactly who we are
Poor Righteous Teachers tribe be PRT for short
Nah, nah, don't want no more, hmm? Am I too much for the mental?
Proceed, teacher, please, just keep it sort of simple
Like hip-hop, yet complicatedly I'll place it
According to the moods of my intellect
Step for step, I'll step a little closer to the point
Rock dis funky joint
But—but I'm your teacher! I teach ya, rockin when I rock ya
The king I vote for needs a different style of hip-hoppa
Smooth like a wise word spoken from a prophet
Rough like the slave trying to get away
See, I combine with two kinds of rhyme tryin to reach ya
The knowledge of myself makes me a Poor Righteous Teacher
Stop to flip the topic, Islamically I drop it
My duty be to teach so keep your pistol in your pocket
I-Self, Lord, and Master
Travelin faster, as I get closer to the point
(Rock dis funky joint)

Stummer step, yeah, yeah, I'm on top of it, I-I have to get
The styles that you be seekin and the words that I be speakin
Poor Righteous Teachers posse teachin
Anyone that lacks this style that I be stylin
Mentally profilin, should I say I'm ...
Smooth with the roughness, just servin justice

Sucker's try to suck this, but-but I be scopin

Never, I'm not sleepin (Because it's Culture Freedom, G)

Whose posse rollin? (PRT)

Word, B, it's sorta simple, see

Now look at me, the holy intellectual type

When I write, the spirit always kick me somethin hype

I grip the mic, yo, 'cause it's my whole life, like

Like I'm creatin, man-I-be-festatin

Can I say I'm great when there's not another brother greater?

Turn to Culture Freedom for support—G, manifest the point

(Rock dis funky joint)

But no excuses, losers never rock this

Snakes try to stop this, purified in holy hip-hopness

Listen to the concepts, sweat tech-technique

Peace be the Lord from the sword when I speak

As-salaam alaikum (Walaikum as-salaam)

A universal greeting from the people of our kind

Step into the realm of my cipher, feel the different type of

Brother stummer slippin steppin Technics

1200s mastered by Devine

He's asking me to rock, so now I'm giving him the spot

Style be the lyrics I be kickin, intelligence be tickin

Somewhat symbolic to a bomb

Many brothers roll and fell a victim

I'm not livin wit' them, because they didn't know the time

Turn to Culture Freedom for support—G, manifest a point

(Rock dis funky joint)

MAKESHIFT PATRIOT
SAGE FRANCIS

[Chorus]

Makeshift Patriot, the flag shop is out of stock

I hang myself at half mast

Makeshift Patriot, the flag shop is out of stock
I hang myself at half mast
Makeshift Patriot, the flag shop is out of stock
I hang myself at half mast
It's the Makeshift, the Patriot, the flag shop is out of stock
I hang myself . . . via live telecast

Coming live from my own funeral, beautiful weather offered a nice shine
Which is suitable for a full view of a forever-altered skyline
At times like these I freestyle biased opinions every other sentence
Journalistic ethics slip when I pass them off as objective. "Don't gimme that
   ethical shit."
I've got exclusive, explicit images to present to impressionable
American kids and it's time to show this world how big our edifice is
That's exactly what they attacked when a typically dark-skinned Disney
   villain
Used civilians against civilians and charged the Trojan horses into our
   buildings
Using commercial aviation as instruments of destruction
Pregnant women couldn't protect their children, wheelchairs were
   stairway obstructions
Now I have to backpedal from the shower of glass and metal
Wondering how after it settles we'll find who provided power to radical
   rebels
The Melting Pot seems to be calling the kettle black when it boils over
But only on our own soil, so the little boy holds a toy soldier
And waits for the suit and tie to come home. We won't wait 'til he's older
Before we destroy hopes for a colder war to end. "Now get a close up of his
   head."

[Chorus]

The city is covered in inches of muck. I see some other pictures of victims
   are up

Grieving mothers are thinking their children are stuck. Leaping lovers are
　　making decisions to jump
While holding hands to escape the brutal heat, sometimes in groups of three
The fallout goes far beyond the toxic cloud where people look like debris
But all they saw after all was said beyond the talking heads
Was the bloody dust with legs looking like the walking dead calling for meds
But all hospitals are overwhelmed, volunteers need to go the hell home
Moments of silence for firefighters were interrupted by cell phones
Who's going to make that call to increase an unknown death toll? It's the
　　one we rally behind
He's got a megaphone promising to make heads roll
We cheer him on, but asbestos is affecting our breath control
The less we know, the more they fabricate, the easier it is to sell souls

*There is a new price on freedom, so buy into it while supplies last. Changes need
　　to be made: no more curbside baggage, seven P.M. curfew, racial profiling will
　　continue with less bitching. We've unified over who to kill, so until I find more
　　relevant scripture to quote, remember: our God is bigger, stronger, smarter,
　　and much wealthier. So wave those flags with pride, especially the white part.*

We're sellin addictive twenty-four-hour candlelight vigils in TVs
Freedom will be defended at the cost of civil liberties
The viewers are glued to television screens, stuck 'cause lots of things seem
　　too sick
I use opportunities to pluck heartstrings for theme music
I'll show you which culture to pump your fist at, which foot is right to kiss
We don't really know who the culprit is yet, but he looks like this
We know who the heroes are; they're not the xenophobes who act hard
"We taught that dog to squat. How dare he do that shit in our own
　　backyard!"
They happened to scar our financial state and char our landscape
Can you count how many times so far I ran back this same damn tape?
While a cameraman creates news and shoves it down our throats on the
　　West Bank

With a ten-second clip put on constant loop to provoke US angst
So get your tanks and load your guns and hold your sons in a family huddle
'Cause even if we win this tug of war and even the score, humanity struggles
There's a need of blood for what's been uncovered under the rubble
Some of them dug for answers in the mess, but the rest were looking for
    trouble

[Chorus]

BROKEN LANGUAGE
SMOOTHE DA HUSTLER & TRIGGA DA GAMBLER

[Trigga]
Uh, base your eyes on the guy that has no kind
Of worries if I die, so, pussy clot, try
Dangerfield step in my way; bodies
Get cremated on a Friday, the do-or-die way
Your death threater, sender, head spinner
Rap beginner, light dimmer, three knockout count winner
The gun reacher, bustin shot teacher
Your funeral service church preacher, your black hearse coffin seeker
The body polluter, the gat shooter
The Brownsville wild Brooklyn trooper, the cock D mountain mover
The face basher, the Mr. Brain Smasher
The ass waxer, the drug money taxer

[Smoothe]
The money stasher, gun blastin razor slasher
The human asthma breath taker, body dump waster
The Glock cocker, the block locker, the rock chopper
The shot popper, the jock cock blocker
The face splitter, human disgrace getter
The lady shitter, phone joneser, sneak over fuck your babysitter
The chronic smokin, gun-totin hearse initiator
Crack supplier, the human drug generator

The honey gamer, the chicken tricker

The slicker, long dick pussy sticker, the ready-to-bust-that-ass kicker

The track manoeuvrer, the box barrier

The off-of-the-dome rapper, the C-74 ox carrier

[Trigga]

The gun seller, the chest sweller

The stickup smack bank teller, the money-back dweller

The stitch provider, the guess rider, the clip inserter

The bullet shooter experter, the man next to murder

[Smoothe]

The ho bitch disser, the cunt man, the I-don't-want clan

The stunt hitter in thirty-four-days-in-a-month man

The front man, the Brooklyn representer, the beat down center

The two brothers the hottest niggas out this fuckin winter

[Trigga]

The girl cheaters, the "be fast" beater

The street sweep keeper, the body to concrete meeter, the blood
    skeeter

The weed smoker, the liver choker, the spot stop broker

The rugged picture poser, the card scrambler

Royal flush, same suit, poker gambler

Nasty amateur damager, snap master without the camera

[Smoothe]

Camera, the beer guzzler, the slug-to-your-mug tussler

The drug juggler, the crazy thug hustler

The Lexus wanter, the chain, ring, and bracelet flaunterer

The chamber smoker, the mansion havin sauna soaker

The corner stander, the style crammer, the takeover

Spot block demander, the Glock on cock handler

The razor spitter, the fast dough, cash flow getter

The transmitter, North Carolina vagina hitter

[Trigga]

The ass kicker, the internal heart dark sticker

The red scope body hitter, hang with Digga and the booty lickers

The trigger-happy, father gun caller pappy

My gun blow out crib wave patterns to keep your hair nappy

To the death thinker, M.O.P. bell ringer

How about some hardcore fan singer, the jam swinger

[Smoothe]

The Nautica wearer, the Karl Kani man

The Mr. Get Jig, the fly man, Notorious ready-to-die man

The knower killer, the expert slayer, the white girl

Gangbanger, the Virgin Mary fucker, the Jesus hanger

The vital kicker, the drug dealer and title stripper

The idol flipper, the cross breaker and Bible ripper

[Trigga]

The black history thriver, the racial thinker

The nine to nine-to-five viber, the jaw sinker

The hell fighter, the Revelation writer

The Egyptian spirit inviter, the black body bag tie-er

The money stasher, the nigga crapper

The AKA cluck basher, my brother got a record racker

[Smoothe (Trigga)]

The battle spinner (the grand prize winner)

The life and death beginner (the ninety-five interstate highway to heaven
    sender)

The cocaine cooker, the hook up on your hooker hooker

The thirty-five-cent shorts on my two for fives overlooker

(The rap burner, the Ike the Tina Turner, ass-whipping learner

The hit man, the money earner)

The 'tologist without the derma', me and my little brother

(The cock me back, bust me off nigga undercover

The Glock to your head pursuer) the Big Daddy Kane

Little Daddy Shane overdoers

I GOT IT MADE
SPECIAL ED

I'm your idol, the highest title, numero uno
I'm not a Puerto Rican, but I'm speaking so that you know
And understand I got the gift of speech
And it's a blessin, so listen to the lesson I preach
I talk sense condensed into the form of a poem
Full of knowledge from my toes to the top of my dome
I'm kind of young, but my tongue speaks maturity
I'm not a child, I don't need nothing for security
I get paid when my record is played
To put it short—I got it made

I'm outspoken, my language is broken into a slang
But it's just a dialect that I select when I hang
I play it cool, 'cause coolin is all that I'm about
Just fooling with the girlies, yes, I'm bustin it out
I'm Special Ed and you can tell by the style that I use
I'm creatively superior, yo, I never lose
I never lost 'cause I'm the boss and never will 'cause I'm still
The champion, chief one, won't lose until
I choose, which I won't 'cause I don't retreat
I'll run you over like a truck and leave you dead in the street
You're inviting me, a Titan, to a battle, why?
I don't need your respect 'cause I got it made

I'm talented, yes, I'm gifted
Never boosted, never shoplifted
I got the cash, but money ain't nothin
Make a million dollars every record that I cut and
My name is Special Ed and I'm a super-duper star
Every other month, I get a brand-new car
Got twenty, that's plenty, yet I still want more
Kind of fond of Honda scooters, got seventy-four
I got the riches to fulfill my needs
Got land in the sand of the West Indies

Even got a little island of my very own

I got a frog, a dog with a solid-gold bone

An accountant to account the amount I spent

Got a treaty with Tahiti 'cause I own a percent

Got gear I wear for everyday

Boutiques from France to the USA

And I make all the money from the rhymes I invent

So it really doesn't matter how much I've spent

Because, yo, I make fresh rhymes daily

You burn me—really?

Think, just blink, and I've made a million rhymes

Just imagine if you blinked a million times

Damn, I'd be paid—I got it made

I'm kind of spoiled, 'cause everything I want I got made

I wanted gear, got everything from cotton to suede

I wanted leg, I didn't beg, I just got laid

My hair was growing too long, so I got me a fade

And when my dishes got dirty, I got Cascade

And when the weather was hot, I got a spot in the shade

I'm wise because I rise to the top of my grade

Wanted peace on earth, so to God I prayed

Some kids across town thought I was afraid

They couldn't harm me, I got the army brigade

I'm not a traitor, if what you got is greater I'll trade

But maybe later, 'cause my waiter made potatoed alligator soufflé

I got it made

TALKIN ALL THAT JAZZ
STETSASONIC

Well, here's how it started

Heard you on the radio, talkin 'bout rap

Sayin all that crap about how we sample

Give an example. Think we'll let you

Get away with that? You criticize

Our method of how we make records

You said it wasn't art, so now we're gonna rip you apart

Stop, check it out, my man

This is the music of a hip-hop band

Jazz: well, you can call it that

But this jazz retains a new format

Point, where you misjudged us

Speculated, created a fuss

You've made the same mistake politicians have

Talkin all that jazz

Talk: well, I heard talk is cheap

But like beauty, talk is just skin deep

And when you lie and you talk a lot

People tell you to step off a lot

You see, you misunderstood, a sample, just a tactic

A portion of my method, a tool

In fact it's only of importance when I make it a priority

And what we sample's loved by the majority

But you a minority in terms of thought

Narrow minded and poorly taught

About hip-hop fame or the silly game

To erase my music, so no one can use it

You step on us and we'll step on you

Can't have your cake and eat it too

Talkin all that jazz

Lies: that's when you hide the truth

It's when you talk more jazz than proof

And when you lie and address something you don't know

It's so wack that it's bound to show

When you lie about me and the band we get angry

We'll bite our pen, start writin again

And the things we write are always true

Suckers, get a grip, now we talkin 'bout you

Seems to me that you have a problem
So we can see what we can do to solve them
Think rap is a fad? You must be mad
'Cause we're so bad we get respect you never had
Tell the truth, James Brown was old
'Til Eric and Ra came out with "I Got Soul"
Rap brings back old R & B
And if we would not, people could've forgot
We wanna make this perfectly clear
We're talented and strong and have no fear
Of those who choose to judge but lack pizzazz
Talkin all that jazz

Now we're not tryin to be a boss to you
We just wanna get across to you
That if you're talkin jazz, the situation is a no-win
You might even get hurt, my friend
Stetsasonic, the hip-hop band
And like Sly and the Family Stone, we will stand
Up for the music we live and play
And for the song we sing today
For now, let us set the record straight
And later on we'll have a forum and a formal debate
But it's important you remember, though
What you reap is what you sow
Talkin all that jazz

Talkin all that jazz [2x]

CHUCK D

We are living in a period of growth for hip-hop culture, led this time not simply by artists but by students and scholars. The word-revolution in rhyme has been reflected in a slew of necessary critical perspectives that shed light on hip-hop's history and development. Books and multimedia on hip-hop culture and rap music have entered a boom period—or should I say BOOM BAP period: a time in which the recorded history and the breakdown of interpretations may be more entertaining than a lot of the new music being made today.

The Anthology of Rap is a landmark text. What makes it so important is that the voices included within it are from the artists themselves, but they are presented in a way that gives the words context and meaning as part of a tradition. Anyone could put together a bunch of lyrics, but an anthology does something more: it provides the tools to make meaning of those lyrics in relation to one another, to think about rap both in terms of particular rhymes, but also in terms of an art form, a people, and a movement. Every great literature deserves a great anthology. Rap finally has its own.

I first heard about The Anthology of Rap after meeting Dr. Adam Bradley at a symposium sponsored by the HipHop Archive at Harvard University. A few weeks later, I interviewed him on my Air America Network radio show, ON THE REAL, about his first book, Book of Rhymes: The Poetics of Hip Hop. I was fascinated by what I would call the emergent "artcademic" perspective he was describing. Here was someone who grew up with the music and had gone on to study it in a social context as well as "gettin down to it" on the level of language. He was spitting out a well-considered, highly analytical point of view to a mass audience that too often defines rap merely by what they hear on radio and see on television. Along with Dr. Andrew DuBois, Dr. Bradley has now brought us a book that just might break the commercial trance that's had rap in a choke hold for the past several years. Rap now has a book that tells its lyrical history in its own words.

My own history in hip-hop goes back decades. I started out in 1979 as a mobile DJ/MC under a crew called Spectrum City in Long Island, New York. Most of the shows we did were in less than ideal acoustic situations. Luckily my partner Hank Shocklee, who is now regarded as a sonic genius in the realm of recording, was just as astute about getting the best sound available out of the least amount of equipment. The challenge for many MCs was figuring out how to achieve vocal projection and clarity on inferior sound systems. I've always had a big voice, so my criteria were different because my vocal quality and power were audible. The content of my rhymes was heady because of what I knew. I'd been influenced by big voices like Melle Mel of Grandmaster Flash and the Furious Five. I studied the rhymes and rhythms that worked and tried to incorporate my voice and subject matter in a similar manner. I had to be distinct in my own identity. That was a very important aspect to propel me beyond the pack.

Most MCs don't listen to enough other MCs. As artists we need to open our ears to as many styles as possible, even—and maybe especially—those that are not commercially successful. In sports you must study the competition. You've got to game-plan. You've got to school yourself not just about the defending champions, but about every team in the league. In these times, the individualization of the MC has often meant isolation—artists focus on a single model, a single sound. Some focus is a good thing, of course, but too much leads to a lot of rappers sounding the same, saying the same things, finding themselves adrift in a sea of similarity.

Having a range of lyrical influences and interests doesn't compromise an MC's art. It helps that art to thrive and come into its own. For instance, my lyrics on "Rebel Without a Pause" are uniquely mine, but even the first "Yes" I utter to begin the song was inspired by another record—in this case, Biz Markie's "Nobody Beats the Biz," a favorite of mine at the time. The overall rhyme style I deployed on "Rebel" was a deliberate mixture of how KRS-One was breaking his rhymes into phrases and of Rakim's flow on "I Know You Got Soul." Although the craft is difficult, the options are many and the limits are few. There are many styles to attend to and numerous ways to integrate them into your own art, transforming yourself and those styles along the way.

That's where *The Anthology of Rap* comes in. It reminds us just how much variety truly exists in this thing we call rap. KRS-One raging against police brutality is far removed from Will Smith beefing about parents that just don't understand or from UGK explaining the intricacies of the street pharmaceutical trade, but all of them are united through rhyming to a beat. We learn more as rap artists and as a rap audience by coming to terms with all those things that rap has made.

In 2006 I did a collaboration with the great conscious rapper Paris. Paris singlehandedly created a Public Enemy album called *Rebirth of a Nation.* At the time, people asked why an MC like me would relinquish the responsibility of writing my own lyrics. My reason was simple: I thoroughly respect the songwriter and happen to think there is a valuable difference between the vocalist and the writer. Rarely are people gifted in both or well trained and skilled enough to handle both at once. The unwavering belief that MCs should always and only spit their own rhymes is a handicap for rap. In my opinion, most writers shouldn't spit and most vocalists shouldn't write unless there is a unique combination of skill, knowledge, ability, and distinction. To have Paris write my lyrics as well as produce the music added a breath of freshness to my voice. I put my ego aside—a hard thing for a lot of rappers to do—and was rewarded with a new weapon in my lyrical arsenal, unavailable had I simply gone it alone.

A lyric requires time and thought if it's going to last. Although top-of-the-head freestyles might be entertaining for the moment, they quickly expire. Even someone like Jay-Z, who claims never to write before rhyming, does his own form of composition. He has the older cat's knowledge, wisdom, and understanding of the many facets of multidimensional life zones and the ability to exercise his quickness of wit and tongue. Few MCs have his particular combination of gifts. Lyricism is a study of a terrain before it's sprayed upon like paint on a canvas. Most MCs would do better to think and have a conversation regarding what to rhyme about before they spit. While the spontaneity of the words to a beat might bring up-to-the-minute feelings to share, one cannot sleep on the power of the word—or in this case the arrangement and delivery of many words in rhythm.

When it comes down to the words themselves, lyricism is vital to rap, and because rap fuels hip-hop, this means that lyricism is vital to hip-hop culture as a whole. A rapper that really wants to be heard must realize that a good vocabulary is necessary, just as a good ball-handler sports his dribble on a basketball court. Something should separate a professional rapper from a sixth grader. Lyricism does that. Even when a middle school kid learns a word and its meaning, social comprehension and context take time to master. Even when a term or a line is mastered, the challenge should be on how many more peaks a rapper can scale to become a good lyricist. We all should know that the power of a word has both incited and prevented war itself.

Good lyrics, of course, existed before rap. They're the lifeblood of song. They direct the music, and the music defines the culture. This is true for rap even though some mistake the music as being all about the beat. People sometimes overrate the beat, separating it from the song itself. I ask folks, would they rather just listen to instrumentals? The general response is no. Listeners want to have vocals driving the beat, but—importantly—not stopping it or slowing it down. It takes a master to ride any wild beat or groove and to tame it. Rakim, KRS-One, André 3000, MC Lyte, Black Thought, and Nas are just a few such masters featured in this anthology. They will make the music submit to their flows while filling those flows with words to move the crowd's minds, bodies, and souls. So reading lyrics on the page gives us a chance to understand exactly what makes these lyrics work. What's their meaning? What's their substance? How do they do what they do?

Like the air we breathe, hip-hop seems to be everywhere. The culture and lifestyle that many thought would be a passing fad has, more than three decades later, grown to become a permanent part of world culture. Hip-hop artists have become some of today's heroes, replacing the comic book worship of decades past and joining athletes and movie stars as the people kids dream of becoming. Names like 50 Cent, P. Diddy, Russell Simmons, Jay-Z, Foxy Brown, Snoop Dogg, and Flavor Flav now ring as familiar as Elvis, Babe Ruth, Marilyn Monroe, and Charlie Chaplin. But keeping in step with straight-up rap, a rapper is not just a celebrity. There still lies a performance factor that must be included before we describe an MC as a lyrical beast.

While the general public knows many of the names, videos, and songs branded by the big companies, it's important to study rap's history. The best place to start is the holy trinity, the founding fathers of hip-hop: Kool Herc, Grandmaster Flash, and Afrika Bambaataa. All are DJs that played the records that moved MCs and dancers to fashion their own art forms. The MC had to go to the rhythm of the DJ, thus creating the atmosphere with words on the beat to music. This background is crucial to the evolution of the MC. But the influence of these hip-hop pioneers often went beyond the realm of art. Bambaataa almost singlehandedly quelled the New York City gang wars of the 1970s with his message of peace, unity, love, and having fun.

Hip-hop is simply a term for a form of artistic creativity spawned in New York City, more precisely the Bronx, in the early to mid 1970s. Amid the urban decay in the areas where black and Hispanic people dwelled, economic, educational, and environmental resources were depleted. Jobs and businesses dried up. Living conditions at times were almost indistinguishable from a developing country, all in the midst of the nation's wealthiest city. Last but not least, art and sports programs in the schools were the first to be cut for the sake of lowering budgets; music classes teaching history and technique were all but lost.

From these ashes, like a phoenix, rose an art form. Through the love of technology and of records found in family collections or discarded on the street, the DJ emerged. Different from the ones heard on the radio, these DJs were innovating a style first popularized on the island of Jamaica. Two turntables kept the music continuous, with the occasional voice speaking or chanting on top of the records. This is the very humble beginning of rap music.

It is important to remember that the thing we call rap is not a music in itself. It becomes music only when two words are combined: rap and music. Rap is the vocal application placed on top of the music. On a vocal spectrum, it falls somewhere between talking and singing and is one of the few new alternatives for vocalizing to emerge in the last fifty years. It is important to realize that inventors and artists are side by side in the importance of music's development. Let's remember that the man who invented the phonograph, Thomas A. Edison, was the first to record a rhyme, with "Mary Had a Little Lamb" in 1877. He did this in New Jersey, the same state that produced the first commercial rap hit, the Sugarhill Gang's "Rapper's Delight," more than a century later.

It's hard to separate the importance of history, science, language arts, and education when discussing music. Because of the social silencing of black people in America from slavery in the 1600s to civil rights in the 1960s, much sentiment, dialogue, and soul is wrapped up in the cultural expression of black music. In eighteenth-century New Orleans, slaves gathered on Sundays in Congo Square to socialize and play music. Within this captivity many dialects, customs, and styles combined with instrumentation, vocals, and rhythm to form a musical signal or code of preservation. These are the foundations of jazz and the blues.

Similarly, it is impossible to separate hip-hop and rap music from the legacy of creativity from the past. Look within the expression and words of black music and you'll get a timeline reflecting American history itself. The four creative elements of hip-hop—MCing (the art of vocalization); DJing (the musician-like manipulation of records); breakdancing (the body expression of the music); and graffiti (the graphic expression of the culture)—have been intertwined in the community before and since slavery. However, just because these expressions formed in the black and Hispanic underclass doesn't mean that they are exclusive to those groups in perpetuity. Hip-hop is specific, but it's universal too.

Hip-hop is a cultural language used best to unite the human family all around the world. Many international rap artists can rhyme in multiple languages and still move crowds with meaning. The world beyond the United States has excelled in hip-hop's fundamentals, perhaps more even than in the country of the culture's invention. To peep rap's global explosion one not even need search very far. Starting just north of the U.S. border, Canadian hip-hop has featured rappers who are infusing different language and dialect flows into their work, from immigrant artists like K'naan rhyming about the "ghosts in my old home" to French flowing cats from Quebec.

Few know that France for many years has been the second largest hip-hop nation, measured not just by high sales numbers, but also by its political philosophy. Hip-hop has been alive and present since the mid-1980s in Japan and other Asian countries. Australia has been a hotbed in welcoming world rap acts, and it has also created its own vibrant scene, with the reminder of its government's takeover of indigenous people reflected in many rappers' flows and rhymes. As a rhythm of the people, the continents of Africa and South America (especially Ghana, Senegal, and South Africa, and Brazil, Surinam, and Argentina) have long mixed traditional homage into the new beats and rhymes of this millennium. Hip-hop and rap have been used to help Brazilian kids learn English when school systems failed to bridge the difficult language gap of Portuguese and patois to American English. It has entertained and enlightened youth, and has engaged political discussion in society, continuing the tradition of the African griots and folksingers.

For decades, hip-hop has been bought, sold, followed, loved, hated, praised, and blamed. History has shown that other cultural U.S. music forms have been just as misunderstood and held up to public scrutiny. The history of the people who originated the art form can be found in the music itself. The timeline of recorded rap music spans more than a quarter century, and that is history in itself. With all this said it might sound like a broken record but the reintroduction must come with the clear definition of what it is. A rapper's style is not to itself. It comes from somewhere. All of these lyrics evolve as the griot-like timeline with the words finally manifesting themselves into a solid testament of the craft. In the words of the Public Enemy song "Bring the Noise," here we go again . . .

COMMON

What you hold in your hands is more than a book. This is a culture. This is hip-hop. This book is Biggie and Pac and Rakim and Lauryn Hill. It's Run-DMC and Public Enemy and the Wu-Tang Clan. It's also Sequence and the Treacherous Three and the Cold Crush Brothers. It's Arrested Development and Goodie Mob and Freestyle Fellowship. It's all of these and so many others. Together, MCs have made music and also poetry. We have created a living language through rap.

Strip all the performance away from rap and what do you have? A new perspective. Reading rap lyrics lets you see familiar things in new ways. Everything that usually captures your attention—the inflections of the MC's voice and the style that somebody's using—fades away and you're left with just the words. You can speed up or slow down, go back or skip ahead. You can take your time and let the words take shape in your mind. When you get down to the bare lyrics, you can tell if there's something deep going on in the words.

So many of the debates about rap today miss the point. People argue without taking the time to listen to what rap is actually saying. *The Anthology of Rap* explodes the myth that MCs rhyme only about money, cars, and women. Think I'm lying? Open up the book and see for yourself. Even open it at random and you'll find lyrics about love and comic books and bicycles, about God and nature and fatherhood. You'll find rhymes, in other words, about life and the art of living.

I wrote my first rap verse when I was twelve. Back then I lived in Chicago and spent parts of my summers in Cincinnati. My cousin and I would hang out with his crew just talking and listening to music. Afrika Bambaataa and Soul Sonic Force. Egyptian Lover. And the biggest group in Cincinnati, the Bond Hill Crew. One night I sat in my cousin's room and tried to rap. He wrote a rhyme about the eighth graders and I wrote one about the Bond Hill Crew. It started out like this:

> Well, let me tell you 'bout a trip, a time ago
>
> I was going there to run a cold-blooded show
>
> When I was there I saw some people jamming, too
>
> They called themselves the Bond Hill Crew
>
> Dr. Ice, Romeo, and Master E
>
> All of the Bond Hill crew rappin to a T
>
> I asked them could they rock with me

I'd write a lot more—and a lot better, I hope—as the years went by, but there was something pure and powerful about that first rhyme. As soon as I finished, my cousin and his friends looked at me, amazed. "Man, that's cold!" They started repeating my lines back to me, memorizing what I had just written. That was deep to me. I loved the way that made me feel. Years later I'd look out into the crowd and see people reciting my words. That's a beautiful thing.

Around 1993, I started writing in my head. I'd be out with my friends and would think of rhymes but wouldn't have a pen and paper. So when thoughts came, I'd just have to remember them. Often, rhymes would come to me in the car. My car became a place of solitude for me. I had a red Toyota Celica GT with no heat and an automatic transmission. I remember driving that car in the wintertime, just trying to wipe the frost off the windshield so that I could see where I was going. That's why I say on *Resurrection,* "cruise the South Side streets with no heat and no sticka." Riding up Lakeshore Drive in Chicago, I'd look at the city and the people, and the lyrics would just . . . flow.

I was attracted to hip-hop because of the rhythm, but the words were the reason I fell in love for keeps. My second album, *Resurrection,* featured a song called "I Used to Love H.E.R.," which tells the story of hip-hop through the guise of a woman. Well, *The Anthology of Rap* makes me fall in love with H.E.R. all over again. I'm reminded of what makes hip-hop so powerful. Lines that rhyme and sometimes don't. Flows on top of flows. Stories about places near and far. Words that people want to memorize and recite. These are the things that drew me to rap from the start and have kept me around for as long as I can remember.

Rap is rhythm and poetry, as Rakim once said. All rap is poetry. That's not to say that all rap is *poetic,* though. Some rhymes just don't quite flow right; some are hard to listen to. But then again, just because it might not sound poetic to me doesn't mean it's not poetry. I get into the things that feel poetic to me—like Nas, Kanye, Eminem sometimes.

Being an MC is about aura and persona. It's a character you inhabit; it's a style; it's a mentality; it's the way you put yourself out there, the way you think and the way you act. It's about lyrics and voice, creativity and showmanship. This book is filled with lyrics from great MCs, whether Rakim or Biggie or Lauryn Hill. And each artist arrives at his or her greatness by mixing the qualities of MCing in different proportions. Rakim has that voice and those rhymes. Biggie has storytelling. Lauryn has some of everything.

I began as a fan of the culture, a fan of rap music. So to be able to participate in making hip-hop culture is a lot like when you were young and the older guys would invite you to join a pickup basketball game. You're watching them from the sidelines, and then they say to you, "Hey, you wanna run?" After a while, you prove yourself. You get to stay on the court. Hip-hop is like that for me. It's an honor to be able to carry on this tradition—not just the tradition of Afrika Bambaataa and Grandmaster Caz and Melle Mel, but the tradition of Miles Davis, James Baldwin, Bob Marley, Fela Kuti, too. We are the children of jazz. We are the children of all black art around the globe.

This book is a testament to the fact that rap is a living tradition told in many voices. Sure, sometimes it fades in and out. But over time, it endures. For me, it taught different spiritualities, different aspects of culture and history, different languages and modes of speech. I hope this book will help more people get back to that.

With *The Anthology of Rap,* Adam Bradley and Andrew DuBois have given us something of great value and great power—if we learn how to use it. For aspiring MCs and established ones too, it can be a tool for the craft, showing you how the best artists throughout rap's history have created their art. For culture warriors, it will give you new ammunition and perhaps new means of finding peace with long-standing debates. For teachers, it offers a way to make the study of literature not only pleasurable but accessible and even cool. For parents, it can suggest new ways of finding common ground with your kids by engaging them on the music they love in terms that you, too, can understand. For anyone with the curiosity to see beyond the stereotype, this book offers a view of rap in full, from the root to the fruit.

ACKNOWLEDGMENTS

AN ANTHOLOGY OF THIS scope necessarily reflects the efforts of a great many individuals, the greatest of whom are the artists who wrote and performed the songs collected here. We thank each of them and offer special thanks to the following for reviewing transcriptions of their lyrics, offering insights into their craft, and generally providing support for this undertaking: Aesop Rock, Bahamadia, Binary Star, Kurtis Blow, Bun B, Camp Lo, Chino XL, Crooked I, dead prez, Del, Digable Planets, DOOM, Edan, Jean Grae, Grandmaster Caz, Immortal Technique, Juba Kalamka, Kool G Rap, MyKa 9, Pharoahe Monch, R.A. the Rugged Man, Ras Kass, Sage Francis, Schoolly D, Sequence, Souls of Mischief, Special Ed, and Speech. A special thanks goes to Chuck D and Common, who contributed tremendous afterwords. We hope this book stands as an appropriate and heartfelt shout-out to all those who've ever picked up a mic to rhyme.

This anthology would not exist without the vision and initiative of Jonathan Brent, former editorial director at Yale University Press. Over the past few years we've had the good fortune of working with a number of tremendous people at Yale. Foremost among them is Sarah Miller, who brought patience, resolve, and insight to her work as editor. Anja Manthey, along with Nathaniel Drake and Jeffery Zuckerman, made heroic efforts in working on the numerous permissions. Senior manuscript editor Jeffrey Schier and his team tackled unprecedented challenges in designing and proofreading this volume. Thanks to Heidi Downey (editorial), Karen Stickler (production), Mary Valencia (design), and Jenya Weinreb (editorial).

We owe a debt of gratitude to Henry Louis Gates, Jr., for

his masterful foreword. From the toasts to 2 Live Crew, he's always been an advocate of outlaw expression. The advisory board, whose names are listed at the front of this book, volunteered their knowledge, opinions, and talents toward making this anthology what it is. We thank them all.

With his cover design and interior images, Justin Francis fashioned a visual feel for the book that is every bit as powerful, stylish, and flavorful as the lyrics themselves. We join Justin in thanking all those who contributed to the book's visuals: Kenneth Barclift, Felton Brown, Dolo, Kareem Johnson, the Retro Kidz, Kyle Mingo, Rebecca Pietri, Samuel T. Ritter, Santiago Siguenza, and Jimmy Silas Ulibarri.

Assembling this anthology required transcribing hours and hours of lyrics as well as writing headnotes and introductions. We had the dedicated assistance of a handful of people. Max Lipset brought his deep knowledge of hip-hop to this anthology in many ways—transcribing lyrics, drafting headnotes, and providing constructive criticism on the collection as a whole. Siavash Khazamipour deciphered some of the toughest lyrical passages; his work was indispensible. Megan Fries brought her rich knowledge of poetry and poetics to her work. A handful of others contributed transcriptions and other assistance to the book: Ezekiel Justice, Mike Lipset, Jake Miller, Julian Padgett, Lance Rutledge, Sydney Schavietello, and Kingston Yogendran. Thanks to David Caplan, Erica Edwards, and H. L. Hix for commenting on drafts of the introduction. Thanks as well to Jayquan and Troy L. Smith of the Web site The Foundation for sharing their copious knowledge of old-school hip-hop.

In addition . . .

Andrew DuBois wishes to acknowledge the support of the UTSC Department of Humanities and of his friends and colleagues in English at the University of Toronto. Deep thanks to Andy and Naomi DuBois, Jay Smith, and Souvankham Thammavongsa, who knows what words can do and how best to make them do it; she listened along to these songs and I love her for that and for everything else.

Adam Bradley wishes to thank his agent, Robert Guinsler of Sterling Lord Literistic. Thanks to the University of Colorado at Boulder for supplying generous grants to support this anthology. Most important, I wish to thank my wife, Anna, who endured the near constant beats and rhymes at all hours of the day and night, whether coming from the car speakers or somehow seeping through my noise-cancelling headphones. You can turn the music down now.

INTRODUCTION

1. KRS-One, *Ruminations* (New York: Welcome Rain, 2003), 217.
2. David Foster Wallace and Mark Costello, *Signifying Rappers* (Hopewell, NJ: Ecco, 1990), 97.
3. Ibid., 96.
4. Marcyliena Morgan, *The Real HipHop: Battling for Knowledge, Power, and Respect in the LA Underground* (Durham, NC: Duke University Press, 2009), 190.
5. Eminem, *The Way I Am* (New York: Plume, 2009), 36.
6. *And You Don't Stop: 30 Years of Hip Hop,* DVD, directed by Richard Lowe and Dana Heinz Perry (n.p.: Bring the Noise LLC, 2004).
7. 50 Cent, *From Pieces to Weight: Once Upon a Time in Southside Queens* (New York: Pocket Books, 2005), 164.
8. Tricia Rose, *The Hip Hop Wars* (New York: Basic Civitas, 2008), 5.
9. Morgan, *The Real HipHop,* 159.
10. Gail Mitchell, "Rapper Medusa Stands Strong in Man's World," Reuters, July 20, 2007.
11. Oliver Wang, *Classic Material: The Hip-Hop Album Guide* (Toronto: ECW, 2003), 24.
12. Paul Edwards, *How to Rap: The Art and Science of the Hip-Hop MC* (Chicago: Chicago Review Press, 2009), 69.
13. Chuck D, *Lyrics of a Rap Revolutionary,* vol. 1 (Beverly Hills: Off Da Books, 2006), xi.

PART ONE: 1978 TO 1984

1. Sacha Jenkins et al., *Ego Trip's Book of Rap Lists* (New York: St. Martin's Griffin, 1999), 22.
2. Jim Fricke and Charlie Ahearn, *Yes Yes Y'all: Oral History of Rap's First Decade* (New York: Da Capo, 2002), 75.
3. Fricke and Ahearn, *Yes Yes Y'all,* 36.
4. *Wax Poetics,* no. 27 (February–March 2008): 109.
5. Jeff Chang, *Can't Stop Won't Stop: A History of the Hip Hop Generation* (New York: St. Martin's, 2005), 130.

NOTES

6. *Wax Poetics,* no. 19 (October–November 2006): 120.

7. Fricke and Ahearn, *Yes Yes Y'all,* 76.

8. Kool Moe Dee, *There's a God on the Mic: The True Fifty Greatest MCs* (New York: Thunder's Mouth, 2003), 117.

9. David Toop, *Rap Attack #3* (London: Serpent's Tail, 1999), 120.

10. *Big Apple Rappin': The Early Days of Hip-Hop Culture in New York City, 1979–1982,* Vol. 2, Soul Jazz Records, 2006, LP liner notes.

11. *Wax Poetics,* no. 24 (August–September 2007): 72.

12. Ibid.

13. Ibid., 74.

14. Fricke and Ahearn, *Yes Yes Y'all,* 71.

15. Chang, *Can't Stop Won't Stop,* 133.

16. The Foundation, http://www.thafoundation.com/sequence.htm.

17. Spoonie Gee, *Spoonie Gee: Godfather of Hip Hop,* Ol' Skool Flava, 1996, CD liner notes.

18. Fricke and Ahearn, *Yes Yes Y'all,* 189.

19. Fricke and Ahearn, *Yes Yes Y'all,* 196.

PART TWO: 1985–1992

1. Jim Fricke and Charlie Ahearn, *Yes Yes Y'all: Oral History of Rap's First Decade* (New York: Da Capo, 2002), 328.

2. Ibid., 329.

3. Ibid.

4. Ibid., 327.

5. Paul Edwards, *How to Rap: The Art and Science of the Hip-Hop MC* (Chicago: Chicago Review Press, 2009), 97.

6. Ibid., 105.

7. D. A. Russell and M. Winterbottom, eds., *Ancient Literary Criticism* (Oxford: Oxford University Press, 1972), 206, 240, 280.

8. Ibid., 241.

9. Terry McDermott, "Parental Advisory: Explicit Lyrics," in *Da Capo Best Music Writing 2003,* ed. Matt Groening (New York: Da Capo, 2003), 20.

10. Kelefa Sanneh, "Rapping About Rapping: The Rise and Fall of a Hip-Hop Tradition," in *This Is Pop: In Search of the Elusive at Experience Music Project,* ed. Eric Weisbard (Seattle: Experience Music Project, 2004), 224, 226.

11. Big Daddy Kane, interview, Werner Von Wallenrod's Humble, Little Hip-Hop Blog, http://wernervonwallenrod.blogspot.com/2007/11/werner-necro-big-daddy-kane-interview.html.

12. Edwards, *How to Rap,* 43.

13. Kool Moe Dee, *There's a God on the Mic: The True Fifty Greatest MCs* (New York: Thunder's Mouth, 2003), 192–193.

14. Chuck D, *Lyrics of a Rap Revolutionary,* vol. 1 (Beverly Hills: Off Da Books, 2006), vi.

15. Moe Dee, *There's a God on the Mic,* 272.

16. Chuck D, *Lyrics of a Rap Revolutionary,* 50.

17. Too $hort, quoted in *Wax Poetics,* no. 22 (April–May 2007): 130.

18. Brian Coleman, *Check the Technique: Liner Notes for Hip-Hop Junkies* (New York: Villard, 2007), 438.

PART THREE: 1993–1999

1. Common, "Why Hip Hop's Square Peg Refuses to Live Up to His Name," CNN.com, October 1, 2007.

2. Peter Spirer, *Thug Angel* (film), 2002.

3. Danyel Smith, "Tupac Shakur," *The Vibe History of Hip Hop,* ed. Alan Light (New York: Three Rivers, 1999), 297.

4. Anthony DeCurtis, "Word," *Vibe History,* 97.

5. Nelson George, *Hip Hop America* (New York: Penguin, 1998), xiii.

6. Jason Tanz, *Other People's Property: A Shadow History of Hip-Hop in White America* (New York: Bloomsbury USA, 2007), xii.

7. Sacha Jenkins et al., *Ego Trip's Book of Rap Lists* (New York: St. Martin's, 1999), 195.

8. *Vibe History,* 332.

9. Roni Sarig, *Third Coast: Outkast, Timbaland, and How Hip-Hop Became a Southern Thing* (New York: Da Capo, 2007), xiv.

10. Tony Green, "The Dirty South," *Vibe History,* 266.

11. George, *Hip Hop America,* x–xi.

12. Paul Edwards, *How to Rap: The Art and Science of the Hip-Hop MC* (Chicago: Chicago Review Press, 2009), 251–252.

13. http://www.sixshot.com/articles/11007/.

14. http://www.planeturban.com.au/node/6337.

15. http://www.hiphop.com/features/78-busta-rhymes-feature-part-two.

16. http://www.riotsound.com/hip-hop/rap/interviews/canibus/index.php.

17. Ibid.

18. Ibid.

19. Michael Eric Dyson and Sohail Daulatzai, eds., *Born to Use Mics: Reading Nas' Illmatic* (New York: Basic Civitas, 2010), x.

20. Brian Coleman, *Check the Technique: Liner Notes for Hip Hop Junkies* (New York: Villard, 2007), 161.

21. DMX and Smokey D. Fontaine, *E.A.R.L.: The Autobiography of DMX* (New York: It Books, 2003), 263.

22. http://www.allmusic.com/cg/amg.dll?p=amg&sql=10:oadnvwxua9uk.

23. Edwards, *How to Rap,* 48–49.

24. http://hiphopruckus.blogsp120t.com/2006/04/e-40-introduces-bay-area-to-rest-of.html.

25. http://www.mtv.com/bands/archive/f/fbrown01/index4.jhtml.

26. Edwards, *How to Rap,* 182.

27. http://www.mtv.com/bands/h/hip_hop_week/2007/groups/index3.jhtml.

28. Sarig, *Third Coast,* 137.

29. Oliver Wang, *Classic Material: The Hip-Hop Album Guide* (Toronto: ECW, 2003), 55.

30. http://www.assatashakur.org/forum/conscious-music-artists-news-views/9432-prophet-lauryn-hill-interview.html.

31. http://www.avclub.com/articles/ice-cube,2139/.

32. http://www.mtv.com/bands/h/hip_hop_week/2006/emcees/index4.jhtml.

33. http://www.avclub.com/articles/ice-cube,2139/.

34. Wang, *Classic Material,* 93.

35. http://www.mtv.com/bands/h/hip_hop_week/2006/emcees/index11.jhtml.

36. *Fade to Black* (film), 2004.

37. Edwards, *How to Rap,* 57.

38. http://www.ilikemusic.com/interviews/mobb_deep_interview_blood_money-2056/4.

39. Ibid.

40. Matt Diehl, "Pop Rap," *Vibe History,* 131.

41. Peter Spirer, *Notorious B.I.G.: Bigger Than Life* (film), 2007.

42. http://www.mtv.com/bands/h/hip_hop_week/2007/groups/index8.jhtml.

43. http://www.hiphop-elements.com/article/read/6/5905/1/

44. Phyllis Croom, "Well Versed in Reality: Scarface May Be Soft Spoken, But His Rap Is Anything But," *Washington Post,* December 19, 1994.

45. Jon Pareles, "Four Hours of Swagger from Dr. Dre and Friends," *New York Times,* July 17, 2000.

46. http://www.mtv.com/bands/h/hip_hop_week/2006/emcees/index12.jhtml.

47. Tabitha Soren, Interview, MTV, 1995.

48. Karolyn Ali and Jacob Hoye, *Tupac: Resurrection, 1971–1996.* (New York: Atria, 2003), 166.

49. Edwards, *How to Rap,* 124.

50. Jon Caramanica, "Bun B," *Believer,* June–July 2006.

PART FOUR: 2000 TO 2010

1. Nas, "Hip Hop Is Dead," *Hip Hop Is Dead* (song), Def Jam, 2006.

2. Michael Eric Dyson and Sohail Daulatzai, eds., *Born to Use Mics: Reading Nas' Illmatic* (New York: Basic Civitas, 2010), xi.

3. Untitled sidebar, *GQ* (February 2010): 55.

4. http://www.forbes.com/2008/08/15/music-media-hiphop-biz-media-cz_zog_0818cashkings.html.

5. David Bry, "New York State of Mind: The Resurgence of East Coast Hip Hop," in *The Vibe History of Hip Hop,* ed. Alan Light (New York: Three Rivers, 1999), 335.

6. Mark Schwartz, "Planet Rock: Hip Hop Supa National," *Vibe History,* 362.

7. David Ma, "Bear Witness: Dilated Peoples' Evidence Testifies to Hip-Hop's Longevity," *Wax Poetics,* no. 26 (December/January 2008): 55.

8. "Resurrection: Common Walks," PopMatters music interview, September 21, 2005, http://www.popmatters.com/music/interviews/common-050921.shtml.

9. Outkast, "Hollywood Divorce," *Idlewild* soundtrack (song), 2006.

10. Paul Edwards, *How to Rap: The Art and Science of the Hip-Hop MC* (Chicago: Chicago Review, 2009), 38.

11. http://www.guernicamag.com/interviews/397/graffiti_or_vermeer/.

12. Edwards, *How to Rap,* 115.

13. Ibid., 8.

14. http://www.hiphopdx.com/index/interviews/id.1309/title.brother-ali-the-truth-teller.

15. http://pitchfork.com/reviews/albums/1791-purple-haze/.

16. http://www.thickonline.com/interviews/index.php?mod=cnt&act=cnt&id=1 143&page=2.

17. John Caramanica, "Keep on Pushin'," *Mass Appeal,* no. 39 (n.d.): 72.

18. *Wax Poetics,* no. 28 (December–January 2008): 52.

19. Ta-Nehisi Coates, "The Mask of Doom: A Nonconformist Rapper's Second Act," *New Yorker,* September 21, 2009, 53.

20. Ross McCammon, "50 Cent: What I've Learned," *Esquire,* January 2010, http://www.esquire.com/features/what-ive-learned/new-50-cent-interview-0110.

21. Eminem, *The Way I Am* (New York: Plume, 2009), 36.

22. http://www.michigandaily.com/content/eyedea-abilities-previewinterview.

23. Ken Capobianco, "Lupe Fiasco Accepts the Outsider Label as a Positive Rap," *Boston Globe,* November 13, 2006.

24. McCammon, "50 Cent: What I've Learned."

25. Ibid.

26. Talib Kweli blog, July 2008, http://www.yearoftheblacksmith.com/profiles/blog/list?user=2cum77csuee8s.

27. http://www.xxlmag.com/online/?p=887.

28. http://www.formatmag.com/features/knaan/.

29. http://www.daveyd.com/interviewtalibkweliaol.html.

30. http://www.popmatters.com/pm/review/47420/talib-kweli-ear-drum/.

31. Edwards, *How to Rap,* 143.

32. http://smokingsection.uproxx.com/TSS/2007/08/tss-presents-smoking-sessions-with-little-brother.

33. http://www.concertlivewire.com/interviews/ludacris.htm.

34. Ludacris, "I Do It for Hip Hop," *Theatre of the Mind* (song), 2008.

35. Edwards, *How to Rap,* 24.

36. Richard Cromlein, "Mos Def Wants Blacks to Take Back Rock Music," *Los Angeles Times,* December 28, 2004.

37. http://www.ugo.com/channels/music/features/youngjeezy/default.as.

SONGS, ALBUMS, MOVIES, AND BOOKS

*(Page numbers in **bold** indicate lyrics)*

INDEX

ARTISTS, AUTHORS, AND LABELS

*(Page numbers in **bold** indicate lyrics)*

INDEX

The editors have made every reasonable effort to secure permissions. If any errors should be noticed, please contact Adam Bradley and Andrew DuBois care of Yale University Press. Corrections will follow in subsequent editions.

CREDITS

INTRODUCTION

Excerpt from "Ice, Ice Baby": words and music by Vanilla Ice, Earthquake, M. Smooth, Brian May, Freddie Mercury, Floyd Brown, Mario Johnson, Roger Taylor, Robert Van Winkle, John Deacon and David Bowie. © 1981, 1990 QPM MUSIC INC., FERN HILL PUBLISHING, ICE BABY MUSIC, AFTERSHOCK MUSIC, SONY/ATV MUSIC PUBLISHING LLC, Johnson Music, Knightlife Productions, Kline Publishing Company, QUEEN MUSIC LTD., EMI MUSIC PUBLISHING LTD., BEECH-WOOD MUSIC CORP., and TINTORETTO MUSIC. All Rights for QPM MUSIC INC., FERN HILL PUBLISHING, ICE BABY MUSIC, AFTERSHOCK MUSIC and SONY/ATV MUSIC PUBLISHING LLC Controlled and Administered by EMI BLACKWOOD MUSIC INC. All Rights for QUEEN MUSIC LTD. in the U.S. and Canada Controlled and Administered by BEECHWOOD MUSIC CORP. All Rights for QUEEN MUSIC LTD. in the world excluding the U.S. and Canada Controlled and Administered by EMI MUSIC PUBLISHING LTD. All Rights for EMI MUSIC PUBLISHING LTD. in the U.S. and Canada Controlled and Administered by SCREEN GEMS-EMI MUSIC INC. All rights on behalf of Johnson Music Co, Knightlife Productions administered by Sony/ATV Music Publishing LLC, 8 Music Square West, Nashville, TN 37203. All Rights Reserved. International Copyright Secured. Used by Permission. Contains elements of "Under Pressure" (Bowie/Mercury/Taylor/Deacon/May). *Reprinted by Permission of Hal Leonard Corporation, Johnson Music, Kline Publishing Company, Sony/ATV Music Publishing LLC and Tintoretto Music admin. by RZO Music, Inc.*

PART I: 1978–1984—THE OLD SCHOOL

"Zulu Nation Throwdown, Pt. 1" used by permission of KLB Productions Inc. and JRL Music, Inc.

"Planet Rock" used by permission of Downtown Music and KLB Productions Inc.

"Rappin' Blow (Part 2)" and "The Breaks" © Neutral Gray Music / Pure Love Music. All rights reserved. Used by permission.

"If I Ruled the World": words and music by Aaron O'Bryant, David Reeves and Kurt Walker. Copyright © 1985 UNIVERSAL—SONGS OF POLYGRAM INTERNATIONAL, INC., KUWA MUSIC, SCRATCH MASTER MUSIC and DAVY-D MUSIC. All Rights Controlled and Administered by UNIVERSAL—SONGS OF POLYGRAM INTERNATIONAL, INC. All Rights Reserved. Used by Permission. *Reprinted by Permission of Hal Leonard Corporation.*

"How We Gonna Make the Black Nation Rise?": Thanks to the kind permission of Lister Hewan-Lowe and Clappers Records. Clappers Music Publishers.

"Live at Harlem World 1981," "Live at the Dixie 1982" and "Weekend" written by Curtis Brown (BMI). Published by GMC Music Publishing (BMI).

"Fresh Wild Fly and Bold": Cold Crush Brothers, (Fisher/Mandes/Harris), Published by Street Tuff Tunes, ℗ & © Tufamerica, Inc. 1984.

"Rappin' and Rockin' the House" written by: Bobby Robinson/Caeser/Green/Myree/Smith/Stone. Copyright Bobby Robinson Sweet Soul Music and JRL Music, Inc. All rights for Bobby Robinson Sweet Soul Music Controlled and Administered by Spirit One Music (BMI). International Copyright Secured. All Rights Reserved. Used by Permission of JRL Music, Inc. and Spirit Music Group.

"That's the Joint" used by permission of JRL Music, Inc.

"Superrappin'" by Williams, Glover, Morris, Wiggins and Glover, Jr. Courtesy of Artists Rights Enforcement Corp. o/b/o Superrappin Music (BMI) and Havnots Music (ASCAP).

"The Message," "White Lines (Don't Don't Do It)," "To the Beat Y'all," "Funk You Up," "And You Know That" and "Simon Says" used by permission of JRL Music, Inc.

"Spoonin' Rap": Spoonie Gee, (G. Jackson), Published by Swing Beat Songs, ℗ & © Tufamerica, Inc. 1979.

"Love Rap" written by: Bobby Robinson and Gabriel Jackson. Copyright Bobby Robinson Sweet Soul Music. All Rights for Bobby Robinson Sweet Soul Music Controlled and Administered by Spirit One Music (BMI). International Copyright Secured. All Rights Reserved. Used by Permission. Spoonie Gee, (G. Jackson), Published by Swing Beat Songs, ℗ & © Tufamerica, Inc. 1980.

"Rapper's Delight": words and music by BERNARD EDWARDS and NILE RODGERS. © 1979 Sony/ATV Music Publishing LLC, Bernard's Other Music. All Rights for BERNARD'S OTHER MUSIC Administered by WARNER-TAMERLANE PUBLISHING CORP. All rights on behalf of Sony/ATV Music Publishing LLC administered by Sony/ATV Music Publishing LLC, 8 Music Square West, Nashville, TN 37203. All Rights Reserved. Used by Permission of ALFRED MUSIC PUBLISHING CO., INC. and Sony/ATV Music Publishing LLC.

"The New Rap Language" written by: Bobby Robinson. Copyright Bobby Robinson Sweet Soul Music. All rights for Bobby Robinson Sweet Soul Music Controlled and

Copyright 2006 Campbell & Co. Limited. All Rights Controlled and Administered by UNIVERSAL—SONGS OF POLYGRAM INTERNATIONAL, INC. All Rights Reserved. Used by Permission. *Reprinted by Permission of Hal Leonard Corporation and Music Sales Corporation.*

"My Melody": words and music by Eric Barrier and William Griffin. Copyright © 1987 UNIVERSAL—SONGS OF POLYGRAM INTERNATIONAL, INC. and ROBERT HILL MUSIC. All Rights Controlled and Administered by UNIVERSAL—SONGS OF POLYGRAM INTERNATIONAL, INC. All Rights Reserved. Used by Permission. *Reprinted by Permission of Hal Leonard Corporation and Robert Hill Music.*

"I Ain't No Joke": words and music by Eric Barrier and William Griffin. Copyright © 1987 UNIVERSAL—SONGS OF POLYGRAM INTERNATIONAL, INC. and ROBERT HILL MUSIC. All Rights Controlled and Administered by UNIVERSAL—SONGS OF POLYGRAM INTERNATIONAL, INC. All Rights Reserved Used by Permission. *Reprinted by Permission of Hal Leonard Corporation and Robert Hill Music.*

"Microphone Fiend": words and music by Eric Barrier, William Griffin, Roger Ball, Malcolm Duncan, Stephen Ferrone, Alan Gorrie, Owen McIntyre and James Stewart. © 1988 EMI BLACKWOOD MUSIC INC., ERIC B. AND RAKIM MUSIC and JOE'S SONGS, INC. All Rights for ERIC B AND RAKIM MUSIC Controlled and Administered by EMI BLACKWOOD MUSIC INC. All Rights for JOE'S SONGS, INC. Administered by WIXEN MUSIC PUBLISHING, INC. All Rights Reserved. International Copyright Secured. Used by Permission. Contains elements of "School Boy Crush": words and music by Roger Ball, Malcolm Duncan, Stephen Ferrone, Alan Gorrie, Owen McIntyre and James Stewart. *Reprinted by Permission of Hal Leonard Corporation.*

"Lyrics of Fury": words and music by Eric B. and Rakim. © 1988 EMI BLACKWOOD MUSIC INC. and ERIC B. AND RAKIM MUSIC. All Rights Controlled and Administered by EMI BLACKWOOD MUSIC INC. All Rights Reserved. International Copyright Secured. Used by Permission. *Reprinted by Permission of Hal Leonard Corporation.*

"Step in the Arena": words and music by Keith Elam and Chris Martin. Copyright © 1991 ALMO MUSIC CORP. and GIFTED PEARL MUSIC, INC. All Rights Controlled and Administered by ALMO MUSIC CORP. All Rights Reserved. Used by Permission. *Reprinted by Permission of Hal Leonard Corporation.*

"Just to Get a Rep": words and music by Keith Elam and Chris Martin. Copyright © 1991 ALMO MUSIC CORP. and GIFTED PEARL MUSIC, INC. All Rights Controlled and Administered by ALMO MUSIC CORP. All Rights Reserved. Used by Permission. *Reprinted by Permission of Hal Leonard Corporation.*

"Words I Manifest (Remix)" used by permission of Frozen Soap Songs.

"6 'N the Mornin'": words and music by Ice-T and Afrika Islam. © 1987 COLGEMS-EMI MUSIC INC., Reach Global Inc., and RHYME SYNDICATE MUSIC. All Rights Reserved. International Copyright Secured. Used by Permission. *Reprinted by Permission of Hal Leonard Corporation and Reach Global Music Publishing.*

"Colors": words and music by Ice-T and Afrika Islam. © 1988 COLGEMS-EMI MUSIC

"Cappuccino": words and music by Lana Michelle Moorer and Marlon Lu Ree Williams. Copyright © 1989 BROOKLYN BASED PUBLISHING, FIRST PRIORITY MUSIC, and MARLEY MARL MUSIC, INC. All Rights for BROOKLYN BASED PUBLISHING Controlled and Administered by UNIVERSAL MUSIC—MGB SONGS. First Priority Music/BMI (admin. by EverGreen Copyrights)/Brooklyn Based Publishing/ASCAP/Marley Marl Music/ASCAP. All Rights Reserved. Used by Permission. *Reprinted by Permission of Brooklyn Based Publishing, EverGreen Copyrights, Inc., and Hal Leonard Corporation.*

"Dopeman (Remix)" written by Leroy Bonner, O'Shea Jackson, Marshall Jones, Ralph Middlebrook, Andrew Noland, Gregory Webster, Andre Young. © 1990 Bridgeport Music, Inc. (BMI). Used by permission of Bridgeport Music, Inc., Downtown Music, Musiranma Comedy Play Music, and Ruthless Attack Muzick.

"Fuck tha Police" used courtesy of Ruthless Attack Muzick.

"Gangsta, Gangsta" performed by N. W. A. Written by Gregory Webster, Andrew Noland, Leroy Bonner, Marshall Jones, Ralph Middlebrook, Walter Morrison, Marvin Pierce, Norman Napier, William Edwards Devaughn, O'Shea Jackson, Lorenzo Patterson, Eric Wright, Andre Young, Roger Parker, Steve Arrington, Charles Carter and Waung Hankerton. © 1988, 1989 Songs Of Lastrada, Deeply Sliced Publishing, Montezk Music, Amazing Love Publishing, Boyz Club Music, Bridgeport Music Inc, Your Mother's Music, Gangsta Boogie Music, Music Sales Corporation (ASCAP), Ruthless Attack Muzick, and Globeart Publishing. All rights on behalf of Songs Of Lastrada, Deeply Sliced Publishing administered by Sony/ATV Music Publishing LLC, 8 Music Square West, Nashville, TN 37203. All rights reserved. Used by permission of Bridgeport Music, Inc., Lastrada Entertainment Company, Ltd., Ruthless Attack Muzick, and Sony/ATV Music Publishing LLC.

"Straight Outta Compton" used courtesy of Ruthless Attack Muzick.

"Miuzi Weighs a Ton": words and music by Carlton Ridenhour and Hank Shocklee. Copyright © 1987 SONGS OF UNIVERSAL, INC., REACH GLOBAL SONGS, TERRORDOME MUSIC PUBLISHING LLC and SHOCKLEE MUSIC. All Rights for REACH GLOBAL SONGS, TERRORDOME MUSIC PUBLISHING LLC and SHOCKLEE MUSIC Controlled and Administered by REACH GLOBAL, INC. All Rights Reserved. Used by Permission. *Reprinted by Permission of Hal Leonard Corporation and Reach Global Music Publishing.*

"Black Steel in the Hour of Chaos": words and music by Carlton Ridenhour, William Drayton, James Boxley III and Eric Sadler. Copyright © 1988 SONGS OF UNIVERSAL, INC., TERRORDOME MUSIC PUBLISHING LLC, REACH GLOBAL SONGS, SHOCKLEE MUSIC and YOUR MOTHER'S MUSIC, INC. All Rights Reserved. Used by Permission. *Reprinted by Permission of Hal Leonard Corporation and Reach Global Music Publishing.*

"Rebel Without a Pause": words and music by Carlton Ridenhour, James Boxely III, Norman Rogers and Eric Sadler. Copyright © 1987 SONGS OF UNIVERSAL, INC.,

PART III: 1993–1999—RAP GOES MAINSTREAM

NIZED NOIZE MUSIC (BMI), BUG MUSIC-HITCO MUSIC (BMI), EMI APRIL MUSIC INC. (ASCAP), BIG SEXY MUSIC (ASCAP), BROWN BRANCHES AND GREEN BOTTLES MUSIC (BMI), GOD GIVEN MUSIC (BMI), MUTANT MIND-FRAME MUSIC (BMI) and T MO 2 MUSIC (BMI). All Rights for ORGANIZED NOIZE MUSIC and BUG MUSIC-HITCO MUSIC Administered by BUG MUSIC. All Rights for BIG SEXY MUSIC Administered by EMI APRIL MUSIC INC. All Rights for BROWN BRANCHES AND GREEN BOTTLES MUSIC (BMI), MUTANT MINDFRAME MUSIC (BMI) and T-MO 2 MUSIC (BMI) Administered by HAVE WE GOT MUSIC FOR YOU, a division of SHELLY BAY MUSIC LLC. All Rights Reserved. Used by Permission. *Reprinted by Permission of Alien Music Services, Hal Leonard Corporation, and Shelly Bay Music.*

Excerpt from "Dirty South" written by Patrick Brown, Raymon Murray, Rico Wade, Frederick Bell, Cameron Gipp and Antwan Patton. © 1995 ORGANIZED NOIZE (BMI), BUG MUSIC-HITCO MUSIC (BMI), COOL PEOPLE MUSIC (BMI), MU-TANT MINDFRAME MUSIC (BMI) and GNAT BOOTY MUSIC. All Rights for ORGANIZED NOIZE (BMI) and BUG MUSIC-HITCO MUSIC (BMI) Adminis-tered by BUG MUSIC. All Rights for GNAT BOOTY MUSIC Administered by CHRYSALIS MUSIC. All Rights Reserved. Used by Permission. *Reprinted by Permis-sion of Cool People Music, Hal Leonard Corporation, and Shelly Bay Music.*

"Tennessee": words and music by Todd Thomas and Tarre Jones. © 1992 EMI BLACK-WOOD MUSIC INC. and ARRESTED DEVELOPMENT. All Rights Controlled and Administered by EMI BLACKWOOD MUSIC INC. All Rights Reserved. Interna-tional Copyright Secured. Used by Permission. *Reprinted by Permission of Hal Leon-ard Corporation.*

"Spontaneity": Antonia Reed p/k/a "Bahamadia," Shades of Brooklyn (ASCAP) c/o The Royalty Network, Inc. Used by permission of The Royalty Network, Inc. and Samadia Music.

"Ebonics (Criminal Slang)": words and music by Rondell Turner, Lester Coleman, Chris Martin and Lamont Coleman. Copyright © 2000 SONGS OF UNIVERSAL, INC., NOTTING HILL MUSIC, INC., BROWZ MUSIC, EMI APRIL MUSIC INC. and GIFTED PEARL MUSIC. All Rights for NOTTING HILL MUSIC, INC. and BROWZ MUSIC Controlled and Administered by SONGS OF UNIVERSAL, INC. All Rights for GIFTED PEARL MUSIC Controlled and Administered by EMI APRIL MUSIC INC. All Rights Reserved. Used by Permission. *Reprinted by Permission of Hal Leonard Corporation.*

"Capital Punishment": Ayatollah Music c/o The Royalty Network, Inc. Used by permis-sion of The Royalty Network, Inc.

"Tha Crossroads": words and music by O'Kelly Isley, Ronald Isley, Rudolph Isley, Ernie Isley, Marvin Isley, Chris Jasper, Bone, DJ U-Neek and Tony C. © 1996 EMI APRIL MUSIC INC., BOVINA MUSIC INC., RUTHLESS ATTACK MUZIC and MO' THUG MUZIC. All Rights for BOVINA MUSIC Controlled and Administered by EMI APRIL MUSIC INC. All Rights Reserved. International Copyright Secured. Used by Permission. Contains elements of "Make Me Say It Again Girl." *Reprinted by Permission of Hal Leonard Corporation and Ruthless Attack Muzick.*

Secured. Used by Permission. Contains a sample of "Allustrious" by Kejuan Muchita and Albert Johnson. *Reprinted by Permission of ALFRED MUSIC PUBLISHING CO., INC. and Hal Leonard Corporation.*

"The Light": words and music by Lonnie Rashid Lynn, James Yancey, Bobby Calwell, Norman Harris and Bruce Malament. Copyright © 2000 SONGS OF UNIVERSAL, INC., SENSELESS MUSIC, INC., UNIVERSAL—POLYGRAM INTERNATIONAL PUBLISHING, INC., E.P.C.H.Y. PUBLISHING, BOBBY CALDWELL MUSIC, THE MUSIC FORCE and BENDAN MUSIC. All Rights for SENSELESS MUSIC, INC. Controlled and Administered by SONGS OF UNIVERSAL, INC. All Rights for E.P.C.H.Y. PUBLISHING Controlled and Administered by UNIVERSAL—POLY-GRAM INTERNATION PUBLISHING, INC. All Rights Reserved. Used by Permission. Contains a sample of "Open Your Eyes" by B. Caldwell/N. Harris. *Reprinted by Permission of Bendan Music, Hal Leonard Corporation, and The Music Force LLC.*

"A Song for Assata": words and music by Lonnie Lynn, James Poyser and Thomas Burton. Copyright © 2000 SONGS OF UNIVERSAL, INC., SENSELESS MUSIC, INC., JAJAPO MUSIC and THOMAS BURTON PUBLISHING DESIGNEE. All Rights for SENSELESS MUSIC, INC. Controlled and Administered by SONGS OF UNIVERSAL, INC. All Rights Reserved. Used by Permission. *Reprinted by Permission of Hal Leonard Corporation.*

"Rebirth of Slick (Cool Like Dat)": words and music by Ishmael Butler and Mary Ann Vieira. © 1993 GLIRO MUSIC, INC. and WIDE GROOVES MUSIC. All Rights Controlled and Administered by EMI BLACKWOOD MUSIC INC. All Rights Reserved. International Copyright Secured. Used by Permission. Contains elements of "Strchin." *Reprinted by Permission of Hal Leonard Corporation.*

"Damien": words and music by Damon Blackman and Earl Simmons. Copyright © 1998 Sony/ATV Music Publishing LLC, Damon Blackman Music, Boomer X Publishing, Inc., EMI April Music Inc. and Dead Game Publishing. All Rights on behalf of Sony/ATV Music Publishing LLC and Damon Blackman Music Administered by Sony/ATV Music Publishing LLC, 8 Music Square West, Nashville, TN 37203. All Rights on behalf of Boomer X Publishing, Inc. Controlled and Administered by Universal Music Corp. All Rights on behalf of Dead Game Publishing Controlled and Administered by EMI April Music Inc. International Copyright Secured. All Rights Reserved. *Reprinted by Permission of Hal Leonard Corporation and Sony/ATV Music Publishing LLC.*

"Who We Be": words and music by Earl Simmons and Mickey Davis. Copyright © 2001 BOOMER X PUBLISHING, INC., DEAD GAME PUBLISHING and FIFTY FOUR VILL MUSIC LLC. All Rights for BOOMER X PUBLISHING, INC. Controlled and Administered by UNIVERSAL MUSIC CORP. All Rights for DEAD GAME PUBLISHING Controlled and Administered by EMI APRIL MUSIC INC. All Rights for FIFTY FOUR VILL MUSIC LLC Controlled and Administered by THE ROYALTY NETWORK. All Rights Reserved. Used by Permission. *Reprinted by Permission of Hal Leonard Corporation and Fifty Four Vill Music LLC (BMI) c/o The Royalty Network, Inc.*

"Sprinkle Me" Words and Music by Michael Mosely, Sam Bostic, Earl Stevens and

William Hart. © 1996 EMI BLACKWOOD MUSIC INC. and WARNER-TAMER-LANE PUBLISHING CORP. All Rights Reserved. International Copyright Secured. Used by Permission. Contains samples of "Story Of Boadicea" by Enya, Nicky Ryan and Roma Ryan © 1987 EMI BLACKWOOD MUSIC INC. *Reprinted by Permission of Brookside Music Corp. (Adm.) / c/o Ocean Drive Music (BMI), o/b/o Nickel Shoe Music Co., Inc. Nickelshoe@aol.com and Hal Leonard Corporation.*

"Cell Therapy": words and music by Robert Barnett, Patrick Brown, Thomas Callaway, Cameron Gipp, Willie Knighton, Raymon Murray, and Rico Wade, and published by Brown Branches and Green Bottles Music/Have We Got Music For You (BMI), God Given Music (BMI), Mutant Mindrame Music/Have We Got Music For You (BMI), T-Mo 2 Music/Have We Got Music For You (BMI). Copyright © 1996 Bug Music-Songs Of Windswept Pacific, Bug Music-Hitco Music, Organized Noize Music and Publisher Unknown. All Rights for Bug Music-Hitco Music and Organized Noize Music Controlled and Administered by Bug Music Songs Of Windswept Pacific. All Rights Reserved. Used by Permission. *Reprinted by Permission of Alien Music Services, Hal Leonard Corporation, and Shelly Bay Music.*

"Classic" by Hieroglyphics from their "Full Circle" CD. Lyrics: Pallo "Pep Love" Peacock, Teren "Del" Jones, Tajai Massey. Music: Damian "Domino" Siguenza. Publishing: Domino Effect Music, Black Magnet Music, Happy Hemp Music, Jhsiri Music, Hiero Imperium Music, Sound Symbol Music.

"Virus" from Deltron 3030 CD. Lyrics: Teren "Del" Jones. Music: Dan "The Automator" Nakamura. Publishers: Happy Hemp Music, Sharkman Songs.

"Doo Wop (That Thing)" Copyright 1998 Sony/ATV Music Publishing LLC, Obverse Creation Music Inc. All rights administered by Sony/ATV Music Publishing LLC, 8 Music Square West, Nashville, TN 37203. All rights reserved. Used by permission.

"Lost Ones" written by Lauryn Hill and Frederick Hibbert. Copyright © 1998 Sony/ATV Music Publishing LLC, Obverse Creation Music Inc., and Universal—Songs Of PolyGram International, Inc. All Rights on behalf of Sony/ATV Music Publishing LLC and Obverse Creation Music Administered by Sony/ATV Music Publishing LLC, 8 Music Square West, Nashville, TN 37203. International Copyright Secured. All Rights Reserved. Contains elements from "Bam Bam" by Frederick Hibbert, published by Universal—Songs Of PolyGram International, Inc. *Reprinted by Permission of Hal Leonard Corporation and Sony/ATV Music Publishing LLC.*

"Final Hour": words and music by Lauryn Hill and Christopher Martin. Copyright © 1998 Sony/ATV Music Publishing LLC, EMI April Music Inc. and Gifted Pearl Music. All Rights on behalf of Sony/ATV Music Publishing LLC Administered by Sony/ATV Music Publishing LLC, 8 Music Square West, Nashville, TN 37203. All Rights on behalf of Gifted Pearl Music Administered by Kobalt Music Services America, Inc. (KMSA) and EMI April Music Inc. International Copyright Secured. All Rights Reserved. *Reprinted by Permission of Hal Leonard Corporation, Kobalt Music Services America, Inc., and Sony/ATV Music Publishing LLC.*

"The Nigga Ya Love to Hate": words and music by O'Shea Jackson, Steven Arrington, Charles Carter, George Clinton, Waung Hankerson, Roger Parker, Eric "Vietnam" Sadler, Garry Shider and David Spradley. Copyright © 1990 UNIVERSAL MUSIC CORP., GANGSTA BOOGIE MUSIC, YOUR MOTHER'S MUSIC, INC., WARNER-TAMERLANE PUBLISHING CORP., AMAZING LOVE PUBLISHING, GLO-BEART PUBLISHING, Songs of Lastrada, Montezk Music, Amazing Love Publishing, DEEPLY SLICED PUBLISHING, BOYZ CLUB MUSIC, BRIDGEPORT MUSIC, INC., SOUTHFIELD MUSIC and WRITER DESIGNEE. All Rights for GANGSTA BOOGIE MUSIC Controlled and Administered by UNIVERSAL MUSIC CORP. All Rights on Behalf of Itself and YOUR MOTHER'S MUSIC Administered by WAR-NER-TAMERLANE PUBLISHING CORP. All rights on behalf of Songs Of Lastrada, Deeply Sliced Publishing administered by Sony/ATV Music Publishing LLC, 8 Music Square West, Nashville, TN 37203. All Rights Reserved. Used by Permission. *Reprinted by Permission of ALFRED MUSIC PUBLISHING CO., INC., Hal Leonard Corporation, Lastrada Entertainment Company, Sony/ATV Music Publishing LLC and Your Mother's Music, Inc.*

"It's a Man's World": words and music by O'Shea Jackson, Anthony (Pka Sir Jinx) Wheaton, James Brown and Betty Newsome. Copyright © 1990 UNIVERSAL MUSIC CORP., GANGSTA BOOGIE MUSIC, WB MUSIC CORP., DYNATONE PUBLISHING CO. and CLAMIKE RECORDS MUSIC. All Rights for GANGSTA BOOGIE MUSIC Controlled and Administered by UNIVERSAL MUSIC CORP. All Rights for DYNATONE PUBLISHING CO. and CLAMIKE RECORDS MUSIC Administered by UNICHAPPELL MUSIC INC. All Rights on Behalf of Itself and GANGSTA BOOGIE MUSIC Administered by WB MUSIC CORP. All Rights Reserved. Used by Permission. Contains elements of "It's A Man's Man's Man's World": words and music by James Brown and Betty Newsome. *Reprinted by Permission of ALFRED MUSIC PUBLISHING CO., INC. and Hal Leonard Corporation.*

"Bird in the Hand": words and music by O'Shea Jackson, Mark Jordan, George Clinton, William Collins, Ronald Dunbar, Garry Shider and Donnie Sterling. Copyright © 1991 UNIVERSAL MUSIC CORP., GANGSTA BOOGIE MUSIC, STREET KNOWLEDGE PRODUCTIONS, INC., Songwriter Services, BRIDGEPORT MUSIC, INC., EMI BLACKWOOD MUSIC INC. and BRITTOLESE MUSIC. All Rights for GANGSTA BOOGIE MUSIC Controlled and Administered by UNIVERSAL MUSIC CORP. All Rights for BRITTOLESE MUSIC Administered by EMI APRIL MUSIC INC. All Rights Reserved. Used by Permission. Contains elements of "Big Bang Theory" Words and Music by George Clinton, Ronald Dunbar and Donnie Sterling and "Bop Gun" Words and Music by George Clinton, William Collins and Garry Shider. *Reprinted by Permission of Hal Leonard Corporation and Street Knowledge Music.*

"It Was a Good Day": words and music by O'SHEA JACKSON, O'KELLY ISLEY, RUDOLPH ISLEY, RONALD ISLEY, ERNIE ISLEY, MARVIN ISLEY, Chris Jasper, Ice Cube, Arthur Goodman, Silvia Robinson and Harry Ray. © 1992, 1993 EMI APRIL MUSIC INC., BOVINA MUSIC INC., GANGSTA BOOGIE MUSIC, GAMBI MUSIC, INC., and WB MUSIC CORP. All Rights for BOVINA MUSIC INC. Controlled and Administered by EMI APRIL MUSIC INC. All Rights on behalf of itself and GANGSTA BOOGIE MUSIC Administered by WB MUSIC CORP. All Rights Re-

"99 Problems": words and music by Norman Landsberg, John Ventura, Leslie Weinstein, Felix Pappalardi, William Squire, Alphonso Henderson and Tracy Morrow. Copyright © 1993, 2003 UNIVERSAL MUSIC—MGB SONGS, UNIVERSAL MUSIC—CAREERS, SONGS OF THE KNIGHT, WB MUSIC CORP., AMMO DUMP MUSIC, CARRUMBA MUSIC, BRIDGEPORT MUSIC, INC., Reach Global Inc., and RHYME SYNDICATE MUSIC. All Rights for SONGS OF THE KNIGHT Controlled and Administered by SPIRIT TWO MUSIC, INC. All Rights for AMMO DUMP MUSIC and CARRUMBA MUSIC Controlled and Administered by WB MUSIC CORP. All Rights on behalf of itself, AMMO DUMP MUSIC and CARRUMBA MUSIC Administered by WB MUSIC CORP. All Rights Reserved. Used by Permission. Contains elements of "The Big Beat," "Long Red," "99 Problems" and "Straight Outta Compton." *Reprinted by Permission of ALFRED MUSIC PUBLISHING CO., INC., Hal Leonard Corporation, Reach Global Music Publishing, and Spirit Music Group.*

"Sound of Da Police": words and music by Rodney Lemay, Lawrence Parker, Eric Burdon, Bryan Chandler and Alan Lomax. Copyright © 1993 LONDON MUSIC U.K., UNIVERSAL MUSIC—Z TUNES LLC, BDP MUSIC, UNICHAPPELL MUSIC INC., SLAMINA MUSIC, LUDLOW MUSIC, INC. and CARBERT MUSIC INC. All Rights for LONDON MUSIC U.K. Controlled and Administered by UNIVERSAL—POLYGRAM INTERNATIONAL PUBLISHING, INC. All Rights for BDP MUSIC Controlled and Administered by UNIVERSAL MUSIC—Z TUNES LLC. All Rights for SLAMINA MUSIC Controlled and Administered by UNICHAPPELL MUSIC INC. All Rights Reserved. Used by Permission. Contains elements of "Inside Looking Out (Rosie)": words and music by Eric Burdon, Alan Lomax and Bryan Chandler. *Reprinted by Permission of Carbert Music Inc., Hal Leonard Corporation, and Ludlow Music.*

"MCs Act Like They Don't Know": words and music by Lawrence Parker and Chris Martin. © 1995 EMI APRIL MUSIC INC., GIFTED PEARL MUSIC and UNIVERSAL MUSIC—Z TUNES LLC. All Rights for GIFTED PEARL MUSIC Controlled and Administered by EMI APRIL MUSIC INC. All Rights Reserved. International Copyright Secured. Used by Permission. *Reprinted by Permission of Hal Leonard Corporation.*

"Afro Puffs": words and music by Robin Allen and Delmar Drew Arnaud. Copyright © 1994, 1998 SONGS OF UNIVERSAL, INC., VRIJON MUSIC, CLARA'S GREAT GRAN', SUGE PUBLISHING, and Robin Allen Pub Designee/ASCAP/Delmar Arnaud Musiq/BMI/Suge Publishing/ASCAP (admin. By EverGreen Copyrights). All Rights for VRIJON MUSIC. Controlled and Administered by SONGS OF UNIVERSAL, INC. All Rights Reserved. Used by Permission. *Reprinted by Permission of EverGreen Copyrights, Inc. and Hal Leonard Corporation.*

"Unfucwitable": words and music by Chris Martin, Robyn Allen and Norman Whitfield. © 2002 EMI APRIL MUSIC INC., GIFTED PEARL MUSIC, STONE DIAMOND MUSIC CORP. and CLARA'S GREAT GRAN'. All Rights for GIFTED PEARL MUSIC Controlled and Administered by EMI APRIL MUSIC INC. All Rights Reserved. International Copyright Secured. Used by Permission. *Reprinted by Permission of Hal Leonard Corporation.*

tered by Universal Music—Careers. All Rights for Senseless Music, Inc. Controlled and Administered by Songs Of Universal, Inc. International Copyright Secured. All Rights Reserved. Used by Permission. *Reprinted by Permission of Hal Leonard Corporation.*

"You Got Me": words and music by Tariq Trotter, Ahmir Thompson, Scott Storch and Jill Scott. Copyright © 1999 by Universal Music—Careers, Grand Negaz Music, Scott Storch Music/Reservoir Media Music (ASCAP), Blues Baby and Blondie Rockwell. All Rights for Grand Negaz Music Administered by Universal Music—Careers. Published by Scott Storch Music/Reservoir Media Music (ASCAP). International Copyright Secured. All Rights Reserved. Used by Permission. *Reprinted by Permission of Hal Leonard Corporation and Reservoir Media Music.*

"Web": words and music by Tarik Collins, Leonard Hubbard, Ahmir Thompson and Robert Dorsey Jr. Copyright © 2004 by Universal Music—Careers, Grand Negaz Music and Brought To Life Music, Inc. All Rights for Grand Negaz Music Administered by Universal Music—Careers. International Copyright Secured. All Rights Reserved. Used by Permission. *Reprinted by Permission of Hal Leonard Corporation and Roots Band/Brought to Life Music Publishing.*

"Mind Playing Tricks on Me": words and music by Isaac Hayes, Brad Jordan, Willie Dennis and Doug King. Copyright © 1991 INCENSE PRODUCTIONS, INC. and N-THE-WATER PUBLISHING, INC. All Rights for INCENSE PRODUCTIONS, INC. Controlled and Administered by IRVING MUSIC, INC. International Copyright Secured. All Rights Reserved. Used by Permission. *Reprinted by Permission of Hal Leonard Corporation.*

"I Seen a Man Die": words and music by Joseph Johnson and Brad Jordan. © 1994 EMI BLACKWOOD MUSIC INC., STRAIGHT CASH MUSIC and N THE WATER MUSIC PUBLISHING. All Rights for STRAIGHT CASH MUSIC Controlled and Administered by EMI BLACKWOOD MUSIC INC. International Copyright Secured. All Rights Reserved. Used by Permission. *Reprinted by Permission of Hal Leonard Corporation.*

"Nuthin' But a 'G' Thang": words and music by Frederick Knight, Leon Haywood and Cordozar Calvin Broadus. Copyright © 1993, 1994 IRVING MUSIC, INC., TWO-KNIGHT PUBLISHING CO., SONGS OF UNIVERSAL, INC., MARI KNIGHT MUSIC, SUGE PUBLISHING, WB MUSIC CORP., and Snoop Doggy Dogg Pub Designee/ASCAP/Suge Publishing/ASCAP (admin. By EverGreen Copyrights)/Jim Edd Music/BMI/Music of the World/BMI. All Rights for TWO-KNIGHT PUBLISHING CO. Controlled and Administered by IRVING MUSIC, INC. International Copyright Secured. All Rights Reserved. Used by Permission. *Reprinted by Permission of EverGreen Copyrights, Inc. and Hal Leonard Corporation.*

"Gin and Juice": words and music by Harry Wayne Casey, Calvin C. Broadus, Richard R. Finch, Cordozar Broadus, Andre Romell Young, Steve Arrington, Steve Washington, Raymond Turner, Daniel Webster and Mark Adams. © 1992, 1993 EMI LONGITUDE MUSIC, WB MUSIC CORP., SUGE PUBLISHING, HARRICK MUSIC, WARNER TAMERLANE PUBLISHING CORP., COTILLION MUSIC, SONY/ATV MUSIC PUBLISHING LLC, and Snoop Doggy Dogg Pub Designee/ASCAP/Suge

"So Many Tears": words and music by Stevie Wonder, Tupac Shakur, Greg Jacobs and Eric Baker. (c) 1995 JOBETE MUSIC CO. INC. and BLACK BULL MUSIC c/o EMI APRIL MUSIC INC., JOSHUA'S DREAM MUSIC, PUBHOWYALIKE PUBLISHING and TRI-BOY MUSIC. All Rights for JOBETE MUSIC CO. INC. Controlled and Administered by EMI APRIL MUSIC INC. All Rights for JOSHUA'S DREAM MUSIC Controlled and Administered by SONGS OF UNIVERSAL, INC. All Rights for PUBHOWYALIKE PUBLISHING Controlled and Administered by UNIVERSAL MUSIC—Z TUNES LLC. All Rights Reserved. International Copyright Secured. Used by Permission. Contains elements of "That Girl" by Stevie Wonder. *Reprinted by Permission of Hal Leonard Corporation and Triboy Music.*

"All Eyez on Me": words and music by Tyruss Himes, Johnny Lee Jackson, James Pennington and Tupac Shakur. Copyright © 1996 by Universal Music—Careers, Universal Music—MGB Songs, Universal Music Corp., Joshua's Dream Music, Songs Of Universal, Inc., Universal Music—Z Tunes LLC and Imperial Loco Entertainment. All Rights for Joshua's Dream Music Controlled and Administered by Universal Music Corp. All Rights for Imperial Loco Entertainment Controlled and Administered by Universal Music—Z Tunes LLC. All Rights Reserved. International Copyright Secured. Used by Permission. *Reprinted by Permission of Hal Leonard Corporation.*

"Changes": words and music by Deon Evans, Bruce Hornsby and Tupac Shakur. Copyright © 1998 by Universal Music—Z Songs, Back On Point Music, Universal Music Corp., WB Music Corp., Joshua's Dream Music, Interscope Pearl Music, and Zappo Music. All Rights for Back On Point Music Administered by Universal Music—Z Songs. All rights on behalf of Zappo Music administered Sony/ATV Music Publishing LLC, 8 Music Square West, Nashville, TN 37203. All Rights Reserved. International Copyright Secured. Used by Permission. *Reprinted by Permission of Hal Leonard Corporation and Sony/ATV Music Publishing LLC.*

"How Long Will They Mourn Me": words and music by Walter Burns, James Gass, Warren Griffin III, Tyruss Himes, Diron Rivers and Tupac Shakur. Copyright © 1994 SONGS OF UNIVERSAL, INC., JOSHUA'S DREAM MUSIC, UNIVERSAL MUSIC—Z TUNES LLC, IMPERIAL LOCO ENTERTAINMENT, DA'GASS CO., WARREN G. PUBLISHING (ASCAP) and WRITER DESIGNEE. All Rights for JOSHUA'S DREAM MUSIC Controlled and Administered by SONGS OF UNIVERSAL, INC. All Rights for IMPERIAL LOCO ENTERTAINMENT Controlled and Administered by UNIVERSAL MUSIC—Z TUNES LLC. All Rights Reserved. International Copyright Secured. Used by Permission. *Reprinted by Permission of Hal Leonard Corporation and Warren G Publishing.*

"Emotions": words and music by Samuel Lindley and Carl Mitchell. Copyright © 1997 UNIVERSAL MUSIC CORP., CREATOR'S WAY MUSIC, INC., STAY HIGH MUSIC and IT'S ALL GOOD! MUSIC. All Rights for CREATOR'S WAY MUSIC Controlled and Administered by UNIVERSAL MUSIC CORP. All Rights Reserved. International Copyright Secured. Used by Permission. *Reprinted by Permission of Hal Leonard Corporation.*

"Murder": words and music by Chad Butler and Bernard Freeman. Copyright © 1996 by Universal Music—Z Tunes LLC and Pimp My Pen International. All Rights Con-

Music—Careers. All Rights Reserved. International Copyright Secured. Used by Permission. *Reprinted by Permission of Hal Leonard Corporation.*

"Brooklyn Zoo": by RUSSELL JONES and DERRICK HARRIS. © 1995 WARNER-TAMERLANE PUBLISHING CORP., WU-TANG PUBLISHING and BRIGHT SUMMIT MUSIC. All Rights on Behalf of Itself and WU-TANG PUBLISHING administered by WARNER-TAMERLANE PUBLISHING CORP. All Rights Reserved. Used by Permission of ALFRED MUSIC PUBLISHING CO., INC. and Bright Summit Music.

"Daytona 500": words and music by Dennis Coles, Robert Diggs, Darryl Hill, Bob James and Corey Woods. Copyright © 1998 by Universal Music—Careers, Ramecca Publishing, Inc., Wu Tang Publishing, Inc., Remidi Music and Writer Designee. All Rights for Ramecca Publishing, Inc. and Wu Tang Publishing, Inc. Controlled and Administered by Universal Music—Careers. All Rights Reserved. International Copyright Secured. Used by Permission. *Reprinted by Permission of Hal Leonard Corporation and Remidi Music.*

"The M.G.M.": words and music by Dennis Coles, Corey Woods and Derrick Harris. Copyright © 1997 by Universal Music—Careers, Wu Tang Publishing, Inc. and Blue Summit Music. All Rights for Wu Tang Publishing, Inc. Administered by Universal Music—Careers. All Rights Reserved. International Copyright Secured. Used by Permission. *Reprinted by Permission of Bright Summit Music and Hal Leonard Corporation.*

"Triumph": words and music by Dennis Coles, Robert Diggs, Gary Grice, Lamont Hawkins, Darryl Hill, Jason Hunter, Russell Jones, Clifford Smith, Elgin Turner and Corey Woods. Copyright © 1997 by Universal Music—Careers, Ramecca Publishing, Inc., Wu Tang Publishing, Inc., Universal Music—MGB Songs and Diggs Family Music, Inc. All Rights for Ramecca Publishing, Inc. and Wu Tang Publishing, Inc. Controlled and Administered by Universal Music—Careers. All Rights Reserved. International Copyright Secured. Used by Permission. *Reprinted by Permission of Hal Leonard Corporation.*

"Shakey Dog": Leon Marcus Michels and Nicholas Anthony Movshon / Kobalt Music Services America, Inc (KMSA). For My Son Publishing (ASCAP) / Wait That's Mine Music (BMI) c/o The Royalty Network, Inc.

PART IV: 2000–2010—NEW MILLENNIUM RAP

"9–5ers Anthem" and "No Regrets" used by permission of Don't Jump! Music

"Fuck You Lucy" and "Sunshine" written by Slug of Atmosphere, S. Davey for Upside-down Heart Music (ASCAP). Used courtesy of Ant Turn That Snare Down and Rhymesayers Entertainment www.rhymesayers.com/atmosphere.

"The Truth": words and music by Dwight Grant, Kanye West and Graham Nash. © 1999 EMI APRIL MUSIC INC., YE WORLD MUSIC, NASH NOTES, BUG MUSIC-MUSIC OF WINDSWEPT, HITCO SOUTH and SHAKUR AL DIN MUSIC. All Rights for YE WORLD MUSIC Controlled and Administered by EMI APRIL MUSIC INC. All rights on behalf of Nash Notes administered by Sony/ATV Music Publishing LLC,

8 Music Square West, Nashville, TN 37203. All Rights for HITCO SOUTH and SHAKUR AL DIN MUSIC Controlled and Administered by BUG MUSIC- MUSIC OF WINDSWEPT. All Rights Reserved. International Copyright Secured. Used by Permission. Contains elements of "Chicago" by Graham Nash. *Reprinted by Permission of Hal Leonard Corporation and Sony/ATV Music Publishing LLC.*

"Alphabet Aerobics" used by permission of Cut Chemist, Songs Music Publishing, LLC o/b/o Ram Island Songs (ASCAP), Gab's Gifted Music (ASCAP), Obrafo Music (ASCAP).

"My Pen & Pad" used by permission of Songs Music Publishing, LLC o/b/o Ram Island Songs (ASCAP), Gab's Gifted Music (ASCAP), Obrafo Music (ASCAP).

"Room with a View" and "Picket Fence" used by permission of Rhymesayers Entertainment, LLC.

"Childz Play": performed by Cee-Lo, Words and Music by Christopher Bridges, Thomas Callaway, Patrick Brown, Raymon Murray and Rico Wade. © 2004 EMI APRIL MUSIC INC., God Given Music (BMI), LUDACRIS MUSIC PUBLISHING INC., CHRYSALIS MUSIC LTD. and ORGANIZED NOIZE MUSIC. All Rights for LUDACRIS MUSIC PUBLISHING INC. Controlled and Administered by EMI APRIL MUSIC INC. All Rights for CHRYSALIS MUSIC LTD. in the U.S. and Canada Controlled and Administered by CHRYSALIS SONGS. All Rights Reserved. International Copyright Secured. Used by Permission. *Reprinted by Permission of Alien Music Services and Hal Leonard Corporation.*

"Grindin'": words and music by Pharrell Williams, Chad Hugo, Gene Thornton and Terrence Thornton. © 2002 EMI BLACKWOOD MUSIC INC., WATERS OF NAZARETH, EMI APRIL MUSIC INC., CHASE CHAD MUSIC, Songs Music Publishing, LLC o/b/o Songs For Beans (BMI), GENMARC and TERRORDOME MUSIC. All Rights for WATERS OF NAZARETH Controlled and Administered by EMI BLACKWOOD MUSIC INC. All Rights for CHASE CHAD MUSIC, GENMARC and TERRORDOME MUSIC Controlled and Administered by EMI APRIL MUSIC INC. All Rights Reserved. International Copyright Secured. Used by Permission. *Reprinted by Permission of Hal Leonard Corporation and SONGS Music Publishing LLC.*

"Police State" used by permission of The War of Art Music (BMI) / Walk Like a Warrior Music (BMI) / Hi Yo Silver Music (ASCAP) / Gold Touch Music (ASCAP) by arrangement with The Royalty Network, Inc.

"Hip Hop" used by permission of War of Art Publishing (BMI) / Walk Like A Warrior Music (BMI) c/o The Royalty Network, Inc.

"Benzi Box": words and music by Brian Burton, Thomas Callaway, and Daniel Thompson. © Copyright 2007 Lord Dihoo Music/Nettwerk One Music A Limited (40%). All Rights Reserved. International Copyright Secured. Used by permission of Metalface and Music Sales Limited.

"Saliva": words and music by Daniel Thompson and R J Krohn. © Copyright 2007 Lord Dihoo Music/Nettwerk One Music A Limited (50%). All Rights Reserved. International Copyright Secured. Used by permission of Metalface and Music Sales Limited.

"Figaro": performed by MF Doom, written by Otis Jackson Jr. and Daniel Dumile

and Wayne Shorter . Copyright © 1991 IRVING MUSIC, INC., MIYAKO MUSIC, FALFURIOUS MUSIC and OMNI FARIOUS MUSIC. All Rights for MIYAKO MUSIC Controlled and Administered by IRVING MUSIC, INC. All Rights for OMNI-FARIOUS MUSIC Administered by FALFURIOUS MUSIC. All Rights Reserved. International Copyright Secured. Used by Permission. Contains elements of "Soul" by Gus Hawkins and Lee Lovett and "Non-Stop Home" by Wayne Shorter. *Reprinted by Permission of Hal Leonard Corporation.*

"Simon Says": words and music by Troy Jamerson. © 2004 EMI BLACKWOOD MUSIC INC. and TRESCADECAPHOBIA MUSIC. All Rights Controlled and Administered by EMI BLACKWOOD MUSIC INC. All Rights Reserved. International Copyright Secured. Used by Permission. *Reprinted by Permission of Hal Leonard Corporation.*

"Desire": words and music by Troy Jamerson, Alan Maman, Luroner Brooksme, Lamont Dozier, Brian Holland and Edward Holland. © 2007 EMI BLACKWOOD MUSIC INC., TRESCADECAPHOBIA MUSIC, SONGS OF UNIVERSAL, INC., GOLD FOREVER MUSIC, INC., A MAMAN MUSIC c/o The Royalty Network, Inc., NOTTING DALE SONGS, INC. and PAT'S SON MUSIC. All Rights for TRESCADECAPHOBIA MUSIC Controlled and Administered by EMI BLACKWOOD MUSIC INC. All Rights for GOLD FOREVER MUSIC, INC. Controlled and Administered by SONGS OF UNIVERSAL, INC. All Rights Reserved. International Copyright Secured. Used by Permission. *Reprinted by Permission of Hal Leonard Corporation and The Royalty Network, Inc.*

"Hip Hop" Words and Music by David Axelrod, Michael T. Axelrod, Mos Def, Joseph Kirkland and Gabriel Jackson. © 1999 GLENWOOD MUSIC CORP., EMI BLACKWOOD MUSIC INC., MEDINA SOUND MUSIC, EMPIRE INTERNATIONAL, DUSTY FINGERS MUSIC and STREET TUFF TUNES. All Rights for MEDINA SOUND MUSIC and EMPIRE INTERNATIONAL Controlled and Administered by EMI BLACKWOOD MUSIC INC. All Rights Reserved International Copyright Secured Used by Permission.—contains elements of "The Warnings" and "Spoonin' Rap". *Reprinted by Permission of Hal Leonard Corporation*

"Mathematics": words and music by Dante Beze and Christopher E. Martin. © 1999 EMI BLACKWOOD MUSIC INC., Sony/ATV Music Publishing LLC, EMPIRE INTERNATIONAL, MEDINA SOUND MUSIC, EMI APRIL MUSIC INC. and GIFTED PEARL MUSIC. All Rights for EMPIRE INTERNATIONAL and MEDINA SOUND MUSIC Controlled and Administered by EMI BLACKWOOD MUSIC INC. All Rights for GIFTED PEARL MUSIC Controlled and Administered by Kobalt Music Services America, Inc. (KMSA) and EMI APRIL MUSIC INC. All rights on behalf of Sony/ATV Music Publishing LLC administered by Sony/ATV Music Publishing LLC, 8 Music Square West, Nashville, TN 37203. All Rights Reserved. International Copyright Secured. Used by Permission. *Reprinted by Permission of Hal Leonard Corporation, Kobalt Music Services America, and Sony/ATV Music Publishing LLC.*

"Dollar Day for New Orleans (Katrina Klap)" performed by Mos Def. Written by Mos Def, Terius Gray & Donald Robertson. Produced by Donald XL Robertson & Terius Gray. Used by permission of No Mistakes Allowed Publishing.

"Auditorium" written by Dante Terrell Smith, Ricky Walters, Otis Lee Jackson, Jr. Pub-

MGB SONGS. All Rights Reserved. International Copyright Secured. Used by Permission. *Reprinted by Permission of Hal Leonard Corporation and Ultra International Music Publishing.*

"Can't Tell Me Nothing": words and music by Kanye West, Aldrin Davis and Connie Mitchell. © 2000 EMI BLACKWOOD MUSIC INC., PLEASE GIMME MY PUBLISHING, TOOMPSTONE PUBLISHING and GOOD SOLDIER SONGS LTD. All Rights for PLEASE GIMME MY PUBLISHING and TOOMPSTONE PUBLISHING Controlled and Administered by EMI BLACKWOOD MUSIC INC. All Rights for GOOD SOLDIER SONGS LTD. in the U.S. and Canada Controlled and Administered by UNIVERSAL—POLYGRAM INTERNATIONAL PUBLISHING, INC. All Rights Reserved. International Copyright Secured. Used by Permission. *Reprinted by Permission of Hal Leonard Corporation.*

"Put On": words and music by Jay Jenkins, Kanye West and Christopher Gholson. © 2008 EMI BLACKWOOD MUSIC INC., YOUNG JEEZY MUSIC INC., PLEASE GIMME MY PUBLISHING, WB MUSIC CORP. and YOUNG DRUMMA. All Rights for YOUNG JEEZY MUSIC INC. and PLEASE GIMME MY PUBLISHING Controlled and Administered by EMI BLACKWOOD MUSIC INC. All Rights on Behalf of Itself and YOUNG DRUMMA Administered by WB MUSIC CORP. All Rights Reserved. International Copyright Secured. Used by Permission. *Reprinted by Permission of ALFRED MUSIC PUBLISHING CO., INC. and Hal Leonard Corporation.*

"My President": words and music by Justin Henderson, Christopher Whitacre, Jay Jenkins and Nasir Jones. Copyright © 2008 SONGS OF UNIVERSAL, INC., NAPPYPUB MUSIC, HENDERWORKS PUBLISHING CO., UNIVERSAL MUSIC CORP., NAPPY BOY PUBLISHING, WEST COAST LIVIN' PUBLISHING, UNIVERSAL MUSIC—Z TUNES LLC, UNIVERSAL MUSIC—Z SONGS, EMI BLACKWOOD MUSIC INC. and YOUNG JEEZY MUSIC INC. All Rights for NAPPYPUB MUSIC and HENDERWORKS PUBLISHING CO. Controlled and Administered by SONGS OF UNIVERSAL, INC. All Rights for NAPPY BOY PUBLISHING and WEST COAST LIVIN' PUBLISHING Controlled and Administered by UNIVERSAL MUSIC CORP. All Rights for YOUNG JEEZY MUSIC INC. Controlled and Administered by EMI BLACKWOOD MUSIC INC. All Rights Reserved. International Copyright Secured. Used by Permission. *Reprinted by Permission of Hal Leonard Corporation.*

LYRICS FOR FURTHER STUDY

"Cadillac on 22's": Crump Tight Publishing (BMI) c/o The Royalty Network, Inc.

"Reality Check" used by permission of Senim Silla.

"Vapors" by Biz Markie is used under license from CAK Music Publishing, Inc.

"The Choice is Yours (Revisited)": words and music by William McLean and Andres Titus. Copyright © 1991 UNIVERSAL—SONGS OF POLYGRAM INTERNATIONAL, INC., PEEP BO MUSIC, IRVING MUSIC, INC. and CHAR-LIZ MUSIC, INC. THE MUSIC GOES ROUND, B.V. dba MUSIC IN ONE c/o THIRD TIER MUSIC, LLC. All Rights for PEEP BO MUSIC Controlled and Administered by UNIVERSAL—SONGS OF POLYGRAM INTERNATIONAL, INC. All Rights Reserved. International Copyright Secured. Used by Permission. *Reprinted by Permission of Hal Leonard Corporation and Third Tier Music.*

"Luchini": words and music by Ricky Smith, Richard Randolph, Kevin Spencer, Saladine Wallace, Salahadeen Wilds and David Anthony Willis. Copyright © 1997 Sony/ATV Music Publishing LLC, My Kinda Music, Universal—Songs Of Polygram International, Inc., RABASSE MUSIC, LTD., UNIVERSAL MUSIC PUBLISHING LIMITED (GB), Biggie Music and Satin Struthers Music. All Rights on behalf of My Kinda Music Administered by Sony/ATV Music Publishing LLC, 8 Music Square, Nashville, TN 37203. All Rights on behalf of Biggie Music Administered by Universal—Songs Of Polygram International, Inc. All Rights on Behalf of RABASSE MUSIC, LTD. Administered by WARNER/CHAPPELL MUSIC LTD. All Rights Reserved. International Copyright Secured. Used by Permission. *Reprinted by Permission of ALFRED MUSIC PUBLISHING CO., INC., Hal Leonard Corporation, Lastrada Entertainment Company, Ltd., and Sony/ATV Music Publishing LLC.*

"They Want EFX": words and music by Andre Weston and Willie Hines. © 1992 EMI APRIL MUSIC INC., SEWER SLANG MUSIC, CELLAR TO THE ADDICT, Donna Dijon Music Publications, Dynatone Publishing Company, and Straight Out Da Sewer. All Rights Controlled and Administered by EMI APRIL MUSIC INC. All rights administered by Sony/ATV Music Publishing LLC, 8 Music Square West, Nashville, TN 37203. All Rights Reserved. International Copyright Secured. Used by Permission. Contains elements of "Blind Men Can See It" by James Brown, Fred Wesley and Charles Bobbit. *Reprinted by Permission of Hal Leonard Corporation and Sony/ATV Music Publishing LLC.*

"For Colored Boys" written by Jerry Brown, Ryan Burke, Essexincantations, Leslie Taylor, Marcus Van, Timothy West. Used by permission of Juba Kalamka/Deep Dickollective.

"Summertime": words and music by Willard Smith, Lamar Mahone, Craig Simpkins, Robert Bell, Ronald Bell, Robert Mickens, Dennis Thomas, George Brown, Alton Taylor, Richard Westfield and Claydus Smith. Copyright © 1991 by Jazzy Jeff And Fresh Prince, ZOMBA ENTERPRISES, INC., WILLESDEN MUSIC, INC., Da Posse Music, Warner-Tamerlane Publishing Corp., Second Decade Music and Gang Music Ltd. All Rights for Jazzy Jeff And Fresh Prince Administered by Universal Music—Z Tunes LLC. All Rights for Da Posse Music Administered by Universal Music—Z Songs. All Rights for Second Decade Music Co. and Gang Music Ltd. Administered by Warner-Tamerlane Publishing Corp. All Rights Reserved. International Copyright Secured. Used by Permission. Contains samples from "Summer Madness" by Alton Taylor, Robert Mickens, George Brown, Richard Westfield, Claydes Smith, Ronald Bell, Dennis Thomas and Robert Bell. *Reprinted by Permission of ALFRED MUSIC PUBLISHING CO., INC. and Hal Leonard Corporation.*

"Fumbling Over Words That Rhyme" used by permission of Edan.

"The Rain (Supa Dupa Fly)": words and music by Ann Peebles, Bernard Miller, Don Bryant, Melissa Elliot and Timothy Mosley. Copyright © 1997 JEC PUBLISHING CORP., WB MUSIC CORP., IRVING MUSIC INC., EAST MEMPHIS MUSIC and MASS CONFUSION PRODUCTIONS. All Rights for JEC PUBLISHING CORP.

Controlled and Administered by IRVING MUSIC, INC. All Rights for MASS CON-FUSION PUBLISHING Controlled and Administered by IRVING MUSIC, INC. All Rights Reserved. International Copyright Secured. Used by Permission. *Reprinted by Permission of ALFRED MUSIC PUBLISHING CO., INC. and Hal Leonard Corporation.*

"Strictly Business" contains a sample from "I Shot The Sheriff" written by Bob Marley. Published by Fifty Six Hope Road Music Ltd/Odnil Music Ltd. All rights administered by Blue Mountain Music Ltd.

"King Tim III (Personality Jock)": written by Bill Curtis, Fred Demery and James Skelton. Published in the USA by Taking Care of Business Music (BMI) and in the rest of the world by Minder Music Ltd (PRS). ℗ © 1979

"Hate It or Love It": words and music by Curtis Jackson, Andre Lyon, Marcello Valenzano, Ronald Baker, Allan Felder, Norman Harris and Jayceon Taylor. Copyright © 2005 UNIVERSAL MUSIC CORP., 50 CENT MUSIC, UNIVERSAL MUSIC—Z SONGS, DADE CO. PROJECT MUSIC, INC., MURED MUSIC CO (BMI), GOLDEN FLEECE MUSIC (BMI), Six Strings Music (BMI), and BLACK WALL STREET. All Rights for 50 CENT MUSIC Controlled and Administered by UNIVERSAL MUSIC CORP. All Rights for DADE CO. PROJECT MUSIC, INC. Controlled and Administered by UNIVERSAL MUSIC—Z SONGS. All Rights Reserved. International Copyright Secured. Used by Permission. Uses a sample of the composition "Rubber Band." *Reprinted by Permission of Each 1 Teach 1, Golden Fleece Music, Hal Leonard Corporation, Mured Music, and Six Strings Music.*

"Why": words and music by Jason Phillips, Pierre Moerlen, Anthony Hamilton and Kejuan Muchita. © 2004 EMI APRIL MUSIC INC., JUSTIN COMBS PUBLISHING COMPANY, INC., EMI VIRGIN MUSIC LTD., SONGS OF UNIVERSAL, INC., TAPPY WHYTE'S MUSIC, UNIVERSAL MUSIC—MGB SONGS and JUVENILE HELL PUBLISHING. All Rights for JUSTIN COMBS PUBLISHING COMPANY, INC. Controlled and Administered by EMI APRIL MUSIC INC. All Rights for EMI VIRGIN MUSIC LTD. in the U.S. and Canada Controlled and Administered by EMI VIRGIN MUSIC, INC. All Rights for TAPPY WHYTE'S MUSIC Controlled and Administered by SONGS OF UNIVERSAL, INC. All Rights for JUVENILE HELL PUBLISHING Controlled and Administered by UNIVERSAL MUSIC—MGB SONGS. All Rights Reserved. International Copyright Secured. Used by Permission Contains sample of "Mandrake" by Pierre Moerlen. *Reprinted by Permission of Hal Leonard Corporation.*

"Uncommon Valor: A Vietnam Story" used by permission of R. A. Thorburn.

"Come Clean": words and music by Chris Martin, Kendrick Davis, Freddie Scruggs, Tyrone Taylor, Kirk Jones and Shelly Manne. © 1994 EMI APRIL MUSIC INC., GIFTED PEARL MUSIC, IRVING MUSIC, INC., PERVERTED ALCHEMIST MUSIC, UNIVERSAL MUSIC—Z TUNES LLC, ILL HILL BILLY Z MUZIK INC., 111 POSSE MUSIC and SITTIN' IN MUSIC PUBLISHING. All Rights for GIFTED PEARL MUSIC Controlled and Administered by EMI APRIL MUSIC INC. All Rights for PERVERTED ALCHEMIST MUSIC Controlled and Administered by IRVING MUSIC, INC. All Rights for ILL HILL BILLY Z MUZIK INC. and 111 POSSE

MUSIC Controlled and Administered by UNIVERSAL MUSIC—Z TUNES LLC. All Rights Reserved. International Copyright Secured. Used by Permission. *Reprinted by Permission of Hal Leonard Corporation.*

"Ha": words and music by Teruis Gray and Byron Thomas. Copyright © 1998 SONGS OF UNIVERSAL, INC., MONEY MACK MUSIC and FRESH IS THE WORD. All Rights Controlled and Administered by SONGS OF UNIVERSAL, INC. All Rights Reserved. International Copyright Secured. Used by Permission. *Reprinted by Permission of Hal Leonard Corporation.*

"BaKardi Slang": by JASON HARROW and SHELDON PITT. © 2000 WARNER CHAPPELL MUSIC CANADA LTD., ONE MAN MUSIC, AND UNKNOWN PUBLISHER. All Rights on Behalf of Itself and ONE MAN MUSIC Administered by WARNER CHAPPELL MUSIC CANADA LTD. All Rights Reserved. Used by Permission of ALFRED MUSIC PUBLISHING CO., INC.

"Everything's Gonna Be Alright (Ghetto Bastard)": by VINCENT "VINNIE" BROWN, KEIR GIST, ANTHONY CRISS and VINCENT FORD. © 1981 WB MUSIC CORP. (ASCAP) and NAUGHTY MUSIC (ASCAP). All Rights on Behalf of Itself and NAUGHTY MUSIC Administered by WB MUSIC CORP. All Rights Reserved. Used by Permission of ALFRED MUSIC PUBLISHING CO., INC.

"Country Grammar (Hot Shit)": words and music by Jason Epperson and Cornell Hayes. Copyright © 2000 UNIVERSAL MUSIC CORP., JAY E'S BASEMENT, D2 PRO PUBLISHING, UNIVERSAL MUSIC—MGB SONGS and JACKIE FROST MUSIC, INC. All Rights for JAY E'S BASEMENT and D2 PRO PUBLISHING Controlled and Administered by UNIVERSAL MUSIC CORP. All Rights for JACKIE FROST MUSIC, INC. Controlled and Administered by UNIVERSAL MUSIC—MGB SONGS. All Rights Reserved. International Copyright Secured. Used by Permission. *Reprinted by Permission of Hal Leonard Corporation.*

"Sometimes I Rhyme Slow" written by: Greg Mays, Dairyl Barnes, Nuno Bettencourt, Gary Cherone, Adam McLeer, Worldwide rights administered by Vanessa Music Inc. o/b/o Nice and Smooth Music. Used by Permission. All Rights Reserved.

"Time's Up": words and music by Anthony Best and Omar Credle. Copyright © 2002 by Universal Music—MGB Songs, Still Digging Music and Organimz Music, Inc. All Rights for Still Digging Music Administered by Universal Music—MGB Songs. All Rights Reserved. International Copyright Secured. Used by Permission. *Reprinted by Permission of Hal Leonard Corporation.*

"They Reminisce over You (T.R.O.Y.)": words by COREY BRENT PENN Music by PETER O. PHILLIPS. © 1992 WB MUSIC CORP. and NESS, NITTY AND CAPONE, INC. All Rights Administered by WB MUSIC CORP. All Rights Reserved. Used by Permission of ALFRED MUSIC PUBLISHING CO., INC. and Smooth Flowing Music c/o The Royalty Network, Inc.

"Passing Me By": words and music by Steve Boone, John Sebastian, Trevant Germaine Hardson, John Manuel Martinez, Emandu Wilcox, Romye Robinson, Derrick Lemel Stewart and Mark Sebastian. © 1992 EMI BLACKWOOD MUSIC INC., BIG BANG THEORY PUBLISHING, BUG MUSIC-TRIO MUSIC CO., INC., ALLEY MUSIC